# ECONOMIC LOGIC

*Revised Third Edition*

# ECONOMIC LOGIC

*Revised Third Edition*

by Mark Skousen
*Benjamin Franklin Chair of Management*
*Grantham University*

Cataloging-in-Publication Data on file with the Library of Congress

ISBN 978-1-59698-545-2

Published in the United States by
Capital Press
An Eagle Publishing Company
One Massachusetts Avenue, NW
Washington, DC 20001

Manufactured in the United States of America

10 9 8 7 6 5 4 3

Books are available in quantity for promotional or premium use. Write to Director of Special Sales, Regnery Publishing, Inc., One Massachusetts Avenue, NW, Washington, DC 20001, for information on discounts and terms or call (202) 216-0600.

Book design by Pitts•LaVigne Associates

Dedicated to two giants

of the 20th Century,

Friedrich Hayek and Milton Friedman.

**OTHER ACADEMIC BOOKS BY MARK SKOUSEN**

Playing the Price Controls Game

The Structure of Production

Economics on Trial

Dissent on Keynes (editor)

The Investor's Bible: Mark Skousen's Principles of Investment

Puzzles and Paradoxes in Economics (co-authored with Kenna C. Taylor)

The Making of Modern Economics

Vienna and Chicago, Friends or Foes?

The Big Three in Economics

Econo Power

*"While the earth remaineth, seedtime and harvest, and cold and heat, and summer and winter, and day and night shall not cease."*

—Genesis 8:22

*"After all, the chief business of the American people is business. They are profoundly concerned with the producing, buying, selling, investing, and prospering in the world. I am strongly of the opinion that the great majority of people will always find these are moving impulses of our life."*

—Calvin Coolidge (1925)

*"No science in the world is more elevated, more necessary, and more useful than economics."*

—Carl Linnaeus, Swedish naturalist

# CONTENTS

# ACKNOWLEDGEMENTS

*Thanks especially to economics professor Brian Addis and Kary Ledbetter of Grantham University and Jeffrey Zucker of McMaster University for editing and updating the New Enlarged Edition of* Economic Logic, *both for micro and macro editions. I also thank Jim Cox at Georgia Perimeter College for preparing the test bank. For a copy of the test bank, instructors should contact Jim Cox at jcox@gpc.edu. I'd also like to thank the following economists, colleagues, and friends who have reviewed, edited, or made suggestions for* Economic Logic. *While their advice has been invaluable, none can be held responsible for the final product. I would especially like to thank my wife, Jo Ann, for her editing of this edition. Her suggestions and changes were invaluable. In addition, I'd like to thank the following for their assistance in this and past editions:*

Martin Anderson, Hoover Institution
Dominick T. Armentano, University of Hartford
Manuel F. Ayau, Universidad Francisco Marroquin
Charles W. Baird, California State University East Bay
Peter Bach, University of Relands Whitehead College
Richard Band, Profitable Investing
P. T. Bauer, London School of Economics
Bret Barker, Schurr High School, California
Bruce Barlett, Alexis de Tocqueville Institution
Robert Barro, Harvard University
Robert Batemarco, Marymount College
Gary S. Becker, University of Chicago
Don Bellante, University of South Florida
Peter L. Bernstein, Peter L. Bernstein, Inc., New York
Mark Blaug, University of London
Walter Block, Loyola University
Peter Boettke, George Mason University
Donald J. Boudreaux, George Mason University
H. L. Brockman, Central Piedmont Community College
Stanley Brue, Pacific Lutheran University
Eamonn Butler, Adam Smith Institute
Roger Clites, Milligan College
David Colander, Middlebury College
Kent Cowie, Henry Hazlitt Foundation
Jim Cox, Georgia Perimeter College
Thomas J. DiLorenzo, Loyola College
Edwin G. Dolan, George Mason University
Peter F. Drucker, Claremont Graduate University
Richard M. Ebeling, Foundation for Economic Education
Kenneth G. Elzinga, University of Virginia

Fred Foldvary, Santa Clara University
Burton W. Folsom, Jr., Hillsdale College
Milton Friedman, Hoover Institution
Lowell E. Gallaway, Ohio University
Roger W. Garrison, Auburn University
Bettina B. Greaves, Foundation for Economic Education
James D. Gwartney, Florida State University
Steve H. Hanke, Johns Hopkins University
G. C. Harcourt, Cambridge University
Fred Harwood, American Institute for Economic Research
Friedrich A. Hayek, University of Freiberg
Robert L. Heilbroner, New School for Social Research
David R. Henderson, Naval Postgraduate School
Paul Heyne, University of Washington
John Hicks, Oxford University
Robert Higgs, Seattle University
Randall Holcombe, Florida State University
John M. Hood, John Locke Foundation
Arthur M. Hughes, University of Maryland
Joseph Kecheissen, Universidad Francisco Marroquin
Matt King, Rollins College
Israel M. Kirzner, New York University
Martin Krause, University of Buenos Aires
Don Lavoie, George Mason University
Stanley Lebergott, Wesleyan University
Dwight R. Lee, University of Georgia
Henri Lepage, Institut Euro 92
John List, University of Chicago
John Mackey, CEO, Whole Foods Market
Burton G. Malkiel, Princeton University
Yuri N. Maltsev, Carthage College
N. Gregory Mankiw, Harvard University
Deidre N. McCloskey, University of Illinois at Chicago
Richard B. McKenzie, University of California, Irvine
Roger LeRoy Miller, University of Texas, Arlington
Hyman P. Minsky, Washington University
Glenn Moots, Northwood University
Charles Murray, American Enterprise Institute
Charles R. Nelson, University of Washington
Gary North, Institute of Christian Economics
E. C. Pasour, Jr., North Carolina State University
Judd W. Patton, Bellevue University

William H. Peterson, Campbell University
Mark J. Perry, University of Michigan, Flint
Madsen Pirie, Adam Smith Institute
Robert Poole, Reason Foundation
Alvin Rabushka, Hoover Institution
Lawrence Reed, MacKinac Center for Public Policy
George G. Reisman
Alan Reynolds, Cato Institute
Benjamin Rogge, Wabash College
Murray N. Rothbard, University of Nevada at Las Vegas
Roy J. Ruffin, University of Houston
Joseph Salerno, Pace University
Paul A. Samuelson, Massachusetts Institute of Technology
Ken Schoolland, Pacific Hawaii University
George A. Selgin, University of Georgia
Hans F. Sennholz, Grove City College
Robert Shiller, Yale University
Gary Shilling
Jeremy Siegel, Wharton School of Business
Julian L. Simon, University of Maryland
Robert Skidelsky, University of Warwick
Royal J. Skousen, Brigham Young University
Gene Smiley, Marquette University
Garvin Smith, Daytona Beach Community College
Robert Sobel, Hofstra University
Jesus Huerta de Soto, Universidad Rey Juan Carlos (Spain)
Thomas Sowell, Hoover Institution
Erich Streissler, University of Vienna
Richard L. Stroup, Montana State University
Richard Swedberg, University of Sweden
Kenna C. Taylor, Rollins College
Timothy Taylor, Macalester College
Glen Tenney, Great Basin College
Paul and Vicki Terhorst
Clifford F. Thies, Shenandoah University
Gordon Tullock, George Mason University
Richard Vedder, Ohio University
Murray Weidenbaum, Washington University
Walter Williams, George Mason University
Larry T. Wimmer, Brigham Young University
Leland Yeager, Auburn University
Harry C. Veryser, University of Detroit-Mercy

*For comments and suggestions, write:*

Professor Mark Skousen

P.O. Box 2488

Winter Park, FL 32790


E-mail: editor@markskousen.com

Webpage: www.mskousen.com; www.markskousen.com

# WHAT'S UNIQUE ABOUT ECONOMIC LOGIC

1. It offers a **logical, step-by-step approach** to economics, starting with the basics of microeconomics (the theory of wealth creation, individual behavior and the firm), and leading into macroeconomics (the theory of economy-wide behavior and government policy).

2. Students can actually predict that the next chapter will be. Hence, the textbook is "econological."

3. It is the first and only textbook to begin with a **profit-and-loss income statement** to demonstrate the dynamics of the economy. The principles of supply and demand are drawn out of the P&L statement. Business students, in particular, find this approach attractive. (See for example figure 4.4.)

4. It integrates other disciplines into the study—finance, business, marketing, management, history, and sociology.

5. It makes frequent references to major economic events in **history**, such as the origin of money and the Great Depression, and the inventors of economic theories and terms (major economic thinkers are highlighted at the end of each chapter). Thus, in this textbook, economic theory is never far from history because new theories almost always develop out of historical events (Adam Smith's competitive model came out of the Enlightenment; Karl Marx's radical distribution economics was in response to the Industrial Revolution; and John Maynard Keynes's aggregate demand model rose out of the Great Depression of the 1930s.)

6. It devotes an entire chapter (13) to the **financial markets**, which are playing a growing role in the expanding global economy. Students must understand Wall Street and the financial world to have a complete education in economics.

7. It introduces a new powerful **four-stage universal model of the economy** (resources, production, distribution, and consumption/investment), and shows how micro and macro are logically linked together. (See for example figure 4.1.)

8. It integrates a new national income statistic called **Gross Domestic Expenditures (GDE)**, which measures total spending at all four stages of production, and shows how it relates to Gross Domestic Product (GDP) and other aggregate business cycle statistics. (See chapter 15.)

8. It introduces a **new "growth" diagram** that improves upon the "circular flow" diagram found in other textbooks, and demonstrates why saving and investing drive the economy, not consumer spending. (See figure 17.7.)

9. It provides a new alternative to the standard Aggregate Supply (AS) and Aggregate Demand (AD) curves, called **Aggregate Supply Vectors (ASV) and Aggregate Demand Vectors (ADV),** which do a better job of explaining the business cycle. (See chapter 14.)

10. It provides a new diagram to show the **optimal size of government**. (See figure 20.1)

For updates on *Economic Logic*, go to www.economiclogic.net.
For a test bank for instructors, email editor@markskousen.com.

For comments and suggestions, write:
Professor Mark Skousen
P. O. Box 2488 • Winter Park, FL 32790
Email: editor@markskousen.com.

Other related websites:
www.mskousen.com • www.markskousen.com

# Introduction to the Second Edition

# A LOGICAL APPROACH TO ECONOMICS

Economics, the youngest of the social sciences, is sometimes described as a difficult subject. "There are so many complicated bits and pieces," Paul Heyne writes in *The Economic Way of Thinking*, "and they are so hard for students to grasp." In the beginning of his textbook, Martin Bronfenbrenner warns students, "You may temporarily find yourself unlearning more than you learn, or operating in a fog of confusion."

But economic science need not be laborious or perplexing. This textbook offers a rigorous course in college economics without unnecessary complications or confusion. It represents a new, integrated approach that establishes the purpose of economics and develops strategies to achieve the economic goals of society. This approach moves from the simple to the complex by systematically building an edifice that, when complete, will be both elegant and practical. It also attempts to integrate disciplines closely associated with economics—business, marketing, management, finance, and sociology.

Today's economics textbooks are often a hodgepodge of esoteric theories, unrealistic graphs, and specialized terms. Chapters are so bewildering that students have no idea what subject matter they are going to study next. Economists argue over which should be taught first, microeconomics or macroeconomics, neither of which is integrated into a whole. Supply and demand are usually introduced at the beginning of a book, and then reintroduced in later chapters. Government policy is mixed throughout. International trade has traditionally been placed in the back of the book, almost as an afterthought, but some recent textbooks have begun to integrate global issues.

## PART I: AN OVERVIEW

This textbook takes a more systematic approach. Part I begins with the fundamental rationale of economics: how wealth is created or destroyed and how the standard of living may improve or decline. Scarcity, choice, and the allocation of resources are important characteristics of economic life and change. Throughout this textbook we emphasize how individuals as consumers, workers, landlords, and capitalists work together to create prosperity, and the extent to which government improves or impedes economic progress. In short, economics concerns itself with wealth, income, choices, incentives, living standards and growth—themes of vital interest to everyone.

In Part I, we discuss the universal characteristics of the world we live in—the limitations of time and resources, the uncertainty of the future, the necessity of work, and the variety of consumer demand. Based on these basic assumptions regarding human behavior, we develop a common-sense model of economic behavior and consumer satisfaction. We show that virtually all usable wealth must go through a series of processes from unfinished resources to final use by consumers and business, a process that takes time and involves numerous stages of production in the allocation of limited resources. The idea that all goods and services take time to produce and consume forms the foundation of our economic model. In this new edition, I replace the industrial four-stage model (natural resources, manufacturing, wholesale, and retail) with a more universal four-stage model of production that includes services (resources, production, distribution, and consumption/investment).

## PART II: MICROECONOMICS AND THE THEORY OF SUPPLY AND DEMAND

To create a complete and praiseworthy edifice, we must build from the ground up. Therefore, Part II begins with microeconomics, the theory of consumer demand, how demands are met by individual producers, and how each firm fits into the stages-of-production model and the time-structure of the economy. Whether involved in mining, insurance, banking, international trade, communications, medical services, or retailing, firms operate on the principle that revenues must exceed expenses over the long haul or they will be forced out of business and into another line of work that better fulfills consumer wants. To be profitable, a firm must set the right prices and control the cost of doing business.

One of the unique features of this textbook is that we begin with a firm's income statement, also known as a profit-and-loss statement. This simple but powerful accounting tool allows us to demonstrate the dynamics of firm behavior. We use the income statement to show downsizing and upsizing, why new products are constantly being developed, and why we see changes in the quantity, quality and variety of goods and services over time. Both students and instructors find that this approach enhances their overall understanding.

Building on the firm's income statement, we then introduce the demand and supply schedules for individual goods and services. We discuss the wants and needs of consumers, how consumer tastes shift, how consumers respond to price changes, how consumer needs are met by suppliers and their factors of production, and how land, labor, capital and entrepreneurship work together to satisfy consumer demands. We also show that the production of all goods requires land, labor, capital and entrepreneurship. Services are, of course, labor-intensive, but land and capital also play pivotal roles in providing services.

Indeed, cooperation among these factors of production is vital, but the conflicts and issues that arise among landlords, laborers, and capitalists are just as vital for a more complete understanding of the process. Therefore, we determine how firms and their inputs respond to changes in supply and demand, and how they create the capital necessary to operate and expand their production, including the development of financial markets. Lastly, various degrees of competition and monopoly are also analyzed.

## PART III: MACROECONOMICS

After analyzing the economic activity of individuals and firms, we shift our attention to macroeconomics—how the economy operates as a whole. Part III examines the Aggregate Production Structure, our macroeconomic model, and various ways to measure economic activity, including Gross Domestic Expenditures (GDE), Gross Domestic Product (GDP), National Income (NI), and other aggregate statistics.

We also introduce an improved version of Aggregate Supply and Demand, which stresses the key role of interest rates in determining macroeconomic equilibrium and growth. After introducing these macroeconomic fundamentals, the discussion shifts to analyzing the impact of changes in saving and technology and their effect on economic growth, as well as the effect of changes in the money supply. Money is introduced as an important ingredient in the economy, followed by a history of the origin of money and banking, and how modern banking works today.

## PART IV: GOVERNMENT POLICY

After we have built the fundamentals of a market economy, Part IV takes a close look at the impact of governmental policies on the economy. What are the legitimate functions of the state? What is the role of government in monetary policy? Other topics include the theory of taxation, the national debt and deficit spending, and the effect that government fiscal and monetary policies have on inflation, recession, and the business cycle. It is in this section that I introduce and critique the basic concepts of Keynesian economics, still popular in the halls of parliament, corporate boardrooms, and Wall Street.

Another important aspect of government policy is regulation and controls—the impact of the state on the environment, international trade, agriculture, housing, and business enterprise.

The final section discusses "macro" government intervention in the form of central planning, socialism, and industrial planning. We discuss the pros and cons, the rejection of socialist central planning in Eastern Europe and China in favor of free markets, and the impact of the financial crisis of 2008.

## A UNIVERSAL APPROACH

The focus throughout the text is on the creation of wealth and expanding the standard of living from the point of view of an individual worker, an entrepreneur, a business, and a government.

Most importantly, we make use of the best thinking from all schools of thought to build a universal model of the economy that is adaptable to cultural differences around the world. As the British economist Lionel Robbins once stated, there are really only two kinds of economics—good economics and bad economics. This textbook is all about good economics for everyone.

One final thought: It is important to remind ourselves what the proper role of an economist is throughout this sojourn in economic theory and application. What are the qualities of a good economist? The brilliant French economist Frederic Bastiat stated in 1850, "There is only one difference between a bad economist and a good one: the bad economist confines himself to the visible effect; the good economist takes into account both the effect that can be seen and those effects that must be foreseen."[1] Thus, the art of good economics is to look beyond the short-term visible effects of a policy, and to foresee the long-term effects not presently visible. It is to trace the consequences of a policy not just on one group, but upon all groups. This is the approach that is incorporated in this textbook—a comprehensive approach to economics that emphasizes all of the effects of economic policy.

1 Frederic Bastiat, "What is Seen and What is Not Seen," *Selected Essays on Political Economy* (Foundation for Economic Education, 1964), p. 1. Originally published in July, 1850.

In this new edition I end with an afterword. Economics has broadened its influence beyond government policy. It is now the imperial science, having an impact in the world of high finance, business management, law, criminal behavior, sociology, religion, and other disciplines. Those interested in pursuing a career in economics will gain some insights into the economics profession in this chapter.

## A PERSONAL NOTE ON WRITING ECONOMIC LOGIC

I firmly believe that economics is one of those subjects that is best taught and understood by those who have had years of experience, knowledge, and wisdom. A thorough grasp of theory is necessary, but it needs to be tempered by on-the-job training in the world of business, finance, history, politics, and sociology. The best teachers and writers in economics are well-read, well-travelled, and well-financed. Too often economics textbooks are written by thirty-something *wunderkinds* who know more about differential calculus than they do about managing a profitable business. That's why I prefer a Principles text written by a 48-year-old Alfred Marshall to one written by a 33-year-old Paul Samuelson. A youthful genius may write a brilliant textbook, but there is no substitute for experience.

*Economic Logic* would be a vastly different textbook if I had written it right after getting my Ph.D. I was tempted on many occasions during my career to write a Principles textbook, but more pressing needs kept me from it. Fortunately, I spent considerable years in apprenticeship running a publishing business, living in six countries, travelling and lecturing in 71 nations, consulting with large and small businesses, writing several dozen books on financial and economic topics, building an investment portfolio, and all the while acting out the role of entrepreneur, capitalist, consumer, and investor. I have also had the opportunity over the past twenty years of testing out my new models and theories before college and graduate students in Florida (Rollins College) and New York (Columbia University). If it hadn't been for these experiences, I doubt that I would have thought of introducing the income statement as a microeconomic technique in *Economic Logic*. In fact, my entire approach to supply and demand, elasticity, cost, competition, entrepreneurship, the stock market, and the very definition of economics itself has been colored by my experiences in the fast-moving world of economics and finance. Even the "problems to ponder" at the end of each chapter were developed over time. In many ways, therefore, *Economic Logic* is not the beginning of a sojourn, but an end-product.

—Mark Skousen
*New York*

*Chapter 1*

# WHAT IS ECONOMICS?

*". . . the desire of bettering our condition . . . comes with us from the womb,
and never leaves till we go into the grave."*

— ADAM SMITH
*The Wealth of Nations (1776)*

*"Capitalism is about turning luxuries into neccesities."*

— ANDREW CARNEGIE
(1873)

Ever since Adam and Eve were cast out of the Garden of Eden, human beings have worked by the sweat of their brow. For the vast majority of people life has been a struggle characterized by hard work and the necessity for problem solving. Few have enjoyed the luxury of extended leisure and material abundance.

Why do humans work? Throughout history, and throughout the world today, humans work to survive. Nature, although beautiful and inspiring, is also a harsh mistress. Very few of wants and needs can be satisfied without transforming natural resources into useful goods and services. Almost everything used or consumed must be made by man. Making raw materials useful and consumable requires dexterity, tools, and thought.

For many people the alternative to work is starvation. This is particularly true in underdeveloped nations. In more advanced nations, and for some fortunate people living in poor countries, citizens work for higher incomes and enjoy a higher standard of living. Higher incomes improve living standards.

The reasons for studying economics are straightforward. Economic desires encourage individuals to seek:

- Improvement in life circumstances
- Acquisition of money
- Having a well-paid and fulfilling job
- Acquiring more leisure time
- Increasing the quantity, quality, and variety of goods and services
- Expanding options for the individual

People living at a subsistence level may not feel these desires. Instead, these individuals may feel fatalistic about their future. The pleasures that may be obtained with money are unavailable to those living in reduced economic circumstances.

The modern world has seen a vast increase in the material well-being of humankind. Dramatic changes in society and city life—in transportation, communications, energy, building, medicine, and entertainment – have occurred in the past century. Per capita income and wages are often used by economists to measure a nation's standard of living. Figure 1.1 shows how dramatically per capita real wages (in constant dollars) have increased in the United States.

**Figure 1.1** *Real wages (excluding company benefits) have dramatically improved since 1890 as hours of work per week have declined.*

However, real wages do not always capture the significance of the dramatic material advances in the past two centuries. Figure 1.2 shows substantial economic progress for Americans, including the poor, into the 21st century. A more recent study by W. Michael Cox and Richard Alm, Figure 1.3, indicates that almost all Americans, including the poor, have advanced materially since the early 1970s.

Evidence of advancement is seen in additional areas. Since the beginning of the 20th century, average life expectancy has risen from 42 years to 75 years of age, while infant mortality has fallen from 200 deaths per 1,000 births to 11 per 1,000 births.

Improvements in sewage systems, water supply, food preparation, and medical technology have sharply reduced death and disease. Worker fatalities have dropped markedly during the past century. The overall accidental death rate has shown a steady decline in the past one hundred years (see figure 1.4).

Vacation time has increased this past century from two days a year to two weeks per year on average. Americans today work half as many hours in factories, farms and stores as they did when this century began. Kitchen appliances, canned foods and other household amenities have dramatically reduced household and family chores from 70 hours per week in 1900 to 30 hours today. In 1900 a typical

## LIVING STANDARDS HAVE RISEN DRAMATICALLY, EVEN FOR THE POOR

| Percentage of Households with . . . | Among all families in 1900 | Among poor families in 1970 |
|---|---|---|
| Flush toilets | 15% | 99% |
| Running water | 24% | 92% |
| Central heating | 1% | 58% |
| One (or fewer) occupants per room | 48% | 96% |
| Electricity | 3% | 99% |
| Refrigeration | 18% | 99% |
| Automobiles | 1% | 41% |

**Figure 1.2**

Source: Stanley Lebergott, *The American Economy* (Princeton, 1976), p. 8.

## MATERIAL ADVANCES FOR THE POOR SINCE 1971

| Percentage of Households with . . . | Poor Households 1984 | Poor Households 1994 | All Households 1971 |
|---|---|---|---|
| Washing machine | 58.2 | 71.7 | 71.3 |
| Clothes dryer | 35.6 | 50.2 | 44.5 |
| Dishwasher | 13.6 | 19.6 | 18.8 |
| Refrigerator | 95.8 | 97.9 | 83.3 |
| Freezer | 29.2 | 28.6 | 32.2 |
| Stove | 95.2 | 97.7 | 87.0 |
| Microwave | 12.5 | 60.0 | <1.0 |
| Color television | 70.3 | 92.5 | 43.3 |
| Videocassette recorder | 3.4 | 59.7 | 0 |
| Personal computer | 2.9 | 7.4 | 0 |
| Telephone | 71.0 | 76.7 | 93.0 |
| Air-conditioner | 42.5 | 49.6 | 31.8 |
| One or more cars | 64.1 | 71.8 | 79.5 |

**Figure 1.3**

Source: W. Michael Cox and Richard Alm, *Myths of Rich and Poor* (Basic Books, 1999), p.15.

housewife had to load her stove with tons of wood or coal each year and fill her lamps with coal, oil or kerosene. Nearly half of all American families drew water from farm wells for washing clothes, for baths, or for gardens. Today almost no one does these chores.[1]

Additional research by Cox and Alm demonstrate advances in practically every economic indicator of household behavior. See figure 1.3.

Even on a global basis, poverty has declined significantly. Figure 1.5 shows what percentage of the world population has lived on $1 a day over the past 200 years. In 1820, over 70% lived in dire poverty, in 1950 the percentage living on $1 a day was down to 50%, and today it's less than 20%.

1 Lebergott, S. *Pursuing Happiness: American Consumers in the Twentieth Century* (Princeton University Press, 1993).

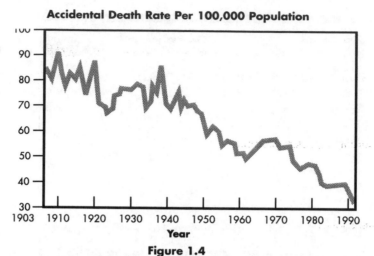

**Accidental Death Rate Per 100,000 Population**

**Figure 1.4**

Source: National Safety Council, *Wall Street Journal*, December 14, 1993, p. A17

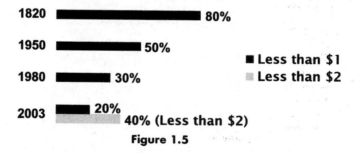

**Percentage World Population
Living on Less Than $1 per Day**

1820 ████████████████ 80%

1950 ██████████ 50%

1980 ██████ 30%

■ Less than $1
▨ Less than $2

2003 ████ 20%
      40% (Less than $2)

**Figure 1.5**

The above indicators of a rising standard of living are often lost in the maze of statistics about rising crime, abortion, unwed mothers, pollution and environmental destruction, the national debt, and so forth.

Not everyone has participated in this miracle of increasing prosperity, including millions of indigent and lower income individuals, but increased economic prosperity, advances in technology, and improved living conditions around the globe make it possible for more people to enjoy an improved living circumstance.

## WHAT IS ECONOMICS? *DEFINITIONS*

Economic science concerns itself with what Alfred Marshall calls "the ordinary business of life." The creation of wealth, income, living standards, and the production and distribution of goods and services—all aimed at improving our lot in life. In the broadest sense, then, economics can be defined as follows:

**Economics is the study of wealth and how it is created or diminished.**

## IMPROVEMENTS IN A VARIETY OF ECONOMIC INDICATORS SINCE 1970

| Item | 1970 | Mid-1990s* (1997) |
|---|---|---|
| Average size of new home (square feet) | 1,500 | 2,150 |
| Average household size (persons) | 3.14 | 2.64 |
| Average square feet per person in the household | 478 | 814 |
| New homes with central heat and air-conditioning | 34% | 81% |
| New homes with a garage | 58% | 87% |
| Housing units lacking complete plumbing[a] | 6.9% | 2.3% |
| Homes lacking a telephone[a] | 13.0% | 6.3% |
| Households with computer | 0% | 41% |
| Households with no vehicle[a] | 20.4% | 7.9% |
| Households with two or more vehicles[a] | 29.3% | 61.9% |
| Households with color TV | 34.0% | 97.9% |
| Households with cable TV | 6.3% | 63.4% |
| Households with two or more TV's | 30.7% | 72.8% |
| Households with videocassette recorder | 0% | 89% |
| Households with answering machine | 0% | 65% |
| Households with cordless phone | 0% | 66% |
| Households with computer printer | 0% | 38% |
| Households with camcorder | 0% | 26% |
| Households with cellular phone | 0% | 34% |
| Households with CD player | 0% | 49% |
| Households with clothes washer | 62.1% | 83.2% |
| Households with clothes dryer | 44.6% | 75.0% |
| Households with microwave | <1% | 89.5% |
| Households with coffeemaker | 88.6% | 99.9% |
| Households with dishwasher[b] | 26.5% | 54.6% |
| Households with vacuum cleaner | 92.0% | 99.9% |
| Households with frost-free refrigerator | <25% | 86.8% |
| Households with outdoor gas grill[c] | <5% | 28.5% |
| Mean household ownership of furniture[b] | $2,230 | $3,756 |
| Mean household ownership of appliances[b] | $943 | $1,547 |
| Mean household ownership of video and audio products[b] | $308 | $2,671 |
| Mean household ownership of jewelry and watches[b] | $728 | $1,784 |
| Mean household ownership of books and maps[b] | $731 | $1,074 |
| Mean household ownership of sports equipment[b] | $769 | $1,895 |
| Mean household net worth[a] | $86,095 | $126,843 |
| Median household net worth[a] | $27,938 | $59,398 |
| Vehicles per 100 persons aged 16 and older[a] | 53 | 94 |
| Work time to buy gas for a 100-mile trip | 49 minutes | 26 minutes |
| Annual visits to doctor[d] | 4.6 | 6.1 |
| Per capita consumption of bottled water (gallons)[b] | <1 | 11.1 |
| Americans taking cruises | 0.5 million | 4.7 million |
| Air-travel miles per capita | 646 | >2,260 |
| Per capita spending on sporting goods[b] | $60 | $213 |
| Recreational boats per 1000 households[a] | 139 | 173 |
| Manufacturers' shipments of recreational vehicles[a] | 30,300 | 281,000 |

*Mid-1990s data are for 1997, except where indicated.
[a]Data for 1995. [b]Data for 1996. [c]Data for 1993. [d]Data for 1994.
All monetary figures are in constant (1997) dollars.

Figure 1.6

Source: Cox and Alm, *Myths of Rich and Poor* (Basic Books, 1999), p. 7.

A central concept, that improved living standards can be achieved through the creation of wealth, will be referred to often throughout this text. How supply and demand, technology, competition, interest rates, employment, or government policy affect economic well-being is the ultimate goal of this discussion. Economic analysis can also be used to determine the cause of wealth destruction and the lowering of living standards by individuals, businesses and nations. Economics provides the tools to analyze negative economic impacts including fraud, theft, crime, false advertising, and government mismanagement.

## WHAT IS WEALTH?

**Wealth consists of goods and services that can be used to fulfill our immediate and future wants.**

Increasing wealth and improving the standard of living means an expansion in three things: the quantity, quality and variety of available goods and services. Increased wealth also means a good job and an enjoyable work environment, though any economic activity that improves the standard of living creates wealth and makes life more interesting, diverse, and fulfilling. In its broadest sense, economic growth signifies an expansion in the quantity, quality and variety of usable goods and services.

All human beings — rich and poor, white and black, male and female — attempt to improve their condition on earth. "If one wants a prosperous society—with resources available for the poor as well as the rich, with rising living standards, with technological progress that does everything from heal the sick to clean the environment—one needs a market economy."[2]

The purpose of sound economics is to outline a blueprint of prosperity for individuals and the world and provide a clear map to avoid the roads that lead to poverty and a lower standard of living. Throughout history, nations have been blessed by periods of prosperity, yet they have also suffered periodically from the pains of depression. By learning the principles of sound economics, stagnation can be avoided and sustained economic growth and improved living standards can be achieved.

## MONEY AND WEALTH

### Is money wealth?

Does a higher income suggest increased wealth? Probably, but only if more goods and services can be purchased with the additional income. If inflation rises and the prices of goods and services increase by more than increased income, a positive benefit does not accrue. In fact, the overall standard of living has declined because real income has declined after taking the loss of purchasing power into account.

2 Bandow, D. and Schindler, D. *Wealth, poverty, and human destiny.* (ISI Books. Willmington, DE., 2003)

Money is not a good or service. Money is a medium of exchange which facilitates the purchase of goods and services. Money has taken many forms including paper, metal, gems, and sea shells. Money can be commodity, fiat, or fiduciary in nature. Fiat money and fiduciary money are tokens and are distinct from commodity moneys. These token monies are the most important kinds of money in modern culture. The exchange of money for goods and services facilitates the wealth-creation process. Money, in any form, is only valuable as long as it has the capability of buying products and services. The value of money changes over time as the rate of inflation goes up and down.

## An experiment with a dollar bill

**Query:** An economics professor asks a student to come forward. In front of the entire class, she is asked to tear up a dollar bill. Following a little encouragement, she commits the deed.

*The question is: Has the student destroyed wealth?*

Some may say "Yes." The dollar bill represents a store of value based on past work, either by the student or perhaps by her father who gave her the dollar bill for lunch. Tearing up the dollar bill destroys the ability of the student to buy a snack. She has lost wealth and her standard of living has declined.

Others will dispute the loss of wealth. Has the destruction of this dollar bill reduced the number of chairs, pencils, or paper in the classroom? Has it eliminated the amount of food, clothing, cars, or buildings in the world? Has the lunch or snack disappeared? Clearly they have not. The snack is still available for someone, though perhaps not for this student. Therefore, they conclude, wealth has not been destroyed.

Who is right?

Both perspectives are correct. Wealth on a global or national scale has not been destroyed. The same amount of goods and services exist after the dollar is destroyed. The student's individual wealth declined, but everyone else's wealth appreciated in value because she tore up a dollar bill. Her wealth has been reduced while the rest of the world's wealth has slightly increased due to the increase in purchasing power caused by the reduction in the total amount of currency on hand. In other words, the tearing up of the dollar bill did not destroy wealth; it merely redistributed it.

What if the student breaks a pencil in half, making it unusable? Such an act would destroy wealth for her and for the community. Everyone is made worse off when goods and services are destroyed.

Focusing on making money instead of producing goods can be a distraction from the goal of increasing the standard of living. There are some cases where money making is not equivalent to increasing the standard of living—business and financial fraud, theft, embezzlement, and occupations that retard productive work. In these cases, people are getting money, but not contributing to the well-being of society.

### How Do the Factors of Production Impact Wealth?

Wealth is defined as goods and services that can be used to fulfill immediate and future wants. This definition implies that goods and services must be useful and practical to consumers in order to be of value. Finished consumer products include food, clothing, cars, houses and musical instruments. Services include medical care, financial services, education, maintenance, and other services that support and improve life.

Value is also placed on unfinished products—raw land, iron ore, forests, and other commodities. Wheat in its raw form is less valuable than the flour that commands a substantial price in the marketplace. Iron ore is useless in its natural state, but steel manufacturers are willing to pay a good price for it. Unfinished products are obtained from the land and are produced using capital goods. Land refers to the ground earth, natural resources and raw commodities that are available. Capital goods are the machinery, tools, and materials used in the production process toward final consumption.

The third factor in the production of goods and services is labor. Land, labor and capital goods are the trinity of the production process. The fourth factor of production, entrepreneurship, brings together the right amount of land, labor and capital to achieve economic goals. These four factors are the essential ingredients in transforming raw commodities and inputs into retail goods and services.

The price and value of labor and the other factors of production are ultimately determined by final consumer demand. This "theory of imputation" is discussed more in chapter 3.

The four factors of production (land, capital goods, labor, and entrepreneurship) impact wealth because they result in derived consumer value. The fact that consumer goods and services command value implies that the means of production also command value, for without land, labor, capital, and entrepreneurship, consumer goods could not be produced. Wealth consists of goods and services which fulfill immediate and future wants. Land, labor and capital also contribute to future needs and wants.

## IS LABOR WEALTH?

Labor is a crucial ingredient in the transformation of materials into finished products. Men and women use their physical and mental powers to produce useful goods and services. Workers supply their services in return for wages or salaries. A nation's wealth is measured in large part by the knowledge, skills and effort of its labor force. Labor is a significant part of wealth.

## HOW WEALTH IS CREATED

The goal of every worker in the economic process is straightforward. The average person works to earn more money so that he can meet his needs and enjoy life. Behind the desire for earning more money are more far-reaching goals: to pay for a child's college education, to have an adequate retirement income, to own a house, to pay off some debts, to have leisure time, or to contribute to a good cause.

Each worker plays a part in moving the production process along its way toward final consumer use and in creating wealth and a higher standard of living for everyone. Output is maximized when workers specialize to do the work they are best suited to do. For example:

Miners dig valuable metals and minerals out of the ground so that these metals and minerals can be manufactured into more usable commodities. Iron ore is made into steel, clay into copper, and rock into gold.

Manufacturers transport raw commodities and other materials and transform them into more usable products.

Chemists, biologists, physicists and engineers analyze the properties of organic and inorganic elements and test them in laboratories to make better and more useful products.

Salespeople make consumers aware of the products that are available for consumption, and facilitate purchasing by providing information to consumers.

Artists create an image for their customers to enjoy.

Bankers provide a variety of services which allow business people to engage in profitable enterprises and they provide a more convenient way for consumers to pay their bills, borrow money, and fulfill their desires.

Teachers help students to acquire useful knowledge and skills.

The list of activities is endless, but the purpose behind these activities is the same—transforming unfinished goods toward final use by consumers.

15

## ETHICS IN ECONOMICS

In every job or profession, there are individuals whose actions are harmful to society. Manufacturers who produce shoddy products, salespeople who defraud, employers who mistreat their workers, doctors who engage in malpractice, lawyers who take advantage of the system. These and others take advantage of their position or skills to harm the public. Ethical practices in business include the following:

- Commitment to customer satisfaction
- Clear, honest, and accurate representation of products, services, terms and conditions.
- Delivery of products and services as represented
- Respectful and courteous communications
- Timely and constructive response to inquiries and complaints
- Implementation of policies and practices to safeguard information and to limit information distribution
- Respect for client rights and requests
- Adherence to the spirit and letter of the law
- Protection of human and environmental rights

## THE PROCESS OF WEALTH CREATION

Economics is concerned with five major questions:

**What** should be produced? (Consumer goods, capital goods?)

**For whom** should the products and services be produced? (Consumers, producers, foreigners?)

**How much** should be produced? (A million cars, a dozen concerts a year?)

**How should** goods be produced? (What materials? What process? How much labor? How much machinery?)

**When** should it be produced? (How long will it take to build that building? Finish college?)

These questions reflect the critical concerns of every producer in the marketplace. Every good and service goes through a basic process. Figure 1.7 illustrates this process.

**NATURAL RESOURCES**

**INTERMEDIATE GOODS AND SERVICES**

**FINAL GOODS AND SERVICES**

**Figure 1.7.** *How wealth is created.*

The basic purpose of economic activity is to turn **unfinished, unusable goods into finished, usable goods**. Cooperation between materials and land owners, producers, those who fund production, and workers is required at every stage of production in order to bring useful goods and services to the consumer.

## IS ECONOMICS ONLY CONCERNED WITH MATERIAL GOODS?

The study of economics has often been criticized as a science of materialism and greed, focusing excessively on material possessions and the philosophy that "more is better." Is this a valid criticism? Economics is concerned with what is produced and for whom. Abraham Maslow defined a hierarchy of needs that must be met in order.

- Biological and physiological needs
- Safety needs
- "Belongingness" and love needs
- Esteem needs
- Self actualization needs

In order to survive, every person must first take care of essential needs such as food, water, shelter, and clothing. These essential needs are material in nature. Once these basic needs are met, however, people are free to seek numerous non-material desires, whether intellectual, social, or spiritual. Most economic concerns are directly related to biological, physiological, and safety needs. However, economic security allows individuals to pursue other needs. Services provided by doctors, lawyers, ministers, educators, entertainers, and sports figures go beyond material needs.

The free-enterprise system, with its constant emphasis on providing and developing products and services meeting new and varied wants, often provides a blizzard of material offerings for the consumer. Becoming caught up in a material world, always seeking and demanding more, is a logical outgrowth of consumerism, but access to more goods and services does not always improve the quality of life.

## MORALITY AND ECONOMICS

The market produces some products and services that may be objectionable to some consumers. For example, there are firms engaged in the production of mind-changing drugs, prostitution, X-rated movies, cigarettes, moonshine, bullfights and illegal weapons. Economists do not justify the public's appetite for these controversial "goods," but believe that an unhampered market does an efficient job in reflecting the wants and desires of the public whether good or bad. Economists tend to avoid making moral judgments, leaving it up to consumers to decide for themselves what to buy or not buy. Economics as a science should be "value free."

At the same time, it is important to note that in a free society, individuals can choose for themselves what kinds of products and services they produce or consume. One person may work at a cigarette factory, another may choose to work for an accounting firm. One person may come home from work, turn on the television and drink a beer, while another may spend the evening as a volunteer at a local hospital. People can choose not to participate in a capitalist world they regard as "greedy and materialistic." Furthermore, a sufficient income and net worth may allow an individual to retire from the world of business and finance and devote more time to charitable, religious, or political causes. The freedom to make choices is essential to economic health.

Issues related to morality and economics include:
- What is produced and for what purpose?
- Who can purchase specified goods and services?
- What consumer protections exist?
- What is the role of government in production?
- How is access to good and services provided to individuals?
- Can quality and safety objectives be met during production?
- How is equitable distribution of goods and services provided?
- Is it possible to balance the needs and wants of a diverse population?

## INCOME AND WEALTH DISTRIBUTION

Economists are also interested in how well individuals and groups participate in the economy. Driving their interest are the questions:

For whom are the goods and services produced?

Can only the wealthy members of the community afford goods and services like automobiles, nice houses, education, or skilled medical care?

Are certain individuals or groups given special privileges and benefits?

Are disadvantaged Americans able to fully participate in the American Dream? (See figure 1.2)

Are the real wages of unskilled workers keeping up with skilled workers?

Are all citizens taxed fairly by the government?

Can the basic needs of middle-class families be met?

Do CEOs get paid too much relative to the average workers of a corporation?

These issues of relative equality of income, opportunity, and wealth are frequently debated and reflect concern about the impact of economics on individuals and groups in an increasingly commercial world.

## WASTE AND POLLUTION

One major area of growing concern is the issue of pollution and the environment. When natural resources are transformed into consumer and capital goods, there are various forms of waste and pollution at virtually every stage of production. As economies have expanded and matured, the management and reduction of waste and pollution have become critical concerns.

## THE ROLE OF GOVERNMENT

A paramount issue relates to the role of government in the economy. Consider the following questions:

Is it possible to produce all the goods and services necessary for a fulfilling life in a completely voluntary society? Or is it necessary to have the government—the agency of force—produce certain goods and services (known as "public goods")?

Can the free-enterprise system provide an adequate supply of roads, utilities, police, prisons, and courts of law?

Can the free-enterprise system produce a sufficient defense system against foreign aggression?

Can the free-enterprise system create its own stable monetary system?

How can the free market deal with the problem of consumer fraud and deceptive business practices?

Can the marketplace and trade operate without strict enforcement of individual property rights?

If government is necessary to produce some public goods, can government expenditures be financed through voluntary contributions instead of coercive taxation?

What kind of government, and how much of it, is optimal?

These issues will be considered in forthcoming chapters.

## MAIN POINTS COVERED IN CHAPTER 1:

1. Very few usable goods are provided by nature; almost all consumer goods (and many services) must be manufactured through production processes.

2. Economics is the study of wealth and how individuals improve their standard of living.

3. Wealth consists of goods and services that fulfill immediate and future wants.

4. Society becomes wealthier by increasing the quantity, quality, and variety of goods and services.

5. Money represents wealth only to the extent that it provides purchasing power to buy goods and services.

6. The creation or destruction of money does not change the amount of wealth in society, but merely redistributes wealth among society's members.

7. The three primary factors of production—land, labor, and capital—constitute wealth because they derive their value from final consumer demand.

8. Actors in the marketplace—landlords, workers and capitalists—do more than merely "make money"—they are helping transform unfinished goods into products and services that consumers can use, and thus enhance people's standard of living.

9. The marketplace does not produce only material goods, but the market also produces non-material services of intellectual, social, or spiritual value.

10. Relative equality of income, wealth and opportunity are controversial issues that concern all members of society, including economists.

11. Waste management and pollution control have become a growing concern as society expands and matures.

12. Government may have to provide certain public goods and services that the private marketplace may not adequately provide for.

## IMPORTANT TERMS

Economics

Wealth

Quantity, quality and variety

Goods and services

Money and exchange

Factors of production

Land

Labor

Capital

Capital goods

Derived value

Means of production

Division of labor

## INFLUENTIAL ECONOMIST

## ADAM SMITH AND THE WEALTH OF NATIONS

**Name: Adam Smith (1723-90)**

**Background:** Scottish philosopher, economist and professor. Considered the founder of modern economics, although physiocrats Richard Cantillon (1680-1734) and Jacques Turgot (1727-81) also qualify as influential "pre-Adamites." Smith is also regarded as the founding father of the British classical school (followed by David Ricardo, John Stuart Mill, and Alfred Marshall).

**Major Work:** Author of the most famous book in economics, *An Inquiry into the Nature and Causes of the Wealth of Nations*. Proclaimed an unabashed endorsement of democratic capitalism, it was appropriately published in 1776, the year of the American Revolution and the signing of the Declaration of Independence. Today a collector might pay over $100,000 for a first edition of the two-volume work, assuming he could find one.

**Strengths:** Adam Smith considered wealth and economic growth to be the focal point of economic analysis, an approach we have appropriately followed. Smith rejected the mercantilist view that wealth arose from the acquisition of gold and silver, but instead arose from the production of goods and services.

Anyone who has taken the time to read Smith's biblical tome can see why it has received widespread praise—it is a grand book, full of interesting facts, cogent criticisms, and fascinating philosophical points.

Smith's strengths lie in his analysis of how individual liberty, economic freedom, and capital investment create wealth, and how government policies of high taxes, deficit spending, and commercial regulations restrict productivity, growth and freedom.

**Weaknesses:** Smith sometimes contradicted himself and led economics down some strange roads—his bias toward agriculture, his bizarre distinction between productive and unproductive labor, and his "labor theory of value," which was fully exploited by Karl Marx, the German economist and father of revolutionary socialism. *The Wealth of Nations* failed to explain the "diamond-water paradox" (why is "useful" water so cheap, while "impractical" diamonds are so expensive?) even though Smith's lecture notes of a decade earlier had solved the theory of value based on the principle of marginal subjectivism. Smith's notorious lapse of memory set the economics profession back generations; it was nearly a century later, in the 1870s, that the marginalist revolution was rediscovered by Carl Menger (Austrian), William Stanley Jevons (British) and Leon Walras (French-Swiss).

**Sample Quotation:** "To prohibit a great people, however, from making all that they can of every part of their own produce, or from employing their stock and industry in the way that they judge most advantageous to themselves, is a manifest violation of the most sacred rights of mankind."

**Most Famous Idea:** The doctrine of "Invisible Hand," that the unintentional acts of self-interest in business lead to the general welfare of the public. "It is not from the benevolence of the butcher, the brewer, or the baker, that we expect our dinner, but from their regard to their own interest."

**Personality:** Adam Smith was the quintessential absent-minded professor. Though a member of many gentlemen's clubs and societies, he never married and never had a serious relationship with any woman. His closest friend was philosopher David Hume (1711-76). Smith was so preoccupied with work that he frequently found himself lost in town or fallen into a muddy hole. He spent ten years writing his 900-page magnum opus after traveling in Europe. Ironically, Smith ended his career as an agent of British customs and contrary to his free-trade beliefs, strongly enforced the mercantilist trade laws and cracked down on smugglers. He died in 1790 and was buried in Edinburgh.

## PROBLEMS TO PONDER

1. Standard of living is reduced when goods and services are destroyed in a society. These questions help to put this statement into perspective:
   - Is war good for the economy?
   - Can you identify advances in medicine and technology as a result of war?
   - Are the tools of modern science still beneficial when converted to instruments of war?

- Is dynamite a benefit to humankind when it helps build a tunnel but harmful when it destroys a bridge?

2. Determine which of the following activities increases or decreases society's wealth:

   a. A lucky person wins five million dollars in the Florida state lottery.

   b. An investor sells a stock and doubles his money.

   c. A thief breaks into a house and steals some jewelry.

   d. Government spends more money on unemployment compensation.

3. Which of the following statements (taken from textbooks) best describes your definition of economics?:

   a. "Economics is the study of choice." (Buchholz)

   b. "Economics is the study of how scarce resources are allocated among competing ends." (Ruffin & Gregory)

   c. "Economics is the study of how societies use scarce resources to produce valuable commodities and distribute them among different groups." (Samuelson & Nordhaus)

   d. "The problem of economic society is, in large part, to change land—that is, natural resources—into finished goods, and to place those goods in the hands of the persons who will consume them." (Gemmill & Blodgett)

   e. Develop your own definition of economics.

4. Contrast our definition of economics (economics is the study of wealth and how it is created or diminished) with the following: "Perhaps the best way to define economics is to pose a series of four basic questions:

   a. Who does the work?

   b. Who owns the factors of production—tools, machines, factories, land and raw materials?

   c. How are the basic economic decisions made about production and distribution?

   d. What are peoples' lives like?"

5. A student is assigned to find out how many different kinds of bread are sold in a local grocery store. Is the number above (a) 20, (b) 30, (c) 40, or (d) 50? Has the variety of goods increased over time?

6. A student is assigned to find out how many different kinds and sizes (packages) of beer are sold in a local liquor store. Have the store manager give the student a printout of all varieties and sizes of beer. Then have the student report to the class. Before the student reports, poll the other students to see how many types and varieties of beer they think are sold.

7. Many people say that their standard of living, as measured by real income or wages, declined over the past decade or two. ~~Is this true?~~ Have the quantity, quality and variety of goods and services declined over the past 10 years? (electronics, office machines, telecommunications, food, clothing, automobiles, etc.)

8. Politicians bemoan the decline in the U. S. manufacturing sector, asserting that it reflects a decline in our nation's standard of living. Is this correct? What other sectors of the economy have counterbalanced this decline?

9. Name some examples of unfulfilled wants and needs in the marketplace. Why are these wants and needs not being met?

10. Give some examples of goods or services which have declined in quality over the past few years. Why is it an exception to the rule that quality increases for goods and services over time?

11. Is one's standard of living the same as one's quality of life? Can a person be materially well-off (high standard of living), but unhappy (low quality of life)?

12. "When a baby dies, the nation's per-capita income rises. When a baby is born, per capita income falls. Death, in sum, reduces poverty and increases per capita welfare." How do these statements relate to the following questions:
    * Does death increase welfare?
    * Does the birth of a child constitute an increase or decrease in a nation's wealth?
    * What are the benefits of an increasing population? What are the disadvantages?
    * On net balance, is population growth good or bad?

13. Suppose Japan's per capita income is twice the United States' per capita income, when both are measured in U. S. dollars.
    * Does this mean that the average Japanese is wealthier than the average American?
    * What factors should be considered in comparing one country's standard of living with another?
    * Are international comparisons legitimate?

14. Figure 1.8 introduces an alternative indicator of economic well-being, "Genuine Progress Indicator," which takes social and ecological factors into consideration (resource depletion, income distribution, unemployment and underemployment, long-term environmental damage, etc.) Evaluate this new definition of economic progress. Do you concur with the proponents of GPI, that "the overall health of the [U. S.] economy shows a steady decline since the 1970s"?

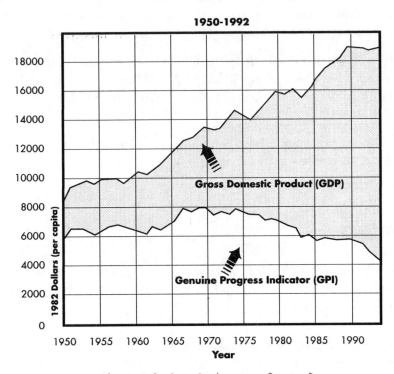

**1950-1992**

**Figure 1.8.** *Gross Production vs. Genuine Progress.*

15. Select a country and determine how much progress has been made over the past fifty 50 years in terms of percentage of citizens having appliances, automobiles, and other consumer goods. How does this country compare with the United States?

16. Textbook writers Ruffin and Gregory state, "Economics cannot teach you how to be rich." Do you agree? If so, what do you hope to gain from your study of economics?

17. British economist David Ricardo attempted to change the approach of economic inquiry. In a letter to Thomas Malthus, he wrote, "Political economy, you think, is an enquiry into the nature and causes of wealth; I think it should rather be called an enquiry into the laws which determine the division of the produce of industry amongst the classes who concur in its formation." What effect would Ricardo's shift away from production and toward distribution have on the world's attitude toward capitalism? How was Karl Marx influenced by Ricardo's approach?

18. Do retired workers create wealth, or are they simply consumers who make no further contributions to productivity? (Hint: Where do retirees invest their retirement funds?)

19. List as many products as you can that did not exist 30 years ago. Then make a list of products that are no longer used. Which list is larger? Why?

20. There was once a billionaire who died single in a small country and requested that all his wealth be converted to cash and burned at a public bonfire, so that he could benefit everyone in his country. What was he thinking? Did he accomplish his goal?

21. John Stuart Mill said, "There is nothing more insignificant than money." Given what was discussed in this chapter, what did he mean?

## FOR ADDITIONAL READING

- Adam Smith, *The Wealth of Nations* (1776). A classic work still worth reading today. Various editions are available, but my favorite is the Modern Library "Cannan" Edition.

- Stanley Lebergott, *Pursuing Happiness: American Consumers in the Twentieth Century* (Princeton University Press, 1993). Lebergott is professor emeritus of Wesleyan University and an expert on the American economy of the 20th century. His book is full of amazing accounts about American households and how living conditions improved dramatically over the years.

- W. Michael Cox and Richard Alm, *Myths of Rich and Poor* (Basic Books, 1999). This is the most optimistic book I've read on new ways to measure economic well-being, the benefits of downsizing, and the dynamics of the U. S. economy. Fascinating reading.

- Nathan Rosenberg and L. E. Birdzell, Jr., *How the West Grew Rich* (Basic Books, 1986). An excellent history of Western economic development from the Middle Ages to the present.

# Chapter 2

# THE FUNDAMENTALS OF ECONOMIC BEHAVIOR

*"I can calculate the motions of heavenly bodies, but not the madness of crowds."*

—Sir Isaac Newton
(1721)

The previous chapter outlined the first law of economic behavior: All human action is aimed at improving one's situation. Every job, every exchange, every production process, and every effort attempts to substitute a better condition for the previous state of affairs. Not everyone succeeds in achieving an improved circumstance goal, and there are numerous failures on the road to success. Ultimately, most people seek and eventually achieve a wealthier state where a greater quantity, quality, and variety of goods and services are at their disposal.

This chapter introduces the fundamental nature of human behavior that forms the foundation of economics and considers the following questions:

- How do people solve the economic problem of transforming natural resources into usable goods and services?
- What goods and services do people desire?
- How can people best acquire wealth and a higher standard of living?
- What limitations and roadblocks exist in human society that make it more difficult to satisfy individual wants and needs?
- How do people choose among a variety of desires, given limited funds and resources?

## BUILDING BLOCKS OF THE WORLD ECONOMY

The world is marked by two essential characteristics that form the foundation of economic activity. These two fundamental characteristics are the critical starting point of economic reasoning.

**The two basic principles of human action are:**

1.  People's wants and desires are virtually unlimited.
2.  Resources for the fulfillment of wants and desires are limited and largely unusable in their natural state.

These two characteristics of the world form the basis of the universal economic problem: How can insatiable desires be fulfilled with the limited resources available on earth?

On the one hand, humans have unlimited wants, needs, and goals. On the other hand, there are limited means—limited time, limited funds, and limited resources—with which to achieve those ends.

Means and ends, constraints and preferences, supply and demand. These are what economics is all about. As the word "economics" implies, the fact that unlimited wants clash with limited means imposes the need to economize, i.e., to use resources judiciously and effectively to achieve as many desires as possible.

## INSATIABLE WANTS

Chapter 1 introduced the purpose of economic activity: to build wealth, as measured by the quantity, quality, and variety of goods and services.

People are constantly striving to achieve, which suggests that needs, wants, and goals remain unfulfilled and that wants and desires are insatiable. People are better off with more wealth (material and immaterial) than less.

## NEEDS vs. WANTS

Are needs and wants different? Needs imply the basics—goods and services everyone demands in order to survive. Food, clothing, and housing represent basic needs. Such basic needs can be fulfilled in this life. We may have enough to eat, all the clothes we need, a car to drive, and a house to live in, and we may not need any more material possessions to be content.

Needs cannot always be precisely defined. It is human nature to expand the definition of "needs." Today's needs may have been luxuries a generation ago. Basic necessities today may include a television, central heating and air conditioning, and a dishwasher. Yesterday's luxuries have become today's necessities. Some economists assert that it is impossible to distinguish in general between needs and wants.

Beyond needs are wants, people want better food and a greater variety to choose from. They want nicer clothes and finer furniture. They sometimes like to go to the movies instead of just sitting at home watching television. They desire leisure time to read, play, travel, spend time with friends and relatives, or help others in need. Once one desire is met, another seems to replace it almost instantly.

People's wants change over time according to income, experience and influence. There is a never-ending process of satisfying infinite wants. The world is full of diversity in individual tastes and desires. As Samuel Johnson said, "We desire, we pursue, we obtain, we are satiated; we desire something else, and begin a whole new pursuit."[1] Finally, people's tastes are different. One person likes to drive a Ford, another likes Toyota. One person likes Chinese food, another likes Italian. The demand for goods and services, both material and ethereal, is unlimited and diverse.

## RESOURCES AND THE PROBLEM OF SCARCITY

First Corollary: Resources are limited.

Availability is one thing that keeps everyone from satisfying all of their wide-ranging desires. Resources include the following:

- Land and natural resources
- Supplies (working capital)
- Equipment, tools, and machinery (fixed capital goods)
- Money (investment capital)
- Labor (human resources)
- Entrepreneurship
- Time

Every productive activity involves the use of the above resources. These resources are used to create goods and services that fulfill wants and needs.

## RESOURCES: ABUNDANT OR SCARCE?

The earth has an abundance of natural resources with which to fulfill needs and wants. The world has the capability of providing food, clothing, housing, and other necessities of life. There are enough crude oil, forests, iron ore, and other natural resources to meet the needs of this, and future, generations. It seems that every time one group of scientists warns about the imminent depletion of an unrenewable

1  Quoted in Walter Jackson Bate, *Samuel Johnson* (New York, 1977), p. 330.

commodity, another group of scientists discovers a new source for that commodity or a substitute for it. In the late 19th century, scientists warned of depleting whale oil as a light source. Entrepreneurs soon discovered petroleum as a more abundant substitute. Necessity is often the mother of invention.

Nevertheless, all resources are limited in one way or another. At any given moment, there is only a certain amount available of crude oil, timber, wheat, or other natural resources.

In addition to limited natural resources, there is also limited time, expertise, ability, and funding. Resources of all types may be unevenly distributed creating advantages for individuals, organizations, or countries that have more resources than others. The need to acquire additional resources results in trade, negotiation, bartering, and other means of getting necessary resources.

## MAKING RESOURCES USABLE:

The second corollary is that almost all resources must be changed in order to be usable. Raw commodities require processing before consumption or use. Processing involves the use of tools to transform raw materials into usable goods. Imagine if you were Robinson Crusoe on an uninhabited island. How could you fish without a fishing pole? You want the bearskin to keep you warm, but how will you kill the bear without a gun or a bow and arrow? You need shelter, but how will you build it without an ax and other tools. Usable tools and finished goods are essential, yet nature does not provide them—they must be manufactured. Your task of creating usable goods from resources unusable in their natural state would be daunting—a painstaking exercise of hard work, intelligence, and trial and error.

Want/need identified
 Raw materials obtained
  Resources (workers) assigned
   Materials transformed into usable goods/services
    Goods/services used
     New wants/needs identified

As the population of the world increases, known reserves of oil, gas, minerals, timber, chemicals, and other basic commodities are being consumed rapidly. New reserves and alternative sources of commodities are always being sought and efforts are constantly made to conserve scarce resources and control consumer demand.

Even though nations such as Russia, Brazil, and South Africa are endowed with abundant natural resources, these resources cannot be made instantly and freely usable. Exploiting natural resources requires investment in infrastructure, equipment, labor, knowledge, and transportation.

## THE COST OF DISTRIBUTION

Moving goods, people and information is critical to fulfilling people's wants and needs. The distribution of goods and services from one stage of production to the next is a major cost factor for any firm. Goods must be transported from where they are produced to where they will be consumed or used. The process of distribution costs money, involves human resources and uses time.

## POLLUTION AND WASTE

Air may be one of the few commodities that is unlimited and considered to be virtually free. But even air is not free in every situation. In outer space, air is not free. Nor is fresh air unlimited in cities where pollution is a problem. Other resources necessary for sustaining human life, such as water, may also be affected by production processes.

Useless by-products and pollution are unavoidable in a world where resources need to be transformed into practical, finished products. An environment completely free of garbage and by-products is impossible to achieve, but pollution can be minimized. For example, used by-products can often be recycled to reduce waste. It is the role of the entrepreneur/capitalist to engage in waste management.

## TIME AND DEPRECIATION

Time is also a precious resource and a critical element in the economic process. Time is a resource which renews itself every 24 hours, cannot be banked for future use, and is available to all in the same increments. The use of time is a controllable factor in the production process, but it may not be slowed down or speeded up. Students are cognizant of how long it takes to graduate from college and graduate school. Engineers measure how many years it takes to construct a building or to manufacture a turbine. Movie producers contemplate how long it takes a film to

31

reach production and distribution, and how costly delays are. When purchasing a new car, customers take into account the average time a car will last. The time it takes to produce and consume products is an essential feature of any economy. The use of time impacts production and cost of goods and services.

Suppose a firm is considering a new process that will cut in half the time it takes to make a television set. Will it adopt this breakthrough process? Not necessarily. What if the new process takes five years to set up and is only marginally more profitable than the current process? The new process might not be worth the time and cost involved to implement it. However, sometimes engineers and political leaders have a hard time understanding the real costs involved in a project. Just because a new process is technically feasible does not mean it is economically justifiable. Effective use of time is measured by what can be done in a given time period balanced against the cost of doing the work in that time period.

Time is a critical element in all economic decision-making. Important questions to ask about time are:

- How much time will the needed activity take? (Duration)
- How much time is available for doing the activity? (Minutes, hours, days, ...)
- How many people will be involved in the activity? (Manpower)
- Must the activity be completed in a certain time frame? (Critical)
- What is the cost for the time?

Time limitations also suggest that man-made capital and consumer goods are always deteriorating—sometimes gradually, sometimes rapidly. Machines, houses, and clothing wear out and need repairing or replacement from time to time. Every successful business puts aside a certain amount of money each year to cover the cost of depreciation.

## THE UNIVERSAL ECONOMIC PROBLEM

The need to balance limited resources and unlimited wants is the hub of economic considerations. How can limited supplies (including resources and time) be used to satisfy unlimited wants? This is the economic problem that all individuals and all societies face. Every participant in the economy must make choices, and every decision has a cost.

Clearly, choices must be made by both the consumer and the producer. The consumer must decide: Should I buy X or Y brand of cereal? Should I work or play? Should I read a book or go to a concert? The producer must decide: Should automobiles be built with workers' hands (labor) or robots (capital goods)? Should television sets be made out of plastic or aluminum? Will a builder use wood or brick in a new housing development? Should a highway construction company use a cheaper asphalt that lasts five years, or an expensive asphalt that lasts 10 years? Should a city build another highway or a subway? Which choice of inputs will best satisfy the demands of consumers? These are the kinds of questions an economic society must address.

Transportation offers a good example of the kinds of choices that both consumers and producers must make. Suppose you live in London and wish to go to Paris. You can fly, take the train and ferry, or take the EuroTunnel (or Chunnel, as it is affectionately called). Flying is faster, but more expensive. As a consumer of this service, you must decide how valuable your time is. Wealthier customers tend to fly, while poorer customers take the train and ferry. The reason? High-income people typically value time more than lower-income people do.

Producers also have to make decisions. Suppose you are the president of EuroTunnel and wish to build a tunnel under the English Channel. By building EuroTunnel, you will provide a third alternative to travelers—a simple train ride between London and Paris. Instead of taking eight hours to travel from London to Paris, EuroTunnel can get your there in three. You know that from an engineering and technical viewpoint, it is feasible to build an underwater tunnel, but what is the cost? Is the risk sufficiently manageable to produce a decent profit, given the alternative ways to travel?

These are the kind of choices producers, consumers and investors need to make. Providers of goods and services balance the cost of production against potential profit while potential consumers balance cost of purchase against the value to them of the good or service vs. the value of alternative goods or services.

## COMPETITION AND COOPERATION

The universal economic problem (the need to balance limited resources and unlimited wants) leads us to two other principles of economics:

1. Competition
2. Cooperation

Competition is the inevitable result of a society facing insatiable demands and limited supply. All societies must choose among a limited number of resources in order to achieve certain goals. Not all goals can be attained; only those that are deemed the most valuable will be fulfilled. If one course of action is chosen, it means giving up another choice, at least in the short run.

33

When you choose a specific action, you must give up doing something else. For example:

| Choice 1 | Alternative 1 |
| --- | --- |
| Go to school full time | Be employed full time at work |
| Marry Sue | Marry Betty |
| Travel to Europe on business | Attend son's soccer match |
| Invest savings in business | Earn 5% in a money market fund |

Economists refer to these decisions as **opportunity costs**. Opportunity cost is defined as the value of the next best alternative or foregone activity.

Cooperation is also universal in the world economy. All factors of production—land, labor, capital and entrepreneurship—are necessary to transform intermediate products into useful final goods and services. Landlords, laborers, and capitalists must work together to make goods usable. This complementary effort requires economic harmony among players. If one player does not cooperate the production process breaks down and work remains undone. Land, labor and capital are complementary factors of production.

The market economy is not just a competitive process—cooperation is just as vital in all aspects of the market economy. The market economy is always both competitive and cooperative. People compete to obtain cooperative relationships.

## INEQUALITY: BOON OR BANE?

Human and capital resources are not only limited, but they are distributed unevenly throughout the world and among people. Tastes, talents, and resources are not equal among individuals and nations. People differ in their intelligence, physical abilities, and circumstances. Some nations, such as the United States and Saudi Arabia, are blessed with an abundance of crude oil, while others, such as Japan and Israel, are not. Each person and each nation has advantages and disadvantages, assets and liabilities.

Society is made of diverse individuals with varied intelligence, talents, and assets who represent different creeds, races, and cultures. What constitutes wealth consists of different goods and services for each individual. People are as different as the cars they drive, the food they eat, and the books they read. People choose their own careers according to their abilities, interests, and qualifications. Such diversity results in a wide degree of specialization and expertise. Without differences and inequalities, our lives would lack diversity, achievement, color and surprise.

Because of inequality and limited resources, human beings are seldom completely self-sufficient. They need the help and expertise of others. Individuals specialize in occupations or businesses, and exchange goods and services according to each participant's ability. Individualized specialization in occupations reflects each individual's abilities and interests. Services are provided to others based on their individual needs and wants by those who have the skills and abilities to meet these needs and wants. Limitations of time and resources result in specialization and division of labor by individuals and firms in the marketplace.

The entrepreneur plays a central role in the creation of wealth based on the underlying axioms of human action referred to above. Individual nations also specialize in certain goods or services. Economists call this comparative advantage.

## THE LAW OF COMPARATIVE ADVANTAGE

The law of comparative advantage allows individuals, businesses and nations to produce goods and services at the lowest cost relative to another. This vital concept was originally developed by David Ricardo in the early 19th century. Comparative advantage allows everyone to play an important role in the economy. Comparative advantage means that economic gain occurs when the items are produced or services are provided that can be most efficiently produced/provided.

To illustrate comparative advantage, suppose a top medical surgeon is also the fastest typist in town. He can type 150 words per minute. Even though he is a superior typist, he is likely to hire a secretary to type for him. Why? Suppose he makes $500,000 a year working full time as a surgeon. If he spends half his time doing secretarial work, he would make only $250,000 a year as a surgeon and $50,000 as a secretary or $300,000, $200,000 less than he would make as a full-time surgeon. But by hiring a full-time secretary for $50,000 a year, he would make $450,000 ($500,000 minus $50,000, the cost of a secretary). His opportunity cost is the lost income from his medical practice, which is substantial.

The medical doctor has a comparative advantage in performing surgeries, while his secretary has a comparative advantage in secretarial work. By hiring a secretary, both the MD and the secretary benefit.

## THE ROLE OF THE ENTREPRENEUR

The entrepreneur also plays a vital role in the economy. The word "entrepreneur" comes from the French word *entreprendre*, which means "to undertake." It forms the basis of the English word, "enterprise." The French economist J. B. Say invented the word to mean "venture capitalist" or "adventurer."

Entrepreneurs are the business owners and producers who assume the risk, uncertainty, and responsibility of running an enterprise. They seek to meet the needs and wants of consumers through innovation, technological change, and increasing capital expenditures. Without this decision-maker, economic performance and living standards would not be advanced. As historian Robert Sobel writes, entrepreneurs are "men and women of vision and energy [who] have seen possibilities where others saw none, seized opportunities when others hesitated, persevered when others gave up."[2]

Entrepreneurs are innovators who reshape patterns of production and distribution, develop new products and processes, open new markets and sources of supply, devise new forms of organizations, and improve existing companies. They are alert to opportunities and new ways of accomplishing tasks. Like all participants in the marketplace, entrepreneurs specialize in what they know best.

Entrepreneurs are also speculators who seek a profit in the stock, commodity, and foreign currency markets, or who take advantage of discrepancies between markets for the same good. They may try to take over existing companies considered to be undervalued or mismanaged. They are opportunity seekers and visionary organizers who bring together capitalists, landlords, workers, and specialized knowledge to create goods and services that they hope consumers will buy. Entrepreneurship is often a discovery process. For the entrepreneur, the future is uncertain and highly risky at times. Many fail, but those who succeed are usually well rewarded.

Speculators are often viewed in a negative light, allegedly causing crises and chaos. But speculators are often the only ones willing to assume the risks of volatile price changes that affect farmers, importers, exporters, and other hedgers in the marketplace.

Entrepreneurs drive the engines of wealth. They are the market decision-makers. In a very real sense, the market process is entrepreneur-driven.

## HUMAN ACTION AND MEANINGFUL BEHAVIOR

People act purposefully to achieve their ends. All human action is purposeful behavior aimed at substituting a more satisfactory condition for a less satisfactory state of affairs. To accomplish their goals, people think, feel, learn, value and act. They produce and consume, buy and sell. Behind every service or commodity are the decisions of numerous individuals who are involved in the economic process, each of whom acted with a purpose in mind.

Behind every price are the buying and selling decisions of numerous individuals, each acting with some purpose in mind. Human action is never random,

2  Robert Sobel and David B. Sicilia, *The Entrepreneurs: An American Adventure*
(Boston: Houghton Mifflin, 1986), flyleaf.

although another person's actions may appear random or irrational because the reasons for their actions are unknown to us.

Purposeful human action is distinct from the actions of plants, animals, and mechanical things. Biological and physical laws appear constant and quantifiable. Physicists and chemists note a regular and repeatable pattern in physical events. Using the scientific method, they can repeatedly perform a controlled experiment and expect that the results are consistent. Animal and plant life also tend to react the same way under the same set of circumstances, like Pavlov's dog or lemmings returning to the sea. The movement of molecules or ping pong balls may seem random, but their movements conform to physical laws.

Not so in economics and other sciences that study human behavior. Humans are not machines or lemmings destined to repeat themselves exactly time after time or respond the same way to specific stimuli. Because human beings possess the ability to think, learn, and change their minds, they cannot be treated as dumb animals or machines. As the Chinese philosopher Lin Yutang puts it, man "does not react to surroundings mechanically and uniformly as animals do, but possesses the ability and the freedom to determine his own reactions and to change surroundings at his will. This last is the same as saying that human personality is the last thing to be reduced to mechanical laws; somehow the human mind is forever elusive, uncatchable and unpredictable, and manages to wriggle out of mechanistic laws or a materialistic dialectic that crazy psychologists and unmarried economists are trying to impose on him. Man, therefore, is a curious, dreamy, humorous and wayward creature."[3]

The creation of wealth requires the assistance of nature—the transformation of the earth's elements, the use of animals, and the aid of tools and machinery. It requires the use of statistics, mathematics and precise formulas. But all efforts are human driven. Man does the acting; land and capital goods are acted upon. Thus, creating wealth ultimately depends on the particular thoughts, emotions, valuations, and purposeful action of human beings.

Economic philosophers refer to this difference between man and nature as "methodological dualism." They make a sharp distinction between the physical sciences and the social sciences, between the world of animals, plants, and inanimate objects, and the world of human beings.

## IS THERE A NEWTONIAN ECONOMICS?

Many economists and social scientists enamored in the past with the precision of the physical sciences have attempted to imitate physics or biology. Economists have borrowed scientific terms such as elasticity, velocity, and equilibrium, and applied them to economics. Even the term "economics" has been made to sound

3  Lin Yutang, *The Importance of Living* (New York: John Day Co., 1937), p. 12.

like physics or mathematics. In the 19th century, it was called "political economy" and was part of the study of logic and natural law. Earlier still, Adam Smith taught economics as a professor of moral philosophy at the University of Glasgow.

Attempts to apply the precision and quantifying characteristics of the natural sciences to economic and financial activity are not always effective. A strict application of the scientific method used in the physical sciences might not always work in economics, even though this method has become a part of the modern economist's toolbox.

## TESTING ECONOMIC THEORY WITH FACTS

Can theories be tested in economics, like an experiment in a laboratory? Not always. The best economists can do is test their theories against historical data or events, and even then the outcome may be uncertain. For example, in 1962, economic advisors to President Kennedy supported the theories of British economist John Maynard Keynes, who argued that running a deliberate federal deficit could stimulate an economic recovery. Congress acted on their advice, cut taxes and ran a deficit in 1964-65. As a result national output (Gross Domestic Product) rose sharply.

However, other economists disagreed with the Keynesian advisors. Followers of the Monetarist (or Chicago) school of economics, led by Milton Friedman, argued that the test was not valid and did not prove the validity of Keynesian theory. Friedman pointed out that during this same period in 1964-65, the Federal Reserve's monetary policy was also active and the rapid growth of the money supply was responsible for the economic recovery.

Who was right? The Keynesians or the Monetarists? The empirical evidence was uncertain because both variables were changing at the same time. This situation is one example of the problem in testing theories with facts in economics. Proving theories in economics is not as easy as proving a laboratory experiment in science class.

Many economists use Karl Popper's methodology in testing theories. Karl Popper, a 20th century Austrian philosopher and author of *The Open Society and Its Enemies*, argued that science could never prove a theory. It could only provide evidence to falsify or disprove a theory. Thus, a theory could be safely dismissed if the evidence contradicts the theory. While this approach is popular among empirical economists such as Milton Friedman and Mark Blaug, Popper's methodology is never fool-proof in economics because the causes of economic events are not always clear.

## SUCCESS AND FAILURE

Another characteristic of human behavior is essential to understanding economics: individuals make mistakes. Before an action is taken, it is assumed that the decision will be positive, but after the action is taken it may be realized that a mistake was made. Decisions are made on the information and analysis available at the time. Results may prove that those decisions were not the best course of action.

The world economy is characterized by frequent individual and business failures. An automobile company may produce a car that does not sell. Investors may make a bad investment. Cereal producers may create a product that tastes terrible. The list of entrepreneurial errors grows every day.

Fortunately, individuals and business leaders can learn from their mistakes and minimize errors. The auto manufacturer can design a more marketable car. The investors can reexamine their strategies and make profitable investments. Taste tests can improve the likelihood that cereal will be palatable. If the same circumstances arise again, individuals are not destined to repeat the same mistakes. If they have learned from the past, they may choose a better course. On the other hand, in the physical sciences, if the same conditions are created in the laboratory, the results will always be the same.

## THE PRINCIPLES OF CAUSALITY AND UNCERTAINTY

Can an economist predict the future? It has been said, facetiously, that economists predicted six out of the last five recessions. One famous story is about Irving Fisher, professor at Yale University and a stock market investor in the 1920s. One week before the 1929 stock market crash, Professor Fisher predicted that "stocks have reached what appears to be a permanent plateau."[4]

In forecasting the future, economists must keep in mind two universal principles:

1.  The Principle of Causality
2.  The Principle of Uncertainty

The Principle of Causality reflects the causal connection between thinking and action. For every cause, there is an effect. Behind every economic event—whether it be a price increase, a currency devaluation, or a decline in employment—there are causes that brought it about.

Often there are multiple causes of economic events and these causes may contradict one another, making it difficult to explain certain phenomenon. Nevertheless, behind every action is economic behavior by human beings. Events

4 *New York Times*, October 16, 1929, p. 1.

may appear to be random and inexplicable at times, but that is only due to the complexity of human behavior.

The second principle of forecasting is uncertainty. The future of human action is uncertain.

Social scientists attempt to study the patterns of human behavior. Psychologists test people's actions and reactions, political scientists investigate the effects of institutions and political parties, historians search for causes, and economists review past data to test their theories. All this social research is done to develop a more accurate portrayal and understanding of human activity.

But no matter how comprehensive their work is, there is always an element of uncertainty and unpredictability in the conclusions of social scientists. For example, no matter how scientific political polls may be in an election year, there is always a certain degree of "statistical error." This "error" is due, in part, to the fact that people are constantly reevaluating their desires and attitudes. They may change their minds in an unpredictable manner.

The Principle of Uncertainty significantly affects the study of economics. While what has occurred can be reported and analyzed, what will occur is less likely to be accurately quantifiable. For example:

- In predicting a nation's economic growth for the next quarter, economists can estimate purchases of goods and services by consumers, business, and government. But these are only "estimates," often based on past relationships or equations which may not hold precisely in the future.

- A futures trader may rely on a computer program to predict the prices of commodities or currencies. These computer-generated buy-and-sell signals are usually based on sophisticated price and volume patterns. Often, however, the pattern breaks down and the futures trader loses money because the factors which determined the movement of past prices may have changed.

- Suppose the world faces a major famine when this year's wheat crop falls in half compared to last year's crop. Economists can say with considerable authority that the price of wheat will rise substantially. But they will have a much more difficult time determining exactly how high the price of wheat will rise. Nor can they predict precisely when the price of wheat will reach a certain price level. They can make educated guesses based on history, but in the final analysis, only today's marketplace of buyers and sellers can determine the outcome of today's prices.

Economists may say "what" will happen, but are often less willing to say "when" and "by how much." Economists differ on how much uncertainty exists in the marketplace. There is always a tug-of-war between the Law of Causality and the Law of Uncertainty.

The British economist John Maynard Keynes (1883-1946) once became so frustrated with the level of uncertainty in the economy that he exclaimed that "our knowledge of the future is fluctuating, vague and uncertain....There is no scientific basis on which to form any calculable probability whatever. We simply do not know."[5] Many economists frequently acknowledge their ignorance about the future course of the economy, interest rates, inflation, and the stock market. Other economists use sophisticated computer models to make forecasts about the economy, interest rates, inflation, and the movement of financial markets.

Uncertainty exists for two reasons: the vast, complex number of factors and players involved in the economy, and the fact that behind the numbers are individuals who are constantly changing and reevaluating their motives. There is always some degree of uncertainty present in human activity. To establish certainty, who, what, when, where, and why questions must be answered; something that is impossible for most human endeavors. The number of individual variables such as when someone will get up or go to bed prohibits certainty.

An astronomer can know the exact time that the sun will come up tomorrow, but can anyone predict when a student will get out of bed in the morning? If he has an eight o'clock class, it may be predicted with some assurance that the student will rise at seven and arrive at school before eight. Studies of his sleeping habits over a period of months based on his regular waking patterns may indicate with some certainty that tomorrow the student will rise at seven and come to class at eight. But there still exists uncertainty. What if the student falls sick and stays in bed, or his alarm clock fails to go off? What if there is a death in the family and he has to go home? There are myriad reasons why the student may not act as expected.

Despite these limits, it is the challenging task of business entrepreneurs to estimate the demand for their products and to set the right prices. The results of estimates are sometimes successful and sometimes not. Henry Ford said, "The best we can do is size up the chances, calculate the risks involved, estimate our ability to deal with them, and then make our plans with confidence."[6]

In sum, while the economic past is precise and quantifiable, the future is always qualitative and inherently imprecise. There are few constants or precise relationships in economics as there are in physics. History and facts are quantitative, but economic theory is qualitative.

---

5 John Maynard Keynes, "The General Theory of Employment," *Quarterly Journal of Economics*, February, 1937.
6 Ford, Henry.
http://thinkexist.com/quotation/the_best_we_can_do_is_size_up_the_chances/296026.html;
Internet

## SUMMARY

### Main points in Chapter 2:

1. Men's wants are infinite. Once one desire is fulfilled, another arises—otherwise, men would cease to act.

2. While the earth provides an abundance of land and natural resources, all resources are limited.

3. Resources require significant work and transformation to be made usable.

4. The universal economic problem is to allocate and transform resources to maximize output of usable goods and services.

5. Competition and cooperation are universal characteristics of all economic activity.

6. Specialization and division of labor are necessary to achieve a high standard of living.

7. Man is seldom self-sufficient and needs to specialize and trade with others.

8. Entrepreneurs, defined as business owners and risk takers, play a critical role in advancing economic performance and living standards. They are responsible for implementing innovation, technological advances, and changes in the economy to better meet the needs of consumers.

9. Inequality of talents, intelligence and property is a given in all societies, leading to specialization by each individual and firm.

10. Behind all economic and financial events is human action, which is always purposeful.

11. The precision of physics and other natural sciences does not normally apply to economics, which involves human behavior.

12. The future of economic events is sometimes predictable according to the law of causality, but because of the complexity of and variability in human behavior, there is always a degree of uncertainty. There are no predictable constant relationships in economics.

13. Economic facts are quantitative, economic theory is qualitative. Entrepreneurs act upon predictions of "when" and "how much," reap rewards when these actions are correct, and suffer consequences when wrong.

14. Waste and pollution are unavoidable, but can be minimized through efforts of the entrepreneur.

15. Time is a major factor in the production and consumption process. Capital and consumer goods depreciate gradually over time and must be repaired and eventually replaced.

Comparative advantage
Depreciation
Distribution of goods
Economics
Entrepreneurship
Inequality
Insatiable wants
Land
Means and ends
Methodological dualism

Opportunity cost
Principle of causality
Principle of competition
Principle of cooperation
Principle of uncertainty
Scarcity of resources
Specialization
Supply and demand
Time
Working capital

**INFLUENTIAL ECONOMIST**

## THE METHODOLOGY OF LUDWIG VON MISES

**Name: Ludwig von Mises (1881-1973)**

**Background:** Taught economics at University of Vienna prior to World War II and at New York University following the war. Considered the dean of the modern Austrian school of economics (followers include Nobel Prize winning economist Friedrich A. Hayek, Israel Kirzner, and Murray Rothbard). Other schools of economics, including the New Classical School and the Public Choice School, consider Mises to be one of their mentors.

**Major Work:** Mises wrote *Human Action* (Yale University Press, 1949; third edition, Regnery, 1966), the first systematic treatise on economics based on the principles of subjectivism and methodological individualism. Mises's analysis of the economy is based entirely on deductive logic rather than on empirical observations or historical studies. Comparing economics most closely to geometry rather than physics, Mises built his system on the logical implications of a few self-evident axioms similar to the ones we have developed in this chapter.

**Sample Quotation:** "Economics...is a deductive system. It draws its strength from the starting point of its deductions, from the category of action. No economic theorem can be considered sound that is not solidly fastened upon this foundation by an irrefutable chain of reasoning."

**Strengths:** Like Adam Smith, Mises emphasized the role of economics as a way to accomplish man's desire for material happiness. "The immense majority of men aim first of all at an improvement of the material conditions of well-being. They want more and better food, better homes and clothes, and a thousand other amenities. They strive after abundance and health." Mises offered the first comprehensive theory of subjective economics. He extended the Austrian tradition (begun by founder Carl Menger in 1871) to money and banking, the business cycle, and government policies. By emphasizing that people are not mechanistic, Mises warned that efforts by dictators and totalitarian regimes to engage in "social engineering" and forced production schemes would not work. Mises was one of the first economists to attack socialist central planning as unworkable.

Mises also condemned most forms of state interventionism as counterproductive to the creation of wealth. He was particularly critical of policies promoting consumption over saving: "The essence of Keynesianism is its complete failure to conceive the role that saving and capital accumulation play in the improvement of economic conditions....It is one of the foremost tasks of good government to remove all obstacles that hinder the accumulation and investment of new capital."

**Weakness:** Mises was often misunderstood during his lifetime. Critics considered him an "extremist" who rejected all forms of empirical work or history. Not many would agree with Mises' statement, "History cannot teach us any general rule, principle, or law." For Mises, facts never speak for themselves. One needs a correct theory to understand historical events.

Mises also denied the value of econometrics and mathematical economics. He used virtually no graphs or statistics in his works. His non-mathematical approach went counter to the profession's trend toward quantitative economics, and the testing of theory with empirical evidence.

**Personality:** Only recently has Mises' prestige risen among professional economists. In Vienna in the early 20th century, he had three strikes against him: he was a Jew, he was an advocate of laissez-faire capitalism, and he was considered dogmatic and uncompromising in his beliefs. In the 1920s and early 1930s, he conducted a famous private seminar in Vienna for a small group of followers. Mises left for Switzerland in 1934 in the wake of Nazism (his entire library was confiscated by the Nazis) and immigrated to the United States in 1940. He lived in New York City for more than 30 years where he taught part-time at New York University, but never accepted a paid, full-time post at any American university. Throughout his life, he was "at war with the spirit of the age," and spoke out regularly against all forms of government interventionism, including socialism, communism, and Keynesianism. When Soviet communism collapsed in 1990, economic historian Robert Heilbroner said that the Austrian economist was vindicated. "Mises was right," Heilbroner said.

Mises died in 1973, pessimistic about the future and the outlook for the Austrian school, but a year later his colleague, Friedrich A. Hayek, won the Nobel Prize in economics.

## PROBLEMS TO PONDER

1. A box of cookies is left on the counter at home, free for the taking, but no one eats them. Does this violate the universal principle of unlimited wants? Explain.

2. Comment on the following: "History repeats itself." To what extent is human nature a constant? A variable?

3. "I predict the Dow Jones Industrial Average will reach 15,000 on December 31." Given what we have just discussed in this chapter, is this an example of sound economic thinking? Explain.

4. "Studies indicate that stock prices are random." Do you agree? What determines the prices of securities?

5. Comment on the following statement by a financial economist: "I cannot tell you what the weather will be on any particular day, but I can tell you the climate of the region." How is an economist like an economic weatherman?

6. Advanced Question: Compare the Principle of Economic Uncertainty with the Heisenberg Principle of Uncertainty in physics. What are their differences and similarities?

7. In light of this chapter's discussion of the social vs. physical sciences, what is your reaction to the following book titles?

    (a) *More Heat Than Light: Economics as Social Physics, Physics as Nature's Economics*, by Philip Mirowski.

    (b) *Bionomics: The Economy as an Ecosystem*, by Michael Rothschild (applies the principles of biology to corporate management).

    (c) *The Golden Constant: The English and American Experience*, 1560-1976, by Roy W. Jastram (seeks to demonstrate that gold has maintained its purchasing power over the past 400 years).

8.  In their textbook *University Economics*, Armen Alchian and William R. Allen argue, "Competition is inevitable with scarcity. Scarcity forces a choice among limited options, and we compete for those options. Hence, in a society of more than one person, scarcity implies competition." Moreover, competition "is not unique to the free-enterprise, private-property system. Competition exists in every social system." How would this statement apply to a socialist economy? What is the relationship between competition and cooperation? Is cooperation more important or prevalent in a market economy or in a command economy?

9.  Comment on the following: "While there often is no clear-cut understanding of what constitutes 'enough,' the simple fact is that there is more than sufficient food to sustain everyone on the planet. The same is true of land and renewable energy. The important question, then, is why the staples of life are so egregiously maldistributed—why, for example, the United States, with a little more than 5 percent of the world's population, uses something like 40 percent of the world's resources. What appears to be a problem of scarcity usually turns out, on closer inspection, to be a problem of distribution."[7] Is scarcity a false issue?

10. Evaluate the following: "Unlimited wants facing limited resources means one universal fact: there is always work to be done. Therefore, there can be no such thing as unemployable labor. If a person is unemployed, it is strictly voluntary. The unemployed can always find something to do."

11. Comment on the following: "Where mainstream economics is based on concepts borrowed from classical Newtonian physics, bionomics is derived from the teachings of modern evolutionary biology. Where orthodox thinking describes the economy as a static, predictable engine, bionomics sees the economy as a self-organizing, 'chaotic' information ecosystem."[8] To what extent is animalistic behavior applicable to economic theory? In what way is the rain forest like a shopping mall?

12. Many social scientists say that poorer Third World countries should reject "models based on economic laws" of universal validity. According to them, there are no universal laws. Do you agree? What laws discussed in this chapter would not apply to poorer nations? Should every nation be democratic and free? Which universal human rights should no government or citizen violate? The right of free speech, religious conscience, a fair trial? Should property rights be enforced everywhere? If so, how?

---

7 Alfie Kohn, *No Contest: The Case Against Competition* (Houghton Mifflin), 1986, p. 72.
8 Michael Rothschild, *Bionomics: Economy as Ecosysem* (New York: Henry Holt, 1995).

13. In a controversial 1953 article, "The Methodology of Positive Economics," Milton Friedman claimed that economic theory does not require realistic assumptions to qualify as a good theory. The important thing is that the theory yield accurate predictions. In fact, Friedman declared, "in general, the more significant the theory, the more unrealistic the assumptions....To be important, therefore, a hypothesis must be descriptively false in its assumptions." Friedman concluded, "the relevant question . . . is . . . whether the theory works, which means whether it yields sufficiently accurate predictions."[9] Do you agree? Can "bad" assumptions lead to "good" predictions?

## RECOMMENDED READING

- Ludwig von Mises, *Human Action: A Treatise on Economics*, 3rd ed. (Regnery, 1966). Mises' magnum opus is heavy reading for the novice economist, but once you pass the early chapters, it is a well-written, thought-provoking treatise.

- Murray N. Rothbard, *Man, Economy and State* (Nash Publishing, 1970). A two-volume treatise on all aspects of economic science. Rothbard writes in a very engaging style.

- Mark Blaug, *Not Only an Economist* (Edward Elgar, 1997). Entertaining essays by a top economic thinker.

- Alfie Kohn, *No Contest: The Case Against Competition* (Houghton Mifflin, 1986). A counter-cultural attack on competition in business, sports and life. Very challenging critique of modern-day society.

9  Milton Friedman, *Essays in Positive Economics* (University of Chicago Press, 1953), pp. 14-15.

# Chapter 3

# PRODUCTION, EXCHANGE AND CONSUMPTION: THE STRUCTURE OF ECONOMIC ACTIVITY

*"All production is for the purpose of ultimately satisfying a consumer....*
*Consumption is the sole end and object of all economic activity."*

—JOHN MAYNARD KEYNES
*The General Theory of Employment,*
*Interest and Money* (1936)

In one television episode of The Twilight Zone, time stood still. All action by machines, animals, and people was halted temporarily, allowing one unaffected individual to move around and observe everything in this motionless world.

If economists could do the same thing, freeze all activity and observe everything in a static, motionless state, what would this snapshot of the economy look like?

If time stood still, goods throughout the world would be frozen in various stages of completion. Many goods would be completely finished and are now in varying stages of use. These goods are being used up, depleted, and consumed to satisfy human needs and wants. These goods include houses that people live in, cars that people drive, food that people eat, machines that manufacture products, and other finished goods in the process of being used up.

Some goods have been completed but are waiting to be sold to final users. These goods are in inventory, about to be sold in retail department stores, grocery stores, and car dealerships. They are ready for use by consumers.

Automobiles are a good example of this frozen economy. Millions of cars have already been built and are being used on the road or parked in the garage. Some are new, others are old. Thousands of new cars are in the showrooms, ready to be purchased. Thousands more are in transit to the car dealers. Others are parked at the production plant waiting to be delivered or to be ordered by the car dealers. And still more cars are coming off the assembly line. Others are sitting in junkyards, ready to be recycled. Like automobiles, other goods produced in the economy also follow the same cycle of creation, purchase, use, depreciation, and recycling.

Services, like goods, are subject to the same laws of supply, demand, and consumption as are tangible goods. Services are the performance of duties or provision of space and equipment helpful to others. Doctors, lawyers, teachers, and garbage collectors are all involved in the provision of services. These services, like products, can be bought and sold.

## THE SUPPLY SYSTEM

Going to the supermarket is a frequent activity for most people. When at the market it is possible to act as an economist seeking an independent view of the economy. First note the myriad products available for purchase. Count the different kinds of bread. Discover how many products are available that one individual might use, but others will not.

How did all these thousands of goods end up on store shelves, all properly packaged and prepared to be accessible to the customer? What has happened behind the scenes to bring about this modern economic miracle?

Thousands of workers in hundreds of organizations are involved in the supply system for the supermarket. The supermarket employs dozens of workers who unload the products, stock the shelves and take orders for more goods. In the backrooms of the supermarket, stockers work supplying shelves and making sure the consumers' needs are met.

The distribution and production system goes much further back than the backroom of the supermarket. The retail part of the economic process is the final stage of production (and the beginning of consumption). Before reaching that stage, time, hard work, and capital are expended to bring those goods to the final retail stage.

Most people will at some time seek the services of a doctor. In order for the doctor to supply his services, he must first obtain the necessary education and credentials allowing him to practice/provide his services. Once he has completed these stages of qualification, which are similar to production of goods, his services are available for consumption by users. Time, work, and capital are also expended to bring the doctor's services to the final retail/user stage.

In the case of both goods and services, the end user/consumer has the ability to purchase those goods and services which meet his wants and needs.

The economic model for goods and services resembles this table:

|  | Goods | Services |
|---|---|---|
| Resources | Raw materials | Individuals |
| Production | Manufacturing, production facilities | Acquisition of knowledge/skills |
| Distribution | Marketing, Transportation | Marketing, transportation |
| Consumption + Investment | Purchase of products/commodities | Selection of needed service providers |

**MANUFACTURER**

**AGENT**

**WHOLESALER**

**RETAILER**

**CONSUMER**

**Figure 3.1.** *A typical portrayal of channel structure for consumer goods.*

## THE WHOLESALE TRADE AND TRANSPORTATION SYSTEM

The supermarket, the shopping mall, the restaurant, and other retail outlets are serviced directly by a group of buying agents, traders, and wholesalers. Agents, traders and wholesalers act as the middlemen between the retail stores and the manufacturers, but are seldom involved in the production of the product itself. Their purpose is to facilitate the buying and selling of finished wholesale goods, to match the needs of the retailer with the manufacturing source, and to make the retailer aware of the variety of products available.

Management experts refer to this wholesale process as "marketing channels. " Figure 3.1 illustrates the potential number of supply stages.

Not every production process involves several levels of wholesaling. For example, if individuals cut their own Christmas trees and sell them on a corner lot, the middleman is left out of the market. Sometimes the manufacturer is the consumer, as in the case of a gardener who consumes the fruits and vegetables from the garden. However, in most production processes, there is at least one middleman between the manufacturer and the retailer.

Service providers also market their services in ways that facilitate matching the needs of the service user with the abilities of the service provider. Marketing tools and techniques for the marketing of goods and the marketing of services are the same. The focus of marketing is on availability, quality, and user satisfaction for both goods and services. Quality for goods relates to tangible items while quality for services relates to skill and ability.

## THE MANUFACTURING SECTOR

Another important stage, the production of the product itself, occurs before wholesale trade. At this stage the automobile is assembled, the clothes are manufactured, the food is processed, and the textbook is printed. The industrial sector of the economy is huge, involving the production of hundreds of thousands of goods each year. It crosses national boundaries, with inputs and manufactured goods being imported from around the world.

The industrial process involves numerous mini-stages of production. In a famous example in the first chapter of *The Wealth of Nations*, Adam Smith describes 18 distinct operations, some occurring simultaneously, in the making of pins. Although he uses the manufacturing of the pin to demonstrate the principle of the division of labor, it also demonstrates the "assembly line" nature of the pin factory. Smith writes, "One man draws out the wire, another straights it, a third cuts it, a fourth points it, a fifth grinds it at the top for receiving the head; to make the head requires two or three distinct operations."[1]

Today, the production of automobiles, computers and other modern-day goods involves complicated procedures and man-made materials. Over time the industrial process has become more complex as scientists and engineers engage in extensive research and collaborate to build advanced machinery and tools.

For example, figure 3.2 illustrates a generic electronics supply chain.

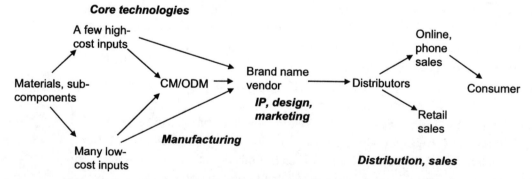

**Figure 3.2.** *Generic Electronics Supply Chain. Source: Greg Linden, Kenneth L. Kraemer, Jason Dedrick, "Who Captures Value in a Global Innovation System? The Case of Apple's iPod," Personal Computing Industry Center (UCIrvine School of Business, 2007), p. 3.*

---

1  Adam Smith. *The Wealth of Nations*. (New York: Modern Library, 1965 [1776]), p.4.

As you can see from this diagram, each producer purchases inputs and adds value, which then becomes part of the cost of the next stage of production. In the first stage, we see that each product contains a large number of low-value components, such as capacitors and resistors, that cost only pennies each. Most electronics products also contain a few high-valued components such as a visual display, hard drive and key integrated circuits. These components have their own multinational supply chains, contract manufacturers (CMs) and original design manufactuers (ODMs). The supply chain is guided by a lead firm (such as IBM, HP, or Apple) to create a brand-name product that distributors sell to retailers and final consumers.

While humans do not "manufacture" their skills and abilities, the concept of production applies to service providers as well as to goods. The acquisition of skills and abilities involves time, money, and the dedication of resources (human) before the service provider is capable of providing the service to the client/consumer. Customers are often willing to pay higher rates for skilled providers of services than those paid for unskilled providers.

## THE EARLIEST STAGE: BASIC RESOURCES

Before manufacturing, the "raw commodity" or "natural resource" stage of the production process must be addressed. Resource suppliers facilitate this earliest stage in the production process. At this stage of production, minerals are mined, crops are grown and harvested, fish are caught from the ocean, and crude oil is pumped out of the ground.

Raw commodities/natural resources are created
↓
Raw commodities/natural resources are obtained
↓
Transportation of raw materials/resources to production facilities
↓
Manufacture of goods/products
↓
Procurement of goods/products
↓
Transportation of goods/products to retail/wholesale stores
↓
Selection and purchase of goods/products by buyer

Between the stages of production, goods are transported from one location to another—from city to city, state to state, or country to country. Transportation of goods and the communication of information are vital aspects of the whole transformation process.

All aspects of the production processes take time, but the production of natural resources can sometimes take the longest period of time. It may take 60 years to grow a tree that can finally be used to make paper. Paper and wood manufacturers plant tree farms using methods that will ensure that trees of varying ages are available for harvesting. Many raw commodities such as crude oil, iron ore and copper are slowly being depleted. Their continued use depends entirely on the ability of capitalists and entrepreneurs to discover new sources of supply, or to develop new methods of extracting natural resources from the earth. Similarly, service providers require the input of knowledge and experience in order to reach the point where they can provide services to the consumer.

Potential service provider identified

Skills and experience are obtained by the service provider

Marketing of services

Procurement of services

## A GENERAL VIEW OF THE ECONOMIC PROCESS

All usable goods originally come from raw commodities in the earth, and services come from human labor. Natural resources are grown or extracted and transformed into manufactured goods, transported and sold in the wholesale trade, and made available in the retail stores for ultimate consumer use. It's a wonder of nature how 90 elements in the earth can, through manufacturing processes, create such a variety of substances for seemingly unlimited uses. All services result from the provider acquiring knowledge and expertise that is marketable.

The economic process described above is the essence of the market economy. Every good used in society goes through this complex production process, from raw commodities through manufacturing to consumer and capital goods. The entire production process and the hustle and bustle of business and trade in the marketplace all have the same effect: fulfilling consumer needs, creating wealth, and increasing everyone's standard of living.

As science writer Ivan Amato states, "Human beings extract about 15 billion tons of raw material—that's 30 trillion pounds—from the earth each year, and from that they make every kind of stuff that you can find in every kind of thing. Mined ore becomes metal becomes wire becomes part of a motor becomes a cooling fan in a computer. Harvested wood becomes lumber becomes a home. Drilled petroleum becomes chemical feedstock becomes synthetic rubber becomes automobile tires. Natural gas becomes polyethylene becomes milk jugs and oversized, multicolored yard toys. Mined silica sand become silicon crystal becomes the base of microelectronic chips. Each kind of stuff is a link to enormous industrial trains whose workers process the world's raw materials into usable forms that constitute the items of our constructed landscape."[2]

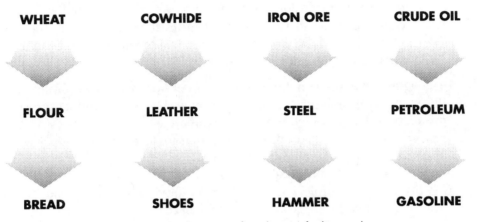

**WHEAT** **COWHIDE** **IRON ORE** **CRUDE OIL**

**FLOUR** **LEATHER** **STEEL** **PETROLEUM**

**BREAD** **SHOES** **HAMMER** **GASOLINE**

**Figure 3.3.** *The stages of production of select products.*

Note that Amato says that the transformation process always goes from raw commodity to intermediate product to final use either as a consumer or capital good—from unfinished, unusable "stuff" to finished, usable "stuff."

## WHAT DETERMINES VALUE?

What determines the prices of labor, capital goods, and other factors in the production process? David Ricardo (1772-1823) and Karl Marx (1818-83) advocated a cost-of-production theory of value, arguing that the amount and cost of labor controlled the output and prices of final consumer goods. But the Marginalist Revolution in the 1870s, led by Carl Menger, William Stanley Jevons, and Leon Walras, dispelled this labor theory of value. They noted that individuals make choices on the basis of preferences and values, and recognized therefore that no amount of labor or production adds value to a product or service unless there is sufficient final demand to warrant the cost. Value consists of the subjective valuations of individual users. In sum, final consumer demand had to be sufficiently high enough before producers would employ productive resources to produce a product or service. Final demand is the ultimate determining factor in what is produced and at what price.[3]

2  Ivan Amato, *Stuff: The Materials the World is Made Of* (Basic Books, 1997), p. 2.
3  For a complete review of this controversy, see Mark Skousen, *The Making of Modern Economics,* 2nd ed. (M. E. Sharpe, 2009), chapter 7.

## ANALYSIS OF INDIVIDUAL PRODUCTS

The following general criteria relate to the economic process of individual goods:

1. The production of each good or service takes time; some products take longer than others to produce.
2. The production of each good or service can take several stages to accomplish.
3. Value is added at each stage of production. As the product moves along each point of the transformation process, the producer applies land, labor, and capital in order to advance the semi-finished good toward the ultimate consumer stage. The factors of production add value to the product as it moves along the production process.

Figure 3.4 is the simplified illustration of how a simple product, bread, is produced over time and how value is added at each stage of production. This stages-of-production diagram incorporates the three basic characteristics of the economic process; production takes time, production involves several stages of completion, and production adds value at each stage.

The vertical axis represents the number of stages needed to produce a commodity. In this example, four stages are required to produce bread. The first or earliest stage (wheat) is listed at the top, with each succeeding stage following below it. The last stage (retail bread) is the completed or finished stage—the consumer good.

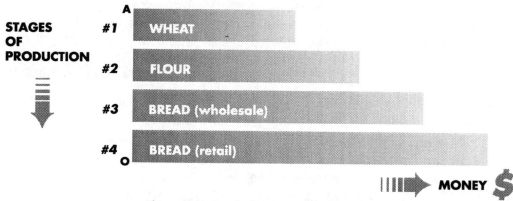

**Figure 3.4.** *Four basic stages of bread production.*

The vertical axis also measures the total amount of time it takes to make bread. Point A represents the time when the wheat is planted by the farmer. Point O represents the time the bread is sold to the consumer in the grocery store.

The horizontal axis measures output in terms of gross revenue or total expenditures at each stage of production. For example, at the final retail stage the horizontal axis measures the gross revenue in one year generated by the grocery store in selling bread. It is not a measure of the number of loaves sold. Revenue is a monetary figure based on dollars, pounds, euros, or whatever medium of exchange is used to buy and sell bread.

## THE BUILDING OF AN ECONOMIC MODEL

The four-stage production diagram discussed above is what economists call an economic model. In economics, a model is a simplified representation of a real-world phenomenon. In the case of bread-making, the real-world process may involve hundreds of stages. But in the simplified model, there are only four simple stages.

A model in economics is not the same as a model in physics or engineering. In the physical sciences, models are closer to being an exact miniature representation of the real thing. But in economics, models are not duplicates of the real world. Rather, they are "heuristic" and involve simplifying assumptions. A heuristic model adopts simplified rules of thumb in order to explain a principle. Simplifying assumptions is frequently necessary in economics in order to make a model useful and manageable. Some assumptions may be unrealistic or even unreasonable, but assumptions are essential in order to glean meaningful results from a model.

## SIMPLIFYING ASSUMPTIONS

Several simplifying assumptions are made in figure 3.4 above:

It is assumed that each stage of production takes the same amount of time. This time schedule is a distortion of reality, since the first stage of bread production, the harvesting of wheat, takes months, while the making of flour and bread takes less than a day.

It is also assumed that only one ingredient goes into the production of bread - wheat. In reality, bread has many other ingredients, including sugar and salt. Also ignored are the materials used for packaging bread. In reality each of these other ingredients and materials also has an economic genealogy, a series of production processes necessary for final consumption.

Third, it is assumed that there is value added at each stage. This assumption indicates that each firm at every stage is making a profit over and above its costs, and that the factors of production—landlords, workers, and capitalists—are all paid sufficiently for their work. This is an assumption that may not always hold true in reality. There are times when firms produce a product at a loss. In most cases if a company produces a product at a loss, eventually it must shut down or shift production to another product.

Fourth, the example of bread assumes the same level of value is added at each stage of production. In the business world, profitability differs considerably from one company to another and among industries. However, over time there is a tendency toward similar rates of profit, adjusted for risk. Why? Because individual and institutional investors will invest in firms earning higher profits and withdraw money from firms earning less profit. Over time, profits tend to adjust.

Fifth, four basic stages of bread making were part of the assumptions of this example. The first stage is the farmer growing wheat. The farmer plants, fertilizes, and harvests the wheat at a certain cost, and sells the wheat to the miller for a profit. The second stage is the miller's threshing of the wheat and grinding it into flour. The miller produces the flour at a basic cost and sells the flour to the baker for a profit. The third stage is the baker, who takes the flour and makes it into bread, and sells the bread to the grocer, again at a price higher than his costs. The fourth and final stage is the grocer who sells the bread to the consumer at still a higher price that ensures a profit for the grocery store.

## A GENERAL MODEL OF THE ECONOMY

This single-commodity model can be extended into a general model of the economy. Figure 3.5 represents this general model.

Note how this general model follows the same pattern developed for individual commodities. Time (the stages of production) is represented on the vertical axis. Output as measured in gross revenue per year is represented on the horizontal axis (money).

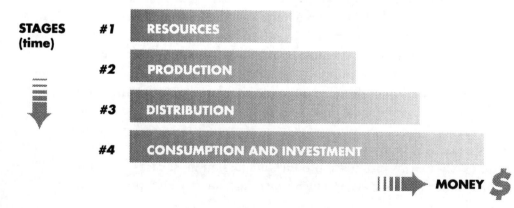

**Figure 3.5.** *A general model of the economy.*

## THE AGGREGATE PRODUCTION STRUCTURE (APS)

The Aggregate Production Structure (APS) is a four sector model. The total of each stage of output represents the dollar amount of all intermediate and final goods and services produced during an entire business year.

All goods and services go through a transformation process in order to become usable by human beings. While some commodities may go through over a thousand steps to reach the final retail stage, in this example the number of stages has been simplified to four general categories to provide a manageable number in order to analyze the economy.

Each stage of production adds value according to the profitability of each producer.

Finally, it takes time to produce and to consume goods and services. Producers must always take into account the time involved in producing a particular product or service, as well as the serviceability of the good when it is produced. The period of production and consumption is vital in any economy.

## APS IS GLOBAL IN NATURE

It is also important to note that the economic model, APS, is interstate global in scope. Iron ore may be mined in Minnesota, made into steel in Indiana, assembled into an automobile in Michigan, and sold to a customer in Florida. Car radios are manufactured in Germany and sold in the United States. Wheat is produced in Canada and exported to Poland where it is made into bread. Televisions are built in Japan and sold in Mexico. Rape seed oil is made into a rubber-like eraser in Indonesia, inserted into the end of a pencil in Oregon, and exported to Indonesia. Some products, such as automobiles, involve so many ingredients that the raw materials and components come from all around the world—rubber from Brazil, copper from Chile, iron ore from Canada, electronics from Korea, leather from Argentina, platinum from South Africa, and airbags from Mississippi. Each material or component is purchased where the highest comparative advantage is given to the manufacturer. A recent advertisement from a car manufactured in Kentucky showed that the parts used in producing the car came from 24 states.

In the past, large electronics and computer firms designed and developed their own products using domestically-produced components. But in recent decades, supply chains in the global electronics industry has steadily moved across borders, especially toward Asian countries. Companies that formerly manufactured most products in-house, such as IBM and Hewlett-Packard, have outsourced production and even product development to global networks of contract manufacturers (CMs) and original design manufacturers (ODMs).

Figure 3.6 illustrates the supply chain of a product (Apple's iPod) involving several input suppliers in China, Taiwan, Korea, and Japan, before being shipped to wholesalers in the United States and ultimately to retail customers.

| Component | Supplier | Company HQ Location | Manu-facturing Location | Estimated Factory Price | Cost as % of all iPod Parts | Gross Profit Rate | Est'd Value Capture |
|---|---|---|---|---|---|---|---|
| Hard Drive | Toshiba | Japan | China | $73.39 | 51% | 26.5% | $19.45 |
| Display Module | Toshiba-Matsushita | Japan | Japan | $20.39 | 14% | 28.7% | $5.85 |
| Video/Multimedia Processor | Broadcom | US | Taiwan or Singapore | $8.36 | 6% | 52.5% | $4.39 |
| Portal Player CPU | PortalPlayer | US | US or Taiwan | $4.94 | 3% | 44.8% | $2.21 |
| Insertion, test, and assembly | Inventec | Taiwan | China | $3.70 | 3% | 3.0% | $0.11 |
| Battery Pack | Unknown | | | $2.89 | 2% | | $0.00 |
| Display Driver | Renesas | Japan | Japan | $2.88 | 2% | 24.0% | $0.69 |
| Mobile SDRAM Memory - 32 MB | Samsung | Korea | Korea | $2.37 | 2% | 28.2% | $0.67 |
| Back Enclosure | Unknown | | | $2.30 | 2% | 26.5% | |
| Mainboard PCB | Unknown | | | $1.90 | 1% | 28.7% | |
| **Subtotal for 10 most expensive inputs** | | | | **$123.12** | **85%** | | **$33.37** |
| All other inputs | | | | $21.28 | 15% | | |
| Total all iPod inputs | | | | $144.40 | 100% | | |

Source: Portelligent, Inc., 2006 and authors' calculations

**Figure 3.6.** The most expensive inputs in the 30GB 5th-generation iPod, 2005.
Source: Greg Linden, Kenneth L. Kraemer, Jason Dedrick,
"Who Captures Value in a Global Innovation System? The Case of Apple's iPod,"
Personal Computing Industry Center (UCIrvine School of Business, 2007), p. 6.

How do land, labor, capital and entrepreneurship fit into this time-oriented model of the economy? The factors of production play an essential role at each stage and in each firm, working toward transforming and distributing goods. Figure 3.7 demonstrates the application of the factors of production in the economic structure.

For example, Exxon, the multinational oil company, extracts crude oil out of the ground and turns it into gasoline and other products to sell to retail customers. Exxon leases federal land in Alaska and acquires capital and equipment to drill the oil and to hire workers to extract the oil and transport it to refineries in the United States. Additional labor and capital are used to refine the oil, and still more labor and capital are required to deliver gasoline and other refined products to gasoline stations and other outlets. In most years, all this cooperative activity is done profitably, adding value to the economic society.

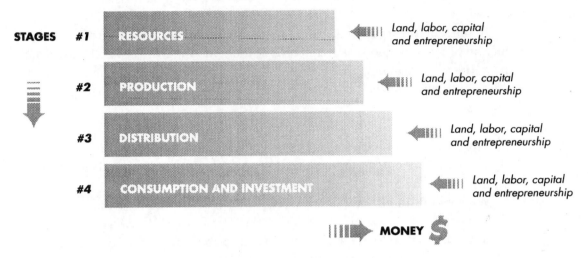

**Figure 3.7.** *Factors used at each stage of output.*

## THE ROLE OF SERVICES

The stages-of-production approach applies to services as well as products. Services exist as both activities that facilitate production processes and as activities that directly meet the needs of individuals. A haircut, for example, may be regarded as a consumer service, while the work of an accountant in an oil company may be considered part of an early stage of production. Services are, in fact, often associated closely with the production of goods.

Economists emphasize that the factors of production—land, labor, capital, and entrepreneurship—work together to transform raw materials into products. Raw materials are known as "stock" in the U. K. or "inventory" in the U. S. Raw materials become goods-in-process or work-in-process and, when transformed, become the firm's products. In a steel plant, goods-in-process are the various forms of steel and other metals being produced. In an automobile plant, goods-in-process are the body parts, tires, textiles and other materials that are used in making a car. In a refinery goods-in-process are the petroleum products being refined.

Fixed capital goods are the machinery and tools used to move goods-in-process along their way toward the next stage of production. Remember the word "fixed" associated with fixed capital—machines and tools stay fixed to the plant and office. They do not move along the next stage of output as goods-in-process do.

## MONEY AND EXCHANGE IN THE PRODUCTION OF GOODS AND SERVICES

In the four-stage model of the economy, money and exchange facilitate the production process for goods. It is conceivable that one single firm could be involved in the entire transformation process from raw materials to retail sales, but most companies specialize in a particular stage of production (remember the law of comparative advantage).

The economic process for products typically follows these steps:
1. The entrepreneur-owner uses his capital to purchase raw materials that will be input into the production process from suppliers.
2. Workers are hired, production space and fixed capital (machines and tools) acquired.
3. Raw materials which have been input into the production system are transformed into a more usable product or service.
4. The capitalist-owner sells these products.
5. At the next level, the previous output product becomes the input product and the process is repeated until the final consumer stage is reached where the product is complete and fully usable.

Money and exchange are an integral part of the global, national and local economy. The supply of goods moves down the production process while money moves upward in payment for the goods. The following diagram demonstrates the direction goods and money flow. (See figure 3.8.)

In the four-stage model of the economy, money and exchange also facilitate the provision of services. The economic process for services typically follows these steps:

The service provider acquires the skills and expertise necessary to provide the service. The input raw materials in this case are knowledge and skills which are acquired from suppliers such as vocational colleges, universities, training programs, and the military.

The service provider markets services as output based on the demand for his skill and knowledge.

## PRODUCTION PROCESS

It is too much for one firm to handle the entire production process for most commodities. Frequently, firms find it convenient and cost-saving to engage in vertical integration whereby they buy a resource supplier or set up their own retail outlet. This is different from horizontal integration where a company buys a direct

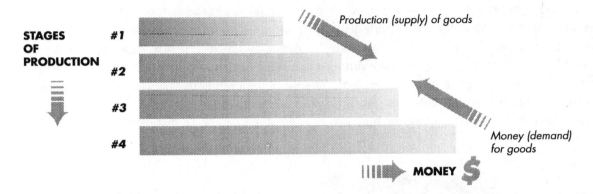

**STAGES OF PRODUCTION**

#1
#2
#3
#4

Production (supply) of goods

Money (demand) for goods

**MONEY** $

**Figure 3.8.** *Goods and money flow in opposite directions in the production process.*

competitor or a company sometimes in a completely unrelated field. General Motors buying Toyota is an example of horizontal integration, but General Motors buying Fisher Body is an example of vertical integration. Several years ago, Philip Morris, a tobacco company, bought Kraft Foods, a food company, in order to diversify—a good example of unrelated horizontal integration, a conglomerate merger. (In 2007, Philip Morris, renamed Altria, divested itself of Kraft Foods.)

Major manufacturers frequently rely on outside suppliers to provide various inputs rather than producing them themselves. The automobile industry is a well-known example of firms depending on outside suppliers for automobile parts and materials, a process referred to as "outsourcing."

## THE IMPORTANCE OF INVENTORIES

Inventories exist at virtually every stage of production, thus significantly reducing the waiting time for a firm to produce its product. An automobile manufacturer does not have to wait for iron ore to be made into steel, or for rubber plants to be planted. It simply orders steel and tires from resource specialists who have them in inventory. Only very expensive and unique items are "made to order." Everything else is in inventory, so that the producers do not usually have to worry much about the production time of inputs. Occasionally there are annoying shortages when unexpected demand occurs, but this occurrence (known as "bottlenecks") is minimized in the marketplace through inventories.

Inventories are not without cost. It costs a great deal of money to maintain a high inventory of supplies, raw materials, and finished goods. Look at a car dealership and note how many automobiles and trucks are in inventory, waiting to be sold. These cars and trucks take up space that could have other uses (remember our concept of opportunity cost). The cars and trucks sitting on the lot represent "accounts payable," meaning that they represent debts owed by the dealer to the automobile manufacturer. Thus, inventories require an investment of capital by businesses. Firms have attempted to reduce the cost of inventories by adopting "just in time" inventory management techniques. Wal-Mart, for example, developed a practice of letting middlemen have direct access to company sales data so as to reduce the amount of inventory held at Wal-Mart stores.

The diagram below demonstrates how inventories play a vital role in production.

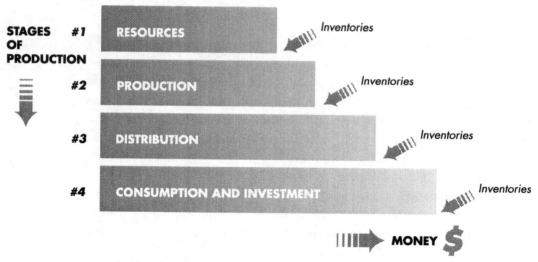

**Figure 3.9.** *Inventories exist at each stage of production.*

## COMPETITION AND COOPERATION

Chapter 2 discussed the fact that competition and cooperation exist in every sector of the market economy. This is evident in the 4-stage model. Cooperation exists among the factors of production. Land, labor, and capital must work together to turn raw materials into usable products and move working capital from one stage of production to the next toward the final user. There is a harmony of interests between landlords, laborers, and capitalists.

There is competition at each stage of production. Competition occurs in several ways. First, there is intrastage competition, i.e., competition within the stages of production. There are usually several possible suppliers of intermediate inputs, all competing to provide their customers with the working capital they need at a decent price. Competitive activity continues all the way down to the final retail customer, where firms market their wares based on price, quality, and volume.

Interstage competition also exists. Since resources are limited (the second axiom of economics), capitalist owners compete for these limited inputs, whether to employ their land, labor, and capital in the "resource" stage or in the "consumption" stage, or any of the stages in between. The level of profit and loss at each stage determines how many resources will be devoted to each stage. If the raw material stage is more profitable than the retail industry, resources will likely be shifted to the earlier stage of production.

Finally, there is competition among the factors of production. One property competes against other properties, wage-earners vie with other wage-earners, and business executives compete with other executives for top positions. Competition is a dynamic process. If Texas experiences an oil boom, the state will attract more workers and new capital, driving up wages, rents, land prices, and executive pay. In short, there is always opportunity cost in competing markets.

Competition also exists among service providers. Intrastage competition is found between providers of the same or similar services. Competitive activity occurs in every stage from acquisition of skills and expertise through the provision of services to the end user where services are marketed based on price, quality, and availability.

## CONSUMPTION AND INVESTMENT

After goods and services are produced, they are used up by consumers (consumer goods) or by business (capital goods). The time it takes to consume goods varies widely—fresh vegetables may last only a few days, canned goods several months, appliances and automobiles a few years, and buildings several decades. The period of consumption varies from one moment to a hundred years or more.

Final retail products are not solely consumer goods, however. There is consumer-good production and capital-good production. Capital-good production includes fixed capital goods such as machinery, equipment, and tools, which are finished goods used specifically to produce other goods in the intermediate stages of production.

The life expectancy of final retail consumer and capital goods is very important. Automobiles that last an average of 20 years are valued more than those lasting only six years. Homes that are built to last 200 years are valued more than homes lasting an average of 30 years.

All durable consumer and capital goods require repairs and upkeep, and eventually need replacing. Chapter 2 introduced the importance of depreciation and the need of rebuilding or replacing depreciated assets, including buildings and machines. All capital and consumer goods have a finite lifetime, and eventually wear out. Even products like computers that do not wear out can lose considerable value due to obsolescence. In short, the value of most products gradually depreciates over time.

Resources have value added as they are produced into usable consumer and capital goods, and then value is gradually (and sometimes rapidly) reduced as these goods are used up. The following diagram (Figure 3.10) reflects this universal phenomenon.

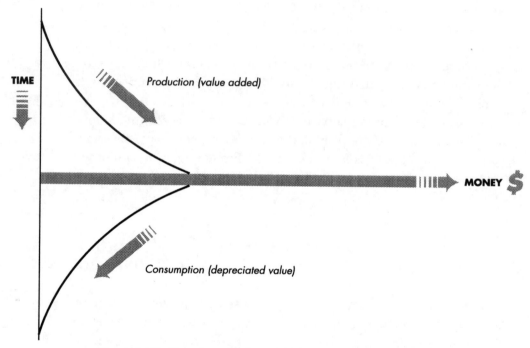

**Figure 3.10.** *The value added in production and value lost in consumption.*

Services, although they are not used up in the same way as goods, are provided on a time-limited or specified criteria basis. It is not possible to buy a doctor, but you can buy an amount of time in which he will exercise his skills. When the time that has been purchased has elapsed, it is necessary to purchase more time in order to use the expertise or knowledge of the service provider.

Those providing services update their skills and expertise to ensure that these have continuing value to potential consumers. Without this update the value of the service provided can diminish.

**SUMMARY**

Main points in chapter 3:

1.  The ultimate purpose of all production and of all provision of services is to satisfy consumer needs. Value of labor, capital, and other factors used in various stages of production are ultimately determined by final consumer demand.

2.  All goods and services go through various stages of production or skill acquisition, exchange and consumption.

3.  Behind every retail outlet and consumer service is a "back up" supply system.

4.  There is an order to the economic process—resources are transformed into production, which are then distributed to the final consumer and investment market.

5.  The Aggregate Production Structure (APS) is an economic model that represents the total dollar value of all intermediate and final goods and services produced in a year.

6.  The APS is interstate and international in scope. Products are transferred to other locations around the world to become inputs in the production process.

7.  The factors of production—land, labor, capital, and entrepreneurship—are crucial to the economic process at each stage of production.

8.  Fixed capital consists of machines, equipment, and tools that are used to assist the transformation of "goods-in-process" toward final use.

9.  Money, exchange, transportation, and inventories at each stage facilitate the production process.

10. Once consumer and capital goods are produced, they are consumed and gradually wear out, and must eventually be replaced. All consumer and capital goods depreciate in value over time.

## IMPORTANT TERMS

| | |
|---|---|
| Aggregate Production Structure | Marketing channels |
| Consumption | Money and exchange |
| Economic model | Natural resources |
| Fixed capital goods | Output |
| Goods-in-process | Retail market |
| Heuristic model | Stages of production |
| Horizontal integration | Supply system |
| Input | Value added |
| Interstage | Value lost |
| Intrastage | Vertical integration |
| Inventories | Wholesale trade |
| Manufacturing sector | |

## INFLUENTIAL ECONOMIST

### CARL MENGER, FOUNDER OF THE "AUSTRIAN" SCHOOL

**Name: Carl Menger (1840-1921)**

**Background:** Born in Neu-Sandez (now in Poland), part of the Austro-Hungarian Empire. Menger studied law and political science at the University of Vienna. In 1873, he became a professor of law and political science at the University and for two years was the private tutor of Crown Prince Rudolf of Austria. He held the chair of political economy from 1879 until 1903.

**Major Work:** In 1871, at the age of 31, he wrote the Grundsatze (translated as *The Principles of Economics*). It was a breakthrough work. Instead of viewing the world horizontally in terms of competitive factors of production (land, labor and capital), he envisioned the world vertically in terms of the cooperative stages of production (higher order capital goods being transformed into lower order consumer goods). His vision of the economy forms the logical approach of this book.

Menger also was one of the three discoverers of the principle of marginal utility (to be explained later), which forms the basis of modern-day microeconomics. He solved the value-exchange debate (diamond-water paradox) that had been a mystery to the classical school of Adam Smith and David Ricardo. The other two co-discoverers were British economist William Stanley Jevons and French-Swiss economist Leon Walras.

In a sense, Carl Menger is the father of both macroeconomics and micro-economics, and thus deserves recognition as one of the greatest economists who ever lived. Adam Smith had the greatest impact in terms of economic policy, but Menger had a far greater understanding of sound economic theory.

**Sample Quotation:** "...should the need of people for the consumption of tobacco cease completely to exist, the tobacco already manufactured into products suitable to human consumption, and probably also the stocks of raw tobacco leaves, tobacco seeds, and many other goods of higher order having a causal connection with the satisfaction of the need for tobacco, would be completely deprived of their goods character. But not all goods of higher order used by the tobacco industry would necessarily meet this fate. The land and agricultural implements used in the cultivation of tobacco, for instance, and perhaps also many tools and machines used in the manufacture of tobacco products, would retain their goods-character with respect to other human needs since they can be placed in causal connection with these other needs even after the disappearance of the need for tobacco." (*The Principles of Economics*, p. 66) Was Menger's classic example of tobacco in 1871 a fortuitous view of the anti-smoking trends of today?

**Most Famous Idea:** Menger introduced two revolutionary concepts in the above paragraph: his theory of imputation and the marginality principle. In the theory of imputation, the price of commodities and capital goods are not determined by their cost of production or labor time, but the demand derived from final consumer use. Menger rejected the labor theory of value. It is final demand by consumers that ultimately establishes the direction of productive activity, not labor and other costs of production. Menger also introduced marginal analysis in economics. When the demand for a specific product declines sharply (such as tobacco in the case above), the factors used to produce this product do not necessarily fall equally. Rather, their price is determined by the next best use of the factors of production.

**Personal Note:** Menger never published a second edition of his *Grundsatze*, even though it was immensely influential. The German historical school, to which Menger's book was dedicated, rejected Menger's claim that economics could be a theoretical science based on logic and laws. Menger's *Grundsatze* was not translated into English until 1950, almost 80 years later!

Menger died in 1921, a pessimist about the future of the West and the future of the school of thought that he founded. Following the First World War, Austria faced starvation, hyperinflation and socialist control. The influence of the Austrian school was on the wane. It would be several generations later before Austrian economics would again be recognized for its positive contribution to mainstream economic thought.

**PROBLEMS TO PONDER**

1.  Identify the general stages in the production of:
    (a)  shoes
    (b)  a hammer
    (c)  gasoline
    (d)  a class lecture
    (e)  a legal case in court
    (f)  a heart operation
    (g)  an economist

2.  Of the four general stages of production (raw commodities, manufacturing, wholesale trade, and retail), identify where the following belong:
    (a)  mining geologist
    (b)  merchant captain
    (c)  steelworker
    (d)  salesclerk at a shopping mall
    (e)  Exxon Corporation
    (f)  airline flight to New York

3.  Determine whether the following products are fixed capital, consumer goods or goods-in-process:
    (a)  air conditioning unit established in an auto factory to make the workplace more comfortable.
    (b)  factory air conditioning unit placed inside an automobile.
    (c)  typewriting paper sold in a college bookstore.
    (d)  typewriting paper used by a paper manufacturing firm for accounting and secretarial needs.
    (e)  corn used by a farmer to plant more corn ("seed corn").
    (f)  cornmeal eaten by the farmer at lunch.

4.  Project: Select a specific item in a retail store and ask the store owner how much it costs to obtain this item wholesale. Why the retail price of a good is usually greater than what it costs in a market economy? Now estimate the cost of running the store. Does the retail price still exceed total costs? Are there any exceptions to this economic law that retail prices must exceed costs, i.e., that the price of outputs must exceed the cost of inputs?

5.  The general model of the economy measures the output of all intermediate and final goods and services produced in a year. How are products which take longer than a year to produce taken into account, such as an office building or dam?

6.  Project: How long does it take for iron ore to become part of a finished automobile that people are driving? For a newly planted tree to become the outside of a house? Contact a local builder and find out how long it takes on average to build an office building, from architectural drawings to moving in.

7.  Describe the major stages of producing a motion picture from the first stage (writing a screenplay) to the final stage (releasing the film in theaters). How important are time and money in film making?

8.  An economist said, "Since the consumer is sovereign, and consumption is the end purpose of all production, therefore the economy is consumer driven, and we must do all we can to stimulate consumption. Production will then follow." Are there any flaws in this economist's logic? Which should government promote first—consumption or production? Or neither?

*Chapter 4*
# THE THEORY OF THE FIRM: THE ROLE OF PROFIT AND LOSS

*"Profits are the ultimate measure of how efficiently we provide customers with the best products for their needs. Profits are required to survive and grow."*

HENRY FORD II—
*Mission Statement, 1984*

Standards of living are increased and economic progress experienced through the transformation of raw commodities into useful goods and services. As a result, individual and national wealth grows as measured by the quantity, quality, and variety of goods and services. In the previous chapter the four-stage model of the economy was presented. This model shows this transformation process, the Aggregate Production Structure (APS). This model is reproduced below.

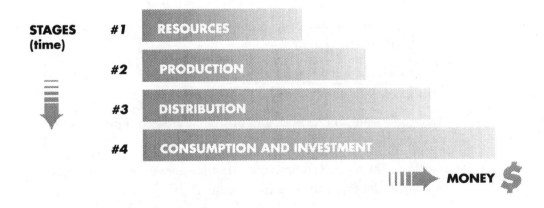

**Figure 4.1.** *The Aggregate Production Structure (APS).*

The APS will serve as our focal point in studying the economics of the whole economy. Macroeconomics is a branch of economics that deals with the performance, structure, and behavior of the economy as a whole.

The APS can also serve as the basis of microeconomics, the theory of consumer demand as it relates to individuals and companies. Microeconomics is the study of the economic behavior of individuals and the companies that serve their needs, as opposed to macroeconomics, which studies the output, prices, profits, money, and trade of an entire nation. The next ten chapters will present microeconomics followed by a discussion of macroeconomics.

## Microeconomics addresses the following questions:

- How do companies set prices for their goods and services?

- What determines consumer demand?

- If the demand for a product increases, should a company raise prices, raise output, or both?

- If the costs of producing a product increases, can a company pass on these costs to consumers by raising prices?

- How are wages, rent and other expenses determined?

- What is the role of profits, and how can profits be maximized or losses minimized by a company?

- Does it make sense for a company to operate a business at a loss over several years?

- What role does opportunity cost play in the company's decision-making, and how can it be measured?

- What motivates businesses to increase the quantity, quality and variety of goods and services?

- What motivates individuals and businesses to economize— to control costs and avoid wasteful spending?

- Is the profit motive sometimes perverse, encouraging a company to make money at the expense of their customers?

- Is it possible to harmonize the interests of shareholders, employees, executives, customers, suppliers, and the community?

## WHAT IS A COMPANY TRYING TO ACHIEVE?

The APS diagram shown in Figure 4.1 shows four stages of production. Each individual company participates somewhere along the production process. A mining company is located in the first stage (resources). An automobile maker is in the second stage (production). A book distributor is in the third stage (wholesale distribution). And a gasoline station is in the fourth and final stage (retail/final consumption). In some cases the stage a company belongs in is difficult to pinpoint. For example, a major oil company may have a place in all four stages—extracting crude oil and natural gas at the well; manufacturing gasoline, motor oil, and other energy products; transporting and wholesaling these energy products; and selling gasoline at the pump.

No matter where a company belongs on the four-sector model, its economic activity is included somewhere in the APS. As a producer, each individual company contributes to the output of goods or services, thus moving the production process forward. The APS is made up entirely of companies that are in the business of moving goods and services down the production line toward final retail use. If added up, the annual revenue of every company would be the total amount of spending in the economy during the year - the total dollar volume of the APS.

When an organization sells services rather than products, the same four stages of production apply, although the terminology differs. Stage one: the organization acquires the needed human resources. Stage two: the organization ensures that these resources have the skills, expertise and abilities to meet customer requirements. This stage is similar to manufacturing in the production of goods. Stage three: the skills, expertise and abilities of the human resource(s) are marketed to end users and, finally, in stage four, services are purchased. Stages three and four in service production are often combined. Each company operates in a similar fashion to the APS model on a smaller scale. Note in the APS model above how each stage of production increases in value as final use (the retail stage) is approached. Value is added at each successive stage. As raw materials are refined into usable products, their value increases. As human resources gain skills, expertise, and knowledge, their value also increases.

The same production flow holds true on a micro scale. A company buys raw materials (inputs), adds value through production processes, and sells the final product (outputs) to its customers. A capitalist-entrepreneur (owner/manager of a company) purchases raw materials from resource owners (suppliers), hires and organizes the factors of production (land, labor, capital), produces a new product or service, and then sells that new product or service to its customers. See figure 4.2.

If the company can sell its products or services for more than it costs to produce them, it makes a profit. If costs exceed revenues the company takes a loss. A profit-and-loss system is the essence of all businesses transactions.

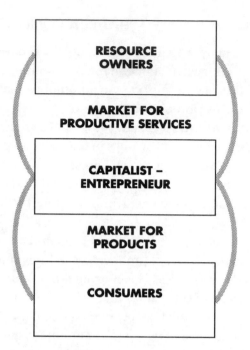

**Figure 4.2.** *The role of the capitalist-entrepreneur (the firm) between resources and customers.*
Source: Israel Kirzner, *Market Theory and the Price System,* p. 19.

## THE CENTRAL ROLE OF THE ENTREPRENEUR

In microeconomics, entrepreneurs are the key players in the company's effort to make a profit. Entrepreneurs are risk-taking businesspersons who initiate or finance new commercial enterprises. They are the idea people behind the company's drive for new products or services.

The term entrepreneur was originally used by J. B. Say. Entrepreneur is a French word meaning one who undertakes a business venture and assumes the risk in order to make a profit. Entrepreneurs initiate production and service process by providing vision and capital. Without entrepreneurs, economic performance could not be improved and living standards would not be advanced.

Who are the entrepreneurs? Robert Sobel says they are "men and women of vision and energy [who] have seen possibilities where others saw none, seized opportunities when others hesitated, persevered when others gave up."[1] Owner/entrepreneurs are innovators who reshape patterns of production and distribution, develop new products and processes, open new markets and sources of supply, devise new forms of company, and improve existing companies. Entrepreneurs are opportunists and visionary organizers who bring together capitalists, landlords, workers, and specialized knowledge to create goods and services

1    Robert Sobel and David B. Sicilia, *The Entrepreneurs: An American Adventure* (Houghton Mifflin, 1986), flyleaf.

that consumers will want. Israel Kirzner describes entrepreneurs as individuals who are alert to opportunities and new ways of accomplishing tasks. Entrepreneurship is also a discovery process.

## CASE STUDY: PORSCHE AUTOMOBILES

There are many examples of the dynamic role of entrepreneurs. For example, Porsche A. G. was founded by German industrialist Ferdinand Porsche in the early 20th century. He invented the Volkswagen, the "people's car," in the 1930s. World War II devastated Porsche's factories and the company had to start from scratch. Porsche defied conventional wisdom by creating an expensive sports car in the country left impoverished by war. From a business viewpoint, Porsche's decision seemed irrational.

In a war torn nation like Germany, where would the demand for an expensive sports car come from? Yet Porsche was successful, due in large part to the owner's racing background. As *The New York Times* (March 28, 1998) reported:

"Porsche's racing acumen brought the car a windfall of free publicity, by word of mouth and in the sports pages. But racing was also the crucible that kept Porsche a technological step ahead of other sports cars. To win races, it was necessary to constantly come up with new ideas about design, fuel efficiency and safety, as well as ways to produce more power from smaller motors."

Over the years, Porsche made improvements such as anti-lock disc brakes, roll bars, higher torque engines, intake and exhaust manifolds, and extra waste gate tailpipes. In the 1990s, Porsche engaged in downsizing to remain competitive, hiring Japanese consultants, slashing the Porsche workforce, and compressing six layers of management into four. As a result, productivity rose sharply.

The two-stage micro model developed in this chapter is a highly flexible way for economists to show the dynamics of a market economy and the role of the owner/entrepreneur in making business and pricing decisions—the creation of new products, the elimination of old lines of production, downsizing and upgrading.

## EXAMPLE: MICROSOFT CORPORATION

The well-known computer software company Microsoft Corporation fits into the APS and the micro models. Microsoft was founded by computer wizard Bill Gates in 1975 and developed into the world's largest software company by the late 1980s.

An examination of Microsoft's economic activity from the accountant's point of view shows how Microsoft has added value to the economy. The following is Microsoft's income statement for 2008 (see the appendix for a discussion of financial statements).

In the following example, Microsoft made a profit of $17.7 billion in 2008. Microsoft added value to the economy because revenues for the company exceeded costs. The company provided a service (computer software) to its customers and wealth was created.

**Figure 4.3**

**INCOME STATEMENT OF MICROSOFT CORPORATION, 2008**

**(U.S. $ millions)**

REVENUES . . . . . . . . . . . . . . . . . . . . . . . . . . . . . . . .$61,742
EXPENSES:
Cost of materials . . . . . . . . . . . . . . . . . . . . . . . . . . . .11,598
Research Development . . . . . . . . . . . . . . . . . . . . . . . .8,164
Wages and salaries/administration . . . . . . . . . . . . . . .18,166
Taxes . . . . . . . . . . . . . . . . . . . . . . . . . . . . . . . . . . . .6,133
TOTAL EXPENSES . . . . . . . . . . . . . . . . . . . . . . . . . .$44,061

NET INCOME (PROFIT) . . . . . . . . . . . . . . . . . . . . . .$17,681

## MICRO MODEL OF AN INDIVIDUAL COMPANY

The microeconomic diagram below is based on Microsoft's financial statement. See figure 4.4 below.

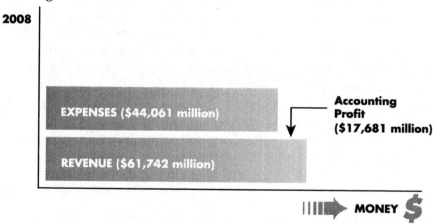

**Figure 4.4.** *Micro Model of Microsoft Corp.*

This diagram coincides with the macro economic model, the APS. In the above model, the two variables of time and money are measured in one year—2008. The vertical axis measures an accounting year, and the horizontal axis represents dollars expended (for expenses and revenues) during the business year. The top rectangle represents total expenses incurred during 2008, amounting to $44 billion. The bottom rectangle represents total revenues for 2008, or $61.7 billion. The difference is a net income (profit) of $17.7 billion.

This diagram is known as an input-output model. The first rectangle represents the "input," the annual expenses of the company, and the second rectangle represents the "output," or the annual revenues of the company.

This diagram is a simplified representation of its income statement. Normally, expenses and revenues occur throughout the year. In this model all the expenses occur first, followed by all the revenues. To repeat what was said in chapter 3, the input-output diagram is a heuristic model, a simplified concept that may not reflect reality perfectly, but is useful in demonstrating a concept.

## LINK BETWEEN MICRO AND MACRO

Note the similarity between the "macro" model of figure 4.1 and the "micro" model of figure 4.4. In each diagram the vertical and horizontal axes are "time" (stages of production) and "money." Both show "value added" from one stage to another. The input-output model of a single company is a microcosm of the APS. The total revenue in the APS can be obtained by adding up the revenues of all companies in a nation during the year. The micro model forms the basis of the macro model. Microeconomics is linked directly to macroeconomics.

There are some differences in the models. The micro model has only two stages, "expenses" and "revenues," while the macro model has four general stages. The micro diagram's vertical axis measures only one accounting year, while the macro diagram's vertical axis represents the entire production process, which may involve many years. The micro diagram's horizontal axis counts the dollar amounts (inputs and outputs) of one company, while the macro diagram's horizontal axis counts the dollar gross output of all companies during the year.

## THE COMPANY'S FINANCIAL STATUS: THREE POSSIBILITIES

Every company's financial status has three possible outcomes:
- The company can make a profit.
- The company can break even.
- The company can lose money.

In the following case, Microsoft Corp. made a substantial profit. In normal economic circumstances, successful companies make a profit in most years.

Comparing the income statements for Wal-Mart, Kmart, and Sears demonstrates these outcomes. Wal-Mart made a profit, Kmart essentially broke even, and Sears lost money. (For comparative purposes, we use the fiscal year 1992 for these three companies. Kmart is now owned by Sears.)

## Figure 4.5

### INCOME STATEMENTS, 1992, FOR U.S. RETAILERS
### (U. S. $millions)

|  | Wal-Mart | Kmart | Sears |
|---|---|---|---|
| Revenue | $ 44.3 | $38.1 | $25.4 |
| Expenses: |  |  |  |
| Wages and salaries | 6.1 | 5.2 | 3.6 |
| Materials | 35.3 | 31.1 | 22.0 |
| Capital costs | 1.3 | 1.7 | 1.0 |
| Total Expenses | $ 42.7 | $38.0 | $26.6 |
| Profit (loss) | 1.6 | 0.1 | (1.2) |

## THE ROLE OF PROFITS AND LOSSES

A market economy is not just an economy of profits. It is an economy of profits and losses. What roles do profits and losses play in the individual company and the economy in general?

Profits and losses are the sine qua non of economic existence. They determine what is produced, when it is produced, how much is produced, and how it is produced.

Companies can continue to produce without making a profit, but not indefinitely. Profits are essential for long-term survival. Without profit, companies will eventually go out of business. Companies can postpone the day of reckoning by borrowing money or selling off valuable assets, but at some point they must return to profitability or else shift labor and resources into another line of business. As British economist John Kay declares, "In the long run, companies that fail to add value in a competitive market will not survive, nor do they deserve to."[2]

Profit and loss are recorded in the company's annual income statement, which lists revenues, expenditures, and net income (or net loss) for the fiscal year. Accountants also find the company's balance sheet, which lists assets, liabilities, and net worth, useful. A third financial statement is the company's cash-flow statement. All three financial statements and how they can help determine a company's financial well-being are discussed in the appendix. Of all the statements, the income statement is most important. Without long-term profitability, no company can survive.

2 John Kay, *Why Companies Succeed* (Oxford University Press, 1995), p. 19.

## THE OPPORTUNITY COST OF CAPITAL

Furthermore, companies need to make enough money to cover the normal return on investment. Business leaders need to be alert to the fact that shareholders and investors must earn enough to compensate them for risking their investment capital. If a profit is not anticipated, investors would be better off investing in a money market fund or a stock market index fund, depending on their tolerance for risk. If a company earns only 2% on its investment capital over the long run, investors and shareholders have been cheated. Yes, they made a profit, but they could have done better earning 5% a year in a bank account. Moreover, the company's capital raised through public offerings on the stock market is competing with other investment capital on Wall Street. The return on capital needs to match the average return of all other stocks or a stock market index. Recently the average long-run return on U. S. stocks has been around 11% a year.

Economists refer to this risk factor as the opportunity cost of capital. A new accounting statistic has been created to quantify the opportunity cost of capital, known as Economic Value Added (EVA). EVA is also known as "super profits" or "residual income." EVA is:

- After-tax operating profits (normal accounting profit)
- Appropriate capital charge for both debt and equity of the company EVA
- EVA is discussed more fully in the appendix to this chapter.

The significant role of profit and loss in the market economy can be explained by examining three potential outcomes—profit, loss and breakeven.

Sears lost money in 1992. This situation is shown in the input-output model. (figure 4.6). Sears' revenues were insufficient to cover costs, including the opportunity cost of capital.

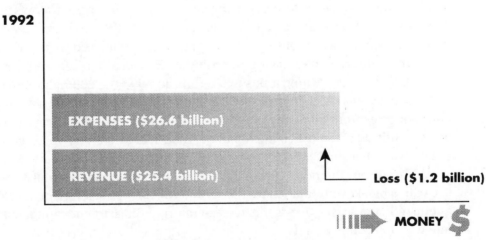

**Figure 4.6.** *Sears loses money in 1992.*

What should company leaders do to regain profitable status and make share-holders happy? There are several alternatives. Sears could continue losing money, while paying workers, rent, taxes and other expenses out of capital, but that is not a viable long-term solution. At some point, the big retailer has to make changes to enhance products or cut costs and become more efficient. Ultimately, Sears must make a profit or it will be forced to close its doors and investors will seek better opportunities with their investment funds.

What about situation #2, where Kmart is breaking even? Figure 4.7 illustrates the case of breakeven.

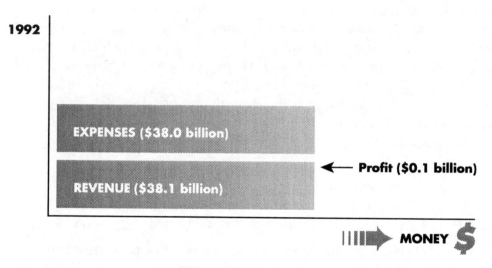

**Figure 4.7.** *Kmart breaks even.*

Is breakeven an acceptable long-term situation for Kmart? Certainly, the company is paying all its bills, including the salaries of its top executives. Kmart is also making enough money to pay for the maintenance of current assets (replacing equipment and other depreciated assets). Yet for 1992 there were no earnings to retain, no accumulation of surplus capital that could be used to expand the business. Why is this not an ideal long-run solution? Because, in essence, the capital tied up in Kmart is not earning a positive return. In 1992 the $38 billion expended in inputs (wages, materials, and cost of capital) resulted in $38.1 billion in output (revenues or sales from company products). If that $38 billion had been invested in a bank certificate of deposit, it might have earned 5, or $1.9 billion in interest income, or better yet in a stock market index fund, it might have earned nearly $5 billion.

A breakeven situation is not an ideal long-term situation. Capitalist-owners can live with a breakeven situation for the short term, but in the long run they must seek a return that at least exceeds the average return of investment capital commensurate with the company's risk.

The minimum acceptable long-run condition for Kmart and other similar companies in the economy is to earn a return better than its competitors. After all, capitalist-entrepreneurs are not interested in risking their money on ventures that cannot promise a better return than they can get elsewhere.

Wal-Mart, like Microsoft Corp., earned a significant profit in 1992. Unlike Kmart and Sears, it added value to its net worth (and to the economy). Figure 4.8 below reflects this profitable situation.

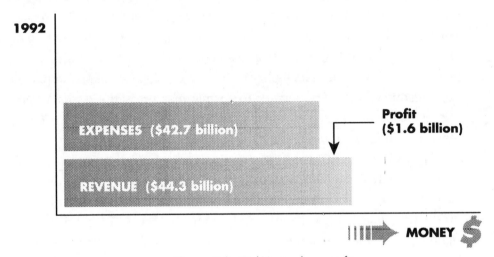

**1992**

EXPENSES ($42.7 billion)

**Profit ($1.6 billion)**

REVENUE ($44.3 billion)

MONEY $

**Figure 4.8.** *Wal-Mart makes a profit.*

Real growth can only take place when a company earns a profit. Value is added, not only to the company, but to the economy. Value is added at the micro level (the company grows), and at the macro level (the APS expands).

A high return of capital also means that the company can expand. It has the funds to buy new equipment, train its employees, adopt new production processes, do research and development, and build new facilities.

McDonald's Restaurants, Inc., is a good example of how long-term profitability can improve the company's prospects. The first McDonald's restaurants were drive-in restaurants. As the company became profitable, it had the funds to offer indoor seating. When it became even more profitable, McDonald's built larger, more spacious restaurants with more inviting surroundings and a wider selection of products, all with an aim to increase sales and customer satisfaction. Today each McDonald's restaurant has its own unique features and furnishings some with playgrounds. McDonald's also expanded rapidly in foreign countries; where most of its profits are now generated. This gradual expansion was due to long-term growth in after-tax earnings.

## THE DISCIPLINE OF THE MARKET

How does profit-and-loss analysis relate to economic well-being? If a company makes an economic profit, it usually indicates that it is responding well to the needs and wants of the public. As David Packard, co-founder of Hewlett-Packard, the electronics company, states, "profit is the best single measure of our contribution to society and the ultimate source of our corporate strength."[3] In the example of companies that make profit and break even above, the customers of Microsoft and Wal-Mart are willing to pay for their products, and these companies can cover all their expenses and more. A higher-than-expected profit means that individuals like the products and want more. A higher profit margin signals the marketplace that even more resources should be devoted to the manufacture of these goods. Wal-Mart and Microsoft ought to expand and the profits these companies earn give them the resources with which to expand.

Losses indicate just the opposite. Customers are not completely satisfied with the way Kmart and Sears were doing business, at least in 1992. In the case of Sears, customers did not purchase enough of their products to cover all of the company's production, marketing expenses, and opportunity cost of capital. The market was signaling that fewer resources should be devoted to companies not operating profitably. Sears' losses indicate that it should find other products, or alternative methods that better serve the customer.

Economic profits and losses are a guide to an individual company's decisions to increase or decrease output according to the desires of its consumers. The market system imposes discipline on companies, making them cost conscious and alert to consumer demands.

MIT Managerial economist Shlomo Maital says "The health and wealth of a large number of individual businesses—small, medium and large—determine the economic health and wealth of a nation. When they succeed, managers create wealth, income and jobs for large numbers of people. When they fail, working people and their families suffer. It is businesses that create wealth, not countries or governments. It is individual businesses that are either competitive in world markets or are unable to sell in them. It is businesses that decide how well or how poorly off we are."[4]

---

3  David Packard, *The HP Way* (Harper, 1995), p. 80.

4  Shlomo Maital, *Executive Economics* (Free Press, 1994), p. 6. Professor Maital lives in Israel and is visiting professor at MIT's Sloan School of Management.

## ACCOUNTING FOR A COMPANY'S PROFITABILITY

A company's profitability is determined in many ways. For example, the following five methods can add to long-term profitability:

(1)  Cut costs
(2)  Increase prices
(3)  Raise output or production
(4)  Expand the product line
(5)  Sell off non-performing assets

Companies have a variety of ways to account for these sources of profitability. They rely primarily on three financial statements required of all corporations each fiscal year: the income statement (also known as the profit-and-loss statement), the balance sheet, and the cash-flow statement. An income statement can indicate reductions in costs or increases in revenues, while a balance sheet shows the sale of an asset. Finally, a fourth financial statement, Economic Value Added (EVA), is helpful in determining true profitability from an economic point of view. Students unfamiliar with these financial statements should study the appendix at the end of this chapter.

## ARE PROFITS ALWAYS A RELIABLE GUIDE?

Profits can also be a misleading guide. Sometimes businesses can be short-sighted, focusing almost exclusively on the short-term bottom line at the expense of its labor force, suppliers, and customers. Executives might short-change their employees, fail to deliver a quality product, squeeze their suppliers, or artificially stimulate customer demand, all in an effort to make a fast buck. Companies sometimes engage in outright fraudulent practices.

Businesses are not clairvoyant. Individuals, including business leaders, make mistakes. Fortunately, the market discourages mistakes. Short-term schemes invariably backfire in the long term and profit margin declines, and the business suffers losses. Those businesses that repeatedly suffer losses eventually go out of business. Short-sighted and dishonest business people lose customers, anger employees, and lose support within the business community.

In the ideal society, capitalist-entrepreneurs must always remember that the needs and wants of the consumer are paramount. The consumer is king in the market economy. The best companies satisfy their customers and develop sound management skills with their employees, suppliers, community, and shareholders in order to produce quality products and services. Honesty is the best policy for long-term survival and profitability.

## HOW TO EXPAND PROFITS OR REDUCE LOSSES

If high profit margins are the key to an expanding economy, what must each company do to increase profits? Or, if a company is losing money, how can it minimize its losses and become profitable again?

The micro model provides insight into these questions. Sometimes business owners think that the primary path to greater profitability is to increase revenues—to expand the "output" side of the business. For instance, Wal-Mart might consider a new marketing campaign for its stores and raising prices. The campaign may be based on the hope that higher prices will not adversely affect sales. Wal-Mart might consider developing its own brand of products, opening more stores, or diversification into other related businesses. These efforts cost money, but they might increase Wal-Mart's sales volume and, therefore, might be marginally successful. If the company increases its revenues in a new campaign, will be it worth the cost? Figure 4.9, demonstrates how a successful new marketing venture pays off.

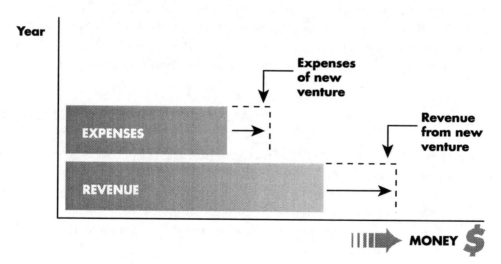

**Figure 4.9.** *Revenues exceed costs in a new business venture.*

The other possibility, sometimes overlooked by companies, is to focus on cost-cutting measures. Rather than increase revenues, why not reduce costs? Companies could concentrate on the "input" side of the company and try the following tactics:

Downsize the company—cut marginal workers, high-priced suppliers, and questionable departments.

- Sell off unprofitable divisions

- Reorganize and become less bureaucratic

- Move to a lower-rent district

The net result may be a smaller but more profitable company that may serve its customers, employees, suppliers, and shareholders better.

The actions of a business can be compared to the actions of a sports team. Suppose a college basketball team had a lackluster season last year, winning 17 games but losing 16 games. Attendance is weak and TV rights are low. What can the coach do to turn his team around next season? Good coaches rely on two factors to win: defense and offense. They can encourage the players to score more points by practicing more often, working on their shot selection and increasing their scoring percentage. They can also improve their defense, working on a full court press, or one-on-one play.

If the coach works only on offense, the benefit may only be marginal. But by improving both offense and defense, the results can be dramatic. The same principles apply to business. A good manager can see dramatic results by focusing on increased sales (offense) and cutting costs (defense) at the same time. By using these principles companies can avoid losses and dramatically increase profits.

The actions of a business can also be compared to the actions of an individual facing financial problems. If an individual faces excessive debt, what is the solution? The simple solution is to earn more money to resolve the financial problems. But earning more money does not resolve the issue in every case. Even millionaires sometimes go broke because they never learn to control their wasteful spending. The more effective solution is to develop ways to control spending rather than earn more money.

The same solutions are true in business. New marketing campaigns and other techniques to increase revenues will not work unless the company imposes a system of controlling the costs of doing business. There is no point in increasing sales if expenses rise by the same amount or more? Figure 4.10 below illustrates the situation where a new venture increases revenues, but the net return is negative because of excessive costs.

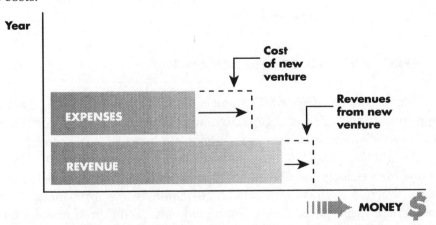

**Figure 4.10.** *Costs exceed revenues in a new business venture.*

## COST-BENEFIT ANALYSIS

Comparing a change in revenue with a change in costs in business is called cost-benefit analysis. Cost-benefit analysis is used in government to determine if building a new dam, highway, or other public project is worth doing. A new venture may raise revenue, but how much does it cost to implement? This is the critical issue. If revenue rise more than costs, then the new venture may be considered a success. But if the new venture costs more than it brings in, it is a failure.

One of the most famous business failures was the introduction of the Ford Edsel automobile in the late 1950s. All the marketing research indicated that the Edsel would be a hit, but when it was introduced to the public, it failed miserably, and many Ford dealers suffered. Another example of a failed product was the New Coke in the mid-1980s. Marketing experts expected the New Coke to be a big hit. New Coke was not a hit, and Coke Classic won out. On the other hand, in 2007 Apple Inc. introduced its revolutionary Iphone, which combines telecommunications with the Internet and numerous other services. Iphone was an expensive investment for Apple, but it turned out to be a huge hit with consumers, especially young people.

Cost-benefit analysis can also be applied within the company, especially in large companies with many departments. Many departments do not know the true costs of their business, because administrative overhead costs such as office space, equipment and other services are shared by everyone. In an effort to control these costs, many office managers now charge each department for a share of the costs. For example, when a department sends out material by an overnight mailing service, the department is charged the fee directly. Or if the department prints material, even though printing is done in-house, the department is charged the cost of printing. This approach allows the department to identify the costs, revenue and value that the specific department has added to the company. Analysis of this type of data and actions taken to improve performance indicated by the data can make the company more efficient and profitable.

## USING EVA TO IMPROVE ECONOMIC PERFORMANCE

Economic Value Added (EVA), an economic measure of profit that includes the opportunity cost of capital, can also dramatically improve a company's profitability and market-share value. (See the appendix for how EVA is calculated.)

Over 300 major U. S. corporations, including Coca Cola, Eli Lilly, and Whole Foods Market, now use EVA as a tool to identify potential acquisitions, expansion plans, and non-performing assets, and to eliminate low profit-margin operations on individual business units within the company. Some divisions of a company are more costly than others. Without taking into account the full cost of capital, a company may be using too much labor and other resources in a specific division. EVA helps determine the right mix of capital in each business unit.

EVA is also being used as an incentive bonus system for managers and employees. Bonuses are linked to economic earnings, not just accounting earnings, and EVA has proven to be an effective tool in boosting productivity.

## TWO CHARACTERISTICS OF THE MARKET ECONOMY

Let's now take an overview of the market economy. Our micro model of the company explains two phenomena of the market economy:

1. The quantity, quality and variety of goods and services tend to increase over time.

2. Waste is minimized and resources tend to be used efficiently.

## HOW QUANTITY, QUALITY AND VARIETY INCREASE

The micro model explains these two phenomena. The "revenue" side of the input-output model demonstrates the tendency toward increased diversity in the marketplace. In the three cases illustrated above, the capitalist-entrepreneur frequently seeks ways to expand revenue in an effort to become more profitable (or avoid losses). The company may create new products, enhance the quality of its current products and services, or expand into foreign markets, all in a strategy to beat the competition and increase the company's profitability. The net result is an increase in the quantity, quality, and variety of goods and services.

Review the past 20 years. Why has there been a tendency toward a wider variety of products, expanded services, and increased quality? Because business entrepreneurs are profit-seeking individuals; they know that by better satisfying their customers, they can achieve greater profits.

Take 3M Company for example. 3M managers have generated so many new products that 30% of its sales come from products that were developed within the past five years. 3M Company now has over 60,000 products compared to only several thousand 20 years ago. Why has 3M Company expanded into so many new and varied products? The long-term effect is to increase its profitability through increased consumer satisfaction.

## INCREASED EFFICIENCY

What about market efficiency? The "expense" side of the input-output model demonstrates the tendency toward efficiency and waste avoidance in the market-place. Considering any of the three examples above (Sears, Kmart, and Wal-Mart), indicates that companies frequently aim at cutting waste and becoming more efficient in an effort to become more profitable or to avoid further losses. Managers are constantly under pressure to make each division of their company more profitable. Each part of the business must add value. Thus, there is a strong incentive to cut costs, eliminate duplicate programs and reduce underemployed resources.

The experience of IBM in the early 1990s provides a good example of the benefits of downsizing and controlling costs. Prior to 1990, IBM had a "hire, never fire" policy combined with a union-management determination to only raise and never lower salaries of IBM employees. This approach at IBM gradually led to a bloated, inefficient workforce that lacked incentives to produce and create new products. Eventually IBM lost its competitive edge, market share, and profitability. Its stock price fell from $140 a share to $40 in the late 1980s.

Finally, in the early 1990s IBM abandoned its lifetime employment policy. The company went through a difficult period of restructuring and downsizing. Cuts were made in management, employees, and bureaucracy. New incentives were established allowing the company to be more responsive to customers. Figure 4.11 reflects the advantage of downsizing:

Downsizing was beneficial to IBM, which is back in the black. Earnings are up and employment is rising again. IBM's stock has more than tripled in price (by 2007).

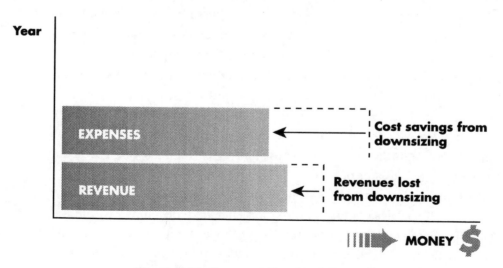

**Figure 4.11.** *The potential benefits of downsizing.*

Inefficiency and waste are present in any economy, but over the long haul, all companies, large or small, must pay attention to their costs or face losing their competitive edge. As shown in later chapters, government operations often do not face the discipline of the market since they do not operate on a profit-loss basis, and thus often become bloated, inefficient, and unresponsive to the needs of customers.

## INTRODUCING SUPPLY AND DEMAND

The models discussed explain the behavior of individual businesses in the market economy and how these businesses respond to profit and loss. But how do the economic laws of supply and demand fit into enterprise calculations? The answer can be derived from the input-output micro model used in this chapter and represented by the diagram reproduced below as figure 4.12.

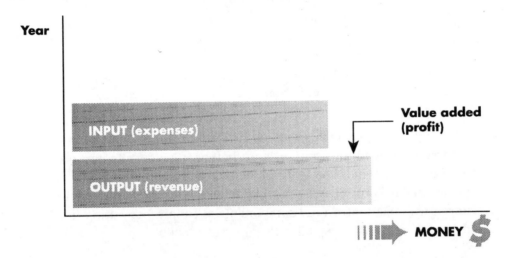

**Figure 4.12.** *Expenses and revenues of a firm.*

The law of supply and demand can be derived from the "output" rectangle, or total revenue of the company, since revenue represents both how much consumers bought and how much suppliers sold.

The law of supply and demand for the factors of production, such as rent or wages, can also be derived from the expense side of the company or the "input" rectangle.

The demand for, and supply of, consumer goods and services is reflected in the revenue side of the company's balance sheet. Revenue is the "price" multiplied by the "quantity" of goods and services sold by the company and bought by customers. In financial terms, total revenue can be stated as follows:

$$TR = P_1Q_1 + P_2Q_2 + P_3Q_3 + \ldots + P_nQ_n, \text{ or}$$

$$TR \sum_{i=1}^{n} = P_iQ_i, \text{ where}$$

| | |
|---|---|
| $P_i$ | = the price per unit, and |
| $Q_i$ | = the quantity of each distinct product or service sold (i=1, ..., n) |

What are supply and demand for wages, rents and other factors of production? Look at the expense side of the company's financial statement. Total costs consist of the prices of each factor of production multiplied by the number of factors involved in the production process. In financial terms, total costs can be broken down as follows:

| | | |
|---|---|---|
| TC | = | L • R + N • W + K • I + S • P, where |
| L | = | Land units, |
| R | = | rents per unit, |
| N | = | labor units, |
| W | = | wages, |
| K | = | capital, |
| I | = | interest rate, |
| S | = | supplies (resources), |
| and P | = | price of each supply unit |

Supply and demand can be determined by breaking down the elements of the company's expenditures and revenue. In the remaining chapters on microeconomics, the components of supply and demand will be presented. The next chapter will be devoted to consumer demand and how prices evolve and function. It will be followed with chapters on the components of supply, presenting the factors of production—land, labor, capital, and entrepreneurship.

## SUMMARY

**These are the main points presented in Chapter 4:**

1. Microeconomics is the study of the economic behavior of individuals and the companies that serve their needs.
2. All companies are similar in that they take inputs, add value and sell outputs that serve their customers.
3. Economic decision-making and the production process are guided by a profit-and-loss system.
4. Companies must earn a rate of return exceeding the return on competitive investment alternatives such as a bank rate of interest or stock market index (depending on the risk) to justify their long-term survival.
5. The capitalist-entrepreneur plays a central role in determining how resources are used to produce capital and consumer goods.
6. Retained earnings from after-tax profits provide the capital for economic expansion and new developments.
7. Short-term profits can sometimes be a misleading guide in satisfying consumer needs and wants.
8. All individuals and businesses must be cost-conscious to achieve long-term survival; increasing income (for individuals) or sales (for companies) is no assurance of success.
9. Every company in the economy engages in a cost-benefit analysis to determine its long-term profitability.
10. The micro model demonstrates two characteristics of a growing economy: an increase in the quantity, quality, and variety of goods and services, and the efficient use of resources.

## IMPORTANT TERMS

Microeconomics

Macroeconomics

Income statement

Profit-and-loss statement

Economic Value Added

Balance Sheet

Breakeven

Capitalist-owner

Cost-benefit analysis

Efficiency

Quantity, quality and variety

Opportunity cost

Cash-flow statement

Downsizing

Supply and demand

## INFLUENTIAL ECONOMIST

### EDWARDS DEMING AND REVITALIZING THE ECONOMIC COMPANY

**Name: W. Edwards Deming (1900-93)**

**Background:** W. Edwards Deming was raised in Wyoming, Deming majored in mathematics and engineering at the University of Wyoming, taught physics at the Colorado School of Mines, and earned his Ph.D. in physics at Yale. During World War II, Deming developed and taught statistical methods of controlling costs in wartime production. After the war he went to Japan and trained industrialists to help rebuild their competitive edge by emphasizing quality control, not just increased production. Until his death at age 93, he was a business consultant.

With a background in the physical sciences, why include Edwards Deming as an economist? Although Deming viewed himself as a statistician, his emphasis on quality control and management techniques have had a large influence on the theory of the company and how companies can be more productive. Deming's approach is a dynamic analysis of the company, never static, and as such, it fits very closely with our approach in *Economic Logic* (emphasis on the stages of production and changes in quantity, quality and variety). Companies should never accept market conditions, but always try to respond to change.

**Major Works:** In his major works, *Quality, Productivity, and Competitive Position* (1982) and *Out of the Crisis* (1982), Deming stresses quality-conscious management and consumer research. Deming is regarded as the father of the Japanese manufacturing miracle, especially in the consumer electronics industry (TVs, cameras, videos, etc.). Since 1951 the Japanese have awarded the Deming Prize for individuals and companies who have advanced the cause of quality control.

**Sample Quotation:** "My job is to find the sources of improvement, sources of trouble....As you improve quality, your costs go down....Better quality and lower price with a little ingenuity in marketing will create a market. Keep the company in business, provide jobs and more jobs....You must carry out consumer research, look toward the future and produce goods that will have a market years from now and stay in business."[5]

5  Mary Walton, *The Deming Management Method* (Mead, 1986) pp. 24-27

**Famous Flow Charts:** Deming is famous for two diagrams. The first is called the "Deming Chain Reaction," reproduced below.

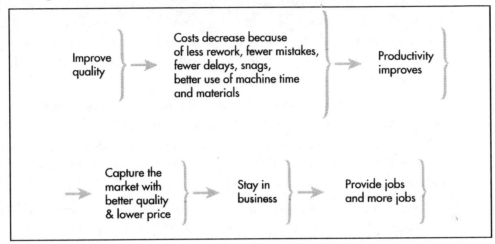

**Figure 4.13.** *The Deming Chain Reaction.*

The second diagram is called the "Deming Flow Diagram," which as you can see has much in common with our stages-of-production approach and our growth model (see chapter 17). It is reproduced below. Referring to the Deming Flow Diagram, Deming states: "The first step is to improve the materials and never stop improving them, and that means that you work with your suppliers....Improve stuff that comes in, adapt it, provide more and more what the customer needs. That requires cooperation, working together....See that upper box—'design and redesign' for the future....The consumer over toward the right [on chart] is the most important part of the production line."[6]

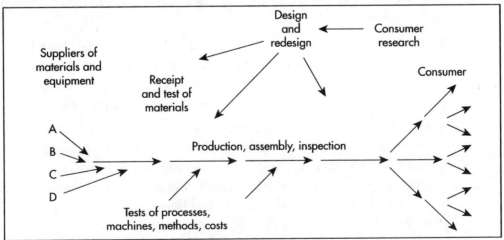

**Figure 4.14.** *The Deming Flow Diagram.*

6  Mary Walton, *The Deming Management Method* (Mead, 1986) pp. 25-29

## PROBLEMS TO PONDER

1. "The purpose of business is to create jobs." Judging from what you have learned in this chapter, is this an accurate statement? What should be done if business fails to generate enough work for everyone? Is chronic unemployment possible in a market economy whose purpose it is to create profits, not jobs? Do more profits necessarily translate into more employment?

2. Hal Rosenbluth, Chief Executive Officer of Rosenbluth Travel, wrote a book entitled *The Customer Comes Second* (William Morrow, 1992). He argues that the key to his company's success has been to satisfy his employees first and his customers second. Do you agree? Will satisfying employees' desires assure customers' satisfaction?

3. Suppose a major component in the manufacturing of perfume—say, alcohol—increases in cost. Such a rise in cost would obviously reduce the profits of perfume manufacturers, but would it affect their revenue? Can perfume companies pass on their cost increase to their customers? Is there any connection between expenses and revenue?

4. The Gannett Co., a publisher, begins a nationwide daily newspaper called USA Today, and continues publishing it for 10 years in a row without making a profit. Is Gannett irrational in its policy? Should shareholders remove the company officers for incompetence?

5. Evaluate this statement by the president of a major corporation: "All great companies are successful because of one simple reason: They are cost conscious!" Is cost containment the only significant factor in long-run corporate profitability and consumer satisfaction?

6. In 1994 during the debate over national health insurance, First Lady Hillary Clinton accused insurance companies of "making profits at the expense of their customers." Do you agree? Can you provide some examples of medical insurance companies being unresponsive to the needs of their customers?

7. In an article on deficiencies in kidney treatment, *The New York Times* (December 4, 1995) accused private health-care companies of mismanaged care of their patients on dialysis machines. "The investigation found an industry that uses equipment and procedures that cut costs and raise profits, often at the expense of patients' health; that operates with few rules to assure high-quality care; and that has induced doctors to play along by giving them a share of the cash." Using our input-output model, demonstrate the short-term advantage of cutting corners on patient care. Does this mean that "for profit" health-care companies are inherently bad? What incentives are there for high-quality health-care services?

8. During the energy crisis in the mid-1970s, a politician remarked, "Excessively high profits do not indicate that the major oil companies are responsive to customers. It means they are gouging the public!" How would you respond to this attack?

9. A major Japanese electronics company is determined to increase its market share in the world, as measured by sales volume. Is this a sound decision? Is market share the same as profitability? How is one related to the other?

10. A company sells off a subsidiary at a substantial profit and consequently reports a profit instead of a loss in its latest quarterly income statement. Has the company added value to the economy by such a financial transaction?

11. In the first quarter of 1998, Apple Computer Inc. reported that revenues declined 12% (from $1.6 billion to $1.4 billion), but Apple reported profits of $55 million, compared to a loss of $178 million in the previous quarter. During this same time, prices of Apple computers and software declined. Analysts were surprised at the announcement, which they say was largely due to "improved profit margins" on Apple products and "sharp cost-cutting." Using a 2-stage income statement, show how this is possible.

12. What is your reaction to the following statement by free-market economist Milton Friedman: "There is one and only one social responsibility of business—to use its resources and engage in activities designed to increase its profits...without deception or fraud....[Charitable] giving by corporations is an inappropriate use of corporate funds in a free-enterprise society." (*Capitalism and Freedom*, University of Chicago, 1962, pp. 133, 135) Should business owners contribute to charity, universities and other good causes? Does charitable giving enhance business's goodwill in the community and, therefore, indirectly enhance their profitability? Or would it be better if companies used their surplus funds to raise wages, increase dividends or lower prices?

13. What do you think Milton Friedman would say to the following statement by David Packard, co-founder of Hewlett-Packard: "We began talking about whether businesses had responsibilities beyond making a profit for their shareholders. I expressed my view that we did, that we had important responsibilities to our employees, to our customers, to our suppliers, and to the welfare of society at large....We stress to our people that each of these communities must be better for our presence. This means being sensitive to the needs and interests of the community; it means applying the highest standards of honesty and integrity to all our relationships with individuals and groups; it means enhancing and protecting the physical environment and building

attractive plants and offices of which the community can be proud; it means contributing talent, energy, and financial support to community projects."[8] In what way do community involvement and other corporate attributes improve the long-term profitability of the company? Or does charitable giving simply reduce profitability as Friedman suggests?

14. Continuing the debate over corporate philanthropy, comment on the following: "With its recently announced 20,000 job cuts, Boeing will have eliminated a total of 48,000 jobs this year. Meanwhile, the company spent $51.3 million on philanthropy in 1997, a year in which it had a $178 million loss....Donating money to a worthy cause bolsters a company's image as socially responsible. But why should it? It's noble to give your own money to a charity, but CEOs are spending other people's money. 'I would not want shareholders to write checks on my bank account for charities of their choice,' says investor Warren Buffett, who, unlike most CEOs, lets shareholders vote on charitable donations."[9] Should companies give money away when they are losing money or laying off workers? Why or why not?

Shareholders often respond favorably to downsizing by major public corporations, but what are the risks and potential dangers of downsizing? What effect does downsizing have on employee morale, the so-called "loyalty factor"? According to business consultant Frederick Reichheld, author of *The Loyalty Effect* (Harvard Business School Press, 1995), the average length of job tenure is only three years in the United States compared with eight years in Japan and Germany. Is it good for employees to change jobs every few years? Are there advantages to establishing long-term relationships with employees, suppliers and consumers? What are the disadvantages? In answering these questions, make a study of companies that have established long-term relationships (e.g., insurance company State Farm, Atlanta-based fast-food chain Chick-fil-A).

15. Why do companies almost always have better kempt lawns and gardens than residential homeowners?

16. John Mackey, CEO of Whole Foods Market, argues that capitalism needs a new brand. He states, "Corporations are probably the most influential institutions in the world today and yet many people do not believe that they can be trusted. Instead corporations are widely perceived as greedy, selfish, exploitative, uncaring-and interested only in maximizing profits. In the early years of the 21st century, major ethical lapses on the part of big business came to light including scandals at Enron, Arthur Anderson, Tyco, the New York Stock Exchange, WorldCom, Mutual Funds, and AIG. These scandals have all contributed to a

---

8  *The HP Way* (Harper, 1995), p. 166
9  *The Wall Street Journal* (Dec. 22, 1998, editorial page)

growing distrust of business and further eroded public trust in large corporations in the United States." Mackey suggests a new business paradigm which he calls "conscious capitalism." According to Mackey, the most successful companies do not focus on maximizing profits as a primary goal, but have more lofty goals such as changing the world for the better and pursuing excellence. He concludes that companies that harmonize the interests of company officials with customers, employees, suppliers, the community and shareholders will maximize profits in the long run. For more information on Mackey's vision of conscious capitalism, go to his blog, http://www.wholefoodsmarket.com/blogs/jm/? Do you agree with Mackey? Why or why not?

## APPENDIX
## UNDERSTANDING BASIC ACCOUNTING

The concept of an annual income statement, the balance sheet, the cash flow statement, and Economic Value Added (EVA) used by companies to determine their financial well-being were presented in this chapter. All four measures of financial corporate well-being are essential in understanding how companies grow and contribute to economic progress.

A company can increase profits in five ways: it can reduce costs, increase its prices, raise output, expand its product line, or sell off non-performing assets. The income statement, balance sheet, cash-flow statement, and EVA all help assist the manager in making the company more profitable.

It is essential that all economics students understand the basic elements of accounting. If you have not had an accounting class, review this material. We discuss the basics of the balance sheet, the income statement, cash flow, and economic value added.

Why are all four of these financial statements valuable to a company? The best way to answer this question is to look at it from an individual's point of view. Suppose you have graduated and after a few years earn a steady income from work. There are four vital ways to examine your financial condition. Let's show why.

Look at your annual income statement. This statement shows how much is earned each year, how it has been spent, and how it was saved, or the level of debt. Inflows and outflows are vital to financial well-being. If more is spent than earned, the individual is in debt. If more is earned than spent, the individual is on the way to financial success.

The income statement does not indicate everything about financial condition. If an individual is in debt and needs to bail himself out, he could sell property or assets to raise the money to pay the debt. The individual's balance sheet, a list of assets and liabilities, tells what assets are owned and what the total debt is. An income statement tells where money is coming from and where it will be going to, while the balance sheet tells what the individual has.

The cash flow statement tells how much money comes in and goes out of an individual bank account. Individuals, like companies, can have cash flow problems. For example, if a real estate agent is only getting paid a commission when he sells a house and if that individual earns an average $60,000 a year as a real estate agent—but may not get paid for six months, he must carefully ration funds over the next six months and may be "cash poor" during the six months until he is paid. He may need to borrow money to last until the next sale. The agent has a cash flow problem.

There is also an opportunity cost associated with income and savings. When take home pay is received there are choices that can be made about the use of the money? If the money is spent, something is conversely being given up. What is given up may be the chance to earn money through savings, in a bank account, the stock market, or by purchasing real estate. If an employee quits a $60,000 job to start his own business, that $60,000 represents his opportunity cost of self-employment. Unless the customer earns $60,000 a year from his new enterprise, he is no better off financially in the new business than he was in the old job.

## THE INCOME STATEMENT: THE BOTTOM LINE

This chapter focused on a company's annual income statement as a way to measure profit and loss. Microsoft, Sears, K-mart, and Wal-Mart served as examples. The income statement serves as a primary yardstick of a company's ability to survive and grow. Without profits, a company can not survive over the long run.

The income statement reports the accounting profit performance of an enterprise. It reflects the ability of the company to make sales, control expenses and earn a profit—just as an individual earns gross income, controls expenses, and saves money. There are several names for the income statement, such as the earnings statement, statement of operations and the profit and loss statement.

A basic income statement summarizes the sales revenue and expenses over a one-year period known as the fiscal year. The fiscal year does not necessarily end on December 31. Most companies operate on a fiscal year different from the calendar year. For example, Microsoft's fiscal year ends on June 30th.

The income statement reads in a step-down format. It can have as many as five lines—gross margin, operating earnings before depreciation, operating earnings, earnings before income taxes, and net income. Some companies combine lines and report only two lines—gross margin and net income.

The income statement for Microsoft for fiscal year 2008 (ending June 30) is shown below:

**Figure 4.15**

## INCOME STATEMENT, 2008
### for Microsoft, Inc (in millions)

Net revenue . . . . . . . . . . . . . . . . . . . . . . . . . . . . . . . . . . .$61,742

Total operating expenses . . . . . . . . . . . . . . . . . . . . . . . . . .$37,928

Operating income . . . . . . . . . . . . . . . . . . . . . . . . . . . . . . . .$22,492

Net income (after income taxes) . . . . . . . . . . . . . . . . . . . . .$17,681

Source: *2008 Annual Report.*

**Net Revenue:** Total amount received from customers from the sales of products and services (such as Microsoft software). "Net" means it excludes sales returns, discounts or other allowances from the original sales price.

**Operating Expenses:** Expenses related to the running of the business, including wages and salaries, sales and marketing, administration, research and development, payroll and non-income taxes, interest payments, and the cost of goods sold (goods missing, stolen, damaged or unusable). Reporting practices are not always uniform.

**Operating Income:** This figure is determined by subtracting the operating expenses from the net revenue figure. It indicates the company's profit level before figuring in depreciation, interest expense and income taxes paid to federal, state and local governments. (Other taxes, such as payroll, property and sales taxes are included in operating expenses.)

**Net Income:** After subtracting the costs of depreciation, interest expenses and income taxes, the net income represents the final profit (or loss) for that fiscal year. In this example, Microsoft earned an after-tax profit of $17.7 billion.

What to do with that $17.7 billion? Microsoft has two choices: It could pay out some of the earnings as dividends to shareholders. Or it could keep the net income as retained earnings to invest in further research, hire more workers, or buy more assets.

All companies function in a basic operating cycle: making products, offering the products for sale, selling the products, waiting to collect the receivables from credited sales and, finally, receiving the cash from the customers.

## THE BALANCE SHEET: DETERMINING NET WORTH

The income statement, vital as it may be, is not the only financial report that company officers examine. Three other financial reports are indispensable: the balance sheet, cash flow, and EVA. An income statement does not reveal the value of the company's receivables, inventory, and assets. It does not tell the manager what the company's liabilities are. To find out this information, the manager looks at the balance sheet of the company. For example, by looking at the balance sheet, a manager can determine if the company is too heavily in debt, which in turn could reduce future profits turning a profitable company into a bankrupt company. A balance sheet can also determine if certain assets should be sold and the funds used in a better way.

The following chart summarizes the balance sheet of Microsoft at the end of fiscal year 2008.

### Figure 4.16

### BALANCE SHEET, 2008
### for Microsoft, Inc (in millions)

| ASSETS | | LIABILITIES | |
|---|---|---|---|
| Current assets . . . . . . .Current liabilities | | | |
| Cash . . . . . . . . . . . . . . . . .$10,339 | | Accounts payable. . . . . . . . $12,830 | |
| Short-term investments . . . . . . .13,323 | | Other . . . . . . . . . . . . . . . . . 17,056 | |
| Accounts receivable . . . . . . . .15,606 | | | |
| Inventories . . . . . . . . . . . . . . . .985 | | Total current liabilities . . . . . . $29,886 | |
| Other . . . . . . . . . . . . . . . . .2,989 | | | |
| **Total current assets . . . . .$43,242** | | **Shareholders' equity . . $36,282** | |
| | | | |
| Property, plant and equipment And other assets . . . . . . . . . .$29,551 | | | |
| | | **Total liability and shareholders'** | |
| **Total Assets . . . . . . . . .$72,793** | | **Equity. . . . . . . . . . . . . . $66,172** | |

Source: *2008 Annual Report.*

Note several characteristics regarding the balance sheet. The left side of the balance sheet lists assets; the right side lists liabilities and owners' or stockholders' equity. The balance sheet was prepared at the end of the fiscal year (June 30 for Microsoft).

The balance sheet represents a fixed point in time. It does not report flows into and out of assets, liabilities and owners' equity accounts. It accounts for those items at only one point in time.

*Current assets* are cash and short-term cash instruments, accounts receivable, and inventories. Accounts receivable are payments due for products purchased or services rendered for customers. Inventories are goods produced that have not yet been sold. Both accounts receivable and inventories play a major role in business activity.

*Property, plants, and equipment* refers to the long-term capital assets used by a business to produce goods and services. In the past, these assets were referred to as fixed assets, even though they may not be permanent (land is fixed, but equipment may be moved).

All capital assets are gradually used up in the production process and, therefore, their value must be depreciated over time. Depreciation must be deducted from the total asset figure each year.

*Current liabilities* are short-term debts, including accounts payable, accrued wages and income tax due. Accounts payable are bills not yet paid by the company (they are typically paid within 60-180 days). Some companies also issue short-term debt such as commercial paper-obligations of major corporations that mature in 3 months or less.

Many companies also have long-term liabilities-debts whose maturity dates are more than one year. Companies that issue corporate notes and bonds have long-term liabilities, and the annual interest charges may be significant. In this example, Microsoft has very little long-term debt. Its operation is almost entirely financed through the issuance of stock.

*Stockholders' equity* represents the assets of the company, net of liabilities. It consists of two parts: capital stock held by the shareholders and retained earnings.

## USING THE BALANCE SHEET DIAGRAM

After-tax profits (net income) provide a regular source of new capital allowing a company to expand its operations, create new products, hire new workers, etc. Net income can be paid out to shareholders or go into retained earnings. Out of retained earnings the company buys more assets and expands its business.

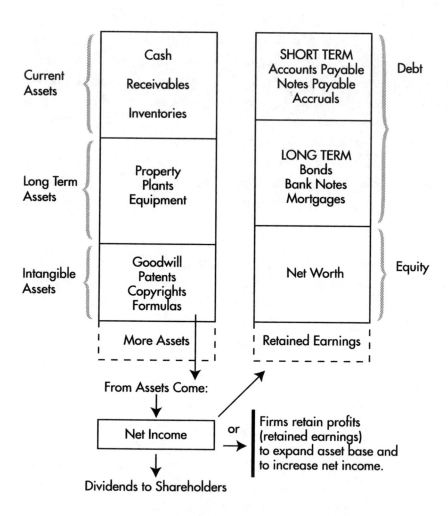

**Figure 4.17.** *Balance Sheet.*
Source: *Mark Perry.*

## CASH FLOW: THE LIFEBLOOD OF THE COMPANY

Cash flow is also important, although it was not required in financial reports until 1987. Many companies are profitable for a while only to end up in bankruptcy because of cash flow shortages. Businesses can be profitable and yet default on their liabilities or miss their payroll because of cash-flow problems. Remember that the real estate agent who got paid infrequently and had to watch his cash flow? The same applies to a business. Cash inflows (cash receipts coming into the company) and outflows (cash disbursements) are the heartbeat of a company, and it cannot afford to skip a beat. Many businesses arrange with commercial banks for a line of credit to cover short-term cash-flow requirements. A line of credit is a pre-approved short-term loan from a bank to pay payroll or other expenses that are due.

Below is the cash flow statement of Microsoft, ending June 30, 2008

### Figure 4.18

### CASH FLOW STATEMENT, 2008
#### for Microsoft, Inc (in millions)

| | |
|---|---:|
| Net cash from operations | $21,612 |
| Net cash used for investments | ($4,587) |
| Net cash from financing | ($12,934) |
| Change in cash and short-term investments | $4,228 |

Source: *2008 Annual Report.*

It is clear from the above statement that Microsoft is in a solid cash position. It increased its cash position during the year and had considerable liquid assets to draw upon to expand and pay expenses.

*Net cash from operations* identifies cash payments from customer sales, minus payments for inventories, depreciation and other current liabilities.

*Net cash from financing* identifies funds coming in from the issuance of new stock, minus repurchasing of stock, etc.

*Net cash used for investments* highlights money used to make short-term investments and to invest in property, plants and equipment.

## SUMMARY

In short, while profit performance is essential in the long run for a company, it alone cannot guarantee company survival in the short run. Assets and liabilities must be managed effectively, and managers must at the same time prevent cash flow shortages. Thus, the job of a company manager is threefold—earning a profit, controlling the financial condition of a company, and preventing cash shortages. Analyzing quarterly financial statements keeps managers, creditors, shareholders, and security analysts abreast of the well-being of the company, both in the short term and the long term.

## AN ECONOMIC VIEW OF ACCOUNTING

Over the years, economists have taken a different view than accountants on the issue of cost accounting. A major concern is the failure of accountants to take into account the full cost of capital. As Peter Drucker states, "Until a business returns a profit that is greater than its cost of capital, it operates at a loss."

For years, economists have complained that conventional accounting distorts the true economics of the company by not including a charge for common stock equity in its earnings reports and balance sheets. General Acceptable Accounting Principles (GAAP) require companies to list interest charges on bonds and other loans on its income statement, but treats equity financing as if it were free. In short, GAAP ignores the full opportunity cost of equity capital (funds invested in a business by owners and shareholders).

Opportunity cost is a term invented by Austrian economist Friedrich Wieser in the early 20th century, and it refers to the universal principle that all human action involves giving up other choices. When an individual invests in a stock, lends money, or creates a new business, he gives up the chance to invest or spend his money elsewhere.

## HOW EVA WORKS

In the 1950s and 1960s, several financial economists, including Merton H. Miller and Franco Modigliani (who later won the Nobel Prize in Economics for their pioneering work), developed models to quantify the opportunity cost of capital. In the 1980s, G. Bennett Stewart III, a financial economist from Chicago, created Economic Value Added (EVA) as a financial yardstick to measure opportunity costs in business.

EVA represents economic profit, which is always less than accounting profit. It is fairly simple to determine: It is after-tax operating profits minus the appropriate capital charge for both debt and equity. The exact formula is:

EVA = NOPAT - C% (TC)

where

| | | |
|---|---|---|
| EVA | = | Economic Value Added |
| NOPAT | = | net operating profits after taxes |
| C% | = | percentage cost of capital |
| TC | = | total capital |

EVA is also known as "residual income"—the residual left over after all costs have been covered.

Here's how EVA is figured for Microsoft for fiscal year 2008, assuming a 8% return on equity capital:

**ECONOMIC VALUE ADDED (EVA)**
**Microsoft Corporation, fiscal year 2008**
**(in millions)**

Net operating profits after taxes . . . . . . . . . . . . . . .$17,681

Equity cost of capital . . . . . . . . . . . . . . . . . . . . . . .$5,028

_____

Economic Value Added (EVA) . . . . . . . . . . . . . . . .$12,653

In other words, in 2008 Microsoft added value beyond the normal rate of investment by $12.6 billion. Clearly, Microsoft was adding value to its shareholders and creating wealth in the global economy.

Accountants still do not require companies to determine their EVA, but EVA is increasing in popularity. All five major accounting companies offer an EVA-type statistic to their clients if they request it. Most accounting textbooks now include a significant section on EVA, economic profit, or residual income. Previous editions did not mention EVA or opportunity cost.

Wall Street analysts, including Goldman Sachs and First Boston, use EVA to evaluate stocks. According to Al Ehrbar, EVA explains stock performance and market value better than any other accounting measure, including return on equity, cash flow, earnings per share, or sales. EVA encourages company officers to focus more clearly on creating shareholder value through higher stock prices.

For more information on EVA, see Al Ehrbar, *EVA: The Real Key to Creating Wealth* (John Wiley & Sons, 1998) or the website, www.eva.com.

## RECOMMENDED READING

- Shlomo Maital, *Executive Economics* (Free Press, 1994). The best book on applying the principles of supply and demand, marginal costs, trade-offs, and other principles of economics to business. Highly recommended, especially for business executives.

- *The EVA Challenge: Implementing Value Added Change in an organization*, by Joel M. Stern and John S. Shiely, and Irwin Ross (New York: Wiley & Sons, 2001). An excellent primer on economic value added (EVA) and how to adopt it.

# Chapter 5

# DETERMINING PRICES AND OUTPUT: THE LAW OF DEMAND

*"The law of demand is a denial of the idea of 'needs.' When someone says there is a 'need' for something, he should always be asked, 'at what cost?'"*

— Armen A. Alchian and William R. Allen
*University Economics*, 3rd ed., p. 67

## Summary of Past Chapters

The step-by-step method of economic analysis began with a discussion of "wealth." Wealth is defined as "usable goods and services that enhance each person's well-being." People of all walks of life desire more wealth, both material and non-material. Individuals create wealth by purchasing raw materials/inputs from suppliers and transforming them into products/outputs for customers. A general four-stage model of the economy was introduced to represent this process.

Each company is involved in this economic process of creating wealth. A two-stage input-output model of the company was introduced to illustrate a company's profit-and-loss income statement. Companies seek to add value to the economy and produce goods and services according to the dictates of the profit-and-loss system.

In the micro model, prices play a role in the output of goods and services in the economy. As noted at the end of Chapter 4, total revenues (TR) or total sales of a company are equal to the price (P) of each item sold times the quantity (Q) sold, for all separate items (n) in the company's financial statement. In other words,

$$TR = P_1Q_1 + P_2Q_2 + P_3Q_3 + \ldots + P_nQ_n = \sum_{i=1}^{n} P_iQ_i$$

## CREATING A DEMAND SCHEDULE

From this equation, a demand and supply schedule can be created for each good or service offered by the company. A demand schedule is the relation between the quantity of a particular good purchased by customers and various prices for that good. The demand schedule represents the price-quantity relationship from the point of view of the buyer. (Later examples will show that the supply schedule represents the P-Q relationship from the viewpoint of the seller.)

Before looking at a specific example, the importance of prices in the economy should be understood. The revenue generated from the sales of a product or service are not only dependent on a good marketing campaign, but on proper pricing as well. Deciding on the right price for a product or service, based on the consumers' demand and the company's competition, is vital to a company's success.

An example from Microsoft Corporation illustrates the relationship between price and the amount sold. One of Microsoft Corporation's products is Microsoft Works, a word-processing software package. If this product normally sells nationwide for $24.95 and computer customers purchased 900,000 units of Microsoft Works in the current fiscal year, the company would generate a total sales revenue of $22,455,000 from this product.

The relationship between price and amount sold can be graphically displayed with a demand schedule. Microsoft Works' price ($24.95) is represented on the vertical line and quantity (900,000 units) on the horizontal line. See figure 5.1 below.

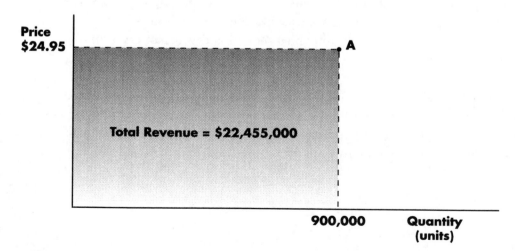

**Figure 5.1.** *Establishing one point on the demand schedule for Microsoft Works software package.*

Point A reflects the fact that customers "demanded" 900,000 units of Microsoft Works software during the year, given the price of $24.95. Total annual revenue is $22,455,000.

If Microsoft Works is appropriately priced at $24.95, the demand for the software package is steady and offers a reasonable profit to the company. Assume that Microsoft is able to fill all the orders it receives and that there is no excess, unfulfilled demand for Microsoft Works.

Now suppose Microsoft decides to raise its price for Microsoft Works from $24.95 to $34.95. What would be the reaction of customers? Would they buy more copies of this product, the same amount, or fewer units of Microsoft Works? Customers will actually buy fewer copies of Microsoft Works if the price is raised. There are several important reasons why the quantity demanded by Microsoft customers would decline if the price were raised by 10 dollars:

1.  **The Budget Constraint:** Individuals earn a fixed amount of income each year. If the cost of a software package goes up, the individual who buys Microsoft Works has less to spend on other goods he desires. Therefore, his budget and his desires limit how much he can afford to pay. Higher prices mean that individuals can afford to buy less, given a fixed income level.

2.  **Principle of Diminishing Marginal Utility:** Diminishing marginal utility is related to the budget constraint. Given a fixed amount of time and income, consumers must rank their wants in order of importance. Their most important wants are satisfied first, followed by the second, then the third, and so forth. This concept of ranking wants is known as the principle of diminishing marginal utility.

    If an individual receives additional funds, he can satisfy the next most important want or need. When people's incomes decline, they have to give up their least important desire. As the price of a good increases, consumers buy less of that good.

3.  **The Substitution Effect:** When Microsoft raises the price for its software package, customers look for substitutes—alternative word-processing programs that offer features similar to Microsoft Works. Consumers are willing to substitute goods with similar or reduced features rather than pay higher prices for the original good or service.

4.  **The Law of Competition:** Apple Computers, Compac, and other competing computer software companies may take advantage of the rise in the price of Microsoft Works and encourage customers to switch to their products.

The above factors will work to reduce the number of purchases made if Microsoft raises its prices. How much less will customers buy? Although purchases will diminish if prices rise, it is highly unlikely that the number will fall to zero. There are several reasons why consumers will continue to purchase the product or service even with a price increase:

1.  Some customers with higher incomes can afford to pay $34.95 and will buy Microsoft Works even at the higher price.

2.  Some buyers have a preference for Microsoft products and have developed "customer loyalty." They are willing to continue buying Microsoft Works software even though its competitors offer lower prices.

Suppose Microsoft raises the price of Microsoft Works to $34.95 and sells 500,000 units the next year. Total sales revenue is $17,475,000.

There is now another point on the demand schedule for Microsoft Works software, Point B. See figure 5.2 below.

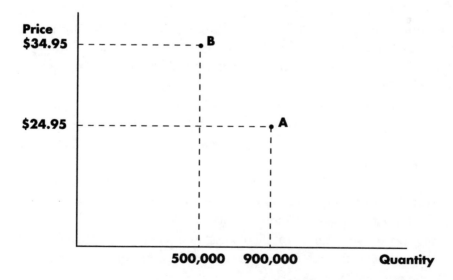

**Figure 5.2.** *Two points on the demand schedule for Microsoft Works software.*

Suppose Microsoft decides to lower its price instead of raising it. It reduces the price from $24.95 to $19.95. Why would it do this? What would be the reaction of customers?

In many ways, the reaction of customers would be just the opposite of the case above. More people could afford to buy Microsoft Works (the budget constraint). Substitutes would appear relatively more expensive (the substitution effect). Competitors would have less advantage over Microsoft (the competition effect). In short, customers would buy more software.

Suppose after lowering the price to $19.95, customers buy 1.5 million copies of Microsoft Works. Gross revenues rise to $29,925,000. Lowering prices adds a third point along the demand curve. See figure 5.3 below.

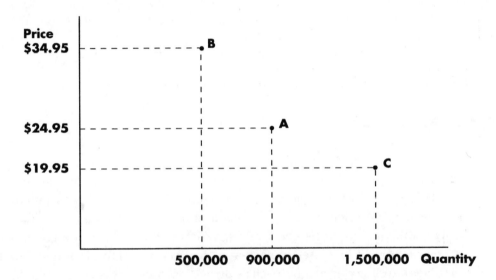

**Figure 5.3.** *Three points on the demand schedule for Microsoft Works software.*

## THE DOWNWARD SLOPING DEMAND CURVE

By linking together these three points on the demand schedule, the law of demand is established. The law of demand says that:

**Other things being equal, consumers will buy more of a good when the price goes down, and less when the price goes up.**

The downward sloping demand curve is illustrated in the example above. As the price of Microsoft Works is lowered from $34.95 to $24.95 and then to $19.95, customers buy greater amounts of software.

Figure 5.4 demonstrates the general design of the demand curve.

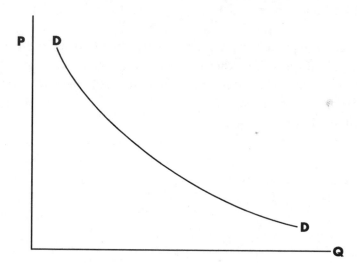

**Figure 5.4.** *The downward-sloping demand curve.*

## "OTHER THINGS BEING EQUAL"

The definition of the law of demand uses the phrase "other things being equal." The Latin version of this phrase is "ceteris paribus," meaning "the rest being equal."

This phrase assumes that people's incomes, tastes, and other factors remain the same when the price changes. The good or service also remains unchanged. The only change made in the economic situation is the price of the good or service. When the price is increased or decreased, it affects the amount purchased. If several things are changing at once such as prices, incomes, or tastes, it would be difficult to establish economic relationships between the variables. So economists assume "ceteris paribus" conditions to isolate the effect of how a change in price affects purchase.

"Ceteris paribus" conditions are also necessary because of the graphical limitations. Since graphs are created in two dimensions, it is only possible to analyze two variables at a time and investigate their relationship. If the graph could be created in three or four dimensions, it would be possible to show how price and quantity are related to income, substitute goods, and so forth, but because graphs are limited to two variables, ceteris paribus conditions are applied.

In the real world it is not always possible to control all other patterns and situations. Companies may be changing prices at the same time that incomes, tastes, advertising and product appearance are changing. Nevertheless, it is a useful exercise to assume "all other things equal." For example, suppose Microsoft raises the price of Microsoft Works and people buy more of this product. Will these purchases affect the law of downward sloping demand? No. This purchase trend simply means that other external factors such as changes in income levels and tastes, called exogenous variables, must be examined to determine what increased the quantity demanded.

The graph of the demand curve can clarify this potential situation. When "all other things remain equal," the effect that a change in price has on quantity demanded can be isolated and all changes as reflected by a movement along the demand schedule can be examined. When ceteris paribus conditions change, the whole demand curve shifts up or down depending on the situation.

Figure 5.5 below demonstrates the two situations.

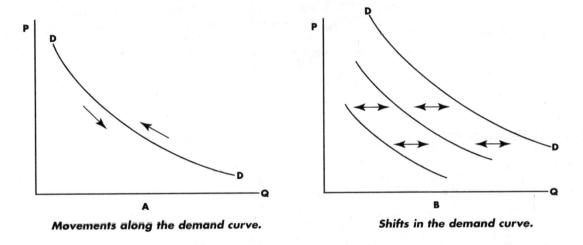

**Movements along the demand curve.**          **Shifts in the demand curve.**

**Figure 5.5.** *Two changes in the demand schedule.*

## ELASTICITY OF DEMAND

Another important concept in economics is known as the elasticity of demand. Elasticity is one of the economic terms that British economist Alfred Marshall borrowed from the physical sciences. In economics, elasticity refers to the impact that price changes have on the company's output and total revenue.

If demand is elastic, a decline in price does not just increase the output of good X, but also increases total revenue. If demand is inelastic, a decline in price still increases output, but total revenue decreases. If the elasticity of demand is unitary (or unitary elastic), a decline or increase in price makes no change in total revenue. If demand is perfectly inelastic, a decline in price has no effect on the quantity purchased, and the quantity sold increases significantly when the price is lowered.

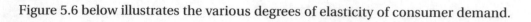

Figure 5.6 below illustrates the various degrees of elasticity of consumer demand.

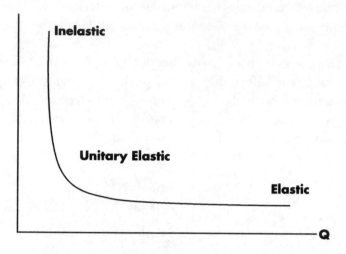

**Figure 5.6.** *Various degrees of elasticity of demand.*

## MEASURING ELASTICITY

Economists have developed a way to mathematically measure elasticity of demand with the following equation:

$$n = \frac{\text{Percentage change in quantity demanded}}{\text{Percentage change in price}}$$

$$= \frac{\% \triangle Q}{\% \triangle P}$$

$$= \frac{\triangle Q/Q}{\triangle P/P}$$

Where

n = elasticity,
Q = quantity, and
P = price

## PRICE ELASTICITY IS NOT SLOPE

The price elasticity of demand is not the same as the slope of the demand curve. Slope is the change in price divided by the change in quantity, or $\triangle P / \triangle Q$.

## THE MEANING OF PRICE ELASTICITY OF DEMAND

The purpose of elasticity is to determine the reaction of a company's total revenue to changes in price.

**There are three possible outcomes as noted above:**

| Elasticity Measure | Meaning |
| --- | --- |
| 0 - 1 | inelastic |
| 1 | unit elastic |
| 1 - ∞ | elastic |

Economists have estimated the elasticity of demand of a wide variety of products. In the example of Microsoft Works, a price rise from $24.95 to $34.95 reduced revenue significantly, from $22.5 million to $17.5 million, a 22% loss.

When Microsoft cut prices from $24.95 to $19.95, revenue rose substantially to $29.9 million, a 32% gain.

**APPROXIMATELY UNITARY**

**INELASTIC**

| | |
| --- | --- |
| Salt | 0.11 |
| Matches | 0.1 |
| Toothpicks | 0.1 |
| Airline travel, short run | 0.1 |
| Gasoline, short run | 0.2 |
| Gasoline, long run | 0.7 |
| Residential natural gas, short run | 0.1 |
| Residential natural gas, long run | 0.5 |
| Coffee | 0.25 |
| Fish (cod), consumed at home | 0.5 |
| Tobacco products, short run | 0.45 |
| Legal services, short run | 0.4 |
| Physician services | 0.6 |
| Taxi, short run | 0.6 |
| Automobiles, long run | 0.2 |

| | |
| --- | --- |
| Movies | 0.9 |
| Housing, owner occupied, long run | 1.2 |
| Shellfish, consumed at home | 0.9 |
| Oysters, consumed at home | 1.1 |
| Private education | 1.1 |
| Tires, short run | 0.9 |
| Tires, long run | 1.2 |
| Radio and television receivers | 1.2 |

**ELASTIC**

| | |
| --- | --- |
| Restaurant meals | 2.3 |
| Foreign travel, long run | 4.0 |
| Airline travel, long run | 2.4 |
| Fresh green peas | 2.8 |
| Automobiles, short run | 1.2-1.5 |
| Chevrolet automobiles | 4.0 |
| Fresh tomatoes | 4.6 |

**Sources:** Hendrick S. Houthakker and Lester D. Taylor, *Consumer Demand in the United States, 1929-1970* (Cambridge: Harvard University Press, 1966, 1970); Douglas R. Bohl, *Analyzing Demand Behavior* (Baltimore: Johns Hopkins University Press, 1981); Hsaing-tai Cheng and Oral Capps, Jr., "Demand for Fish," *American Journal of Agricultural Economics,* August 1988; and U.S. Department of Agriculture.

**Figure 5.7.** *Estimated price elasticity of demand for selected products.*
*Source:* Gwartney & Stroup, *Economics,* 8th ed., p. 453.

This exercise indicates that Microsoft Works software is highly elastic - very responsive to price changes.

In the case of the higher price, elasticity of demand (n) is determined as follows:

$$n \quad = \quad \%\triangle Q \ / \ \%\triangle P$$

$$= \quad \frac{400,000/700,000}{10/29.95}$$

$$= \quad \frac{0.57}{0.33}$$

$$= \quad 1.73$$

In the case of the lower price,

$$n \quad = \quad \%\triangle Q \ / \ \%\triangle P$$

$$= \quad \frac{600,000/1,200,000}{5/22.45}$$

$$= \quad .5/.22$$

$$= \quad 2.27$$

This exercise indicates that the demand for Microsoft Works is elastic overall and becomes even more elastic as the price declines. This example suggests that Microsoft is in a rapidly expanding market characterized by falling prices and increasing revenue.

## ELASTICITY AND PROFITABILITY

How important is elasticity of demand? Chapter 4 noted that profitability is the most important factor in the long-run survival and prosperity of a company. How does elasticity fit into the profit equation?

The elasticity of demand helps a company decide how raising or lowering prices affects total revenue, the first half of the profitability equation. If the demand for Microsoft Works is highly elastic, Microsoft could lower the price of Microsoft Works 20% and expect to increase revenue 32%. But the real question Microsoft wants answered is, "How will a 20% cut in price affect profit?" Revenue increases 32%, but will profit also increases?

The effect on profit depends on the cost of producing the additional units of Microsoft Works. If the average cost stays the same or even declines (due to economies of scale), total profits will also increase. If, on the other hand, the increased sales of Microsoft Works squeezes the production schedule at Microsoft's plant, requiring Microsoft to pay its workers overtime or to hire additional workers at higher wages, the company's costs will increase. In this case, the effect on profit-sis uncertain.

The next two chapters discuss how "supply" responds to "demand" or changing demand and, how price is established on the open market.

These chapters also present how the cost of production relates to the laws of supply and demand.

## SUMMARY

**These are the main points covered in Chapter 5:**

1.  Each company's revenue is determined by the quantity of individual products and services it sells multiplied by its prices.

2.  Each company seeks to determine the best price and output combination for profit maximization and customer service over the long run.

3.  The level of demand for a company's products and services is limited by the budget constraint of potential customers, the availability of substitutes, customer loyalty, and the policies of competitors.

4.  The law of demand states that other things being equal, customers will buy more of a good when the price goes down and less when the price goes up.

5. The elasticity of demand helps a company decide how a price increase or decrease would affect total revenue and ultimately the profitability of a company.

6. Elasticity of demand tells us how price changes affect revenue, but this alone cannot determine whether a company should raise or lower prices. Costs must also be figured into the profitability equation.

## IMPORTANT TERMS

Budget constraint
Ceteris Paribus ("other things being equal")
Demand schedule
Economies of scale
Law of competition
Law of downward-sloping demand curve
Marginal utility
Perfectly elastic
Perfectly inelastic
Price elasticity of demand
Substitution effect
Unit elasticity

## INFLUENTIAL ECONOMIST
## ALFRED MARSHALL, THE FATHER OF MICROECONOMICS

**Name: Alfred Marshall (1842-1924)**

**Background:** Born in London in 1842, Alfred Marshall studied mathematics at St. John's College, Cambridge, graduating in 1865. After teaching at the University of Bristol and Oxford College, he returned to Cambridge in 1885 as professor of political economy.

**Major Work:** Marshall is considered the dean of the British school of economics, following in the footsteps of Adam Smith, David Ricardo, Thomas Malthus, and John Stuart Mill. In 1890, at the age of 48, he wrote *Principles of Economics*, which became the principal textbook in economics for the next 40 years, going through 12 editions. More than anyone, he attempted to make "political economy" a science like the physical sciences of chemistry, physics and mechanics. He introduced many mechanical and mathematical terms such as "elasticity of demand," and he changed the name of political economy to "economics."

**Sample Quotation:** "Thus progress itself increases the urgency of the warning that in the economic world, Natura non facit saltum. Progress must be slow." (*Principles of Economics*, 1890)

**Most Famous Idea:** His grand theme was that price is always determined by demand and supply. Like the blades of the scissors, both are essential to determine price. "We might as reasonably dispute whether it is the upper or the under blade of a pair of scissors that cuts a piece of paper, as whether value is governed by utility or cost of production." (*Principles of Economics*, 1890) He was critical of the marginalist revolution of the Continental economists such as Carl Menger, Leon Walras, and Eugen Böhm-Bawerk.

**Personal Note:** Marshall lived a quiet life in Cambridge, so quiet in fact that a definitive biography of his life was not written until 1995 (*A Soaring Eagle: Alfred Marshall*, by Peter Groenewegen, economics professor, University of Sydney). Mark Blaug comments, "He never expressed an opinion, whether on pure theory or on questions of practical policy, without an almost endless list of qualifications. In short, he was a very complex, contradictory economist and perhaps that is the secret to his long-lasting appeal." (*Great Economists Before Keynes*, p. 151)

## PROBLEMS TO PONDER

1. A mail order publisher tests two prices for the same book, "How to Get Rich in Real Estate," at $15 and $25. He mails each ad to 5,000 randomly selected names from a list of book buyers. 150 people order the book for $25, while 250 people respond to the $15 offer. The mail order publisher decides to advertise all future books for $25. Did he make a mistake? (Hint: How much does it cost to produce and fulfill the orders for the book? What is the value of the book buyers list?)

2. If the price of a good is raised, people will buy less of it. In the above case (problem #1), the publisher decides to change the format of the book to a "special executive report," and to title the report "How to Make a Million Dollars in Real Estate in 30 Days in Your Spare Time," and charge $100. However, the content of the "special report" is the same as the earlier book. Nevertheless, when the publisher advertises his new report to 5,000 randomly selected book buyers, he sells 100 copies. Does this case violate the law of a downward-sloping demand curve?

3. During the Irish famine of the 1840s, the price of potatoes skyrocketed, but the poor ate less meat and more potatoes. So claimed Sir Robert Giffen, who was the first to observe this phenomenon. Does the case of a "Giffen good" violate the law of demand?

4. "Diamonds are expensive, but they have little practical value; water is cheap, but has great utility in everyday life." Adam Smith was perplexed by this diamond-water paradox. Using price and demand curves, show how you could explain this diamond-water dichotomy to Adam Smith.

5. "The demand for money is always infinite. Obviously, everyone wants as much money as they can get." Do you agree? If you were to draw a demand schedule for money, what would be on the horizontal and vertical axes? What is the price of money?

6. People cannot live without water. No one will reduce his use of water just because the price goes up. Therefore, it will do no good for the utility company to raise the price of water during a water shortage. Water must be rationed. Are necessities like water subject to the downward-sloping demand curve? What is the elasticity of demand for water? Elastic or inelastic? Check the library to see if any studies have been made on the price elasticity of water.

7. David Packard, co-founder of Hewlett-Packard, wrote in his autobiography, *The HP Way* (HarperBusiness, 1995) about the success of the LaserJet printer in the early 1990s. It was priced $1,000 less than its predecessor and was so popular that he said, "We couldn't make them fast enough." How can you illustrate this situation using a demand schedule for the LaserJet printer? They were making a good profit at this price, but should they have raised the price?

8. Prior to 1996, Upjohn Company's hair regrowth product, Rogaine, required a prescription. It retailed for approximately $50 a bottle (2 fl. oz.). Then in early 1996 Upjohn obtained approval from the Federal Drug Administration to sell Rogaine without a prescription. The retail price was reduced sharply to approximately $30 a bottle. Using the principles of elasticity, draw a demand schedule that justifies Upjohn's decision to cut the price from $50 to $30.

## RECOMMENDED READING

James Gwartney, Richard L. Stroup, and Dwight R. Lee, *Common Sense Economics* (New York: St. Martin's Press, 2005). An excellent primer on supply and demand and basic economics.

*Chapter 6*

# SUPPLY AND DEMAND

*"The invisible hand [of supply and demand] has an astonishing capacity
to handle a coordination problem of truly enormous proportions . . . "*

—WILLIAM BAUMOL AND ALAN BLINDER
(*Economics*, 6th ed., p. 251)

Following World War II the German economy was in shambles. Berlin and other major cities had been destroyed by Allied bombing and fires. Production of coal, automobiles, and food was low, and basic necessities were in desperately short supply. Personal savings had disappeared and the German currency was worthless. Barter and black markets became the only means of survival. The new Allied-controlled regime in Germany maintained strict central planning with price controls, rationing, and industrial regulations.

In June of 1948 economic minister Ludwig Erhard made a dramatic, controversial decision to end virtually all price controls, rationing, and regulations of business, while establishing a sound currency reform. Erhard was heavily criticized for making this bold one-man decision; most bureaucrats wanted to try a piecemeal reform.

The results were described in vivid detail by economist Jacques Rueff:

"The black market suddenly disappeared. Shop windows were full of goods; factory chimneys were smoking; and the streets swarmed with lorries [buses]. Everywhere the noise of new buildings going up replaced the deathly silence of the ruins. If the state of recovery was a surprise, its swiftness was even more so. In all sectors of economic life it began as the clocks struck on the day of currency reform....One day apathy was mirrored on their faces while on the next a whole nation looked hopefully into the future."[1]

---

1  Quoted in Ludwig Erhard, *Prosperity Through Competition: The Economics of the German Miracle* (New York: Praeger, 1958), p. 13.

By the next decade the war-torn nation had been completely rebuilt, workers' real wages had increased dramatically, and West Germany was on its way to achieving the highest standard of living in Europe. This dramatic economic improvement was accomplished because of Erhard's brave experiment in Martwirtschaft, the market economy.

The market economy can be defined as a private enterprise system where decisions are made by individuals who set prices and determine production of goods and services according to supply and demand. As the post-war German case proved, the effects of changes on the market economy can be rapid and successful.

## HOW SUPPLY FULFILLS DEMAND

Prices are found everywhere in a market economy and at every level of production. They are essential in determining what is produced, how much is produced, and when goods are produced. Prices determine profitability and help coordinate where scarce resources should be allocated.

Chapter 5 described the demand curve and its role in the determination of price. But demand is only half the equation in our search for the correct price for a specific product or service. Can producers supply the products and services demanded? Something must also be known about the suppliers of goods and services. This chapter examines the supply curve, how it relates to the demand curve, and ultimately how the supply curve relates to the price of a good or service.

Figure 5.4, the downward sloping demand curve for Microsoft Works is reproduced below as figure 6.1.

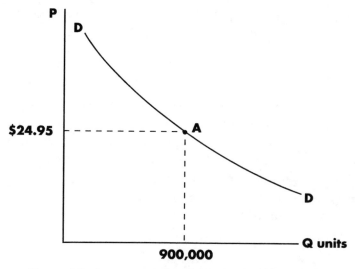

**Figure 6.1.** *Downward sloping demand curve for Microsoft Works.*

Notice point A, the original price of Microsoft Works ($24.95) and quantity sold (900,000 units). Point A represents the actual annual revenue from the sale of Microsoft Works and is the amount demanded by Microsoft customers during the year at a specified price.

Point A, the total annual revenue from the sale of Microsoft Works, also equals the total quantity supplied by Microsoft. Point A represents one point on the supply curve as well as one point on the demand curve. Point A represents both the amount demanded and the amount supplied.

## WHAT IS THE SUPPLY CURVE?

The demand schedule is the amount of goods customers are willing to buy at various prices. In contrast, the supply schedule is the quantity of goods the producer is willing to sell at various prices. How is a supply curve developed?

Suppose the word spreads that Microsoft Works is the best computer word processing program available, causing interest in Microsoft Works to increase dramatically while the interest in other programs drops off. Because tastes have changed in favor of Microsoft Works, the demand schedule shifts outward to the right at every price level. (See figure 6.2 below)

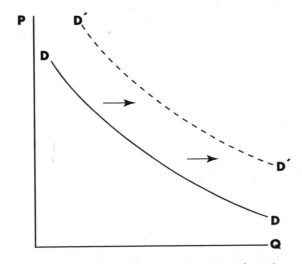

**Figure 6.2.** *Shift in demand for Microsoft Works.*

With the growing popularity of Microsoft Works, Microsoft will undoubtedly respond by increasing production to thereby gain more profits. Employees will work overtime, new workers will be hired, and Microsoft will produce more Microsoft Works packages. There is no question that Microsoft will increase the quantity of software packages in response to this shift in demand because expanding output increases profits.

Will Microsoft also raise its price for Microsoft Works? A price increase is a definite possibility depending on several factors:

1. Level of inventories. If inventories disappear quickly and Microsoft Corporation cannot keep up with demand, there may be no choice but to raise prices. If Microsoft fails to raise prices, there could be shortages of Microsoft Works, and retailers may raise prices on their own, leaving retailers with excess profits rather than Microsoft. Car dealers, for example, often add surcharges to the sticker price as a method of rationing and increasing profits.

2. Higher costs. Profits might be squeezed if the costs of overtime work rise and plant capacity reaches its limits. The only solution may be to raise prices to help offset cost increases.

3. Concern about competition. Microsoft may not want to raise prices too much for fear that competitors will imitate the software and steal business away.

If Microsoft sees a steady demand for its products and believes it can preserve its brand name loyalty, it will raise both the quantity produced and its prices. Suppose it raises the price of Microsoft Works by $10 to $34.95 and is able to sell 500,000 more units for a total output of 1,400,000 units the following year.

Figure 6.3 illustrates the effect of a shift in demand for the amount supplied:

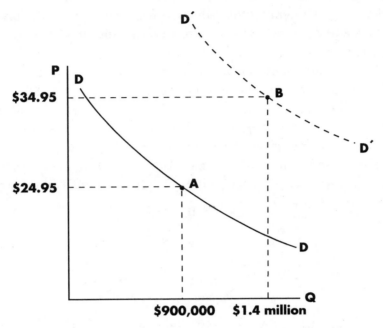

**Figure 6.3.** *Effect on supply when demand shifts forward.*

If the demand shifts away from Microsoft Works in favor of products offered by competitors the demand curve shifts backwards to the left. See figure 6.4 below.

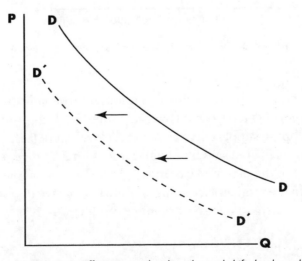

**Figure 6.4.** *Effect on supply when demand shifts backward.*

What will happen if demand decreases? The first reaction would be for Microsoft Corporation to reduce its production schedule—to produce fewer Microsoft Works packages. Implementing the reduction will probably require Microsoft to lay off workers and cut orders to suppliers, or switch production to other more popular product lines.

If Microsoft hopes to maintain market share, it may reduce prices again in an effort to keep loyal customers from going to competitors. Sometimes a company tries to compensate for falling revenue (and higher per unit costs) by raising prices, but clearly such an approach would be counterproductive if the demand curve has definitely shifted downward at every price level.

If Microsoft Corporation cuts its price to $19.95 and is only able to sell 500,000 units, the results can be shown on the graph as point (C) on the supply schedule.

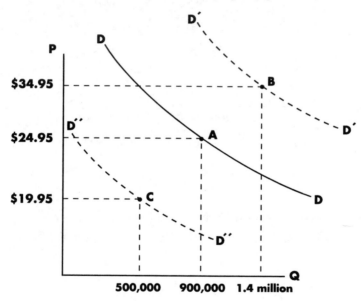

**Figure 6.5.** *Effect of a shift in demand on prices and production.*

Three points (A, B and C) on a supply schedule, represent what a firm is willing to produce at a variety of prices. A supply curve can be formed by connecting the three points in the demand curves. The result is an upward-sloping supply curve as shown below (figure 6.6).

An upward-sloping supply curve says that higher prices for X induce producers to expand production and supply more X to the marketplace. Equally, lower prices for X lead producers to cut back output and supply less X to the marketplace. Suppliers are responsive to price signals. Market prices serve as an incentive mechanism to increase or reduce production.

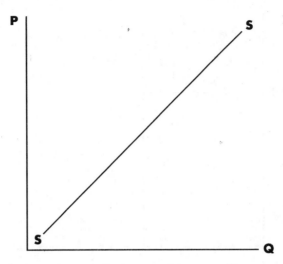

**Figure 6.6.** *The upward-sloping supply curve.*

## ELASTICITY OF SUPPLY

Chapter 5 introduced elasticity of demand. Elasticity of demand indicates how sensitive consumers are to changes in price. If a price rise increases revenue, the demand for the good is "price inelastic." If it reduces revenue, the demand for the good is "price elastic."

As in the case of demand elasticity, supply elasticity is linked to total revenue. What is the effect on total revenue of movement up or down the supply curve?

For example, U. S. farmers produce 2 billion bushels of wheat this year and the going price is $4 a bushel. It is late fall and the harvest is complete. Suddenly a famine strikes the rest of the world and foreigners come into the U. S. market to demand wheat. From an economic point of view, the demand curve for U. S. wheat has shifted outward while the supply of U. S. wheat is severely limited. The supply of U. S. wheat is not completely inelastic because some additional wheat may be available from granaries.

Figure 6.7 demonstrates the situation.

As the graph shows, the short-term supply of U. S. wheat is highly inelastic. Supplies cannot be increased at this point, so they must be allocated through an adjustment in price. The rise in demand pushes the price of wheat from $4 to $10 a bushel, and the dollar revenues to U. S. farmers increase dramatically. While the short-term supply curve for wheat may be highly inelastic and not very responsive to increased demand, next year's crop is a different story. Encouraged by higher prices, U. S. farmers are likely to increase wheat output substantially by allocating

129

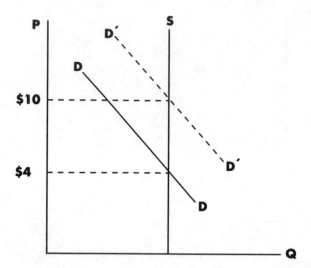

**Figure 6.7.** *An increase in demand faces a limited supply.*

more land to wheat production. The long-term supply curve is usually much more elastic. (See figure 6.8 below.)

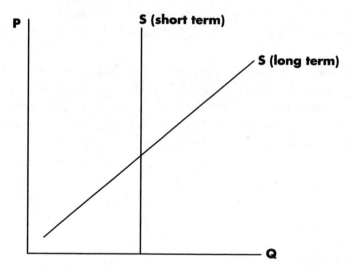

**Figure 6.8.** *Short term and long term supply curves for wheat.*

In manufacturing, the supply curve is normally elastic and sometimes even perfectly elastic. That is, an increase in demand can result in increased supplies within a very short period of time if it does not take much time to manufacture more products. Figure 6.9 demonstrates the highly elastic supply curve in response to an increase in demand.

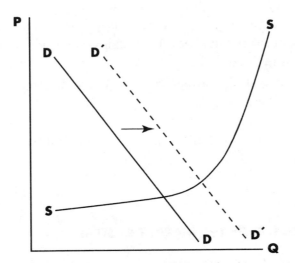

**Figure 6.9.** *Effect of increased demand for elastic supplies.*

In the above graph, the manufacturers can handle increased orders rather easily and without raising prices—at least until the point where plant use is maximized. As output reaches plant capacity, the supply becomes inelastic and prices start to rise-until another plant can be built. Elasticity on both the demand and supply side tends to be even more flexible given more time.

## SUPPLY, DEMAND AND PRICE

In a free market, prices tend to stabilize at the point where supply equals demand as shown in figure 6.10 below.

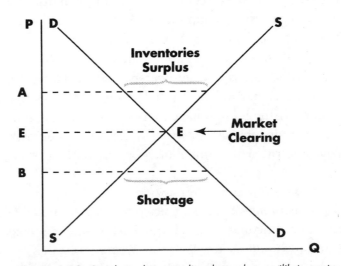

**Figure 6.10.** *Supply tends to equalize demand at equilibrium price.*

131

Figure 6.10 indicates three possibilities.

At point A, quantity supplied exceeds quantity demanded, causing a surplus of inventory. Companies cut back production—and prices tend to fall toward point E, the equilibrium price.

At point B, quantity demanded exceeds quantity supplied, causing a shortage in inventories. Companies increase production and raise prices to meet the excess demand.

Prices tend to rise toward point E, the equilibrium price. Only at point E is quantity supplied equal to quantity demanded.

## THREE ESSENTIAL PRINCIPLES OF THE MARKET SYSTEM

Three main characteristics of the market system are vitally important and highly useful in analyzing economic issues. These principles are non-discrimination, the market as an incentive system, and the benefit principle.

### The Principle of Non-discrimination

In the marketplace, everyone tends to pay the same price no matter what his or her ethnic, religious, racial, political and financial background. Note the tendency toward one price in figure 6.10. Black or white, male or female, rich or poor, Baptist or Buddhist, everyone pays the same price for a loaf of bread in the grocery store or for a refrigerator at the appliance store. This is why the market is often described as blind or impersonal.

It is true that there is a certain amount of price discrimination in the marketplace, with businesses attempting to charge different prices to different people. Price discrimination does happen. For example, some car dealers try to charge wealthier clients more money. Airlines are notorious for charging a wide variety of prices on flights. Hotels, movie theaters, and amusement parks give special discounts to children and senior citizens. Firms are always trying to discover distinct markets offering them the chance to charge higher prices for select customers. But such methods do not always work. As society becomes more competitive and knowledgeable, price discrimination becomes more the exception than the rule.

### The Market as an Incentive System

As a consequence of the one-price rule, it is clear that a free market favors those who earn more income because they have greater purchasing power. The more money an individual makes, the more resources he can command and the more goods and services he can obtain. Is this a bad thing?

Clearly, the free market is an incentive system, always encouraging individuals to work hard, save, and become more educated. More productive workers are rewarded in a market economy. If there were few rewards for doing better, how well would people and products perform?

Many utopian societies have attempted to devise ways to live and work without financial rewards, and some have been successful in the short run. But the vast majority of these efforts have ultimately failed. Monetary incentives are an important element of human motivation. Without financial rewards, individuals are discouraged from working and producing quality goods and services.

The market does provide low-priced goods and services for lower-income people just as it provides high-priced items for high-income people. The marketplace offers McDonald's as well as Ruth's Chris Steak House, Holiday Inn as well as Hyatt Regency Hotels, and Chevrolets as well as Cadillacs. In virtually every area of society, there are markets for every income group.

When the price increases, people demand less of a product or service. They are more careful how they use a scarcer resource. Conversely, when the price declines, people use more of a product or service. They can be more generous in their use. From the producer's point of view, the economic incentives are different. When the price of a good or service increases, producers are encouraged to produce more of it. When the price declines, they have an incentive to produce less of it.

The market sends vital signals out to all producers and consumers to ration scarce resources. When the market is interfered with and prices are not allowed to fluctuate according to supply and demand, the incentive system breaks down.

Rewards and punishments affect behavior. Gary Becker, University of Chicago professor and Nobel laureate (see biography in this chapter), has emphasized this point repeatedly in areas beyond traditional economic research. For example, if society raises the cost of crime, individuals will commit less crime. This is not to say that other cultural and social factors do not affect crime. But costs and benefits do play a role.

### The Benefit Principle

The Principle of Accountability, also known as the benefit principle, says that those who benefit from a good or service should pay for it. If a loaf of bread is consumed it should be paid for. If two loaves of bread are purchased, twice as much should be paid.

This accountability principle is important for a variety of reasons. First, since individuals are buying the goods or services they use, they are more conscientious as consumers. The market system encourages individuals to shop around for the best price, to demand quality in the good or service, to insist on full disclosure from the seller, and to demand money back if they are not pleased with the product or service. In many ways, the "consumer is king" in this competitive environment.

Second, waste and inefficiency are minimized. If someone else (the government, the insurance company, your boss, or a rich uncle) is paying for the goods or services used, an individual may care very little about the price he pays. Someone else is paying, so why shop around for the best deal? When the benefit principle is not in operation, there is a tendency toward overuse and waste of resources.

The closer government comes to adopting competitive market approaches in providing public services such as schools, roads, bridges, highways, welfare, and medical care, the more efficiently and effectively these services run. As government moves away from free-market principles, the more problems it faces in terms of shortages and waste.

## LIMITATIONS OF SUPPLY AND DEMAND ANALYSIS

Supply and demand analysis can be applied to many situations, but supply and demand does have its limitations. Note that each supply and demand diagram applies to only one product, and there is no way to show graphically how or why a producer may improve or change the quality of this product, or why a company may create a whole new product. The two stage model presented in Chapter 4 demonstrates "The Theory of the Firm," or the income statement.

Despite the limitations of the supply and demand model, supply-and-demand analysis can tell a great deal about markets.

## SHORTAGES AND SURPLUSES

One thing that supply and demand curves can demonstrate is how the market solves problems of shortages and surpluses. The market has a wonderful corrective mechanism that responds quickly to changes in supply and demand. Prices are the signals in the marketplace that tell firms what, where, when and how much to produce.

It should be pointed out that the market is not some impersonal machine that automatically solves coordination problems in the economy. Rather, the market consists of individual consumers and producers who make decisions about prices and production based on available information. These individuals are entrepreneurs who act in expectation of making profits and avoiding losses. Successful entrepreneurs may make mistakes from time to time, but they learn from their mistakes and eventually solve the problem.

## HOW THE MARKET RESPONDS TO SHORTAGES

The following examples show how supply and demand problems are solved. The first example looks at a shortage situation in the economy. Suppose that a war breaks out in the Middle East and Saudi Arabia, Iran and Kuwait stop exporting oil. Figure 6.11 illustrates a short-term shortfall in oil supplies.

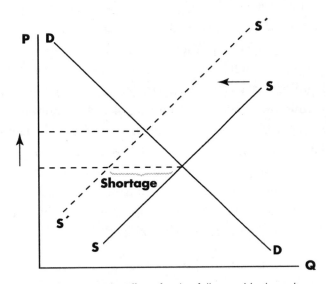

**Figure 6.11.** *Effect of a shortfall in world oil supplies.*

The oil supply curve shifts to the left while the demand schedule remains the same. At current prices a major shortage arises—demand exceeds supply. But if market prices are allowed to rise, a shortage will not exist. Instead, consumers will choose to use less oil because the price has increased.

The market responds differently in the short run and the long run.

In the short run, producers of oil and gas will respond to the war environment and oil stoppage by quickly raising prices at all levels of production—oil, gas, and gasoline at the pump. Futures prices for oil and gasoline will jump immediately, and buyers and sellers will struggle to identify the right amount of price increase. The war will cause oil and gasoline prices to rise, but by how much or for how long prices will stay up can not be specified. (Chapter 2 discussed this aspect of uncertainty.) Decisions about price will be made daily by producers, consumers, and speculators.

Higher prices result in consumers with the most capital to spend and/or the highest user demands able to purchase the most of a limited product. Higher prices send signals to consumers that they should reduce consumption of oil, gasoline and natural gas. Household and commercial users will cut back on their energy uses. Over time the amount demanded declines to match the reduced amount supplied.

The short-term increase in oil prices will solve the immediate shortage problem. If the price mechanism is working properly, there need not be any lines at gasoline stations or severe shortages in the pipeline or in storage tanks, although supplies may be tight at times since the market is not perfect and cannot foresee all circumstances.

The Middle East producers are the financial losers if they stop producing. Higher oil prices will create a gigantic increase in earnings of major oil companies outside the Middle East. This windfall profit is not to be taken lightly. Windfall profit brings into play the market's long-term solution to the oil shortage.

If major players in the energy field conclude that the Middle East war will continue indefinitely, they will be encouraged to use the additional profits to expand exploration and production of oil and gas elsewhere around the world. New oil and gas discoveries will be sought. Marginal wells that had been closed down will be reopened in an effort to draw out oil. The cost of exploration, development, and re-engineering will suddenly be profitable at the higher prices the product now demands. The effect should be an increase in oil output from non-Middle East sources over the next few years. The supply curve will shift back to the right, causing prices to fall, much to the relief of consumers.

## CASE STUDY: THE ENERGY CRISIS

A similar scenario took place in the 1970s and early 1980s. The Organization of Petroleum Exporting Countries (OPEC) imposed an oil blockade that drove up oil and gasoline prices in 1973-74 and again in 1979-80. The market responded with producers and entrepreneurs searching for and finding new oil fields in Alaska, Mexico, Indonesia, and other places around the world. By the early 1980s the world was flooded with oil and prices plummeted, causing OPEC to have a difficult time maintaining its cartel status.

Note: Why didn't the market prevent these shortages and eliminate the consumer needs illustrated by pictures of long gas lines in 1974? Although gasoline prices skyrocketed in the 1970s, prices were not allowed to rise to their full market level. The Federal government imposed price ceilings on gasoline and oil products. As a result, shortages continued and long lines at gasoline stations lasted for months. Figure 6.12 below illustrates the effect of a government-imposed price ceiling.

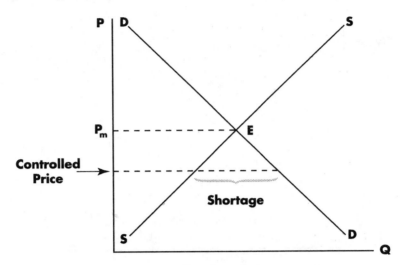

**Figure 6.12.** *Effect of price ceiling on gasoline.*

While oil and gasoline prices were allowed to rise, they were not allowed to rise enough to eliminate the difference between quantity supplied and quantity demanded. The impact? Gasoline had to be rationed, black markets developed, and oil companies were deprived of some additional revenue which could have been used for further exploration and production.

During this era of energy crisis, the government and the media attacked oil companies for price gouging and consumers for wasteful overconsumption of energy products. However, when the government keeps prices from rising to their market levels, it sends a conflicting message to the public. Public officials may tell the public that they are consuming too much, but the controlled price, which is below the market price, is telling them that energy is relatively less expensive, and that consumers should continue to spend at previous levels. Only when prices were allowed to reach market levels did this conflict disappear and consumers could once again find ample supplies at gas stations, albeit at higher prices.

## HOW THE MARKET RESPONDS TO SURPLUSES

Real estate provides an example of how the market deals with surpluses. During the oil boom of the late 1970s, real-estate developers in the Houston area built thousands of new homes, apartments and commercial buildings in expectation that the oil boom would continue for a long time. When the oil bust came in the early 1980s, it became clear that developers had overbuilt in the Houston area. The supply of housing exceeded the demand for both residential and commercial property. Figure 6.13 illustrates the situation.

137

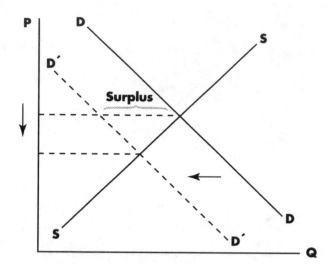

**Figure 6.13.** *Effect of an excessive supply on demand.*

When supply exceeds demand the market responds by cutting prices. Developers slashed prices for homes and offered reduced rental rates for office properties. In the early 1980s some developers in Houston were so desperate that they offered six months free leasing of office space.

Problems in real estate are not solved as quickly as the oil shortage case described above. Getting rid of overbuilt properties is not easy. In order to resolve problems in real estate, prices are cut, rents are reduced, office buildings and apartments are auctioned off, and developers go out of business. It may take years before the real-estate market is back to normal and supply equals demand.

Surpluses in commodities are much easier to deal with than surpluses in real estate. For example, if farmers produce a bumper crop of wheat in one year, the price goes down sharply. If the price falls below the cost of production, some farmers may go out of business or shift to another crop next year. As a result, the crop in the following year will be substantially less than the previous year. Consequently, prices for wheat will rise in the next year, restoring profitability to the wheat farmers.

If there are surplus service providers, either costs for services must go down or some providers must cease to provide their services. If demand for their services increases in future years, those providers who still provide the service can increase their prices and a demand for additional providers is created.

## FOUR SUPPLY AND DEMAND SCENARIOS

There are four possibilities when it comes to changes in supply and demand. Figure 6.14 below illustrates these four alternatives.

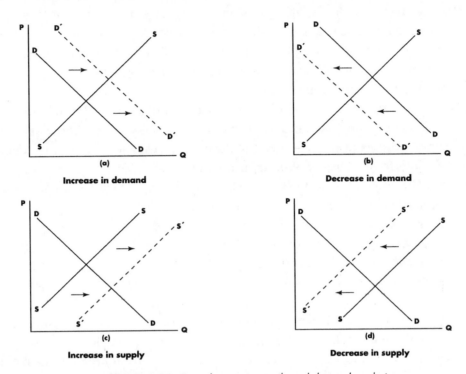

**Figure 6.14.** *Four changes in supply and demand analysis.*

1. **An increase in demand.** Example: People in a Texas community hit a big oil well, increasing dramatically the income of all its residents. Demand for consumer goods in the area increases, and so does the price and amount supplied.

2. **A decrease in demand.** Example: A major textile manufacturer in a New York town decides to move its plant to Mexico, affecting over half of the town's residents. Their income falls sharply as they scramble to find other jobs or to move to other communities. Demand for goods and services falls across the board—many supermarkets and shopping malls put their merchandise on sale at substantial discounts.

3. **An increase in supply.** Example: A new nickel mine is discovered and starts producing, doubling the amount of nickel available at market in a couple of years. As the supply increases, the price of nickel falls by 30%.

4. **A decrease in supply.** Example: A strike at the Chilean copper mines cuts off new supplies, forcing inventories to fall and sharply raising prices of copper on the world markets.

## THE ROLE OF THE PRICE SYSTEM

In each of the examples above, pricing performed a valuable service. The price system offers several benefits to individuals and the public. First, prices ration scarce resources. They inform business how much of a product or service should be produced relative to other products and services, keep costs under control and discourage waste (the discipline of the market). No economy can produce everything people want. The fact that prices are still positive suggests that resources are limited and need to be used efficiently.

Second, prices influence human behavior. Prices tell how much something costs and help potential buyers decide whether to purchase the product or service. Every time a product or service is bought, the costs are weighed against the benefits. Prices are determined based on this consideration.

Although a single price is decided in any voluntary exchange, the perceived value is different for buyer and seller. One price for each exchange may suggest that there is equality of value, but that is not the case. In fact, every voluntary exchange suggests an inequality of value. For example, vine-ripe tomatoes are for sale at the farmer's market. The farmer charges the customer $2 for four tomatoes. Is there equality of value? The customer would rather have the four tomatoes than the $2. He purchased the tomatoes at the price of $2 for four tomatoes because he perceived the value was higher than $2; otherwise, he would not have bought them.

For the seller the situation is just the opposite. He would rather have the $2 than the four tomatoes. For the farmer, the money is worth more than the commodity.

There is inequality of value in every exchange, which allows both the buyer and the seller to gain.

## CONSUMERS' SURPLUS

The net benefits buyers receive from exchange is called "consumers' surplus" and can be expressed graphically in figure 6.15 below.

In the diagram, the triangle PAE represents consumers' surplus. It represents the value to consumers who valued the product more than the cost to buy it (P). For example, in the case of the tomatoes at the farmer's market, there may be a few individuals willing to pay $3 for those four vine-ripe tomatoes, but they only had to pay $2. Their consumers' surplus was $1. When items are sold for less than the consumer expected to pay, as is the case with sale items, the consumer feels that he has received a gift. This is the meaning of consumer's surplus.

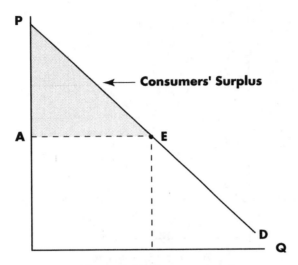

**Figure 6.15.** *Consumers' surplus.*

Consumers' surplus is a theoretical concept. Given that the entire demand schedule for a particular good is not generally known, how much consumers' surplus exists cannot be determined.

On the other hand, there are many customers who, for one reason or another, either cannot afford or do not desire to purchase an item or service at the current price P. However, if the price were reduced, more of them would buy.

Consumers' surplus is a measure of economic well-being. If producers are able to reduce the price of goods and services they sell to the public, consumers' surplus increases and more people can buy their products and their standard of living rises.

As pointed out earlier, the price system is an incentive/disincentive method and affects human behavior in all areas of activity. Prices help consumers and producers measure costs and benefits. Higher prices encourage consumers to buy less; lower prices encourage consumers to buy more.

## SELLERS' RENT

The opposite side of consumers' surplus is known as "sellers' rent." Sellers' rent refers to the benefits producers enjoy when they can sell a product or service at a price higher than they expect or substantially higher than their cost. Figure 6.16 measures sellers' rent.

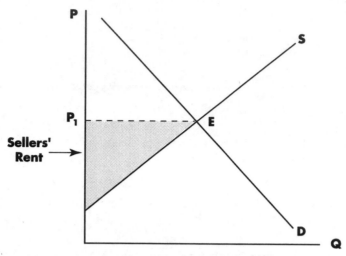

**Figure 6.16.** *Sellers' rent.*

The shaded area below price P represents sellers' rent. When sellers are able to get a higher price than they intended to charge for their products, that extra price is seller's rent – a free gift to the company/seller. If a farmer comes to market expecting to sell vine ripe tomatoes for $1.50 for four tomatoes and discovers that other farmers are selling their tomatoes for $2 for four, it is possible for a seller's rent of $.50 to be realized by raising the price to equal that of the other farmers.

If a service provider is searching for a new job and hopes to earn $50,000 a year, but is offered $70,000 a year by a prospective employer, the $20,000 difference between desired income and offered income is seller's rent.

The supply curve below the price P represents prices that producers are willing to accept and still earn a profit. It suggests that lower-cost producers exist and could survive if prices for their goods or services were driven lower.

Now look at the supply schedule above the price P. A higher price suggests that current producers would supply more goods and new suppliers might come on board. These new suppliers may be high-cost producers who, at the higher price, can now afford to be in business.

Chapter 7 will introduce the role of cost and how it affects supply and prices.

## PRICES ARE DETERMINDED AT THE MARGIN

Another important characteristic of the price system is that prices are determined at the margin. Prices are based on the number of buyers and sellers in the exchange marketplace at any particular time. But this is typically a small percentage of the number of individuals in a community. How many consumers buy a car or a major appliance during the year? No doubt thousands do each year, but as a percentage of the local total population, the number represents a minority.

General Motors typically sells 80,000 Buicks a year at an average price of $24,000 per car. What would happen to the price if suddenly an additional 10,000 car buyers wanted a Buick? There would be a temporary shortage in the dealers' lots as the Buick division of GM geared up to build more Buicks. Meanwhile, Buick dealers would demand a premium for Buicks currently on the lot and would likely raise the price.

The same is true if there were suddenly a decline in Buick sales by 10,000. Car dealers would offer "specials" on Buicks, trying to reduce their inventory by cutting their prices.

In Winter Park, Florida, where Rollins College is situated, the average home price is approximately $300,000. What determines this price? The average price of $300,000 is based on current demand for Winter Park homes, given the normal number of homes for sale (the supply). Typically, only 5% of all Winter Park homes are for sale—one out of 20.

If suddenly 10% of all homes in Winter Park were for sale, assuming that the demand remains the same, would the price of the average home stay constant? The price would fall sharply. In this example the supply would exceed the demand and drive prices down.

In the stock market, millions of shares trade hands every day on the New York Stock Exchange. Sometimes 1 billion shares are exchanged. But this large number of transactions is still a very small percentage of the total number of shares held by individuals, banks, insurance companies, pensions, and other financial institutions. If an additional 10% of all stockholders decided to sell, given no change in the demand for shares, prices would plummet.

Prices are determined by the number of buyers and sellers in relation to the amount of product or service available.

Pricing at the margin is a two-edged sword, with both advantages and disadvantages. The advantage: A small number of consumers can make a difference between a profit and a loss in a specific product. So retailers tend to be conscientious about consumer complaints. The disadvantage: A small number of sellers can sharply reduce the value of an investment or other asset that you are holding.

## SUPPLY AND DEMAND ONCE AGAIN

This chapter has shown how the basic ingredients of the marketplace—supply, demand and price—offer stability and flexibility in the global economy. In normal times, prices equalize supply and demand so that shortages and surpluses are minimized. Consumers are able to obtain what they wish at prices most can afford. Prices teach responsibility and respect and minimize the waste of valuable resources. In periods of crisis, crop failures, or shifting tastes, the market proves itself to be highly flexible. In times of shortages, for example, prices increase, additional resources enter the market, and new supplies are provided in the next season or long term. In times of surplus, prices decline, resources leave the market, and remaining companies survive. In short, the unhampered market economy is flexible and dynamic, bringing order out of chaos.

## SUMMARY

Main points covered in Chapter 6:

1.  The law of supply: When prices rise, suppliers respond to higher profits by increasing production; when prices fall, suppliers cut back on output.

2.  The elasticity of demand is low in the short run, but high in the long run.

3.  Supply and demand tend to force a single price in equilibrium.

4.  There are three essential principles of the market economy: non-discrimination (the tendency toward "one price" for all), an incentive system (rewarding higher incomes and providing a rationing device), and accountability (those who benefit pay).

5.  The market economy provides affordable goods and services for almost every class of income.

6.  Shortages and surpluses are temporary if prices are allowed to fluctuate freely and producers are permitted to enter or leave markets.

7.  Windfall profits are necessary to finance increased future production.

8.  Prices are signals in the marketplace that tell firms what, where, when and how much to produce, and help consumers relate costs to benefits.

9.  Lower prices benefit consumers and increase the size of the marketplace (consumers' surplus). Higher prices benefit producers, attract new suppliers and increase sellers' rent.

10. Prices are determined the marginal number of buyers and sellers in relation to the amount of product or service available.

## IMPORTANT TERMS

Consumers' surplus
Cost-benefit analysis
Elasticity of supply
Incentive or reward system
Marginal exchange
Microeconomics
Non-discrimination
Price gouging
Sellers' rent
Shortages and surpluses
The law of supply
Upward-sloping supply curve
Windfall profits

## INFLUENTIAL ECONOMIST

### GARY BECKER AND MICROECONOMICS

### Name: Gary S. Becker (1930- )

**Background:** Becker is considered one of the brightest and most creative geniuses in economics today. He is a primary proponent of the Chicago School of Economics, with a special emphasis on applying microeconomics (supply and demand theory) to some unusual areas such as sociology and criminal behavior. He was honored with the John Bates Clark Award (given to economists under 40 years of age), served as president of the American Economic Association, and won the Nobel Prize in Economics in 1992. Becker received his Ph.D. from the University of Chicago, and, except for teaching at Columbia University from 1957 to 1969, he has been a lifelong faculty member at Chicago.

**Major Works:** Almost all Becker's writings are written for a professional audience, much of it mathematical. His dissertation examined the economics of discrimination against blacks, which formed the basis of a book, *The Economics of Discrimination* (1971). Becker demonstrated that contrary to the Marxist view, discrimination does not favor the employer who discriminates, but rather costs the employer, since he loses out on a valuable employee. Other professional works include *Human Capital* (1975) and *Treatise on the Family* (1981).

In 1985 Becker began writing for *Business Week*, which expanded his influence to the general layman. His columns applied supply and demand theory to the issues of baseball, affirmative action, immigration, Social Security, religion, the

145

drug war, the homeless, and the feminist movement. His columns have recently been published in the book, *The Economics of Life* (McGraw-Hill, 1997), co-authored with his wife Guity Nashat Becker. His basic thesis is that all forms of human behavior respond to rewards and punishments, and changes in the net benefits or net costs can significantly change behavior for better or for worse. If society raises the cost of crime, criminals will commit fewer crimes. If students have a greater choice in which schools they attend, competition will enhance the level of education.

**Sample Quotation:** "Everyone recognizes that most people respond to costs and benefits in deciding how much to buy of simple goods such as fruit, clothing, or a car. I claim that this common-sense idea applies to all human decisions....For example, this view implies that criminals also respond to incentives, so crime increases when potential miscreants believe they won't be punished much for robbery and other crimes....The number of children a couple has depends on the costs and benefits of child rearing: Therefore, couples tend to have fewer children when the wife works and has a better-paying job, when subsidies from the government through child allowances and tax deductions for dependents are smaller, when the cost of educating and training children rises, and so forth."[2]

## PROBLEMS TO PONDER

1. Some economists such as William Baumol and Alan Blinder, criticize the market economy as pro-wealthy. They declare, "This rationing process does favor the rich, and is a problem that market economies must confront." They suggest high progressive tax rates on income to "equalize incomes," and "let the market mechanism distribute goods in accord with preferences." Is it possible for the tax system to redistribute income from the rich to the poor without affecting incentives?

2. Cite examples where the market economy provides low-priced goods and services for lower-income individuals and does so profitably. Think of specific examples in the following areas: hotels, air travel, restaurants, clothing, groceries, drinks, entertainment, and vacations.

3. Have you ever walked into a store and not been able to find an item you were looking for? How often do shortages appear? At what time of the year (Christmas holidays, for example)? How does the free market deal with shortages?

2  Gary Becker and Guity Nashat Becker, *The Economics of Life* (New York: McGraw Hill, 1997), p. 308

4. If a store is offering a free sample, does this indicate unlimited supply?

5. During the energy crisis of the 1970s, Congress bemoaned the "price gouging" and "windfall" profits of the major oil companies and imposed an "excess profits tax." Was this act of Congress justifiable? If "excess profits" are taxed away, where will oil companies get the money to fund new exploration and development of oil properties?

6. The American Economic Association, the largest professional organization of economists, charges three different prices for itsannual membership fee: $54 for members earning $37,000 a year or less; $64 for members making between $50,000 and $37,000 a year; and $75 for members earning more than $50,000. Students pay only $27 a year. Is this form of price discrimination justifiable? Do you think this encourages economists to lie about their income?

7. Of the four diagrams in figure 6.14, select the appropriate diagram for each of the following supply and demand scenarios:

   (a) Labor market: The government increases the cost of labor when it raises the minimum wage by 50%.

   (b) Stock market: A publicly-traded company declares a 10% stock dividend and the price of the shares drops 10% overnight.

   (c) Imported goods: when a government devalues its currency by 40%, the price of imported goods rises.

   (d) Oil market: War ends in the Middle East so Iraq begins exporting oil again.

   (e) Capital market: The Federal Reserve reduces interest rates and floods the capital market with new money.

   (e) Consumer goods market: Following a depression, people buy fewer consumer goods.

8. How would you respond to the following: "When producers reduce prices for goods and services, it increases consumers' surplus and everyone's standard of living. Therefore, it behooves government to impose below-market price ceilings on consumer goods, thereby increasing consumers' surplus and making everyone better off." What would be the effect of this policy?

9. In 1979 two major U. S. airlines handed out free "half fare" coupons to travelers. These coupons entitled customers to half-regular fares on future flights for the next six months. This could mean savings of between $25 and $300. Millions of these coupons were handed out. The coupons were trans-

ferable. What do you think happened to the coupons? Would the market set a single price for all coupons, or would the price of the coupon depend on the destination? What would happen to the price of coupons as the expiration date approached?[3]

10. Evaluate the following statement: "The more one makes, the less he responds to the competitive marketplace. A millionaire artist no longer plays what the public wants to hear, but writes songs that please only him. In the same vein, big business has made so much money that it doesn't respond to public desires anymore." Does an artist or a big company become unresponsive to the public once successful?

11. You are an economist working as a consultant to a small company. Suddenly a recession hits and demand falls. The company president comes to you for advice: Should you raise prices to offset a falloff in sales or reduce prices to increase volume? Using supply and demand curves, suggest which route is best for the business leader.

12. Artists and composers often complain that the marketplace forces them to produce according to "crass" public demands rather than art for its own sake and beauty. Is this a logical criticism of the free market? How can there be sufficient demand for "higher arts" in the marketplace, or must it be subsidized by government? Why are so many artists and musicians thought to be anti-market?

13. In their book, *Down the Tube: An Inside Account of the Failure of American Television*, authors William F. Baker (president of a public television station) and George Dessart characterize television programming as immature and mediocre, like an undisciplined child. They blame lack of proper regulation for TV's downfall. TV does not serve the "public interest" because "commercial television must appeal to the majority in order to survive." Based on what you have learned in this and earlier chapters, is there any way to satisfy demand for television programs for minority interests? To what extent has the television industry increased the quantity, quality and variety of television programs?

14. The President of the United States declares a national emergency and pronounces an edict that from this time onward all citizens and residents of the country should pay according to their ability. He mandates that all prices will now be quoted as a percentage of income, e.g., 10% for rent, 40% for automobiles, 0.01% for bread. Prices will be replaced with percentage marks in all retail outlets. What effect will this new declaration have on the economy? Productivity? Unemployment? Honesty? Black markets?

3  Paul A. Samuelson, *Economics*, 6th ed. (New York: McGraw Hill, 1964), p. 254)

15. Sellers of art and collectibles often say that prices can only rise because of limited supply. "They aren't making any more of these," they claim. They argue that the supply of rare coins, Masters' paintings, and Babe Ruth autographed baseballs are forever fixed. Hence, the supply curve is perfectly inelastic. After studying this chapter on supply and demand, show how prices can still fall with a perfectly inelastic supply curve. Also, given that the supply curve represents the number of buyers and sellers at any given time, and not the total of owners of collectibles, explain why the supply curve may in fact, be elastic. [Hint: If the price of an art work or collectible becomes extremely high, will new sellers enter the market?]

16. Economist Ronald H. Nelson has criticized Gary Becker and the Chicago School as being too economic in focus. He states, "According to Becker, criminals do not prey upon victims because the criminals are bad people — 'fallen people' — who simply cannot resist the immediate temptation to steal. Rather, they are responding to their economic incentives — for example, whether a life of crime, considering the risks of punishment by the criminal justice system, maximizes their prospective economic benefits minus the costs. A marriage, according to Becker, reflecting the value system of the Chicago school, is not a sacred trust formed by two people in love. It is instead a contract to perform mutually beneficial services that, if it is to succeed, maximize the independent utility of each marriage partner."[4] Do you agree? How important are economic factors in crime, marriage, etc.?

## RECOMMENDED READING

Gary Becker and Guity Nashat Becker, *The Economics of Life* (McGraw-Hill, 1997). These are columns that Gary Becker wrote, with the help of his wife, in *Business Week*. They include many examples of applied microeconomics.

Steven Landsburg, *The Armchair Economist: Economics and Everyday Life* (Free Press, 1993). A delightful book that applies economics to everyday situations.

4  Ronald Nelson, *The Theology of Samuelson's Economics* [manuscript, 1997], pp. 115-116)

*Chapter 7*

# HOW COSTS AFFECT PRICES

*"Business decisions are built on three pillars –
cost, value and price."*

—SHLOMO MAITAL
*Executive Economics,* p.6

Chapters 1 – 6 have explained the basics of how prices are determined in the global economy through supply and demand and how an equilibrium price is established, the dynamics of the marketplace, and how prices change when supplies change or demand shifts. The importance of changing the product or service itself to enhance value to the customer and hence increase profitability of the firm has also been discussed.

Price and value are extremely important in the world economy. One more element in pricing in the economy—how costs affect prices – must also be considered. When a company's costs of production rise, can the company simply pass on these cost increases to their customers by raising prices? Frequently workers negotiate higher wages, or input suppliers raise their prices, or landlords raise their rent. How do these cost increases affect prices and profit margins? Can there be such a thing as "cost push" inflation where prices rise in response to higher costs?

Can cost reductions result in lower prices for consumers? How do lower costs affect profit margins? What incentive do producers have to reduce prices if their costs go down? Why have the prices of televisions, computers, and ballpoint pens fallen sharply over the past half century? If a clothing manufacturer builds a factory in Latin America to take advantage of cheap labor, will this result in lower clothing prices for consumers in the United States?

Chapter 7 will answer these questions and show how costs affect the supply curve and the price of goods and services, and how price changes affect costs. Chapter 7 will also address the question: When demand rises for a good or service, do the prices of outputs affect the prices of inputs?

## BACK TO THE MICROSOFT EXAMPLE

The Microsoft example presented in Chapter 6 helps to answer these questions. Recall that an equilibrium price of $24.95 had been established for the Microsoft Works software package resulting in sales of 900,000 units. Below is a diagram of this equilibrium condition:

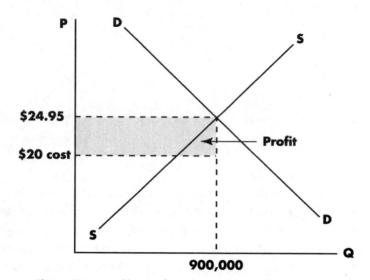

**Figure 7.1.** *Equilibrium of supply and demand for Microsoft Works.*

The total revenue generated by the sales of Microsoft Works for the most recent fiscal year is $22,455,000.

Assume that the cost per unit of producing Microsoft Works is $20. Costs include research and development, materials and supplies, labor, rent, and overhead. The total cost of producing 900,000 units is $18,000,000. The addition to the company's bottom line is $4,455,000 before taxes.

Suppose that a new technology permits Microsoft to produce Microsoft Works software for only $15 per unit as a result of an engineering breakthrough, or suppose Microsoft starts producing software diskettes in Latin America with substantially lower labor costs. The costs of production fall sharply to $15 per unit.

How will this cost reduction affect the price of Microsoft Works?

The first impact will be seen in the profits of Microsoft. The market has already established that it can still sell 900,000 units a year at $24.95 irrespective of the cost to produce it. (Remember, the demand schedule is separate from the supply schedule.) At the same time, costs have fallen from $20 to $15 a unit, thereby increasing the annual before-tax profit from $4,455,000 to $8,955,000.

Is there any reason to change Microsoft's pricing strategy? If Microsoft has a long-term monopoly on this new cost-saving technology or labor-saving strategy, the company would probably not cut prices because there is no incentive to do so. Microsoft will continue to enjoy even higher levels of profit.

However, historically, companies facing lower costs tend to cut prices. Why? Two reasons: First, to capture a wider market, especially when demand is relatively elastic. This means that Microsoft could expand its campaign into many new markets at lower prices. Many companies attempt to increase market share as a way to maximize long-term profitability.

Second, competition can quickly catch up with Microsoft if it does not stay ahead of the game. Suppose Microsoft stubbornly refuses to cut prices and enjoys abnormally high profits for the next year. Other firms may adopt the new technology if it is available, or they may follow Microsoft's path and open factories overseas. By cutting their costs, they can then reduce prices quickly and cut into Microsoft's market share. To counter this anticipated strategy, Microsoft wisely keeps ahead of its competition and cuts prices.

By how much? It is difficult to say whether Microsoft will reduce prices by as much as the per unit cost savings. Much depends on the capacity of competitors and their cost structure and on differences in demand for various brand names. The only certainty is that Microsoft will probably cut retail prices as production costs decrease.

## HISTORICAL EXAMPLES OF COST-INDUCED PRICE CUTTING

There have been numerous examples of products whose prices have fallen sharply as the costs of production have declined.

In the early 20th century, the price of automobiles fell steadily and dramatically. Figure 7.2 illustrates the decline in Henry Ford's Model T car prices between 1908 and 1916.

Price declines were accompanied by huge increases in car sales. Clearly the long-run demand curve for automobiles was highly elastic in the early 20th century. The main source of creating such a large market was Ford's cost-cutting methods. Henry Ford created the mass market for automobiles through assembly-line manufacturing. When he started making the Model T in 1908, it took more than half a day—a full 12 1/2 hours—to produce one car. Ford knew that he had to cut this time dramatically to create a car market for the masses. His goal was to make one car a minute, and he eventually achieved this goal in 1918. By 1925 his Michigan plant was producing one Model T every 10 seconds. The price of his car fell to one-tenth of its starting level, and over 15 million cars were sold in 1925.

Ford's assembly-line methods reduced the time and cost to build a car dramatically, and allowed Ford to cut retail prices accordingly.

153

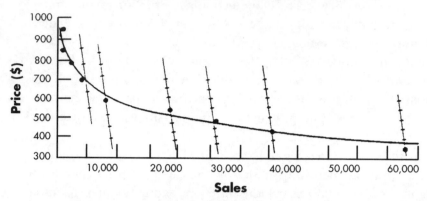

### Model T Touring Car

| Year | Price ($) | Unit Sales |
|------|-----------|------------|
| 1908 | $850 | 5,986 |
| 1909 | 950 | 12,292 |
| 1910 | 780 | 19,293 |
| 1911 | 690 | 40,402 |
| 1912 | 600 | 78,611 |
| 1913 | 550 | 182,809 |
| 1914 | 490 | 260,720 |
| 1915 | 440 | 355,276 |
| 1916 | 360 | 577,036 |

**Figure 7.2.** *Demand for Model T Touring Cars, 1908-1916.*

*Source:* Richard S. Tedlow, *New and Improved: The Story of Mass Marketing in America* (Basic Books, 1990), p. 125. See also Shlomo Maital, *Executive Economics* (Free Press, 1994), p. 189.

## ECONOMIES OF SCALE

Another vital factor in the reduction of per-unit costs and prices is economies of scale achieved through mass production. Certainly Ford was able to take advantage of economies of scale in producing millions of Model T's.

Here's why the increased production of a single product creates economies of scale. Production costs of a single product can be divided into two types: fixed costs and variable costs.

**Fixed costs** are defined as the short-run expenses of a firm that do not vary with output, sometimes called "overhead" or "sunk costs." Examples of fixed costs include office rent, payments for equipment, interest payments on debt, and research and development expenses. In the long run, however, fixed costs are not so fixed. Businesses can relocate and pay less rent or wages, for instance. But in the short run, fixed costs are not very flexible.

**Variable costs** are the firm's costs that do vary with output. Examples of variable costs include labor, electricity, and materials from suppliers. The greater the output, the higher the variable costs.

**Total cost** is simply defined as the sum of **fixed costs** and **variable costs**.

To illustrate the advantage of economies of scale, return to the Microsoft Works example. The average cost of producing Microsoft Works is $20 per unit. This cost is based on the production of 900,000 units per year for a total cost of $18,000,000.

Of the $18 million in total costs to produce Microsoft Works, fixed cost including research & development, floor space, and overhead, amount to $1 million, and variable costs are $17 million. The fixed costs are built into the firm's operations; they are "sunk" costs. But the variable costs vary with the level of production.

The following table (figure 7.3) illustrates the relationship between fixed, variable, and total costs.

**Microsoft Works Cost Structure**

| Units Produced | Fixed Cost | Variable Cost | Total Cost |
|---|---|---|---|
| 0 | $1,000,000 | 0 | $1,000,000 |
| 100,000 | 1,000,000 | $4,600,000 | 5,600,000 |
| 300,000 | 1,000,000 | 11,300,000 | 12,300,000 |
| 500,000 | 1,000,000 | 14,000,000 | 15,000,000 |
| 700,000 | 1,000,000 | 15,800,000 | 16,800,000 |
| 900,000 | 1,000,000 | 17,000,000 | 18,000,000 |

**Figure 7.3.**

Total costs change as production increases. The diagram below illustrates how the **marginal cost** of producing an additional 200,000 units of Microsoft Works declines.

In figure 7.4 (including the graph), the **marginal cost** (the amount necessary to produce one more software diskette) declines dramatically, pushing the average unit cost of production down. The marginal cost has fallen from $46 to $6 per software unit and the average per unit cost from $56 to $20.

Given a $24.95 retail price, Microsoft Works does not make a profit until at least 700,000 units are sold in a year. When the retail price equals the average total cost (or ATC), a profit will be made.

Why do the marginal and average costs decline with increasing output? There are two reasons. First, suppliers of input materials in manufacturing software offer bulk discounts on larger orders, thus reducing per unit costs. Second, a large production schedule also ensures that machinery and labor are used optimally.

**Marginal and Average Cost**

| Total Cost | Marginal Cost | Marginal Cost (per unit) | Average Cost (per unit) |
|---|---|---|---|
| $1,000,000 | $1,000,000 | — | $1,000,000 |
| $5,600,000 | $4,600,000 | $46.00 | $56.00 |
| 12,300,000 | 6,700,000 | 33.50 | 41.00 |
| 15,000,000 | 2,700,000 | 13.50 | 30.00 |
| 16,800,000 | 1,800,000 | 9.00 | 24.00 |
| 18,000,000 | 1,200,000 | 6.00 | 20.00 |

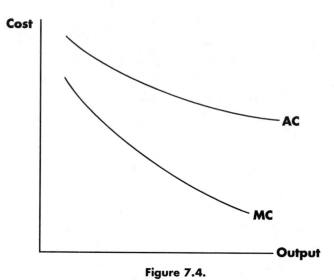

**Figure 7.4.**

## CAN UNIT COSTS RISE?

There might come a point when marginal and average costs of production start rising. Why? When plant capacity reaches a maximum, resources are strained and quality may be sacrificed. Workers may have to be paid overtime. New staff may be hired, which requires training and other expenses. Facilities may have to be expanded. This additional investment to expand output may increase the per-unit costs.

Economists talk a great deal about the possibility of increasing costs based on the law of diminishing returns. Normally, a plant is fixed in terms of size and the number of machines and equipment. Adding additional workers will undoubtedly increase output as these workers specialize and produce more. However, the production process reaches a point of diminishing returns as more workers use the same machines and work in the same space. As a result, hiring more workers continues to increase output but by smaller amounts. In other words, marginal returns decline. See figure 7.5.

156

The law of diminishing returns and increasing costs says that as a firm uses more of a variable input (such as labor) with a given amount of fixed input, the marginal product eventually declines.

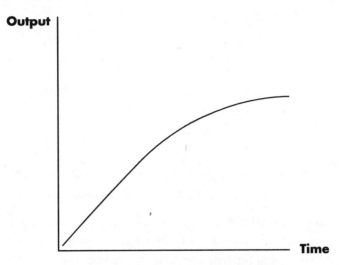

**Figure 7.5.** *The law of diminishing returns states that output increases at a decreasing rate.*

## SONY AND THE U-SHAPED COST CURVE

Akio Morita, the founder of Sony Corp., raised the specter of a rising cost curve in his 1987 autobiography, *Made in America*. When his company was in its infancy in 1955, he began taking orders for a small transistor radio. Then Bulova, a large watch and appliance firm, ordered 100,000 radios. Sony also received other large orders.

Morita was in shock. "We did not have the capacity to produce one hundred thousand transistor radios a year and also make the other things in our small product line," he wrote. He added: "Our capacity was less then than a thousand radios a month. If we got an order for one hundred thousand, we would have to hire and train new employees and expand our facilities even more. This would mean a major investment, a major expansion, and a gamble."

Morita drew a U shaped curve (see figure 7.6). "The price for five thousand would be our regular price. That would be the beginning of the curve. For ten thousand there would be a discount and that was at the bottom of the curve. For thirty thousand the price would begin to climb. For fifty thousand the price per unit would be higher than for five thousand, and for one hundred thousand units the price would have to be much more per unit than for the first five thousand."

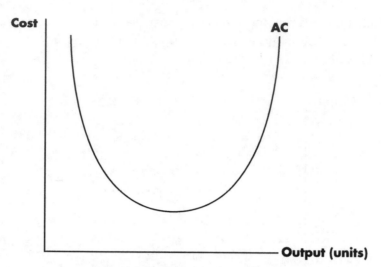

**Figure 7.6.** *Morita's U-shaped cost curve.*

Morita explained further: "My reasoning was that if we had to double our production capacity to complete an order for one hundred thousand and if we could not get an order the following year we would be in big trouble, perhaps bankrupt, because how could we employ all the added staff and pay for all the new and unused facilities in that case?"[1]

Clearly, the risk of expanding too quickly is a problem facing many growth companies. But failing to expand for fear of having unused capacity is just as dangerous. Overused facilities can cut deeply into profits and can lose business. Morita declined the huge order and instead developed longer term contracts with retailers that provided a steady, rising production. Gradually Morita expanded his plant operation, and today Sony is one of the world's largest industrial firms.

## DOES THE U-SHAPED COST CURVE EXIST IN THE LONG RUN?

Nobel Prize winning economist Herbert Simon denies the existence of any U-shaped cost curve in the long run. "Empirical studies show the firm's cost curves not to be U-shaped, but in fact to slope down to the right and then level off, without a clearly defined minimum point." According to Simon, "such a curve implies decreasing costs in all sizes, with no upper boundary on the size of the firm."[2]

Generally, U-shape cost curves exist only in the short term. Over the long run, firms with rising costs and over utilized capacity build new facilities to handle increased demand. Bureaucracy is a major source of rising costs in large corporations, but the inefficiencies of bigness can be overcome through the creation of separate profit centers within the organization.

1  Akio Morita, *Made in America* (Fontana: New York, 1987).
2  Herbert Simon, interview, in *Challenge*, Nov.-Dec. 1986, p. 24.

## DECREASING COSTS AND INCREASING THE STANDARD OF LIVING

Ultimately, declining costs of production push the supply curve downward, thus increasing "consumers' surplus" and raising a nation's standard of living. Figure 7.7 illustrates this effect:

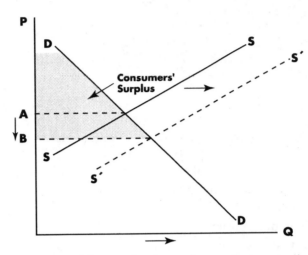

**Figure 7.7.** *Shift outward in the supply curve due to cost reductions.*

Cutting costs, in addition to improving quality, is essential to an advancing economy and an increasing standard of living. The job of entrepreneurs and business leaders is to build and operate businesses by selling goods and services that provide value at a reasonable price and an acceptable cost. If firms create more value by improving quality and lowering prices, their businesses will prosper and expand. And the entire nation—consumers and businesses—will benefit. That is the essence of the capitalist system.

### ARE COSTS AND REVENUES CONNECTED?

Until now, supply and demand have been viewed as two separate entities. A firm's expenditures (the supply side) are separate from a firm's revenues (the demand side). Figure 7.8 illustrates this firm's basic income statement (see chapter 4, "The Theory of the Firm").

If a firm's costs suddenly rise, will that affect revenue? It will definitely cut into profits, but will it increase revenue? Microsoft's customers are usually not aware of Microsoft's costs in producing its software programs. All customers know is that the price, $24.95, fits their budget and their demand schedule. If Microsoft raises its price to offset rising costs, say to $29.95, some customers will still buy Microsoft Works, but many thousands will go elsewhere, possibly to a competitor, or they may not buy at all.

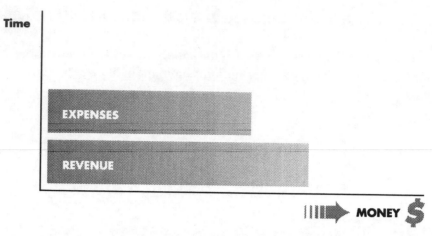

**Figure 7.8.** *Expenses and revenues of a firm.*

Clearly, this analysis makes sense at a microeconomic level. If one firm's per-unit costs rise, it will be difficult to pass these costs on to customers. It can do so depending on its level of goodwill and customer loyalty, but not without risking lost sales to other competitors.

It should be possible to distinguish between the supply schedule of a firm and the supply schedule of the entire product or industry. What if every firm's costs go up? Can firms raise prices and maintain their profit margins? Rising costs will cut into profits, as figure 7.9 demonstrates.

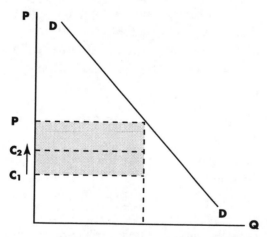

**Figure 7.9.** *Rising costs reduce profits.*

Rising costs for only one firm will not alter the supply curve for the entire industry. But if costs affect all industries, what then? Suppose a major component of the cost to produce software packages for sale in the United States is the cost of software in Japan. If the Japanese yen increases in value against the dollar, the cost of producing software packages, including Microsoft Works, goes up for American companies. How will software companies respond to this cost increase? Figure 7.10 illustrates the effect:

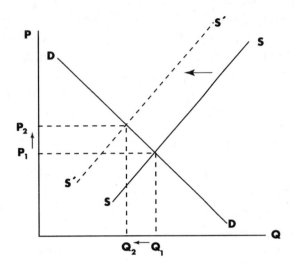

**Figure 7.10.** *How rising costs push prices up.*

In the above example, the final effect of an industry-wide cost increase is shown. Output declines from $Q_1$ to $Q_2$, prices rise from $P_1$ to $P_2$, and profit margins are relatively unchanged. Changes in the industry bring about higher prices, lower output, and relatively unchanged profit margins.

First, rising costs (due to the appreciation of the yen) squeeze profit margins. As a result, higher-cost producers go into other markets or go out of business. The remaining software businesses raise their prices (from $P_1$ to $P_2$) to offset the higher costs. At higher prices, customers buy fewer software packages and will reduce the amount purchased from $Q_1$ to $Q_2$.

Can producers raise retail prices equal to the cost increase and completely pass on their rising costs to their customers? It depends on the degree of competition in the industry—sometimes they are able to pass on all the increased expenses, but other times only a small portion is passed on to their customers.

Firms often raise prices immediately when costs go up, making a public announcement explaining their increase in prices in terms of "unavoidable cost increases." However, they are generally only able to do so when the increased costs affect the entire industry. Moreover, the price increase is a test of how responsive customers are to a price increase. Sometimes customers accept the higher price, but sometimes they balk and the firm may have to rescind the price increase.

## "PRICE SEARCHERS" vs. "PRICE TAKERS"

In dealing with changing costs and shifting demand, owner/operators of firms engage in price searching. Setting prices is a discovery process based on trial and error in an effort to find the right price. Clearly, setting prices is an entrepreneurial activity. Competition makes it easier to set prices, but setting prices is in no way automatic. Sometimes the market is so large that owner/operators can act as "price takers," rather than "price searchers," but this is the exception to the rule. The prices of agricultural products and major publicly-traded stocks fit into this category of "price taking." But in most markets, firms are "price searchers."

## RISING PRICES: COST PUSH OR DEMAND PULL?

In times of inflation, when the general price level is rising for all goods and services, firms frequently announce price rises in response to cost increases. During these times economists speak of "cost push" inflation.

How does "cost push" differ from "demand pull"? Higher prices can only be maintained if consumers are willing to pay the higher prices. Costs of production may indeed rise, but consumers may not be willing to pay the higher prices.

For example, suppose the cost of oil rises due to an oil crisis in the Middle East. Exxon, Texaco and Chevron attempt to pass along the higher oil costs by raising gasoline prices. Suppose crude oil rises from $20 to $40 a barrel. Can the big oil companies also double gasoline prices from $1.20 a gallon to $2.40? Probably not. Consumers will respond to higher gas prices by traveling less or by purchasing cars that get better gas mileage. Of course, some driving is essential and will be done even at higher prices. But the oil companies will undoubtedly raise prices to less than $2.40 a gallon depending on consumer demand.

Each situation is different. In some cases, firms may be able to increase prices equal to cost changes; in other cases, they may raise prices by less.

During a period of general inflation, incomes are also rising. That in turn means the ability of consumers to buy more gasoline and other products at every income level. The result? Rising consumer demand for all goods and services. In short, during a general inflation, "cost push" and "demand pull" inflation are both at work.

## DO HIGHER OIL PRICES RAISE COSTS?

Can retail prices affect the cost of production? Surprisingly, yes.

The oil industry during the 1970s and 1980s provides a good example of how higher prices affect the costs of production and exploration. During the energy crisis of the 1970s, oil prices skyrocketed due to the oil embargo by the Organization of Petroleum Exporting Countries (OPEC). How did rising oil prices affect the costs of producing oil—the refineries, oil rigs, exploration activities and labor? Rising oil prices had two effects:

1. Rising oil prices dramatically increased the efforts of non-OPEC producers to find new petroleum fields; and
2. Rising oil prices put considerable pressure on the resources devoted to oil production and exploration.

In an effort to increase the production of oil and oil products, costs were squeezed. The prices of land, labor and capital involved in the oil refinery, production and exploration rose dramatically. In oil-rich Texas, real estate, oil-related wages, and oil rigs skyrocketed in price during the late 1970s. Of course, costs did not increase as much as the price of oil, but they did increase. Profit margins for the oil industry rose dramatically in the initial phase. Then increasing costs cut into the profit margins. Still, the profit margins stayed at above average levels, providing an incentive for non-OPEC producers to find and produce more oil.

Figure 7.11 shows the relationship between prices and costs during the energy crisis of the 1970s.

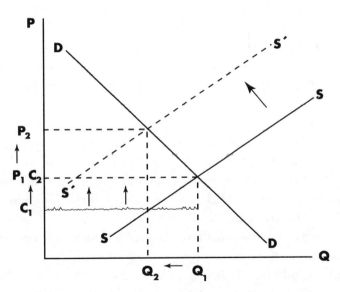

**Figure 7.11.** *Supply, demand and costs during an energy crisis.*

The incentives to find new oil fields and new production were so successful that by the early 1980s, a flood of new oil hit the markets and the price of crude plummeted from $45 a barrel to $10 a barrel. Gasoline and other petroleum-related products dropped accordingly. And the OPEC cartel collapsed.

But note what happened to the cost of oil rigs, salaries and wages of oil workers, and other costs associated with production. These costs also fell significantly. The price of oil properties in Texas and other oil-rich states fell. Rigs sat idle, and a general recession hit major cities in Texas.

163

The link between costs and prices definitely exists, at least on an industry-wide basis. The link is essentially tied to profit and loss. Cost and price are sufficiently intertwined so as to assure long-term profitability and adjustment in the marketplace.

## THE PRINCIPLE OF DERIVED DEMAND

The energy crisis of the 1970s illustrates another vital principle of economics: the concept of derived demand.

**Derived demand refers to the fact that the costs of production are linked to the demand of consumers or final users.**

The concept of derived demand was originally developed by Carl Menger, the founder of the Austrian School. In his classic work, *Principles of Economics* (published in 1870), Menger divided all goods into categories based on their distance from final consumption, from "higher order" capital goods to "lower order" consumer goods. He stated, "The goods-character of goods of higher order is derived from that of the corresponding goods of lower order."[3]

To demonstrate this concept, he used the example of tobacco. Suppose people stopped smoking (a prophetic example by Menger). What effect would that have on the factors of production used in the production of tobacco: the raw tobacco leaves and seeds, the labor services, tools and appliances used to produce tobacco products, and tobacco farmland? The value (price) of these goods and services would fall, probably drastically.

The price of tobacco-related factors of production is derived from the demand for tobacco by end users.

Suppose smoking became popular again and the demand for cigarettes, cigars and chewing tobacco rose. How would that affect the factors of production for tobacco products? These costs would also rise in value or price. How high? Ultimately to the point where a normal, long-run competitive profit margin was achieved in the tobacco industry.

Derived demand shows us that the price of materials, labor, land and other factors is directly linked to the price of the final good or service demanded by consumers.

---

3  Carl Menger, *Principles of Economics*, translated by James Dingwall and Bert F. Hoselitz (New York University Press, 1976), p. 63.

## PRICING IS EQUAL TO MARGINAL USE

Another vital concept in economics emerges from this concept of derived demand. In Menger's example of tobacco, the price of the factors used to produce tobacco fell when people decided to stop smoking. But do the prices of all inputs fall to zero? Perhaps the price of tobacco seeds will fall to zero unless the seeds have another useful purpose. But what about the farmland used to grow tobacco? Clearly, price of farmland will not fall to zero. As Menger notes, "The land and agricultural implements used in the cultivation of tobacco, for instance, and perhaps also many tools and machines used in the manufacture of tobacco products, would retain their goods-character with respect to other human needs since they can be placed in causal connection with these other needs even after the disappearance of the need for tobacco."[4]

The farmland could now be used to produce another crop such as wheat, barley, or soybeans. Or perhaps the farmer will use the land to raise cattle, or maybe even sell the property to a residential builder.

The value of the farmland will fall to its next best use, or marginal utility. Prices are determined at their margin, or their next best use.

## THE PRINCIPLE OF OPPORTUNITY COST

Menger's concepts of derived demand and marginal utility also lead to another powerful principle known as "opportunity cost." This concept was introduced in Chapter 4 in connection with a firm's financial statements. Friedrich von Wieser, one of Menger's students who became a professor at the University of Vienna early in the 20th century, invented the term.

**Opportunity cost is defined as the next highest valued alternative sacrificed by consumers or producers when making a choice.**

Examples of opportunity cost abound in life. When farmers produce tobacco leaves, they give up the use of the land for wheat, corn, soybeans, or other crops. Reading this textbook means giving up the opportunity to play sports, watch TV, or read another book. If business employees work late at the office, they give up time with their spouse and family. If an individual quits a $50,000 job to start his own business, the "opportunity cost" of running his own company is $50,000 a year. If the firm is a publicly traded company, the return of the firm's investment capital needs to exceed alternative uses.

4 Ibid., p. 66.

The appendix of Chapter 4 discussed opportunity with regard to the role of alternative investments in cost accounting.

Chapter 8 will discuss the issue of monopoly and competition—the ability of individual firms to set prices and control output with or without the help of government.

## SUMMARY

### Chapter 7 covered these main points:

1. The three pillars of profitability are cost, value, and price.

2. Costs affect prices and profitability. New technology causes firms to cut prices of new products, as in the case of automobiles, computers, televisions, and ball point pens.

3. Large-scale production can also reduce per-unit costs, and firms are likely to reduce retail prices for their products further to increase market share and meet competition, especially when the demand curve for those products is elastic.

4. Increased costs are possible in the short run due to the law of diminishing returns; however, in the long run most "fixed" costs become "variable" costs.

5. Lower costs result in a higher standard of living and greater consumers' surplus.

6. Rising costs may result in higher prices, but for different reasons. A single firm may not be able to pass on higher costs if competition is stiff and there is little brand loyalty. However, if rising labor or supply costs affect the entire industry, profits are squeezed, marginal firms go under, and the remaining companies are able to pass along higher costs to their customers.

7. During a period when the general price level is rising, both "cost push" inflation and "demand pull" inflation are at work to push prices higher. Ultimately it is consumers, as a group, who decide how high prices go.

8. Changes in prices throughout an industry can have an impact on the costs of production. Prices of inputs are derived in part by demand for final products. Thus, supply is linked to demand for products.

9. Prices are determined by their marginal use, or by the highest valued use.

10. Opportunity costs exist throughout economic life. Consumers, through choice, are forced to give up alternative uses of time, productive effort, money, or resources.

## IMPORTANT TERMS

Cost push inflation
Customer loyalty
Demand elasticity
Demand pull inflation
Derived demand
Economies of scale
Fixed costs

Law of diminishing returns
Marginal cost
Opportunity cost
Price searchers
Price takers
Variable costs

## INFLUENTIAL ECONOMIST

## WILLIAM STANLEY JEVONS AND THE THEORY OF VALUE

**Name: William Stanley Jevons (1835-82)**

**Background:** Jevons, along with Alfred Marshall, was one of the founders of the British School of Economics. Born in Livermore, England, Jevons studied chemistry and botany at the University College of London, but became assayer at the Mint in Sydney, Australia, during 1854-58. He later returned to England and became Professor of Political Economy at University College. After retiring at the youthful age of 44, he drowned while swimming two years later.

**Major Works:** His most important book is *The Theory of Political Economy*, published in 1871. This work established Jevons as one of the three discoverers of the marginalist revolution (the other two being Carl Menger in Austria and Leon Walras in Switzerland). Jevons disproved that price (or value) was determined by the labor costs involved in the production of a good or service, but rather that price was determined by the marginal utility of consumer use. "Value depends entirely on utility," Jevons declared. Cost, then, became more a function of final value rather than the other way around. Menger made the same point.

The issue of cost came up in conjunction with the coal issue in late 19th century England. In his book *The Coal Question* (1865, 1906), Jevons predicted that Britain would decline because of its dependence on coal, which was gradually depleted. As coal reserves ran out, the price of coal would rise. Economic power would shift to America where coal was abundant. Jevons was proven right in his prediction of the decline of Britain and the rise of America, but not due to the coal question. As the price of coal rose, demand shifted toward alternative energy sources such as oil and natural gas, and dependence on coal waned.

Jevons, influenced by Menger, developed an economic model based on a period of production. He wrote extensively about the "orders of industry" and the "classification of trades" according to the stages of industrial production, from dealers in raw materials to final retail users. Ultimately, however, he rejected the period-of-production concept as "hopelessly" complex.

167

**Note:** Economists William Breit and Ken Elzinga are the authors of a series of mystery fiction, *Murder at the Margin* (1978), *The Fatal Equilibrium* (1985), and *A Deadly Indifference* (1995). Their pen name, Marshall Jevons, draws from two British economists, Alfred Marshall and Stanley Jevons. All three novels creatively use the basic principles of economics to solve a murder mystery and are highly recommended.

## PROBLEMS TO PONDER

1. "An upward-sloping demand curve doesn't make sense in my business. All I know is that if I raise my prices, revenue doesn't go up, it goes down. I don't sell more products, I sell less." Can you straighten out this businessman's thinking?

2. Suppose the demand for an artist's paintings declines due to a nationwide recession. To offset the lost revenue, should the artist raise the prices he charges his current clients? What alternatives does he have to survive the recession?

3. Referring to problem #2, suppose the suppliers of painting materials—the paints, the brushes, the canvases, etc.—raise their prices. Should the artist pass on these costs to his customers by charging more? Show what is happening using supply, demand and profit margin. What should he tell his customers?

4. Compare the market for gasoline and the market for oil rigs: Show the effect of (a) an energy crisis where oil prices double, (b) an energy glut where oil prices fall in half, and (c) a general rise in nominal incomes due to monetary inflation.

5. Interview five other students and ask them what their opportunity cost is of (a) going to college, (b) going to medical school, (c) getting married, (d) not getting married, (e) drinking at a late night party, (f) traveling to Europe on a vacation, and (g) sleeping at night.

6. Explain the meaning of the following two statements in terms of opportunity cost: (a) "Either you spend it or someone else will." (b) "If you spend it now, you can't spend it later."

7. Why are the prices of wheat and corn the same throughout the country, but the costs of producing wheat and corn vary considerably from farm to farm? Why are some farmers able to survive a depression in agricultural prices better than other farmers?

8.  Is the price of chicken lower than the price of beef because beef is preferred over chicken (the demand factor), or because it is cheaper to produce chicken (the supply factor)? Is the cost of producing chicken lower than the cost of producing beef because chicken is considered an inferior good?

9.  An airline ticket costs the same from Casper, Wyoming, to Denver, Colorado, and from Denver to Orlando, Florida. Does this make economic sense? Explain the rationale behind equal prices for unequal distances in air travel using supply, demand and cost curves.

10. Given what we have shown in this chapter relating costs to final demand (derived demand), evaluate the following statement by British economist P. T. Bauer: "Once it is recognized that current and prospective product prices affect costs, it is not legitimate to treat supply as independent of demand (as is the standard practice in microeconomics)." (*The Development Frontier: Essays in Applied Economics*, p. 202)

## RECOMMENDED READING

- Carl Menger, *The Principles of Economics* (New York University Press, 1976). Originally published in 1871, Menger's classic work created the marginalist revolution in economics. It contains the foundation of microeconomics and macroeconomics as well as an excellent chapter on the origin of money.

- Shlomo Maital, *Executive Economics* (Free Press, 1994). This book on applied economics has a sizeable section on the relationship between costs, prices and values. Highly recommended.

*Chapter 8*

# MONOPOLY AND COMPETITION

*"Competition is a tough weed, not a delicate flower."*

— GEORGE J. STIGLER

D oes the size of a firm make any difference in terms of its ability to raise prices, cut costs, or improve the product line? Does big business have market power over its customers? What role has government played and what role should government play in regulating commerce? Should government grant special privileges to firms and, if so, what are the consequences?

This chapter analyzes monopolies and the impact, if any, of large firms or a group of big companies on supply and demand. Using the Microsoft example provided in Chapter 6, suppose that the cost of producing each Microsoft Works software package is $20 per unit and that Microsoft can produce any number of units at the same $20 per unit price. Currently Microsoft sells 900,000 units of the software for $24.95, and grosses $22,455,000. Net income—revenue minus expenses—is $4,455,000.

Suppose also that Microsoft has a patent on its software program for another 50 years, and there are no substitutes available in the marketplace. Microsoft has no fear of the competitors coming in and stealing away customers. It can charge any price it wants and maximize profits. In short, Microsoft is a monopoly—a single seller with no serious competition.

What could Microsoft do? Chapter 6 demonstrated what the revenue would be if Microsoft charged $34.95 for Microsoft Works instead of $24.95. Many customers would decide to do without the product rather than pay the higher price. Microsoft would sell fewer units, only 500,000, and the gross revenue would fall to $17,475,000. However, given the per unit cost of $20, the total cost of producing 500,000 units of the software amounts to $10,000,000, giving Microsoft a substantial increase of profit to $7,475,000, almost double the profit level from when the price was $24.95. It should also be noted that per unit costs may be substantially higher when fewer units are produced.

171

Figure 8.1 below illustrates the benefits of raising the price in the case of monopoly power.

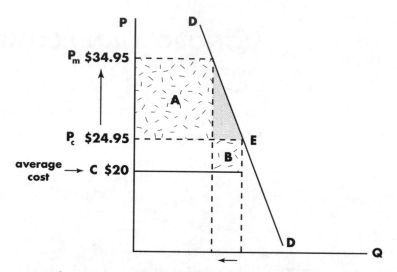

**Figure 8.1.** *Increased profitability due to single monopoly power.*

Note several points about figure 8.1. $P_m$ is the monopolist's price of $34.95. $P_c$ is the competitive equilibrium price of $24.95. C is the per unit cost of producing Microsoft Works.

There are several comments worth noting about the above example of monopoly power.

First, monopolies are still subject to the law of consumer demand which dictates that at higher prices consumers buy less. Monopolies cannot raise prices without losing some business, even if they are natural monopolies providing "essential" services. In the above case, consumers bought only half a million units compared to 900,000 at the lower price. Clearly there is a limit to their price gouging, based on the elasticity of demand. (See the discussion on natural monopolies later in the chapter.)

Second, in order for a monopolist to raise prices, the demand curve above the competitive level must be inelastic. The product or service must be something that people consider necessary enough that they are willing to pay for it even though the price is higher. In the above diagram, rectangle A must be larger than rectangle B. If the demand for the product is elastic at higher prices, a rise in prices would be counterproductive—the firm would earn less revenue rather than more.

Having made these two points, this example shows that monopoly power — raising prices and reducing output — benefits the producer, but clearly hurts the consumer or society's welfare (well-being). As George Stigler, economist at the University of Chicago (see biography at the end of this chapter), states, "When the monopolist raises prices above the competitive level in order to reap his monopoly profits, customers buy less of the product, less is produced, and society as a whole is worse off. In short, monopoly reduces society's income."[1]

Figure 8.1 demonstrates the net loss to society. Consumers lose because they have to pay $10 more for each software package. As a result of the increased cost consumers will purchase fewer copies. This consumer loss is made up in part by increased profits of the corporation. In this case, Microsoft earns monopoly profits of $10,000,000. (Monopoly profits are also refered to as economic rent. The net loss to society, welfare loss, or deadweight loss, is equal to the shaded area in figure 8.1.

How much is this welfare loss? As noted above, the corporation makes $10 million in monopoly profits. Customers would be willing to buy an additional 400,000 software packages from Microsoft if the price came down to $24.95, the competitive price. Assume these additional 400,000 units have an average value of $30 for customers. An additional $12 million in potential consumer satisfaction is not satisfied by the market because of the monopoly status of the company. Because the monopolist corporation would cover its costs and earn a decent profit in producing the additional 400,000 units, it would lose nothing. Producing the extra 400,000 units, therefore, would benefit society on a net basis to the tune of $2 million ($12 million in foregone consumer satisfaction minus $10 million in monopoly profits).

## DO MONOPOLIES EARN ABOVE-AVERAGE RETURNS?

A third issue regarding monopoly power considers if monopolistic firms earn above-average profits. In the example above, Microsoft's profits jump from $4 million to $7 million by cutting output and boosting prices. But that action assumes that costs remain the same ($20 per unit). This is a significant assumption that may not always hold true. Big corporations that have government privileges, special patents, or other guarantees often ignore labor and supply costs. Without market competitiveness, they may pay excessive wages and high management bonuses, or run their operations in a bureaucratic and inefficient manner. As a result, costs may creep up and eat away at profit margins. Instead of "mean and lean," they become "big and fat."

Historical studies have shown that monopolies and oligopolies have a limited ability to earn higher than competitive rates of return on capital. There is no close relationship between the rate of return on investment and the degree to which industries are concentrated (measured by share of the industry sales by the four largest firms, for example). Less than 25% of the variation in the profitability across industries can be attributed to concentration.[2] In short, monopoly results in higher prices and higher costs, but it does not guarantee high profits.

George J. Stigler, "Monopoly," *The Fortune Encyclopedia of Economics*, ed. by David R. Henderson (Warner Books, 1993), p. 400.
2  Ibid., p. 401.

## HOW PREVALENT IS MONOPOLISTIC POWER?

The monopoly example above demonstrates how monopolistic power raises prices, reduces output, encourages inefficiency, and causes social welfare loss. This theoretical example raises a number of practical issues for economists and public officials: Is there a way to determine monopolistic power in an economy? What policies can be taken to minimize monopoly by encouraging large firms to reduce prices, expand output, and eliminate waste?

## DEFINITIONS OF MONOPOLISTIC POWER

In the example above, monopoly is defined as a situation in which one company controls an industry or is the only provider of a product or service. Examples include a local electric utility or a town with only one drugstore. If there are a small number of sellers—2 to 6, say—with considerable barriers to entry, economists call the industry an **oligopoly**. If there are a large number of buyers and sellers in an industry, the industry is called pure or perfect competition.

## SEARCHING FOR THE IDEAL COMPETITIVE MODEL

Economists have searched for an ideal competitive model from which all degrees of competition and monopoly can be judged. The optimal level of competition should be one that produces the greatest benefit to consumers and to society at the lowest possible cost. According to this optimal condition, scarce resources would be allocated at their highest value use, and no alternative outcome could make anyone else better off without making someone else worse off. Economists call this situation **Pareto optimality**, named after the Italian economist and engineer Vilfredo Pareto (1848-1923).

Pareto worked out a general equilibrium theory of economics and demonstrated that "perfect competition"—defined below—achieved an optimal solution. Perfect competition is defined as a market with the following conditions:

1. Large number of buyers and sellers so that no one individual producer or buyer has any control over price. In a perfectly competitive market, all firms are relatively small and are "price takers" rather than "price makers."

2. No product differentiation. All products are homogeneous.

3. No barriers to entry or exit. Anyone can enter or leave this industry without any significant costs.

4. Information is well-known and relatively free (thus, advertising is unnecessary).

174

Two examples of perfectly competitive industries are agriculture and the financial markets. Of course, these industries are far from "perfectly competitive," but they fit the definition better than most other markets.

According to the perfectly competitive model, any market or industry that lacks the above four characteristics is "imperfect," and can be improved upon (usually through anti-trust measures and other forms of government authority). Imperfect competition includes industries where product differentiation, price discrimination, and concentration exist. By definition, firms have some degree of monopolistic power, and therefore are relatively inefficient and misallocate scarce resources. According to advocates of this model, these industries can be forced to be more efficient and competitive by various forms of government policy.

## DRAWBACKS TO PERFECT COMPETITION

The problem with the perfectly competitive model is that it is not applicable to all markets, and should not be used as an ideal model to judge efficiency.

Take product differentiation, for example. Should all headache medicine be generic? Should automobiles be required to maintain the same style for decades? The advocates of perfect competition suggest that a great deal of waste and inefficiency (including advertising) could be eliminated from society if firms sold homogeneous products rather than brand name products that frequently change. Society could move toward Pareto optimality.

Other economists disagree, arguing that the market critics have the cart before the horse. According to these market defenders, many goods are not homogeneous precisely because people demand variety. If consumers do not prefer style changes or brand names, will not new competitors enter the market and offer more homogenous goods? The fact that some large supermarket chains offer their own generic products suggests that there is demand for basic, non-brand products. However, these supermarkets also offer brand names. Why? Because customers demand those products, too, and judging from the number of sales, they demand them more than the generic products.

According to this argument, product homogeneity does not necessarily represent the optimal use of resources. Commercially successful product differentiation clearly reflects the preferences of consumers in open markets.

## ECONOMIES OF SCALE

Advocates of the perfect competition model also complain that big firms gain an unfair advantage over small firms because they realize lower average costs due to larger volumes and supplier discounts, a phenomenon economists call "economies of scale." This is the tendency of average costs and marginal costs to decline with greater output. However, market critics note that economies of scale make it harder for smaller, higher-cost firms to enter the market. Thus, competition is allegedly reduced in industries that require bigness to operate on a large scale.

This debate goes to the heart of what a free market economy is all about. If competition means anything, it rewards the producers with the lowest cost and best products and services for consumers. Bigness or smallness is not the issue. The issue is low cost versus high cost producers. Clearly, consumers prefer the lower-cost producers. Consumers are willing to pay for higher-cost products only if these products offer greater benefits. Therefore, consumers often favor bigger companies.

## THE ISSUE OF CONCENTRATION

How do economists determine whether an industry is highly competitive or monopolistic? One traditional method is the concentration ratio. The concentration ratio measures the percentage of assets or sales held by the largest firms in an industry. The Big Three in the automobile industry (General Motors, Ford, Chrysler) and the Seven Sisters in the oil industry (Saudi Aramco, Russia's Gazprom, CNPC of China, NIOC of Iran, Venezuela's PDVSA, Brazil's Petrobras and Petronas of Malaysia) are examples. The level of concentration is meant to reflect certain degrees of monopolistic power, competition, and social welfare. The higher the ratio, the greater the concern that firms may collude or limit production as a cartel.

Economists have pointed out a number of drawbacks to the use of a concentration ratio to determine the degree of competition in an industry. In many ways the ratio is arbitrary and may have little to do with the intensity of competition or the dynamics of the marketplace. Two firms may dominate an industry, yet the rivalry can be so strong as to suggest a high degree of competition rather than collusion. Coca Cola and Pepsi are two examples.

Concentration could also increase because one or two firms produce products that are highly innovative and responsive to consumer needs. Alcoa dominated the aluminum market following World War II. IBM controlled 85% of the computer industry in the 1960s. Why? Because they were clearly ahead of everyone else in offering the best aluminum and the most advanced computers.

## COMPETITION IN THE COMPUTER INDUSTRY

The story of IBM illustrates the need to take a long-term view of the competitive process. For many decades IBM controlled the computer industry, but, gradually, market forces diminished its supremacy. Today IBM is still a major company in the computer industry, but now there are dozens of rivals for IBM. Figure 8.2 below shows how the various players in the computer industry changed places from 1967 to 1997.

**ELECTRONICS, OFFICE EQUIPMENT AND SOFTWARE INDUSTRY**
Assets in Constant 1997 Dollars (billion)

**1967**

| | |
|---|---|
| International Business Machines (IBM) | $170.3 |
| Xerox | 32.2 |
| Radio Corp of America (RCA) | 16.1 |
| Sperry Rand | 10.5 |
| Honeywell | 7.7 |
| Burroughs | 7.4 |
| National Cash Register | 5.7 |
| Texas Instruments | 5.7 |
| Zenith Radio | 5.2 |

**1987**

| | |
|---|---|
| IBM | $137.8 |
| Digital Equipment | 29.1 |
| Hewlett-Packard | 23.7 |
| Xerox | 11.0 |
| Motorola | 10.3 |
| NCR | 9.9 |
| AMP | 8.6 |
| Unisys | 7.9 |
| Intel | 7.3 |

**1997**

| | |
|---|---|
| Microsoft | $129.5 |
| Intel | 112.1 |
| IBM | 69.7 |
| Hewlett-Packard (HP) | 50.7 |
| Lucent Technologies | 34.4 |
| Motorola | 33.6 |
| Cisco Systems | 32.1 |
| Oracle | 24.4 |
| Compaq Computer | 19.7 |
| Electronic Data Systems | 19.1 |
| Xerox | 19.0 |
| Computer Associates | 15.8 |
| Texas Instruments | 15.6 |

**Figure 8.2**
Source: *Forbes*, July 7, 1997.

The chart above tells quite a tale. IBM, the dominant computer company for most of the last half of the 20th century, lost market dominance due to intense competition from Microsoft, Intel, and other major computer companies. Bigness does not guarantee staying on top. Witness the demise of Xerox. Xerox was #2 in assets in 1967. 20 years later, Xerox had fallen to #4 and by 1997, Xerox was no longer in the top 10. Sic transit gloria mundi! (Fame is fleeting.)

Since 1997 IBM has regained its glory and exceeds Microsoft again in assets. However, Lucent Technology, fifth in size in 1997, fell 97 percent in value and was merged with Aloatel in 2006

Figure 8.3 lists the top companies in 1917, 1967, 1997, and 2007.

### TOP U.S. COMPANIES IN VARIOUS CATEGORIES

| Year | Financial Services | Food | Aerospace |
|---|---|---|---|
| 1917 | National City Bank | Armour & Co. | NA |
| 1967 | Bank of America | General Food | Litton Industries |
| 1997 | AIG | Campbell Soup | Boeing |
| 2007 | Bank of America | Kraft Foods | Boeing |

| Retailing | |
|---|---|
| 1917 | Sears, Roebuck |
| 1967 | Sears, Roebuck |
| 1997 | Wal-Mart Stores |
| 2007 | Wal-Mart Stores |

**Figure 8.3**
Source: *Forbes*, July 7, 1997; Yahoo Finance.

Of course, some big companies have stayed on top throughout the last half of the 20th century—in chemicals, Dupont; in automobiles, General Motors; in film, Eastman Kodak; in communications, AT&T; in oil, Exxon. Even in these examples, rivals — including foreign competition — have significantly penetrated the company's stronghold on the industry. Recently Toyota exceeded GM in car sales.

A review of the 20th century shows a dynamic, evolving and sometimes revolutionary economy. Very little can be taken for granted. Competition is fierce, even among billion-dollar corporations. Many major companies that used to be household names have disappeared (Pan American Airlines, Studebaker). Others have suddenly appeared and become giants (Microsoft, Toyota, MCI, Home Depot).

In this context, market concentration looks ominous in the short run, but may mean little in the long run.

Joseph Schumpeter, the Austrian-born economist who later became a professor at Harvard, best summed up the dynamics of the market economy by characterizing it as "creative destruction." As the tables above indicate, the 20th century has seen the creation of many new companies, products and services, as well as the destruction of same.

Schumpeter himself was highly critical of the perfect competition model. He concludes, "perfect competition is not only impossible but inferior, and has no title to being set up as a model of ideal efficiency. It is hence a mistake to base the theory of government regulation of industry on the principle that big business should be made to work as the respective industry would work in perfect competition."[3]

Edward Chamberlin was equally critical of the perfect competition model. He wrote, "pure competition may no longer be regarded as in any sense an ideal for purposes of welfare economics....Differences in tastes, desires, incomes, and locations of buyers, and differences in the uses which they wish to make of commodities all indicate the need for a variety and the necessity of substituting for the concept of a 'competitive ideal' an ideal involving both monopoly and competition."[4]

## WHAT IS THE CORRECT MODEL OF COMPETITION?

If this perfect competition model is not an ideal standard, what model should be used? Economists argue that the best model is the "market test." The market test is not a perfect model, by any means, yet through trial and error, optimal market size and competitive prices can be determined. This model allows any firm with sufficient capital and ability to enter the industry and create whatever products and services are desired by customers. While the market test allows for market barriers to entry (minimum capital requirements), there should be no artificial barriers to entry imposed by government, including special licenses, imports and quotas.

The result of the market test will be some markets with few differentiated products, a diversity of buyers and sellers, and few barriers to entry; and other markets with only a few players, high capital and technological requirements, and considerable economies of scale resulting in barriers to entry. In this approach, the optimal number of firms, the level of concentration, and minimal capital requirements will vary almost arbitrarily and unpredictably from industry to industry. This market trial-and-error model suggests that competition is a dynamic process that cannot be measured by conventional methods such as concentration ratios. The market is always imperfect in one way or another, and perfection is never an option or even a goal.

## THE ROLE OF GOVERNMENT: ANTI-TRUST LEGISLATION

Over the years, government has adopted two methods of encouraging competition: Anti-trust legislation and deregulation.

The Sherman Anti-Trust Act of 1890 and other anti-monopoly legislation grew out of the "Gilded Age" of John D. Rockefeller, Andrew Carnegie, J. P. Morgan and

---

3   Joseph A. Schumpeter, *Capitalism, Socialism and Democracy*, 3rd ed. (New York: Harper and Row, 1976[1950]), p. 106.
4   Edward H. Chamberlin, *The Theory of Monopolistic Competition* (Cambridge University Press, 1948), p. 214.

other business titans at the turn of the 20th century. Contemporary historians and politicians view this period of consolidation, cutthroat competition, and collusion in a highly negative way. Paul Samuelson and Bill Nordhaus describe these legendary figures as "brilliant, inventive, unscrupulous, and often dishonest robber barons...driven by visions that created entire industries like railroads, oil, and steel, provided their finance, developed the western frontier, destroyed their competitors, and passed on fabulous fortunes to their heirs."[5] Books were written about them, such as Thorstein Veblen's *The Theory of the Leisure Class* (1899) and Matthew Josephson's *The Robber Barons* (Harcourt, Brace, 1934).

Federal legislation was passed during this time to protect consumers and business from big business trusts and unfair practices, and to restore competition in the market economy. The major laws include:

(1.) The Sherman Antitrust Act of 1890, which made it illegal to conspire to restrain trade;

(2.) The Clayton Antitrust Act of 1914, which made it unlawful to engage in most forms of price discrimination, tying agreements (requiring customers to buy one product in order to have another), and mergers that reduce competition;

(3.) The Federal Trade Commission Act of 1914, which made it unlawful for business to engage in unfair or deceptive methods of competition, and prohibited false and misleading advertising.

## FAMOUS ANTITRUST CASES

The antitrust division of the Justice Department has prosecuted a number of famous cases, including the following court decisions:

**Standard Oil:** (1911) required Rockefeller's giant oil company to be split up.

**Alcoa:** (1945). Alcoa had gained 90% market share in aluminum by anticipating growth and keeping prices low. The Supreme Court ruled that Alcoa violated the Sherman Act, even though its practices were lawful, because monopoly power constitutes an economic evil.

**IBM:** (1969-82). By the late 1960s, IBM dominated the computer industry with 76% of the market. The Justice Department sued IBM for maintaining monopolistic pricing practices. IBM vigorously denied the charge, arguing that it achieved its dominance through "superior skill, foresight, and industry." If the government's case had merit, argued IBM, business would have no incentive to be the best. The anti-trust suit against IBM lasted for more than a decade. In 1982 the Reagan administration dropped the suit, saying the government case was "without merit."

5  Paul A. Samuelson and William D. Nordhaus, *Economics*, 16th ed. (Irwin McGraw-Hill, 1998), p. 167.

**Microsoft:** (1997). Microsoft's anti-trust case is similar to IBM's. The government sued Microsoft for creating a monopoly in its Windows' operating software. Microsoft, the world's largest software company, controlled more than 80% of the world's computer operating systems. Microsoft counters that it offers a superior consumer product, and if the Justice Department wins out, customers will get fewer options and inferior products.

The antitrust division of the Justice Department has also frequently denied certain mergers and acquisitions, arguing that such business connections reduce competition in an industry. Generally it is much easier to acquire companies in other industries than it is to acquire companies in related businesses.

However, when Exxon merged with Mobil Oil in 1998, the Justice Department did not object. Exxon and Mobil were part of the original Standard Oil Company when it was broken up in 1911. What made the difference? Today global competition requires companies to be huge. The Exxon-Mobil merger means lower costs and economies of scale and thus an ability to compete better against foreign competition.

## THE CASE AGAINST ANTITRUST

Over the years, economists have gradually shifted ground on the issue of market power and antitrust. In the first half of the 20th century, most economists favored strong action against big business and market cartels. Joan Robinson and Edward Chamberlin developed their theories of imperfect and monopolistic competition in the 1930s. Even the Chicago School, a bastion of free-market capitalism, favored antitrust action. Conservative economist Henry C. Simons advocated nationalization of railroads, utilities and all other "uncompetitive" industries in his book *Economic Policy for a Free Society* (1948).

This view has changed, even among free-market advocates at Chicago. Competition is no longer viewed as a static condition, but as a dynamic process that changes over time. Witness the dramatic change in listings of major companies in electronics, telecommunications, automobiles, and other industries from decade to decade. Concentrated power in the short term is no guarantee of concentrated power in the long run.[6]

Game theory, which is mathematical theory primarily concerned with determining an optimal strategy for situations in which there is competition or conflict, has also shown that collusion cannot last because it pays for an individual company to cheat by acting independently. For example, if major airline executives decide to raise prices all at the same time, it pays for one airline to break the agreement and reduce prices.

6  The best summary of antitrust can be found in Dominick T. Armentano's Antitrust and *Monopoly: Anatomy of a Policy Failure* (Holmes & Meier, 1990).

The Organization of Petroleum Exporting Countries (OPEC) has proven this to be the case. Initially, in the early 1970s, the cartel agreed to cut production and thereby raise prices dramatically. But two things worked against OPEC's power: First, non-members such as the United States, Mexico, and Indonesia discovered new oil fields and increased output. Second, OPEC members had an incentive to cheat on the agreement. By increasing output, they could profit handsomely. Not surprisingly, OPEC today has far less influence in raising oil prices and controlling production.

Regarding the expensive antitrust case against IBM, Lester Thurow, former dean of the MIT Sloan School of Management, concluded, "The millions spent on the IBM case would have been better spent if they had been plowed back into research and development on keeping America No. 1 in computers."[7]

Richard Posner, formerly a law professor at the University of Chicago and now a federal judge, has concluded, "The only truly unilateral acts by which firms can get or keep monopoly power are practices like committing fraud on the Patent Office or blowing up a competitor's plant, and fraud and force are in general adequately punished under other statutes."[8]

## DEREGULATION

If antitrust legislation is largely counterproductive, is there anything the government can do to encourage competition? How can the legislature change the rules and regulations so that competition increases, output expands, prices fall, and social welfare rises? Deregulation of an industry is a possible way to encourage competition.

Historical examples demonstrate the impact of deregulation. Prior to deregulation of the airline industry in the late 1970's, the Civil Aeronautics Board, a government agency, controlled ticket prices, the number of new airlines, and the routes of carriers. In 1978 the U. S. Airline Deregulation Act decontrolled prices and routing. Airlines were free to set fares and traffic schedules. Following deregulation the airline industry went through a chaotic period. Some companies failed and merged with bigger airlines. Airlines moved to hub-and-spoke operations, which increased efficiency, but made some airports more crowded. Prices rose and fell, depending on rapidly changing conditions of supply and demand. There were demands for re-regulation. But two decades later, deregulation is viewed largely as a success. Recent studies have shown the following:

7  Quoted in Samuelson and Nordhaus, *Economics*, 6th ed., p. 318.
8  Richard A. Posner, *Antitrust Law: An Economic Prospectus* (University of Chicago, 1976), p. 212.

(1.) Average fares have declined 30% in real, inflation-adjusted terms since deregulation, saving travelers between $5 billion and $10 billion each year.

(2.) The average number of airlines per route has increased by 25% despite mergers. Examples: Between 1979 and 1988, American Airlines increased the number of airports it serves from 50 to 173, and United Airlines from 80 to 169.

(3.) Years after deregulation, the airline industry employed 65% more people and logged 70% more domestic passenger-miles.

(4.) Contrary to skeptics' concerns, air service for small towns and rural communities has improved. Small towns have, on average, experienced a 35-40% increase in the number of flights and available destinations.

(5.) Airlines have become more productive by increasing the size of planes and the number of seats.

While the road to deregulation has been bumpy, freeing the airline industry has been a success.[9]

Other U. S. industries have been deregulated, including trucking, railroads, buses, cable television, oil and gas, telecommunications, financial markets, and even local electric and gas utilities. The net effect of deregulation is shown in diagram 8.4 reproduced below. Average prices in these industries have declined and output has increased.

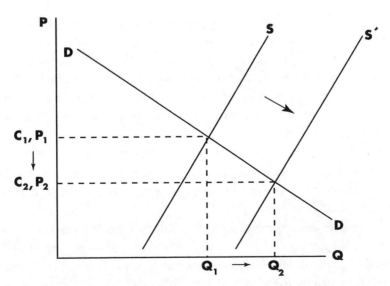

**Figure 8.4.** *Effect of deregulaton: lower prices, higher output, greater efficiency.*

9  For further information, see Alfred E. Kahn, "Surprises of Airline Deregulation," *American Economic Review* 78:2 (May, 1988), pp. 316-322, and his article, "Airline Deregulation," in *The Fortune Encyclopedia of Economics*, pp. 379-84.

Not all markets have been completely deregulated. Currently controlled markets include cable television, cellular telephone services, exclusive franchises of public utilities and radio and television stations, and first-class mail. Governments also license and franchise professional groups such as lawyers and medical doctors, sometimes resulting in higher salaries and fewer professionals than in an unregulated free market.

In short, efforts to deregulate industries have achieved most of the goals desired by economists—an expanding market, lower prices, and increased social welfare.

## NATURAL MONOPOLIES

One final issue needs to be addressed regarding monopoly—the case of "natural monopolies" such as public utilities, dams, lighthouses, telephone service, and roads and highways. Should natural monopolies be regulated, and are there ways to encourage competition?

Natural monopolies are industries in which the market can support only one firm efficiently. A natural monopoly occurs when a single producer is the most economical and when competition would result in duplication and wasted investment. In such cases, firms offer products or services in an industry where the total cost would rise if competitors entered the market. Thus, natural monopolies enjoy considerable economies of scale.

For example, the local water supply has always been viewed as a natural monopoly. A water utility must dig up the streets, lay the water pipes, and maintain them. A local telephone company or electric utility faces the same situation. It appears inefficient to have two utility firms or telephone companies supplying the same neighborhood with two sets of wires. Covering the country with power lines, cable television connections and telephone exchanges costs billions of dollars. Clearly, a single supplier is more efficient than two or three suppliers in these situations due to considerable economies of scale. Moreover, granting a monopoly means that a utility can invest in the company infrastructure and product improvement instead of marketing and sales.

If only one firm is granted the right to deliver water, electricity, or telephone services, the community has a right to be concerned about the possibility of monopolistic behavior—of the business earning excessively high rates of return at the expense of consumers.

It is worth noting, however, that public utilities are not entirely immune to competition. If they set prices too high, residents may move to another city, county, or state. Industrial customers can sometimes buy electricity from out-of-state rivals.

Higher prices for water or electricity can also influence consumer behavior. Water is normally considered "essential" for life and its demand rather inelastic. Yet, studies indicate that the average per capita daily purchase of water varies considerably from city to city—230 gallons in Chicago, 150 in New York and Los Angeles,

120 in San Diego and 110 in Boston. Armen Alchian and William Allen state, "The quantities reflect, for one thing, differences in industrial use. Chicago has steel- and oil-refining industries, which use a great deal of water; New York City businesses — finance, retail, apparel — are light water users."[10]

Despite these examples, most economists consider competition in utility industries to be weak and the community is left with two options: public regulation or public ownership and operation. Over the years, cities and states have gravitated toward public regulation rather than public ownership. And some publicly owned utilities have recently been privatized.

Public utilities are typically regulated by a state utility board, which must approve or disapprove all rate increases. One of the drawbacks to regulatory price controls is that utility profits can be so squeezed that capital improvements and research and development are retarded. An alternative is to deregulate utilities so they are allowed to charge whatever the market will bear. Utilities may use excessive profits to invest heavily in research and development and technological advances, make capital improvements, enhance the physical surroundings, benefit public charities and community services, or pay out liberal dividends to shareholders.

## INCREASED COMPETITION AMONG UTILITIES

One of the remarkable events in recent years has been the introduction of competitive practices in many areas that were once deemed natural monopolies. Conventional wisdom once dictated that only one telephone company could serve a community, but now we see intense competition for long distance and even local service among several carriers. Before AT&T was broken up in the 1980s, prices for long distance remained high and the price of AT&T stock was stagnant.

After the break-up, prices for long distance have fallen sharply and stock prices for AT&T and baby bells, regional Bell operating companies, skyrocketed. (Most of the baby bells have since merged togegher to form the new AT&T.) Local leaders used to grant one contract to a single garbage collection service, but now some local communities allow competing garbage collectors to provide services and these companies are typically privately owned. In the 1960s, only the U. S. Postal Service delivered mail and packages. Now regular mail and package service is provided by several competitors such as United Package Service (UPS), Fedex, and DHL. The U. S. Postal Service still has a monopoly on first class mail, but this monopoly is largely in name only as many other forms of communication are now available and being used to replace first class mail. These forms of communication include fax machines and e-mail.

In today's competitive global economy, pure natural monopolies may no longer exist.

10 Armen Alchian and William Allen, *University Economics*, 3rd ed. (Wadsworth Publishing, 1972), pp. 64-65.

## SUMMARY

**The main points of Chapter 8 are:**

1.  A monopoly occurs when a single provider has no rivals. It results in higher prices, reduced output, and higher costs. Monopolistic power reduces the general welfare.

2.  Monopolies are not assured above-average profits due to the waste and inefficiency that result from being insulated from competition.

3.  Perfect competition — defined as a large number of buyers and sellers who cannot influence prices — is not an ideal economic model of a market.

4.  Many economists regard the market test model as the optimal number of competitors in each industry. In an unregulated market, the number of firms that survive is optimal.

5.  Governments use antitrust measures and deregulation as two ways to increase competition.

6.  Natural monopolies, such as public utilities, are usually subject to government regulation. Increased competition has reduced the number of pure "natural" monopolies—in utilities, communications, and transportation.

## IMPORTANT TERMS

Antitrust laws
Concentration ratio
Creative destruction
Economies of scale
Monopoly
Natural monopoly
Oligopoly
Pareto optimality
Perfect competition
Welfare loss

MONOPOLY AND COMPETITION • CHAPTER 8

## INFLUENTIAL ECONOMIST

### GEORGE J. STIGLER

**Name: George J. Stigler (1911-91)**

**Background:** Economist, professor, author and one of the principal spokesmen for the Chicago School of free-market economics. Stigler taught at Columbia University (1947-58) and the University of Chicago (1958-91) and was a long-time colleague of Milton Friedman. He received the Nobel Prize in economics in 1982 for his work on regulation and competition.

**Important Contribution:** Like many economists from Chicago, Stigler emphasized the importance of empirical studies to support their theories. His main focus was industrial organization, and the theories of competition and monopoly, including the impact of government regulation. His well-used textbook, *The Theory of Price*, is full of practical examples. He urged economists not to just assume the effects of regulation, but to study the actual effects of government intervention. *The Journal of Law and Economics*, started in 1958 at Chicago, and *Regulation*, published by the Cato Institute, are examples of empirical studies of government behavior. In 1971 Stigler wrote an article entitled "The Theory of Economic Regulation," arguing that government agencies tend to be captured by firms in the regulated industry and are frequently used to prevent rather than encourage competition. As a result of Stigler's work, today's economists are much more skeptical of government regulation.

As a result of his own research in industrial organization, Stigler gradually shifted ground regarding antitrust. In the 1940s and 1950s, he was a staunch defender of antitrust laws. He would appear before Congress advocating the breakup of "concentrated" industries, at one point proposing that U. S. Steel Corporation be broken up. But by the early 1970s, he had changed his mind. The evidence suggested that even a small number of rivals may bring prices down to competitive levels.

**Quotation:** "More recently, and at the risk of being called fickle, many economists (I among them) have lost both our enthusiasm for antitrust policy and much of our fear of oligopoly."

**Personality:** Stigler stood tall (over 6'5"), in contrast with his friend Milton Friedman (5'2") on the campus of the University of Chicago. Always known for his humor and wit, Stigler objected to economics being called the "dismal science." He once recommended that students read Adam Smith's *Wealth of Nations* except for page 720 (a section where Smith criticizes professors!). His most popular books are: *The Theory of Price* (1966, 3rd ed.) and *Memoirs of an Unregulated Economist* (Basic Books, 1988).

## PROBLEMS TO PONDER

1. You walk into a store to buy some AA batteries for your transistor radio, and the store offers you two choices, Duracell and Eveready. Both charge the same price—$3.99 for a package of four. Is this situation a sign of dual monopoly or perfect competition? What criteria would you use to determine the difference?

2. "People cannot live without water. No one will reduce his use of water just because the price goes up. Therefore, it will do no good for the utility company to raise the price of water during a water shortage. Water must be rationed." List ways that consumers would use less if the price of water were raised. Demonstrate that water has a downward demand curve like all other commodities. What is the elasticity of water demand?

3. Paul Terhorst, author of *Restoring the American Dream* and graduate of Stanford Business School, states: "In business school we used to say, 'The best patent protection you can have is 80% of the market.' Monopoly power comes from market acceptance, not from a patent, a prettier product, a slick advertising campaign, or anything else. So rather than spend your time in court, you should be out there drumming up business." Do you agree? How important is defending patent rights?

## RECOMMENDED READING

* Dominick T. Armentano, *Antitrust and Monopoly: Anatomy of a Policy Failure* (Holmes & Meier, 1990). The best summary of the issues regarding monopoly, competition and anti-trust.

* Joseph A. Schumpeter, *Capitalism, Socialism and Democracy* (Harper & Row, 1976 [1950]). Schumpeter, the Harvard economist, makes the case favoring big business and the dynamics of the entrepreneurial marketplace.

* John Kenneth Galbraith, *The New Industrial State* (Houghton Mifflin, 1967). Galbraith is a powerful writer who scrutinizes the influence of big business and monopoly power in a mixed capitalist economy.

*Chapter 9*

# THE FACTORS OF PRODUCTION: LAND, RENT AND NATURAL RESOURCES

*"Land is the only thing in the world that amounts to anything, for 'tis the only thing in this world that lasts, and don't you be forgetting it! 'Tis the only thing worth working for, worth fighting for—worth dying for."*

—GERALD O'HARA
in *Gone With the Wind*
by Margaret Mitchell

*"Arizona is my land, my home, my father's land, to which I now ask to be allowed to return. I want to spend my last days there, and be buried among those mountains. If this could be, I might die in peace...".*

—GERONIMO, *Apache Chief (1877)*

Continuing our logical approach to economic science, the next four chapters deal with the cost side of the company, specifically the factors or inputs that create the final product or service. This chapter deals with the most basic of all inputs, land and the natural resources it contains.

Past chapters began with a discussion of the goal of economics which is to study how wealth is created. The simple 4-stage macro model of wealth-creation demonstrates how all goods and services go through a series of stages of production, from the unfinished to the usable, from natural resources to final goods and services.

The 4-stage model shown as figure 9.1 on the following page shows how the factors of production operate.

As noted in the diagram, land, labor, and capital goods exist at every stage of output. Completing the four stages successfully is impossible without the effort of all three factors of production: land, labor and capital goods working together. One of the fundamental features of the market system is cooperation.

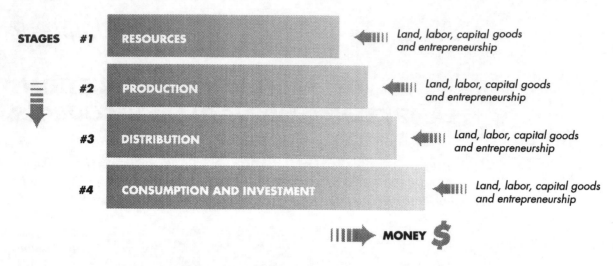

**Figure 9.1.** *The factors of production at the four stages.*

## THE TRADITIONAL COMPETITIVE VIEW

In traditional classical economics, the factors of production have typically been viewed in a competitive light. Landlords, wage-earners and capitalists compete in a contest to increase their individual market share in the distribution of factor income. Each group competes with the other two. Adam Smith and David Ricardo, co-founders of the classical school, often focused on the distribution of income and how it was divided. If landlords increased their share of the national income, it meant less income was available for workers or capitalists. If capitalists and landlords earned more, it meant that the wage fund was reduced for workers.

Karl Marx went further and considered that any share taken by capitalists and landlords was tantamount to theft, and resulted in exploitation of the working class. According to the Marxists, any fight over national income was nothing less than class warfare. As Marx states, "Wages are determined by the fierce struggle between capitalist and worker. The capitalist inevitably wins. The capitalist can live longer without the worker than the worker can live without him. Combination among capitalists is habitual and effective, while combination among the workers is forbidden and has painful consequences for them....So, for the worker, the separation of capital, ground rent and labor, is fatal."[1]

---

1  Karl Marx, "First Manuscript: Wages of Labor," *Economic and Personal Manuscripts* (April-August 1844), p. 1.

In this early classical model, the national income was viewed as an apple pie. The focus was not on the production of the apple pie, or how to make it bigger, but on how it was divided up. If one class received a bigger piece, it meant less pie for the weaker class, which was invariably the working class, according to Marx.

## NEW FOCUS ON COOPERATIVE NATURE OF THE ECONOMY

The four-stage model in this textbook offers a new approach. Land, labor and capital goods work together to move the production process along toward the next stage of output. Resources are acquired and the factors of production act upon these resources to transform inputs into output. In this model, if one element of the group does not cooperate, the production process stops dead in its tracks. Nothing is accomplished. If landlords refuse to rent their buildings or property, if workers go on strike, or if capitalists refuse to apply their capital goods or lend their funds, the company does not achieve its ends. Final goods and services are no longer produced, and factories remain idle. This situation is like the situation described in Poor Richard's Almanac, "For want of a nail the shoe was lost, for want of a shoe the horse was lost, and for want of a horse the rider was lost."

In the past the market economy has been viewed as a competitive system in both the product and factor markets. Now, at least in the factor markets, we see that there are significant levels of cooperation between landlords, workers, and capitalists. Without each contribution, nothing can be accomplished.

The market system is a model involving both competition and cooperation.

## IDENTIFYING THE FACTOR MARKET IN THE MICRO MODEL

The factors of production are also identified in our 2-stage micro model. This 2-stage model reflects a company's annual profit-and-loss income statement. The dynamics of an individual company in terms of changing costs, prices, and revenues and their effect on the bottom line were previously discussed. To review, see figure 9.2 below.

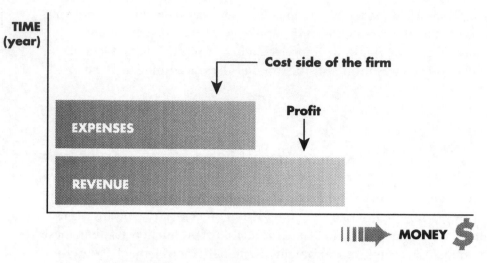

**Figure 9.2.** *A two-stage model income statement of a firm.*

What are the components of the cost side of economic transactions as illustrated by a recent income statement from Microsoft Corporation? Figure 9.3 shows the income statement.

**Figure 9.3.**

**INCOME STATEMENT OF MICROSOFT CORPORATION, 2009**
**(U.S. $ millions)**

REVENUES . . . . . . . . . . . . . . . . . . . . . . . . . . . . . . .$61,742
EXPENSES:
Cost of materials . . . . . . . . . . . . . . . . . . . . . . . . . . .11,598
Research Development . . . . . . . . . . . . . . . . . . . . . . . . .8,164
Wages and salaries/administration . . . . . . . . . . . . . . . .18,166
Taxes . . . . . . . . . . . . . . . . . . . . . . . . . . . . . . . . . . . .6,133
TOTAL EXPENSES . . . . . . . . . . . . . . . . . . . . . . . . .$44,061

NET INCOME (PROFIT) . . . . . . . . . . . . . . . . . . . . . .$17,681

The cost side of any company such as Microsoft can be divided into four major categories:

1. Materials and supplies (inputs to be acted upon or transformed)
2. Land and rent (real property, factories, and buildings)
3. Labor (wages, salaries, and consulting fees)
4. Capital goods (machinery, equipment, and office supplies)

In the basic input-output model, the company applies land, labor and capital goods to the inputs (goods-in-process) and transforms them into outputs that are then sold to customers at the next stage of use.

This chapter discusses how land and economic rent are priced and what use land and economic rent serve in the marketplace.

## LAND, PROPERTY RIGHTS AND DEMOCRACY

Land! The natural resources of an abundant earth.

Land! Man has possessed it, fought for it, and exploited it. The Communist revolutions of Russia, China and Cuba succeeded in part because the public's demand for democratic land reform. America was able to avoid national socialism, in part, because property ownership was widespread.

Land is the most fundamental of all factors of production. Without land, there would be nothing to act upon—no materials, supplies, goods or services. In fact, there are only two original means of production—land and labor. All tools, equipment, capital goods and goods-in-process came originally from the ground. Labor applied to the creations acquired or developed from the land gave humans their first tools from which other capital goods were created.

## LAND AND PROPERTY RIGHTS

Land is inevitably linked to property and the issue of property rights. Who owns the land? William Blackstone declared, "The earth, and all things therein, are the general property of all mankind, from the immediate gift of the Creator." But today the vast majority of land is owned privately by individuals or companies (stockholders). The public (government) owns roads and highways, parks and wilderness areas. How much acreage is privately owned varies from country to country. In the United States, real estate has been widely dispersed over the centuries. Home ownership, which usually includes a plot of land, is almost universal in the U. S., while in Latin America, whose landlords were granted huge areas by Spain and other colonial powers, land reform has been necessary to build up a large middle class.

One of the fundamental principles of the market economy is the establishment in the legal system of well-defined property rights. Without these rights to ownership of land and property, legal disputes can curtail the efficiency of an economy.[2] Property rights are discussed further in Chapter 20, "Fiscal Policy and the Role of Government."

## WHAT IS LAND?

Land is defined in the broadest way possible as the physical space necessary for the operation of an economic activity. Land can be urban property—a barren lot, useful only for building a residential or commercial building. Or land may be agricultural land where a farmer raises crops or animals. Land can be a mining property, where iron ore, copper, or precious metals are mined. Land can be a lake or river, providing water or means of transportation, or land can be a forest used as a source of timber or an animal retreat.

Land provides the natural resources—minerals, forests, water resources—as well as properties where permanent improvements have been made. Land cleared of a swamp, for example, may be considered permanently changed. The criteria of permanent change distinguishes land from capital goods. Capital goods, including buildings and machinery, may be added to an empty lot, but are not a permanent part of land. Buildings and machinery deteriorate and must be depreciated and replaced over time. Land always exists and is permanent. Land is a non-exhaustible resource.

## IS THE SUPPLY OF LAND PERFECTLY INELASTIC?

A common refrain referring to land or real estate is "They aren't making any more of it." Therefore, the argument goes, the supply of land is fixed and hence the price of land is determined solely by demand. Michael Parkin expresses this standard textbook view of land as follows: "The quantity [of land] supplied cannot be changed by individual decisions....The aggregate quantity of land supplied of any particular type and in any particular location is fixed, regardless of the decisions of any individual. This fact means that the supply of each particular piece of land is perfectly inelastic....Because the supply of land is fixed regardless of its price, price is determined by demand. The greater the demand for a specific piece of land, the higher is its price."[3]

2 For an excellent discussion of the importance of property rights, see Tom Bethell, *The Noblest Triumph: Property and Prosperity Through the Ages* (St. Martins Press, 1998).
3 Michael Parkin, *Economics*, 4th ed. (Addison-Wesley, 1998), p. 331.

The following graph illustrates a perfectly inelastic supply schedule where demand alone determines the price of land (figure 9.4).

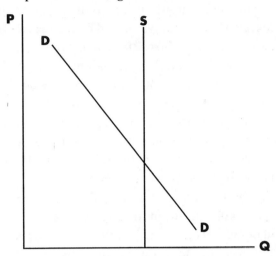

**Figure 9.4.** *A verticle supply curve for land.*

## HENRY GEORGE AND THE SINGLE TAX ON GROUND RENT

Relying on the alleged inelastic supply curve for land, many economists have written in favor of Henry George's celebrated policy of a single tax on land as an optimal economic and fiscal solution to public finance, one that is both efficient and equitable.

Henry George (1839-97) was a newspaperman in California who wrote his masterpiece, *Progress and Poverty*, in 1879.

His book serves as his philosophy of social justice. Henry George believed in competition and free-market capitalism and at the same time distrusted government. However, he claimed that capitalism had one serious flaw—the monopoly of land ownership—which he regarded as the root of all evil. All increases in the value of land are "unearned" according to George, creating "unjust" inequalities of wealth and poverty. "But all other monopolies are trivial in extent as compared with the monopoly of land," he declared.[4] George particularly attacked land speculators, who, he maintained, served no social function.

The idea that land generates "unearned" surplus goes back to the classical economists Adam Smith and David Ricardo, who viewed land rent as pure profit to landowners for nature's bounty rather than human effort. The amount of rent paid to a landlord may bear no relation to the landlord's costs. Therefore, land rents were condemned as unearned incomes.

4  Henry George, *Progress and Poverty* (New York: Robert Schalkenbach Foundation, 1942), p. 412.

To solve the problems of inequality and other economic evils, Henry George did not follow the advice of socialists in advocating nationalization of land, but instead favored a single tax on economic ground rent. Whatever the landord charged in rent for the land (exclusive of buildings) would be the tax bill. George considered this the ideal tax. "Taxes levied upon the value of land cannot check production in the slightest degree," he argued, "for unlike taxes upon commodities, or exchange, or capital, or any of the tools or processes of production, they do not bear upon production."[5]

George proposed a single tax on ground rent only, not on capital or land improvements. As long as the tax was on pure economic rent only—the value of the property without improvements or buildings—the owner's tax would allegedly have no negative effect on productive activity. No private land titles would be disturbed. No land would be expropriated—just taxed.

In addition, the ground tax policy would attack land speculators and force them to abandon their selfish profit motives. George argued that the single land tax had the additional benefit of encouraging idle land to be put to productive use.

Henry George spent the rest of his life crusading for social justice through the single tax movement. He ran for mayor of New York City in 1897, but died during the campaign and was accorded one of the biggest funerals in New York history. His legacy lives on. Today, several economists, including Paul Samuelson, have agreed with George that only landlords would bear the burden of a single tax on land and agree that a tax on ground rent would be a good idea. The following diagram (figure 9.5) demonstrates their interpretation of the benefits of a single land tax.

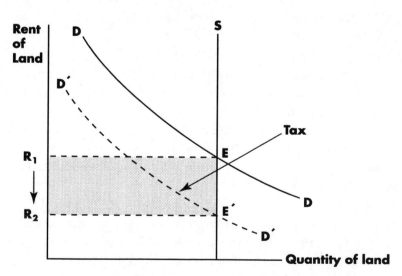

**Figure 9.5.** *Effect of a tax on land: landlords bear the burden.*

5  Henry George, Progress and Poverty (New York: Robert Schalkenbach Foundation, 1942 [1879]), p. 328.

According to Samuelson and Nordhaus, "The whole of the tax has been shifted backward onto the owners of the factor in inelastic supply....The striking result is that a tax on rent will lead to no distortions or economic inefficiencies." Why not? "Because a tax on pure economic rent does not change anyone's economic behavior. Demanders are unaffected because their price is unchanged. The behavior of suppliers is unaffected because the supply of land is taxed and cannot react."[6]

## THE DEBATE OVER GEORGE'S SINGLE LAND TAX SCHEME

Other economists disagree with the concept of a single land tax. A vocal critic was Murray N. Rothbard, who objected to Henry George's attack on land speculation. According to Rothbard, land speculators serve a useful economic function. Rothbard applied the principle of marginal analysis, which was developed in the 1870s by Carl Menger, Leon Walras and William Stanley Jevons (during the marginalist revolution). According to this principle, a piece of property is allocated according to its most value-productive bidders representing the highest possible marginal productive use.

Property prices vary considerably from city to city, state to state, and country to country.

Imagine if each property were valued at the same price around the world no matter where an individual lived. What would the effect be? In some locations, there would be massive shortages (prices would be too cheap); in others, there would be empty apartments (prices would be too expensive). The market price helps allocate land to its most valued use irrespective of its original cost or possible windfall profit or losses to landlords.

Rothbard also disagreed with Samuelson and other economists who contend that a tax on pure land or ground rent would not create any distortions or inefficiencies. On the contrary, Rothbard argues, "If the Henry George scheme went into effect, there would not only be complete misallocation of sites to less productive uses, but there would also be great overcrowding in the downtown areas."[7] Why? Since landlords would no longer earn any income from ground rents, they would need to increase their profits on the building rents by building larger and taller buildings. It would pay them to build buildings on empty lots rather than sell the land, since selling would result in heavy losses and no gain whatsoever. Landlords would be encouraged to build bigger and taller buildings (skyscrapers) on each property, thus diminishing the negative impact of earning nothing on their ground rent. The result would be more overcrowding in downtown areas.

6  Paul A. Samuelson and William D. Nordhaus, *Economics*, 16th ed. (Irwin McGraw-Hill, 1998), p. 250.
7  Murray N. Rothbard, *Power and Market* (Institute for Humane Studies, 1970), p. 96.

Georgists respond by contending that ground rents optimize land use and building construction, and therefore do not involve a deadweight loss. If a property is idle, a land tax would encourage the landowner to develop the land. Fred Foldvary, a Santa Clara University professor, provides two contrasting examples in American history. After the 1906 great earthquake, San Francisco residents quickly rebuilt, since they had to pay a property tax regardless of whether the land remained empty or was rebuilt. On the other hand, New Orleans residents enjoyed a substantial $75,000 real estate tax exemption, and after the 2004 hurricane, thousands of properties remained broken down and uninhabited for years to come.

Georgists also note that the price of land and rental values are affected by what Mason Gaffney, professor of economics at University of California at Riverside, calls "municipal mercantilism." Zoning, wasteful open spaces, and subsidies in building golf courses, and other government-imposed regulations on land use cause prices of land and rents to be substantially higher. For example, land values are higher in the San Francisco Bay area than other areas in the United States with similar population density, because the development is more restricted.

## SUPPLY CURVE IS NOT PERFECTLY INELASTIC

It is also possible to dispute the assumption that a fixed amount of land necessarily means a perfectly inelastic supply curve for land. Is it true that no matter what the price, the same amount of land will be offered on the market? The market for land is not based on the total amount of land, but on the amount of land available for sale at any one time. The price of land is determined by marginal buyers and sellers.

This marginalist principle can be applied to collectibles. Many collectibles such as Babe Ruth baseballs, Morgan silver dollars, or 19th century paintings, are not being made any more. The total number of items for sale at any one time varies considerably depending on the price. Price is heavily influenced by consumer demand. While it is true, for example, that there are a fixed number of baseballs Ruth signed over his lifetime, the number for sale at any one time varies considerably. Figure 9.6 illustrates the elasticity of the supply schedule for Babe Ruth autographed baseballs.

Note in the example below that if the price is high enough, virtually every Ruth baseball is available for sale, and clearly at that point the supply curve is perfectly inelastic. But until that point (Z) is reached, the supply schedule is relatively elastic. The price of collectibles is determined by marginal sales, not by the number of collectibles made.

Chapter 6 referred to the real estate market in Orlando, Florida, where typically one of every 20 residential homes is for sale, and the average home price (approximately $200,000) is based on that equilibrium condition. But suppose that suddenly Orlando becomes a less desirable place to live because crime increases or a major

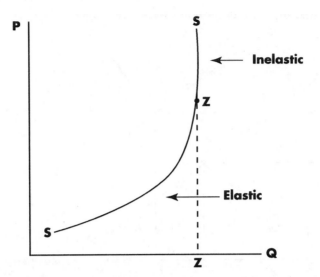

**Figure 9.6.** *Elastic supply curve for Babe Ruth autographed baseballs.*

theme park decides to leave the area. Now the number of homes for sale doubles. One out of every 10 is for sale. The marginal number of homes for sale has increased. Even though the total amount of housing remains the same in Orlando, the price of the average house is likely to fall substantially.

In the same way, the supply of land — though fixed in its totality — changes with price. The higher the price, the more lots will be offered for sale. The lower the price, the fewer lots will be offered.

Chapter 6 concluded that prices for goods and services are determined at the margin. The same is true for land and the factor markets in general (land, labor, and capital). The principle of marginal productivity of the factors of production will be discussed in Chapter 10.

## THE CONCEPT OF ECONOMIC RENT

To understand economic rent, review supply and demand in figure 9.7.

Chapter 6 introduced the concepts of consumer's surplus and seller's rent. Consumers' surplus for each individual is the maximum price someone is willing to pay, minus the actual price paid. For example, a car buyer may be willing to pay $25,000 for a Mustang, but is able to buy one for only $20,000. He enjoys a $5,000 consumers' surplus. Many, if not most, consumers enjoy consumers' surplus for most of the goods and services they buy.

Sellers' rent is similar to consumers' surplus, but represents a surplus for the seller. A landowner may be willing to part with his property in New York City for $250,000, but he sees that the going market price is $400,000, so he receives economic rent of $150,000. Economic rent is the difference between the market price an

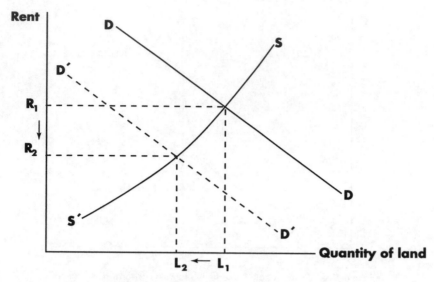

**Figure 9.7.** *Effect of a tax on ground rents.*

owner can receive for an asset or service and the price he would be willing to accept. In the diagram in figure 9.8, economic rent is shown in the area between the supply curve and the market price.

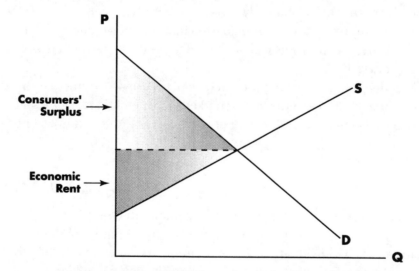

**Figure 9.8.** *Consumers' surplus and economic rent in supply and demand.*

Economic rent applies to all aspects of the marketplace, not just land. For example, a baseball player may be willing to play baseball for only $100,000 a year, but the New York Yankees offer him the market price of $3 million a year. In this situation, almost his entire salary is economic rent. Economic rent can be huge when it applies to individuals with unusual talents in sports or entertainment. They might be willing to work for much less than their true market value.

## THE CONCEPT OF RENT SEEKING

Economists have also extended the concept of economic rent to government policy and public-choice theory. Gordon Tullock, professor of economics at University of Arizona, invented the term rent seeking to refer to the use of political influence (lobbying) to secure protection and artificially high profit margins in the marketplace for products or services. Just as landlords benefit from an unexpected rise in rents without any effort on their behalf, so new government laws can artificially benefit certain groups in society. Economist David Henderson calls it "privilege seeking." Rent-seeking or privilege-seeking activities are common in agriculture, the military, the post office, and trade protection, for example. Companies involved in these industries or markets will lobby politicians to pass legislation favorable to their special interest group. The intriguing concept of rent-seeking is discussed in detail in Chapter 20, "The Role of Government," and Chapter 23, "Government Regulations and Controls."

## SUMMARY

**The main points covered in Chapter 9 are:**

1.  The free-enterprise economic system is composed of both competitive and cooperative elements. Landlords, workers, and capitalists must work together to create usable wealth.

2.  Effective property rights to land and other resources are essential to exchange, trade, and economic activity.

3.  Even though the total amount of land may be fixed, the supply curve represents the amount of property available for sale at a given point in time and therefore is not strictly inelastic.

4.  Rent—the price of land—serves a useful purpose in allocating property to its most valued and productive use.

5.  Economists debate the impact of taxes on ground rent. Some economists argue that it causes overcrowding. Georgist economists content that it is the optimal tax in social development.

6.  Major companies may enjoy the benefits of rent seeking by obtaining subsidies and special privileges from government. Examples include farm subsidies, import duties and restrictions, and other types of corporate welfare.

## IMPORTANT TERMS

Competition
Consumers' surplus
Cooperation
Economic rent
Economies of scale
Factors of production
Ground rent
Land

Lobbying
Monopoly
Perfectly inelastic
Privilege seeking
Property rights
Rent seeking
Sellers' rent

## INFLUENTIAL ECONOMISTS

### THOMAS MALTHUS and DAVID RICARDO

**Names:**  **Thomas R. Malthus (1766-1834) and
David Ricardo (1772-1823)**

**Background:** Malthus and Ricardo were founders of the classical school, and followers of Adam Smith. They had much in common. Both were friends who generally favored *laissez faire* policies but had a pessimistic view of the future, such as the threat of overpopulation and the subsistence theory of wages.

Malthus graduated in 1788 from Jesus College at Cambridge with a degree in mathematics, and was a minister for a brief period (thus known as Reverend Malthus). He married in 1804 and became a professor of history and political economy for the East India Company's College at Haileybury.

Ricardo was born in a Jewish family, but married a Quaker against the wishes of his parents. He accumulated a fortune speculating in the London stock market. In addition to his writing career, he obtained a seat in the House of Commons in 1819. He died in 1823, leaving a wife, seven children, and an estate worth 750,000 pounds, making him the wealthiest economist who ever lived.

**Major Works:** Robert Malthus wrote *An Essay on the Principle of Population* (1798), one of the most influential works in economics and social science. He warned that the growth of population is limited by the food supply (the bounties of land). According to Malthus, population naturally grows geometrically (1, 2, 4, 8, 16...), while food supply tends to increase arithmetically (1, 2, 3, 4...). The result could be mass starvation and the subsistence of wages. Malthus also wrote *Principles of Political Economy*.

David Ricardo's most famous book is *Principles of Political Economy and Taxation* (1817). Ricardo introduced several concepts in economics, among them: law of diminishing returns, comparative advantage in international trade, and the labor theory of value.

**Strengths:** Although Malthus failed to foresee the technological advances in agricultural production and efficiency, his Malthusian theory of population raised doubts about the panaceas of visionary reformers who sought to ban poverty overnight. Malthus also questioned the ability of the economy to recover immediately from "general gluts" or depression. Keynes hailed Malthus as a forerunner of his own attack on Say's law of markets and the virtue of saving.

Ricardo is considered the founder of economics as a rigorous science, although many critics think Ricardo took economics down the wrong road (see the "Ricardian vice" below). Ricardo was a strong defender of the gold standard, a critic of inflation and the welfare state, and a proponent of free trade. He argued ably that two countries would both benefit from lower tariffs. He supported the elimination of the "corn laws," which imposed tariffs on imported wheat.

**Weaknesses:** Both Malthus and Ricardo had dim views of land and of the earth's ability to produce enough to keep up with the world's population. Malthus and Ricardo argued that as more land was cultivated, farmers would have to start using less productive land. As a result, rents for more productive land would favor the idle landlord. Malthus' and Ricardo's negative views on land and landlords gave support to the Georgist attack on rental income.

Ricardo also invented what economists term the Ricardian vice whereby theorists build models based on false and misleading assumptions that lead inexorably to the desired results. In his principles, Ricardo used this technique to "prove" the labor theory of value. Some critics blame Ricardo as the source of today's highly abstract, mathematical, and ahistorical theoretical model-building. Ricardo also furthered the cause of Marxism by implying that profits could only increase at the expense of workers' wages, which tended toward the subsistence level.

The theories of Malthus and Ricardo caused Thomas Carlyle to label economics "the dismal science."

## PROBLEMS TO PONDER

1. In this chapter, Murray Rothbard contends that the Henry George tax on ground rent would lead to overcrowding in major cities. But according to standard supply and demand, higher taxes raise costs and reduce the amount demanded. As a result, would high real estate taxes cause businesses and residents to leave the city? Would a ground tax result in fewer city residents and more people moving to the suburbs?

2. Give some historical examples of landlords and speculators earning "windfall" or "monopoly" profits.

3. A farmer owns several acres of land known as Tysons Corner, Virginia. The land is used to produce agricultural products and is worth little. Suddenly the I-495 Beltway is built right next to the property and the value of the land skyrockets as builders contemplate developing a major shopping center known as Tyson's Corner Shopping Mall. Should the farmer be allowed to make 100 fold profit on his property by selling it to developers? Do unexpected windfall profits serve any useful function in an economy or should these profits always be taxed away?

4. When oil prices increased 10 fold during the 1973-80 energy crisis, many oil companies made huge profits. During this energy crisis, Congress considered imposing an "excess profits" tax on oil companies. If you were in Congress, would you vote for such a tax? Do unexpected monopolistic profits serve any useful function in a market economy? (Hint: Could additional oil revenue be used to explore and develop new oil fields?)

5. Comment on this statement by Walter A. Weisskopf, author of *The Psychology of Economics* (University of Chicago Press, 1955): "Ricardo and Malthus both attribute a peculiar role to land. For them it is the source of all economic ills, the evil principle in their universe of discourse. Malthus believed that population growth outruns the production of food with the inevitability of a natural law. This implies an unfavorable comparison of the fertility of the earth with the fertility of the human female....In a similar fashion Ricardo considers the 'female' land as the ultimate factor which causes all the unfortunate results expounded in his long-run dynamic theory of economic development. Ricardo's pessimistic forecasts rest on three assumptions: (1) the law of diminishing returns, (2) the principle of population, and (3) the subsistence theory of wages....All three of these assumptions have to do with the scarcity of fertile lands." (pp. 125-127) Was the Malthus-Ricardo "dismal science" essentially anti-female?

6.  Socialists have argued that any annual income ("economic rent") exceeding that which would keep an individual working should be taxed away since it has no effect on effort. For example, if a player is willing to play professional baseball for $100,000 a year, any salary beyond $100,000 could conceivably be taxed without affecting his performance as a ballplayer. What effect on incentives would a 100% marginal tax rate beyond a certain base salary (say $100,000) have for baseball players, actors or other celebrities? Is "sellers' rent" the same for every celebrity or sports figure? Would you favor such a progressive tax on celebrity income? On your own income?

7.  In the 18th century, America was said to have plenty of cheap land; the real problem was a shortage of labor. Europe was said to have plenty of labor and not enough land. Were wages higher in Europe or America during the colonial period? What about land prices during that same time period?

8.  California's Proposition 13, enacted in 1978, limits the property tax on real estate to one percent of the market value when purchased, and a maximum annual increase in the tax amount of two percent. Followers of Henry George contend that Prop 13 deprived local government of its most suitable tax base, real estate taxes, and forced the state to increase other taxes that hurt business activity, and shifted power from local government to the state. According to the Georgists, Prop 13 did not constrain state spending and caused the budget deficit to grow so that California was hit with a fiscal crisis in 2008-09. What could be done to solve California's financial crisis?

## RECOMMENDED READING

- Tom Bethell, *The Noblest Triumph: Property and Prosperity Through the Ages* (St. Martins Press, 1998). An excellent discussion of property rights, including the issue of land reform.

- Henry George, *Progress and Poverty* (Robert Schalkenbach Foundation, 1942). George is an eloquent critic of landlords and a fervent advocate of the single tax on land. A classic in social economics.

- Fred E. Foldvary, *The Ultimate Tax Reform: Public Revenue from Land Rent* (Santa Clara University, 2006). A Georgist economist makes the case for tax reform.

# Chapter 10

# THE FACTORS OF PRODUCTION: WAGES AND THE PRODUCTIVITY OF LABOR

*"Higher wages come from increased output per hour of work."*

—F. A. HARPER, *Why Wages Rise* (1957), p. 19

*"Unemployment is considered a social evil that must be kept at an 'acceptable' level."*

—ROBER LeROY MILLER

Most individuals spend more time in their waking hours toiling at jobs than anything else. Some people enjoy their work, others hate their job. Some have to deal with tough bosses and unreliable workers. Not every job is pleasant. Yet others can not wait to get up in the morning and start working. Many employees fret about not getting paid enough, and wonder if they will get a raise next month. Others are anxious about the company stock they hold in their pension plan. There is the fear of getting fired or losing one's job. Maybe it is time to return to school.

This chapter deals with the economics of labor and wages and considers the following questions:

1. What determines wages and a country's standard of living?
2. How can more income be earned?
3. Do labor unions help workers, raise wages, and improve the environment for employees?
4. What causes unemployment?

Recall that labor is one of the means of production—land, labor and capital. Chapter 9 covered the vital role of land and natural resources. In this chapter, income and work will be discussed. Payment in wages, salaries, and other forms of income determines the standard of living. The more money earned each year, the more things can be bought and done, and the more leisure time can be enjoyed.

## REAL WAGES SKYROCKETED IN THE 20th CENTURY

Historically, real income (after inflation) has risen spectacularly for most people living in the industrial world, especially in the 20th century. Germany, Japan and other industrial nations have also enjoyed a tremendous rise in wages and living standards, and now the rest of the world is catching up rapidly.

Prior to the 20th century, there was very little economic progress for the average worker. (See Figure 10.1) Real wages began rising significantly with the Industrial Revolution in the early 19th century and took off in the 20th century with the advent of major breakthroughs in energy production, communications, and transportation.

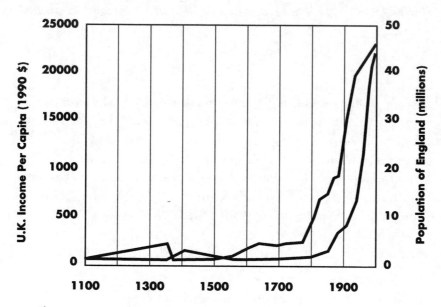

**Figure 10.1.** *Real income didn't rise much until the 19th century; then it took off.*

Figure 10.2 demonstrates the sharp rise in real wages in the United States from 1890. Note also the decline in the average working hours, indicating more leisure time for American workers. In the 20th century, Americans reduced official working time by 50% while increasing their real income eight fold. This is a remarkable achievement.

Other statistics indicating rising living standards are found in Chapter 1. Today's generation has much to be grateful for compared to those living a century earlier, at least in terms of material wealth.

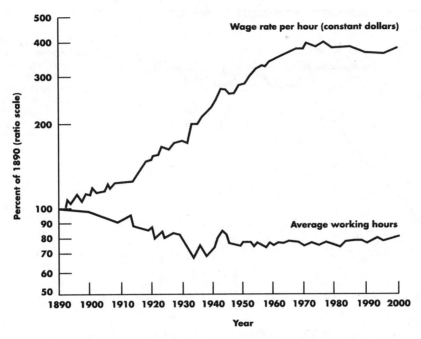

**Figure 10.2.** *Improved real wages and declining work hours for Americans.*

## SLOWDOWN IN AVERAGE REAL WAGE GROWTH?

Readers may note that real wages appear to have leveled out since the early 1970s. One reason is that worker benefits—including medical insurance plans, paid vacations, and pensions, have increased significantly over the past 35 years. Figure 10.3 demonstrates that total real compensation per hour, which includes worker benefits, has continued to rise during this period. However, even when worker benefits are included, the graph indicates that total real compensation per hour has slowed remarkably since the early 1970s. Why?

**Economists point to several possible explanations:**

(1) Foreign competitors have dramatically caught up with American productivity,

(2) increasing the demand for foreign products and raising foreign wages while slowing growth for U. S. wages.

Taxes and inflation have eroded corporate profits and reduced real take-home pay resulting in an increasing number of American families where both parents work or take second jobs to meet financial needs.

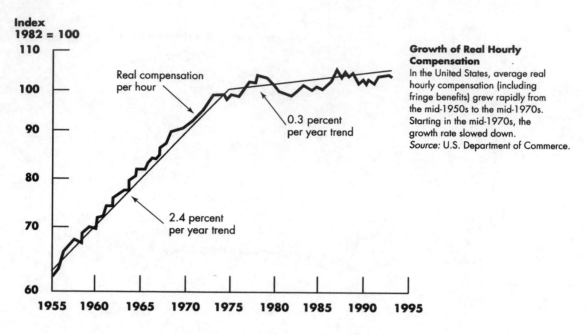

**Figure 10.3.** *Growth of real hourly compensation in the U.S. (including worker benefits)*

## THE ROLE OF LABOR IN BUSINESS

From a business point of view, labor is a critical element. Often in major corporations, wages and salaries are the biggest expense as shown in Microsoft's income statement for 2006, reprinted in figure 10.4. After the cost of materials, the cost of labor represented the biggest item in Microsoft's budget, a total of $3.8 billion in 2006.

How does labor play a role in the profitability of a firm? Figure 10.5 shows that labor is involved in both the cost and revenue side of the firm's business.

What does labor do? In a work environment (land, factories, or offices), workers take tools and equipment (capital) and transform inputs (goods-in-process) into outputs (final goods and services). Labor is an essential ingredient in the production process.

Entrepreneur-owners also play a vital role. As owners/operators, entrepreneur-owners make the critical decisions and give the instructions of what products are produced, how the production process takes place, and who is involved. Entrepreneur-owners are the ones directly in charge. Normally the role of the entrepreneur-owners is separated from labor. Employers and employees serve different functions, but both are labor—workers who accomplish a variety of tasks. (Entrepreneurship will be the subject of Chapter 12.)

**Figure 10.4.**

**INCOME STATEMENT OF MICROSOFT CORPORATION, 2008**
**(U.S. $ millions)**

REVENUES . . . . . . . . . . . . . . . . . . . . . . . . . . . . . . .$61,742

EXPENSES:
Cost of materials . . . . . . . . . . . . . . . . . . . . . . . . . . .11,598
Research Development . . . . . . . . . . . . . . . . . . . . . . . .8,164
Wages and salaries/administration . . . . . . . . . . . . . . . .18,166
Taxes . . . . . . . . . . . . . . . . . . . . . . . . . . . . . . . . . . .6,133

TOTAL EXPENSES . . . . . . . . . . . . . . . . . . . . . . . . .$44,061

NET INCOME (PROFIT) . . . . . . . . . . . . . . . . . . . . . .$17,681

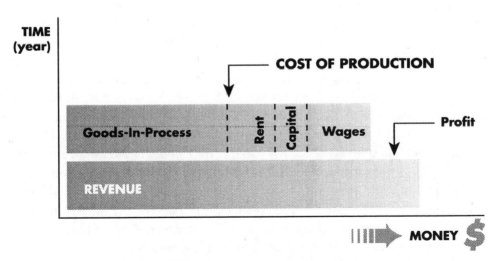

**Figure 10.5.** *A firm's profit-and-loss income statement.*

Once again, the cooperative nature of the capitalist system is important to emphasize. Without labor, final goods and services cannot be made available to consumers. Without capital and capitalists, labor would be handicapped from completing their task. Both labor and capital complement each other and work together to achieve goals. In fact, workers have greatly increased their compensation over the years due to the availability of expensive capital equipment provided by the entrepreneur and money. Without advanced capital, workers' wages would be meager.

## WAGES, DERIVED DEMAND AND THE MARGINAL PRODUCTIVITY OF LABOR

What determines wages, the price of labor? Why have wages risen over time? To answer these questions, review the dynamic two-stage model of a firm's income statement shown in Figure 10.5.

As discussed in the Chapter 4 discussions on profit and loss, a firm seeks to maximize profits by buying (or hiring) additional inputs—land, labor and capital—and thereby increasing revenue. The firm engages in cost-benefit analysis. A cost-benefit analysis identifies all the positive factors – benefits. The negative factors are identified and subtracted from the benefits. The difference between the two indicates whether the planned action is advisable.

Is the additional cost (in wages, rents and interest) worth the benefit of higher revenue? If the new marketing plan or new product line is sufficiently profitable to cover costs plus a reasonable profit, then the firm's executives have made the right decision. If increased revenue does not match the additional cost, the decision was a wrong one.

The price (or cost) of the factor market is derived from final consumer demand. What does "derived demand" mean? The demand for land, labor and capital is determined by the final revenue and hence profitability of the products the firm sells to its customers. The firm continues to demand more factors of production until revenue meets costs after achieving a reasonable profit.

Use labor as an example. Let's suppose the demand for software is rising and Microsoft sees an opportunity to expand its market position by hiring more computer software technicians. Assume that the going wage for software technicians with several years experience is $100,000 a year. Why would Microsoft hire more technicians? One reason for hiring more technicians is because of the potential additional income the company could earn. The benefit to Microsoft of hiring these workers is the extra revenue generated by these employees. The additional output generated by the extra worker is called the marginal productivity of labor.

How many workers will Microsoft hire? Theoretically Microsoft will hire more labor up to the point where the value of its marginal product (the marginal benefit) is equal to its price; i.e., the wage of software technicians.

In general, the theory of marginal productivity of labor suggests a close connection between workers' income and profitability of the firm. Wages, salaries and bonuses are inexorably linked to profitability. Broadly speaking, the same principle applies to all factors of production. The value of office space, wages, equipment and other factors of production are directly related to the company's profitability. If the company is doing well, it will demand more office space, more workers, and more capital to expand—and may even pay more to get these resources, depending on the competition and how fast the economy is growing. If the company is doing poorly, it will sell off office space, let workers go, and cut back on supplies and equipment.

Figure 10.6 demonstrates the supply curve for labor, which slopes upward. The supply curve tends to be relatively flat at first as firms can initially hire more workers without requiring them to pay higher wages. As the economy reaches full employment of resources and competition becomes more keen for skilled workers such as software technicians, firms have to pay higher wages to attract good workers.

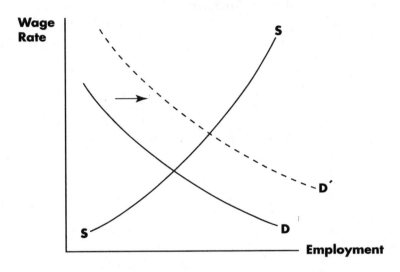

**Figure 10.6.** *Upward-sloping supply curve for labor.*

## WORK vs. LEISURE: BACKWARD-BENDING SUPPLY CURVE FOR LABOR?

Normally, the supply curve for labor is upward sloping. Higher pay encourages more employment and a willingness to work long hours. However, leisure is also highly desirable, and some individuals may choose to work fewer hours even if offered higher levels of compensation. Economists cannot always tell for sure how powerful this effect is on workers, but leisure is a strong influence, especially on doctors, lawyers, other professional groups, and the younger generation.

## THE DEMAND FOR LABOR

What about the demand for labor? In the above example the supply curve is developed by shifting the demand curve for software products upward and seeing how workers responded. As figure 10.6 indicates, by changing demand, an upward sloping supply curve is created. Increasing labor demand caused the supply of workers to increase at generally higher wages.

To develop the demand curve for labor, the supply curve must be shifted. How? Suppose computer-industry forecasters are predicting a huge shortage in software technicians over the next decade due to increasing demand for computers. Millions of students switch from other majors to computer science, graduating in four years. More foreign workers with computer skills immigrate to the U. S. The effect will be to shift the supply curve outward and downward. The large increase in the number of computer graduates and foreigners will create greater competition among workers, and computer firms such as Microsoft will be able to hire more workers at lower wages. Figure 10.7 illustrates the effect of this increasing supply of software technicians.

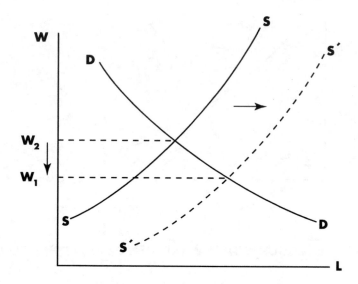

**Figure 10.7.** *Effect of increasing supply of computer workers.*

Shifting the supply curve allows the basic supply and demand factors for labor to be derived. Increasing demand and profitability for final products causes wages to rise, while increasing supply of new workers causes wages to fall. The equilibrium wage rate tends to equal the marginal productivity of labor. That is, wages rise or fall based on changes in the buying and selling of labor.

The concept of marginal productivity of labor was first proposed around the turn of the 19th century by John Bates Clark, a professor of economics at Columbia University (see biography in this chapter). Clark reasoned that in a competitive economy, firms will not hire workers if the market wage exceeds a worker's marginal product, i.e., a worker's ability to produce a profit for the company. It would be unprofitable for a firm to hire such a worker. Moreover, the market wage for all workers would have to be what new employees (equal in experience and training to current workers) are willing to work for—the marginal or last worker who enters the labor force. Hence, wages will rise or fall with the marginal value of labor. There is a tendency for all wage rates to rise or fall depending on the wage demands of additional workers—those who are entering the labor force. The wage rate of these additional workers affects all workers' wages, not just new workers, just as a change in property values affects all existing real estate in the area, not just the new buyers or sellers entering the market.

## THE PRINCIPLE OF ONE WAGE RATE

Figure 10.8 shows the supply and demand for a specific labor market. Note the tendency for the equilibrium wage. Chapter 6 demonstrates the tendency for one price to prevail in the product market. "Equal pay for equal work" is not just a political slogan, but a general characteristic of the labor market. Labor mobility is one reason why wage rates tend to equalize. If one region of the nation generally begins to pay higher wages, workers will tend to move to that region, bringing wages down to the average level in that area.

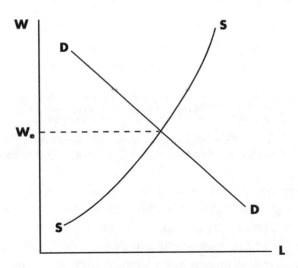

**Figure 10.8.** *Supply and demand for labor.*

It is true that wages for similar work do vary to some extent in the marketplace. Reasons include differences in experience, age, sex, transportation costs, and the cost of living in various communities. For example, accountants in Manhattan are usually paid more than accountants in Kansas City due to both higher demand for accountants and higher living expenses in New York City.

## JOB DISCRIMINATION AND "EQUAL PAY FOR EQUAL WORK"

Social commentators note that wages differ on the basis of race and sex, which raises the emotionally-charged issue of discrimination in the marketplace. Studies indicate that blacks and women have often been paid less for comparable work. Figure 10.9 summarizes sex and race differentials in wages.

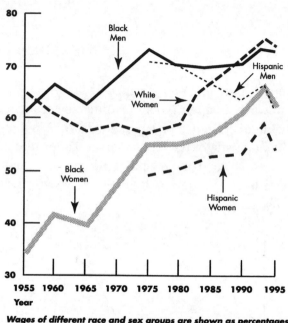

*Wages of different race and sex groups are shown as percentages of white male wages. These differentials have persisted over many years, but their magnitudes have changed.*

**Figure 10.9.** *Wages of different race and sex groups as a percentage of white male wages.*
*Source:* U.S. Bureau of the Census, *Statistical Abstract of the United States,* 1996, 116 ed. (CD-ROM), Table 663

The overall differentials in wages between blacks and whites and men and women have gradually closed as indicated in Figure 10.9. A study by the American Enterprise Institute (Washington, D. C.) determined that the wage gap for younger women has virtually closed and that they are now earning 98% of men's wages. The same study also indicates that the gap is rapidly closing for older women and that there are now more women than men in higher education. If these improvements in wage differentials are occurring, why should discrimination exist at all in the labor market, and what, if anything, should be done about it?

Economists disagree about the race and sex differentials in wage rates and whether they reflect discrimination or other factors. Wages are determined in part by (1) years of education, (2) years of work experience, and (3) number of job interruptions. Traditionally, employers have paid women, blacks and other minorities less than their white male counterparts because, in general, minorities may not have had the same level of education or years of experience. Until recently, blacks have had less educational opportunities than whites. Similarly, job interruptions have been more frequent for women because women's careers may be shortened or interrupted for bearing and rearing children. Employers usually hire full-time workers on a long-term basis, and if they think that long-term employment may be interrupted, wages may be reduced. Now that maternity leave and child-care facilities are more common, the differential in wages has narrowed.

## DISCRIMINATION AND AFFIRMATIVE ACTION

What about discrimination against blacks, Hispanics and other minorities?

The government imposes penalties on discrimination and the market also imposes a penalty on prejudice. A consumer who refuses to buy from a black, Hispanic, or Jew restricts his choices of products and stores. An employer who refuses to hire a minority limits his choice of qualified workers. Milton Friedman states, "The man who exercises discrimination pays a price for doing so."[1] Friedman points out that the development of capitalism has been accompanied by a major reduction in religious, racial, and sexual discrimination, even without the help of government.

Usually we think of government as an opponent of racial discrimination. Yet, the state has sometimes imposed discriminatory laws. In the early 1900s in South Africa, mine owners sought to replace higher-wage-earning white workers with lower-wage-earning black workers. In response, the South African government imposed economic restrictions on black workers. In the United States the southern states also passed laws limiting the opportunity for blacks to work and vote. In many southern cities, streetcar companies refused to enforce desegregation laws for as long as 15 years after they were passed.[2]

Since the passage of the 1964 Civil Rights Act, the federal government has made discrimination and segregation illegal and has enforced anti-discrimination authority. In addition to desegregating schools and other public facilities and outlawing discrimination in the workplace, the federal government has gone further and imposed "affirmative action" programs on colleges and government agencies. Affirmative action requires employers to favor the hiring of minority groups to remedy the imbalances of the past. Critics call affirmative action "reverse discrimination" and claim it is unconstitutional to impose racial quotas and force companies to hire unqualified workers which may result in inefficient and uncompetitive performance. The debate over affirmative action argues that reverse discrimination in the workplace results in a trade-off between equality and efficiency.

1  Milton Friedman, *Capitalism and Freedom* (University of Chicago Press, 1962), p. 110.
2  Linda Gorman, "The Market Resists Discrimination," *The Fortune Encyclopedia of Economics*, ed. by David Henderson (Warner Books, 1993), pp. 474-475.

## THE DEBATE OVER COMPARABLE WORTH LAWS

Over the years, the U. S. government has imposed "equal pay for equal work" laws, starting with the Equal Pay Act of 1963 and the Civil Rights Act of 1964. In extending this principle, the U. S. Supreme and federal courts have ruled that employees have a right to equal pay for "comparable worth." Washington, Minnesota, and other states as well as the Canadian province of Ontario, have passed laws imposing "comparable worth" requirements. Rather than allowing market factors such as ability, education, experience, and job reliability to establish wages, the government sets criteria to determine wages. A committee assigns points to each job based on the factors influencing the job, including knowledge and skills, the mental demands of the work, supervisory relationships, and work conditions. According to this approach, nurses in Washington state were rated above computer systems analysts, and, therefore, should be paid more, quite the opposite of the market test.

Like many policy issues in economics, the comparable worth test has unintended consequences. The results go counter to the state's good intentions. Comparable worth requirements forced secretaries to be paid more than the market rate, leading to too many applicants and a shortage of positions in the state of Washington. Another study indicates that Minnesota's comparable-worth law has reduced employment growth in jobs traditionally held by females. These laws also discourage women from breaking into higher-paying professions dominated by men because of the government-mandated higher pay in jobs traditionally held by women. This practice increases the dominance of women in the secretarial field as they choose those professions with the highest wage. Figure 10.10 illustrates a government-imposed wage rate for secretaries and computer analysts.

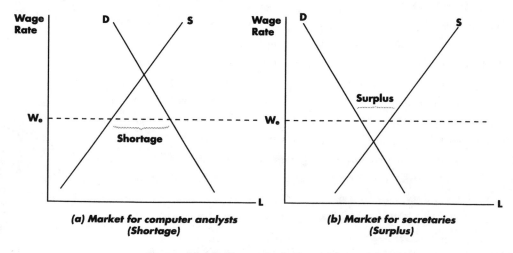

**(a) Market for computer analysts (Shortage)**

**(b) Market for secretaries (Surplus)**

**Figure 10.10.** *The result of comparable worth laws.*

## THE VALUE OF HIGHER EDUCATION

One of the most important survey findings is that formal education increases a worker's chance of higher lifetime income. According to the most recent studies, a male college graduate will earn on average $4.5 million before retiring at the age of 65 (in today's dollars). A male high school graduate will earn about $2.5 million over his career, and a high school dropout will make on average $1.8 million. Figure 10.11 illustrates the significant difference education can make in lifetime earnings. The earnings differential between a "skilled" (educated) worker and an "unskilled" worker is increasing. In the late 1970s a college graduate earned an average 45 % more than a high school graduate with the same background, but by the late 1990s the earnings difference grew to 85 % . There is an increasing premium in the labor market for staying in school and becoming educated or obtaining a skill.

There is a cost for receiving more education which involves foregoing current income while in school in expectation of higher future earnings. These costs include tuition, college expenses, living away from home, and putting off gainful employment. The cost for college can be $100,000 or more.

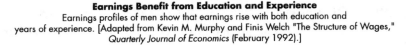

**Earnings Benefit from Education and Experience**
Earnings profiles of men show that earnings rise with both education and years of experience. [Adapted from Kevin M. Murphy and Finis Welch "The Structure of Wages," *Quarterly Journal of Economics* (February 1992).]

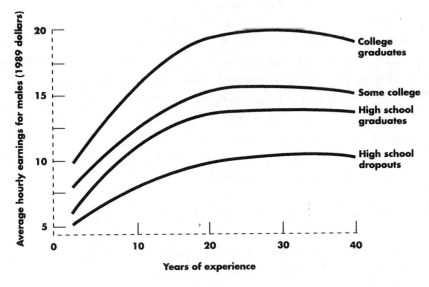

**Figure 10.11.** *Earnings by education and experience.*

## WHY WAGES RISE

Why have real wages risen a remarkable eight-fold in the past century in the United States? F. A. Harper wrote a small book in the 1950s on this subject: *Why Wages Rise* (Foundation for Economic Education, 1957). In his book, Harper makes an important distinction between legitimate ways to raise the average wage and artificial means of raising workers' income. According to Harper, real wages rise primarily because of the critical role of production and worker productivity. "Production comes first," he explains. "Higher wages come from increased output per hour of work."[3] Harper produced a graph showing a close relationship between wages per hour and output (GDP) per hour, expressed in constant dollars, between 1910 and 1960. The close relationship between wages and worker productivity has continued throughout the rest of the 20th century.

Harper's theory of wages is not new. Basically, wages have risen because U. S. businesses have increasingly earned higher profits by creating and selling more and better products and services. Rising wages result from the use of more and better tools and equipment through increased capital and technology. Capital and technology will be discussed in Chapter 11. As a result, business owners and executives have been paid record compensation and ordinary workers have also benefited. Profitable companies have reinvested much of their earnings into more capital, more training and better working conditions, and thus raised the marginal productivity of their workers—and their wages.

Higher profits translate into higher wages for workers. Suppose the labor market for software technicians is relatively close to equilibrium at $50,000 a year per worker, and Microsoft is making above average profits. Microsoft executives could keep these profits to themselves through increased salaries, bonuses, and stock options, but such a policy would be short-sighted. Successful companies recognize that their businesses must constantly reinvest their earnings and keep their best workers happy, or lose success in the long run. Microsoft, like many other companies, is in an intensely competitive industry, and workers will move to other companies if Microsoft's salaries are not competitive.

**When firms increase their profits, workers benefit in four ways:**

(1) Workers receive higher wages and more compensation, including training, better equipment, and benefits

(2) More funds are available from retained earnings to pay workers and to improve tools, equipment and training.

3  F. A. Harper, *Why Wages Rise* (Foundation for Economic Education, 1957), p. 19.

(3) Stock prices tend to rise with earnings over the long term, so that workers who participate in company stock purchase plans will see an increase in their wealth, and,

(4) More and better products and services are sold to workers as consumers.

**What are the advantages to management and owners of giving higher compensation to their workers?**

(1) Less employee turnover resulting in retention of an experienced workforce

(2) Creation of a stable corporate culture

(3) Less need for initial employee training, allowing more focus on enhanced training

## THE FORD $5-A-DAY STORY

One of the best examples of how workers benefit from capitalism is the story of Henry Ford and his decision in 1914 to pay his workers a minimum wage of $5 a day, more than double the prevalent wage rate. As a result of the huge success of the Model T, the Ford Motor Company in 1913 had doubled its profits from $13.5 million to $27 million. With these profits, Ford asked the Board to consider sharing the wealth with his employees. For four hours the Board members discussed how profits would be affected by wage increases. Charles Sorensen wrote on a blackboard a computation of cost, sales, and profit data based on wage step increases of 25 cents from the existing range of $2 to $2.50 until $5 was reached. Finally, Ford exclaimed, "Stop it Charlie, it's all settled. Five dollars a day minimum and at once."[4] The announcement made the front page and made Henry Ford an industrial messiah.

The effect of the instant pay raise was nothing short of sensational. There was a tremendous surge in product output and morale skyrocketed among Ford workers. Thousands of potential employees moved to Detroit in hopes of getting a job. Ford argued that the higher wage had two major benefits: increased efficiency at the automobile plant, and increased buying power for his workers. He was right on both counts. Employee turnover dropped significantly, and workers became more productive. The $5 wage permitted Ford workers to buy their own cars for the first time. Sales of Model Ts continued to soar as wages went up and prices declined. By 1916, over half a million cars were sold.[5]

4 Quoted in Jonathan Hughes, *The Vital Few* (Oxford University Press), p. 302.
5 For a complete retelling of the $5-a-day story, see Jonathan Hughes, *The Vital Few*, pp. 301-304.

## LABOR PRODUCTIVITY RAISES ALL WAGES:
## THE PRINCIPLE OF "MISES' BUTLER"

Ford's famous pay raise not only improved the financial condition of Ford workers, but wage levels also rose gradually throughout the U. S. during this period. As previously noted, the change in wage rates for additional workers affects the wage rates of all workers in that particular labor market. In the case of Ford's workers, new workers were not the only beneficiaries of the higher wage. All Ford workers received a raise avoiding the resentment that could occur if only new workers got $5 a day. Marginal productivity combined with total productivity raises wages.

Both total and marginal productivity result from an increase in wages. Ludwig von Mises points out this principle in his example of what is now known as the "Mises' Butler" Principle. Mises notes that many jobs, including those of barbers and butlers, have not changed over the years yet these professions have benefited tremendously from higher wages due to labor competition.

As Mises states, "That the increase in wage rates does not depend on the individual worker's 'productivity,' but on the marginal productivity of labor, is clearly demonstrated by the fact that wage rates are moving upward also for performances in which the 'productivity' of the individual has not changed at all. There are many such jobs. A barber shaves a customer today precisely in the same manner his predecessors used to shave people two hundred years ago. A butler waits at the table of the British prime minister in the same way in which once butlers served Pitt and Palmerston. In agriculture some kinds of work are still performed with the same tools in the same way in which they were performed centuries ago. Yet the wage rates earned by all such workers are today much higher than they were in the past. They are higher because they are determined by the marginal productivity of labor. The employer of a butler withholds this man from employment in a factory and must therefore pay the equivalent of the increase in output which the additional employment of one man in a factory would bring about. It is not any merit on the part of the butler that causes this rise in his wages, but the fact that the increase in capital invested surpasses the increase in the number of hands."[6]

---

6  Ludwig von Mises, *The Anti-Capitalist Mentality* (Libertarian Press, 1972), pp. 88-89.

## THE MINIMUM WAGE CONTROVERSY

Despite the tremendous rise in real wages for the average worker in the U. S. and other industrial nations, and the fact that higher marginal productivity has raised the wages of all employees, social reformers are always concerned that some workers will be left behind. To remedy this situation, legislators in many countries have passed minimum wage laws. In the United States the minimum wage has gradually been increased from 25 cents an hour in 1938 to $5.85 per hour in 2007. The federal minimum wage provisions are contained in the Fair Labor Standards Act (FLSA).

In addition, many states and localities have passed minimum wage laws above the federal rate, and some communities have imposed a "living wage" on businesses.

### What is the effect of a minimum wage?

According to standard economic analysis of the labor market, minimum wages should cause income for those still employed to increase, while at the same time putting some people out of work. Employed workers definitely benefit from a hike in the minimum wage, as long as they remain employed. A rise in the minimum wage may raise the compensation for higher-paying jobs. This is one reason why labor unions have traditionally supported minimum wage legislation. Figure 10.12 demonstrates the positive impact of a minimum wage on employed individuals and the negative impact on the unemployed.

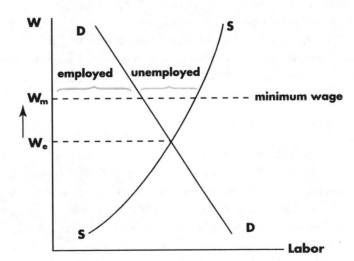

**Figure 10.12.** *Minimum wage legislation rasies wages for some—and unemployment for others.*

Nevertheless, minimum wage laws tend to hurt the younger, unskilled and inexperienced workers, depending on the level of the minimum wage. Studies have shown that the unemployment rate for teenagers, black youth, and unskilled workers in general have been consistently higher since minimum wage legislation has been in effect. The unemployment rate for U. S. teenagers is triple the national rate. (The teenage rate of unemployment was about the same as the national rate before the minimum wage law took effect in the 1930s.) Many economists blame the minimum wage, in part, for raising unemployment among the disadvantaged, emphasizing the unintended consequences of social legislation. The goal was to pay the working poor a decent wage; however, the end result is more unemployment for the working poor.

The modern welfare state has also had a tremendous impact on incentives to work, especially among the poor and minorities. Interestingly, prior to the imposition of welfare measures in the 20th century, there was no significant racial differential in unemployment.[7] The minimum wage in the U. S. had been low compared to the median wage. Today the new $5.85 minimum wage represents only 40% of the median wage in the United States of $13 an hour. France has a minimum wage representing 60% of the French median wage. Because the minimum wage in the United States rate is relatively low, studies indicate that total employment has not suffered much. In France, however, the government-mandated minimum wage may have a greater effect. France has been suffering from double digit unemployment for several years.

The rising cost of labor makes it necessary for companies to devise ways to balance the cost of meeting the minimum wage with expense reductions obtained by reducing benefits, cutting hours, reducing on-the-job training, cutting back on new employees (often indirectly discriminating against minorities), and adopting mechanized labor-saving production processes.

Legislators have considered ways to minimize the distortions of minimum wage laws, such as adopting lower minimum wage rates for teenagers or part-time workers. But such measures have been opposed by labor unions and other special interest groups.

## CAN LABOR UNIONS RAISE WAGES?

There is little doubt that unions have won higher wages and better working conditions and benefits for their members. Several studies by labor economists have concluded that unions have raised members' wages 15 to 30% higher than similar non-union workers, depending on the industry. But there's a downside. By artificially raising wages, business costs increase and the number of jobs declines. Union benefits come at the expense of consumers, non-union workers, the jobless, and owners of corporations.

7   Richard K. Vedder and Lowell E. Gallaway, *Out of Work: Unemployment and Government in Twentieth-Century America* (Independent Institute, 1993), p. 294.

The impact of labor unions is not much different from minimum wage legislation, except that it affects more workers. Unions have been celebrated as fearless champions of the downtrodden worker against the faceless, cold-hearted big corporation, but in economic terms, unions are defined as monopolistic cartels that raise wages above competitive levels. Figure 10.13 illustrates the impact of labor unions.

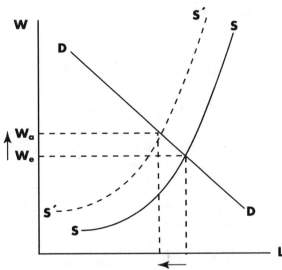

**Figure 10.13.** *Unions limit employment and increase wages.*

Labor unions have relied heavily on government protection to raise wage rates and establish rigid work rules. The first major union movement came in 1881 when the American Federation of Labor (AFL) was organized under Samuel Gompers. Instead of promoting socialism and nationalization of American big business, Gompers favored business unionism, with an emphasis on improving the economic status of workers: higher wages, shorter hours, more vacations, and better working conditions. He also pushed for collective bargaining, requiring corporations to negotiate agreements for the entire workforce exclusively with a single union.

Gompers created the AFL with high-minded ideals. In an 1898 speech, he declared:

> "To protect the workers in their inalienable rights to a higher and better life; to protect them, not only as equals before the law, but also in their health, their homes, their firesides, their liberties as men, as workers, and as citizens; to overcome and conquer prejudice and antagonism; to secure to them the right to life, and the opportunity to maintain that life; the right to be full sharers in the abundance which is the result of their brain and brawn, and the civilization of which they are the founders and the mainstay....The attainment of these is the glorious mission of the trade union."

Worker unions, including the Congress of Industrial Organizations (CIO), grew rapidly, first as a result of violence against workers at Carnegie's Homestead plant in Pittsburgh in 1892, and later during the two world wars and the Great Depression of the 1930s. The monopoly power of the unions was enhanced by a series of Federal interventions:

- The Railway Act of 1926
- The Davis-Bacon Act of 1931
- The Norris-LaGuardia Act of 1932
- The National Labor Relations Act of 1935
- The Walsh-Healy Act of 1936
- The Fair Labor Standards Act of 1938

These legislative acts required business and government to deal with unions rather than their non-union competitors, and confirmed the right to strike. In many states, all workers at a company are required to join a union. Union officials can force payment of compulsory union dues, which can be used for political purposes.

Unions became so powerful and so big under these series of government acts that Congress became concerned with the increasing number of strikes and violence associated with the unions. Moreover, unions did not appear to do much for the advancement of blacks, women, and other minorities. In fact, the "union label" started in the 1880s as a backlash against garments being made by the Chinese. Economist Ray Marshall, secretary of labor under President Jimmy Carter, noted that unions excluded blacks from membership in the 1930s and 1940s. Booker T. Washington opposed unions and W. E. B. DuBois called unions the greatest enemy of the black working class.[8]

In response to cited "unfair labor practices" and excessive power being granted to unions, Congress passed the Taft-Hartley Act in 1947. Specifically, the act permits state governments to ban the union shop, which requires employees to join a union. Known as the "right to work" law, workers are not required to join a union in certain states. The Taft-Hartley Act also provides for court injunctions and an 80-day "cooling off" period to delay strikes that threaten the national interest.

---

8   Morgan O. Reynolds, "Labor Unions," *The Fortune Encyclopedia of Economics*, ed. by David R. Henderson (Warner Books, 1993), p. 496.

Labor unions have gone through a rise and fall. See figure 10.14 below.

In 1930, unions had enrolled just under 7 percent of the U.S. labor force. By 1933 this figure had slipped to barely above 5 percent. Unionization took off with the New Deal, reaching almost 16 percent of the labor force by 1939. It then drifted irregularly upward to a peak of about 25 to 26 percent of all workers in the mid-1950s from which it has since fallen more or less steadily back to 16 percent in 1991.

*Source:* U.S. Department of Labor, Bureau of Labor Statistics. *Employment and Earnings,* January issues, various years.

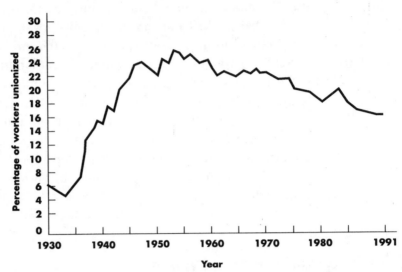

**Figure 10.14.** *The rise and fall of union membership in the United States.*

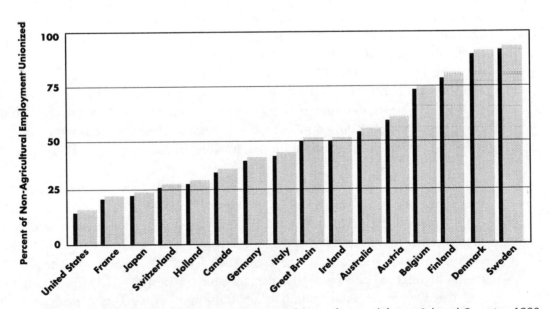

**Figure 10.15.** *Union membership as a percentage of the nonfarm work forces: Selected Countries, 1993*
*Source:* Bureau of Labor Statistics, *Employment and Earnings,* January 1988 and *The Economist,* August 1980.
Total union membership in the United States has been falling in recent years and union membership as a percentage of the work force has been declining for over three decades.
These trends in the United States are counter to those occurring in several other developed nations.

The influence and membership of labor unions increased sharply during the 1930s and 1940s and, for a while, appeared to be headed toward total dominance of the U. S. labor market as in other countries. However, since the 1950s, union membership has gradually deteriorated, and since the 1980s, has fallen sharply. Unions have tended to do best in heavily regulated, monopolistic environments. Unions represent garment and textile workers, building trades people, airline pilots, merchant seamen, teamsters, rail workers, postal employees, auto and steel workers, teachers, and public servants. But unions have a harder time organizing among small businesses, those who are self-employed, and the service industry. These areas have all grown dramatically since the 1970s. As a result, union power has been undermined, and today only an estimated 10% of the U. S. workforce belongs to a union. Union power is much stronger in Europe and Latin America than in the United States.

## EMPLOYMENT AND UNEMPLOYMENT

In a free economy, change is inevitable. The freer the economy, the more changes occur. A dynamic economy witnesses new goods replacing old products, new companies competing against established firms, businesses expanding and contracting. Harvard economist Joseph Schumpeter called this process of expansion and contraction "creative destruction."

When it comes to jobs, Schumpeter's label is appropriate. The dynamic market economy is not only a job creator, it's also a job destroyer. With frequent changes in technology, consumer preferences, competition between domestic and foreign companies, and shifts in population, it is natural to expect some workers to be displaced, transferred, fired, and retired as businesses come and go, expand and contract.

In a growing, dynamic economy, total employment is usually on the rise. Good economists not only watch the unemployment figures, they also check the total employment figures as an indicator of national well-being. Often the establishment media tends to ignore the positive employment news and focus on the negative unemployment figures. "AT&T to Cut 20,000 Jobs," the headline might read. The media highlighted corporate "downsizing" during the 1990s. Layoffs are big news, and can have a devastating impact on thousands of workers getting pink slips. Meanwhile, many companies may be adding jobs, a few hundred here and there. At the same time, small business and self-employed businesses may grow rapidly with little publicity. It all adds up to a net increase in national employment, but the media tend to favor the big downsizing events rather than the small-but-more-common upsizing. (For more discussion of corporate downsizing, see Chapter 4.)

## JOB CREATION AND DESTRUCTION IN THE UNITED STATES

| Industry | Downsizers | Jobs Lost | Upsizers | Jobs Gained |
|---|---|---|---|---|
| General Merchandisers | Sears<br>K-Mart | −131,000<br>−65,000 | Wal-Mart<br>Dayton Hudson<br>J.C. Penney | +624,000<br>+90,000<br>+59,000 |
| Specialist Retailers | Woolworth | −37,000 | Limited<br>Gap | +97,800<br>+55,000 |
| Mail, Package, and Freight Delivery | Federal Express | −33,988 | UPS | 183,600 |
| Food and Drugstores | Safeway | −45,385 | Publix<br>Food Lion<br>Albertson's<br>Walgreen<br>Kroger | +62,902<br>+56,081<br>+61,000<br>+39,800<br>+33,849 |
| Telecommunications | AT&T<br>GTE | −207,200<br>−81,033 | Lucent Technologies<br>MCI<br>Sprint<br>Bell South | +124,000<br>+42,840<br>+20,609<br>+14,259 |
| Computers, Software, Data processing | IBM | −164,920 | Seagate Technology<br>Intel<br>Microsoft<br>Sun Microsystems | +82,300<br>+27,200<br>+19,563<br>+16,300 |
| Aerospace/Defense | | | Lockheed Martin<br>General Dynamics | +102,200<br>+80,200 |
| Electronics and Electrical Equipment | General Electric | −65,000 | Motorola | +48,800 |
| Entertainment | | | Viacom<br>Disney | +79,100<br>+75,000 |

Source: Michael Cox and Richard Alm, *Myths of Rich and Poor,* Table 6.1.

The news media are also short-sighted when they highlight job losses due to military cutbacks or plant closings. They focus on the market's ability to destroy jobs, but not the market's ability to create jobs. Recent studies by the General Accounting Office demonstrate that regions with high plant closings are also regions with high rates of plant openings. The net effects of job destruction/creation activity are better working conditions, more enjoyable jobs, and a higher standard of living. As Richard B. McKenzie concludes, "The day the country no longer has to face adjustment problems will probably be the day its people can no longer look forward to a better economic future."[9]

9   Richard B. McKenzie, *The American Job Machine* (Universal Books, 1988), p. 15.

## TEMPORARY UNEMPLOYMENT AND THE NATURAL RATE

When supply and demand shift in a dynamic economy, jobs come and go. Cars replaced the horse and buggy. Oil took over the petroleum market from kerosene. Personal computers took the place of typewriters. Volumes of mail are sent electronically over the Internet rather than through the post office. Television sets are made in Asia rather than the United States. New technology, changing tastes, and new competitive forces, both here and abroad, will continue to disrupt the labor market.

A changing economy also results in changes in the job market which results in temporary or permanent unemployment for millions of citizens. It may take a few weeks, several months or longer for an unemployed person to find another job. The percentage of temporarily unemployed workers looking for a job is known as the natural rate of unemployment. The natural rate of unemployment is a term coined by Milton Friedman to refer to the lowest sustainable unemployment rate in an economy.

In the Employment Act of 1946, Congress supported the goal of full employment, but obviously full employment is impossible in a free society. Even in a robust, growing economy, where plenty of work is available, people will be changing jobs, either through career changes, downsizing, new hires, firings, etc. Most economists now agree that there exists a certain level of temporary, unavoidable unemployment that government cannot and should not eliminate however painful as it may be for individuals. It is from this pool of labor that workers in new occupations are taken. Some economists favor institutional changes designed to lower the natural rate of unemployment, but such changes may be difficult and even detrimental.

No one knows for sure exactly what this natural rate is, but most economists think the rate is around 3-4%.

## PROBLEM IN DEFINING UNEMPLOYMENT

When the unemployment rate exceeds the natural rate, government leaders and the media express alarm, worrying that the nation might be hit with a recession or that job opportunities may dry up. Consequently, the monthly unemployment rate is highlighted in the news.

How is the unemployment rate detrimental? Each month the U. S. Department of Labor conducts a random sampling of about 60,000 households. Anyone 16 or older who is actively looking for work during the most recent four weeks is considered unemployed. That number is divided by the total labor force. The total labor force includes all those who currently have jobs, plus the unemployed.

The national unemployment rate has been as low as 4% (during the 1950s-60s) and as high as 25% (during the Great Depression of the 1930s). In the 1990s the U. S. unemployment rate steadily declined to under 5%. However, unemployment in Europe — which used to be substantially less than the U. S. rate — rose dramatically during most of the 1990s and reached double-digit levels in the mid-1990s.

Many economists are critical of the way the national unemployment rate is calculated. First, they point out that the unemployment rate may understate the true level of unemployment because it does not include discouraged individuals who have stopped looking for jobs.

In many countries, individuals may be listed as employed who are, in fact, underemployed. The underemployed are either working unproductively, or people who are working part-time but want to work full-time. This criticism applies to employment statistics in developing nations where governments often hire citizens to work at useless jobs in order to meet their public goal of full employment. For years, the leaders of the Soviet Union proudly proclaimed full employment in their nation, but we now know that much of the work was anything but gainful in the sense of meeting employee requirements for earning enough money to meet basic needs.

On the other hand, unemployment statistics may overstate the level of unemployment because official statistics often ignore the underground economy, black markets, and small businesses. Many underemployed workers may actually have moonlight jobs or other sources of income, but keep it quiet in order to qualify for unemployment compensation or welfare.

Another criticism of the official unemployment rate is that it provides only one simple statistic to reflect what is happening in a dynamic economy. Aggregate economic statistics such as Gross Domestic Product (GDP), the official interest rate, or unemployment rate often do a poor job of telling the complete economic story. For example, while the nation's GDP may be flat, the state of California may be booming. The prime rate (the interest rate banks charge big corporations) may be 8%, but what the mortgage rate, the auto car loan rate, or the interest rate charged on credit cards may reflect a different economic picture. All these interest rates may give a better indication of economic activity than a simple aggregate statistic. Instead of a single unemployment rate, perhaps a better indicator of job-seeking is to know what the unemployment rate is for those seeking jobs for various lengths of time: how many people are unemployed for a month, six months, or a year? Surprisingly, in periods of expansion and contraction the rate of long-term unemployment (those searching for a job for a year or more) is relatively low and stable (around 1% of the labor force). Such a statistic gives the unemployed some comfort in knowing that almost everyone (99%) who loses a job finds another one within a year as long as they don't get discouraged and stop looking. (See figure 10.16)

231

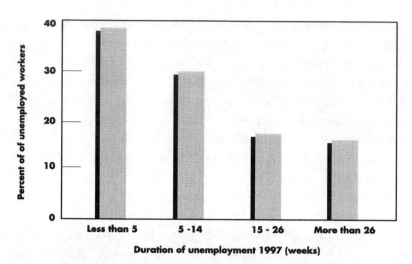

**Figure 10.16.** *Most unemployment in the United States is short-term.*

## REAL WAGE RATES AND THE THEORY OF UNEMPLOYMENT

In their study, *Out of Work*, economists Richard Vedder and Lowell Gallaway demonstrate that persistently high unemployment is due to real wage rates being kept artificially above the market (natural) rate. "Just as a surplus of wheat exists if the prevailing price is above the equilibrium level that equates the quantity supplied with the quantity demanded, so there is a surplus of labor—unemployment—when the prevailing price, or wage, of labor exceeds the equilibrium level that eliminates unemployment."[10]

Figure 10.17 below demonstrates the classic model of unemployment.

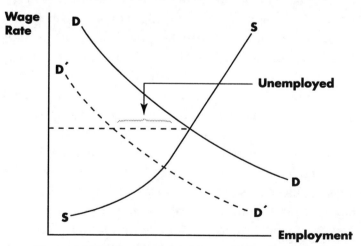

**Figure 10.17.** *Real wages and the market for unemployed labor.*

10  Vedder and Gallaway, *Out of Work* (Independent Institute, 1993), p. 14. For an earlier treatment of the classical model of unemployment, see W. H. Hutt, *The Theory of Idle Resources*, 2nd ed. (Liberty Press, 1977).

Vedder and Galloway developed an econometric model that predicts rates of unemployment in the U.S. during the 20th century based upon above-average real wages. Figure 10.18 below, indicates that their model is accurate.

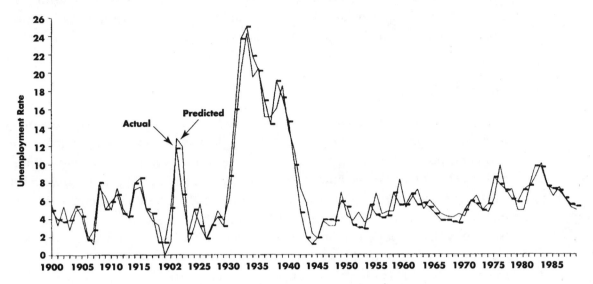

**Figure 10.18.** *Actual vs. predicted unemployment, 1900-1990.*
*Source: Vedder and Gallaway,* Out of Work.

## "STICKY WAGES": WHO'S TO BLAME?

In a free labor market where wages are flexible, unemployment tends to disappear fairly quickly during a recession. The key factor here is wage flexibility. In the past, wages have been known to be "sticky," and do not fall sufficiently during a recession to restore full employment.

The question is, who is responsible for wage stickiness? Government policies often encourage wage inflexibility through pro-union legislation, unemployment compensation and welfare plans.

It is important to note that of the three factors of production—land, labor and capital—labor is inherently the most adaptable to a changing economic climate. Capital goods are designed to be specific and heterogeneous. A tractor does not have too many alternative uses. Tractors cannot be easily converted into sedans to take the children to school. Similarly, an oil rig can be used for only one purpose. If there is no demand for it, it may sit idle for years. Land may be more flexible and non-specific, but there is a limited possibility of alternative use if there is a building on it. An office building cannot suddenly be converted to a factory.

233

But labor is different. Human capital is always relatively nonspecific. Though wage-earners and professional workers are trained to handle specific tasks, they can also perform a variety of additional tasks and can be retrained to accomplish other jobs more fitting to the new economic situation. Human capital is not inflexible the way fixed capital and land are. In an unregulated market, the unemployment rate of labor may recover much more quickly in a recession than either land or capital.

## LABOR-MANAGEMENT RELATIONS

The level of unemployment is also affected by the type of labor-management relations. Companies and countries differ in their approach to employment and compensation of employees. There seem to be several options, each with benefits and disadvantages. On the one extreme, labor-management policies in some countries favor fixed high wages, generous benefits and guaranteed lifetime employment. In an economic downturn, workers under this system get the same wage and benefits with no layoffs. On the other extreme, some companies favor flexible wages and the right to hire or fire workers at will. In a recession they may opt to reduce wages and benefits, or layoff workers, or do a combination of both.

Which is the best policy? Among large U. S. corporations, such as the automobile industry, the traditional labor-management approach has been to establish inflexible wages/salaries through long-term contracts with labor unions while permitting temporary layoffs during downturns.

IBM used to be an exception. Until the early 1990s, "Big Blue" had a strict policy of paying high salaries and never laying off workers. IBM used to boast that it had never fired a full-time employee since its inception in the 1930s. But IBM, losing its competitive edge in the 1980s, was forced to alter its long-standing labor policy and dismissed thousands of workers. Its downsizing decision worked, and now IBM is profitable and hiring employees again.

## THE JAPANESE MANAGEMENT MODEL

The Japanese management model is also flexible, but in a different way. Major Japanese corporations hire workers for life, but wages/salaries vary depending on the profitability of the company. Through their bonus system, total compensation in Japan fluctuates with the company's profits. Bonuses are paid in cash every six months in addition to wages. Bonuses increase when the company is doing well and decrease when the company is doing poorly. Flexible compensation through the bonus system allows Japanese companies to minimize layoffs. During a recession, if the Japanese company is losing money, employees maintain employment, but earn less. According to economist Robert Osaki, the Japanese bonus system is superior to the American labor-management system because it encourages company loyalty. Workers share in the fortunes of the company, in both good and bad times. "Semiannual adjustment of bonuses enables [Japanese workers] to operate under a flexible-wage system instead of the more constricting fixed-wage associated with American management."[11]

Some U.S. corporations have adopted this Japanese-style approach. For example, Magma Copper, one of the largest copper mining companies in the U. S., adopted a policy of linking employee compensation to the price of copper; the higher the copper price, the more workers were paid. The idea is that higher copper prices mean higher profits for the company (assuming costs stay constant). As the company earns more, it can afford to pay its workers more. In return for a flexible wage policy, Magma Copper employees are guaranteed employment without the threat of future layoffs.

In reviewing the various approaches to labor-management relations, the lesson is clear: in a dynamic, global economy, firms must not be restricted by inflexible labor rules. The worst condition and a recipe for failure is where workers are guaranteed a fixed wage and employment for life. It is better to have either a variable wage policy or temporary layoff plan, or both.

## THE STATE'S ROLE IN UNEMPLOYMENT

What role does government play in reducing or increasing unemployment? According to Vedder's and Gallaway's classic labor model, only government policies can create an environment of excessive unemployment—due to unemployment insurance, social security, minimum wages, trade-union collective bargaining, affirmative action, and other forms of activist interventionism. Monetary and fiscal policies can also contribute to employment disequilibrium. According to Vedder and Gallaway, in all four cases of high unemployment during the 20th century (1920-21, 1929-33, 1937-38, and 1981-82), "all may be traced in some substantial way to the effects of government interventionism."[12]

## CASE STUDY: THE UNEMPLOYMENT CRISIS IN EUROPE

The recent steady rise in the unemployment rate in Europe has worried economists and government leaders. Europe used to have extremely low rates of unemployment, lower than the U. S., but that changed in the 1990s. By the late 1990s the average unemployment rate in Europe exceeded 11% compared to 5% in the U. S. and 3% in Japan. (See figure 10.19.) What is the cause of this increase? Economists point to several factors at work.

11  Robert Osaki, *Human Capitalism: The Japanese Enterprise System as World Model* (Kodansha International, 1991), p. 103.
12  Vedder and Gallaway, *Out of Work*, p. 292.

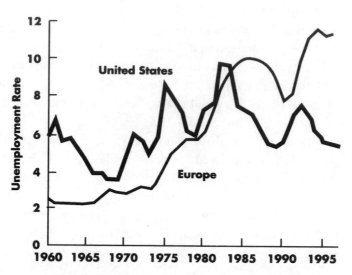

**Figure 10.19.** *Unemployment in the U.S. and Europe.*

First, Europe has some of the strictest labor laws and regulations, including minimum wages, collective bargaining, and labor-management restrictions. In Belgium the minimum wage is E1,210 per month; Germany and France have recently reduced the official work week; and Spain and Italy impose severe restrictions against firing workers. In Italy an employer must give up to six months notice before dismissal. In order to protect workers from sudden unemployment, Spain passed legislation making it virtually impossible for employers to fire workers. The unintended effect is unemployment. If workers cannot be fired, there is a risk associated with hiring them. Spain's labor law dealing with employers' obligations to the workforce is 600 pages long. Spain's unemployment rate rose to 25% in the mid-1990s. Portugal, on the other hand, has a less regulated labor market and an unemployment rate of less than 5%.

Second, European governments raise labor costs for companies in the form of mandatory benefits such as health care, pensions, unemployment and disability compensation, and paid vacations. European payroll taxes, including social security and personal income tax, are some of the highest in the world. High labor costs discourage businesses from hiring new workers. As Edmund S. Phelps, economics professor at Columbia University, states, "Nearly every European country has brought much of its unemployment on itself—through its punishing taxation of labor....Big increases in payroll and personal income taxes in most countries have been mass job-killers."[13] There is a silver lining to this unemployment cloud: a dramatic increase in small business, self-employment, and the underground economy, all in an effort to beat the taxman and regulators. This same phenomenon occurs in the U. S., Canada and Latin America.

13 Edmund S. Phelps, "Summiteers: Your Taxes Kill Jobs," *Wall Street Journal*, March 14, 1994.

Third, Europe offers one of the most generous welfare programs in the world, encouraging citizens to stay on welfare and avoid looking for work.

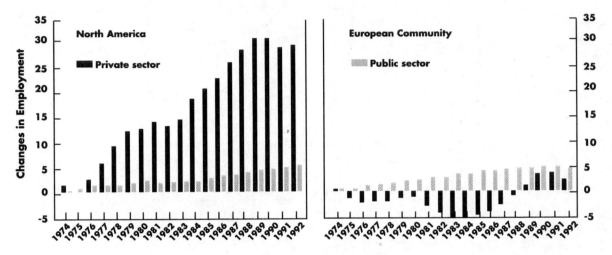

**Figure 10.20.** *Cumulative employment growth in the public and private sectors, United States and Europe. (change in millions since 1973)*

## CYCLICAL UNEMPLOYMENT AND THE PHILLIPS CURVE

Since World War II it has been the policy of the U. S. government to guarantee full employment. The Employment Act of 1946 and the Full Employment and Balanced Growth Act of 1987 have committed the government to this goal. As Campbell McConnell writes, "The government's obligation is to augment private spending so that total spending—private and public—will be sufficient to generate full employment."[14]

The idea that government needs to inflate its spending and employment in order to stimulate the private economy has its modern origin in Keynesian economics (see Chapter 22, "National Debt and the Federal Deficit"). In the late 1950s, British economist A. W. Phillips developed a model showing an inverse relationship between unemployment and changes in nominal wages in the United Kingdom over a hundred year period.[15] His model, now known as the Phillips Curve, created a sensation in the 1960s, giving support to Keynesian policies of deficit spending to reach full employment. The Phillips Curve (Figure 10.21) suggests that increasing money wages through inflation could reduce unemployment. Or, conversely, any effort by government to curtail inflation would pay a price—higher unemployment, at least in the short term.

14  Campbell McConnell and Stanley Brue, *Economics*, 11th ed. (McGraw-Hill, 1989), p. 93.
15  A. W. Phillips, "The relationship between unemployment and the rate of change of money wage rates in the United Kingdom, 1861-1957," *Economica* (November, 1958).

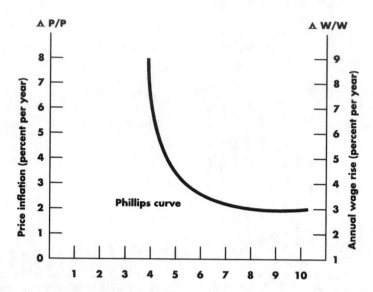

**Figure 10.21.** *The Phillips Curve: The alleged trade-off.*

## BETWEEN INFLATION AND UNEMPLOYMENT

The idealized Phillips Curve seemed to explain the economy in the 1960s in the U. S. and Europe. Inflation rose in the 1960s and unemployment stayed low. The inflationary recession of the 1970s changed everything. Unemployment rose along with inflation, an event the Phillips Curve failed to predict. The Phillips Curve broke down and became the Phillips Confusion (Figure 10.22), showing either no relationship at all or multiple relationships between inflation and unemployment.

Why did the Phillips Curve fall apart? In the short term, the Phillips Curve can accurately predict the effects of an inflationary boom. If the economy is coming out of a recession with some level of unemployed resources, an inflationary government policy can cause rising prices and falling unemployment during this economic boom and recovery. Eventually the boom in production and employment must end as the government stops its inflationary process. In the short run, higher inflation reduces unemployment, but in the long run it causes higher unemployment.

In the late 1960s, Milton Friedman argued that in the long term the Phillips Curve is an illusion. A dose of inflation can cut unemployment temporarily, but as soon as people become aware of what is happening and anticipate rising prices, inflation loses its power to stimulate economic activity. Empirical work done by Milton Friedman and Edmund Phelps confirmed this effect. "In my opinion," Friedman concluded, "there is no perpetual trade off between inflation and unemployment. The trade off is between acceleration of inflation and unemployment, which means that the real trade off is between unemployment now and unemployment later."[16]

16 Milton Friedman, *Dollars and Deficits* (New York: Prentice-Hall, 1968), p. 159.

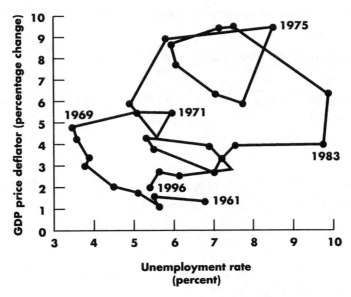

**Figure 10.22.** *The undoing of the Phillips Curve.*

## THE PHILLIPS CURVE AND THE NEW ECONOMY

Since the early l990s, advocates of the Phillips Curve have made a new argument: lower unemployment and stronger-than-expected economic growth must cause a return of price inflation in the United States. Keynesian economists and the established media constantly warn that a booming economy will put pressure on wages and reignite price inflation. Yet so far, price inflation has not occurred. Supply-side economists have pointed out that increased global capacity, worldwide competition and productivity gains occurring from the use of the Internet and telecommunications have created an economic boom without consumer price inflation.

## SOUND LABOR ECONOMICS

This long chapter has only scratched the surface of the issues of labor and its role in the economic process. The essential principles of sound labor economics have been well established:

(1) Ample work and jobs will always be available as long as the market for labor is free and unregulated, so that wages can reach their market level.

(2) Real wages rise through increased productivity of labor—through education, training, technology, and capital investment.

(3) Government intervention imposes restrictions on the labor market and can only make matters worse in the long run.

## SUMMARY

**These are the main points covered in Chapter 10:**

1. Average real wages (after inflation) for Americans rose eight-fold in the 20th century, while working hours declined 50%, reflecting a sharply rising standard of living for most Americans.

2. Wages are determined at their marginal productivity of labor; that is, how much each additional worker contributes to the final product. Higher productivity comes from higher profits, education and training, and investment capital.

3. Leisure is a desirable good. Workers must engage in a trade-off between more work and more leisure time.

4. A competitive labor market tends toward "equal pay for equal work" — a uniform wage rate for similar occupations.

5. Labor-management relations need to be flexible, either in the form of variable wage rates or hiring/firing policies. Guaranteed wages and lifetime employment are likely to undermine company profitability in the long run.

6. Comparable worth, minimum wage laws, pro-labor legislation and other interferences by government benefit some at the expense of others; such actions cause disequilibrium and unemployment in the labor market.

7. There is an increasing premium for education in the labor market, and the lifetime income differential is widening between educational levels.

8. The market is both a job creator and a job destroyer, but on net balance it is a job creator. It is impossible to achieve full employment at all times in a dynamic economy.

9. There may be a short-term trade-off between inflation and unemployment (the Phillips Curve), but in the long run, more inflation means more unemployment down the road.

## IMPORTANT TERMS TO KNOW

Creative destruction

Classic model of unemployment

Comparable worth

Japanese bonus system

Keynesian economics underemployment

Marginal productivity of labor

Mises' butler

Natural rate of unemployment

Phillips curve

Sticky wages

## INFLUENTIAL ECONOMIST

### JOHN BATES CLARK AND THE MARGINAL PRODUCTIVITY OF LABOR

**Name: John Bates Clark (1847-1938)**

**Background:** This long-time professor of economics at Columbia University (1896-1923) was the leading American economist at the turn of the century, famous for developing the marginal productivity theory of labor. Born in Providence, Rhode Island, he studied at Amherst College and went to Germany for three years where he came under the influence of the German Historical School. After teaching at Smith College and Johns Hopkins University, he began his professorship at Columbia.

**Major Works:** Clark's most important textbooks are *The Distribution of Wealth* (1899) and *Essentials of Economic Theory* (1907), wherein he develops the marginal productivity theory of income distribution.

**Contributions:** Clark argued with other economists and social thinkers, including Karl Marx, Eugen Böhm-Bawerk, and Henry George. His marginal productivity theory was a rebuttal of Karl Marx's exploitation theory. Marx argued that capitalism robs labor of its rightful fruits. Clark responded by saying that payment to capital, like land and labor, is determined by its marginal productivity and, therefore, there is no surplus value expropriated from labor as Marx alleged.

241

Clark took issue with Böhm-Bawerk and the Austrian theory of capital. The Austrians viewed capital as a heterogeneous stock of intermediate goods used to produce final consumer goods over time. By contrast, Clark envisioned capital as a permanent fund, like a reservoir, providing a perpetual income stream. Clark argued that there was no "waiting" in the production process, no "period of production" and, therefore, no "business cycle" as the Austrians maintained. Today the time-structure of the capital stock is considered a significant element in business-cycle theory, and as Mark Blaug points out, "Clark's theory of the perfect synchronization of production and consumption now seems to be untenable." (*Economists Before Keynes*, p. 52.)

Finally, Clark was a chief critic of Henry George's land tax idea. Land, like the other factors of production, earns its own marginal product and does not deserve to be singled out as monopolistic. Interestingly, Clark was one of those economists who gradually shifted ground over his career from a socialist sympathizer to a believer in free-market capitalism.

**John Bates Clark Medal:** Clark, one of the founders of the American Economic Association, is the namesake for one of the most prestigious awards in economics. Each year an up-and-coming economist under the age of 40 is given this award. Paul A. Samuelson was awarded the first medal in 1947, given on the 100th anniversary of Clark's birth. Others to receive the award have included Kenneth Boulding, Milton Friedman, James Tobin, Kenneth J. Arrow, Lawrence R. Klein, Robert M. Solow, Gary Becker, Martin Feldstein, Joseph Stiglitz, Paul Krugman, Lawrence Summers, and David Card. Many of these economists later earned the Nobel Prize.

## PROBLEMS TO PONDER

1. Paul Krugman, an MIT economist, states, "At the heart of capitalism's inhumanity—and no sensible person will deny that the market is an amoral and often cruelly capricious master—is the fact that it treats labor as a commodity." (*The Accidental Theorist*, Norton, 1998, p. 15) Is it true that capitalist employers treat their workers as "commodities"? In what sense is the marketplace "cruelly capricious"? Give examples.

Contrast Professor Krugman's views with those of Bill Marriott, president of Marriott Corporation, who said:

"One of the important things...is [to] counter the notion that big corporations are faceless machines....When employees know that their problems will be taken seriously, that their ideas and insights matter, they're more comfortable and confident. In turn, they're better equipped to deliver their best on the job and to the customer. Everyone wins: the company, the employee, the customer. The philosophy of putting employees first is particularly important in our industry, because Marriott is in the people business, not just the service business....I've said again and again that our associates [employees] are number one. It won't hurt to say it one more time. Without the hard work and dedication of our team, Marriott wouldn't exist. Period. That's why taking care of our employees is a top priority for the organization." (*The Spirit to Serve*, HarperBusiness, 1997, pp. 5, 35, 126-127)

Are employees treated as "commodities" at Marriott? Is their labor policy "cruelly capricious" or "caring"? Is Marriott the exception to the rule among big companies?

2. Paul Krugman also argues, "An unsold commodity is a nuisance, an unemployed worker a tragedy; it is terribly unjust that such tragedies are created every day by new technologies, changing tastes, and the ever-shifting flows of world trade." (*The Accidental Theorist*, p. 15). Is losing one's job a "tragedy" or is it an "opportunity" to change jobs? Interview several people who have lost their jobs over the years. Ask them if their job loss was a "tragedy" or "blessing in disguise." Can people gain through adversity?

3. In 1998, actor Jerry Seinfeld allegedly turned down $5 million per episode of the popular TV show, *Seinfeld*, because he wanted to do something else, probably less profitable. Did Seinfeld make a rational economic decision?

4. Following the success of the $5-a-day wage, Henry Ford became an advocate of so-called "Vulgar Keynesianism," the idea that increasing the wage bill would stimulate spending and bring the economy out of a slump. In 1930, during the Great Depression, Ford was a strong supporter of maintaining wages. As he had written earlier, "If we can distribute high wages, then the money is going to be spent and it will serve to make storekeepers and distributors and manufacturers and workers on other lines more prosperous, and their prosperity will be reflected in our sales." (Henry Ford, *My Life and Work*, 1922, p. 124) However, Ford's plan failed in the early 1930s, and his company eventually had to reduce wages and lay off workers.

Why did Ford's wage increase work in 1913, but not in 1930? (Hint: Which comes first, increased wages or increased profits? See a discussion of this issue in Mark Skousen, *The Structure of Production* (New York University Press, 1990, pp. 340-341).

6. Does every citizen have a "right" to a job? A right to education, to health care, or to food? How should economic rights be defined? Charles W. Baird, an economist at California State University East Bay, states, "Is there any job-related human right in the Jeffersonian sense? Yes. It is the right of all individuals to offer to buy or sell labor services at any terms they choose....Suppose Jones claims a right to a job. If that claim means that Jones will be employed anytime he wishes to be (on whatever terms he wishes?), there must be some other person, Smith, who has the duty to provide the job. But, then, Smith does not have the same right." (*The Freeman*, October, 1996, p. 667)

   How do you respond to Professor Baird's assertion that people have a right to offer their services, but can't demand that someone hire them?

7. Ludwig von Mises declares, "Unemployment in the unhampered market is always voluntary....There is always for each type of labor a rate at which all those eager to work can get a job." (*Human Action*, 1966, p. 599) Do you agree? If a worker is fired, what would it take for him to get another job the next day? In a recession or depression, is it possible for all workers to obtain work by lowering their wage demands sufficiently? Since there is always work to be done (remember what we said in chapter 2 about unlimited wants and limited resources), how can unemployment ever be involuntary?

8. *The New York Times* (January 14, 1987) ran an editorial with a startling headline: "The Right Minimum Wage: $0.00." It stated: "The idea of using a minimum wage to overcome poverty is old, honorable—and fundamentally flawed." The Times noted that minimum wages often go to teenagers who do not come from poor households. The editorial suggested that a minimum wage law simply raises the cost of labor, amounting to a hidden tax. A better solution, it opines, would be an anti-poverty program that deals directly with individuals making less than the poverty level. Do you agree? How would you seek to help the working poor?

9. In his book, *Rewarding Work: How to Restore Participating and Self-Support to Free Enterprise* (Harvard University Press, 1997), economist Edmund Phelps offers this plan to help the working poor: apply tax credits for "qualified employers" or hire disadvantaged people for "eligible jobs." Evaluate this plan in terms of market incentives to work and current welfare programs. Is the Phelps' plan an improvement over current government policies?

10. In her provocative work, *The Overworked American: The Unexpected Decline in Leisure* (Basic Books, 1991), Harvard economist Juliet B. Schor states, "In the last twenty years the amount of time Americans have spent at their jobs has risen steadily. Each year the change is small, amounting to about nine hours, or slightly more than one additional day of work." She says that U. S. manufacturing employees work 320 hours longer a year—the equivalent of two months—than their counterparts in Germany and France. She blames the demands of employers and the addictive nature of consumption for the decline in leisure. Her solution is for the government to intervene, cutting back the work week, requiring corporations to pay overtime in time off, not money, and enhancing the feasibility of part-time work. Are people you know spending more time at work? Why do they work overtime? Survey several workers and see what their reaction would be to these proposals. To what extent is government policy such as higher taxes responsible for less leisure time and both husband and wife working?

11. *The Economist* (May 30, 1998, p. 74) states: "Secretaries in investment banks tend to earn far more than secretaries in hotels....Numerous studies, looking as far back as the 1920s, show that industries where profits and average productivity are higher tend to pay all their workers more." Does this violate the principle of one-wage in economics, that all firms should pay workers doing identical jobs the same wage? How do you explain this disparity? Consider the Japanese bonus system in your answer.

## RECOMMENDED READING

- Richard K. Vedder and Lowell E. Gallaway, *Out of Work: Unemployment and Government in Twentieth-Century America* (Independent Institute, 1993). Vedder and Gallaway apply the classic model of marginal productivity to the U. S. labor market in the 20th century. Superior work.

- Hans Sennholz, *The Politics of Unemployment* (Libertarian Press, 1987). A revealing discussion of wage levels, the cause of unemployment, the role of labor unions, and labor laws. Professor Sennholz has a fascinating chapter on how unemployment is treated in college textbooks.

- Robert Osaki, *Human Capitalism: The Japanese Enterprise System as World Model* (Kodansha International, 1991). Professor Osaki raises several major points about the benefits of the bonus system, permanent employment, and other aspects of the Japanese labor-management relationship.

*Chapter 11*

# CAPITAL AND INTEREST

*"A country becomes more prosperous in proportion to the
rise in the invested capital per unit of its population."*

— LUDWIG VON MISES
*Economic Policy*, p. 14

During World War II, Japanese Emperor Hirohito asked his Naval Chief of Staff, Admiral Nagano, "Why did it take the Americans only a few days to build an airbase and the Japanese more than a month?" The answer was clear. The Americans had the capital necessary to build an airbase, while the Japanese only had manpower. The United States had a vast array of bulldozers and earth-moving equipment, while Japan had to rely on muscle-power.[1] This advantage became more apparent as the war progressed, and it is the primary reason why the Americans eventually claimed victory.

This story demonstrates the value of capital in a wartime economy.

## THE STORY OF HONG KONG AND SWITZERLAND

The economic histories of Hong Kong and Switzerland also illustrate the value of capital.

Hong Kong in 1842 had been involved in years of Chinese efforts to keep British merchants from smuggling opium into China which led to the Opium War in 1839. When Great Britain won the war, the Chinese were glad to hand over to Britain the "useless" rock called Hong Kong. The Hong Kong Islands consisted of 33 square miles populated by 5,000 Chinese. The islands had virtually no natural resources.

Population in this British colony grew rapidly, mainly due to immigrants and refugees from mainland China. Today six million Chinese live in Hong Kong, Kowloon and the New Territories, making this the most densely populated area in the world. Hong Kong imports its oil and raw materials and most of its food and even

---

1  This story is retold in Paul *Johnson's A History of the American People* (HarperCollins, 1997), p. 782.

water. Hong Kong's trading partners are thousands of miles away. Given its severe limitations of land and natural resources and its crowded population, the economic prospects for Hong Kong look dim.

Yet, Hong Kong's income per capita now ranks second (behind Japan) in the Far East. China was delighted to get back a much wealthier Hong Kong in 1997.

What is the source of the Hong Kong economic miracle? Land? There are few natural resources. Population? Most demographers would consider Hong Kong with its 6 million people overpopulated.

The answer to Hong Kong's success is found in its factories, skyscrapers, ports, roads, banks, telecommunications, retail outlets, and the entrepreneurial spirit of its people. Hong Kong has succeeded because of human and physical capital and the ability to trade goods and services freely with the rest of the world.[2]

The economic history of Switzerland demonstates the value of capital. In the center of Europe lies the small mountainous country of Switzerland. Like Hong Kong, Switzerland has very few resources. There are no coal mines, no minerals, and few natural resources. Yet the Swiss have developed one of the most prosperous nations on earth with the highest standard of living in Europe. How? Switzerland has had a stable, limited government over the centuries, and people devoted to free enterprise, education and technical knowledge. Through Swiss banking and finance, the Swiss have attracted capital from all over the world, and they have specialized in unique products such as chocolate and watches.

## THE MEANING OF CAPITALISM

There is a reason Karl Marx named the free-enterprise system *capitalism*. The most essential ingredient to economic growth is capital—specifically, the tools, equipment, and know-how that advance civilization to a higher standard of living. Without modern-day capital, the backward age of feudalism would be common. Marx noted in 1848 that capitalism "during its rule of scarcely one hundred years, has created more massive and more colossal productive forces than have all the preceding generations together. Subjection of nature's forces to man, machinery, application of chemistry to industry and agriculture, steam navigation, railways, electric telegraphs, clearing of whole continents for cultivation, canalization of rivers, whole populations conjured out of the ground—what earlier century had even a presentiment that such productive forces slumbered in the lap of social labor?"[3] Marx was a bitter critic of the capitalist system, but he understood the importance of "capital" as the lifeblood of a nation.

2  For a fascinating account of Hong Kong, see P. T. Bauer, "The Lesson of Hong Kong," *Equality, the Third World and Economic Delusion* (Weidenfeld and Nicolson, 1981), pp. 185-190.
3  Karl Marx and Friedrich Engels, *The Communist Manifesto* (Verso, 1998 [1848]), pp. 40-41.

Return for a moment to our definition of economics in Chapter 1 (see p. 17): Increasing the standard of living requires transforming natural resources into usable goods and services. This transformation takes landlords, workers, capital goods, and owner-entrepreneurs to create usable wealth.

Among these factors of production, physical and human capital play a critical role in achieving this goal. Capital is the most important element in achieving a higher standard of living. Capital is more important than natural resources and a large population.

## WHY SOME COUNTRIES ARE RICH AND OTHERS ARE POOR

China posseses vast lands, natural resources, and the world's largest population, yet China has one of the lowest standards of living in the world. Why? It has a low standard of living because it lacks capital—specifically, capital goods—to transform its natural resources into usable goods and services.

Next to China are two neighbors who have advanced far ahead of China—Japan and Hong Kong. Aside from some farm land, Japan has few natural resources. Japan must import all its oil. Equally, Hong Kong imports all of its oil and raw materials, and most of its water, and is thousands of miles away from its primary markets. Yet, Japan and Hong Kong have the highest standards of living per capita in Asia and rivals the United States and Europe in per capita production. Why are Japan and Hong Kong so rich and China so poor? The answer is simple: Japan and Hong Kong have capital in abundance; China does not (at least, until recently).

There are many examples around the world where two cities or countries lie next to each other, similar in culture and climate, yet exhibit stark contrast in terms of wealth. Such a rich-poor dichotomy can be found between San Diego, California, and Tijuana, Mexico, and between South Korea and North Korea. Why? One encourages capital formation; the other does not.

## WHAT IS CAPITAL?

Capital has many definitions.

Capital can mean capital goods—tools, equipment, machinery, plants, buildings, infrastructure and technological know-how. Examples of this type of capital are jet airplanes, trucks, mainframe computers, hammers, telephone lines, roads, and highways.

Capital also refers to the research and development efforts used to improve the productivity of capital and labor. Private businesses and governments spend billions of dollars each year to develop new products and technology.

249

Capital also includes human capital, the knowledge and skills of the workforce. Textbooks like this one serve as capital. Education and training play a major role in increasing worker productivity and raising our standard of living.

Another form of capital is goods-in-progress: the inventory of raw materials and semi-finished goods that are transformed into goods and services further along the supply pipeline. (Recall the four-stage model of production outlined in Chapter 2.)

Capital also refers to investment capital, or the funds used to finance the purchase of real estate, build a factory or fund other business projects. (See also Chapter 13, *Financing Capitalism*.)

## CHARACTERISTICS OF FIXED CAPITAL GOODS

Capital investment funds finance capital assets. Once capital funds are invested, they are transformed from a homogeneous stock into heterogeneous goods to be used for specific needs. If an airport is built, the funds and resources going into the airport can not be used to build roads, automobiles or houses. Capital goods are also durable and usually last for years. For example, a truck may be usable for five years and a building may last for over a hundred years. Capital goods are fixed, durable, heterogeneous assets created for a specific use.

**Capital goods are durable goods that are used to further the production process.**

Like all goods, capital goods go through a production process—from raw commodities to final output—but then are used once again to make other goods and services. A truck is produced from capital and then becomes a capital good used to produce other products, including trucks. Oil is converted to gasoline, which is then used in a variety of businesses, including the oil business. Capital goods are both an output and an input unlike consumer goods such as food or clothing which are typically only outputs.

## WHY IS CAPITAL SO BENEFICIAL?

Why are capital goods so useful in achieving a higher standard of living?

The clothing and textile industry demonstrates the power of capital resources in the creation of wealth. Prior to the inventions of the power loom, the cotton gin, and the sewing machine, millions of women, seamstresses and tailors spent their working lives stitching clothing, boots, and uniforms. Hand-made clothing has always been a highly laborious task involving hours of needlework. Sewing was a major part of the labor-intensive textile industry prior to these inventions. Clothing was expensive for consumers who usually limited themselves to only two or three outfits per year.

The situation changed dramatically with a series of new mechanical textile devices, including:

- Hargreave - Spinning Jenny (1770)
- Cartwright – power loom (1785)
- Slater – cotton-spinning loom (1790)
- Whitney – cotton gin (1794)

Raw cotton was produced on southern plantations and exported to England where it was used to make clothes. Prior to the cotton gin, the cotton textile industry was growing but cotton was expensive due to the cost of tediously separating the cotton lint from the seeds by hand. Whitney's machine was simple, cheap, and efficient. Using a gin, a plantation could now process 50 pounds of cotton per day instead of one.

The final leap in productivity in the clothing and textile industry came with the refined development of the sewing machine in the 1830s and 1840s. Several entrepreneurs were responsible for developing a workable sewing machine: Barthelemy Thimonnier in France, and Walter Hunt, Elias Howe, Jr., and Isaac Singer in the United States. These inventors spent years of their time and invested large sums of capital in developing a workable machine. Why? Because the sewing machine sharply reduced the time and expense of sewing clothing and textiles. Howe demonstrated his sewing machine in a competition against the best professional seamstresses, and his machine won handily. As a result of Singer's improvements upon Howe's methods, there has been, until recently, a sewing machine in practically every house and community in the world. (Today fewer women sew because ready-made clothing has become so inexpensive.)

## THE ECONOMICS OF CAPITAL TECHNOLOGY

These technological advances impacted the clothing and textile industry in the following ways.

1. It took time, money, and creativity to invent these new technologies.

2. The inventions were superior to the previous methods of production. These inventions increased productivity tremendously.

3. They expanded the textile industry and consumer market, which in turn reduced the costs of production, reduced prices and raised the general standard of living.

4. These revolutionary technologies replaced the old styles of production, causing antagonism among workers as they adjusted to the new production system.

5. The new technologies made the inventors wealthy men, while financially hurting those firms using the old forms of production.

Figure 11.1 illustrates the net benefit achieved through labor-saving devices. In this diagram, the line X represents the profit or net income over time using the old production method. Time t represents the time it takes to create a new technology. Line Y represents the increased profit achieved from the new technology.

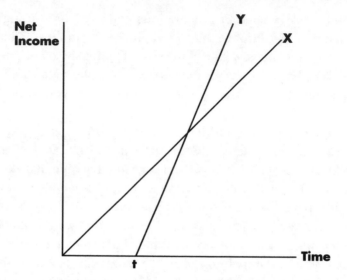

**Figure 11.1.** *The productivity of capital technology.*

There is always a trade-off between the current plan and a new production method. A capitalist-entrepreneur must determine if the new technology is sufficiently profitable over the current production process to pay for the time and capital necessary to develop the invention. What is the breakeven point? Line Z in Figure 11.2 below represents the minimal profitability the new technology must provide to be worth the development cost and achieve profitability.

In Figure 11.2 Line Z slopes upward, representing the time value of money, or the general interest rate. This is the minimum rate of return an investor can expect on his investment if he puts the investment in the bank or in money market instruments. If the interest yield is 5%, the rate of return must be higher than the current mode of production with a minimum return of 5% for investment to be worthwhile. The total annualized return must include the time and capital used in developing the invention.

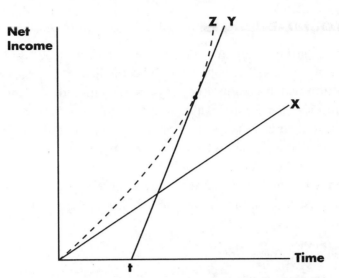

**Figure 11.2.** *Breakeven point for a new capital technology.*

## THE PRODUCTIVITY OF CAPITAL

A standard two-stage income model illustrates the benefits of investing in a new project. See Figure 11.3 below.

In the two-stage model, a new technology has a cost and a benefit. The cost is the monetary investment needed to create a workable innovation and the value of the time vested in research and development which could have been used in current production or other alternative uses (opportunity cost). The benefit is the stream of additional future revenues or cost savings gained once the innovation is put into production. If revenue exceeds the opportunity cost over the long run, the project is profitable. If the costs exceed revenue, the project is a mistake.

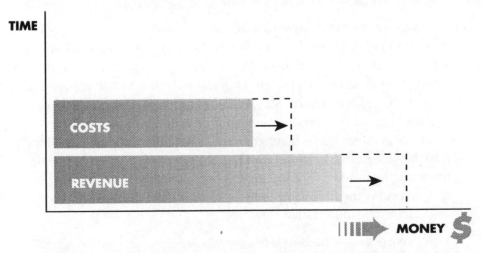

**Figure 11.3.** *A successful new project means additional revenues exceed marginal costs.*

## THE BENEFITS OF "ROUNDABOUTNESS"

The Austrian economist Eugen Böhm-Bawerk (see "Influential Economist" at the end of this chapter) referred to the capitalistic process as an indirect method of production which uses indirect or circuitous methods to increase production and consumption. For example, a man can try to catch fish with his hands, but he can catch more fish if he takes the time to build a boat and a fishing pole. As Böhm-Bawerk states, "roundabout methods are more fruitful than direct methods in the production of consumers' goods."[4]

Böhm-Bawerk's concept of roundaboutness is inherent in our four-stage model of the industrial economy, reproduced below in Figure 11.4:

**TIME**

 MONEY $

**Figure 11.4.** *Four-stage model of the economy demonstrates a long series of indirect methods of production.*

In order to obtain consumer goods, the producers must convert raw materials into manufactured goods and transfer them to the wholesaler and retailer before selling them to the final user. Machines and other capital goods are necessary throughout production. The four-stage model confirms Böhm-Bawerk's theory that the creation of final consumer goods involves "a long series of tools and buildings, and these in turn demand a great amount of preliminary work."[5]

Time and money are required to build either a boat and/or a fishing pole. People must be willing to forego present consumption in order to produce the tools, equipment and technology to increase future consumption. They must be willing to save and invest for the future. Chapter 17, "Saving, Technology and Economic Growth," will discuss the importance of saving.

4  Eugen Böhm-Bawerk, *The Positive Theory of Capital* (Libertarian Press, 1959), p. 12.
5  Böhm-Bawerk, *Positive Theory of Capital* (Libertarian Press, 1959), p. 12.

## THE PRINCIPLE OF CAPITAL DEEPENING

Böhm-Bawerk also asserted that capitalistic methods increase the **period of production**, the time it takes for goods to be transformed from raw commodities to final consumable products. This is known as **capital deepening**, an increase in the number of stages needed to produce final goods. When Ford created his assembly line, the line may have involved as many as 200 steps to build an automobile. Today, building a Ford car requires thousands of stages of production.

The building of a city's water system is another example of capital deepening. Turning on the tap produces water from the faucet. But how is this convenience possible? In early days it was a simple, though laborious, process to carry buckets of water from a well to the house. To provide water for a modern city, the process is infinitely more complex and expensive. Using extensive tools and machinery, city engineers devise a plan to build reservoirs, pumping stations, and an extensive line of pipes, sewers and plumbing fixtures. Years elapse between the first steps in the conception of a water system and the flow of water to every home.[6]

Peter F. Drucker states, "It is the essence of economic and technological progress that the time span for the fruition and proving out of a decision is steadily lengthening....Edison, in the 1880s, needed two years or so between the start of a laboratory work on an idea and the start pilot of pilot-plant operations. Today it may well take Edison's successors fifteen years. A half century ago a new plant was expected to pay for itself in two or three years; today, with capital investment-per-worker twenty times that of 1900, the payoff period often runs to ten or twelve years. A human organization, such as a sales force or a management group, may take even longer to build and pay for itself."[7]

Consumers do not notice the lengthening of the capitalist project because of inventories at each stage of production. It is of no concern to the consumer how long it takes for a good to be produced as long as it is available when they want to purchase it.

## REDUCING COSTS AND EXPANDING THE MARKET

Another benefit of a new technology is that it expands the market and allows production costs to be cut. The impact of the cotton gin demonstrates this principle. Prior to the invention of the cotton gin in the late 1700s, Britain imported a few million pounds of raw cotton per year. Very little raw cotton originated in the American colonies. Following Whitney's invention, U. S. cotton output and trade skyrocketed. By 1810, Britain was consuming 79 million pounds of cotton, mostly from the U. S.

6  A fuller discussion of capital deepening and other concepts of capital are found in Mark Skousen, *The Structure of Production* (New York University Press, 1990).
7  Peter F. Drucker, *Management: Tasks, Responsibilities, Practices* (Harper & Row, 1985), p. 44.

By 1830, total cotton imports to Britain amounted to 248 million pounds, and by 1860, cotton imports reached over 1,000 million pounds. The cost of raw imported cotton fell from 45 cents a pound to as low as 28 cents. Figure 11.5 illustrates this effect.

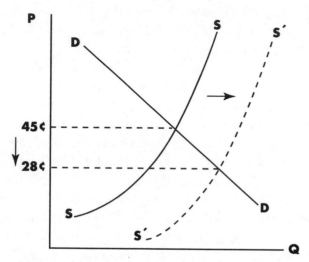

**Figure 11.5.** *How the cotton gin increased supplies and reduced the price of cotton.*

The cotton gin is an expensive machine that cuts costs for processing cotton dramatically and vastly expands production. The supply and cost schedule for raw cotton shifted to the right, showing increasing production, lower costs and lower prices. As a result, consumers' surplus (a measure of standard of living) expanded across the economy.

There are numerous other examples of how advancing technology and use of capital in the 19th and 20th centuries expanded markets and reduced costs. The steel industry in the late 19th century presents a classic case of accelerating output and declining prices. Prior to the application of the Bessemer process, the pig iron and steel industries were struggling. The Bessemer process was installed at a plant in Pittsburgh in 1875 and the steel industry exploded in the U. S. Output climbed rapidly from 69,000 tons in 1870 to 1.3 million tons in 1890, and to 10 million tons in 1900, surpassing British production. Steel rail production rose from 84,000 tons in 1872 to 291,000 tons in 1875, and over 3 million tons in 1900. Along with the huge increases in steel output, prices plummeted from $106 a ton in 1870 to $17 a ton in 1898.

The petroleum business is another example of the importance of innovation and capital investment. The cracking of oil was introduced in 1875, and the minimum size of an efficient refinery was increased to over 1,000 barrels a day. Economies of scale definitely favored the large oil refiners like Rockefeller, because huge capital requirements were necessary to build large refineries. Between 1870 and 1885, the price of refined kerosene dropped from 26 cents to 8 cents per gallon. The price of refined oil per gallon fell from 9.33 cents in 1880 to 8.13 cents in 1885 to 7.38 cents in 1890, and to 5.91 cents in 1897. During this period, petroleum prices fell, costs declined, output expanded, and product quality improved. Despite criticisms of the "robber barons" of this period, the public benefited from increased output, improved quality, wider variety of products, and lower prices.

The automobile went through a similar transformation. Henry Ford's revolutionary assembly line system in Detroit resulted in increased production of Model Ts and lower prices. Figure 11.6 shows the dramatic change that occurred in the early 1900s.

**Demand for Model T Touring Cars, 1908-16**

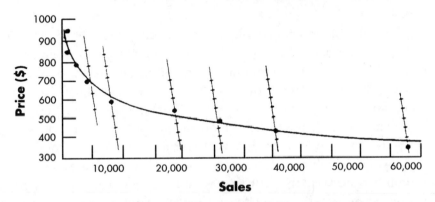

**Figure 11.6.** *Increased output of Model Ts and lower prices.*

The application of technology and capital has been responsible for an enormous rise in the standard of living. Revolutions in the production and distribution of textiles, oil and gas, iron and steel, and automobiles are just a few examples. Electricity transformed the 20th century for all people, rich and poor. Electricity extended the hours of recreation and work and opened stores, parks, restaurants, and clubs at night. The telephone reduced the need to send messengers, while the automobile and the airplane sharply reduced distances. Technology in household products and appliances such as the washer and dryer, the dishwasher, the stove, vacuum cleaners, hot water heater, central heating, and bathroom fixtures sharply reduced the hours and toil spent on chores. Television and radio provided cheap and expanded entertainment. Medical breakthroughs such as drugs, penicillin, x-rays, open-heart surgery, and vaccines helped increase life spans in the United States to over 70 years.[8]

These advances were born of capital investment and entrepreneurship and have enhanced the material lives of all.

8 For a fascinating review of advances in consumer satisfaction in the 20th century, see Stanley Lebergott, *Pursuing Happiness: American Consumers in the Twentieth Century* (Princeton University Press, 1993).

## DOES AUTOMATION CAUSE PERMANENT UNEMPLOYMENT?

New technologies are often labor-saving devices that disrupt the labor market in the industry where the invention is used. When the sewing machine was introduced, a mob in France destroyed 80 machines used to make uniforms for the French Army. The mob was worried that the sewing machines would destroy the livelihood of French tailors.

The sewing machine, along with the other labor-saving devices in the textile industry, dramatically increased the output of clothing and the number of workers needed in the industry. Many workers were changed to other assignments in foreign countries. The significant long-term benefit of this example may be hidden or not apparent in the short term. To quote Frederic Bastiat, "the good economist takes into account both the effect that can be seen and those effects that must be foreseen."

The fear that machines will put people out of work has existed for years, yet it has never materialized as a real outcome. Machines have displaced workers, but the effect has typically been temporary. Technology expands the market and reduces the cost of production. The secondary effect of new technology is to reduce the cost of living and put more money into the hands of consumers, allowing them to buy either more of the same good or more of other goods and services.

If the demand for a product is elastic, a cost-saving invention can create more employment. Such has been the case in clothing, steel, automobiles, and gasoline. Colonists feared that the cotton gin would put people out of work, but the labor-saving device did just the opposite—it created a whole new industry for the South and increased the demand for labor. In the case of the automobile, even though the worker-hours per car fell by 25% between 1920 and 1930, employment in the automobile industry rose by approximately 50%.

If the demand for a product is inelastic, and consumers buy less as a result of the innovation, consumers then have more funds in their budget to purchase other goods and services. The net effect is to create more jobs in the marketplace by stimulating other industries. These may not be the same jobs, but they are jobs nevertheless. Labor is always more flexible and non-specific than capital or land. As long as consumer wants are insatiable and labor is scarce, there will always be work and jobs available.

## THE ROLE OF CAPITAL FUNDS

Technological advances improved the standard of living for consumers and investors around the world in the 20th century. But technology is only half the equation for economic success. Technology also requires capital investment—pools of money made available to implement technologies. Without an adequate pool of investment capital, many advanced technologies go unused.

This requirement was made clear to travelers from the west who visited China. As recently as the early 1980s, Chinese farmers still relied on oxen to till the land. Nowhere did visitors see tractors or other farm machinery that are so common in the West. Were the Chinese farmers so isolated from civilization that they were unaware of agricultural technology? The Chinese were quite familiar with western technology. The problem was not lack of technology; it was lack of capital. The Chinese farmers lacked the money necessary to pay for tractors. Technology and advances in a nation's standard of living are only limited by a country's capital, and China lacked the capital necessary to buy modern farm equipment. The problem was not ignorance of the technology available, but supply of capital with which to purchase it.

**There are many sources of investment capital:**

1.  Domestic savings from individuals, institutions and businesses

2.  The stock market

3.  Government funds

4.  Foreign investment

When domestic savings are insufficient for domestic investment, foreign investment can make up the difference and accelerate capital-intensive production. With the exception of Great Britain, foreign investment has played a key element in the development of all nations. Foreign investment has led to charges of "capitalist imperialism" by the critics of capitalism, yet foreign investment has advanced the standard of living in most nations. Ludwig von Mises calls foreign investment "the greatest event in the history of the nineteenth century."[9]

Investment capital is the pool of funds available to finance investment projects in the capital-goods industries. Banks, insurance companies, federal agencies, and other financial intermediaries may also finance consumer purchases, but most of the funds are normally used to finance business operations and long-term projects.

Loans, leasing or other financial arrangements are also made in the great majority of cases for durable consumer goods such as houses, furniture, automobiles and appliances. From an economic point of view, these durable consumer goods can be treated as investment capital because these goods take a long time to consume. Houses, for example, may last for hundreds of years, while automobiles may last for 10 years. Consumer durables are just as interest-sensitive as business capital goods. How long a durable consumer good is expected to have useful life is a factor in pricing.

---

9  Ludwig von Mises, *Economic Policy* (Gateway Editions, 1979), p. 78.

## DEPRECIATION AND INFLATION

Capital goods and consumer durables are used up over long periods. **Depreciation** is used to determine the value lost each year as a capital good or consumer durable is used. According to acceptable accounting practices in most countries, capital goods are depreciated over long periods of time. A rental house may be depreciated over a 28-year period for income tax purposes; an automobile over 5 years. Businesses normally set aside large sums to replace worn out machinery, equipment, and buildings. To fail to adequately fund the depreciation of company assets is to invite a cash shortage and can lead to bankruptcy.

One of the difficulties facing accountants is to properly estimate the value of replacing an asset in the distant future. Inflation can cause financial officers to grossly underestimate replacement costs. Firms have wisely adopted "inflation accounting," but due to the fickle nature of inflation, this process is still more an art than a science.

## INTEREST RATES

Interest rates have a significant impact on capital expenditures for several reasons. First, most big businesses are capital-intensive, requiring plants, heavy machinery, and real estate in the production process. This is especially true in the raw commodities and manufacturing sectors of the economy. Multi-million-dollar projects and capital goods are usually financed by banks and other financial institutions. Leasing and borrowing are common in capital-intensive businesses. A small change in interest rates can make a difference between profit and loss over the long run.

The capital-goods market is far removed from final consumption. The further assets and production are removed from final consumption, the more volatile the industry tends to be. Interest rates play a major role in this volatility.

Final consumption goods that are consumed in a short period of time are hardly affected by changes in interest rates. Food, clothing, and gasoline are examples of consumables that are not normally interest-rate sensitive. However, demand for durable capital goods such as machinery used in mining or manufacturing is highly volatile. The price of these goods is determined in part by the interest rate. Suppose the interest rate on a leased oil rig jumps from 6% to 12%. This dramatically raises the total cost of the oil rig, and there's no assurance that future earnings from the oil rig will cover those expenses. As a result, demand for new oil rigs will fall sharply. On the other hand, if interest rates fall from 12% to 6%, the demand for new oil rigs will rise because costs have fallen dramatically.

Volatility can be expressed in many ways. There can be volatility of:

- Annual production

- Profitability

- Employment and unemployment

- Inventories

- Costs of production

- Prices of capital goods

- Stock prices

Commercial and residential real estate is another industry greatly affected by the volatility of interest rates. Why? Because housing is so durable, only a small percentage of commercial buildings or residential homes is consumed each year. Therefore, changes in interest rates have a magnified effect on the price of real estate.

Figure 11.7 shows the general model of volatility in capital assets based on their distance from final consumption.

As noted above, assets that are immediately consumed do not fluctuate as much as assets further removed from consumption. The further capital assets are from final consumption, the more volatile these assets are in prices and output.

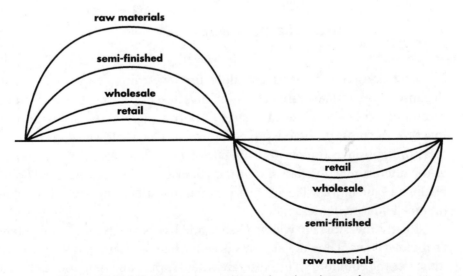

**Figure 11.7.** *Volatility in prices and output based on distance from consumption.*
*Source: Lawrence K. Frank, "A Theory of Business Cycles," Quarterly Journal of Economics (August, 1923), p. 347.*
*Reprinted by permission of John Wiley and Sons, Inc.*

Capital, or investment spending, has always been the most unstable sector of the national economy. Consumer spending has always been more stable than capital spending. Interest rates are the key factor in this inherent instability.

## INTEREST RATES AND THE LOANABLE FUNDS MARKET

The demand for investment capital is closely linked to the demand for loanable funds. The demand schedule slopes downward as figure 11.8 indicates.

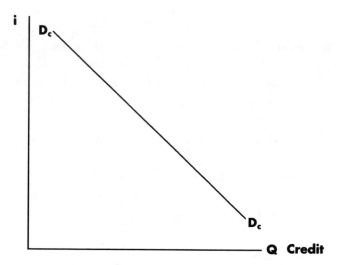

**Figure 11.8.** *The demand for loanable funds.*

Why does the demand schedule for investment capital slope downward? Because as the interest rate falls, more investment projects become profitable, and more businesses become interested in borrowing. Financial institutions tend to invest in the most profitable projects first, working their way down toward less and less profitable investments until the rate of return on investment projects approaches the interest rate, the rate of return on bank deposits. As the interest rate declines, businesses are more willing to finance their investment projects through banks and financial intermediaries.

Clearly, investors are willing to save and banks are more willing to lend at higher interest rates. Thus the supply curve for loanable funds is positive. Figure 11.9 indicates the equilibrium interest rate where supply and demand for loanable funds match.

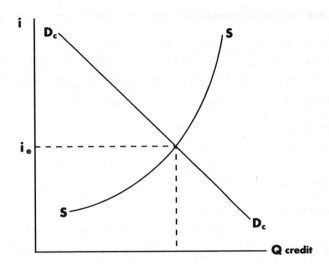

**Figure 11.9.** *The supply and demand for loanable funds.*

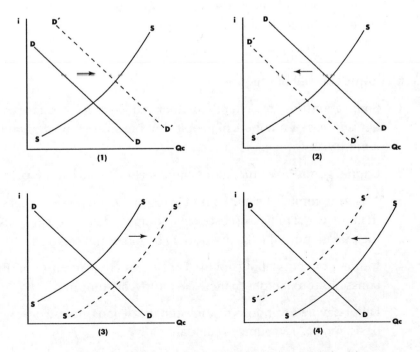

**Figure 11.10.** *Four scenarios in the investment capital markets.*

263

**Four scenarios for examination:**

(1.) Outward shift in the demand for capital occurs in an economic boom when increased construction of plants, buildings, and other capital-intensive business activities requires huge outlays of investment. In this situation, interest rates tend to rise along with capital invested.

(2.) Decreased shift in the demand for capital occurs in an economic downturn or recession. The economy stops growing, the real estate market collapses, and new building permits drop. The result? Lower interest rates and less capital invested.

(3.) Outward shift in supply of capital occurs in situations where new sources of capital enter the market, either from domestic savings (people desire to save more) or foreign investment sources. The greater supply of capital requires banks and other intermediaries to reduce interest rates and encourage more borrowing. Net result: lower interest rates and more capital invested.

(4.) Inward shift in the supply of capital occurs when people decide to cut back on their savings or foreigners withdraw investment capital. With fewer loanable funds available, banks and other financial institutions must ration the funds, causing interest rates to climb and fewer investment projects. Net result: higher interest rates, less capital invested.

**Main points covered in Chapter 11:**

1. Some countries are richer than others not so much because of greater natural resources or numbers of people, but because of the availability of physical and human capital.

2. Capital goods take time, money, and technology to develop.

3. Adopting capitalistic methods of investment and production benefits nations in many ways: reducing costs, expanding markets, creating jobs, and increasing the quantity, quality and variety of goods and services.

4. Indirect or roundabout methods of production require sacrifice of present consumption in order to increase future consumption.

5. Labor-saving inventions destroy and create jobs and businesses, but on a net basis, increase a country's standard of living.

6. The capital-goods industries are highly sensitive to interest rates and are more volatile in prices, output, employment, and inventories than consumer goods industries.

Capital deepening
Capital good
Capital-goods industry
Consumer-goods industry
Depreciation
Inflation accounting

Inventories
Investment capital
Loanable-funds market
Period of production
Roundaboutness

## INFLUENTIAL ECONOMIST

### EUGEN BÖHM-BAWERK AND THE POSITIVE THEORY OF CAPITAL

**Name: Eugen von Böhm-Bawerk (1851-1914)**

**Background:** At the turn of the century, this Austrian-born economist was probably the most famous economist in Eastern Europe. He was a student of Carl Menger, the founder of the Austrian school. Böhm-Bawerk was appointed Minister of Finance of Austria three times (1893, 1896, and 1900), and is the only economist to appear on a nation's currency (the Austrian 100-schilling note). After a distinguished political career, he was appointed chair of economics at the University of Vienna. His lectures attracted many famous students, including Ludwig von Mises, Joseph Schumpeter, and Otto Bauer.

**Major Works:** Böhm-Bawerk made three major contributions to economics. First, he was a strong defender of the virtue of saving in a period of increasing animosity toward the traditional value of thrift. Böhm-Bawerk contended that increasing savings by postponing consumption is essential to economic growth and is more productive than consumption. Public and private saving provided the source of funds for investing in new businesses, technology, and capital formation.

Second, he developed the classical theory of economic growth based on the superiority of "roundabout" capitalistic methods of production. The capitalist system involves indirect methods of producing consumer goods. This process requires longer, more productive techniques, but once they are in place, they increase the quantity, quality and variety of final consumer goods and services. According to Böhm-Bawerk, the key to economic growth is to save more, and to use those additional savings to invest in research and development, new technologies, and advanced production processes. His classic work on the subject of capital and economic growth is *The Positive Theory of Capital*, first published in 1889. He also wrote about and criticized the various theories of capital and interest.

Third, Böhm-Bawerk was the first economist to attack Karl Marx's theories of surplus value and exploitation. Marx argued in *Das Capital* that profit and interest paid to capitalists constituted "surplus value" that rightly belonged to the workers. Böhm-Bawerk countered that capitalists should be compensated for two distinct reasons: First, capitalist-owners must wait for their goods to be sold while they advance wages to labor. In other words, wage-earners are paid regularly (monthly or weekly) irrespective of when the firm's goods are sold. The payment of interest compensates capitalist-owners for waiting to receive their funds.

Second, capitalist-owners take greater risks than wage-earners with their funds. Wage-earners may continue to receive regular payments for their efforts at a time when the company is losing money. Therefore, capitalist-owners deserve to earn profits on their investments as a reward for greater risk-taking.

Böhm-Bawerk's critique of Marxism is found in his book, *Karl Marx and the Close of His System* (Orion Editions, 1984). Oddly enough, it is published only by Marxists who offer rebuttals to Böhm-Bawerk's criticisms.


## PROBLEMS TO PONDER

1. Using the four scenarios referred to in this chapter (see page 247), choose periods when each scenario has occurred in the U. S. or other countries:

   a. higher interest rates, more capital invested
   b. lower interest rates, less capital invested
   c. lower interest rates, more capital invested
   d. higher interest rates, less capital invested.

2. Which scenario is most conducive toward economic growth? Which scenario is the most normal historically?

3. Suppose you own a company that makes fishing poles. Business is good with annual revenue of $1 million and profits of $100,000. One day a bright young employee comes to you and says he has developed a better fishing pole that will increase profits by 50% a year. You test the new pole and are convinced the pole is superior. However, you estimate it will require an investment of $200,000 in new machinery and equipment, marketing, etc., to start producing the new pole. You figure it will take a year before the new fishing pole is selling 50% more than the old fishing pole. Should you take the gamble? Create a graph to demonstrate the costs and benefits. What is the minimum annual return you require to invest in this new fishing pole?

4. Which of the following products have become more complex (judging from their internal physical structure) over the past 30 years:
   a. Radio
   b. Stereo
   c. automobile engine
   d. television
   e. computer
   f. pencil?

Do these examples confirm or deny the principle of capital deepening in the production process?

## RECOMMENDED READING

- Sidney Homer, *A History of Interest Rates*, 2nd ed. (Rutgers University Press, 1977). The role of rising and falling interest rates over the centuries in capitalist development.

- Mark Skousen, *The Structure of Production* (New York University Press, 1990) paperback edition published in 2007 with a new introduction. An historical survey and theory of the role of capital in the marketplace and its critical role in macroeconomics.

*Chapter 12*

# THE ROLE OF ENTREPRENEURSHIP

*"What is happening in the United States is . . . a profound shift from a 'managerial' to an 'entrepreneurial' economy."*

—PETER F. DRUCKER[1]

Probably no scientist had a greater impact on the daily lives of Americans — and the rest of the world — than Thomas A. Edison. The Wizard of Menlo Park patented over a thousand inventions in his lifetime. His greatest brainchild was the electric light, which replaced other forms of artificial lighting. As historian Stanley Lebergott states, Edison's light bulb "extended the hours of sensation and recreation. It made plays and movies visible after sunset. It opened libraries, restaurants, bowling alleys, baseball parks, and clubs in the hours of darkness....By 1990, American households consumed 10,000 kilowatt hours per capita, over forty times as much as Soviet households. Did that profusion help explain the excessive cheerfulness that foreign visitors attributed to Americans?"[2]

Edison improved the telephone, the typewriter, the motion picture, the electric generator, and the electric-powered train. He also developed the first mimeograph machine and the phonograph. Many scientists proclaim him the greatest inventor in history.

Edison was also a businessman who organized many companies to manufacture and sell his inventions, including General Electric, one of the largest companies in the world.

**Thomas A. Edison was an inventor-entrepreneur.**

John D. Rockefeller was not an inventor, but a producer and manager. He founded the Standard Oil Company, which by 1900 had captured 90% of America's oil refining. Benjamin Silliman, Jr., a professor of chemistry at Yale, discovered how

1 Peter F. Drucker, *Innovation and Entrepreneurship* (Harper & Rowe, 1985), p. 1.
2 Stanley Lebergott, *Pursuing Happiness: American Consumers in the Twentieth Century* (Princeton University Press, 1993), p. 39, 121.

crude oil could be distilled and purified into kerosene. But it was Rockefeller who transformed the oil industry from a volatile, risky business into an orderly, expanding market. He took control of the refining end of the oil business, cut production and transportation costs, raised capital and built bigger and better equipment to produce gasoline and other petroleum products. Rockefeller's goal was to provide "cheap and good" gasoline for the consumer, "the best...at the lowest price." His capitalistic methods reduced the price of gasoline from 58 cents to 8 cents a gallon and made Rockefeller the richest man in the world.

**John D. Rockefeller was a capitalist-entrepreneur.**

In September, 1992, a European currency crisis developed. Despite the wreckage that left institutional investors with devastating losses, financial entrepreneur George Soros, legendary chairman of the Quantum group of funds, made an incredible $1.2 billion in just one month.

How did George Soros achieve such a spectacular return on his investment? He profited from a defective Exchange Rate Mechanism (ERM) that the European Union had created to stabilize its members' currencies. Soros engaged in an arbitrage technique of selling weak currencies and buying strong currencies. In short, he used sound economic thinking to take advantage of government policies that attempted to contradict the laws of the market. When the ERM fell apart in September, 1992, Soros and his partners profited handsomely.

**George Soros is a financial-entrepreneur.**

The examples of Thomas A. Edison, John D. Rockefeller, and George Soros demonstrate that the world economy is run by inventors, capitalists, and speculators. Each of these men is an entrepreneur.

## THE CENTRAL ROLE OF ENTREPRENEURSHIP

Used originally by J. B. Say, *entrepreneur* is a French word meaning one who undertakes a business venture and assumes the risk in order to make a profit. Entrepreneurs assume the risk, uncertainty, and responsibility of running an enterprise—whether it be an invention, a production process, or an investment fund.

The four-stage model of the economic process is shown in figure 12.1 below.

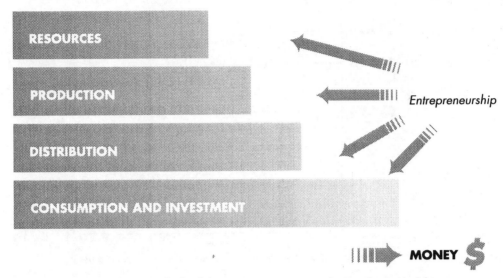

**TIME**

**Figure 12.1.** *Central role of the entrepreneur-owner in the Four-Stage Model.*

How is the final stage of production—consumer goods and services—reached? Who brings together the production factors of land, labor, and capital? How are determinations made about the final product or service made? Ultimately, it is the entrepreneur-owner of the business who makes these critical decisions:

- what product to make
- what price to charge
- whom to hire
- where to operate the business
- how much capital to raise

These are tough decisions that can result in spectacular profits or massive losses. Without the decision maker, economic performance and living standards could not advance.

## MOVING TOWARD EQUILIBRIUM

Economists have traditionally viewed the entrepreneur in two ways. First, the entrepreneur acts in the production process, moving the market toward equilibrium, a state where where supply equals demand. In this role the individual acts as an arbitrage-entrepreneur.

Second, the entrepreneur creates new markets and disrupts the old products and production processes where new supplies and new demands occur in the marketplace. In this role the individual acts as an innovator-entrepreneur.

Imagine the market for software packages in which Microsoft and other computer companies compete. Suppose the supply and demand for software is in disequilibrium, as drawn below in figure 12.2.

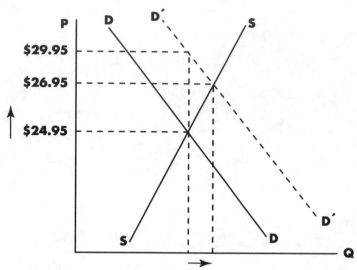

**Figure 12.2.** *Demand exceeds supply in software programs.*

In the above case, suppose the market for software has been in relative equilibrium for a year, but there is an unexpected increase in demand for software packages. The initial effect is that software on the shelves and inventories start to shrink. Alert suppliers and marketing specialists note this shortage. Microsoft and other software firms quickly make the decision to produce more software packages. The market tells them to produce more, but at what price? Should Microsoft continue to charge $24.95 for its *Microsoft Works*, or should it raise the price to $29.95 due to the increased demand? What impact would a price increase have on competitors? In the end, software firms, always interested in maximizing their profits, increase output and raise the price to $26.95 as figure 12.2 indicates.

In referring to the entrepreneur as an arbitrager of supply and demand, Israel M. Kirzner, economics professor at New York University, states, "the entrepreneurial role...has an equilibrating influence; it is entrepreneurial alertness to unnoticed opportunities...."[3] Furthermore, he states, "I view the entrepreneur...as being alert to the opportunities that exist already and are waiting to be noticed...The entrepreneur is to be seen as responding to opportunities rather than creating them; as capturing profit opportunities rather than generating them."[4]

Another form of arbitrage-entrepreneurship occurs when capitalists shift resources from losing or low-profit sectors of the economy to more profitable markets. For example, in the 1980s and 1990s the computer industry offered extremely high rates of return, while the mining industry, suffering from low commodity prices, was relatively unprofitable. Entrepreneurs took advantage of this variation in

3  Israel M. Kirzner, *Competition and Entrepreneurship* (University of Chicago Press, 1973), p. 81.
4  Ibid., p. 74.

profitability by transferring capital and assets from the mining industry and other low-profit sectors to the computer market and other high-profit sectors of the economy. J. B. Say emphasized this role when he wrote, "The entrepreneur shifts economic resources out of an area of lower and into an area of higher productivity and greater yield."

When supply and demand are in perfect equilibrium, where supply equals demand, according to Kirzner, there is no role for the entrepreneur as arbitrager. In these circumstances the innovator-entrepreneur sees new markets, new alternative products, or new cost-cutting techniques.

## AN ALTERNATIVE ROLE: MOVING AWAY FROM EQUILIBRIUM

While there may be no role for the arbitrager when supply equals demand, this is when the role of the innovator-entrepreneur comes alive.

Supply and demand never stay equal for long. There are always entrepreneurial forces at work to increase revenue or reduce costs, and hence change the profit picture of a product or industry. The two-stage income statement demonstrates the effects of arbitrage. (See figure 12.3 below).

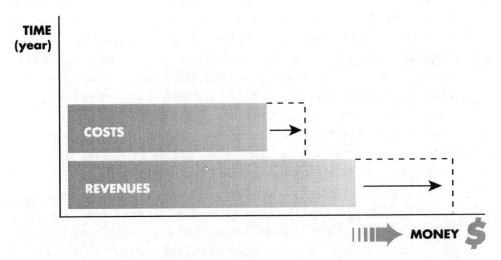

**Figure 12.3.** *Two-stage income statement shows the incentive of the entrepreneur to create new, better products at cheaper prices, thus increasing profits.*

The owner-capitalists of the firm are responsible for both the revenue and cost side, which determine whether a company earns a profit or loss. They determine the mix of land, labor and capital, the type of goods and services which will be produced, and the prices associated with these items.

The market encourages the successful innovator-entrepreneur. Money-seeking capitalists may attempt to increase revenue (through new or improved products, or new marketing techniques) more than to reduce costs. Or they may seek to engage in a cost-cutting campaign that reduces expenses more than revenue, or engage in a combination of the two. Either way, the result is higher profitability for the firm.

In the example of the computer software industry, Microsoft may choose either approach to enhance company profitability, even though the company is currently in temporary equilibrium.

## SCHUMPETER AND THE CONCEPT OF "CREATIVE DESTRUCTION"

Joseph A. Schumpeter (1883-1950), an Austrian economist who taught at Harvard, looked at entrepreneurship in a different way than Kirzner. He envisioned the innovator-entrepreneur. Schumpeter insisted that innovation, the process of transforming old and obsolete methods into new and more productive techniques, is the very essence of the modern economy. The capitalist-entrepreneur is always seeking new ideas, new products, and new markets which make the current capital equipment and production processes obsolete.

In this sense, free-market capitalism is engaged in a process known as "creative destruction." In creating new markets and products, the capitalist system destroys old markets and products. As Schumpeter declared, "Capitalism, then, is by nature a form or method of economic change and not only never is but never can be stationary....The opening up of new markets, foreign or domestic, and the organizational development from the craft shop and factory to such concerns as U. S. Steel illustrate the same process of industrial mutation—if I may use that biological term—that incessantly revolutionizes the economic structure from within, incessantly destroying the old one, incessantly creating a new one. This process of creative destruction is the essential fact about capitalism."[5]

Schumpeter's concept of creative destruction was also discussed in Chapter 8 and Chapter 10. Schumpeter's dynamic model of the economy is in sharp contrast to the static model of perfect competition where there are no incentives toward innovation or change. As Schumpeter notes, the perfect competition model is an inferior model of the capitalist process. Moreover, in properly describing a dynamic economy, economists and financial journalists should highlight the "creative" and

5 Joseph A. Schumpeter, *Capitalism, Socialism and Democracy*, 3rd ed. (Harper & Row, 1950), pp. 82-83.

not just the "destructive" nature of the economy. An objective reporter should announce a company's new hirings as well as layoffs, new pay raises as well as pay cuts, the employment rate as well as the unemployment rate, and the number of new businesses as well as the latest bankruptcies. As part of a dynamic process, entrepreneurs can make profitable decisions, not just mistakes.

## THE ECONOMICS OF INFORMATION

In analyzing the role of the entrepreneur, we need to keep in mind several important points:

1. Information is imperfect and often inaccurate in the marketplace. There is no such thing as "perfect knowledge."
2. Ignorance is commonplace in the marketplace.
3. The future is often uncertain and risky.

Imperfect knowledge, ignorance, uncertainty and risk are potential liabilities to the market's players: capitalists, workers, and consumers alike. Everyone makes mistakes despite the best of intentions. Successful entrepreneurs seek to minimize their level of imperfect knowledge, ignorance, uncertainty and risk.

## UNCERTAINTY AND THE DISCOVERY PROCESS

Professor Israel Kirzner states that entrepreneurs must be "alert" to change and new information. But they can never be sure of the outcome. There is always uncertainty. Even if a major company does extensive research and consumer surveys, it has no guarantee of success. Why? Because of the principle of uncertainty — human beings are not entirely predictable despite the techniques of sampling and polling. One classic example of uncertainty and risk occurred in the early 1980s when Coca Cola introduced the New Coke. Despite guarantees from the marketing department that the New Coke would be a hit, it was a dismal failure.

Kirzner calls this aspect of the marketplace the "discovery process." He states, "Entrepreneurship is required for the discovery of the profit opportunity."[6] Business people and marketing experts anticipate a certain outcome, but the result is not always what was expected. Sometimes an expected profit turns into an unanticipated loss. The market is a discovery process.

6  Israel M. Kirzner, *Competition and Entrepreneurship* (University of Chicago Press, 1973), p. 38n.

## PRICE AS A MEANS OF COMMUNICATION

Prices, including selling prices, costs of production, and wages, play a critical role in the decision-making process for capitalists, workers and consumers. Prices, costs and wages serve as a message center for the economy. Prices send out signals to capitalist-owners who want to know what to produce, what price to pay, and how many to produce. Prices send signals to consumers who want to know what to buy, what the cost of the product or service will be, and how much they can afford.

In a classic article in 1945, Fredrich A. Hayek highlighted the role of prices as transmitters of information to producers, buyers and sellers in the marketplace. He stated, "We must look at the price system as a mechanism for communicating information if we want to understand its real function..."[7] Hayek uses the example of tin. Suppose a new use for tin is discovered which increases the demand for tin. The resulting higher price forces tin users to economize, to use less tin, even though they may not know about the new use for tin. Price provides a valuable signal of the best marginal use of a commodity or product by an entrepreneur.

## ADVERTISING AND ITS CRITICS

Kirzner notes that "market disequilibrium is characterized by widespread ignorance."[8] Market participants need the most reliable information possible to decide what to produce and to consume. Market participants need to know prices, wages, rents and the costs of supplies. They need to know what kinds of consumer and producer products are available and what these products can do. Information about the markets is not always conveniently available or cheap. The goal of having perfect information and perfect understanding of the competition is absurd. Information, like all other scarce commodities, has a price, and, in fact, the prices for various types of information vary considerably. Information, like other goods and services, can be both marketed and purchased.

Providing information about goods and services, financial markets, and companies requires marketing and advertising. Producing products or services does no good if potential consumers do not know about them, or are if they are misinformed about prices and alternatives. Companies work to put products or services into the hands of consumers, and advertising and marketing campaigns are the way that consumers are informed about product or service availability.

---

7 Friedrich A. Hayek, "The Use of Knowledge in Society," *American Economic Review* (September, 1945), pp. 519-30. Reprinted in *The Essence of Hayek* (Hoover Institution, 1984), p. 219.
8 Kirzner, *Competition and Entrepreneurship*, p. 69.

Critics of the market often complain about the waste and misinformation in advertising and product differentiation. Advertising and other marketing methods account for approximately 10% of total consumer costs. See figure 12.4 below.

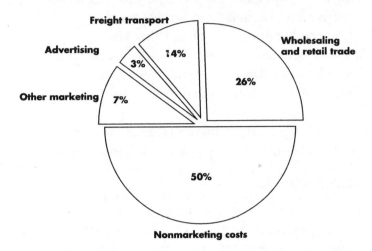

**Figure 12.4.** *Marketing and retail costs in the United States (2000).*

As the above chart indicates, the cost of producing the good or service accounts for half of the final amount spent by consumers. Then it costs an average 14% to transport the product to its destination. Another fourth is spent for wholesaling and retail trade such as purchasing agents and the cost of retail outlets. And the remaining 10% is for advertising and other marketing expenses.

## THE PURPOSE OF ADVERTISING

Are advertising and marketing campaigns a waste of money or do they serve a useful purpose? Companies advertise to provide information to consumers about their product or service, and to persuade consumers to buy.

## ADVERTISING AS AN INFORMATION PROVIDER

Most economists support efforts to increase the education of consumers. Customers frequently end up overpaying and getting the wrong product if they are not conveniently provided with basic information such as price and product differentiation. Store displays, classified ads, and billboard advertising usually provide this kind of essential information. Such advertising helps the customer test and compare products and services. Imagine the expense a car buyer might have to go through if car dealers were not allowed to advertise their prices in the classified ads or on radio and television.

Studies have demonstrated the benefits of advertising in the sale of eyeglasses and legal services. A study was made in 1972 that compared the price of eyeglasses in states that restricted advertising with the price in states that allowed advertising. The study found that price of eyeglasses in states without advertising were more than twice as high as in those with advertising .[9]

In 1977 the Supreme Court ruled that lawyers have a constitutional right to advertise their services. In a 1983 study, the Federal Trade Commission concluded that fees for legal services such as wills, bankruptcies, undisputed divorces and accident cases were 5 to 13% lower in the cities that had fewer restrictions on advertising.

In these examples, the evidence is strong that advertising has had a beneficial effect on the economy—lower prices and increased services.

## THE CRITICS OF ADVERTISING

The second purpose of marketing campaigns is to persuade consumers to buy brand-name goods and new products. Advertising informs consumers, shapes their tastes, and creates new consumer desires. Procter & Gamble, Coca Cola, and Budweiser spend millions of dollars per year advertising their products. In the words of Vance Packard, advertisers have market power and are the "hidden persuaders." John Kenneth Galbraith's thesis is that Madison Avenue has created a "dependence effect" in consumers, and hence threatens consumer sovereignty. "As a society becomes increasingly affluent," Galbraith states in *The Affluent Society*, "wants are increasingly created by the process by which they are satisfied....Producers may proceed actively to create wants through advertising and salesmanship."[10] According to Galbraith, big corporations gain monopolistic power through advertising, brand names and product differentiation. He blames the excesses of the consumer society (consumer debt and frivolous consumer products) on Big Business's ability to manipulate the public.

Huge advertising budgets and brand name recognition make it more difficult for rivals to enter the market, or for a small entrepreneur to introduce a new product. This circumstance is especially true in large consumer industries such as breakfast cereals, automobiles, cigarettes, and household appliances.

Studies have shown that advertising is highly profitable. Industries with high advertising outlays are generally more profitable than companies that do not put money into advertising. Marketing campaigns lead consumers to buy brand names at substantially higher prices even though generic products are virtually identical (aspirin, shampoo, etc.).[11]

9   Lee Benham, "The Effect of Advertising on the Price of Eyeglasses," *Journal of Law and Economics* 15 (October 1972): 337-52.

10  John Kenneth Galbraith, *The Affluent Society* (Houghton Mifflin, 1958), p. 158.

11  W. S. Comanor and T. A. Wilson, "Advertising, Market Structure, and Performance," *Review of Economics and Statistics* 49 (November 1967).

## THE HIGH FAILURE RATE OF NEW PRODUCTS

Have consumers lost all consumer sovereignty as a result of clever advertising? After all, despite extensive promotional campaigns, Ford's Edsel in the late 1950s and the New Coke in the mid-1980s failed miserably to attract new buyers. AcuPoll indicates in a 2006 study that somewhere between 80 percent and 95 percent of new product introductions fail. [12]

Product differentiation is not forced on the public. Clearly, product differentiation is what the public wants. In order to achieve the optimal level of product differences, marketing departments have to promote a huge number of products, most of which will fail.

## SUMMARY

**Main points covered in Chapter 12:**

1. The entrepreneur plays a critical role in the economy, bringing together land, labor and capital to create wealth and improve the standard of living.

2. The entrepreneur is the steering wheel of the economy, whether playing the role of the driver maintaining the course toward a goal (Kirzner's equilibrium model) or steering in a new direction to avoid an accident or discover a new destination (Schumpeter's disequilibrium model).

3. The entrepreneurial economy is always dynamic, a system both of creative destruction (Schumpeter's term) and a discovery process (Kirzner's term).

4. Advertising serves two purposes: to provide vital information to customers, and to persuade customers to buy. The first is considered essential and useful for an efficient economy, but the second is more controversial. Some critics consider advertising and product differentiation a monopolistic practice and a barrier to entry by competitors.

## IMPORTANT TERMS

Arbitrage entrepreneurship

Barriers to entry

Dependence effect

Enterpreneurship

Innovative entrepreneurship

Kirzner's discovery process

Monopolistic power

Schumpeter's creative destruction

12Jack Gordon, "Returning Insight to the Consumer" *New Products Magazine* (December 2006).

## INFLUENTIAL ECONOMIST

### PETER F. DRUCKER, MANAGEMENT GURU

**Name:  Peter F. Drucker (1909 - 2005)**

**Background:** Peter Drucker, the world's most famous management guru, is a household name among MBAs, corporate executives and business students. Although he did not earn a degree in economics and did not consider himself an economist, he wrote extensively on economic topics, emphasizing entrepreneurship and investment capital while denouncing big government, excessive taxation, and Keynesian economics. His accomplishments were multifarious: lawyer, journalist, political theorist, economist, novelist, futurist, and philosopher. As one admirer remarked, Drucker was an "iconoclast—the smasher of idols, seeker of proof, demander of evidence, gadfly, thorn in the side, tough and hard-nosed commentator on problems faced by our society."

Born in Vienna, Austria, Drucker earned a law degree at the University of Frankfurt, refused to work for the Nazis, and immigrated to England and to the U. S. in the 1930s. He lived the rest of his life in the United States, writing numerous books and articles on corporations, management and economics.

**Major Works:** *The Concept of the Corporation*, a study of General Motors, put Drucker on the map. He discovered an alternative to big government (which Drucker considered inherently inefficient and wasteful) as a social welfare institution: the multinational corporation. By assuming social responsibilities such as job security, training and educational opportunities, health care, retirement and other benefits, big business offers a "non-revolutionary" alternative to government. Initially, GM rejected his vision of the corporation as a social entity, but eventually all major companies have moved in the direction of social organizations.

Drucker's favorite economist was Joseph Schumpeter. According to Drucker, Schumpeter—not Keynes—is the economist of the future. Drucker liked Schumpeter's emphasis on dynamic disequilibrium, the vital innovative role of the entrepreneur, and his defense of big business. In his 1985 book, *Innovation and Entrepreneurship*, Drucker focused on the impact of technological change, innovation, the unexpected and new knowledge of business and the world economy.

**Critic of Keynesian Economics:** According to Drucker, government officials and policymakers have been afflicted by Keynesian thinking. John Maynard Keynes (see chapter 22) was a British economist who introduced a theory favoring deficit spending and other short-term inflationary policies during an economic downturn.

According to Drucker, government can do only two things effectively—wage war and inflate the currency. He states, "Indeed, government is sick—and just at a time when we need a strong, healthy, and vigorous government."[13] Drucker advocated privatization (a word he invented in his 1969 book, *The Age of Discontinuity*) of government services, especially Social Security. Echoing Hayek, Drucker claimed that no public institution can operate in a businesslike manner because "it is not a business."

Drucker blamed Keynesianism for an unhealthy anti-saving mentality, causing "undersaving on a massive scale" among the western nations, especially the U. S. Moreover, "Keynes is in large measure responsible for the extreme short-term focus of modern politics, of modern economics, and of modern business....Short-run, clever, brilliant economics—and short-run, clever, brilliant politics—have become bankrupt."[14]

**Personality:** Peter Drucker published over 25 books in his lifetime, in addition to his writing and consulting activities. He was famous for using no secretary or supporting organization. He answered the telephone himself.

Drucker was largely optimistic about the future of the expanding global economy, especially after the collapse of Communism and Soviet central planning. Multinational corporations, both large and small, are far more important than foreign aid or domestic spending programs, Drucker stated. Companies must be entrepreneurial, not just administrative, he argued.

## PROBLEMS TO PONDER

1. In Germany the law requires a public company's board of directors to include labor representatives, not just management. Do you think it is a good idea to include labor in the decision making role of the business? Should it be mandatory or voluntary?

2. In this chapter, two kind of entrepreneurs were discussed, the Kirznerian entrepreneur moving toward equilibrium and the Schumpeterian entrepreneur moving away from equilibrium. Give real-life examples of each. Which type of entrepreneur is more common in business life?

3. John D. Rockefeller, Andrew Carnegie, J. P. Morgan and other big business entrepreneurs in the late 19th and early 20th centuries were called "robber barons" by Matthew Josephson and other critics. Defenders of big business have argued otherwise. Compare Matthew Josephson's original work, *The Robber Barons* (Harcourt, Brace, 1934) with Burton W. Folsom, Jr.'s book, *The Myth of the Robber Barons* (Herndon, Virginia: Young America's Foundation, 1996). Which author is right in your judgment?

13 Peter F. Drucker, *The Age of Discontinuity* (Harper & Row, 1969), p. 212.
14 Peter F. Drucker, *Toward the Next Economics and Other Essays* (Harper & Row, 1981), pp. 1-21.

4. After reviewing the above books, which statement is more accurate? Why?

   A. "Behind every great fortune is a crime" (Honore de Balzac)
   B. "Great inequality and concentration of business are essential for the future progress of the race" (Andrew Carnegie).

5. Suppose the state of Florida responds to the demands of nature-lovers and bans all billboards along the roads and highways. What effect would such a ban have on the prices of motels, restaurants and other services previously advertised on billboards? Would such a ban increase the amount of time travelers take to find a place to eat or sleep?

6. One of the reasons Joseph Schumpeter argued that capital was doomed was because he predicted that big corporations would naturally shift away from risk-taking entrepreneurship in favor of low-risk managerial strategies. Has this happened? Have major corporations been unwilling to adapt to the times and meet competition head on? Are corporate executives better described as risk-averse managers than entrepreneurs willing to take a chance?

## RECOMMENDED READING

- Peter F. Drucker, *Innovation and Entrepreneurship* (Harper & Row, 1985). The world's best-known management expert explains the role of entrepreneurship in the marketplace.

- Israel M. Kirzner, *Competition and Entrepreneurship* (University of Chicago Press, 1973). The classic work on entrepreneurship, the discovery process, and disequilibrium in the capitalist economy.

- Charles R. Morris, *The Tycoons: How Andrew Carnegie, John D. Rockefeller, Jay Gould, and J. P. Morgan Invented the American Supereconomy* (New York: Times Books, 2005). An up-to-date objective review of the lives and ideas of the great albeit flawed capitalists of the 19th century.

# Chapter 13

# FINANCING CAPITALISM: STOCK AND BOND MARKETS

*"There was nothing basically wrong with the American economy
nor the vast majority of companies whose stocks were listed on the
New York Stock Exchange...I'd be foolish not to buy."*

—J.Paul Getty (1962)

*"Although it's easy to forget sometimes, a share of stock is not a lottery ticket.
It's part ownership of a business."*

—Peter Lynch

The story of Bill Gates, the richest man in the world, worth over $50 billion, and his software company, Microsoft, is a perfect example of microeconomics or the theory of the firm in action, and the vital role of the financial markets in the economy.

Gates and Paul Allen, his business partner, went to high school together in Seattle and were enthusiastic adventurers and entrepreneurs. Gates went to Harvard, but dropped out. In 1974, Gates (19 years old) and Allen (21 years old) created a company that read computer cards from machines monitoring traffic flow for local municipalities. Traf-O-Data, the company that ultimately became Microsoft, made $20,000 in revenue the first year.

When minicomputers were developed in the late 1970s, Gates and Allen wrote a successful software and began selling it to other companies in the growing personal computer business. By 1980, their Albuquerque, New Mexico firm had eight employees and $8 million in revenue.

Their big break came in 1980 when Gates received a call from IBM, asking him to write an operating system for its new personal computer. The result was MS-DOS (DOS stands for "disk operating system"), which went on to dominate the personal computer software market. Microsoft's revenue topped $100 million in 1984.

By 1985, Microsoft's market was expanding so rapidly that Gates and Allen decided they needed to issue stock to the public in order to raise more capital. Reaching his 30th birthday, Gates announced he was taking the company public, meaning he would offer shares of Microsoft to outside investors for the first time. For several years, Microsoft had been distributing private stock to its staff under an employee stock ownership plan (ESOP), but it was about to introduce the new Windows software worldwide, which required a huge amount of investment capital. Gates chose investment bankers Goldman Sachs and Alex Brown to underwrite the public offering. The stock began trading on the NASDAQ market on March 12, 1986, priced at $21 a share. Microsoft raised $690 million from the IPO (initial public offering). Owning 45% of the stock, Bill Gates suddenly had a net worth of $311 million, on paper anyway. His annual salary at the time was only $122,000.

One hundred shares of the original Microsoft stock cost $2,100 in 1986. Today those 100 shares are worth over $500,000. And Bill Gates, now in his fifties, owns stock valued at over $50 billion at today's market valuation (2009).

Microsoft is, of course, a fantastically successful entrepreneurial venture. It demonstrates the role the financial markets play in the market system. The aim of this chapter is to explain the stock and bond markets, and how they help finance capitalism. How important are Wall Street and the securities market? Are options and futures markets, known as the derivatives market, beneficial or harmful to the economy? Can an investor beat the market, i.e., outperform the Dow Jones Industrial Average or the S&P 500? What role should the government play in controlling Wall Street and the commodity exchanges, and in protecting investors? Economists have a great deal to say about these issues.

## THE STOCK MARKET AS A SOURCE OF CAPITAL

The most important point in this chapter is that the stock market serves as a major source of new capital in achieving our goal of creating wealth and pursuing a higher standard of living.

Bill Gates and Paul Allen developed new software and computer services that individuals and companies demanded. These products served a growing need. Gates and Allen formed a company which was later incorporated as Microsoft. They hired workers, rented space, bought supplies, tools, and equipment, and developed new products that they sold to their customers (such as IBM). They acted as entrepreneurs, putting together the right amount of land, labor and capital (the factors of production) to make a product to sell to consumers. And they accomplished their goal at a substantial profit.

## TRADITIONAL SOURCES OF CAPITAL

Gates and Allen could not have done all this without outside capital. Few businesses succeed without help from financial institutions and individual investors.

To start a new business requires money to hire workers, rent an office, and buy supplies. Bill Gates and Paul Allen started out with little personal savings.

**Five traditional sources of capital are:**

(1.) Use personal savings

(2.) Borrow money from close relatives or friends

(3.) Borrow money from banks, insurance companies or other financial institutions

(4.) Issue notes or bonds, i.e., short-term or long-term debt obligations

(5.) Sell shares of the company to the public

Most start-up businesses rely on the owner's savings and personal loans from friends, relatives and banks to raise funds. Only when a business is in full operation for several years, profitable and expanding, is "going public" or issuing debt instruments considered.

## THREE LEGAL FORMS OF BUSINESS

A new business venture may operate as a sole proprietorship in the early stages of development, filing a schedule C (unincorporated) business tax return each year. Such a legal form is a simple, inexpensive way to operate a business. However, the firm faces unlimited liabilities. If the company loses money or gets sued, the company owner may have to sell the home or other family assets to pay off the company debts.

Normally after a business grows, it switches from a sole proprietorship to either a partnership or a corporation. A partnership may involve a small business owned by only two people, or it may be more sophisticated involving hundreds of individuals, as in the case of many law or accounting firms. In partnerships, each partner is liable for all the liabilities or debts of the company. If two individuals open a pet shop in a mall and each puts up $10,000 to get the store going, and they borrow $100,000 from the bank and various other sources to pay for inventory and other costs, both partners are liable for the entire amount if the store closes.

Accounting and law firms believe that a partnership is a more appropriate legal form to assure clients that the firm is backed by the resources of all the partners. In the 1980s, most Wall Street investment firms switched from partnerships to corporations because of the increasing liability and risk associated with underwritings and global investments.

## BENEFITS OF INCORPORATION

What are the benefits of incorporation? Incorporating is the most common form of business ownership. When incorporated, a business is owned by the shareholders in percentages based on the number of shares they own. In the case of Microsoft, Gates and Allen started their business in 1974, not as a publicly traded corporation, but as a privately held corporation.

Anyone can incorporate a business simply by registering with a state government and issuing shares to various company officers. Corporations do not have to be registered in the state in which they reside. Delaware and Nevada are the most popular states for incorporating because of certain tax advantages. Even a single person can incorporate a business or service company. The corporation must register with the Securities and Exchange Commission as well as state securities commission(s) if the company exceeds a specific number of shareholders. The registered corporation issues private stock to shareholders. Private stock is not traded on a formal exchange. To sell the stock would require finding a willing buyer—either a company officer or another private investor wanting to invest in the company.

Corporations benefit from limited liability. In the case of the bankrupt pet shop, the partners were personally liable for the entire debt, $100,000. If they had incorporated, only the company's cash and assets could have been used to pay off the debts. They personally would not be liable unless they put up personal assets such as home, car or, other tangible goods, as collateral.

When Pan American went bankrupt in the early 1990s, none of the airline's shareholders were liable for Pan American's debts. These shareholders lost their entire investment in the company, but did not lose personal assets. Whether a firm is a public or private corporation, liability is limited to the investment of the shareholders.

## FINANCING A FIRM

A growing corporation often needs additional funds to expand—to increase its marketing efforts, to build a new plant, to hire more workers, and so forth. In fact, without outside capital, most big businesses would never grow. Where does the corporation get this fresh capital?

A company can generate investment capital by retaining corporate earnings rather than paying these earnings out as dividends. Many companies have financed expansion plans through internal financing this way.

Second, a company can borrow funds from a bank, insurance company, or other financial institution. Financing through intermediaries requires extensive paperwork and disclosure of a company's financial condition. Once a loan or credit line is approved, the corporation will have to pay interest on the loan.

Third, a major company has the option of issuing debt instruments to the public in the form of commercial paper, notes or bonds.

Finally, a firm can issue new shares of stock to current or new shareholders. Most big businesses are publicly-traded companies, but there are exceptions such as Koch Industries, a major commodities firm based in Wichita, Kansas, or Mars, the famous candy maker (M&Ms). These remain private corporations.

Suppose Microsoft incorporated by issuing 100,000 shares at $1 a share, thus raising $100,000 from Bill Gates, Paul Allen, and their associates. Suppose Gates and his partners decide they need more money to expand, so the company issues another 100,000 shares at $5 a share for a total of $500,000 in new investment capital. This new issue dilutes the number of company shares, increasing the outstanding stock from 100,000 to 200,000, but it also injects fresh cash into the company, an additional $500,000 that can be used to expand operations.

Throughout this expanding development, Microsoft remained a privately-held corporation. No shares traded on NASDAQ or other stock exchanges. If any partner wanted to sell shares of Microsoft, he had to find another willing investor to pay an agreed-upon price.

## GOING PUBLIC

For the vast majority of small corporations, issuing public shares is the way to finance growth.

In 1986, Microsoft decided to go public, in part because of the huge capital requirements needed to introduce Windows software. In order to go public, Microsoft chose an investment banker to underwrite the sale of the stock to the public in an Initial Public Offering (IPO). Well-known investment bankers include Salomon Brothers, First Boston, Merrill Lynch and Goldman Sachs. Microsoft used Goldman Sachs and Alex Brown.

Taking a new stock public requires extensive experience. The investment banker helps the company officers decide how much stock to issue, the price, and when to sell the stock to investors. Sometimes warrants are attached to the stock (the stock and the warrant are sold together as a "unit"). Warrants give shareholders the right to purchase a certain amount of stock at a specific price within a specified time. Warrants, however, are usually only issued if the underwriter thinks the company needs to make the deal more attractive in order to get investors to buy the stock.

287

Setting the right price for a new issue is extremely important. If the price is considered too high, brokers will not be able to sell the entire issue to their customers. Or if it does sell out and the price declines right after the IPO, investors may become discouraged. Making shareholders unhappy right after an IPO is not considered good public relations.

If the IPO price is set too low, the stock becomes too attractive and the entire issue sells out quickly, forcing brokers to ration the hot issue to their favored customers. Sometimes this practice of favoritism creates ill-will among would-be shareholders who now have to wait to buy it on the open market. Moreover, the company ends up giving a windfall to speculators who buy the new issue and sell it immediately in the secondary market for a quick profit. Instead of the additional funds going to the company to expand business, the profits go to speculators.

Rising stock prices (known as "bull markets") are the most favorable environment for new issues. More IPOs come out during times when the market is "bullish". The worst time to promote a new issue is during and right after a crash or bear market. It can ruin the prospects of a new issue even though the company is fundamentally sound.

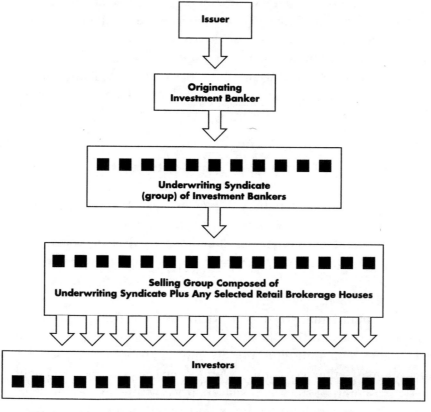

**Figure 13.1.** *The issuance process for new securities in the primary market.*

Apparently Microsoft had some smart underwriters. The stock came out at $21 a share, which offered a substantial profit to company insiders who had purchased privately-held stock earlier at much lower prices. Shareholders who received the IPO price were happy to see their investment increase gradually and substantially over time.

The IPO for Microsoft raised $690 million, minus the costs of underwriting, in new growth capital for Microsoft. Underwriters and stockbrokers typically share around 10% of the investment capital in an IPO. Hence, Microsoft received approximately $621 million with which to expand their business.

## SHOULD INVESTORS BUY NEW ISSUES?

IPOs are effective ways to raise money for companies and their employees who own stock. By going public, company officers can more easily sell their stock at substantially higher prices. Insiders sell to diversify their wealth. Prior to going public, stock held by company officers and insiders were tied up in privately-issued stock, and the only way they could liquidate their position was to search for another private investor to buy this stock. After the IPO, this stock is traded every day on the exchange, allowing them to sell fairly easily.

Secondly, the firm now has substantial funds with which to expand its business. Moreover, the company is under no obligation to return the money to shareholders. Company officials do not have to declare a dividend, nor do they have to pay interest every six months as they are required to do with bonds or interest on any bank loan. In short, issuing publicly-traded stock is the cheapest form of capital formation.

Many Wall Street observers recommend against buying "new issues" or IPOs by pointing out that purchasers are buying an unknown commodity without any track record. Purchasers do not know whether the price of a new issue is a bargain or not until it starts trading on the exchange (the secondary market). Even a so-called "hot issue" may be deceiving. The stockbroker may say that the stock is heavily oversubscribed, but then the new issue comes out and the stock fails to go to premium as predicted, and the price drops quickly.

In a bull market, most new issues increase in price, then fall back. *Forbes* magazine recently found that the average IPO rises in price on average for two years, then falls back to its original price. Despite this, new issues can be a good investment if the purchaser looks at the fundamentals closely. Some underwriters are better than others in selecting the right companies to take public. Careful research (called "due diligence" in the industry) instead of simply relying on hot tips provides a solid foundation for making good money in new issues.

Microsoft stock is an example of a major success, increasing 20 times its original IPO price by 2009. Microsoft has announced several stock splits over the past 20 years, a bullish indicator. (The last stock split came in 2003.) In 1998, when Microsoft was selling for about $160 a share, it declared a 2-for-1 stock split, instantly doubling the number of shares. If an investor owned 1,000 shares at $160 a share, he would now have 2,000 shares at $80 a share. The total value is still the same ($160,000), but the investor now has twice the number of shares at half the price. If the value is still the same, why do companies announce stock splits? By cutting the price in half, the stock appears more affordable to smaller investors, which in turn encourages more people to buy the stock. This is a marketing ploy.

All stocks trading on the exchanges today were once new issues: IBM, McDonald's, Xerox, General Motors, General Electric, and the other household names.

## THE ABCs OF THE STOCK EXCHANGE

Once Microsoft issued its new securities and qualified for a listing on NASDAQ in 1986, investors began buying and selling Microsoft shares on the secondary market. Thousands of stocks trade on official exchanges in the U. S. and around the world.

Several thousand companies trade on the New York Stock Exchange (NYSE). Located at Broad and Wall Streets in Manhattan, the NYSE is the oldest and largest exchange in the U. S. and the world. Founded in 1792, NYSE started out with bond brokers meeting under a buttonwood tree on Wall Street. Soon they met in the Tontine Coffee House where memberships were called "seats." In 1817 it took the name New York Stock Exchange Board. A new building was constructed and completed in 1903, which is in use today. Today the "Big Board" is responsible for over half the dollar volume of securities traded in the U. S.

Other regional stock exchanges exist in the U. S., but the fastest growing exchange is the National Market System, listing over 3,200 companies. NASD stands for the National Association of Securities Dealers, a self-regulatory body of brokers and dealers. The Automated Quotation System (NASDAQ) offers up-to-the-minute stock quotes via computer to thousands of broker/dealers around the country. The most frequently traded NASDAQ stocks are traded on the computerized National Market System and are followed regularly on computer and in the financial media.

In the early days of NASDAQ, successful companies would typically graduate to the "Big Board," the New York Stock Exchange, which was considered the most prestigious stock exchange in the world. For example, almost all the Dow Jones 30 industrial stocks are listed on the NYSE. However, several major companies recently chose to remain on NASDAQ. Microsoft and Apple Computer are two examples. As a result, NASDAQ is gaining a reputation as a prestigious stock exchange on par with the NYSE.

There is talk that eventually the NYSE will switch to a pure computerized system similar to NASDAQ. Currently the NYSE relies on specialists on the floor of the exchange who act as broker/dealers and are required to make a market of their assigned stocks at all times in order to maintain an orderly market. This requires specialists to maintain adequate cash and capital reserves during bear markets and crashes.

## WORLD STOCK MARKETS

The stock markets outside the United States have been booming since World War II. Major exchanges exist throughout Europe, Asia and Latin America. The Nikkei Index in Tokyo has grown so rapidly during the post-war period that by the late 1980s, the Japanese market nearly equaled the NYSE's dollar volume, though it has since retreated.

Today's financial markets are global. The financial media keep a close watch on individual markets in Asia, Europe and Latin America, and how these markets might affect the U. S. market. Long gone are the days when the U. S. was insulated from foreign markets. Today an investor in Kansas can pick up the phone, call a broker, and buy stocks immediately in London, Zurich, Johannesburg, or Hong Kong. Investors can buy individual foreign stocks or country funds, investment companies that invest exclusively in a foreign nation. Foreign markets are covered extensively on television (such as CNBC), the Internet (such as Yahoo Finance), and financial newspapers (such as *The Wall Street Journal, Barron's, The Financial Times* and *Investor's Business Daily*).

## STOCK INDICES

One way to gauge what the market is doing is to look at market indices.

The Dow Jones Industrial Average (DJIA) is the most well-known stock market index. It a price-index consisting of the 30 largest blue-chip companies in the U. S. The Dow Jones Company publishes its list of 30 industrials in each issue of *The Wall Street Journal*, and the Dow is monitored continually on the financial news networks.

Note that in figure 13.4, some of the companies—American Express, Citigroup, and JP Morgan Chase—may not be regarded as industrial firms. Nevertheless, the 30 Dow Jones Industrial Average (DJIA) stocks are the most watched U. S. indicator of stock activity, although they represent only a fraction of all transactions on the NYSE. The S&P 500 Index, which measures the market value of the top 500 companies in the U. S., is probably a better all-around stock market indicator.

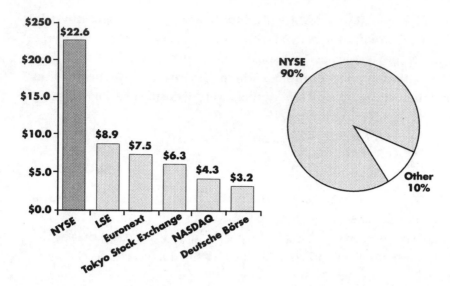

**Figure 13.2.** *Total Market Capitalization of World Stock Markets, 2006 (in $trillion).*
*Source:* World Federation of Exchanges.

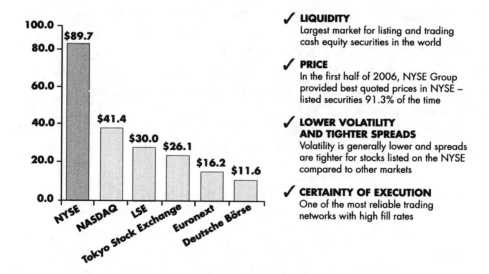

✓ **LIQUIDITY**
Largest market for listing and trading cash equity securities in the world

✓ **PRICE**
In the first half of 2006, NYSE Group provided best quoted prices in NYSE – listed securities 91.3% of the time

✓ **LOWER VOLATILITY AND TIGHTER SPREADS**
Volatility is generally lower and spreads are tighter for stocks listed on the NYSE compared to other markets

✓ **CERTAINTY OF EXECUTION**
One of the most reliable trading networks with high fill rates

**Figure 13.3.** *Average Daily Volume of Trading in World Stock Exchanges, 2006 (in $billion).*
*Source:* World Federation of Exchanges.

**Figure 13.4**

## DOW JONES INDUSTRIAL AVERAGE INDEX (2010)

| | | |
|---|---|---|
| Alcoa | Exxon Mobil | Merck |
| American Express | General Electric | Microsoft |
| AT&T | Hewlett Packard | 3M |
| Bank of America | Home Depot | Pfizer |
| Boeing | IBM | Procter & Gamble |
| Caterpillar | Intel | Travelers Companies |
| Chevron | Johnson & Johnson | United Technologies |
| Cisco Systems | J. P. Morgan Chase | Verizon |
| Coca Cola | Kraft Foods | Wal-Mart |
| DuPont | McDonald's | Walt Disney |

The DJIA list has changed many times over the years as some companies expand and others decline in a dynamic economy. Charles Dow created the Dow Index in 1884 and listed 11 stocks, a combination of mostly railroad companies and a few industrial companies. They included Union Pacific and Western Union. The list included 12 stocks between 1896-1916, changing companies as the market grew. U. S. Steel, American Sugar, People's Gas, General Motors and General Electric were added. The Dow grew to 20 stocks between 1916-28, and finally the popular series of 30 industrials began in 1928. Since then the Dow has been modified over 18 times and has involved over 50 companies. Only two big companies have survived during the entire period: General Electric and Standard Oil (now Exxon Mobil). AT&T almost lasted the entire time, but was briefly dropped in 2004 and then reinstated as the new name of SBC Communications. Major names such as Westinghouse, Sears, Woolworth, and U. S. Steel (now USX) had been on the list for decades but were finally dropped in the 1990s, replaced by Wal-Mart, Hewlett-Packard, and Disney, and the financial crisis of 2008 caused Dow Jones to drop Citigroup, AIG, and General Motors and add Bank of America, Cisco Systems and Travelers Companies. This is clearly a case of Schumpeter's "creative destruction" at work.

## WHAT IS THE BEST WAY TO INVEST IN THE STOCK MARKET?

The creation of the stock market from the firm's point of view is a superior way to raise capital and expand the business. Company founders and officers also use the stock market as a way to sell their company at a substantial profit and move on to other work. What is the best way to make money in the stock market from the investor's point of view?

293

Whole books and numerous courses are offered on strategies for investing in the market. This chapter will focus on a few traditional techniques followed by some of the world's most successful investors and money managers such as Warren Buffett, John Templeton, Arnold Bernhard, and J. Paul Getty. All four men are known as fundamental analysts—investors who look closely at a company's income sheets and balance statements.

These successful investors look for publicly-traded companies that are highly profitable and expanding over the long run. They look at sales figures, costs of production, payables and receivables, profit margins, return on equity (after-tax profit/net worth), book value, and so forth. They search for companies with strong management skills. As J. Paul Getty states, "...no one should ever buy a stock without knowing as much as possible about the company that issues it. In more cases than legitimate brokers would care to count, such so-called investors have insisted on buying large numbers of shares in companies without having the foggiest notion of what those companies do or produce."[1]

John Templeton adds that a global approach allows investors to find more opportunities for good investments. "It's not easy, but if you're going to buy the best bargains, look in more than one industry, and look in more than one nation." Templeton is considered the father of international investing. The Templeton Growth Fund was founded in 1954 and is considered one of the best performing funds in global investing.

Templeton also emphasizes the need to invest in countries that favor free enterprise. "Avoid investing in those countries with a high level of socialism or government regulation of business. Business growth depends on a strong, free-enterprise system."[2]

Once the earnings picture — now and in the future — has been established by an investor, the next most important issue is the price. A company can be highly profitable, but if speculators have driven the price too high, it may no longer be a bargain or fairly priced. In fact, it may be highly overpriced.

Ideally, investors want to buy a highly profitable company at a cheap price. Bargain hunting is a popular strategy among stock-pickers. But there is no easy formula for finding a bargain.

---

1  J. Paul Getty, *How to Be Rich* (Jove, 1965), p. 156. "The Wall Street Investor" is an excellent summary of the fundamental approach of investing.
2  John Templeton, quoted in William Proctor, *The Templeton Prizes* (Doubleday, 1983), p. 71.

## PRICE/EARNINGS RATIO

One method of finding a bargain stock is to look at the price-earnings ratio (P/E), defined as follows:

$$P/E = \frac{\text{price per share}}{\text{earnings per share}}$$

There are several kinds of P/E ratios, such as the trailing 12-month P/E which is based on the earnings per share of a company over the previous four quarters or past year, and the projected P/E which is based on predicted earnings per share over the next four quarters or next year.

By looking at the P/E ratio of a company and comparing it to the rest of the companies in the industry and the general market, analysts can get a good idea of how overvalued or undervalued a stock is. Recently, companies in high growth industries such as computers, semi-conductors, and the Internet have extremely high P/E ratios because investors have pushed their prices sky high in anticipation of high company earnings. On the other hand, companies growing slowly or not at all such as banks and utilities have low P/E ratios because analysts do not expect future earnings to accelerate.

Arnold Bernhard founded the Value Line Investment Survey, a popular rating service of individual U. S. stocks. Since 1965, Value Line has offered a one-page summary of a company's fundamentals followed by a ranking of stocks from one to five based on timeliness and safety (recently adding technical ratings as well). Bernhard's service has done an admirable job of selecting top rated growth companies and avoiding companies with poor prospects. Value Line's #1 rated stocks for timeliness have generally outperformed the market averages, a difficult achievement. (See the section below, "Can you beat the market?")

## BUYING AND SELLING: THE BROKERAGE BUSINESS

Stocks and other investments are bought and sold through stockbrokers whose reputations vary considerably with the public. Brokerage firms with high reputations are usually those offering nationwide services such as Merrill Lynch, Morgan Stanley, Smith Barney, and discount brokerage firms such as Charles Schwab, E-Trade, and Fidelity. Commissions vary among brokers, although the competition has driven the rates down in recent years, especially with Internet trading.

Merrill Lynch was a pioneer in the early 1950s to dispel the notion that stockbrokers were simply incompetent salesmen who switched customers in and out of stocks just to make high commissions. Charles Merrill, the founder, tried to change

Wall Street's tarnished image by instituting rigorous training programs and by putting brokers on salary, not just commission. Merrill Lynch published research and market letters which they offered free to customers. Merrill's policies of "People's Capitalism" paid off—by the late 1950s he had over half a million customers. Most other brokerage firms have since imitated Merrill Lynch's methods.

Still, investors have to be careful whom they are dealing with. Stockbrokers must take a Series 7 examination administered by the National Association of Securities Dealers (NASD), but the test does not guarantee competence or experience. Becoming a broker does not require a college degree, although most major brokerage firms now insist on one.

## BUYING ON MARGIN

Brokerage firms are also a place where more aggressive investors can borrow money and buy more stock. Investors who are extremely optimistic about a stock's prospects can purchase shares "on margin," i.e., with borrowed money, using their existing stocks as collateral.

Since the 1930s the margin requirement for stocks has been 50%. (By comparison, the margin is 30% for high-grade corporate bonds and only 10% for government bonds.) The margin requirement is not set by the Securities & Exchange Commission or NASD, but by the Board of Governors of the Federal Reserve Board. Until the 1930s, margin requirements were set by brokerage firms and the major stock exchanges. During the Roaring Twenties bull market, stocks could be bought with as little as 10% down. When the market crashed in 1929-32, so many investors were hurt by being overleveraged that the Federal Reserve raised the margin requirement to 50%.

A 50% margin requirement means that investors can buy $10,000 worth of stock with only $5,000 in their investment account. If the price of the stock declines too much, the investor can get a margin call from his broker asking him to put up additional cash to maintain his position. If he does not meet the margin call, the broker will sell his stock.

## SELLING SHORT

Brokerage firms also allow investors to "sell short," a way of profiting from *declining* stock prices. When stock is "sold short," the stock is borrowed from another investor or the brokerage firm and sold. When the stock declines, brokers go back into the market, buy the stock again and return the stock to the original owners. Selling short reverses the normal trade. Instead of buying low and selling high, investors sell high and buy low. If the stock goes up instead of down, the investor can get a margin call.

## WHEN TO SELL

How long should investors hold onto their stocks? Opinion varies, but most fundamental investors like Bernhard and Templeton hold stocks for six or seven years. When Warren Buffett was asked, "How long do you plan to hold onto Coca Cola?", he responded, "Forever." However, there are better times to sell than others such as when the stock's price has clearly climbed sharply and may be overvalued, or when the money is needed for other purposes such as retirement or to buy a house. Or a company's growth prospects may turn negative, warranting a sell.

## THE GROWTH IN MUTUAL FUNDS

Many investors do not feel comfortable buying and selling individual stocks, given that there are over 10,000 publicly traded stocks in the U. S. alone, and many thousands more overseas.

A popular alternative to buying individual stocks is mutual funds. These are investment companies that offer to select and manage stocks for investors. The mutual fund industry has grown dramatically in the past 50 years.

The concept of mutual funds is not new. The first funds were formed in the British Isles and were called investment trusts. One of the first, the Scottish-American Investment Trust, was formed in 1873 and invested in American railroad bonds. All Scottish and British trusts were of the "closed end" variety: they were capitalized with a fixed number of shares which traded regularly on the stock exchange, with prices varying according to supply and demand.

This same type of closed-end investment trust also became a popular vehicle in the United States for small investors during the 1920s. At the height of the bull market in 1929, there were 19 such investment trusts in operation with assets totaling $140 million. The big four trusts — Goldman Sachs Trading Corporation, United Founders, American Founders, and Lehman Fund — were the darlings of the small investors. It was through the investment trusts that Wall Street insiders lured the public to speculate in the bull market of the 1920s. The minimum investment was low, and small investors believed this was the best way to get a piece of Radio Corporation of America (RCA), American Telephone and Telegraph (AT&T), U. S. Steel, and Standard Oil of New Jersey, which sold at high prices individually. Moreover, the trusts were viewed as an ideal way to maximize one's profits since the trusts had a specific number of shares outstanding and could sell far above their net asset value or NAV (the value of the underlining shares). Investment trusts traded just like common stocks, and often sold for more than their book value during the 1920s.

Then the stock market crash hit in late October 1929. The crash wrecked the majority of the investment trusts, which fell far below their NAV after the crash. Some never recovered.

## THE RISE OF THE OPEN-ENDED MUTUAL FUND

During the 1920s a new investment vehicle was created, which became known as an "open-ended mutual fund." Unlike the older trusts, these were "open-ended" operations which agreed to sell shares at their NAV plus a small commission, and to redeem them at a later date at their NAV. The first such open-ended fund was Massachusetts Investors Trust created in 1924. It is still in existence today with $2 billion under management, one of the largest "load" mutual funds. ("Load" refers to the commission charged when mutual funds are bought or sold.)

Massachusetts Investors Trust and the other mutual funds suffered along with the closed-end investment trusts during the stock market crash, but survived because it was not tainted with the speculative fever of the other trusts. Sales grew slowly through the Great Depression so that by 1940 the net assets of mutual funds reached $500 million.

After World War II, mutual funds grew dramatically. By 1950 there were nearly 1 million accounts with net assets of $2.5 billion. Still, they represented only 1% of all purchases on the NYSE. By 1960, mutual fund net assets had climbed to $25 billion.

The 1950s and 1960s were the "go go" years of mutual fund investing, but it all changed in the late 1960s when the Dow Jones Industrial Average stalled around 1,000 for the next 15 years. The public became disenchanted with investing in stocks in general, whether through mutual funds or individual shares.

It was not until the 1980s that mutual funds hit the jackpot again. Net assets grew from $50 billion to $450 billion, a tenfold increase. Institutions dominated the purchase and sale of individual stocks, but mutual funds represented the individual investor. All varieties of new funds were created to respond to the needs of the investor, especially the creation of money market mutual funds which became a popular alternative to checking accounts and passbook savings accounts.

Throughout the 1990s and 2000s, mutual funds have continued to grow at a torrid pace, and today there are over 8,600 funds with net assets exceeding $9 trillion (compare that figure with $140 million in the 1920s!). There are all kinds of funds to choose from—funds that invest in blue chips (stocks in the S&P 500), growth, utilities, dividend-paying stocks, bonds, real estate, foreign markets, individual countries, and precious metals. There are balanced funds (funds that invest in a variety of sectors), index funds, and growth-plus-income funds.

How do funds make their money? They charge a variety of fees and commissions. Some have no upfront commissions ("no load"), but charge an annual administrative fee that covers the expenses of managing the fund (typically 1-2% a year). Others charge a front-end or back-end "load" which can vary from 1% to 5%. (Load funds used to charge as much as 8 1/2%, but competition has driven down the load commissions.) "Front end" load means a commission is charged when the stock is first purchased; "back end" load means a commission is charged when the stock is sold. Many full-service brokerage firms are now offering funds with no front-end load, but with a back-end load that declines each year (from, say, 4% to 0% over five years). These kinds of funds are designed to compete against the pure no loads, but still allow them to pay commissions to brokers for selling the fund to clients.

## CLOSED-END FUNDS MAKE A COMEBACK

Closed-end funds have also increased in popularity, though not as much as the open-ended funds. As we mentioned earlier, closed-end funds are investment companies that trade like common stocks on the exchanges. They have a fixed number of shares, and the price of the fund is determined daily through supply and demand. Unlike open-ended funds, closed-end funds can trade above or below their net asset value (NAV) just as companies trade above or below their book value.

Many fund managers prefer closed–end funds because their portfolios are insulated from market gyrations. For example, during a stock market crash, open-ended funds often have to dump shares quickly to meet redemptions by investors. Not so with a closed end fund. The fund manager can hold onto all securities in the fund's portfolio if necessary. If shareholders want out, they simply sell the fund on the stock exchange to a new investor. But selling or buying the fund has no effect on the portfolio itself. This is especially valuable in cases where the fund manager holds securities that are relatively illiquid at times. Almost all country funds, funds that invest in highly volatile securities in foreign countries (especially emerging markets), are of the closed-end variety.

Closed-end funds frequently sell at significant discounts to the NAV, sometimes as high as 30%. Bargain hunters often look for closed-end funds as opportunities to buy stocks at a discount, and during a rising market, closed-end funds normally outperform open-ended funds.

## THE NEW WORLD OF EXCHANGE TRADED FUNDS (ETFs)

A new development is Exchange Traded Funds (ETFs). ETFs are open-ended mutual funds that trade throughout the day on major exchanges. They are a low-cost, diversified way to invest in stocks, bonds, commodities, foreign markets, and specific sectors (utilities, technology, country funds, etc.). A popular ETF is the S&P

500 Index Fund, symbol SPY. It trades upwards of 200 million shares a day. ETFs have proliferated fast with over 400 on the market today. Some have poor liquidity, however.

ETFs are index-linked rather than actively managed, and therefore minimize their taxes. Unlike most mutual funds, they can be bought and sold throughout the day.

## CAN THE MARKET BE BEATEN?

How well do mutual funds and professional money managers do compared to the market indices such as the DJIA or S&P 500? Several services rate mutual funds, such as Morningstar, Lipper Services and Forbes magazine. Generally they conclude that the vast majority of mutual funds (at least two-thirds) consistently under perform the stock market averages. Why do professional fund managers do so poorly?

The reason is simple: competition. With thousands and thousands of securities analysts and investors combing the markets for the best stocks, the market quickly adjusts to new information. In this age of computers, technology and competition, information moves very quickly to wipe out undervalued and overvalued situations within a short period. In sum, the markets are relatively efficient.

The hypothesis that the market can not be beaten is known as the **efficient market hypothesis**. The efficient market theory was first raised by academic economists in the 1960s such as Eugene Fama at the University of Chicago. Burton G. Malkiel, professor of economics at Princeton University, wrote a book on the subject in 1973 called *A Random Walk Down Wall Street*, which has since gone through nine editions. Malkiel sums up the efficient market theory as follows:

"It means that short-run changes in stock prices cannot be predicted. Investment advisory services, earnings predictions, and complicated chart patterns are useless....Taken to its logical extreme, it means that a blindfolded monkey throwing darts at a newspaper's financial pages could select a portfolio that would do just as well as one carefully selected by the experts."[3]

The efficient market proponents were labeled "random walkers" because of their belief that short-term movements in the stock market appeared unpredictable and random, like a drunken sailor meandering down Wall Street.

Taking a cue from Malkiel's book, the editors of *The Wall Street Journal* used to engage in a contest every six months between the editors who chose stocks by throwing a dart at the stock listings, and professional analysts who selected their favorite stocks. (Interestingly, the professionals won most of the contests.)

3 Burton G. Malkiel, *A Random Walk Down Wall Street*, 5th ed. (Norton, 1990), p. 24. See Peter L. Bernstein, *Capital Ideas* (Free Press, 1992), chapters 2, 7.

What do the random walkers propose? They argue that fund managers trading stocks are not likely to beat the market. In addition to increasing the likelihood of losing money, traders face transaction costs (commissions, bid-ask spreads, and taxes) when they trade. The academic economists suggest an alternative: be a passive investor. Buy a large selection of individual stocks, or a stock index fund, and hold for the long term, taking dips and bear markets in stride. As simplistic as it may seem, such a strategy has been highly profitable since the early 1980s, with S&P 500 index funds returning 10% per annum.

The random-walk theories of academia created a furor on Wall Street when they introduced their ivory-tower theory. Highly-paid securities analysts and fund managers felt that their careers were threatened by evidence that they underperformed the market averages. Nevertheless, it was hard to contradict the evidence. Few professional investors have been able to top the return on the S&P 500 stock index since 1980 (about 10% per annum). See figure 13.5.

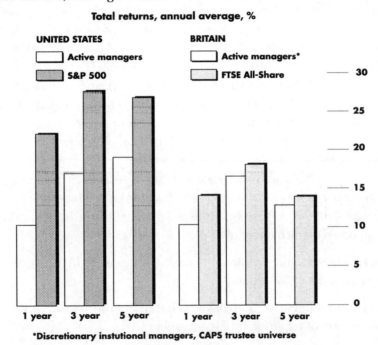

**Figure 13.5.**

*Source:* The Economist, *(29 May, 1999).*

As a result, Wall Street has joined the ivory tower professors of finance, and stock market index funds have become very popular in recent years. The Vanguard group of mutual funds, based in Valley Forge, Pennsylvania, was the first to offer an index fund, and the Vanguard Index Trust 500 Portfolio remains the largest index fund today with $35 billion in assets under management. Now there are hundreds of index funds, including international index funds.

Active fund managers still try to beat the indexes, and some of them have been successful, including Warren Buffett, Peter Lynch, Michael Price and Value Line. Warren Buffett's closed-end fund, Berkshire Hathaway, is without question the most successful fund to outperform the indexes over the long run. (The fund traded for $20 a share in the early 1970s and recently was selling for over $100,000 a share in 2009!) The Omaha billionaire has been a sharp critic of the efficient market theory. Berkshire Hathaway as well as earlier partnerships he was involved in with his mentor, Benjamin Graham, the father of fundamental analysis, consistently beat the averages. The problem with the efficient market hypothesis is that it always assumes efficiency. Warren Buffett states, "Observing correctly that the market was frequently efficient, they [the academic random walkers] went on to conclude incorrectly that it was always efficient. The difference between these propositions is night and day."[4]

Arnold Bernhard's Value Line Investment Survey has also produced a consistent record of selecting above-average stocks. In general, stocks ranked #1 in timeliness by Value Line have outperformed the market. Professor Fischer Black, an earlier proponent of the random walk theory, makes an exception for Value Line. He states, "Actively-managed portfolios do not do better than buy-and-hold situations." But he adds, "The Value Line Ranking System is one of the only two or three clear examples I have seen that show significant performance over a reasonable period of time. It still appears that most investment management organizations would improve their performance if they fired all but one of their security analysts and then provided the remaining analyst with the Value Line service."[5]

Then too there are innumerable cases of technical futures and options traders who have dramatically outperformed the market averages over many years. Jack D. Schwager of the New York Institute of Finance illustrates the ability of a few to turn a small bankroll into a fortune:

- A trader who, after wiping out several times early in his career, turned a $30,000 account into $80 million.

- A fund manager who achieved what many thought impossible—five consecutive years of triple-digit percentage returns.

- An electrical engineering graduate from MIT whose largely computerized approach to trading has earned his accounts an astounding 250,000 percent return over a sixteen-year period.[6]

4 Warren Buffett, 1998 Annual Report to Shareholders, Berkshire Hathaway.
5 Fischer Black, "Yes, Virginia, There is Hope: Tests of the Value Line Ranking System," cited in Arnold Bernhard, *How to Use the Value Line Investment Survey*, p. 20. Black's article appeared in 1971.
6 Jack D. Schwager, *Market Wizards: Interviews with Top Traders* (Simon & Schuster, 1989), p. ix.

Schwager points out, "only a handful of individuals" have this capability.

In sum, competition and entrepreneurship are in a constant battle in the financial markets. Entrepreneurs seek to outperform other investors and managers, but competition is so strong in this highly efficient field that it is difficult, though not impossible, to beat the averages.

The financial markets are neither perfectly efficient nor totally irrational. The truth lies somewhere in between; what we might label "imperfectly efficient." Undervalued and overvalued conditions exist in the marketplace. If investors do not take advantage quickly, the opportunities will disappear.

Similarly, our knowledge of the financial markets and the future is not perfect, but neither is it totally imperfect. Economic events and investment prices are not always predictable, but sometimes they are quite predictable. Markets are not totally efficient, but neither are they completely inefficient. This middle-ground position is similar to Friedrich Hayek's view of money in the economy. Hayek asked the question, "What is the relationship between changes in the money supply and economic activity?" He concluded that the relationship was neither a "tight joint" nor a "broken joint," but a "loose joint." By the same token, our knowledge of the future stock prices is neither perfect nor completely lacking, but somewhere in between—"imperfect."[7]

## ARE COMMON STOCKS A GOOD INFLATION HEDGE?

Common stocks and stock mutual funds are, in general, a good long-term investment. All stock indices during the 20th century show a general upward trend. Jeremy Siegel, finance professor at the Wharton School, has done more historical work on U. S. stock prices and other financial assets than anyone else. His book *Stocks for the Long Run* covers financial assets since 1802. See figure 13.6.

Siegel found that the total real return (including dividends and capital gains after inflation, as measured by the Consumer Price Index) for common stocks between 1802 and 2001 was approximately 7.0% per annum. The annual return on stocks has been even more pronounced since the bull market of 1982, with an average annual compounded return in this period of 10%.

Siegel concludes, "It can be easily seen that the total return on equities dominates all other assets. Even the cataclysmic stock crash of 1929, which caused a generation of investors to shun stocks, appears as a mere blip in the stock return index. Bear markets, which so frighten investors, pale in the context of the upward thrust of total stock returns."[8]

---

7  Friedrich A. Hayek, *The Pure Theory of Capital* (University of Chicago Press, 1941), p. 408. The idea of a "loose joint" in economics is more fully developed in Roger Garrison, "Time and Money: The Universals of Macroeconomic Thinking," *Journal of Macroeconomics* (Spring, 1984) and Mark Skousen, "The Economist as Investment Advisor," *Economics on Trial* (Irwin, 1991), pp. 261-63.

8  Jeremy J. Siegel, *Stocks for the Long Run*, 4th ed. (McGraw-Hill, 2008), p. 6.

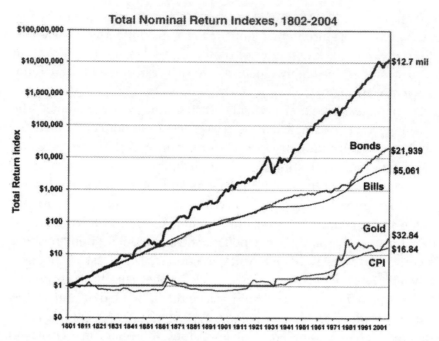

**Figure 13.6.** *Total real return indices, 1802-2004, for stocks, bonds, bills, gold and the U.S. dollar. Source:* Jeremy Siegel, *Stocks for the Long Run.*

How do stocks compare with bonds and gold? Stocks far outperformed both according to Siegel. Gold maintains its purchasing power in the long term, while bonds just barely stay above a positive real return. Stocks are the only clear winners.

Does this mean that stocks are a better inflation hedge than gold? Not necessarily. One must be careful with statistics. Stock prices may rise over the long term, overcoming periods of inflation or deflation, but another question is, how well or poorly did stocks behave during periods of rising inflation? During the double-digit inflationary era of the 1970s, for example, stocks did not do well. In fact, when price inflation accelerated in 1973-74 and 1979-81, many stock prices fell sharply. After an extensive study of inflation and stock values, economist Charles Nelson concludes, "When inflation [as measured by the Consumer Price Index] is on the rise, stay out of stocks; when it is on the decline, buy stocks."[9]

Siegel adds, "stocks are not good hedges against inflation in the short run," (p. 167) but adds that "no financial asset is." Gold and gold stocks usually advance when price inflation heats up. Gold is not a pure inflation hedge, though. The Midas metal fares well when the rate of inflation accelerates, but cannot maintain its return when the rate of inflation falls.

9  Charles R. Nelson, *The Investor's Guide to Economic Indicators* (Wiley, 1987), p. 123.

## THE BOND MARKET AS ANOTHER SOURCE OF CAPITAL

At the beginning of this chapter we listed several popular ways to raise capital for an expanding business. For corporations large enough to seek capital from the public, the capital raised from issuing bonds and other debt instruments is larger than the equity market. Analysts believe that the debt market is 10 times larger than the stock market. During the past two decades, bonds supplied 75% of external corporate financial needs, even at a time when the stock market was having its best years ever and IPOs were growing rapidly.

From a cost point of view, corporations would prefer to issue stock rather than bonds. Bonds are an extremely expensive source of capital because the firm must pay a fixed-interest payment every six months on its bonds, or every three months in the case of commercial paper, although the interest payments are tax deductible. Corporations do not have to pay interest or even dividends on their common stock.

**Preferred stock** is less expensive than bonds, but it is more expensive than common stocks. Preferred stock pays the stockholder a fixed dividend every quarter or whenever dividends are declared. Preferred stock has traditionally paid slightly less interest than bonds. Almost all corporations now have a **call provision** on their bonds and preferred stock. A call provision allows a firm to call in the old bonds and issue new ones at a lower interest charge or dividend. If interest rates are declining, more companies will "call" their bonds and issue new ones.

Corporations sometimes issue **convertible bonds** and **warrants** as a way to also reduce their costs. Convertibles give investors the chance to buy the issuer's stock at a fixed price while they continue earning interest on the bond. Traditionally, convertibles pay a slightly lower coupon rate because they are willing to accept a lower rate in exchange for the convertible feature. Warrants do not pay any interest income, but give the shareholder the right to buy the common stock at a fixed price during a specified period of time.

If common stock is the cheapest source of capital, will corporations avoid the headaches of issuing bonds and preferred stock and simply issue common stock? Corporations do not take this action because the market (the investing public) may not respond favorably to a large stock issue. The majority of investors tend to be older risk-averse individuals such as retirees who demand regular income. They may be conservative investors who prefer income to capital gains, even though history demonstrates that the total return on stocks is better than bonds. Therefore, traditional investors demand fixed-income instruments such as bonds, money market funds, and bank certificates of deposit. They may hold common stocks, but they prefer a majority of their portfolio to be in debt instruments. Therefore, corporations issue bonds not because they want to, but because the market demands it.

305

## THE ESSENTIALS OF THE BOND MARKET

Debt instruments represent contractual obligations of a corporation or government agency to pay interest to the bondholder, usually every six months, and the face value of the bond at maturity. The length of the debt instrument can vary between a day and 30 years. Recently a few brave companies such as Disney have issued bonds maturing in 50 years or longer. During the gold standard era of the late 19th century, railroads issued gold-backed bonds for 100 years. The classic gold standard (1867-1914) provided long-term stability unmatched in today's world of volatile interest rates.

In today's world of inflation and uncertainty, the average distance to maturity of debt instruments has gradually declined. The majority of Treasury debt is now medium- to short-term. Money market funds, which invest in short-term debt instruments such as Treasury bills, bank certificates of deposit, commercial paper, banker's acceptances and Eurodollars, are growing rapidly because their principal is relatively secure. Falling markets (called "bear" markets) and occasional crashes in stocks force many corporations to curtail their long-term financing.

## THE GROWTH OF MONEY MARKET FUNDS

Money market funds were created in the early 1970s as part of the financial revolution. They afforded the opportunity for the average investor to participate in the various money markets that previously required large minimums ($25,000 to $1 million) and were limited to institutions and wealthy individuals. Previously, the small investor who wanted complete liquidity was limited to investing in low-yielding passbook savings accounts at a local bank or savings and loan association.

The Reserve Fund was the first money market fund established in the U. S. Started in 1972, assets exceeded $9 billion until it was forced to liquidate during the financial crisis of 2008. The Reserve Fund was quickly imitated and today there are over 1,000 money market funds, many of them larger than the Reserve Fund. Merrill Lynch's Cash Management Account has over $100 billion in assets.

One of the greatest innovations by the Reserve Fund was to make money market funds instantly accessible through checking accounts. Thus, money market funds became in essence a high-yielding checking account.

Money market funds are not insured by the Federal government, although money market accounts at commercial banks are FDIC-insured.

## NOMENCLATURE OF BONDS

Corporate bonds with maturities ranging from 7 to 30 years are issued in units of $1,000. Municipal bonds are issued in units of $5,000, and Treasury bills mature at $10,000. Bonds are quoted based on a system of points. "100 points" represents a face value of $1,000. Thus, a one-point drop in bond prices represents a $10 decline in the value of the bond.

If a bond is selling at **par**, it is selling for 100 points or $1,000 face value. Below par means under 100, i.e., the bond is selling at a discount from its face value, less than $1,000. Above par means over 100, i.e., the bond is selling at a premium over its face value, above $1,000.

Bonds consist of two parts: the bond itself, which matures at face value, and the coupons or interest payments. Bonds offer a **coupon** payment every six months. The coupon is attached to the bond and is "clipped" on the due date (every six months) and redeemed at its face value.

If interest rates have risen since the bond was issued, the **current** rate of interest will exceed the coupon rate and the price of the bond declines. On the other hand, if interest rates have fallen since the bond was issued, the current rate will be less than the coupon rate and the price of the bond goes up. Thus bond prices and interest rates always move in opposite directions, assuming there's no change in the safety rating of the issuer. To repeat: If interest rates rise, bonds go down. If interest rates fall, bonds go up in price.

**Zero coupon bonds** are bonds without coupons or interest payments. Merrill Lynch was the first to develop the use of "zeroes" as a financial vehicle in the early 1980s. A Merrill Lynch broker cleverly separated the coupons from the bonds, creating an ideal security for certain investors. Today many companies issue zero coupon bonds, a way of raising capital without having to pay interest for 30 years. Moreover, because these zero bonds make no interest payments, they cost investors substantially less. Investors may only pay $150 for a zero coupon bond worth $1,000 in 30 years (at maturity).

## THE GROWTH OF DEBT: GOOD OR BAD?

The debt market—including corporate, municipal and federal government issues—has grown dramatically over the past 30 years. Is the exponential increase in private and public debt as bad as critics claim it to be?

It is important to get an accurate picture of what debt is all about. People often forget the other side of the debt coin—the credit side. Creditors include savers, banks, corporations and other institutions that lend money to debtors. These individuals and institutions do not always want to take an equity position in capital-seeking enterprises.

They are willing to lend money to them only after carefully considering the borrowers' credit-worthiness. In sum, lending and borrowing money is an essential characteristic of a growing capitalistic system. Of course, there will always be businesses that run into trouble and debtors who cannot pay back their loans. Inability to pay back loans is an unavoidable risk in a world where the future is uncertain. In many ways the huge growth in the private debt market is a reflection of a rapidly growing economy, not a society overwhelmed by consumer and corporate debt.

## THE IMPACT OF A LARGE TREASURY DEBT MARKET

The main issue regarding the debt pyramid is the potentially unstable role of government which has often been responsible for excessive debt creation through deficit financing. We will discuss the benefits and disadvantages of the government's creation of debt instruments in chapter 22, "Deficit Financing and the National Debt."

Suffice it to say for now that the U. S. Treasury market is by far the largest debt market in the U. S. and the world. The Treasury market is the only market large enough to handle the huge supply of capital and credit of foreigners (such as the Chinese). It is also the most liquid of debt markets (meaning easy to sell). The corporate and municipal bond markets are relatively illiquid compared to the Treasury market. Many municipal bonds do not trade daily or even weekly. Meanwhile the Treasury market is extremely active with T-bills, T-notes and T-bonds trading every business day. The Treasury market represents the vast majority of the liquid debt market today.

The existence of a large Treasury market cannot be underestimated in its effect on corporate and municipal bond markets. The size, liquidity and safety of the Treasury market have forced other issuers to pay extremely high interest rates on their lower-grade bonds and debt instruments. The government bond market is so large and active that it crowds out numerous capital projects by private firms and municipalities. The Treasury may pay 4-5% on its 30-year bonds, while private corporations must pay 8-12% depending on their safety ratings. There is no doubt that less creditworthy corporations who issue high-yielding (known as "junk") bonds have had a much harder time raising capital than otherwise would be the case if the government did not take most of the fixed-income market.

## WHAT MAKES THE MARKETS TICK?

How important are the stock and bond markets in the economy? For years the traditional view was that the financial markets were relatively unimportant and had little effect on the real economy, such as the day-to-day production process, consumer spending, and exchange of goods and services. Sometimes the Dow might fall 20%, as it did in 1990, or 30% as in 2000-03, while the economy continued to grow. As one cynic put it, "The stock market has predicted seven out of the last three recessions."

However, there is a growing sense among economists that the financial markets are playing a more serious role in the world economy today. The financial crisis of 2008 made that clear. Certainly the stock and bond markets have always played a major role as a source of investment capital for an expanding economy, both here and abroad, and that role may be increasing. In addition, millions more Americans are investing in the stock market as a form of saving or as a retirement plan. More companies are offering 401(k) plans, stock options and other forms of securities investments to employees and executives. Around the world, privatization of government-owned enterprises has put shares of publicly-traded companies into the hands of millions of citizens. All this has a "wealth effect" on individuals, and changes in that wealth effect can have significant impact on consumer buying decisions and business expectations.

The stock market index is a leading indicator of economic activity. In many ways, stock prices are an indicator of future plans by business and consumers. These plans reflect business and consumer sentiment about the prospects for economic growth. If those expectations are dashed due to higher interest rates, a financial panic in Asia, a collapse in the demand for U. S. exports, or a war breaking out in the Middle East, a sudden drop in the stock market might portend a recession or worse.

Ultimately the performance of any stock market depends on the viability of the free-enterprise economy. After all, the stock market represents the fortunes of the individuals and companies that make up the economy. There is nothing magical about stocks being a good investment over the long term in the United States. It all depends on the creative ability, hard work and able administration of its players.

Markets may appear irrational and volatile at times, but the long-term trend of the market is based on the entrepreneurial spirit of the people behind the companies that make up the markets. Stock prices rise over the long run because publicly-traded firms expand their markets, improve their products, and increase their profits. Prices fall over the long run when firms do not respond to customer needs or fail to create new consumers, and hence experience a decrease in their profits or lose money outright. This fundamental principle explains why McDonald's stock has skyrocketed over the years while Western Union has collapsed. As investment analyst David Dreman summarizes, "Research has demonstrated that earnings and dividends [profits] are the most important determinants of stock prices over time."[10]

10 David Dreman, *The New Contrarian Investment Strategy* (Random House, 1982), p. 40.

Obviously, stock prices sometimes exceed or fall below their long-term trend line. Investment psychology can drive stock prices to undervalued or overvalued situations. Short term market movements are frequently unpredictable and erratic. A company's earnings may be rising, but the stock price may decline over the short run. Eventually, if earnings continue to do well the stock will rebound, but it is often impossible to predict when. In short, Wall Street exaggerates everything.

## IS THE STOCK MARKET A GIANT CASINO?

Volatility and irrationality in the financial markets have worried investors and economists over the years. In the early 1990s, *Business Week* ran a cover story labeling the financial markets part of a "Casino Society" in the U. S., where Americans bet on anything without regard to fundamentals and real values. Is Wall Street just another Las Vegas as some analysts have suggested? Stock market expert Nicolas Darvas calls the market "a gambling house peopled with dealers, croupiers and touts on the one side, and with winners and suckers on the other."[11]

John Maynard Keynes, a British economist who was an avid speculator himself, regarded the stock market as a game of chance whose outcome was unpredictable and often irrational. Market uncertainty led to excessive pessimism and optimism which could be damaging to expectations in the real economy. Referring to the stock market, Keynes remarked, "For it is, so to speak, a game of Snap, of Old Maid, of Musical Chairs—a pastime in which he is victor who says *Snap* neither too soon nor too late, who passes the Old Maid to his neighbor before the game is over, who secures a chair for himself when the music stops."[12] Keynes recommended the introduction of a "substantial government transfer tax" on all stock transactions to discourage speculative fever. Other Keynesian economists recommend a higher tax on short-term capital gains.

Believing the stock market is essentially a gambling hall that serves no social or economic function, some social philosophers have urged that the stock market be abolished or at least highly taxed and regulated. The Marxists see no value in the stock exchange, which they regard as a bourgeois pleasure dome. The old stock exchange in Leningrad became a museum when the Marxists took over Russia in 1917, although the stock market, risky and unpredictable as it is, is now back in style in post-Soviet Russia.

Is the stock market a casino as the Keynesians and the Marxists have alleged? Outward appearances can be deceiving. Certainly the financial markets can be used as a gambling vehicle, and many technical systems are based on mathematical formulas similar to betting schemes. Trading no-load mutual funds, switching in and

11  Nicolas Darvis, *Wall Street: The Other Las Vegas* (Lyle Stuart, 1964), dustjacket.
12  John Maynard Keynes, *The General Theory of Employment, Interest and Money* (Macmillan, 1936), pp. 155-56.

out of the market based on moving averages and volume figures, and other charting devices have very little in common with the long-term value of the company's profitability. Yet there are a number of differences between the stock market and a game of craps or blackjack.

There is not necessarily a winner for every loser in investing. An investor may hold a stock for a year and sell it for a 30% profit to another investor, who may in turn hold it for a year and sell his shares for a 30% profit. This can continue indefinitely if the stock price continues to rise as in a major bull market. (A "bull" market is defined as a rising market.)

Second, in gambling, such as slot machines or craps, the odds are set, in every case slightly in favor of the house, while an investor seeks to minimize his risks or change the odds through superior knowledge or technique. Admittedly, gamblers can increase their chances of winning through card-counting methods and other techniques, but such methods, if successful, will force the house to deny the player an invitation to gamble. In the investment markets, a top-performing speculator is not limited in his success.

Third, investors can make money in the stock market over the long term, while gamblers tend to lose the longer they stay in a game. Eventually, the odds favor the house in a game of craps or blackjack so that the longer a gambler stays at the table, the greater the chances of losing. Experienced gamblers walk away from the table once they achieve their goal. In the U. S. stock market, the average investor made 10% per annum on his money over the past 70 years.[13] Stock markets in other countries have sometimes done even better.

Fourth, the gambling industry is in large measure a consumer industry, while the stock market represents the capital markets which are crucial to a modern developing nation. Invariably, countries without a stock market are backward and underdeveloped in their standard of living. If the stock market were abolished in major industrial nations, there would undoubtedly be considerable layoffs and a recession as sources of capital dried up. Many new company expansion plans would come to a halt. Granted, many companies could raise funds from the bond and commercial paper market or through bank loans, but the cheapest and most liquid form of capital, issuing stock to the public, would no longer exist.

Despite some appearances of a gambling mentality in the financial markets, the securities industry plays a crucial role in a nation's capital development and business expectations.

13See Jeremy J. Siegel, *Stocks for the Long Run*, 4th ed. (McGraw-Hill, 2008), for returns on stocks, bonds, and gold over the past 200 years.

## THE ROLE OF GOVERNMENT IN SECURITIES BUSINESS

What is the role of government, if any, in regulating the securities industry? Government policy on the state and federal level plays a key role in maintaining a beneficial climate for investors and business, but like any government activity, it can over regulate and cause unintentional consequences.

Following the stock market crash of 1929, Congress investigated fraudulent practices on Wall Street and concluded that the Federal government needed to play a more active role in regulating the securities business. The New York Stock Exchange had already imposed its own regulations on its members and the companies that traded on its exchange, but Congress went further. Over the years, it has passed a series of regulatory acts. Here are the highlights:

- The Security Act of 1933 established the Securities and Exchange Commission which consists of five members appointed every five years by the President of the U. S. (Its first chairman was Joseph P. Kennedy, who had firsthand experience with dubious securities practices, but, nevertheless, took a strong stand against securities fraud.) The Act outlawed certain stock manipulation practices, imposed "full disclosure" in prospectuses, and required all stock exchanges and all new stock issues to be registered with the SEC.

- The Securities Exchange Act of 1934 required all publicly traded companies, not just new ones, to be registered with the SEC.

- The Investment Advisors Act of 1940 required individuals and firms who sell investment advice to the public to register with the SEC (major publications such as The Wall Street Journal and Forbes were exempted).

- The Securities Acts Amendment of 1975 abolished fixed brokerage commissions, creating a whole new industry of discount brokers and lower commissions and mutual fund loads by major brokerage houses.

- The Insider Trading Act of 1986 prohibited company executives and other insiders from trading on corporate information not generally available to the public. Fines can be up to three times the profits insiders make on illegal trading. (Company executives can still legally buy and sell stock under certain circumstances, but they must disclose their trades to the SEC.)

- The Public Company Accounting Reform and Investor Protection Act of 2002 (known as "Sarbanes-Oxley" or Sarbox for short) introduced a whole new set of accounting rules and onerous regulations on all U. S. publicly-traded company boards, management and accounting firms. (See chapter 23 for more information.)

In addition to the SEC, Congress has established the Commodity Futures Trading Commission to regulate commodity futures trading in the United States. Sometimes the SEC and the CFTC fight over which agency is going to regulate the futures and options markets, which sometimes involve both securities and commodities such as options on the S&P 500 futures index.

## THE SEC: COSTS vs. BENEFITS

Regulation is not free. Though there are benefits to government regulation, the cost can be high. In the U. S. it costs over $1 million to take a company public, especially since the adoption of Sarbox. Thousands of young growth companies would like to go public and expand their operations, but cannot afford the expense. Not only do they have to register with the SEC, they have to gain approval of all 50 states before their stock can be sold to individuals in those states. Usually it takes up to a year to become registered on the federal and state levels.

As a result, many new U. S. companies go to Canada or London to become listed first because registration is faster and much cheaper (usually less than $200,000). After achieving success in Canada or London, they can afford to become listed on the NASDAQ, AMEX, or NYSE in the U. S.

Most foreign stocks and mutual funds do not register with the SEC because of the burdensome costs and regulations. Americans can still purchase unregistered foreign stocks and mutual funds, but an unregistered foreign company cannot solicit business in the U. S.

## FALSE SENSE OF SECURITY?

The SEC's job is to establish the rules of the transaction and to prevent fraud, but the task is not easy to fulfill. Since the SEC's creation, there have been many cases of fraud and abuse missed by the SEC. Two classic examples in the early 1970s are the Bernie Cornfield IOS fraud and the Equity Funding scandal. Millions of dollars were lost by the public as the SEC looked on. In fact, in the case of the Equity Funding scandal, the SEC criminally indicted Ray Dirks, an independent securities advisor, for exposing the Equity Funding fraud! SEC attorneys indicted Dirks for insider trading. Finally, after Dirks had spent 10 years and half a million dollars in legal fees, the Supreme Court ruled against the SEC and found Dirks innocent.

Following the collapse of the technology bubble in the early 2000s, there were an unprecedented number of corporate scandals and bankruptcies, including Enron, Tyco, Global Crossing, and Worldcom. The SEC failed to protect investors from these scandals. To boost government authority, Congress passed the Sarbanes-Oxley law that established onerous new rules and regulations on publicly-traded companies and their employees.

The financial crisis of 2008 revealed the worst case of SEC negligence — money manager Bernie Madoff confessed to embezzling up to $60 billion in investor funds in an incredible Ponzi scheme that defrauded non-profit organizations, hundreds of

313

investors in the Jewish community and quite a few celebrities. The massive cover-up was accomplished despite numerous warnings from the Wall Street community to SEC lawyers that Madoff was promising impossible returns every year.

One of the unintended consequences of the SEC is that the existence of a powerful government agency can create a false sense of security among investors. Customers may think that the government will keep the fraud-peddlers outside the legal playing arena, and may not pay attention to potential abuse, misleading information or outright fraud. Fortunately, many financial publications offer an alternative to the SEC through their intense investigative reporting on publicly-traded companies and brokerage houses. *Forbes, Business Week* and other establishment publications have written a series of reports on potential shams, boiler room operations, and swindles. The financial media and security analysts were the first to draw attention to the corporate scandals of the early 2000s, and the Madoff Ponzi scheme in 2008.

Financial newsletters have flourished in a free market of financial information. Under the Investment Advisory Act of 1940, the SEC regulated financial newsletters. However, in 1985 the Supreme Court ruled in *SEC vs. Lowe* that the SEC does not have the right to regulate independent newsletter writers or publishers unless they manage money.

## SUMMARY: FINANCIAL CAPITALISM IS GROWING

Clearly the financial markets play a significant role in the growth of an economy. In the new global economy, financial markets are growing rapidly and new ones are being created in developing nations. The stock market is clearly the most efficient way to raise capital. Governments can provide a useful service by clearly establishing the ground rules for securities transactions while discouraging fraudulent activities. But ultimately investors are on their own.

## IMPORTANT TERMS

| | |
|---|---|
| Bear market | Margin requirement |
| Bid-Ask spread | Modern portfolio theory |
| Bull market | Open-end mutual funds |
| Closed-end mutual funds | Partnership |
| Covered shorts | Price-earnings ratio |
| Efficient market theory | Private corporation |
| Equity | Publicly traded corporation |
| Exchange traded funds (ETFs) | Sarbanes-Oxley law |
| Hot issue | Secondary market |
| Initial Public Offering (IPO) | Selling short |
| Investment banker | Single proprietorship |
| Investment trusts | Stock split |
| Limited liability | Warrants |
| Liquidity | |

**HARRY MARKOWITZ AND MODERN PORTFOLIO THEORY**

**Name: Harry M. Markowitz (1927 - )**

**Background:** Markowitz is considered the father of modern portfolio theory which favors the efficient market theory and diversification of investment choices. Born in Chicago, Markowitz was a 25-year-old graduate student at the University of Chicago when he wrote his 14-page paper, "Portfolio Selection," for the March 1952 issue of the *Journal of Finance*. It was this article that won him the Nobel Prize in economics in 1990, which he shared with two other colleagues, Merton Miller and William Sharpe.

**His contribution:** Prior to Markowitz and modern portfolio theory, investors had no scientific method for measuring risk. Markowitz's primary contribution was to quantify risk and develop ways to reduce risk while increasing investment return. Modern portfolio theory is highly mathematical, but essentially Markowitz and other founders of the theory (Merton Miller, William Sharpe, Franco Modigliani, Myron Scholes, Paul Samuelson, James Tobin, Fischer Black, Eugene Fama, and Burton Malkiel) make three general recommendations for investors:

(1.) Diversify as much as possible. Diversification reduces risk and increases return. Financial economists usually recommend a broad-based index fund such as the S&P 500 stock index.

(2.) If high returns are sought, expect to take high risks. This concept is known as the "efficiency frontier" (see figure 13.7). If low-risk Treasury bills or money market funds are invested in, the principal will not be lost, yet a large profit will not be made. Putting money in aggressive growth stocks (such as technology stocks or gold shares), results in a higher rate of increase.

(3.) Do not try to beat the market. Only a handful of investors can consistently outperform the overall market such as the S&P 500. This is implied by the efficient market theory which we discussed earlier in this chapter. It argues that "high return/low risk" situations are hard to find and when they occur they disappear quickly due to competition in the financial marketplace.

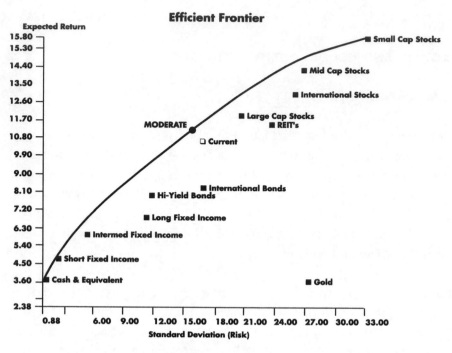

**Figure 13.7.**

**Background:** Modern portfolio theory and efficient market theory have come under criticism recently. Markowitz and his colleagues use past prices on stocks, bonds, real estate and other assets to measure risk, but past performance may not be a reliable indicator of future performance. Two top financial economists (Robert Merton and Myron Scholes, 1997 winners of the Nobel Prize in economics) became involved in Long Term Capital Management, a hedge fund that lost over 90% of its value in 1998. The hedge fund lost money primarily because it relied on past relationships that did not hold up.

## PROBLEMS TO PONDER

1.  How would you respond to the following: "The stock market does not create new capital, it just redistributes it. When a saver decides to invest in the stock market, he buys stock from another investor, and the money goes to another investor, not a company. Therefore, Wall Street is a zero sum game and the economy is no richer because of it." Is this view correct? (Hint: If new buying leads to a rising stock market, what effect will that have on new public offerings?)

2. Economist Milton Friedman maintains that stock market activity has little to do with the real economy: "The stock market is grossly overrated as it affects the economy," he statesd. Is he right? Why or why not?

3. Given the statement that the stock market is not the same as Las Vegas, how do you respond to the following report taken from the 1990 edition of the *Forbes 400 Richest People in America* issue: "Successful business people often turn out to be avid gamblers. Whether the game is poker, bridge, blackjack or the horses doesn't matter, what matters is the game itself. The essence of these games—the systematic weighing of risks against rewards against mathematical probabilities—is the essence of business itself." If stock market speculation is not gambling, why do so many players in the stock market also gamble? Of the types of games—casino gambling, poker, chess, horses, or blackjack—which one best imitates the ups and downs of the financial markets?

4. After reading this chapter, what is your reaction to the following statement in an economics textbook? "Economics cannot teach you how to be rich. It doesn't supply magic formulas that tell you what stocks to pick, whether or not interest rates will rise, or if the dollar will fall. It doesn't predict which of today's businesses are the IBMs of tomorrow." (Roy Ruffin and Paul Gregory, *Principles of Economics*, 3rd ed., p. 2.) If economics can not do any of the above, why study economics?

5. Below is the income statement of a publicly-traded biotech company from 2004 until 2007:

| | 2004 | 2005 | 2006 | 2007 |
|---|---|---|---|---|
| Revenue...... | 0 | 0 | 0 | 0 |
| Expenses..... | $0.2 million | $0.7 million | $2.2 million | $4.8 million |

The company's stock was trading for $2 in 2004 and is now trading for $7. Are investors irrational? Should the stock be sold short? Is it possible for a company in the biotech business to be worth something even though it has no current sales? What can justify the billion-dollar values of technology companies which have yet to earn any profits?

6. What causes stock markets to crash? Evaluate the causes of the stock market crashes in 1929, 1987, and 2008 in the United States and the Asian markets in 1997. How can future crashes be prevented?

7. Early in the 21st century in the United States, mortgages and mortgaged-backed securities became valuable financial assets that increased dramatically in volume during the real estate boom. In 2008-09 the real estate market fell, bankruptcies rose sharply, and the market for mortgage-backed securities (especially sub-prime mortgages) collapsed, threatening the entire financial system. The Federal Reserve and other central banks had to intervene to bailout the credit markets. How important is the mortgage-backed securities market as a financial asset? What role does the Fed have in maintaining stability in the mortgage and credit markets?

## RECOMMENDED READING

- Jeremy J. Siegel, *Stocks for the Long Run*, 4th ed. (McGraw-Hill, 2008). An historical comparison of various investments—stocks, bonds, gold and cash—by one of the top financial economists.

- Burton G. Malkiel, *A Random Walk Down Wall Street*, 9th ed. (Norton, 2007). A full discussion of the contribution of financial economists in developing the efficient market hypothesis.

- Peter L. Bernstein, *Capital Ideas Evolving* (Wiley & Sons, 2007). An engaging history of modern portfolio theory through the eyes of their inventors.

- Mark Skousen, *Investing in One Lesson* (Regnery, 2007). The lesson is "Wall Street exaggerates everything."

# PART III
# MACROECONOMICS

# Chapter 14

# UNDERSTANDING THE MACRO ECONOMY

*"One cannot eschew studying the microcosm if one wants to
understand properly the macrocosm of a developed country."*

—EUGEN BÖHM-BAWERK (1891)

A tale of two countries, Venezuela and Ireland, illustrates macroeconomics. The first country is Venezuela, the richest oil-based economy in Latin America and the largest supplier of crude oil to the United States. During the 1990s, Venezuela suffered from low oil prices and rising inflation but made gradual progress in per capita income. Adjusted for inflation, Venezuelans earned $4,000 per person in 1985, and by the late 1990s, the figure had reached $5,600 per person. Things were going well. Then in 1998 Hugo Chavez, a Marxist military leader, became Venezuela's 53rd president and immediately began a campaign to combat poverty, illiteracy and other social ills through democratic socialism. At the same time, he imposed new taxes and restrictions on the wealthy classes and on trade, including foreign exchange controls and higher taxes on the oil companies. Chavez also joined Cuban Fidel Castro in attacking U. S. foreign policy as imperialistic.

Since Chavez took office, Venezuela's economy has floundered, despite higher oil prices that should have improved the GDP. Many wealthy Venezuelans have left their country for the United States, and per capita real GDP has declined. From 2005 – 2007 the real GDP declined nearly 20%, while price inflation climbed to 24% a year. Chavez won re-election in 2004, but he has been accused of electoral fraud, human rights violations, and assaulting democracy in favor of dictatorship. The *2009 Index of Economic Freedom*, issued annually by the Heritage Foundation and the *Wall Street Journal*, now lists Venezuela in the "repressed" category.

The economic history of Ireland is a distinct contrast to the economic history of Venezuela. For years Ireland was known as the stepchild of Britain, suffering from rigid controls, underdevelopment, stagnation, violence, political instability, and even famine. As late as 1987, the unemployment rate in Ireland was 17%. But then things suddenly changed. Ireland joined the European Community, including the adoption of the new euro currency, created a free-trade zone and worked out a deal with the trade unions to create a flexible, highly skilled labor force. Irish leaders aggressively courted multinational corporations in the United States and Europe by providing a well-educated but relatively cheap labor workforce and offering substantial tax breaks to businesses. Today Ireland has the lowest corporate tax rate (12.5%) in Europe. Ireland recruits immigrants with advanced skills from other countries, especially those of Irish descent. Ireland offers a stable, healthy government and an excellent infrastructure. EC subsidies of up to 1.2 billion euro a year also helped.

The results of these actions have been exceptional. For the past decade, the economy of the Republic of Ireland has grown three times faster than the rest of Europe and twice as fast as that of the U. S. In the last half of the 1990s, real Gross Domestic Product grew at a 10% annual rate. Employment growth was even more spectacular, rising 50% over the past decade. Unemployment, once 17%, fell sharply, although it has risen again due to the financial crisis of 2008. Wages are also on the rise, and today the average income of the Irish worker is on par with the rest of Europe. The only economic downside is price inflation, which is double the European rate. Ireland used to be considered a place to escape from. This is no longer true.

## WHY MACROECONOMICS MATTERS

These two stories of tragedy and hope are a good introduction to the topic of macroeconomics. Note the points of discussion: GDP growth, the unemployment rate, price inflation, wages, and immigration. Macroeconomic issues affect almost everyone in the economy. The purpose of the macro chapters of *Economic Logic* is to introduce macroeconomic theory, and to illustrate how the global economy works.

Macroeconomics is not just for policy makers. Macroeconomics provides the information that enables employment choices and illustrates whether the economy is going to keep growing or whether the economy is headed for a recession. Macroeconomics demonstrates how price inflation cuts into earning power and provides the basis for determining if prices of most goods and services will rise or fall and by how much.

Macroeconomics can help to determine:

- Whether interest rates for purchases, like buying a house or a car, will rise or fall

- Whether the dollar will rise or fall against other major currencies

- Where the stock market is headed

- The outlook for the economy and jobs

**Macroeconomics** is the study of economy-wide and world-wide events and models. Certain actions affect not just one individual, company or industry, but many sectors of the economy. Changes in interest rates, the national debt, inflation, saving rates, taxes, business regulations, and monetary policy can dramatically affect businesses, government, and individuals. The business cycle and government regulations can have a dramatic impact on wages, profits, trade, and stock prices. Macroeconomics plays a significant role in society. The study of macroeconomics is useful to anyone interested in business, finance, public policy, history, engineering, or psychology.

## A LOGICAL APPROACH TO MICRO...AND MACRO

The first volume of this textbook presented **microeconomics**, the economic behavior of individuals, firms, and groups, which includes consumer behavior, supply and demand, the cost of labor and other factors of production, entrepreneurship and the financial markets. Microeconomics was introduced in a logical way—using a profit-and-loss income statement. How "wealth" (the quantity, quality and variety of goods and services) is created by each firm was demonstrated in the Aggregate Production Structure. How price and cost work together to maximize consumer demand, given the limits of supply and technology, and how new products and services are created in a dynamic process was discussed. The final "micro" chapters focused on the factors of production — how land, labor, capital and entrepreneurship operate together to maximize economic growth and a rising standard of living.

Chapters 14-27 will present macroeconomic theory and data by covering the fundamentals of macroeconomic behavior, ways to measure the whole economy, aggregate supply and demand, the role of savings and technology in economic performance, the effects of economic activity on income and wealth, and the function of money and banking in the macroeconomy. The next part introduces government policy and its effects, both good and bad, on the economy. In this section of the textbook the positive role of government is presented using an econological approach to current debates while considering the questions: What can the state do better than private enterprise? How should these projected be financed? How can government be made more efficient?

Government has expanded its functions far beyond its limited role of the past. These chapters will apply the principles of public choice theory to issues of chronic deficit spending, taxes, the national debt, government regulations and controls, environmental policy, and inflation. The expected purpose of the welfare state will be discussed, and experiments in totalitarian central planning, socialism and communism in the 20th century will be examined. The new phenomenon of denationalization and privatization in the post-socialist era of the global economy will be explored. Finally, the impact of the financial crisis of 2008 on the global economy and the role of government will be examined.

## A GENERAL MODEL OF THE ECONOMY: A REVIEW

To grasp the importance of macroeconomics, recall the basics of the production process in chapter 1 of *Economic Logic*. Humans have always faced a difficult task: wants are unlimited, while resources to achieve those wants are limited. Goods and services are created through time and effort because the earth's basic resources are scarce, and often unusable and unfinished in their natural state. Land, labor and capital must be applied to these unfinished resources in order to make them usable by the consumer. Wealth is created and acquired through this universal economic process. All goods and services from clothing to the theater — require expenditures of time, capital, and labor. During this process, businesses must determine which goods and services to provide the consumer based on the degree of customer demand and the cost of producing the products or providing the services.

## THE PRODUCTION PROCESS: A MICRO EXAMPLE

The production process involved in providing of a cup of coffee at a popular coffee-house is a micro example. Figure 14.1 shows the value added at each stage of production, from acquisition of beans to brewing espresso.

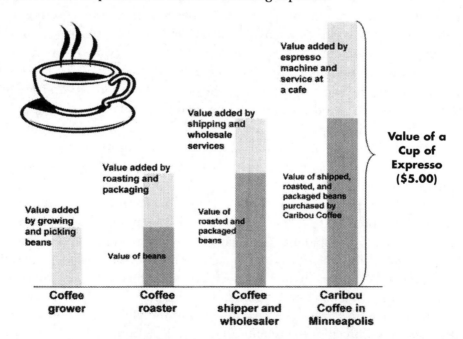

**Figure 14.1.** *Valued Added in Supply Chain for Coffee: From Beans to Expresso.*

Figure 14.1 represents the supply chain for the making of coffee. This figure represents the following stages:

Commodity stage: the coffee grower in Brazil grows and harvests the coffee beans

Manufacturing stage: the coffee roaster adds value to the product by roasting and packaging the coffee beans

Distribution stage: the coffee supplier and wholesaler ship the prepared beans to the retailer

Retail stage: the retailer grinds the beans and brews the coffee in an espresso machine and serves the customer

Note that each producer adds value to the production process and each is paid as value is added.

## CHARACTERISTICS OF THE ECONOMIC PROCESS

Every supplier of goods and services in an economy follows a similar process, whether producing coffee, trying a court case, or playing a baseball game. The following generalizations about the economic process may be made:

1.  Production and consumption take time.

2.  Producers and providers seek a profit by adding customer value at each stage of production. If their attempts fail they experience a loss. Risk always exists in the production process or when providing services.

3.  Factors of production (land, labor, capital, and entrepreneurship) must cooperate at each stage in order to produce usable, finished goods and services at the retail (final) stage.

4.  Competition and cooperation exist throughout the production process.

5.  Inventories exist at each stage to facilitate the production process.

6.  Goods depreciate and lose value over time as they are consumed.

7.  Money, exchange and trade are an integral part of the production process.

Chapter 3 introduced a general model of the economy, the Aggregate Production Structure (APS), to describe this process.

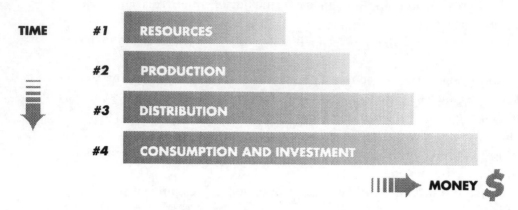

**Figure 14.2.** *A general model of the economy.*

This general model applies to all goods and services produced in an economy. The brewing of an espresso coffee is just one of millions of possible examples of activities performed within the APS. Time (the structure of production) is represented on the vertical axis. Money (nominal output) is measured on the horizontal axis. The monetary expense can be reflected in dollars, euros, yen, pounds, pesos and other national currencies.

## CHARACTERISTICS OF THE 4-STAGE MODEL

The 4-sector model is called the **Aggregate Production Structure** (APS). It measures the nominal output at all stages of production of goods and services sold during the calendar year. The APS can be calculated on a local, regional, national, or global level. The four stages are:

1. **Resources**: These inputs include raw commodities as well as expenditures on research and development and education/training. The resource stage is the earliest stage of production and refers to the raw materials used in producing goods and services. In manufacturing, resources may include iron ore, timber, other natural materials, or research and development. In services, it may include training, consulting, and machinery. The key focus is on the behavior of prices, employment, wages, profits, and output at the **resource** level.

2. **Production**: At this stage, resources are gathered and mixed with land, labor and capital (the factors of production) to transform a good or service into a more useful, finished product. The key focus here is the behavior of prices, employment, wages, profits, and output at the **producer** level.

3. **Distribution**: Once a product is made, it must then be transported or distributed to the final user. Here marketing and shipping play a key role. The principal focus is on prices, employment, wages, profits and output at the **wholesale** level.

4. **Consumption and Investment**: The final stage of the APS occurs when the good or service reaches the final user. "Final use" may occur at the consumption stage, such as an appliance, clothing, or a car for household use, it may be used for investment in business at an earlier stage of production, such as a truck, computer, factory, or even education. In the case of consumption, which normally represents the largest sector of final use, the focus is primarily on prices, employment, wages, profits and output at the **retail** level.

The value of each stage increases over time. The resource sector is the smallest part of the economy, and final output (retail) is the largest. As noted with the coffee example, **value is added** as products move toward final usability. On a micro basis, many businesses continue to manufacture products at a loss, but on a macro level the majority of producers make money if the economy is to continue growing.

Once a product becomes a finished good and is purchased and used by a customer (whether it be a final consumer or a producer), it starts losing value over time, what is called **depreciation**. After a consumer or capital good is sold, it no longer earns added value, but loses value as the product is used up. The depreciation schedule varies with each product—an apple may be consumed in a few minutes, a truck in 15 years, and a house may depreciate in value over a hundred years before being replaced or repaired.

The only exception is an important one for economic growth. **Capital investment** that is reintroduced into the production process has the potential of continuing to add value by increasing the **productivity** of workers and entrepreneurs involved in the production process. Investments in better tools, machinery, processes, training and education can also potentially increase **output per man hour**.

The **cooperative** nature of the production process is a crucial concept to understand. Although competition is important for stimulating innovation and reducing costs, all the factors of production — entrepreneurs, capitalists, workers, landlords, and suppliers — must work together in order to meet the needs of customers. If Starbuck's didn't have the cooperation of each supplier within the supply chain, the coffee would never make it to the customer. While the market system is highly **competitive** it is not solely a competitive model. The market is also a **cooperative** model, and in some ways, may be more cooperative than competitive. If, for example, labor refuses to work with company managers, the production process comes to a standstill and no final product is made.

**Inventories**, goods being held by producers at each stage of production in expectation of being sold, facilitate a more efficient and expanding economy, and play a key role in avoiding bottlenecks in the economy and reducing the time it takes to produce products.

The APS is often a global activity involving the importing and exporting of commodities, manufactured products, whole goods, and even services (through outsourcing) to create cheaper and better products and services.

## MEASURING THE ECONOMY: GDE AND GDP

Economists use the APS as a way of measuring not only the economy, but the economic well-being of its citizens as well. Measuring the well-being of an individual, the value of a particular good or service, or a nation's standard of living can be measured in many ways including; life expectancy, literacy, average work hours, amount of leisure time, availability of services, the condition of the environment. Economists usually focus on some key financial statistics to measure material well being. For example, **per capita income and wealth** are vital statistics that provide a way of comparing living standards from country to country.

On a national scale, economists rely on the dollar value of the Aggregate Production Structure (APS) to measure spending in the economy and the world. First, they may choose to measure spending at all four stages of output, which we call Gross Expenditures. Measuring gross expenditures for a nation is called **Gross Domestic Expenditures (GDE).**

Or, the economist may wish to disaggregate the economy, and measure output, prices, and profits at each stage of production, to see which direction the production process is headed. An economist may look at the **Commodity Price Index**, **the Producer Price Index**, and the **Consumer Price Index** to see if any trends can be spotted. For example, if commodity and producer prices are rising sharply, the economist may anticipate a rise in the CPI. Disaggregating the economy in this way can help economists forecast the direction of final consumption, investment, and prices.

Economists are also interested in measuring final output, which represents all goods and services sold to consumers, business, and government. This is an important yardstick for measuring a nation's current standard of living. Final output is represented by the **last stage** of production only—the nominal value of consumption and investment. This statistic is called the **Gross Domestic Product (GDP).** The difference between Gross Domestic Expenditures (GDE) and Gross Domestic Product (GDP) is **Intermediate Business Expenditures (IE),** comprising the first three stages. Figure 14.3 illustrates the three concepts.

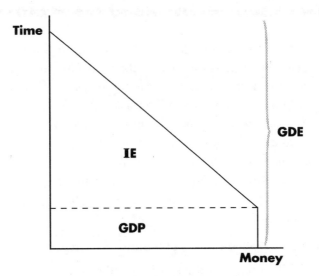

**Figure 14.3.** *GDE, IE, and GDP.*

Chapter 15 will introduce specific ways to measure national output, wealth, and the standard of living including:

1. **Gross Domestic Expenditures (GDE),** a measure of total spending in the economy in one year.

2. **Gross Domestic Product (GDP),** the value of *final* goods and services produced in a year. (This is the most common measure but not necessarily the best one.)

3. **National wealth**, as determined by the estimated net worth of private and public interests. Net worth is the market value of all assets minus liabilities. Per capita wealth is another important measure of well-being. After all, a poor nation may grow very fast, with a GDP growth rate of 10% a year, and yet its citizens may still be suffering.

4. **Market capitalization** monitors changes in various country stock indexes, the broad baskets of publicly-traded stocks offered in each major country. There are many such country indexes: In the US, the S&P 500 or the Wilshire 5000; in London, the FTSE 250; in Paris, the CAC 40; in Japan, the Tokyo Nikkei 300; in Australia, the S&P/ASX 200; in South Africa, the Johannesburg All Share index.

## MONEY, EXCHANGE AND TRADE: THE BUILDING BLOCKS OF GLOBALIZATION

Money, exchange, and trade are critically important to a well-functioning production process. It's almost inconceivable to imagine how individuals and businesses could transform resources into final goods and services without money and exchange, although it has happened occasionally. Ancient Egypt, for example, developed a fairly significant economy largely without a monetary unit, but these advances were dependent on slave labor. Under most circumstances, money and exchange develop naturally because of the inherent disadvantages of barter, and have developed historically in almost all civilizations. (More on the origin of money in chapter 18.) Once a monetary unit has been established, all kinds of advances are possible including:

- sophisticated accounting of commercial success or failure
- the establishment of values, prices and costs
- the replacement of barter with productive indirect exchange
- liquid wealth and financial markets can be created
- international markets can be established.

Chapter 3 explained how the production process is international in scope, taking advantage of each nation's comparative advantage. Figure 3.5 below illustrates this concept.

**TIME (Stages of Production)**

#1 IRON ORE (Canada)

#2 STEEL (Ohio)

#3 AUTOMOBILE (wholesale) (Japan)

#4 AUTOMOBILE (retail) (United States)

MONEY $

**Figure 14.4.** *The global nature of the Aggregate Production Structure.*

This figure illustrates how an automobile in an American showroom is produced:

- Iron ore is mined in Canada
- The ore is converted to steel in Ohio
- The steel is shipped to Japan

- The car is produced

- The Japanese car is sold to an American consumer

Exchange and foreign trade offer many benefits to business, consumers, and society:

- Economic Growth: Buyer and seller/producer and consumer improve the situation (achieve their goals) through exchange and trade.

- Specialization: Trade encourages individuals, companies and nations to specialize.

- Efficiency: Increased competition between communities, states and nations keeps costs and prices down, and increases volume of transactions.

- Social welfare ("invisible hand" doctrine of Adam Smith): Law of comparative advantage suggests that less qualified individuals can survive and prosper in the marketplace. Trade increases comparative advantage of relatively poor nations.

## AGGREGATE SUPPLY AND DEMAND

Chapter 3 discussed how the supply of goods and services move downward along the production function, while the funds to pay for these goods and services flow upward. Figure 14.5 reproduces this diagram.

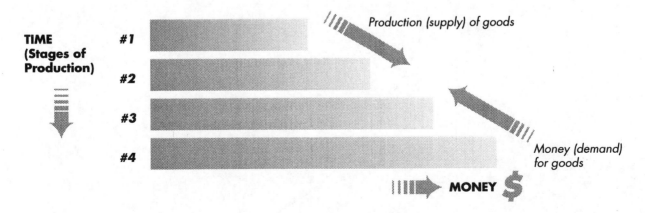

**Figure 14.5.** *Goods and money flow in opposite direction in the production process.*

In the 4-stage model, the supply chain of goods and services moves gradually downward from "resources" to "consumption." The downward supply-of-goods movement can be expressed as a vector. A vector shows distance and direction over time. The supply chain shown in figure 14.6 is called the **Aggregate Supply Vector (ASV).**

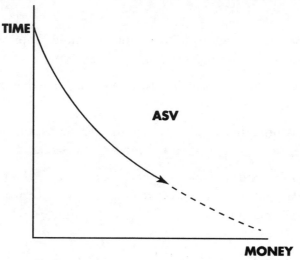

**Figure 14.6.** *The Aggregate Supply Vector (ASV).*

The direction and the ASV are determined by productivity and the profit margins at each stage of production, known as the "supply side" of the economy. At the same time, payment for these goods and services at each stage moves upward as the suppliers are paid. The upward payments vector is called the **Aggregate Demand Vector (ADV).** See figure 14.7 below.

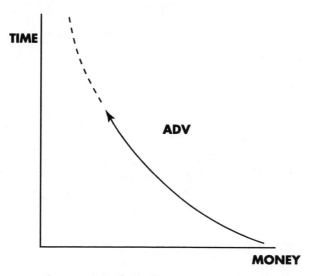

**Figure 14.7.** *The Aggregate Demand Vector (ADV).*

The direction of the ADV is influenced largely by the savings rate in the economy, the decision of consumers whether to save or spend their income. When the ASV and ADV are parallel and equal at each stage of production, macroeconomic equilibria , or a "steady state" is achieved. When the ASV and ADV separate and move in different directions, macroeconomic disequilibria occurs. Traditionally, interest rates serve as the pricing and rationing system that achieves equilibrium at each stage of production.

## SUMMARY

Chapter 14 covered these main points:

1. Macroeconomics is the study of economy-wide and world-wide events and models.

2. Changes in interest rates, the national debt, inflation, saving rates, taxes, business regulations, monetary policy, and other macroeconomic phenomenon can dramatically affect all businesses, government, and individuals.

3. All goods and services must go through four cooperative stages of production in order to become useful products for business and consumers: resources, production, distribution, and final consumption. These can be divided into two general stages: intermediate production and final output (Gross Domestic Product or GDP).

4. Money, exchange, foreign trade, and specialization play critical roles in advancing the prosperity of any civilization.

5. Aggregate Supply Vector (ASV) represents the supply chain of goods and services along the production process from resources to final consumption, and Aggregate Demand Vector (ADV) represents the payment schedule for goods and services produced along the production process.

6. When the ASV and ADV are parallel and equal at each stage of production, we achieve macroeconomic equilibria, or a "steady stage." When the ASV and ADV separate and move in different directions, a unstable boom-bust business cycle is created.

333

## IMPORTANT TERMS

Aggregate Demand

Aggregate Demand Vector (ADV)

Aggregate Production Structure (APS)

Aggregate Supply

Aggregate Supply Vector (ASV)

Business cycle

Capital investment

Commodity Price Index

Comparative advantage

Consumer Price Index (CPI)

Consumption

Distribution

Factors of production

Gross Domestic Expenditures (GDE)

Gross Domestic Product (GDP)

Inputs

Intermediate Domestic Output (IDO)

Inventories

Investment

Macroeconomics

Market capitalization

Microeconomics

National wealth

Producer Price Index (PPI)

Productivity

Retail

Stages of production

Value added

Wholesale

## INFLUENTIAL ECONOMIST

### WASSILY LEONTIEF AND INTERWORKINGS OF A DYNAMIC ECONOMY

**Name: Wassily Leontief (1906-1999)**

**Background:** Born in St. Petersburg, Leontief lived in Russia until 1925, when his parents moved to Germany to escape Communist oppression. He earned his Ph. D. in economics from the University of Berlin, and after a year in China, in 1931 moved to the United States. He worked as a researcher for the National Bureau of Economic Research (NBER) and taught at Harvard University. It was in the 1930s that he developed the idea of "input-output models," a way to describing the inner workings of a growing economy. In 1970, he was elected president of the American Economic Association, and in 1973, was awarded the Nobel Prize for his work in input-output analysis. In 1975, he took a position at the Institute of Economic Research at New York University. He died in 1999.

**Major Works:** *The Structure of the American Economy, 1919-29* (Harvard University Press, 1941) and *Input-Output Economics*, 2nd ed. (Oxford University Press, 1966, 1986)

**Major contributions:** Wassily Leontieff was critical of GDP, the general price level, and the generally excessive aggregative approach by Keynesian economists. He favored a more realistic micro-economic approach that involved the "intervening steps" between inputs and outputs, steps which involved "a complex series of transactions among real people." Leontieff's invention was the construction of **input-output tables** for the United States and other industrial countries.

I-O tables are more sophisticated than our simple 4-stage model of the economy. In an input-output table, the horizontal rows show how the output of each sector or industry (agriculture, apparel, and vehicles) is used by the other sectors, while the vertical columns show how each sector obtains from other sectors its needed inputs of goods and services. For example, the vertical column for the automobile industry shows such inputs as ferrous metals, rubber, electrical equipment, and textiles. The horizontal rows indicate which are the final users of automobiles, trucks, and other vehicles: construction, manufacturing, and consumers. In general, sectors above any row are *customers* of that industrial group, and industries below any row are *suppliers.*

**Strength:** By describing in mathematical form the interrelationships among the different sectors or industries of an economy, Leontieff was able to show has goods and services are produced and how economies work. I-O tables show how shortages and bottlenecks can be created, or how the inflationary process can work through the economy.

**Weakness:** In the 20th century, central planners in totalitarian regimes (USSR, China) used I-O tables to determine the exact inputs necessary to produce the output required by "five year plans" — without the need of prices. However, such static models failed to anticipate changes in technology and provide the incentives to improve the efficiency and changing demands of the production process. Leonteif was critical of such unrealistic formal model building.

## PROBLEMS TO PONDER

1.  Some economists say there's no such thing as macroeconomics, only individual and firm behavior (microeconomics). Do you agree?

2.  Identify ways of measuring a nation's standard of living other than per capita income.

3.  Professor Israel Kirzner (New York University) says that it is impossible to determine whether an American businesssman earning $100,000 a year is necessarily better off than a French peasant earning $200 a year. Are interpersonal utility comparisons valid?

## FOR ADDITIONAL READING

• Mark Skousen, *The Structure of Production* (New York University Press, 1990). The 2007 paperback edition has a new introduction.

• James Gwartney, Richard L. Stroup, and Dwight R. Lee, *Common Sense Economics: What Everyone Should Know About Wealth and Prosperity* (New York: St. Martin's Press, 2005). An excellent primer on macroeconomics, plus a chapter on personal economics.

*Chapter 15*

# MEASURES OF ECONOMIC ACTIVITY, INCOME AND WEALTH

*"A balanced Input-Output framework...*
*provides a more accurate and consistent picture of the U. S. economy."*

—*Survey of Current Business*, June 2004

*"When you cannot express it in numbers,*
*your knowledge is of a meager and unsatisfactory kind."*

—LORD KELVIN, inscription on the front of the
Social Science Building, University of Chicago

How is the economy made visible? What is the best measure of an individual's or nation's standard of living? Is a particular economy growing or shrinking? How wealthy are individuals, families and nation?

These are the questions Chapter 15 will address. Chapter 15 focuses on several important concepts:

1. **Spending activity at various stages and industries in the economy**. The total value of spending in the **Aggregate Production Structure (APS)** during a calendar year is called **Gross Domestic Expenditures (GDE).** The chapter will concentrate on how spending patterns change within the supply chain or industries, and how these factors influence wages, profits, prices, inventories, and stock values at each stage of production or in each industry. Input-output data created in the 1960s by Russian economist and Nobel laureate Wassily Leontieff provides such a framework.

2. **Final output of goods and services**. Final output of goods and services allow the material well-being in society to be measured. These statistics represent the value of goods and services that are usable to consumers, business and government.

    Economists have developed several quantitative tools to measure living standards. On a national scale, the most common yardstick is **Gross Domestic Product (GDP)**, which is the value of final, usable goods and services produced in a year. Since countries vary in population, economists focus on per capita GDP, which allows for comparisons between nations, and indicates how well each nation is advancing in a material world. A digital reference to GDP data can be found at http://www.nationmaster.com.

Another measurement is per capita real income, or average income levels, adjusted annually for inflation, or per capita income in **Purchasing Power Parity** (expressed normally in U. S. dollars). PPP is defined as the amount of income it takes to purchase an equal basket of goods and services in each nation.

3. **The level of national wealth and per capita wealth.** An extremely wealthy nation may be able to withstand a temporary recession or unemployment more easily than a nation with fewer resources, just as a wealthy person may be able to survive for a longer period of time without work than an individual without savings. A report by the Economic Policy Institute points out that 57.5% of the population was in the bottom 90% of income and wealth distribution in 2004.[1]

4. **Market Capitalization.** Economists have started to look at a new measurement of economic activity, growth and wealth. **Market capitalization** is the total market value of individual stocks traded in a broad-based index, such as the S&P 500, or Russell 5000. These market statistics may best reflect the dynamics and outlook of the future economy or financial sector.

## MEASURING SPENDING IN THE ECONOMY

Chapter 14 divided the economy into four general stages (figure 15.1).

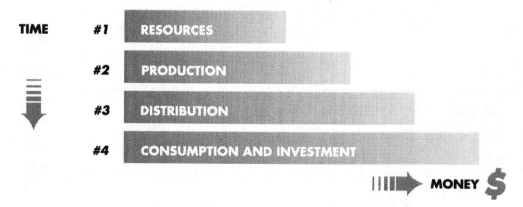

**Figure 15.1.** *The Aggregate Production Structure in Four Stages.*

1  Economic Policy Institute, *Wealth: Unrelenting Disparities.* (Cornell U. Press, 2006-07), Chapter 5.

Each stage represents the total amount of gross expenditures incurred by each business during the year, and demonstrates that total spending increases with each stage as final output (consumption and investment) is approached.

The micro example of the processes involved in producing a cup of espresso coffee will illustrate how the aggregate production structure works. Figure 15.2 notes the cost of the ingredients at each stage of production:

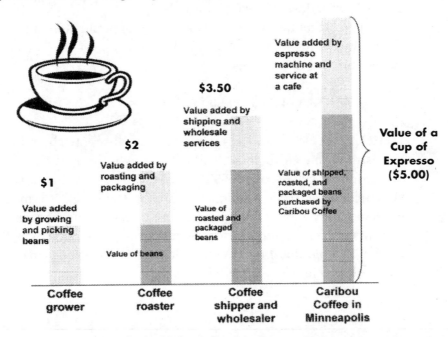

**Figure 15.2.** *Valued Added in Coffee: From Beans to Expresso.*

## LOOKING AT EACH STAGE OF PRODUCTION

In the first stage of production the coffee grower expends $1 in labor, supplies, agricultural land and other costs in growing and picking coffee beans in order to produce enough beans to make a cup of coffee. This $1 includes the coffee grower's profit, or return on capital, per unit.

In the second stage, the coffee roaster expends $2 in labor, supplies, building expenses, and other costs to roast and package the beans (which includes the purchasing the beans from the coffee grower). This $2 includes the coffee roaster's profit.

In the third stage, the coffee shipper/wholesaler expends $3.50 per unit in labor, supplies, and other costs to transport and provide wholesale services to the retailer. The distributor's costs include the $2 already paid to the coffee roaster for the roasted beans. His $3.50 price charged to the retailer includes the amount that will he will earn as profit as well as the profit included in the $2 paid to the coffee roaster.

339

In the fourth and final stage, the retailer charges the customer $5 for one cup of espresso. This charge reflects the capital expenditures for the espresso machine, service at the café, and all other costs of doing business at the retail level, and includes the $3.50 cost per cup of shipped roasted beans as well as a reasonable return on the retailer's capital.

The total spending pattern in this production process for making a cup of coffee can be broken down in several ways.

The total amount spent at all four stages of production to produce a cup of coffee can be examined. The total cost of production results from adding up the gross expenditures of all four stages:

$1 + $2 + $3.50 + $5 = $11.50

$11.50 was spent by the entire commercial supply chain to produce a cup of espresso for one customer at Starbucks. Why is this cost so much larger than the final price of a cup of coffee of $5? The $11.50 represents the real costs of production per cup of coffee. Each business as a capitalist/entrepreneur must raise the capital necessary to pay for gross expenditures—to pay for the rent, labor costs, and supplies to produce the product for the next stage in the supply chain. The $11.50 also involves **double counting.** For example, the $11.50 includes the cost of growing and picking beans (the first, or agricultural, stage) four times.

## TOTAL SPENDING VS. VALUE ADDED

To see why the price of a cup of espresso at Starbucks is only $5, double counting should be eliminated and each producer's contribution to the final product should be counted once. The focus will be on the **value added** at each stage of production.

This equation represents the value added by each producer:

$1 + $1 + $1.50 + $1.50 = $5

The value added is equal to the $5 retail price the customer pays for the final product. Note that the $5 retail price includes all the costs of production at each stage — counted only once — plus the profit earned by each producer. Everyone in the production process benefits, and the consumer gets what he wants, a cup of coffee.

We gain two insights into the economic process from this simple micro exercise:

**First, the total value added by all producers is equal to the final price paid by the consumer**. The value of final output of any good or service is equal to the value added of the inputs, no matter how many stages of production are involved.

**Second, gross business investment is typically larger than the final output**. This is a more subtle concept. In the example above, note that the total spending is $11.50, while final output (the cup of coffee) is valued at $5.

$11.50 (total spending) - $5 (consumer/retail price) = $6.50

By subtracting the value of the consumer product of $5 from total spending at all stages of production, the value of intermediate spending, $6.50 is obtained. Thus, the second proposition is confirmed, business investment is a larger segment of the economy than spending by the final consumer. There may be times when the value of a retail product may be worth more than the gross intermediate expenditures. For example, when there is a sudden demand for a product driven by a fad and the price for the product skyrockets beyond the costs of production. This situation is highly unlikely to last on a macro scale for all goods and services.

The point of this exercise is to emphasize the relative importance of business investment in the economy, which is much more significant than commonly recognized. The standard established view is that consumer spending (the final retail stage) is the largest and most important sector in the economy rather than business investment. However this may not be the case after all. Business investment may be more important than consumer spending. (See also Chapter 17.)

## MEASURING THE MACRO ECONOMY

Statistics on spending have been compiled for many years. Gross Domestic Product (GDP), which measures spending on final goods and services, is reported quarterly and provides the most up to date data. Harvard economist Simon Kuznets, highlighted at the end of this chapter, invented GDP in the 1940s. The GDP overemphasizes the relative size of consumer spending in the economy. GDE, total spending at all stages of production, is a new statistic based on data from the annual input-output tables compiled by the **Bureau of Economic Analysis** and annual gross business receipts compiled by the Internal Revenue Service. Recently the government has also attempted to broaden output figures beyond GDP. Their latest data is Gross Output (GO) a measure of total spending by industry. Neither GDP or GO data includes non-reported transactions or black-market activities, which may make up a considerable part of the economy.

Unfortunately, because many firms are involved in more than one stage of production, an exact value for each stage of intermediate production (resources, production and distribution) is difficult to determine. For example, Exxon engages in the entire supply chain, from exploration and production of oil products to selling gasoline to retail consumers. To simplify matters the first three stages are combined into intermediate expenditures (IE). See figure 15.3 for the estimated figures for GDE, IE and GDP for 2008.

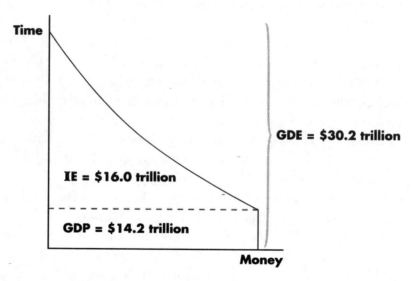

**Figure 15.3.** *Breakdown of total spending in the economy in 2008 by three categories: GRE, IE, and GDP (estimated). Source: Bureau of Economic Analysis; Internal Revenue Service; Statistical Abstract of the United States.*

Total spending in the economy reached approximately $30 trillion in 2008. Of that spending total, $16 trillion constitutes intermediate business spending (the first three stages of production), and $14 trillion represents final output, or Gross Domestic Product (GDP) in 2008.

## THE IMPORTANCE OF INTERMEDIATE BUSINESS SPENDING (IE)

Intermediate business expenditures, or IE ($16 trillion) is slightly larger than final output or GDE ($14 trillion) in 2007. Intermediate business spending is an important indicator to watch, especially in the early stages of production. These early indicators inform us about the future expectations of economic activity. Market data tends to be more volatile the further the product is from final consumption.

## THE IMPORTANCE OF GROSS DOMESTIC PRODUCT (GDP)

**Gross Domestic Product (GDP)** is the most publicized indicator of national economic performance. GDP is reported quarterly in industrial nations and annually in developing countries. GDP in the United States is compiled and reported quarterly by the Bureau of Economic Analysis (BEA) of the Department of Commerce; the Organisation for Economic Co-operation and Development (OECD) compiles and reports GDP, on a quarterly basis for 30 industrial countries, and estimates this data for an additional 70 countries on an annual basis.

GDP is the best single measurement of goods and services used to improve the standard of living. Intermediate production measures non-finished goods on their way to final use. But retail goods and services are products at the finished stage that serve direct use.

## GDP IS FINAL OUTPUT ONLY

GDP is defined as the value (in dollars, Euros, yen, pesos, or the currency of the country) of <u>final</u> goods and services produced or bought within a country in a year. Journals and economic commentators often mistakenly state that GDP represents total spending in the economy. Total spending in the economy, GDE, is more than double GDP in most nations.

## THREE WAYS TO MEASURE GDP

GDP can be measured in three ways: by purchases, by value added by industry, and by national income.

**Purchases made by consumers, business, and government**: Here GDP is divided into four categories, according to the following equation:

GDP = C + I + G + (X - M)

where,

C = Personal consumption expenditures
I = Gross private domestic investment
G = Government consumption expenditures and gross investment
X = Exports
and   M = Imports.

Here is the break down for GDP in 2008:

**Figure 15.4.**
GROSS DOMESTIC PRODUCT (2008) IN CURRENT DOLLARS
(in billions of US dollars)

Personal Consumption Expenditures . . . . . . . . . . . . . . . . . . $9,927.9
    Durable goods . . . . . . . . . . . . . . . . . . . . . . . . . . . . . . . . $946.3
    Non-durable goods . . . . . . . . . . . . . . . . . . . . . . . . . . $2,839.0
    Services . . . . . . . . . . . . . . . . . . . . . . . . . . . . . . . . . . $6,142.5

Gross private domestic investment . . . . . . . . . . . . . . . . . . . $1,906.1
    Residential. . . . . . . . . . . . . . . . . . . . . . . . . . . . . . . . . $ 438.4
    Non-residential . . . . . . . . . . . . . . . . . . . . . . . . . . . . $1,504.3

Government consumption expenditures and gross investment . $2,911.4
    Federal . . . . . . . . . . . . . . . . . . . . . . . . . . . . . . . . . . . $1,107.0
    State and local . . . . . . . . . . . . . . . . . . . . . . . . . . . . . $1,804.4

Net Exports . . . . . . . . . . . . . . . . . . . . . . . . . . . . . . . . . – $545.1

    Exports . . . . . . . . . . . . . . . . . . . . . . . . . . . . . . . . . . $1,724.7
    Imports . . . . . . . . . . . . . . . . . . . . . . . . . . . . . . . . . . $2,269.7

GROSS DOMESTIC PRODUCT (GDP) . . . . . . . . . . . . . . . $14,200.3

*Source: Bureau of Economic Analysis (www.bea.gov).*

**Personal consumption expenditures (C)** is defined as the dollar value of final goods and services bought by consumers in a year. It includes durable goods such as cars, appliances and furniture; non-durable goods such as food, clothing and gasoline; and services such as utilities, medical care, and entertainment.

**Gross private domestic investment (I)** is the value of all final fixed investment goods purchased by business in a year: tools, equipment, machinery, and buildings. It includes residential housing because housing is seen as an investment rather than a consumer good. It also includes changes in business inventories, an important factor in the business cycle.

**Government Consumption Expenditures and Gross Investment (G)** are the value of goods and services that the government (federal, state, and local) purchases each year from business. Note that G does not include transfer payments for welfare, food stamps, Medicaid, and other social programs. Consumption expenditures include wages and salaries for government employees; gross investment includes payments for building highways.

**Net exports (X-M)** is exports minus imports, a figure that has been negative since the 1980s. Imports are subtracted from exports because they are already accounted for in GDP in Personal Consumption Expenditures (C). Thus they are subtracted from exports to avoid double counting.

Which of these four sectors are the most important in the United States? In percentage terms, GDP is broken down as follows:

| | |
|---|---|
| C = $9,927.9 | 69.9% |
| I = $1,906.1 | 13.4% |
| G = $2,911.4 | 20.5% |
| X - M = $ – 545.1 | – 3.8% |
| GDP = $14,200.3 | 100% |

**Figure 15.5.** *GDP by Category, 2008.*

Personal consumption represents the largest sector of final output, while government purchases and investment capital are a distant second and third. This chapter and Chapter 17 demonstrate that the resultant emphasis on consumer spending as the largest part of GDP has led to much mischief in public policy.

**World GDP**
Dec 29th 2004
From *The Economist*

How fast is the world economy growing? From this week *The Economist* will track global GDP growth each quarter. We will estimate global growth based on 52 of the economies that we track each week in the paper or on this website. These countries account for about 90% of world GDP. Each new quarter's global growth rate will be published as soon as figures for about 80% of world GDP are available, and be updated as more countries publish their data.

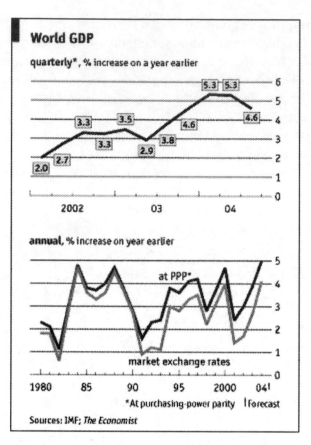

**Figure 15.6.** *World GDP. Sources: IMF; The Economist.*

Each country's GDP growth is weighted by its share in world GDP, valued not at market exchange rates, but at purchasing-power parity (PPP), which takes account of differences in price levels between countries. This is the method used by the IMF in its *World Economic Outlook*. It avoids the distortions caused by the volatility of market exchange rates. The prices of non-traded goods tend to be much cheaper in poorer countries, so exchange rates also misleadingly reduce the weight of their economies in global GDP.

At market exchange rates the rich developed economies account for 77% of global output, but using PPP, they account for only just over half. As a result, the weights used make a big difference to global growth rates. Over the past 25 years, global GDP growth using PPP has averaged 3.3%, but only 2.7% at market exchange rates, which give a much smaller weight to fast-growing economies such as China. And the gap is widening: in 2004, the IMF estimates that global GDP growth at PPP was 5.0%—its fastest for almost 30 years; but at market exchange rates, estimated growth was only 4.1%.

## GDP BY VALUE ADDED

**A second way to measure GDP is by adding up the value added at each stage of the economy.** Here is the estimated breakdown for GDP in 2008:

Gross Domestic Product (GDP) ...........................................$14,200.3
    (in billions of U. S. dollars)
    Agriculture, forestry, fishing & hunting ...............................$157.7
    Mining .................................................................................$325.3
    Utilities .................................................................................$306.0
    Construction ........................................................................$581.5
    Manufacturing ...................................................................$1,637.7
        Durable goods....................$914.7
        Nondurable goods..............$723.0

    Wholesale trade ..............................................................$818.8
    Transportation and warehousing ......................................$419.9
    Retail trade........................................................................$885.5

    Information ........................................................................$622.0
    Finance, insurance, real estate, leasing..........................$2,848.4
    Professional and business services...................................$1,805.8
    Educational services, health care, etc. ...........................$1,157.9
    Arts, entertainment, recreation, food...............................$536.3
    Other services except government.....................................$326.8

    Government, federal, state and local..............................$1,840.0

**Figure 15.7.** *Gross Domestic Product, Valued Added by Industry, 2008 (est.).
Source: Survey of Current Business.*

By categorizing GDP according to value added by industry, economists can identify which sectors of the economy are growing the fastest, and which are falling. For example, during 2007-08, the economy headed into recession and GDP grew only 1% in real terms (after inflation). Revenues from construction fell 5.6%, manufacturing dropped 2.7%, and financial services declined 3%. On the other hand, information businesses grew 5.2%, professional and business services climbed 5.5%, healthcare expanded by 4.6%, and government — which never declines — increased 3%.

## GDP BY INCOME

Another way of looking at economic growth is by measuring income recipients in terms of wages, rents, profits, and interest. See figures 15.8 and 15.9 below.

Gross Domestic Income ...................................................$14,007.3
    (in billions of U. S. dollars)

    Wages, salaries and other compensation........................$8,091.6
    Rental and proprietors' income ....................................$1,152.0
    Corporate profits...........................................................$868.6
    Net interest.................................................................$963.1
    Taxes on production and imports .................................$1,026.1
    Less: subsidies..............................................................$51.2
    Consumption of fixed capital ........................................$1,850.1
    Other items, including statistical discrepancy.....................$193.0

**Figure 15.8.** Gross Domestic Income by Type, 2008 (est.).
Source: Survey of Current Business.

**Figure 15.9.** *Gross Domestic Income by Type, 2008. Source: Survey of Current Business.*

The pie chart (figure 15.9) illustrates that employee compensation (wages and salaries) represent by far the largest income generator in the economy (58%), followed by profits and interest (13%), and rents (8.2%).

## WHAT DOES GDP LEAVE OUT?

GDP currently serves as the important measurement of economic performance in each nation, so significant that the GDP is updated quarterly in industrial nations. But how reliable is it as a macroeconomic indicator? To answer this question, consider the list of items that are left out of GDP.

1. **Intermediate production**: First, GDP leaves out spending at the intermediate level, before we reach the final retail stage of consumption. This fact is often ignored when journalists and commentators refer to GDP as "total spending" in the economy. In fact, it represents only **final** spending in the economy at the retail level. And since consumption represents 70% of GDP, journalists often make the mistake of assuming that the economy is "consumer driven" rather than "investment driven." In reality, business spending, defined as intermediate business spending (IE) and private capital investment (I), represents over half of total economic activity in the United States and other industrial countries. Hence, supply-side business investment, broadly defined, is far more important than demand-side consumer spending in the economy. For more detail, see chapter 17.

2. **Black Market Activities:** GDP also leaves out many transactions that are hard to measure. For example, non-reported and tax-free black market activities are difficult to quantify, and are largely ignored if they aren't part of the official accounting system as reported to tax authorities. When taxes and regulations are low, black market activities are low and create little distortion in government data. But when taxes and regulations are burdensome, non-reported transactions can represent 30-40% of the economy, and the distortion is significant. Countries in Latin America and Europe (e.g., Italy) are famous for black market activity, and reporting agencies attempt to estimate these informal transactions in GDP data.

3. **Household Work:** Some analysts complain that if GDP is supposed to measure output in the economy, it should include an estimate of household work. Recent studies show that unpaid household work accounts for up to 44% of GDP.

   Regardless of the actual figures, the key point to understand here is that GDP is not actually a measure of total production in the economy. GDP represents final transactions — that is, goods and services that are bought and sold using money in an exchange. Since household work is largely "unpaid," household work is not included as an output, or service, even though it introduces value in the economy.

4. **Used goods:** GDP measures only transactions for new, finished goods and services. Yet in any economy, used goods play an increasing role, especially during a recession, when used products can be purchased at much lower prices than new. Thus, used cars, appliances, tools, and computers represent an important and growing sector of the economy. The success of eBay is a good example, where millions buy and sell used products every year. GDP does estimate the output and income accrued by workers, capitalists/entrepreneurs, and suppliers in the used product market but not the value of the used goods themselves.

## OTHER IMPORTANT NATIONAL INCOME STATISTICS

Governments compile other important national accounting statistics, such as Gross National Product (GNP), Net National Product (NNP), National Income (NI), and Personal Income (PI). See figure 15.10 for the latest breakdown, and how they are determined.

Gross Domestic Product (GDP), 2008 .............................. $14,200.3
    (in billions of U. S. dollars)
    Plus: Income receipts from the rest of the world...................$843.2
    Less: Income payments to the rest of the world...................$705.1

Equals: Gross National Product (GNP) ...............................$14,289.0
    Less: Consumption of fixed capital ...............................$1,477.5

Equals: Net National Product (NNP) ...................................$12,511.1
Less: Statistical discrepancy.......................................$63.4

Equals: National Income................................................$12,477.6
    Less: Corporate profits ...................................................$1,593.5
    Plus: Personal income receipts on assets ........................,$1,999.6

Equals: Personal Income ...................................................$12,144.4

**Figure 15.10.** GDP, GNP, NNP, NI, and PI for 2008 (est.).
Source: Bureau of Economic Analysis, www.bea.gov.

How important are these other national accounting statistics?

**Gross national product (GNP)** is the market value of goods and services produced by residents, regardless of where they are located around the world. It was used as the primary measure of U.S. production prior to 1991, when it was replace by GDP. Economists believe that GDP better reflects what is being produced inside each country.

**Net domestic product (NDP)** is the market value of the goods and services produced in a country, less the value of the fixed capital used up in production. As every household and business knows, durable goods depreciate in value as they are used up over time. Both consumer goods (cars, appliances, computers) and producer goods (tools, equipment, buildings) are used up and eventually need to be replaced. In 2008, the government estimated that $1.48 trillion in fixed capital was used up, and needed to be replaced.

Replacing depreciated fixed capital each year is vital to a vibrant growing economy. If a nation consumes its capital, the result is a gradual decline in its standard of living and economic growth. The depreciation figures compiled by government agencies are only an estimate of the gradual using up of fixed capital.

**National Income (NI)** is the sum of all incomes, net of depreciated fixed capital, earned in production by employees, capitalists/entrepreneurs, landlords, and government.

**Personal Income (PI)** is income received by persons from all sources, including income earned from participation in production as well as from government and business transfer payments.

The following diagram summarizes the relationship among all the various national accounting figures used in this chapter.

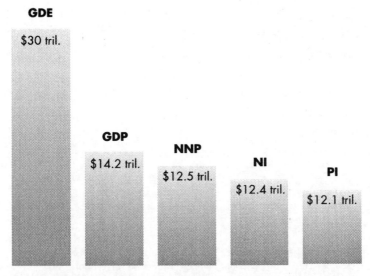

**Figure 15.11.** *The relationship of Gross Domestic Expenditures (GDE), Gross Domestic Product (GDP), and other national accounting statistics for 2008.*

351

## MEASURING WEALTH AND INCOME

Every three years the Federal Reserve Board issues its "Survey of Consumer Finance," which measures per capita income, family net worth, and consumer debt levels. The latest figures are for 2007 (see figure 15.12 on net worth).

### Average U. S. Family Net Worth, by Selected Characteristics of Families, 2007

All families.....................................................................$556,300

Percentile of income
   Less than 20% ..........................................................105,200
   20-40%.....................................................................134,900
   40-60%.....................................................................209,900
   60-80%.....................................................................375,100
   80-90%.....................................................................606,300
   90-100%................................................................3,306,000

Education of Head of Household
   No high school education ..........................................142,900
   High school diploma ..................................................251,600
Some college ...............................................................365,900
   College degree.......................................................1,097,800

Race or ethnicity
   White non-Hispanic...................................................692,200
   Nonwhite or Hispanic................................................228,500
Current work status of head
   Working for someone else..........................................350,100
   Self-employed .......................................................1,961,300
   Retired ....................................................................543,100
   Other not working ....................................................124,100

Housing status
   Owner ....................................................................778,200
   Renter or other..........................................................70,600

**Figure 15.12.** Average Net Worth by Selected Characteristics, 2007
Source: Survey of Consumer Finance, Federal Reserve Board, 2009

What can be learned from this survey of net worth? First, it pays to get an education, and the more the better. As demonstrated in Chapter 10 on wages (see figure 10.11), an individual who has a college degree has a much better chance of succeeding financially than high school graduates and dropouts. Second, it pays to be self-employed. Third, buy a house as soon as practical. Finally, the survey shows that minorities still have a long ways to go to catch up with the majority Caucasian population in the United States.

## HOW IMPORTANT IS STOCK MARKET PERFORMANCE?

Recently some economists have suggested that stock market behavior, as measured by a country stock index, might serve as an indicator of national well-being and its outlook for the future. For example, the following chart (figure 15.13) indicates the market capitalization of stock indexes since 1970 in the United States, the United Kingdom, Germany and Japan.

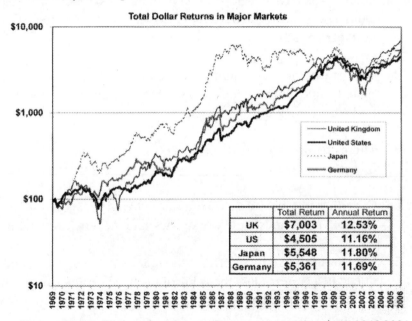

**Figure 15.13.** *Stock market returns in Germany, Japan, US and UK, 1969-2006*
*Source: Jeremy Siegel, Stocks for the Long Term, 3rd ed. (2002), p. 167. Data updated by Jeremy Schwartz.*

Several conclusions can be drawn from looking at this long-term comparison graph. First, both recessions and inflation hurt the stock market and the economy. Stocks fell sharply during the 1973-75, 2001-03, and 2008-09 global recessions. The 1970s was also a period of rapid inflation, and all markets struggled except Japan. Second, note the long decline in Japanese stocks during the 1990s, a reflection of the low-growth malaise Japan suffered from during this time. Finally, losing a war can be devastating. Although figure 15.13 doesn't go back to the 1940s, Wall Street declined slightly during World War II, but Germany and Japan, the two big losers in the war, saw their stock markets collapse.

In short, country stock indexes can reveal a lot to say about economic performance.

In the next chapter, we will discuss the importance of price inflation, the various ways to measure inflation, and the impact it has on GDP and our standard of living.

## SUMMARY

Chapter 15 presented the following main points:

1. Economists have developed several measures of national well-being: Gross Domestic Expenditures (GDE), Gross Domestic Product (GDP), and stock market capitalization.

2. GDP is the most common measure of economic activity. GDP is the estimated value of final goods and services purchased by consumers, business and government during the year.

3. There are three ways to determine GDP: buy purchases, by value added, and by national income.

4. GDP does not measure all economic activity. It leaves out intermediate production, most household work, black market activities, and used goods.

5. Net Domestic Product (NDP) is the market value of goods and services produced in a country, less the value of the fixed capital used up in production. Replacing depreciated fixed capital each year is vital to a vibrant growing economy.

6. Other national statistics such as wealth and stock market indexes are valuable tools to assess national well-being. The stock market, in particular, is a valuable indicator of a country's economic future.

## IMPORTANT TERMS

Aggregate Production Structure (APS)

Black market

Double counting

Government consumption expenditures

Government gross investment

Gross Business Investment

Gross Private Domestic Investment

Gross Domestic Expenditures (GDE)

Gross Domestic Product (GDP)

Gross National Product (GNP)

Intermediate Expenditures (IE)

Intermediate production

International Monetary Fund (IMF)

Market capitalization

National Income (NI)

Net exports

Net Domestic Product (NDP)

Net worth

Personal Consumption Expenditures

Personal Income (PI)

Purchasing Power Parity (PPP)

Standard & Poors Stock Index

Value added

World GDP

## INFLUENTIAL ECONOMIST

### SIMON KUZNETS AND THE INVENTION OF NATIONAL INCOME ACCOUNTING

**Name: Simon Kuznets (1901-1985)**

**Background:** Like Leontief, Simon Kuznets was born in the Soviet Union (modern day Belarus) but the Kuznets family fled Russia after the Communist revolution and eventually moved to the United States, where he worked closely with the National Bureau of Economic Research (NBER). With a Ph. D. from Columbia University in 1936, he went on to become a professor of economics at the University of Pennsylvania, Johns Hopkins University, and Harvard University. He was elected president of the American Economic Association in 1954, and won the Nobel Prize in economics in 1971 for his work on national income accounting, economic growth, and income inequality.

**Major work:** *National Income and Capital Formation, 1919-1935* (Princeton: NBER, 1937).

**Major contribution:** Prior to Kuznets, only rudimentary efforts had been made to measure national economic activity. At NBER, Kuznets quickly became the leader in collecting national income data, starting with the United States. He was the first to develop estimates of national income for the 1929-32 Great Depression, and from 1919 to 1938, and eventually provided estimates going back to 1869, and was an important contributor to *Historical Statistics of the United States, Colonial Times to 1970*, published by the U. S. Commerce Department.

Kuznets also focused on the causes of economic growth, business cycles, and changing income inequality.

**Strength:** Kuznets set the highest standards in collecting economic data, and the foundation of national income accounting in the 20th century. He also understood the severe limitations of GDP and per capita real GDP as an indicator of national well-being. High GDP growth may not benefit all citizens. Kuznets was always concerned about income and wealth inequality, and how the poor survived and improved their living standards compared to the rich.

Kuznets also questioned the Keynesian theory that wealthy people save at higher rates. Looking at long-term data, he discovered that savings rates were relatively constant, despite higher economic growth.

**Weakness:** Despite some criticisms of the Keynesian theory, Kuznets helped advance the Keynesian revolution by creating Gross National Product as a measure of final goods and services only. It was Kuznets who, under the influence of Keynes and his belief that all that mattered was "final effective demand," decided to measure final goods rather than intermediate goods plus final goods in determining "total economic activity." Kuznets's focus on GNP (or today's GDP) as THE measure of economic activity helped encourage today's overemphasis on consumer spending as the driving force in the economy rather than supply-side capital investment and productivity.

## PROBLEMS TO PONDER

1.  Where does the government classify the following purchases in GDP statistics: (C, I, or G?)
    A.  A consumer buys a Toyota Camry.
    B.  A corporate executive buys a sports truck for his business, but uses it also for personal use.
    C.  A couple buys a new home.

2.  Why is the purchase of residential housing included in I while automobiles are included in C? What is the logic of this difference? Are not both capital goods?

3.  Currently government (G) amounts to approximately 20% of GDP. Yet many studies show that government spending in the economy represents 35% or more of the US economy. How do you explain this large discrepancy?

4.  We have learned in this chapter that consumer spending represents 70% of GDP, by far the biggest sector. Yet economists contend that saving and investment, not spending, are the primary key to economic growth, and bemoan the low saving rate in America. How do you reconcile this apparent paradox? (More on this debate in chapters 17 and 25.)

5. According to official GDP statistics, the American economy suffered another "great depression" in the year following World War II, with GDP declining 17% in 1946. Yet all economists report a booming economy in construction, employment, capital and consumer spending during that time. How do you explain this anomaly? (After attempting an answer, see Richard K. Vedder and Lowell Gallaway, "The Great Depression of 1946," Review of Austrian Economics 5:2 [1991], for an explanation.)

6. In Venezuela, the government uses oil revenues to build a 4-lane superhighway into the hinterlands of the country, where only a few hundred cars use the road daily. Should the construction of this highway be included as investment spending (I) in GDP? Using a cost-benefit analysis on this project, determine if, on balance, it increases or decreases the Venezuelan standard of living.

7. Labor unions often complain about the excessive power and influence of big business. In this chapter, we learn that workers earn by far the biggest share of national income, approximately 58%, compared to 13% for corporations, and only 8% for landlords. How would you address the unions' criticism of corporate power?

8. How much in durable goods did consumers and businesses purchase in the past year? Was it sufficient to replace the depreciated goods? Is America increasing its capital investment base, or consuming it?

9. Respond to the following criticism of GDP by the creators of the Genuine Progress Index (see p. 25): "Giving no value to unpaid work creates accounting absurdities and social inequities. Hire a housekeeper to wash your dishes and do your laundry, and it's counted as part of the economy. Marry your housekeeper, and the GDP goes down. Eating out is good for the economy. Home cooking has no value in our accounts. Pay someone to look after your child, and it registers as economic growth and progress. Look after your own child, and it's invisible, counted nowhere. In fact, eating out or hiring a housekeeper or child care service is not increasing production, but merely shifting it to that part of the economy that's measured. By measuring the value of unpaid household work, the Genuine Progress Index remedies this flaw and allows us to track important trends and shifts between the household and market economies." Should the Bureau of Economic Analysis include unpaid work in its GDP figures? How accurate are these figures?

10. Should government collect economic statistics at all? Milton Friedman wrote in the *Wall Street Journal* (October 6, 2006): "Though a colony of socialist Britain, Hong Kong followed a laissez-faire capitalist policy, thanks largely to a British civil servant, John Cowperthwaite. Cowperthwaite was so famously laissez-faire that he refused to collect economic statistics for fear this would only give government officials an excuse for more meddling. His successor, Sir Philip Haddon-Cave, coined the term "positive nonintervention-tionism" to describe Cowperthwaite's approach. The results of his policy were remarkable. At the end of World War II, Hong Kong was a dirt-poor island with a per-capita income about one-quarter that of Britain's. By 1997, when sovereignty was transferred to China, its per-capita income was roughly equal to that of the departing colonial power, even though Britain had experienced sizable growth over the same period. That was a striking demonstration of the productivity of freedom, of what people can do when they are left free to pursue their own interests." Should government pursue Cowperthwaite's "positive noninterventionist" approach by not collecting economic statistics? If government doesn't keep statistics, who would? Why would private companies and organizations keep industry or country wide economic statistics?

11. In the March 13, 2008, issue, the Economist asked this question: "Which economy has enjoyed the best performance over the past five years: America's or Japan's?" Based on real GDP figures, the answer would be America. Average annual real GDP growth was 2.9% in the United States during this 5-year period, much faster than Japan's 2.1%. However, per capita real GDP is a better gauge of economic performance. Thanks to immigration and a higher birth rate, the population of the United States grew much faster than Japan's. The result? The Economist states: "Japan's GDP per head increased at an annual rate of 2.1% in the five years to 2007, slightly faster than America's 1.9% and much better than Germany's 1.4%." Was Japan's "Lost Decade" of stagnation and deflation as bad as the media makes it out to be?

## ADDITIONAL READING

- Jeremy Siegel, *Stocks for the Long Run*, 4th ed. (McGraw Hill, 2008). An excellent historical review and insights into the stock market and economic growth.

- Stanley Lebergott, *The American Economy: Income, Wealth, and Want* (Princeton University Press, 1976). A well-researched description of various measures of economic progress in the 20th century.

# PRICE INFLATION AND THE PURCHASING POWER OF MONEY

*"Fiat money and fiduciary credit are the pillar and post of our age of inflation."*

—HANS F. SENNHOLZ
*The Age of Inflation* (2006)

In 2004 the gross domestic product (GDP) in Mexico reached US$1 trillion, a monumental achievement. The GDP in the United States stood at almost $12 trillion in 2004. The value of final output of Mexican goods and services had climbed 10% from the previous year to reach this milestone. Yet the average Mexican may not have felt much richer upon hearing the news because the cost of living in Mexico rose by more than 6% at the same time, giving the average Mexican only a 4% increase in real purchasing power terms.

To provide a more accurate measure of material well-being, income must be translated into real terms, taking into account actual purchasing power. This chapter focuses on the value of the goods and services produced in a country in "real" terms, after price inflation. The contrast between what is earned and the cost of goods is explored. For example, if an individual receives a 10% raise but the price of goods, on average, are up 10%, that individual has not increased his purchasing power. To determine the value of "real" income a variety of price indexes provided by government and private economists are used to determine real value. These indexes cover various stages of production, as follows:

— **Commodity price indexes**, such as the CRB Commodity Index, determine price changes at the earliest stage of production

— **Producer Price Index (PPI)** measures price changes at the manufacturing and wholesale level

— **Consumer Price Index (CPI)** measures price changes at the consumer or retail level

— **GDP deflator**, a composite of price indexes that make up GDP (prices of final goods and services paid for by consumers, business, government, and exporters/importers)

## COMMODITY PRICES: THE MOST VOLATILE

The Reuters/Jefferies CRB Commodity Index is a 22-commodity price index compiled daily by the Commodity Research Bureau, in conjunction with Reuters and Jefferies Financial Products. The CRB Commodity Index has existed in one form or another since January, 1934. Commodities include foodstuffs, such as hogs, steers, corn and wheat; industrial metals such as copper, zinc, lead and tin (but not gold or silver); and raw industrials such as hides and rubber. Historically, the price of raw commodities, being further away from final consumption and capital-intensive, tend to be the most volatile.

## PRODUCER PRICE INDEX (PPI)

The Producer Price Index (PPI) is released monthly by the Bureau of Labor Statistics in the U. S. The PPI tracks the change in prices of domestic goods at the production stage, from the early-stages in agriculture, forestry, fisheries, mining, to manufacturing and construction, to service sectors such as transportation, wholesale and retail trade, insurance, real estate, health, legal and professional services. The PPI includes input from over 25,000 organizations providing approximately 100,000 price quotations per month. Economists and financial experts follow the PPI closely as a forecaster of general price inflation that might lead to rising pressure on consumer prices.

## CONSUMER PRICE INDEX (CPI)

The Consumer Price Index (CPI), released monthly by the Bureau of Labor Statistics, is a government-generated tool used to measure the rate of price inflation. The CPI tracks the prices of a theoretical group of goods and services that most households need to purchase each year. This selection of goods and services includes such necessities as gasoline, food, housing, and movie tickets. Over the course of a year, some of these items remain the same in price, while others rise significantly, and some may drop in price. The CPI aims to measure the overall rate of price inflation as an estimate of the cost of living.

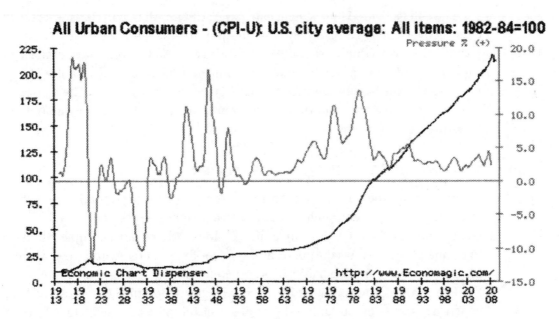

**Figure 16.1.** *Changes in the Consumer Price Index for Urban Americans, 1913-2008. Source: Economagic.com*

Government salaries, welfare benefits, unionized wages, and many other payments rely on CPI figures to determine cost-of-living adjustments (COLA), so getting an accurate picture of the cost of living is important. For example, over 2 million labor union workers are covered by collective bargaining agreements whose wages are tied to the CPI. Monthly benefit checks of almost 80 million people are linked to this price index, including 47.8 million Social Security beneficiaries, about 4.1 million military and Federal Civil Service retirees and survivors, and about 22.4 million food stamp recipients. Changes in the CPI also affect the cost of lunches for the 26.7 million children who eat lunch at school. Some private firms and individuals use the CPI to keep rents, royalties, alimony payments and child support payments in line with changing prices. And since 1985, the CPI has been used to adjust the Federal income tax structure to prevent inflation-induced increases in taxes. The U. S. Treasury also issues I-bonds, or TIPS (Treasury Inflation Protected Securities), which are linked to the CPI. The CPI is the most widely used measure of inflation used by government officials, business executives, labor leaders and private citizens as a guide in making policy and economic decisions.

The CPI is determined each month by a survey of 87 urban areas of prices of 364 items that compose a typical bundle purchased by urban consumers during the base period, 1982-84. Items include food and beverages, housing (including owner's equivalent rent), apparel, transportation, medical care, recreation, education, and communications. The CPI includes taxes that are linked to goods and services: sales taxes, automobile registration fees, excise taxes, user fees, and property taxes.

The CPI is divided into several categories: CPI for All Urban Consumers (CPI-U), which covers approximately 87% of the population, and a CPI for Urban Wage Earners (CPI-W), which covers 32%. The CPI is a market basket index of these items, valued according to a weighted average. For example, the price of an apple should not be given the same weight as a T-bone steak or a refrigerator. The weight for an item is derived from reported expenditures on that item as estimated by the Consumer Expenditure Survey.

## IS THE CPI A GOOD MEASURE OF THE COST OF LIVING?

Over time, the CPI has added more items to its representative sample in an attempt to be more comprehensive. However, some essential items are still excluded and therefore, the CPI is more a "price" index rather than a complete "cost of living" index. No one buys the goods and services that exactly match the government's formula for the spending habits of an urban family.

For example, according to government surveys, college tuition and related expenses have risen at double-digit rates over the past decade or two. But the CPI largely ignores college expenses, such as tuition, even though these expenses affect many Americans.

Many Americans travel frequently outside the United States for business or pleasure. Overseas the dollar has lost much of its purchasing power during the past 30 years. How does the CPI reflect the dollar's decline? It doesn't.

Crime is a problem in many communities, so homeowners often buy expensive security protection plans for their homes. The CPI doesn't include this expenditure in its consideration of services. Nor does the CPI include accountants who prepare their tax returns. Some people also go out to restaurants that the average person may not frequent. The government's hypothetical selection of goods and services is not necessarily representative of actual household expenditures.

The CPI also does not cover the value of securities and other investment prices: stocks, bonds, life insurance, and some types of real estate. Some economists consider this a serious omission because increases in the cost of living that limit the ability to buy investments may have a significant overall "wealth effect" compared to the cost of basic necessities.

The biggest defect in the CPI may be its omission of the largest item in nearly everyone's household budget—Social Security and income taxes. Today, government taxation represents over 32% of GDP. The CPI recognizes taxes linked to the buying of goods and services (sales taxes and user fees), but ignores Social Security and Medicare taxes as well as federal, state and local income taxes that households must pay. Furthermore, income taxes have been rising as inflation pushes taxpayers into higher tax brackets, and as states and local governments have increased their levies.

In short, some economists argue that the CPI underestimates the actual increase in the cost of living each year by several percent.

## COULD THE CPI OVERESTIMATE THE COST OF LIVING?

Other statisticians contend that the CPI consistently overestimates price inflation in the United States because it does not sufficiently account for several other factors:

1. **Quality improvements**. New technology constantly improves the quality and utility of various products, including televisions, computers, cell phones, and cars. Camcorders, for example, are usually priced the same each year, but the quality of the product has increased tremendously (from black and white viewfinders to LCD viewfinders).

2. **New products**. It always takes time for new products to be included in survey. For years the CPI basket did not include computers, despite their growing use by individuals and businesses. Meanwhile computer prices continued to fall, usually by 10-15% a year. By not accounting for this drop in prices, the CPI over-estimated the cost of living.

3. **Discounts and substitutes**. Consumers are constantly bargain shopping, taking advantage of discounts and sale prices. With the internet, comparison shopping has been taken to a whole new level, and today consumers can find superior bargains on airline tickets, cars, and many other products. An individual's "personal CPI" may be declining in certain areas, while the official CPI remains constant or even rises.

## UNDERSTANDING CHAIN WEIGHTED PRICED INDEXING

As a result of these omissions and distortions, economists have recently created a new CPI statistic, the **chain weighted price index**. The chain weighted CPI accounts for substitutions of goods and other changes in consumer spending habits each year, and is considered more accurate than the fixed weighted CPI.

This example illustrates the difference between fixed weighted CPI and the chain weighted CPI. Assume that Harold has purchased two similar products in the past two years, basketball shoes and tennis shoes, according to the following price and quantity changes during this 2-year period.

363

## HAROLD'S GOODS

2008: 2 basketball shoes, 2 tennis shoes

2009: 3 basketball shoes, 1 tennis shoes

Prices

2008: basketball shoes cost $55, tennis shoes cost $40

2009: basketball shoes cost $50, tennis shoes cost $55

Here is the difference in how the CPI is figured:

## FIXED WEIGHT APPROACH

In the fixed-weighted CPI, we assume Q stays the same from one year to the next; only prices vary.

Therefore, changes in "fixed weight" CPI are as follows:

$$\frac{2 \text{ basketball shoes} \times \$50 + 2 \text{ tennis shoes} \times \$55}{2 \text{ basketball shoes} \times \$55 + 2 \text{ tennis shoes} \times \$40} = 10.5\%$$

According to the fixed weight approach, the CPI increased 10.5% from 2008 to 2009. Note that the fixed weight CPI does not acknowledge the change in the quantity of shoes purchased from 2008 and 2009. In the fixed weighted CPI, the quantity remains theoretically fixed from year to year. Now let's look how the chain weighted CPI gives a more accurate picture of the change in Harold's purchasing power or CPI.

## CHAIN WEIGHTED APPROACH

In the chain-weighted CPI, assume Q and P change from one year to the next.

Thus, changes in the chain weighted CPI are as follows:

$$\frac{3 \text{ basketball shoes} \times \$50 + 1 \text{ tennis shoes} \times \$55}{2 \text{ basketball shoes} \times \$55 + 2 \text{ tennis shoes} \times \$40} = 7.9\%$$

Under the chain weighted approach, the CPI increases only 7.9%, much less than the fixed weighted method. Note the difference. The chain weighted CPI is considered more accurate because it takes into account quantity changes from 2008 to 2009. Because basketball shoes declined in price while tennis shoes went up in price, Harold decided to buy more pairs of basketball shoes and fewer pairs of tennis shoes. The chain weighted method takes this quantity change into account and is considered more accurate.

Many economists believe that the fixed-weighted CPI tends to overestimate the cost of living by a percentage point or so. After conducting an exhaustive study of the CPI, Professor Michael Boskin (Stanford University) concludes that without using the chain weighted method, "The Consumer Price Index overstates increases in the cost of living by about 1.1 percentage point a year."[1]

There are two major deficiencies in the CPI, one that the CPI underestimates the cost of living (omitting payroll taxes) and another that the CPI overestimates changes in quality, quantity and variety. Which force is more powerful? Without further empirical work it is hard to know which is most powerful but it would be national folly to include the former and ignore the latter. Probably Ludwig von Mises said it best when he wrote, "These index numbers are at best crude and inaccurate illustrations of changes which have occurred."[2]

## GDP Deflator

Economists and government officials sometimes refer to the GDP Deflator, which is not the same as the Consumer Price Index. The GDP deflator is not based solely on a fixed selection of consumer goods and services. Like the chain-weighted CPI, the selection is allowed to change with people's consumption and investment patterns each year. The big difference between the GDP deflator and the CPI is that the GDP Deflation includes the price of investment goods as well as consumption goods. (Recall that GDP represents final goods and services purchased by consumers, business, and government.)

The formula used to calculate the deflator is:

$$\text{GDP Deflator} = \frac{\text{Nominal GDP}}{\text{Real GDP}} \times 100$$

---

1  Quoted in *Wall Street Journal*, February 25, 1997, p. A24. Professor Boskin headed a government panel investigating the CPI.
2  Ludwig von Mises, *Human Action*, 3rd ed. (Chicago: Regnery, 1966), p. 222.

The GDP Deflator is used to calculate real GDP, as follows:

$$\frac{\text{Nominal GDP}}{\text{GDP Deflator}} = \text{Real GDP}$$

Dividing the nominal GDP by the GDP deflator gives the figure for real GDP deflating the nominal GDP into a real measure.

## VOLATILITY AND THE STRUCTURE OF PRODUCTION

One of the curious features of the economy, both domestically and globally, is that price indexes tend to be more volatile the further removed they are from final consumption. The following graph in figure 16.2 illustrates this fact:

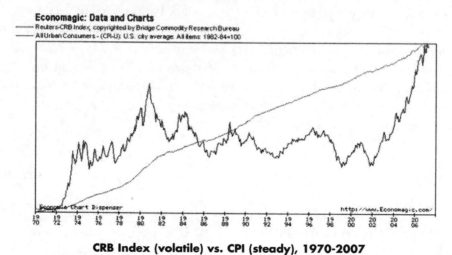

**CRB Index (volatile) vs. CPI (steady), 1970-2007**

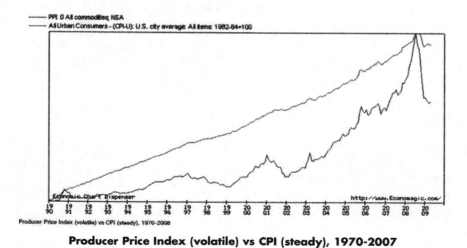

**Producer Price Index (volatile) vs CPI (steady), 1970-2007**

**Figure 16.2.** *Changes in price indices over time: Commodity, Producer, and Consumer Price Indexes (1970-2008).*

1. What accounts for this increasing volatility further from final use? Discuss this issue with several economists and business people. [Hint: Consider the impact of changes in interest rates and financing on various price indexes, or how distant each index is from final consumer use.]

2. Volatility along the supply/production chain is not limited to prices. Over the entire business cycle, greater volatility in employment, inventories and corporate profit statistics exist the further away from the final consumer stage. In the commodity markets greater volatility in employment, inventories and profits exists compared to the manufacturing industries and the consumer goods sector. Why?

**SUMMARY**

Chapter 16 covered these main points:

1. Price indexes are helpful in determining the "real" value of the purchasing power of money.

2. Private institutions and government agencies rely on a variety of price indexes, including those the CRB Commodity Index, the Producer Price Index, and the Consumer Price Index.

3. The GDP Deflation is a composite price index consisting of prices for goods and services paid by consumers, business, government, and exporters/importers.

4. The Consumer Price Index (CPI) is the most popular price index, but the CPI is not a complete indicator of general price inflation, nor is it a true cost of living index. The CPI leaves out payroll taxes, and may not reflect actual spending habits of many Americans.

5. The CPI may not reflect changes in quality, new products, discounts, and substitutions over time. Chain-weighted CPI is an improvement over the traditional fixed-weighted CPI because chain-weighted CPI takes into account substitutions of goods and other changes in consumer spending habits from year to year.

## IMPORTANT TERMS

Chain-weighted CPI
Commodity price index
Consumer Price Index (CPI)
Fixed-weighted CPI

GDP Deflator
Producer Price Index (PPI)
Purchasing Power Parity (PPP)


## INFLUENTIAL ECONOMIST

### IRVING FISHER, THE FATHER OF MONETARY ECONOMICS AND PRICE INDICES

**Name: Irving Fisher (1867-1947)**

**Background:** Irving Fisher is the father of monetary economics, and considered by many economists (James Tobin and Milton Friedman) to be the greatest American economist who ever lived. Born in 1867 in New York to a clergyman, Fisher excelled at mathematics and graduated first in his class at Yale University. Under the influence of social Darwinist William Graham Sumner, he developed an interest in economics, devoting the rest of his life to the study of money, prices, and the economy. After obtaining his Ph. D. from Yale, he married, had children, and settled down to living the life of a professor and author. He authored dozens of books on monetary economics, healthy living (having survived tuberculosis), and investing in the stock market. In 1918 he was elected president of the American Economic Association, and later helped found the Econometric Society. A creative mind, he invented a card index system (today's Rolodex), which he sold to Remington Rand. At the height of the Wall Street bull market, his Remington "A" stock was valued at $10 million. In addition to teaching economics at Yale, Fisher became a financial advisor and became known as the "Oracle on Wall Street," and was quoted frequently in the financial media. But he failed to predict the October 1929 crash and was wiped out, never to recover. He died in 1947.

**Major work:** *The Nature of Capital and Interest* (Macmillan, 1906), and *The Purchasing Power of Money,* 2nd ed. (Macmillan, 1911, 1922).

**Major contribution:** Fisher devoted his life to studying money, prices and business cycles. His most important contribution is the Quantity Theory of Money and the development of price indexes. Fisher created a mathematical equation to symbolize the close relationship between price inflation and the money supply, known as monetarism. (See chapter 19 for an explanation of the Quantity Theory of Money.)  Fisher, like Milton Friedman a generation later, was convinced that a rising cost of living was caused primarily by an excessive expansion of the money supply. Fisher invented the first price indices that formed the basis of the producer price index and the consumer price index.

**Strength:** With his Quantity Theory of Money, Fisher confirmed mathematically what other economists knew (such as David Hume and David Ricardo), that a general rise in prices was caused by an expansion of money and credit through the banking system, not by labor unions, commodity shortages, or other forms of "cost-push" inflation. Fisher also helped advance the gathering of macro-economic data in pioneering the use of price indexes.

**Weakness:** Fisher's main weakness was his dependence on excessive macroeconomic concepts. His Quantity Theory failed to predict the Great Depression, because he firmly believed in the long-run neutrality of money, that is, an increase in the money supply would result in higher prices but not any structural imbalances or other ill-effects. As an optimist who believed in a "new era" in the Roaring Twenties, he ignored the signs of an economic storm brewing in the late 1920s. He had blind faith in the ability of the Federal Reserve to provide liquidity in times of monetary crisis. He was devastated financially when the Fed refused to reverse the tide of deflation and depression.

## PROBLEMS TO PONDER

1. According to Ludwig von Mises, inflation should be defined as increases in the supply of fiat money currency by government, not increases in a price index. And deflation should be defined as decreases in the money supply. Should inflation be defined as a change in the money supply rather than prices? What are the advantages of this approach? The disadvantages? If monetary inflation (measured by a broad monetary index such as M2) goes up 100%, but the CPI only 60%, which inflation index should be used? Is it possible to have 100% increase in the money supply and only 60% increase in prices?

2. The Golf Players' Price Index (GPPI) is based on a survey of people who regularly play golf throughout the year. Information on the market basket for the GPPI and the prices for each of the goods in 2008 and 2009 are given below.

| Product | 2008 | | 2009 | |
| --- | --- | --- | --- | --- |
| | Quantity | Price | Quantity | Price |
| Golf shoes | 2 | $50 | 3 | $50 |
| Clubs | 3 | $400 | 4 | $430 |
| Golf balls | 200 | $0.50 | 150 | $1.00 |
| Membership | 1 | $500 | 1 | $650 |

Based on this survey, calculate:

    A.  The cost of these goods and services in 2008.

    B.  A fixed-weighted GPPI for 2009.

    C.  A chain-weighted GPPI for 2009.

    D.  Which price index is more accurate, fixed or chain? Why?

3.  In the late 19th century, many railroad companies issued long-term bonds guaranteed to be repaid at maturity in a fixed amount of gold bullion. Do some research on these bonds and see what interest rate they were able to pay because of these gold-backed bonds. Was the interest paid on these gold railroad bonds higher or lower than the then-current interest rates on regular corporate bonds? Was it higher or lower than government bonds? What accounts for this difference? When the bonds came due in the 20th century, after the U. S. went off the gold standard, did the railroad companies honor these bonds in gold? Why or why not?

4.  Which would be a better way for the government to protect its investors from inflation: offer a bond linked to changes in the CPI, or a bond guaranteed to pay its principal in a fixed amount of gold bullion?

5.  The Consumer Price Index is not considered a complete "cost of living" index. The CPI does NOT include which of the following items (there may be more than one correct answer):

    A.  Sales taxes

    B.  Imported goods

    C.  Cost of housing

    D.  Stock market prices

    E.  Cost of business machinery

    F.  Personal income taxes

6.  Government officials often consider the "core inflation rate," defined as the CPI excluding food and energy. Food and energy are the most volatile of the CPI goods, and therefore, according to officials, often distort the long-term inflation levels. Do you agree with this official view? Should basic necessities such as food and energy be excluded from the "core inflation rate," or is this a political device to disguise higher inflation rates?

7.  In 2003-04, Fed chairman Alan Greenspan pushed short-term interest rates down to 1% because he feared a "Japanese-style deflation" of falling prices. Is fear of deflation a legitimate concern?

8.  In 2008-09, the Consumer Price Index (CPI) actually fell for a few months in a row. Berkeley professor Brad DeLong argues that the public should fear price deflation (when average prices fall): "The root reason to fear deflation is that the nominal interest rate is bounded below at zero. Significant deflation — even completely anticipated deflation — thus generates high real interest rates and large transfers of wealth from debtors to creditors. Deflation's high real interest rates depress investment, lower demand, and raise unemployment. Deflation's transfers of wealth from debtors to creditors diminish the economy's ability to keep the web of credit and financial intermediation functioning. Such disruption of the financial system puts additional downward pressure on investment, demand, and unemployment." Do you agree? Is price deflation always bad? Should the federal government fight deflation? Can you think of times when falling prices helped the economy? What about the 1920s?

## FOR ADDITIONAL READING

*   Hans Sennholz, *The Age of Inflation*, 2nd ed. (Libertarian Press, 2006). An excellent analysis of the causes of inflation.

*Chapter 17*

# ECONOMIC GROWTH:
# SAVING, INVESTMENT AND TECHNOLOGY

*"In short, the way to wealth, if you desire it, is as plain as the way to market. It depends chiefly on two works, industry and frugality."*

— BENJAMIN FRANKLIN
"The Way to Wealth" (1758)

The first three chapters on macroeconomics discuss the various ways to measure economic performance. These are crucial questions to answer: How can a nation increase its wealth, its income (GDP) and its quality of life? Why are some countries rich and others poor? And can understanding and applying sound macroeconomic principles help poor countries become wealthier?

## WHAT IS THE KEY TO ECONOMIC SUCCESS?

The wealth of a nation can be enhanced in the same way that an individual's wealth is improved. This question is frequently asked, "How can I, as an individual, achieve financial success in life, starting out from scratch?" Assuming that the individual did not inherit a large sum of money, and that his parents or a rich uncle do not plan to subsidize his lifestyle, how can the individual achieve financial independence?

Benjamin Franklin wrote a pamphlet outlining the basic principles of personal economics called "The Way to Wealth." He emphasized three grand principles; industry, frugality, and prudence.

Industry means finding a suitable occupation or career and working industriously at it. Frugality requires being economical and thrifty. It means living within individual means, watching expenses, and avoiding waste. Frugality might mean buying a used car instead of a new one, or renting rather than buying a house. Frugality means avoiding consumer debt as much as possible. Frugality also includes saving regularly by spending less than is earned each month. When Franklin said, "A penny saved is a penny earned," he meant that whether you earn a penny more or spend a penny less, you will put another penny in your pocket. Most people think the only way to increase wealth is to earn more, but spending less is just as effective, and is less difficult.

Here's another way of looking at Franklin's adage: Suppose an individual earns $1,000 a month in income, and over the year he saves $1,000. Now suppose he becomes ill and must convalesce at home for a month. That $1,000 he has in his savings account can be drawn upon to replace what he would have otherwise earned. Thus, $1,000 saved is indeed exactly equal to $1,000 earned. Smart people make it a habit to save regularly and live within their means.

Prudence means wisdom. Prudence requires that savings be invested wisely. This can be done by advancing education and training, investing in a new business venture, or profiting from other people's successful businesses via the stock market. Prudence means more than working hard; it means working smart, exhibiting self-control, and spending prudently.

## SAVING AND CLASSICAL GROWTH THEORY

The classical economists Adam Smith (1723-90), David Ricardo (1772-1823) and John Stuart Mill (1806-73) emphasized these same virtues in what is now considered the classical model for advancing the wealth of nations. Theoretically, if industry, frugality and prudence were sources of progress for an individual, so should they be for the nation. This may seem self-evident today, but at the time governments believed that a finite amount of wealth existed throughout the world, and that the only way for a country to increase its wealth was to take from another country. Adam Smith rejected this mercantilist philosophy. "What is prudence in the conduct of every private family can scarce be folly in that of a great kingdom," declared Smith.[1] His principle focus throughout his magnum opus, *The Wealth of Nations*, was the "improvement" of the individual through "frugality and good conduct," saving and investing, exchange and the division of labor, education and capital formation, labor-saving technology, and enlightened self-interest. After introducing the management technique of division of labor, Smith emphasized the need for saving and frugality as essential keys to economic growth. In addition, a growing economy required stable government policies, a competitive business environment, and sound business management. "Little else is required to carried a state to the highest degree of opulence from the lowest barbarism, but peace, easy taxes, and a tolerable administration of justice."[2]

1  Adam Smith, *The Wealth of Nations* (New York: Modern Library, 1965 [1776]), p. 424.
2  Quoted in Clyde E. Danhert, ed., *Adam Smith, Man of Letters and Economist.* New York: Exposition, 1974, p. 218.

Another economist who advanced the classical theory of economic growth and the importance of saving/investing is the Austrian economist Eugen Böhm-Bawerk (1851-1914), whom we introduced in chapter 11. In his book, *The Positive Theory of Capital* (1890), he explained that capital in its many forms — saving, investing, labor-saving technology, capital goods, productivity, knowledge, education — is the key to fulfilling Adam Smith's world of universal prosperity, for capitalists as well as laborers. He pointed out that if laborers wished to surpass a subsistence wage, they must recognize that simple labor or hard work was not enough to achieve a higher standard of living. "It is simply not true that the man is 'merely industrious.' He is both industrious and thrifty," he wrote, echoing Franklin. Böhm-Bawerk described three possible scenarios:

1. **Positive saving rate**: Suppose a country has an average saving rate of 25%, i.e., the average citizen saves a fourth of his earnings each year. What would be the effect? Bohm-Bawerk declared: "An economically advanced nation invests its savings. It buy securities, it deposits money at interest in savings banks or commercial banks, which puts it out on loan. In other words, there is an increase in capital, which rebounds to the benefit of an enhanced enjoyment of consumption goods in the future." The result, he said, would be positive economic growth.

2. **No net savings**: Now suppose another alternative, that a country on average has no new net savings beyond the payment for depreciation or upkeep of buildings, tools, and equipment. That is, the average citizens spend all their income, and save nothing. The result would, according to Böhm-Bawerk, be a nation that does "no more than preserve its capital." Growth would be zero.

3. **Negative savings**: Finally, what if the nation on average consumed 25% more than its income; instead of saving, the citizens use up their stock of wealth. By consuming their capital, the result would be negative economic growth, a lower standard of living.

## THE KEYNESIAN PARADOX OF THRIFT:
## DOES MORE THRIFTINESS CAUSE A RECESSION?

What if citizens decide to reduce their consumption and increase their savings? Here Keynesian economists[3] are often critical of consumers who retrench and increase their savings at the expense of consumption, concluding that the net effect is lower consumer spending and lower economic growth, or even recession. Is this an accurate view of higher saving?

If the standard 4-stage macro model is reduced into 2 stages the Keynesian model supports this anti-saving thesis. Normally intermediate production consists of three stages — resources, production and distribution — but if these three stages are combined in the investment stage production, there are only two stages of production, "investment" and "consumption." Figure 17.1 illustrates the effect of increased savings, which has the same effect as reduced consumption.

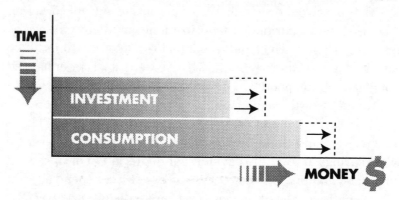

**Figure 17.1.** *A Keynesian model of economic growth:*
*Two-stage macro model showing investment and consumption moving together.*

In the Keynesian model above, investment, i. e., business activity, depends entirely on demand for consumer goods. Investment and consumption move up and down together. If society demands more consumer goods, investment will increase. What happens when consumers cutback **and** save more? According to figure 17.1, the result will be less investment, less business spending, unemployment and recession. Keynesians deny the universal virtue of thrift as espoused by Ben Franklin and Adam Smith. As William Baumol and Alan Blinder, both Keynesian economists, have written, "While savings may pave the road to riches for an individual, if the nation as a whole decides to save more, the result may be a recession and poverty for all."[4]

3  Keynesian economics is discussed here in this chapter and in more detail in chapters 19-22. See in particular chapter 22, where John Maynard Keynes is highlighted as an "influential economist."
4  William J. Baumol and Alan S. Blinder, *Economics: Principles and Policy* (New York: Harcourt, Brace and Jovanovich, 1988), p. 192.

In some ways, the Keynesian view appears to make common sense. After all, does it make sense for people to buy fewer cars (reducing consumption) so that manufacturers can build more auto factories? If people save more and cutback on buying cars and going to the mall, won't business suffer? Keynesians such as Paul Samuelson argue that increasing saving may result in less saving if income falls as a result of less business activity.

## THE CLASSICAL DEFENSE OF SAVINGS

Classical economists, including Böhm-Bawerk, John Stuart Mill and J.-B. Say, give several arguments in response to the Keynesian challenge. According to them, the Keynesians fail to recognize another form of demand that increased savings generates — *the increase in demand for future consumption*. In mathematical form, total output or income (Y) is a function of current demand (C, which stands for consumption) and future demand (I, which stands for investment):

$$Y = f\,(C) + f\,(I)$$

Two forms of demand are always at work in the economy: the demand for current consumption (e.g., the current demand for automobiles) and the demand for future consumption (e.g., the future demand for automobiles).

If the public decides to save more, demand for current consumption will indeed fall; however, demand for future consumption will rise, countering the fall in current consumer demand. Meanwhile savings do not disappear from the economy, but move to a different stage of production, responding to the demand for investment.

Böhm-Bawerk describes how this works: "The truth is that a curtailment of consumption involves, not a curtailment of production generally, but only, through the action of the law of supply and demand, a curtailment in certain branches....There will not be a smaller production of goods generally, because the lessened output for immediate consumption may and will be offset by an increased production of 'intermediate' or capital goods."[5]

## THE EXAMPLE OF BUILDING A BRIDGE

A hypothetical example illustrates the benefits of increased savings. Suppose the two parts of a community, such as Minneapolis-St. Paul, Minnesota, are separated by a river and the only transportation between the two sides is by barge. Travel between Minneapolis and St. Paul is expensive and time-consuming. The two town leaders call a meeting and recommend the building a bridge, to be paid for

5 Eugen Böhm-Bawerk, "The Positive Theory of Capital," cited in Richard Ebeling, ed., *Austrian Economics: A Reader* (Hillsdale College Press, 1991), pp. 405-06.

by a temporary 5-year increase in the sales tax. The sales tax increases the price of consumer goods across the board including the price of cars, appliances, clothing, food, and other goods — causing retail sales and consumer spending to fall, which in turn reduces the profits and employment in local department stores and other retail outlets. On the other side of the ledger the decline in consumer spending is off-set by a rising in investment spending. New construction workers are hired to build the bridge, and a whole new building industry is created in the town. These workers spend their income in the city, boosting retail sales. They may also save some of their earnings, boosting deposits at local banks. In the aggregate, is there any reduction in output and employment? No, only a change in the composition of the output and employment.

Moreover, once the bridge has been built, the community, made up of consumers, business, and government officials, benefits greatly from the lower travel costs and increased competition between the two sections of town. In the end, the community's short-term sacrifice has been transformed into a higher standard of living. In more general terms, a higher saving rate means an increase in the supply of savings and a fall in interest rates. Figure 17.2 illustrates this effect of increased savings.

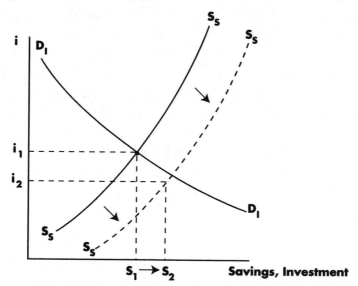

**Figure 17.2.** *Increased savings rate will lower interest rates.*

Lower interest rates means that banks and finance companies can offer cheaper business and consumer loans, thus reducing the overall cost of financing producer and consumer goods. In addition, lower rates may encourage an increase in spending on retooling, upgrading or building new plants, and developing new, better products. Individuals spend less now in order to increase their consumption a few years later….perhaps on the new, better consumer products.

The problem with the Keynesians is that they fail to incorporate in their two-stage model a capital structure that is time-using and multi-stage. In other words, "investment" is not simply one stage removed from final consumption. Investment is multi-layered, where changes in interest rates affect the composition of the intermediate stages of production. Figure 17.3 illustrates this complex structure using a 4-stage model.

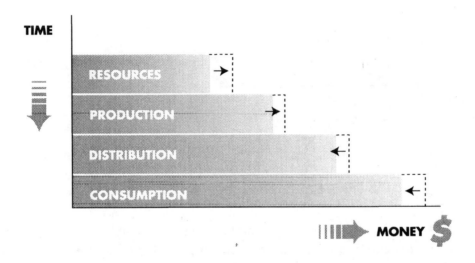

**Figure 17.3.** *A shift in the structure of production due to an increase in saving.*

In this diagram consumers cut back and the increased savings and lower interest rates affect the entire structure of intermediate production. There is a cutback in production in the second stage but not as much as final consumption. In the third stage (production), the decrease in demand from the later stage is offset by an increase in demand from the earlier stage, due to lower interest rates. In the earliest fourth stage, the resource stage (which includes research & development) rises, where the interest-rate effect far outdistances the consumer demand effect.

Chapter 11 introduced the economics of capital technology, demonstrating how a technological advance increases output. Figure 17.4 shows the breakeven point for a new capital technology.

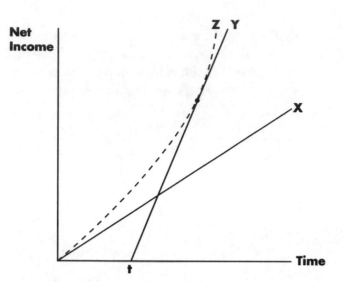

**Figure 17.4.** *Breakeven point for a new capital technology.*

In the above diagram, the line X represents the profit or net income over time using the current production method. Time t represents the time it takes to create a new technology, Y, and line Y represents the increased profit achieved from the new technology.

As noted in chapter 11 a trade-off between the current plan and a new production method always exists. Company leaders must determine if a new technology is sufficiently profitable over the current process to warrant the time and expense in developing the new technology. What is the breakeven point? Line Z in figure 11.2 above represents the minimal profitability the new technology must provide; otherwise, the invention isn't worth development cost and is not sufficiently profitable.

Note that the new process Y may be profitable but still not worth pursuing if it doesn't exceed the opportunity cost of money. Y must exceed Z in order to make it worth adopting. In this case, it does.

But suppose **a**nother new technology represented by Line A, which is profitable but not as profitable as technology Y exists. Figure 17.5 demonstrates this situation.

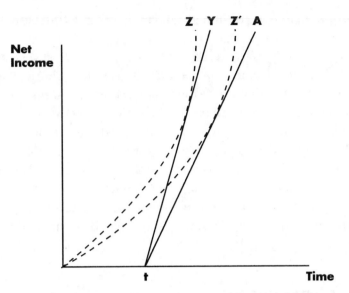

**Figure 17.5.** *Two production processes, Y and A.*
*Process A becomes viable when interest rates fall, so that Z shifts to Z´.*

Given the current level of interest rates and opportunity cost of capital, A would not be pursued. But suppose interest rates decline because of an increase in the public savings rate. Line Z now shifts downward and to the right in figure 17.5, sufficiently to touch Line A. Now suddenly because of the lower rates and increased savings, a company can adopt and benefit from this new technology.

A cutback in consumer spending and an increase in saving can cause production, especially intermediate output, to rise. Higher saving rates cause an increase in the supply of savings and a reduction in interest rates. This in turn encourages increased output at the earlier stages of production, graphically a broadening and deepening of capital. Business upgrades and purchases new equipment, builds new plants and production processes, and invests more in R&D. In a few years, the economy enjoys the benefits of this new capital investment, and we witness an improvement in the quantity, quality and variety of goods and service…..and even lower prices. In real terms, consumption in the future is better and cheaper.

## WHAT ABOUT SAVING DURING A SLUMP?

Modern economists accept classical growth theory as a long-term strategy, but worry more about the short-term effect of increased saving on production and income during a slump. Spending on goods and services is a positive act, they say, but during a downturn increased saving may be detrimental if savings are not invested either, that is, consumers hold cash, or banks increase bank reserves rather than invest the savings when investment opportunities are scarce. Keynes himself feared this "liquidity trap" in the 1930s, and lashed out at savers and hoarders during the 1930s Great Depression and their "fetish for liquidity." The Great Depression was an unusual situation where the public was wary of banks and the monetary system. Over a third of American banks either closed or consolidated. Most economists agree today that once the government removed this public fear of monetary instability, the positive virtues of saving and investing were restored.

In a normal slowdown, it is doubtful that increased savings would have a negative effect on business. Banks and other financial intermediaries are always alert to business opportunities, and during the slump, if interest rates decline, business may be willing to borrow in order to invest, or upgrade their production processes and equipment.

## EMPIRICAL EVIDENCE SUPPORTS A LINK BETWEEN SAVING AND GROWTH

Empirical evidence supports the classical model, demonstrating a connection between saving and economic growth over the long term. Figure 17.6 presents a scatter plot of annual average savings rates (as a percentage of real GDP per worker) and real GDP per worker growth rates across countries over the period 1950 through 2000.

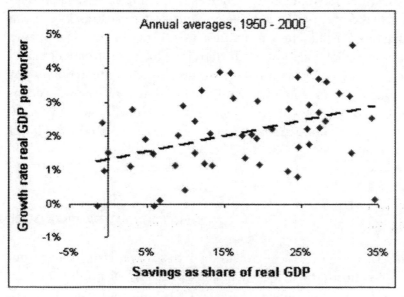

**Figure 17.6.** *Relationship between savings and growth rate of real GDP per worker. Source: Penn World Tables (http://datacentre.chass.utoronto.ca/pwt/alphacountries.html).*

The dashed linear regression line in Figure 17.6 indicates that each 10% increase in the average savings rate increases the growth rate of real GDP per worker by 0.45%. The United States falls right in the middle of the graph with an average savings rate of 19.2% and a real GDP per worker growth rate of 1.95%.

Obviously, other factors are also important in raising GDP growth, such as technology and a stable government policy. But the relationship between saving and growth is positive.

The fact is that in real life consumption, saving and investment do tend to increase together, and it's possible for an increase in saving to occur at the same time consumption rises also. In a sense this reality reinforces both the classical and Keynesian models of economic growth. In the same way, a wage-earner who received a 10% raise can do both—increase his consumption by 5 percentage points and increase how much he saves each month by an equal 5 percentage points.

## WHICH IS MORE IMPORTANT? CONSUMPTION OR INVESTMENT?

This is an appropriate time to revisit a major philosophical debate over the balance between consumption and investment. In chapter 15, it was noted that personal consumption expenditures represent 70% of the final output in the United States, a fact that has led to a popular view that consumer spending is the kingpin of an advanced economy. Yet in this chapter investment and technology are the primary tools of economic success. Is the economy consumer-driven? Or is it investment driven?

## KEYNES AND THE ANTI-SAVINGS MENTALITY

A pro-consumption bias began in the 1930s and was reflected in the writings of the British economist John Maynard Keynes (1883-1946). Keynes spoke out against the traditional virtue of thrift during an economic downturn. During the Great Depression of the 1930s, Keynes lashed out at frugal savers as hoarders. The conventional wisdom in bad times has always been to cut costs, get out of debt, build a strong cash position, and wait for a recovery. Yet Keynes opposed this approach, reasoning that savers were hurting the economy by withholding their money. He was joined by other economists who encouraged consumers to spend and governments to go on a building binge. In his classic work, *The General Theory* (1936), Keynes referred to saving during a downturn as "absurd." He boldly wrote, "The more virtuous we are, the more determined by thrift, the more obstinately orthodox, in our national and personal finance, the more our incomes will fall."[6]

6 John Maynard Keynes, *The General Theory of Employment, Interest and Money* (New York: Macmillan, 1936), p. 111, 211.

According to Keynes, if saving ended up under the mattress or languishing in bank accounts, the economy would suffer. Only money spent on goods and services constituted "effective demand." Keynes also expressed concerned with what he called a "psychological law" that the "marginal propensity to save" tends to increase with income. That is, as individuals earn more income and become wealthier, they tend to save a greater percentage of their income. Thus, there is a strong tendency for savings to rise disproportionately as national income increases. But what if a growing economy can't invest productively all those increased savings? Keynes and his followers worried about the possibility of a dearth of investment opportunities, and supported progressive taxation to reduce this risk and increase "more dependable" consumer spending.

For decades, members of the media, the financial community and the government have fallen under the Keynesian spell, emphasizing the importance of macro demand over supply, of deficit spending over surpluses (especially during a recession), of debt over equity in corporate finance, and of consumption over saving. For them, the key to prosperity is found in encouraging a high level of consumption, even if it means going deeply into debt. The established news media are so enamored with consumption that they highlight monthly changes in consumer spending (C), retail sales, consumer prices, and surveys of consumer confidence, looking for any encouraging signs.

After all, they say, doesn't consumer spending represent more than two thirds of total economic activity?

## WHICH IS BIGGER: CONSUMER SPENDING OR BUSINESS INVESTMENT?

The idea that consumption is the largest sector of the economy is based on a misreading of Gross Domestic Product (GDP). In figure 15.5, indicated that personal consumption expenditures (C) represent 70% of GDP in the United States, nearly four times more than gross private investment (I). Government spending is even slightly larger than private investment. By making the standard assumption that GDP measures total economic activity, the unsophisticated journalist has concluded that consumer and government spending are by far the most important sectors of the economy, while investment rates a poor third.

| | |
|---|---|
| C = $9,927.9 (million) | 69.9% |
| I = $1,906.1 | 13.4% |
| G = $2,911.4 | 20.5% |
| X - M = $ – 545.1 | – 3.8% |
| GDP = $14,200.3 (million) | 100% |

Many problems in government policy have resulted as a consequence of this misinterpretation of national income statistics. Many lawmakers have passed legislation encouraging consumption at the expense of investment. At the same time, they see no reason to cut capital gains taxes or corporate income taxes, since the business investment sector appears to be relatively small and unimportant.

## THE SOURCE OF THE FALLACY

What's gone awry? The source of the error is that GDP is *not* a measure of total economic activity. GDP measures the purchase of final goods and services only. The GDP deliberately leaves out spending by business in all the intermediate stages of production before the retail market.

To determine total spending in the economy at all stages of production, look at **Gross Domestic Expenditures (GDE),** which seeks to measure gross expenditures at all stages of production, from resources to finished products.

As noted earlier,

$$GDE = IE + GDP$$

As noted in chapter 15, here are the government estimated statistics for 2007:

$$
\begin{array}{lll}
C = \$9,927.9 \text{ (million)} & 69.9\% \\
I = \$1,906.1 & 13.4\% \\
G = \$2,911.4 & 20.5\% \\
X - M = \$ - 545.1 & -3.8\% \\
\hline
GDP = \$14,200.3 \text{ (million)} & 100\% \\
+ IE = \$16.0 \text{ trillion} \\
\hline
GDE = \$30.2 \text{ trillion}
\end{array}
$$

Therefore,

Of the total spending in the economy (GDE), consumption (C) represents approximately 33%, not 70% as normally quoted. For gross business investment, add together I + IE, gross private investment of $1.9 trillion and intermediate production (IE) of $16 trillion, for a total of $17.9 trillion. Roughly 59% of the economic activity involves business spending.

In conclusion, business investment spending constitutes a much larger sector of the economy than consumer spending, quite the opposite conclusion of the modern Keynesian model and the general media.

## SAY'S LAW VERSUS KEYNES'S LAW

Jean-Baptiste Say (1767-1832), known as the "French Adam Smith," devoted his career to the benefits of saving and economic growth. In Chapter 15 of *A Treatise on Political Economy*, in which he introduced his famous "law of markets," Say contends that the key to prosperity is production, not consumption. Say's law is generally interpreted as "supply creates its own demand."

Sometimes, demand leads to supply. For example, disposable diapers have improved immensely since their introduction 40 years ago, largely as a result of mothers' complaints. On the other hand no consumer thought of a tiny device that could contain 10,000 songs, but once the iPod was invented (supplied), every young adult bought (demanded) one.

Question: Which is more accurate? Does supply create its own demand (Say's law)? Or does demand create its own supply (Keynes's law)?

One can find examples which contradict both laws. For example, an inventor can produced an unlimited supply of widgets, but if customers won't buy (demand) his product, his brilliant production scheme is all in vain. On the other hand a transportation system to transport travelers from San Francisco to New York in an hour is greatly needed but so far no one has invented (supplied) this desirable good. Clearly, the simplified versions of Say's and Keynes's laws often fail to reflect reality.

The problem with Say's law is that the law is often misunderstood. He illustrated this law using a simple agricultural example, the case of a bumper crop. A good harvest is favorable. The greater the crop, the larger are the purchases of growers. In other words, a good harvest gives farmers the means to buy a wide variety of other commodities, resulting in widespread prosperity for the entire community, not just the farmers. On the other hand suppose the farmers have a poor crop. Even though scarcity may cause prices to rise, the community will struggle. A poor harvest hurts the sale of commodities at large.

Say extends his agricultural example to commerce in general. "The success of one branch of commerce supplies more products to all the other branches; on the other hand, the stagnation of one channel of manufacture, or commerce, is felt in all the rest."[7]

Say draws several conclusions. Production and productivity are the keys to prosperity across the board. Increased output leads to higher consumer spending, while decreased output leads to lower consumption. This is true only *if the product produced is sold*, a very key point. A more accurate rendering of Say's law of markets is, "the sale of X creates the demand for Y." A seller who produces and sells a product suddenly becomes a potential buyer with expendable income.

7 J.-B. Say, *A Treatise on Political Economy*, 4th ed. (New York: Augustus M. Kelley, 1971), p. 135.

Say concludes that production, not consumption, is the catalyst to economic performance. Consumption is the effect, not the cause, of prosperity. Production, productivity and supply are the key ingredients to economic growth.

## HOW CAN YOU HAVE A SALE WITHOUT A WILLING BUYER?

How can you have a sale without a willing buyer? Clearly the sale of a bumper crop presupposes the community's propensity to consume. To sell is to buy, and vice versa. Is Say's law merely a tautology?

Expanding production through technological advances and an expanding market create new and better products at lower costs, which in turn open new markets and increase consumption. The focus of Say's law is on the producer and the entrepreneur, not the consumer per se. Entrepreneurs and inventors are the catalyst of new products and new processes, not consumers. Consumers are, by and large, less active, less dynamic. They tend to be passive, not so much demanding new products as responding to new products and services placed before them by marketers and innovators. Marketing studies have demonstrated this principle time and time again. Consumer surveys are no guarantee of success in the marketplace of new products. The success formula for the introduction of new products is invariable: entrepreneurs come up with an idea that they think consumers will want, and they test it. Did consumers know they wanted a Dodge Minivan before it was created in the early 1980s? Did customers demand the Internet, e-mail, and iPod? They never dreamed of these products. But when the products were offered by innovative scientists, consumers could not get enough of them. Israel Kirzner states. "Entrepreneurship is required for the discovery of the profit opportunity."[8]

In conclusion, capital investment in its many forms — saving, loanable funds, education (human capital), and technology — drives the economy to new heights and a higher standard of living for consumers. Figure 17.7 illustrates this growth process.

8 Israel M. Kirzner, *Competition and Entrepreneurship* (Chicago: University of Chicago Press, 1973), p. 38n.

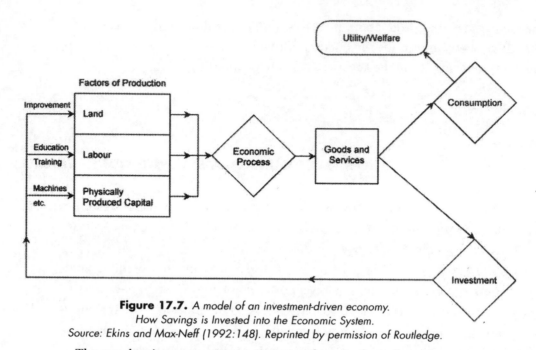

**Figure 17.7.** *A model of an investment-driven economy.
How Savings is Invested into the Economic System.
Source: Ekins and Max-Neff (1992:148). Reprinted by permission of Routledge.*

The production process creating two forms of goods, either consumption or investment goods, is illustrated above. Consumption leads to direct utility by the consumer, utility that is used up over time. However, investment — in the form of capital (liquid assets such as loanable funds, bonds, and stocks) and capital goods, comes back around and feeds into the production process in the form of education, training and new technology. The next round of production leads to more, better and cheaper consumer goods. The process is never ending.

Personal computers are a good example of this dynamic process. When PCs first became available in the early 1980s, they were big, bulky, and expensive — $15,000 was a typical price. Over the next two decades personal computers became smaller, faster, better, and cheaper. But the high price in the early years was essential for future innovation. Pioneers in the computer industry needed those wealthy consumers who could afford the big expensive models in order to have sufficient capital and feedback to continue their innovations and production. Eventually, mass production led to lower prices and availability of former luxuries to all consumers.

## WHAT CAUSED THE WEST COAST BOOM?

An historical example may be helpful in explaining this point. Why did the west coast of the United States (San Francisco, Portland and Seattle) boom in the 1990s? New technology in telecommunications and the Internet created a whole new level of wealth and prosperity in the region. Intel, Cisco Systems, and Microsoft became household names. Note that only after the technology boom began did consumer spending on cars, housing, travel, jewelry, and entertainment move sharply higher. Consumption is the effect, not the cause, of prosperity, in the long run. The key to the economic boom of the 1990s was increasing technology, productivity, and entrepreneurship, what economists call the "supply side" of the economy. Advances in technology, production processes and entrepreneurship create new and better products for consumers at lower costs, which in turn open up new markets, increases income, and benefits consumption. However, when the technology boom ended in 2000, business investment fell, unemployment rose, and consumer spending slowed. During the 2000-03 recession, it was consumer spending that kept the economy from falling further (Keynes's Law).

Throughout the business cycle, investment spending tends to be more volatile than consumer spending. Retail spending by consumers tends to be relatively steady throughout the ups and downs of the economy. Thus, it was not surprising that consumer spending held up well during the 2000-03 global recession. The recession was primarily a business recession. And when the economy recovered in 2003, it was business spending that finally made it happen.

Studies in business cycles and marketing demonstrate repeatedly that CEOs, entrepreneurs, capitalists and other business decision-makers are the primary activators of the economy, and determine when to start investing in capital again and turn the economy around. Government leaders cannot depend on consumers to lead the recovery. They tend to be passive, responding to past events rather than creating new products and services.

In normal times, increased savings expands the pool of capital investment, lowers interest rates, and allows firms to adopt new production processes, new technologies, and create new jobs. Thus, saving is just as much a form of spending as consumption is, only a different form of spending, and in some cases, a better form of spending when it fulfills a need for more capital and investment.

## LEADING INDICATORS CONFIRM SAY'S LAW

Interestingly, business cycle statistics appear to confirm Say's law and question the whole notion of the importance of consumption as a dynamic leading indicator of economic performance. Business investment and early-stage production statistics are a more reliable predictor of the business cycle than consumer spending and retail trade alone. Let's take a closer look at the Index of Leading Indicators in major industrial nations. The compiler of these business cycle indicators is the Conference Board, a nonprofit impartial statistical service.

Of the 10 leading indicators measured by the Conference Board, only one, the index of consumer expectations, appears to be related to final consumption, and even then when the questions the survey asks consumers are examined, they are more about job dependability than current consumer spending patterns. The other nine indicators are far removed from final use, highlighting such factors as building permits, average weekly manufacturing hours, manufacturer's new orders for consumer goods and materials, new orders for non-defense capital goods, and stock prices. Retail sales is not considered a leading indicator by this service.

Similarly, of the nine leading indicators in Germany, only two are linked loosely to consumer spending: the consumer-confidence index and the consumer price index for services. The rest are connected to earlier-stage production, such as inventory changes, new purchases of capital equipment, and new construction orders. Among France's 10 leading indicators, two are consumer related, and all the rest are tied to stock prices, productivity, building permits, the yield spread and new industrial orders. The UK's leading indicators are linked to export volume, new orders in engineering industries, inventories, housing starts and money supply, as well as to consumer confidence. None of Japan's 10 components are consumer related. They include overtime work in manufacturing, business conditions survey, labor productivity, real operating profits and new orders for machinery and construction. In all five nations, retail-sales figures do not show up as leading indicators at all.

## SAVING SUBJECT TO LAW OF DIMINISHING RETURNS

Over the years, researchers have uncovered growing evidence of the importance of saving and capital formation in promoting economic growth. In the 1950s and 1960s, MIT professor Robert Solow, who won the Nobel Prize in economics in 1987, developed what is now known as the Solow growth model. The Solow model attempts to determine the relative importance of varying determinants of growth, such as natural resources, population, capital formation, and technical progress. He came to two conclusions, based on empirical work with input-output models.

First, he concludes that increased saving has a positive impact on economic growth, but saving is subject to the law of diminishing returns. In other words, increased savings encourages economic growth in the initial stages, but eventually its impact diminishes. Figure 17.8 illustrates the diminishing returns of saving.

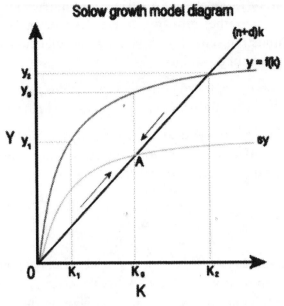

**Figure 17.8.** *According to the Solow growth model, increased saving has diminishing returns on national output.*

Second, Solow calculated that about four-fifths of the growth in US output per worker was attributable to technical progress. Technology seems to be more important to economic advancement than public saving, labor, or natural resources.

## SUMMARY

These are the main points discussed in Chapter 17:

1.  The classical model of Adam Smith, David Ricardo, and John Stuart Mill emphasized the benefits of saving, investing, and capital formation as the keys to economic growth.

2.  Eugen Böhm-Bawerk, the Austrian economist, added the vital ingredient of labor-saving technology to saving and capital formation as an essential key to economic growth.

3.  An increase in the national saving rate tends to reduce long-term interest rates and encourages the financing of new capital projects, new technologies and production processes.

4.  Classical economists, especially Böhm-Bawerk, Mill and J.-B. Say, countered the Keynesian argument that business investment depended on consumer spending (known as Keynes's law), noting that the Keynesians fail to recognize the importance of demand for future consumption. Demand for intermediate output can offset a temporary decline in present consumption.

5. Contrary to Keynesian doctrine, consumer spending does not drive the economy; rather, gross business investment is larger than consumption in an industrial economy. Say's law states that consumption is the effect, not the cause, of prosperity.

6. Economic history and business cycle indicators confirm Say's law that production leads the economy, consumption follows.

7. Solow's growth model demonstrates that an increase in savings is subject to the law of diminishing returns. Technical progress is essential to maintaining a high level of economic performance.

## IMPORTANT TERMS

Classical economists
Classical growth theory
Consumer Confidence Index
Consumption
Gross Domestic Expenditures (GDE)
Gross Domestic Product (GDP)
Human capital
Index of Consumer Expectations
Index of Leading Economic Indicators
Intermediate production
Investment
Keynes's law

Keynesian economics
Keynesian model of economic growth
Labor productivity
Liquidity trap
Marginal propensity to consume
Real GDP
Real operating profits
Regression line
Say's law
Solow growth model
Structure of production

## INFLUENTIAL ECONOMISTS

### J.-B. SAY, ROBERT SOLOW, AND ECONOMIC GROWTH

**Name: Jean-Baptist Say (1767-1832)**

**Background:** As the author of Say's law, J.-B. Say became the father of supply-side economics. He invented the term "entrepreneur" in economics and business. Born in Lyon, France, Say was an entrepreneur himself (cotton producer) who served as a member of Napoleon's government. Spending two years in London, he became a fan of Adam Smith's *Wealth of Nations* (1776), and through his writings became known as "The French Adam Smith." However, his *Treatise on*

*Political Economy* (1803) offended Napoleon's interventionist policies and was banned. The textbook became the most widely used textbook in economics and went through several editions, including an English translation, until it was surpassed by John Stuart Mill's *Principles of Political Economy*. Say became the first professor of economics in France. He was friends of David Ricardo and Thomas Malthus in England. He died in 1832 at the age of 65.

**Major work:** *A Treatise on Political Economy*, 4th ed. (New York: Augustus M. Kelley, 1971 [1880]).

**Major contribution:** Say made two major contributions to economics, the introduction of entrepreneurial decision-making in the economy, and Say's law. Say's law, usually described as "supply creates its own demand," focuses on the direction of economic performance. The key to a rising standard of living is on the supply side: saving, investing, entrepreneurship, technology, and productivity. Consumption is not the cause of prosperity, but the effect. Production and productivity must come before consumption.

**Name: Robert Solow (1924 - )**

**Background:** Solow, the author of the Solow growth model, was born in New York City in 1924 and earned three degrees, including his Ph. D., from Harvard University. He studied under Wassily Leontief (see chapter 14), and became a long-time professor at MIT. He won the John Bates Clark Award in 1961, given to the best economist under the age of 40, and became president of the AEA in 1979. He received the Nobel Prize in Economics in 1987.

**Major work:** *Capital Theory and the Rate of Return* (1963), and *Growth Theory* (Oxford University Press, 1969).

**Major contribution:** Prior to Solow's writings, most economists believed that the main causes of economic growth were increases in capital and labor. But Solow demonstrated that over half of growth was caused by technological innovation, now known as the "Solow residual."

## PROBLEMS TO PONDER

1.  Economists state that the ultimate purpose of investment and production is to fulfill the needs of consumers. But if the purpose of business to fulfill the needs of consumers, why then do we conclude in this chapter that the economy is more "investment driven" than "consumer driven"?

2.  Several years ago during an economic downturn, Range Rover, a British maker of sports-utility vehicles, ran an ad campaign in USA Today. It announced its formula for ending the recession: "Buy Something." Range Rover wanted you to buy their car, but in any case, purchase something. "Buy a microwave, a basset hound, theater tickets, a Tootsie Roll, something." Anything to get the economy going again. After studying this chapter, how would you respond to the Range Rover ad? What would be the effect if consumers bought stocks or put their money into a bank account instead of consumer products?

3.  In 2001, when President George W. Bush signed into law a tax rebate, he encouraged citizens to "spend" rather than "save" their tax refunds. "Take your tax rebates to the mall, not the bank," he declared. Some analysts on CNBC contended that "if consumers saved their refund checks, it would do nothing to stimulate the economy." In what way can increased saving and investing cause an economic recovery?

4.  In light of the discussion about Say's law in this chapter, evaluate the following statement by Say: "Thus, it is the aim of good government to stimulate production, of bad government to encourage consumption." In what ways do governments encourage consumption? Do they also encourage production? How do tax laws and subsidies influence consumption or investment?

5.  The Reverend John Wesley, founder of the Methodist Church, gave a famous "Sermon on Money" in 1743. He emphasized three grand principles to his Methodist listeners: Earn all you can; save all you can; give all you can. Why did he leave out "spend all you can"? Research and determine historically how financially well off the Methodists were in the 18th century.

6.  Are thrifty people necessarily penny-pinching misers? Consider this statement from George Clason's description of Arkad from the classic book on the virtue of saving, *The Richest Man in Babylon*, "Far and wide he was famed for his great wealth. Also was he famed for his liberality. He was generous in his charities. He was generous with his family. He was liberal in his own expenses. But nevertheless each year his wealth increased more rapidly than he spent it." How was this possible? (To answer this question, you will need to read Clason's classic work. Highly recommended.)

7. MIT economist and Nobel laureate Franco Modigliani reverses the classical model of saving by contending that the "key to saving is growth, not thrift." He uses postwar Japan as an example: "One of the interesting implications of the life-cycle theory suggests that when a country needs capital to drive rapid growth, capital will be forthcoming. The growth process itself generates saving. Once Japan's growth engine got going, it produced enormous saving, at times amounting to one quarter of annual national income." And Robert Eisner, who called himself an "unreconstructed Keynesian," argues similarly: "To raise the saving rate, try spending." Examine other countries' growth histories to see if they match the conclusions of Modigliani and Eisner.

8. The motto of a flamboyant salesman, who might be labeled a Keynesian businessman, is "what goes around, comes around." He advocates aggressive spending on advertising, and a high-profile lifestyle of big houses, expensive automobiles, and lavish promotion, which he says will pay off in more sales from customers down the road. Will his strategy work, or could he cause his company to go bankrupt?

9. Based on the empirical work of Richard Thaler, a behavior economist at the University of Chicago, Congress passed the Pension Reform Act of 2006. This law requires private companies to automatically enroll their workers in 401k saving plans, unless they opt out. Having a 401k plan is still voluntary, but the new law encourages workers to save more. Do you think this is a good idea? What has been the effect of the law since it was passed?

## ADDITIONAL READING

- Steven Kates, *Say's Law and the Keynesian Revolution* (Edward Elgar, 1998)

- Steven Kates, ed., *Two Hundred Years of Say's Law* (Edward Elgar, 2003).

- Jerry J. Jasinowski, ed., *The Rising Tide* (New York: John Wiley & Sons, 1998). A series of essays by top economists, including Jack Kemp, Nobel Prize winner Robert Mundell, Cato Institute chairman William A. Niskanen, on how to increase the secular rate of growth in the United States and elsewhere.

- William Easterly, *The Elusive Quest for Growth: Economists' Adventures and Misadventures in the Tropics* (MIT Press, 2001). Fascinating account by a former World Bank economist on what works and doesn't work when it comes to fostering economic growth in developing countries.

# Chapter 18

# MONEY AND THE COMMERCIAL BANKING SYSTEM

*"The origin of money is entirely natural and thus displays legislative influence in the rarest instances. Money is not an invention of the state. It is not the product of a legislative act."*

— CARL MENGER

*"The king reigns but the bank rules."*

— JACOB FUGGER

This book is based on an important assumption: the existence of a monetary system allows modern economy to trade goods and services at a particular price, establishes a way of accounting for costs, and creates a store of value in a medium of exchange. Establishing prices, costs and values is possible because of a monetary system that is readily acceptable throughout the modern economy. Money is the lifeblood of the economy, and without it, it would be difficult to maintain an advanced civilization.

## THE MYSTERY OF MONEY

Money is in many ways a mystery. Money is unlike any other commodity. In physical form, money is merely specially-manufactured paper bearing printed numbers and images that discourage counterfeiting. This special paper has no intrinsic value. Unlike most other goods in the marketplace, there is no relationship whatsoever between the cost of its production and the value or price of money. Exactly the same amount of labor and material is taken to produce a $1 bill as to produce a $100 bill. The Treasury pays a few pennies to produce a banknote that can carry a value of $1, $20, or $100.

How is it possible to create a product whose price is unrelated to its cost of production?

**Exercise**: To understand the mystery of money, consider the following exercise. Suppose a teacher and some students are on a field trip and get stranded on an island for several years. The teacher becomes the leader and organizes the group. The leader takes several pieces of paper and writes on them "Teacher 10" and

"Teacher 20" and uses these special notes to go around and demand from each member of the group certain labor tasks, such as cooking meals, starting a fire, or building a house, in return for one of the notes. How many students will accept these notes as payment for the work demanded?

Now suppose all of the students refuse to receive the notes as payment for the work required. A change to the contract is offered. This time the students are told that a "Teacher 10" represents 10 hours of hard work on the instructor's part for any purpose the students desire, and a "Teacher 20" equals 20 hours of instructor labor. Would this make it a better trade? A point of negotiation for the work the students were asked to do now exists. Will the students be willing to work in return for payment in other forms? For example, will the students work if the "Teacher 10" is a warehouse receipt equal to 10 fish? Would the students be willing to do the work in return for payment in a certain number of pineapples? What if the currency is backed by pineapples or fish?

Teacher notes or bills created out of thin air, with no backing, may fail as money, while a note with a real contract backed up by labor or a valuable commodity may be functional currency.

At one time, all banknotes issued by governments were backed by silver and gold or other valuable commodities, but this practice ended in 1933 when Franklin Roosevelt took the United States off the gold standard. Now the currency of the United States is backed by the "full faith and credit" of the government. This type of currency is called "fiat" currency.

How can governments get away with unbacked currency? Why do citizens everywhere, even in foreign countries, accept fiat paper banknotes issued by their governments with faith that this unbacked currency has, and will continue to have, value?

## THE REGRESSION THEOREM

Ludwig von Mises, a 20th century Austrian economist, provides an answer to this question, in his "Regression theorem." He contends that today's paper money has value because of its history. If the value of the money is observed from the past by regressing a few generations — to 1933 in the United States, to be precise — banknotes were "backed" by gold or silver bullion, a specified amount of precious metal, a valued commodity. For every $20 "gold certificate" issued by the U. S. Treasury, the government had a $20 double-eagle gold coin on reserve for when the gold certificate was redeemable by its bearer. Anyone could take the $20 banknote to a commercial bank, Federal Reserve, or U. S. Treasury, and demand a $20 gold coin for the banknote. Prior to 1933, the United States and most of the world operated on the international gold standard, when currencies and government banknotes were promises to pay in gold or silver, or actual warehouse receipts of gold or silver stored in bank vaults or the government mint. Further back in history, there was a time when there were no paper currencies in existence, only coins in various sizes.

When the United States went off the gold standard in 1933, the banknotes that were issued appeared the same except the small print changed. The U. S. Treasury no longer promised to redeem the paper money in gold or silver, but the public accepted the banknotes because they had confidence that the government and other customers would accept the notes as a medium of exchange.

## CAN CIVILIZATION EXIST WITHOUT MONEY?

Can a civilization exist solely on the basis of production, without money, exchange, or trade? Believe it or not, it can, but its economy is not likely to advance in a modern sense. Examples include ancient Egypt, ancient China, the Inca civilization, monasteries, medieval manors, feudal estates, tribal communities and frontier farms. In essence, these include any community that operated as an extension of the household model. Norman Angell writes, "There have been great and elaborate civilizations, before whose art and industry the world today stands in wonder, managing to maintain an active and continuous industry without that system of constant —daily and hourly— exchanges by means of money... outstanding types of a form of social organization which might be described as an enlargement of the household, operating by what some writers have called the 'natural' economy as distinct from the money economy; societies often highly complex in their division of labor, in which neither money nor exchange nor barter entered any more than it need into the relationships between members of the family."[1]

Generally, moneyless civilizations are only possible in authoritarian regimes, where there is concentrated power and citizens are subject to custom and law, and assigned specific tasks for which they are paid in goods and services. Angell continues, "All these cases tell the same story: Where men are guided unquestioningly by authority, by custom or habit, particularly where those factors are buttressed by religious tradition, it is possible to secure both a very elaborate and a very stable civilization, sometimes with marvelous art and handicraft, without resorting to trade, exchange, or money....Those things are no more needed in that type of civilization than they are needed in the extremely elaborate social organization of the beehive— which some ancient civilizations in their utter lack of freedom and individuality astonishingly resembled....In the case of the beehive or the ant-hill, these processes attain a complexity and delicacy which no human society has ever been able to duplicate....If an elaborate civilization is to exist without money it must be by rigid rules that rob the individual of freedom. If the individual is to be free and at the same time industrious, the money economy is indispensable."

1  Norman Angel, *The Story of Money* (London: Cassel & Co., 1930), p. 35.

## HOW TRADE DEVELOPED

A moneyless, production-only economy has severe limitations, however. Inevitably, some communities or nations produce a surplus in some commodities, while others incur shortages, resulting in a wasteful, imbalanced economy. How does one minimize these surpluses and shortages?

Trade develops naturally when production exceeds needs or when the need for a good or service exceeds the value of the item produced. Surplus goods and services are created, by one group or individual, which in turn leads to exchange and trade. For example, a farmer might have several hens that produce far more eggs than the farmer's family can consume. Rather than let the eggs go to waste the farmer sells them and uses the money to acquire goods and services that he does not produce but does need.

## BARTER AND DIRECT EXCHANGE

Barter or direct exchange has been in existence throughout history. The Bible tells stories of tribute and tithes paid "in kind," meaning in goods, not money. For example: without money a farmer may barter his eggs. He may take a dozen eggs to a market and seek out an individual who has something to sell that the farmer needs, such as a dozen apples. If he can find another farmer who has apples and who also needs eggs, there is a basis for exchange.

Farmer A has a dozen eggs to sell and wants to buy a dozen apples.

Farmer B has apples to sell and wants to buy eggs.

These farmers have what Carl Menger calls a "mutual coincidence of wants."

But what if Farmer B wants bread, not eggs? He is out of luck with Farmer A and must look for another supplier. If Farmer A has a creative attitude, he will locate Farmer C, who is willing to exchange 3 loaves of bread for a dozen eggs. Thus, A buys bread (even though he wants apples) with his eggs, then turns around and sells the bread to B in exchange for apples. A and B achieve their goals by making "bread" a **medium of exchange**. In this transaction, A doesn't need bread but he buys it anyway in order to facilitate the sale of his eggs.

| Farmer A | | Farmer C | | Farmer B |
|----------|---|----------|---|----------|
| 12 eggs | = | 3 loaves of bread | = | 12 apples |

## HOW DIFFICULT IS INDIRECT EXCHANGE?

The major question is: How difficult is it to find a transaction with an indirect exchange or medium of exchange?

**Menger's thesis** is this: There will be a tendency to seek out goods that are more universally marketable as a medium of exchange. "Different goods have degrees of marketability." If it turns out that bread is frequently used by suppliers as the "medium of exchange," it rapidly becomes the standard currency or money, and demand for bread increases far beyond its normal demand as food. This phenomenon is often seen in prisons, where inmates use tobacco as medium of exchange.

The development of a common medium of exchange is an evolutionary process, where, through trial and error and communication, goods with the highest degree of marketability will become more suitable as a medium of exchange. Eventually, when one type of good becomes the most suitable as a medium of exchange, it becomes "money."

Without the guidance of a central authority, money emerged in a gradual, natural, unpredictable evolution. Money was not created by a legislative act. This process is an example of Adam Smith's "invisible hand" doctrine. "The origin of money," declared Carl Menger, is "entirely natural and thus displays legislative influence in the rarest instances. Money is not an invention of the state. It is not the product of a legislative act."[2]

## CHARACTERISTICS OF NATURAL MONEY

Traders will seek to acquire marketable goods they do not need to exchange for the goods they wish to consume. These are the characteristics of most useable currency:

1. Usable
2. Recognizable
3. Indivisible
4. Uniform in quality
5. Fungible (one piece of money is exactly like another)
6. Portable
7. Durable

---

2 Carl Menger, *Principles of Economics* (New York University Press, 1981), p. 262

The following commodities are examples of items that have been used for money over the centuries:

| | |
|---|---|
| Cattle | Feathers |
| Tobacco | Porpoise teeth |
| Wampum (Indian beads) | Blankets |
| Shells | Salt |
| Stones | Precious metals |

Eventually, precious metals won out as the primary monetary unit, especially gold, silver and copper. [Why?] As Stanley Jevons states, "Some of the metals seem to be marked out by nature as most fit of all substances for employment as money, at least when acting as a medium of exchange and a store of value."[3]

## THE BENEFITS AND USE OF MONEY

The creation of money as a medium of exchange creates a system of exchange where many advantages in handling the wealth of an advancing civilization can occur. These advantages include include:

1.  The establishment of prices for goods and services, allowing choice, comparison pricing, and competition

2.  Having a uniform medium of exchange allows for the creation of the banking ledger and cost accounting.

3.  Store of value — saving and wealth building. Gold and silver are particularly useful because they are durable, portable and fungible.

4.  Facilitating the creation of commercial banking and financial institutions to facilitate saving, investing and borrowing.

5.  The increase of government power, especially its taxing and spending authority.

---

3  W. S. Jevons, *Money and the Mechanism of Exchange* (London: Kegan Paul, 1905), p. 40.

## THE DEVELOPMENT OF COINAGE

Precious metals became the standard medium of exchange or money, with values varying according to scarcity and use. Gold was the most highly prized, and ideal for large transactions; silver as more plentiful and useful for the most common transactions; and copper/bronze was ideal for small change and token coins. Coins became the most common form of money, convenient for transactions and storage.

The first coins in Greece and Rome were made of gold, silver, and bronze. Images were stamped on the coins to reflect the political culture. These images evolved from animals to the Greek and Roman gods to the heads of dead emperors and finally to the heads of living emperors. Sometimes the coins would celebrate an important event or anniversary. The history of coins often reflects the history of a nation.

In early days, coins would be divided into smaller denominations. Initially, money in its various forms traded according to fineness and weight of the precious metal, in grams, ounces and pounds. For example, a talent in the Bible was defined as 60 pounds of copper. (A talent was never a circulating coin, but served rather as a unit of account.) The Roman denarius coin was a specified weight of silver, and the aureus and the solidus were certain weights of gold. Members of the society understood the value of specific coins and accept the coins as a medium of exchange for other goods and services. The value of money varied by the impact of events on society.

In Rome's case, following Caesar's reign, coins were constantly debased as the state took on more burdens—the expense of the Roman army, welfare and subsidies, and the cost of public buildings. Diocletian declared severe price controls and rationing on penalty of death in his famous "Edict of Prices" in 301 AD. But not even the death penalty could stop the rampant inflation, where the gold solidus became 30 million denarii by the mid-4th century.

Many of the terms used for money or currencies came from ancient times. Libra, a bronze Greek coin, is the origin of the Italian lira. "Salary" comes from the Latin word "salarium" or salt, once used as money to pay Roman armies. "Money" and "mint" come from the Latin goddess "Moneta," whose temple was used to mint Roman coins.

An early monetary debate occurred over the definition of a coin. Should the national monetary unit be identified by **weight** or **tale** (name only)? For example, when the original Roman Denarius silver coin — the standard coin in the Roman empire for 5 centuries — was first minted in 215 BC, it was defined as 4.5 grams of pure silver. But by the early third century AD, it has been reduced by 50% to around 2.2 grams of silver, yet it was still called the denarius. Identifying the monetary unit by tale (name) instead of weight allows the government to have greater control over the value of money and makes it easier to debase.

**Figure 18.1.** *Roman coins*

## BIMETALISM AND GRESHAM'S LAW

Another issue concerns whether gold and silver should be traded at a fixed or floating exchange rate. As the most highly valued precious metal, gold has been the premier money and eventually became the monetary unit of account or numeraire among Western nations. Most national currencies on the gold standard eventually defined their currency in specified weights of gold (see chapter 19). However, silver has always been a leading contender, and before the gold standard was established in the 19th century, most countries preferred silver as the legal tender metal because it was the most common medium of commercial exchange. With both metals in circulation at the same time, how should they be valued and exchanged? Should silver be tied or fixed in exchange for gold, or should it be allowed to fluctuate according to market forces of supply and demand?

Bimetallism, the system where the government fixes the exchange rate between gold and silver, has been a convenient practice for centuries but not without creating shortages from time to time. In fact, bimetallism can cause what is known as **Gresham's law**, "bad money drives out good." Gresham's law is named after Sir Thomas Gresham (1519-79), founder of the English Royal Exchange in the 16th century. He noted the poor state of England's coinage following the great debasements of Henry VIII and Edward VI, which reduced the metallic value of the English silver coins to a small fraction of their value at the time of Henry VII. The kings required citizens to accept these smaller and clipped coins in equal value to the full-sized coins. Consequently, citizens hoarded or sold abroad the larger silver coins and spent the smaller and clipped coins. Thus bad money (smaller coins) drove out the good (larger coins). Restated in a broader sense, Gresham's law states that with fixed exchange rates, undervalued coins will be hoarded and overvalued coins will circulate.

Gresham's Law can apply to bimetallism. For many years, silver traded for gold at approximate 16 to 1. That is, it took 16 ounces of silver to equal in trade 1 ounce of gold. When governments fixed the exchange rate at 16 to 1, the supply of silver increased dramatically, so that it took 20 ounces of silver to equal 1 ounce of gold.

Suddenly individuals found gold more valuable and would start hording the gold coins, while silver (the cheaper metal) continued to circulate. Governments could postpone the breakdown of its bimetallic standard by absorbing most of the silver on the market at the fixed rate, but if citizens demanded too much gold from the Treasury, the state mint would have to default and establish a new rate of exchange.

The most recent example of Gresham's Law occurred in 1964-65, when the industrial value of silver crept over $1.23 an ounce. At this point the silver content of the U. S. coins (dollars, half-dollars, quarters, and dimes) exceeded their face value, and Americans started hoarding coins. The government responded by issuing coins with only 40% silver, and later no silver — prompting US silver coins to disappear entirely into the hands of investors or manufacturers who melted down the silver coins.

## ORIGIN OF MONETARY UNITS

The names of national currencies, such as the pound and the dollar, originated from certain weights in silver. The British pound sterling was defined as one "Saxon pound of standard sterling silver" (a unit of account). Charlemagne minted silver coins that totaled a pound weight, and 240 pennies were cut from a pound weight. The Spanish dollar originated from a high quality one ounce silver coin produced by a Bohemian Count in Joachimsthal, or Joachim's valley. These were reputable coins known for their uniformity and fineness. Spanish called them "Thalers"; in colonial America they became "dollars." The Spanish dollars were cut into eight parts, or "pieces of eight," and thus "two bits" was a colloquial term used in the 19th and 20th century to designate a quarter of a U. S. dollar.

**Figure 18.2.** *Spanish dollars*

## THE ROLE OF PAPER MONEY

Paper money was introduced as a "warehouse receipt" for the gold or silver placed in storage with goldsmiths or bankers. As these warehouse receipts were more convenient to carry around than the heavy metal coins and bars, it became common to pay for goods and services with the "banknotes" (certificates issued by the banks) rather than go to the bank and withdraw or deposit coins and bars.

The Treasury, and later, central banks, operated under the same "warehouse receipt" system into the 20th century under the Gold Standard. For example, until 1933, all United States Treasury $20 Gold Certificates stated on the front: "This certifies that there has been deposited in the Treasury of the United States of America Twenty Dollars in Gold Coin Payable to the Bearer on Demand." In other words, for every U. S. gold certificate issued, the U. S. Treasury was required to have on deposit a $20 St. Gauden's Double-Eagle Gold Coin, and the bearer of the $20 banknote could at any time go to the U. S. Treasury or a commercial bank, turn in his banknote, and receive a $20 gold coin.

## INTRODUCTION OF CHECKING ACCOUNTS AND CHEQUE BOOKS

Commercial banks went beyond the issuance of gold and silver certificates or banknotes. They also developed the use of personal checking accounts and cheque books as a convenient way to transact business. Instead of paying in cash (coins or banknotes), customers could purchase goods and services by writing a check against their deposit account at the bank. The merchant then redeemed the check at the customer's bank, or deposited it in his own bank, which in turn would send the check for payment. In some cases, the merchant might use the check to make his own purchases elsewhere by endorsing the check over to another merchant. It was not uncommon in the 19th and early 20th century to see checks pass through several hands before ultimately being redeemed by the bank (with up to a half dozen signatures appearing on the back of a check). Such a practice has been discontinued.

## FRACTIONAL RESERVE BANKING
## AND THE FRAGILITY OF THE MONETARY SYSTEM

It was not long before bankers took advantage of the "law of large numbers" and the "fungibility" of money. They noted that only a small percentage of customers came into the bank to withdraw their funds or claim their gold or silver. Deposits largely offset withdrawals, and because every banknote and coin were interchangeable or "fungible," banks no longer felt the need to maintain 100% reserves to convert notes to coin, or checking accounts to cash. "Fractional reserve" banking was the result. Deposits became promissory notes representing a claim on the bank. Banks began loaning out money on deposit, and issuing banknotes far exceeding the amount of metal in the bank's vaults.

Fractional reserve banking became a standard practice in the 18th century, although banks differed on the level of reserves they held. By expanding the availability of credit through fractional reserves, the natural effect was an inflationary boom, followed by a financial crisis, and ultimately bank runs as depositors rushed to the banks to claim their assets, an event that occurred all too often during economic crises. Chapter 19 will address how the money supply multiples under fractional reserve banking. Bank runs became so common from the 17th century to the Great Depression in the 1930s that the term "***bank***ruptcy" (a rupture in the bank) became the common word for financial ruin.

## THE CURRENCY SCHOOL VS. THE BANKING SCHOOL

The instability of the banking system and the suspension of specie payments (money with intrinsic value, such as gold and silver coins) caused a strong backlash against paper money and the fractional reserve system in Britain and the United States. During the early 19th century, Thomas Jefferson and Andrew Jackson, among others, led an anti-banking movement arguing for the restoration of "constitutional money" (gold and silver), and the elimination of the Bank of the United States.

At the same time, the Currency School developed in England named after their support of the "currency principle," a 100% hard-money standard. They were influenced by the economist David Ricardo, who argued in 1810 for the resumption of specie by the Bank of England. The cardinal tenet of the Currency School was that to safeguard the value of the gold standard and to prevent runaway inflation, the quantity of paper money and coin in circulation should never exceed the amount of gold and silver on deposit.

The Banking School, led by James Wilson, founder of the *Economist* magazine, opposed the Currency Principle, which they regarded as an unnecessary interference in the banking business. The Banking School favored "free banking" as long as convertibility was maintained. Competition between banks would limit the amount of credit in the economy while providing the necessary "elasticity" to adjust favorably to the borrowing needs of business and trade (known as the "real bills" doctrine). According to the Banking School, financial institutions which engaged in excessive credit expansion (lending more money than there is gold backing) would see their banknotes redeemed by creditors. An over issue of banknotes would be controlled by the "invisible hand" of bank competition and was therefore unlikely.

The views of the Currency School prevailed in the passage of the Peel Act of 1844, which called for all future issues of money and currency to increase or decrease in the amount equal to the changes in the country's bullion reserves. This law was passed to prevent banks from inflating the money supply and reducing the value of the currency. However, the Peel Act did not cover checking accounts, and was never a true 100% gold deposit system. As a result, banking instability and bank runs continued to menace the financial landscape, culminating in the 1930-33 Great Depression, when thousands of commercial banks and savings institutions failed in Europe and America. When times are good fiat currency is an acceptable currency but, when times are difficult, it is more likely that bank balances will be exchanged for cash.

After the Great Depression, most governments guaranteed bank deposits through federal deposit insurance (FDIC) and thus sharply curtailed the number of bank runs, but fractional reserve banking is still the norm in today's global economy and subjects the monetary system to instability if the public loses faith in the monetary system.

## THE EVOLUTION OF MERCHANT BANKING AND FINANCIAL CAPITALISM

The first commercial banks were developed in Greece and Italy and took in deposits for safekeeping and loaned money at interest. However, the unrestrained banking practices of the private Italian banks often led to reckless credit arrangements, bankruptcies and loss of funds. As a result, "continental banks of deposit" developed in the 17th century with more stringent requirements. The Bank of Amsterdam was created by the Dutch government as a "bank of deposit" in 1609 and was a precursor to the first central bank. The bank's founders insisted on a strict separation of the lending and deposit functions, and maintained a full 100% reserve on its capital stock. Unfortunately, the Bank of Amsterdam did not live up to its charter, and later was accused of surreptitiously loaning 9 million guilder to the city of Amsterdam. The Bank of Amsterdam failed in 1791 after 182 years of existence.

International traders also became merchant bankers. The famous House of Medici in Italy, the Fuggers of Germany, the Rothschilds of Europe, and the House of Morgan in the United States were involved in international trading. The old political system in Medieval Europe consisted of three estates: Clergy, Nobility, and the Army, but by the 19th century, the merchant bankers had become so powerful that they replaced the clergy as the "Third Estate."

## THE HOUSE OF MEDICI AND THE FUGGERS OF GERMANY

A romantic enchantment is associated with the stories of the merchant bankers of the 18th and 19th century as the capitalist system gradually transformed itself from commodity-based capitalism to a money-based system. The House of Medici was the first banking family dynasty. Founded by Giovanni de Medici in 14th century Italy, the Florence-based bankers were traders, lenders, manufacturers, and investors. It took the Medicis three generations to become the most important banking house in Italy, and they became highly influential as political leaders in Florence and supporters of Renaissance art.

Another important merchant banking family was the Fuggers of Germany. Jacob Fugger (1459-1526) — "Fugger the Rich" — was a textile manufacturer based in Augsburg, Germany. He was a devout Catholic who embraced two forbidden activities, money leading at interest, and currency exchange. An expert in double-entry bookkeeping, trade, mining, international finance, and courier service ("letters of credit"), he became the Pope's banker. His most famous saying was "The king reigns but the bank rules." Some historians suggest that the collapse of his fortune in 1607 led to the Protestant Reformation by Martin Luther. Today the "Fuggerei" — a housing development for low-income poor people in Augsburg — is a standing monument to Fugger's influence.

## THE ROTHSCHILDS OF EUROPE

European Jewish merchant bankers became prominent in late 18th century as bond traders; international financiers of wars and business; lenders to trading companies, kings and counts; and gold traders. The founding father was Meyer Rothschild (1743-1812), a merchant/money changer in the Frankfurt ghetto specializing in rare coins, medals, and second-hand goods. With his success, he became the private banker for Wilhelm IX, a Prussian nobleman.

The family symbol was a small oval sign embossed by five gold arrows, representing Rothschild's five sons: Nathan in London, Jakob (James) in Paris, Amschel in Frankfurt, Salomon in Vienna, and Kalmann in Naples. By establishing roots throughout Europe, the Rothschilds gained an advantage over other merchant bankers, becoming rich and famous by financing the Napoleonic Wars. It is believed that the Rothschilds were the first to know that Wellington had won the Battle at Waterloo in June 1815, and profited handsomely from this insider information. The Rothschilds became the most powerful private banking family in Europe and maintained that height of influence until their downfall in World War II as a result of Nazi persecution and taxation. Today's Rothschild & Co. serve as investment bankers and, as the official gold broker, set the official gold price from London.

## THE HOUSE OF MORGAN

The most distinguished merchant banker in the United States was J. P. Morgan (1837-1913), known as the bulbous tycoon of Wall Street. Morgan was a cantankerous investment banker who controlled one third of America's railroads, and an estimated 6% of the stock market. His early exploits included refunding the Civil War debt, financing and merging American railroads, and twice rescuing the U. S. Treasury from a drain on gold in 1895. In 1901, he put together the first $1 billion IPO, U. S. Steel. During the Panic of 1907, Morgan acted as quasi-central banker by forcing fellow bankers to raise the funds to keep the markets and the banks from failing. It was his finest hour as a public citizen. His heroics led to the creation of the Federal Reserve Act of 1913. As Senator Nelson Aldrich, a sponsor of the bill, stated, "Something has got to be done. We may not always have Pierpont Morgan with us to meet a banking crisis."

Morgan never lived to see the Federal Reserve in action. His son, Jack (J. P. Morgan Jr.), lived through the 1929 crash and Great Depression and saw his firm split into two organizations, J. P. Morgan and Morgan Stanley, in consequence of the Glass-Steagall Act, which was part of the Banking Act of 1933 that separated commercial banking from investment banking.

Chapter 19 examines the forces that transformed the international monetary system from the gold standard to central banking and the story of the Federal Reserve and its role today in stabilizing or destabilizing the global economy.

## SUMMARY

1.  Money, or a medium of exchange, is necessary to establishing prices, costs, a store of value, and financial accounting in a dynamic global economy.

2.  Irredeemable fiat paper money could only be established because the official government money (banknotes) used to be redeemable in gold, silver or other commodity (Mises regression theorem).

3.  Money came into being through the natural evolution of useful commodities that enjoyed a growing degree of marketability. Gold, silver and copper gradually developed into the primary medium of exchange.

4.  Fractional reserve banking developed naturally due to the law of large numbers and the fungibility (similarity) of money. Debates developed over what constitutes a safe level of bank deposits. The Banking School, led by merchant bankers such as the Fuggers, the Rothschilds, and the House of Morgan, favored a "real bills" doctrine, that credit expansion should be limited to the needs of business, while the Currency School favored "constitutional money," that is, 100% backed by specie (gold and silver). The creation of central banking placed the decision on the level of bank deposits and credit expansion in the hands of government-controlled bankers.

## IMPORTANT TERMS

Banking Act of 1933

Banking School

Barter

Bimetallism

Constitutional money

Continental banks of deposit

Currency principle

Currency School

Direct exchange

Federal Deposit Insurance Corp. (FDIC)

Federal Reserve Act of 1913

Fiat money

Fractional reserve banking

Fungible, fungibility

Glass-Steagall Act

Gresham's law

Gold certificate

Invisible hand doctrine (Adam Smith)

Medium of exchange

Merchant banking

Mutual coincidence of wants

Peel Act of 1844

Real bills doctrine

Regression theorem

Tale

Third estate

Specie

Suspension

Warehouse receipt

**INFLUENTIAL ECONOMIST**

**MURRAY ROTHBARD AND SOUND MONEY**

**NAME:   Murray N. Rothbard (1925-95)**

**BACKGROUND:** Murray Rothbard was the premier libertarian economist of the 20th century.  Raised in New York City by secular Jewish parents, Rothbard earned his Ph. D. in monetary economics in 1956 at Columbia University.  He taught economics at the Brooklyn Polytechnic Institute from early 1960s until the 1980s, and University of Nevada at Las Vegas from 1986 until his death in 1995. He wrote prolifically on Misesian economics, especially a treatise called *Man, Economy, and State* (1962) and *America's Great Depression* (1963).  These scholarly works broadened Austrian themes into a full-scale alternative to standard neo-Keynesian economics.  *Man, Economy, and State* is often called an Americanized version of Mises's *Human Action*.  It dissected Keynesianism and introduced an Austrian version of micro and macro economics.  He helped found the Cato Institute in 1977 and the Mises Institute in 1982.

**MAJOR CONTRIBUTION:**  Rothbard was a highly influential American economist, historian and natural law theorist belonging to the Austrian School of economics (followers of Ludwig von Mises and Friedrich Hayek) who helped define modern libertarianism.  Rothbard took on the Keynesians, Marxists, and socialists of all stripes, and later on, the Chicago monetarist school.  His lucid, powerful polemics attracted a large number of libertarians, gold bugs, and free-market economists.  His pamphlet, *What Has the Government Done to Our Money?* (1964), touched the hearts of followers as much as *The Communist Manifesto* had affected the minds and hearts of Marxists.  His pamphlet on money was something every intelligent layman could comprehend about the origins of money, the gold standard, and central banking.  The mystery of money was no more.  (Much of this chapter has been drawn from Rothbard's pamphlet.)  Rothbard made the case for a natural law in monetary economics — the classical gold standard.  He fiercely opposed Keynesian and Chicago-school economics and was critical of government intervention in the economy. He demonstrated that central bank inflation created the boom-bust business cycle, and supported a return to a strict gold standard.  Rothbard was also an economic historian and philosopher who made significant contributions to the modern libertarian movement.

**QUOTATION:** "We can look back upon the 'classical' gold standard, the Western world of the nineteenth and early twentieth centuries, as the literal and metaphorical Golden Age.....The international gold standard meant that the benefits of having one money medium were extended throughout the world. One of the reasons for the growth and prosperity of the United States has been the fact that we have enjoyed one money throughout the large areas of the country.....One money facilitates freedom of trade, investment, and travel throughout the trading and monetary area, with the consequent growth of specialization and the international division of labor." (*What Has Government Done to Our Money?*, 4th ed., 1990, pp. 91-92)

## PROBLEMS TO PONDER

1. Barter — the trade of goods for goods — is booming. According to the U. S. Department of Commerce, barter accounts for 30% of the world's total business, and experts estimate that 65% of Fortune 500 companies engage in barter to one degree or another. If a medium of exchange clearly has advantages over barter, why does barter exist today?

2. To what extent is a nation's standard of living reflected in the quality of its coinage? Historian Michael Grant demonstrates the rise, decline and fall of the Roman empire through the gradual deterioration of its coinage. Can one say the same about modern coinage? Give a report on the changes in the types of coins and banknotes in various countries from the 19th and early 20th century under the International Gold Standard to coins and banknotes created in the late 20th century.

3. To what extend is a central bank necessary? Describe the conditions of banking in the United States and other countries when a central bank did not exist. Was the monetary system adequate for the commercial needs of the nation, or did the nation inevitably fall into crisis and instability?

## FOR ADDITIONAL READING

- Murray N. Rothbard, *What Has Government Done to Our Money?* 4th ed. (Mises Institute, 1990). The most revealing book about money ever written.

- Michael Grant, *Roman History From Coins* (Cambridge University Press, 1958). How Roman coins tell the rise and fall of the Roman Empire. Amazing.

- Pierre Vilar, *A History of Gold and Money* (London: Verso Books, 1976)

*Chapter 19*

# INFLATION, CENTRAL BANKING AND MONETARY POLICY

*"The establishment of Central Banking removes the checks of bank credit expansion, and puts the inflationary engine into operation."*

—MURRAY N. ROTHBARD

*"Inflation is everywhere and anywhere a monetary phenomenon."*

—MILTON FRIEDMAN

This chapter begins with a tale of two monetary events. The first occurred on December 11, 1930, when the Bank of the United States closed its doors. The bank's name suggested both at home and abroad that it was an official bank. Technically the Bank of the United States was not a public bank, yet as the largest commercial bank in the country, and a member of the Federal Reserve Bank, the demise of the bank was devastating to the rest of the country. When the Federal Reserve Board failed to live up to its charter as a lender of last resort and save the Bank of the United States, financial havoc occurred. December 11, 1930 became a day of monetary infamy, the beginning of four banking crises that eventually carried America and the world into the worst economic collapse in history. The bankruptcy was symbolic of bad faith on behalf of the U. S. government, especially the Federal Reserve Bank, the central bank that had been established in 1913 specifically to be a "lender of last resort" and prevent this kind of banking crisis.

A few years later, the Bank of the United States paid off 83.5 percent of its liabilities. If the Federal government had lent some funds to the Bank of the United States, perhaps the Great Depression would have been merely another recession in American history rather than the economic catastrophe that caused so much misery.

The next generation of Federal Reserve Bank chairmen thought they had learned how to handle a monetary crisis as a result of the Great Depression. The Federal Reserve Board acted very differently during the second monetary event that occurred in the fall of 2008. A financial panic in inter-banking lending occurred in September, 2008, as the US real estate boom collapsed and sub-prime loan losses exposed other risky loans and over-inflated asset prices around the world. Wall Street and global stock prices plunged 30% or more. Investment and commercial banks in the United States and Europe suffered massive losses and even faced bankruptcy. Lehman Brothers, one of the world's largest investment banks, collapsed, and AIG, the world's largest insurer, was threatening failure. The global economy, which had enjoyed remarkable growth during the new century, suddenly faced the worst recession since the Great Depression, with a serious drop in international trade and a sharp rise in unemployment.

Under Fed chairman Ben Bernanke, the Federal Reserve acted quickly on several fronts as a lender and even buyer of last resort. It injected billions of new dollars in liquidity to the threatened financial community, doubling the Fed's balance sheet. It guaranteed commercial paper and worked with the FDIC to assure the public that money market funds were safe. Bernanke worked closely with the Bush administration to bail out brokerage firm Bear Sterns and AIG. Congress and the President worked with the Fed to inject billions of taxpayers money into Citibank, Bank of America, and other major commercial banks.

When the International Monetary Fund and other economic advisors warned of "worrisome parallels" between the current global crisis and the Great Depression, Ben Bernanke, a student of the Great Depression, took the controversial step of buying $300 billion directly from the US Treasury, the first time to do so since World War II. The Fed also agreed to buy up to $700 billion in mortgage securities. Critics complained that such extreme measures destroyed the independence of the central bank from the executive branch in government, enlarged the size of government far beyond its legitimate role, and threatened the future of a global free-market economy. The outcome of this monetary crisis has yet been decided.

## THE NEED FOR A CENTRAL BANK

These two stories illustrate the impact of central banking or government-controlled banking. It was created for two purposes:

- to provide a lender of last resort during a banking crisis
- to facilitate the growth of government power.

Central banks are distinct from private commercial banks. Central banks are public or quasi-public institutions with monopoly powers to control and manipulate money and credit through a variety of tools not available to the private banking community.

Banks with central authority were created in Amsterdam in 1609 and Sweden in 1668, but the most significant financial institution with state powers was the Bank of England ("The Old Lady") created in 1694. The Bank of England was privately chartered with a £1.2 million loan to the British government to help finance its continuous wars with France and other European powers. The bank also functioned as a commercial bank until the end of World War II. The Bank of England managed the national debt of England throughout this period. Financial trouble caused the government to suspend gold payments from 1797 until 1821 due to the excessive cost of foreign wars. When the Bank renewed specie payments, Parliament passed the 1844 Bank Charter Act, which tied the issuance of banknotes to gold reserves (100% gold reserve standard) and gave the Bank the sole right to issue banknotes. Older private banks continued to issue banknotes until the 1930s. Britain remained on the gold standard until 1931. The Bank of England was nationalized in 1946 when it became exclusively a central bank.

Other European central banks were chartered in the 19th century. The Bank of France ("Napoleon's Bank") was established in 1800, and the Bank of Germany ("The Reichsbank") was established in 1876. In 1957, the name of the German central bank was changed to the Bundesbank. The Bank of Japan, established in 1882, became the fiscal agent of the Emperor of Japan. Most nations, including developing countries, now have a central bank.

## THE ORIGIN OF CENTRAL BANKING IN THE UNITED STATES

There were two attempts to establish a public bank in the United States prior to the Federal Reserve Act of 1913. The first Treasury Secretary, Alexander Hamilton, proposed the creation of the first Bank of the United States as part of his overall financial plan to establish public credit. The Bank's charter lasted from 1791-1811. The Bank of North America, established in 1781 by Robert Morris, preceded the public bank. The creation of a national bank was controversial. Critics viewed it as an unconstitutional act giving monopoly power to wealthy commercial interests. Thomas Jefferson and other political leaders mistrusted paper money and considered the Bank of the United States as an engine of inflation. But with George Washington's support, the Bank was established. Based in Philadelphia with eight branches, the Bank of the United States was capitalized with $10 million in stock owned by individuals, corporations, and the Federal government. It acted as both a commercial and national bank, issuing coins and currency. The Bank had five functions:

1. Manage government accounts
2. Make loans to the Treasury
3. Deal in bullion
4. Discount bills of exchange
5. Serve as a redemption center for other banknotes at par

The Bank of the United States was a huge success. The stock was heavily oversubscribed and Hamilton's grand plan to combine the national and state debts with a central bank and sinking fund (to pay off the debt) proved a stabilizing influence in the struggling new nation. The Bank's charter was renewed in 1816, capitalized with $35 million in its 29 branches. Its director, Nicholas Biddle (1786-1844), appointed at the age of 33, was a Princeton graduate, scholar, diplomat, and lawyer and was regarded as a successful banker. When the charter for the Second Bank of the United States came up in 1832 Biddle faced strong opposition from President Andrew Jackson. Jackson, a Tennessee democrat, hated all forms of banking and paper money. He ultimately vetoed renewal of the second charter of the Bank of the

417

United States, which forced it to be converted into a private bank, the US Bank of Pennsylvania, in 1836. Immediately following the demise of the Bank of the United States, Jackson, reflecting his hatred of paper money, required all payments for Federal land to be purchased with gold and silver only. Customers ran to their banks demanding gold and silver, and the Panic of 1837 ensued.

Between 1836 and 1913, the United States operated on a state-chartered private banking system with no functioning federal bank. However, except during the "greenback" era of the Civil War (1861-70), the country operated on a gold standard with state-chartered banks required to redeem their banknotes in gold or silver. The banking system was characterized by an era of gold rushes, inflationary booms, deflationary busts, wildcat banking, and threats to the Treasury. It was an unstable monetary era.

In the early 20th century, bankers, politicians and economists saw the growing need to create a central bank for four reasons:

1. Fear of another panic, following the Panic of 1907.

2. The need for an "elastic" or flexible currency more responsive to commercial needs (the "real bills" doctrine).

3. The desire to stabilize a haphazard national banking system.

4. The need to strengthen and improve the international gold standard.

## THE CLASSICAL GOLD STANDARD (1816-1914)

The International Gold Standard served as the primary monetary system during the 19th and early 20th century. Great Britain served as the creator and center of the classical gold standard when Britain — at the time the world's economic and political superpower — passed the Coinage Act of 1816. This act established the gold standard as the "numeraire" or monetary unit, following the Napoleonic Wars. It was adopted throughout the United Kingdom, which covered most of the globe at the time. Following the gold rushes in the United States, Australia, and South Africa, gold gradually became the monetary standard of all industrial nations by the 1890s.

A de facto gold standard existed prior to 1816, when banknotes were redeemable in gold or silver (see chapter 18). In fact, the price of the pound sterling was fixed to gold bullion based on the rate set by Sir Isaac Newton, Master of the Mint, in 1717, where one troy ounce of gold was defined as £3.17s.10p. The Peel Act of 1844 solidified the international gold standard by linking the increase of British pound notes to the amount of specie on reserve.

The United States used a silver standard from 1792 until 1834. In 1834, it followed Britain's lead by adopting gold from 1834-1861 and 1879-1914 at $20.67 per ounce, except during the Civil War and for nine years after, when the U. S. suspended specie payments.

France adopted the international gold standard in 1850, Germany in 1871, and the rest of Europe, including Austria-Hungary and Russia, by 1880. After the Civil War, the U. S. rejoined in 1879. Japan went on gold in 1897.

By defining a nation's currency in terms of a set amount of gold, fixed exchange rates were established between currencies of different countries on the international gold standard. For example, in 1900, President McKinley defined the US dollar as equal to 1/20th ounce of gold, while Queen Victoria defined the pound sterling equal to 1/4th ounce of gold. Thus, under the fixed exchange system, £ = $5. This system made it much easier for producers and consumers to participate in global markets.

## THE CASE FOR GOLD

The international gold standard provided a stable monetary framework from which economies could grow rapidly. By defining a nation's currency in terms of a set amount of gold, prices for goods and services could remain relatively stable, and with exchange rates fixed, trade and production flourished. As Murray Rothbard comments, "The international gold standard meant that the benefits of having one money medium were extended throughout the world. Money facilitated freedom of trade, investment, and travel throughout that trading and monetary area, with the consequent growth of specialization and the international division of labor."[1] John Maynard Keynes notes, "For a hundred years the system worked, throughout Europe, with an extraordinary success and facilitated the growth of wealth on an unprecedented level."[2]

Advocates of the gold standard indicate that these benefits accrue:

1. **Stable money**: little or no monetary deflation. As figure 19.1 demonstrates, monetarized gold — the amount of gold bullion on deposit at banks and government — gradually increases and never declines. Gold production can decline from time to time, but since gold is largely indestructible, production only adds to the monetary hoard.

---

1 Murray N. Rothbard, *What Has the Government Done to Our Money?* (Auburn, AL: Mises Institute, 1990), pp. 91-92.
2 John Maynard Keynes, *A Tract on Monetary Reform* (New York: Prometheus Books, 2000 [1923]), p. 7.

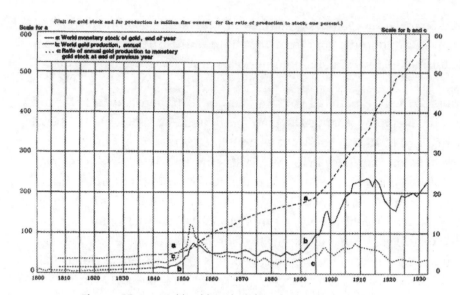

**Figure 19.1.** *World gold stock and production, 1800-1932.*
Source: Rufus S. Tucker, "Gold and the General Price Level," *Review of Economic Statistics*, July,1934.

2. **An inelastic currency leads to "iron discipline" on government**: Under a true gold standard, where the amount of currency in circulation is directly linked to the amount of gold on deposit, the "rules of the game" inhibits deficit spending and inflation. For example, if Britain inflates the money supply by printing more pounds, the Hume-Ricardo specie flow mechanism (named after British economists David Hume and David Ricardo) eventually forces the government to retrench. How? The process works as follows:

   • Inflation increases domestic incomes
   • Imports increase faster than exports
   • The trade imbalance causes gold to leave the country (as importers exchange gold for British pounds)
   • The decline in gold stocks causes the money supply to decline at home
   • The fall in the money supply causes a recession and retrenchment.

Under the Hume-Ricardo specie flow mechanism, inflation cannot last and inevitably causes deflation.

3. **Price stability**: there is a tendency toward long-run price stability under gold. Keynes notes that the classical gold standard enjoyed a "remarkable feature....the relatively stability of the price level," adding, "Approximately the same level of price ruled in or about the years 1826, 1841, 1855, 1862, 1867, 1871, and 1915." Compare that record to the price of a new suit in 1926, 1941, 1955, 1962, and today. In terms of gold, the real price of a suit remains the same.

Figures 19.2 and 19.3 show the effect of the gold standard on the price level during the 19th century compared to the price level during the 20th century, when the world gradually went off gold.

**FIGURE 11–3A**
**Wholesale Price Index, United Kingdom, 1800–1979**

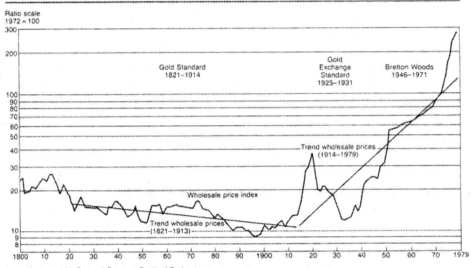

Note: Prepared by Federal Reserve Bank of St. Louis.

Source: Reprinted with the permission of the Pacific Research Institute for Public Policy. From: Bordo, David. "The Gold Standard." In *Money in Crisis*, edited by Barry N. Siegel. San Francisco: Pacific Research Institute, 1984.

**FIGURE 11–3B**
**Wholesale Price Index, United States, 1800–1979**

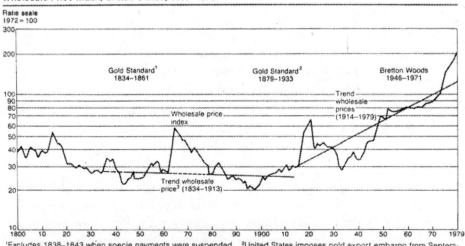

[1]Excludes 1838–1843 when specie payments were suspended. [2]United States imposes gold export embargo from September 1917 to June 1919. [3]Broken line indicates years excluded in computing trend.
Note: Prepared by Federal Reserve Bank of St. Louis.

Source: Reprinted with the permission of the Pacific Research Institute for Public Policy. From: Bordo, David. "The Gold Standard." In *Money in Crisis*, edited by Barry N. Siegel. San Francisco: Pacific Research Institute, 1984.

**Figure 19.2 and 19.3.** Wholesale Price Index in England and the United States, 1880-1979. Source: Michael David Bordo, "The Gold Standard: Myths and Realities," in *Money in Crisis*, ed. (Pacific Institute for Public Policy Research, 1984), pp. 212-13.

4. **Economic growth**: The gold standard encouraged international trade and rapid domestic expansion.

5. **Low and stable interest rates**: Under gold, companies made long-term contracts and made extensive use of gold-linked bonds. For example, American railroad companies issued 100 year old gold bonds at extremely low interest rates. The railroads were able to obtain low interest loans by promising to pay back the bonds in 100 years in a fixed amount of gold.

Milton Friedman and Anna J. Schwartz conclude, "The blind, undersigned, and quasi-automatic working of the gold standard turned out to produce a greater measure of predictability and regularity—perhaps because its discipline was impersonal and inescapable—than did deliberate and conscious control exercised within institutional arrangements intended to promote stability."[3]

## THE DANGERS OF AN IRREDEEMABLE PAPER MONEY SYSTEM

Adherents to the gold standard contend that without the gold standard as an anchor and discipline, government will be tempted to resort to excessive and sometimes even runaway inflation. While there are a few cases of excessive inflation during gold rushes (such as in California in 1848), there are a large number of irresponsible inflationary episodes in history. Examples include:

— John Law and the Mississippi Bubble
— Continentals and the American Revolution ("Not worth a Continental")
— Assignats and the French Revolution
— Greenbacks and the Civil War
— The Great German Hyperinflation, 1920-23
— Post-World War II hyperinflations in Eastern Europe and Africa
— Latin American hyperinflations ( For example: Peru, Argentina and Bolivia.)
— Post-Berlin Wall hyperinflations in Eastern Europe

Runaway inflation occurred in Eastern Europe, Africa, and Latin America in the 1990s and in Zimbabwe in 2008-09. Runaway inflation destroys the lifelong savings of average citizens and disrupts the social fabric of a nation and can lead to the creation of dictatorships and tyranny. As John Maynard Keynes observed, "There is no subtler, no surer means of overturning the existing basis of society than to debauch the currency."[4]

3 Milton Friedman and Anna J. Schwartz, *A Monetary History of the United States, 1867-1960* (Princeton University Press, 1963), p. 10.
4  John Maynard Keynes, *Economic Consequences of the Peace* (New York: Penguin, 1971 [1920]), p. 236.

History identifies a number of reasons for government leaders to resort to printing currency and for reckless depreciation of currency.

1. **American Revolution inflation, 1776-83**: Unable to raise sufficient funds from colonial taxes and duties, Congress and the 13 colonies resorted to printing the "Continental" currency. Not backed by gold or silver, and easily counterfeited, it quickly lost value, giving rise to the phrase "not worth a Continental." Because of their bad experience with paper money, the Constitutional Convention included in the U. S. Constitution a requirement that "no state shall....make anything but gold and silver coin a tender in payment of debts" (Article I, section 10).

2. **German hyperinflation, 1920-23:** Following the First World War, the Versailles Treaty imposed draconian reparations on Germany—up to $5 billion to pay for the war, to be paid in "gold, commodities, ships, securities or otherwise" before May, 1921. Germany paid by printing Reichmarks that gradually and dramatically lost value. In his brilliant report, *The Economic Consequences of the Peace* (1920), Keynes warned that the reparations demands on Germany would lead to hyperinflation. At the height of the debacle in 1923, the exchange rate between the dollar and the Mark was one trillion Marks to one dollar, and the press showed pictures of Germans carrying wheelbarrows of banknotes into stores to buy a sack of food.

3. **Yugoslovia hyperinflation, 1989-94:** This Soviet satellite went through hyperinflation when the Soviet model collapsed and Yugoslovia, like other Eastern countries behind the Iron Curtain, had to adjust to the new realities of competitive capitalism. Because they were unable to finance public spending with taxes, they paid for government services and public works through the printing press. The highest denomination printed in 1988 was 50,000 dinar; by 1989 it was 2,000,000 dinars. In the early 1990s, Yugoslavia reformed its currency, loping off 4-5 zeroes. But they continued to inflate the money supply, and by 1993, the largest denomination was 10,000,000,000 dinars. Then the government lopped off another six zeroes. But before the year was over, the highest denomination was 500,000,000,000 dinars, the largest single denomination in modern history.

## THE CASE AGAINST GOLD

Despite these extreme cases of hyperinflation that occur without gold as a discipline, many economists, bankers and politicians have expressed reservations about gold as a monetary numeraire. Reasons include:

423

1. **High resource costs:** Economists such as Milton Friedman have estimated that it costs 3-4% of GDP to produce monetary gold and silver. However, Roger Garrison (Auburn University) has shown that since abandoning the gold standard in 1971, mining companies are still mining gold and silver; consequently the 3-4% resource cost of GDP is still born by the economy, although under a fiat money standard, the cost is born by private enterprise, not the government.

2. **Instability in domestic economies during "gold rushes" and "silver rushes."** Gold discoveries have increased the world money supply by no more than 5% a year, even in the 19th century, but the impact on local gold-producing economies in California, Australia or South Africa can be significant as prices skyrocketed.

3. **A gold standard links the internal economy (prices and real output) to external rules (balance of payments).** Under a gold standard, trade/payments deficits would cause deflation domestically (specie-flow mechanism), cutting off a rising inflation. Of course, this is also an argument for the gold standard, as it imposes the cost of recession if a government embarks on an inflationary path under gold.

4. **Periodic panics and crisis**: During gold standard, US still experienced economic crises in 1884, 1890, 1893, and 1907. In other words, governments found ways around the gold standard to create boom-bust.

5. **"Inelastic" currency**: Because the supply of gold is so restrictive (averaging an increase of only 1-2% a year), the gold standard fails to keep up with real economic growth and cannot provide an elastic money and credit system for trade and industry.

Monetary historian Michael David Bordo concludes that a monetary system controlled by a central bank could provide greater flexibility than a gold standard. He states, "A fiduciary money standard based on a monetary rule of a steady and known rate of monetary growth could provide both greater price level and real output stability than a return to the gold standard."[5]

---

5 Michael David Bordo, "The Classical Gold Standard: Some Lessons for Today," *St. Louis Federal Reserve Review* (May 1981), p. 16.

## THE STORY OF THE FEDERAL RESERVE BANK

The U. S. political system experienced three revolutionary changes that significantly increased and centralized the power of the Federal government in 1913. The first was the ratification of the 16th Amendment, which instituted an income tax. As a result the Federal government would have an increasing interest in the occupations and income of American citizens. The second was the adoption of the 17th Amendment, which allowed for the direct election of senators (prior to this amendment, senators were elected by state legislators). Finally, the Federal Reserve Act of 1913 established a central bank in the United States.

The origins of the central bank are shrouded in mystery and are the delight of conspiracy theorists. Why did the backers of the Federal Reserve Bank meet in secret at the Jekyll Island Club in Georgia? Some suggest that the bankers, including representatives of Morgan and Rockefeller interests led by Paul Warburg, the father of the Federal Reserve Bank, "met in secrecy because of the long standing tradition against central banking, and its opposition from 'big bankers, money trusts, and Wall Street interests.'"[6] Warburg and his colleagues intended to create a European-style central bank, partially independent of government. Their plans did not result in the creation of such a bank. The Federal Reserve Bank Act that became law December 23, 1913 put the Secretary of the Treasury in charge, uniting the power of the government with the power of the central bank. Only later (1933) would the Federal Reserve Bank chairman become independent of the Treasury. The act stated that the functions of the Federal Reserve Bank were to:

1. Act as a clearinghouse for commercial banks
2. Provide loans at interest (known as the "rediscount rate") to member banks
3. Become a lender of last resort in times of crisis
4. Maintain the Gold Standard Act of 1900

The original Federal Reserve Bank Board consisted of 7 members; the Treasury Secretary, Comptroller of the Currency, and five members appointed by the President and confirmed by the Senate to serve for 10 years.

Twelve regional Federal Reserve banks (with only one in the West, in San Francisco) were established for check-clearing services and the rediscount window. To become a member of the Federal Reserve Bank, private commercial banks had to invest 6% of bank reserves (earning interest) in non-tradable stock.

---

6 See for example, G. Edward Griffin, *The Creature from Jekyll Island*, 3rd ed. (California: American Media, 1998).

## THE FEDERAL RESERVE BANK DURING WORLD WAR I AND THE 1920s

The Federal Reserve Bank was immediately tested during the First World War. With heavy gold inflows flowing in from Europe, the US money supply rose 70% between 1914-18, creating a huge domestic inflation. When the war ended, the 1920-21 depression followed. Fortunately, the economy rebounded quickly, and the Federal Reserve Bank in the 1920s witnessed a booming economy known as the Roaring Twenties.

Andrew Mellon, then Treasury Secretary, served also as the Chairman of the Federal Reserve Bank, although Benjamin Strong, the president of the Federal Reserve in New York, quickly established the New York branch as the most influential. Strong started "open market" operations in New York in 1923, allowing the buying and selling of government securities. There was still a high level of bank failures, especially in rural areas, with over 500 failures in 1921 alone, but no serious collapse occurred until 1929.

Economists take two views of the 1920s and the Federal Reserve. The first view was held by the Monetarists and Keynesians, including Irving Fisher (Yale), Frank Taussig (Harvard), and John Maynard Keynes (Cambridge), and later Milton Friedman (Chicago). They contended that the Federal Reserve Bank made few mistakes during the 1920s, and everything justified the "New Era" optimism of the Roaring Twenties, with stable growth and no price inflation. The 1920s was, according to Friedman, "the high tide of the Federal Reserve Bank System."[7]

The second view holds that the Federal Reserve Bank was an engine of "easy money" through low interest rates during the 1920s, creating an artificial, debt-driven boom in real estate, manufacturing, and the stock market. This "easy money" era was the catalyst for the collapse in 1929-33. Advocates of this view include American hard-money economists such as H. Parker Willis (Columbia) and European economists Ludwig von Mises and Friedrich A. Hayek (Vienna).

Who was right? Both sides make good points in this debate. The Federal Reserve Bank did artificially reduce the discount rate in an effort to help out Britain in the mid-1920s, but the money supply did not increase dramatically during the 1920s. Most economists agree that the overwhelming deflationary forces of the early 1930s was due to blunders by the Federal Reserve Bank in the 1930s, not the 1920s.

## THE GREAT DEPRESSION: THE FEDERAL RESERVE BANK'S GREAT BLUNDER

The turning point in the history of the Federal Reserve Bank resulted from the worldwide 1929-33 economic depression, which continued unabated in most countries until World War II. The 1929-33 crisis, starting with the October 1929 stock market crash and the December 1930 demise of the Bank of the United States, was the

---

7 The title of chapter 6 of Milton Friedman and Anna J. Schwartz's *A Monetary History of the United States*.

most traumatic economic event of the 20th century, causing industrial output to decline 30%, unemployment to soar to over 25%, and stocks to collapse by 90%. The prolonged depression fostered criticism of classical economics and laissez faire, and encouraged favoritism toward the Welfare State and Big Government in Europe and the United States.

For years after the Great Depression, most economists believed that the Federal Reserve Bank did everything it could to avert disaster but was unable to stem the deflationary tide. The Federal Reserve Bank provided needed liquidity, but still a third of the banks and saving institutions went bankrupt or merged. Policy makers concluded that monetary authorities had been incapable of reversing the depression and the collapse of the banking system and were exonerated. This historical interpretation also led policy makers and economists to accept the original Keynesian idea that "money doesn't matter," that somehow an aggressive expansion of the money supply during a recession or depression would not have a negative effect. Monetary policy, they said, was like a string; you could pull on it but you can't push on it. Central banks can stop a boom but are incapable of igniting a recovery. According to the early Keynesians, using open-market operations (buying Treasury bonds) and lowering interest rates would only lead to hoarding or a build-up of cash reserves at banks due to what Keynes called a "fetish for liquidity." Only an aggressive fiscal policy — deficit spending and tax cuts — could stimulate spending and recovery, they said.

However, this Keynesian view of monetary policy changed dramatically due to the scholarly statistical work of Milton Friedman and Anna J. Schwartz in their massive work, *A Monetary History of the United States, 1867-1960*, published in 1963. They demonstrated that the Federal Reserve Bank, far from being benign during the early 1930s, was devastatingly effective in a negative way. In the most important chapter, "The Great Contraction," the authors report that money stock had fell over a third from 1929 to 1933, the worst in U. S. history. (See figure 19.4.) The indictment of the Federal Reserve Bank is unmistakable: "….it is crystal clear that at all times during the contraction, the Federal Reserve Bank had it within its power to prevent the decline in the quantity of money and to produce an increase."[8] Furthermore: "Far from being a testimony to the irrelevance of monetary forces in preventing depression, the early 1930s are a tragic testimony to their importance in producing depression" by ineptly turning a garden-variety recession into the worst economic calamity of the century.[9]

Further work by monetarist economists show that the Federal Reserve Bank largely ignored its mandate to be a lender of last resort because of the "real bills" doctrine. This is the view that the Federal Reserve Bank should extend or restrict

8  Milton Friedman and Anna J. Schwartz, *A Monetary History of the United States*, p. 299, 391.
9  Milton Friedman, *Dollars and Deficits* (New York: Prentice-Hall, 1968), pp. 78-79.

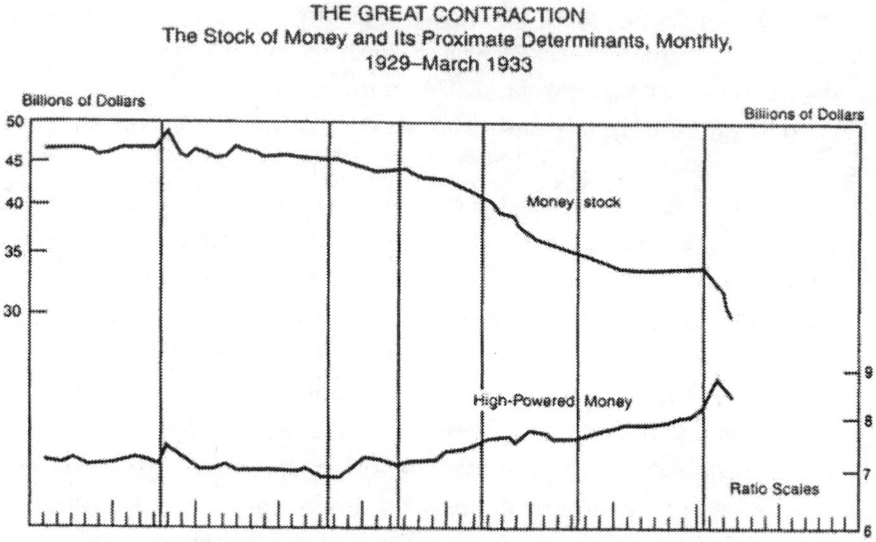

THE GREAT CONTRACTION
The Stock of Money and Its Proximate Determinants, Monthly,
1929–March 1933

**Figure 19.4.** *Graph of Money Supply, 1929-33.*

credit only according to the growth of the real economy, meaning actual production and marketing of goods and services, rather than for speculative investments in stocks and real estate. Real bills makes sense as a commercial bank practice, but fails as a central bank policy. As Federal Reserve Bank member Charles O. Hardy stated in 1932, "It is not the business of the Reserve system to stimulate business by making money artificially cheap in periods of depression or dear in periods of boom, but merely to adapt itself to conditions as it finds them," heading off panic or bankruptcy whenever it might occur.[10]

## THE FEDERAL RESERVE BANK SYSTEM TODAY

Since the Great Depression, the Federal Reserve Bank has gradually regained its influence in the world and today is considered more important than Congress or the President in terms of stabilizing the business cycle. As Paul Samuelson recently stated, "Fiscal policy [government spending and taxes] is no longer a major tool of stabilization policy in the United States. Over the foreseeable future, stabilization policy will be performed by the Federal Reserve Bank monetary policy."[11]

When the Federal Reserve Bank was reorganized in the mid-1930s, the Treasury Secretary was replaced by a private citizen (usually with banking or Wall Street experience) as chairman of the Federal Reserve Bank. The Board of Governors consists of

10 Charles O. Hardy, *Credit Policies of the Federal Reserve* (1932). For more informaton on the role the "real bills" doctrine played, see Richare Timberlake, *Monetary Policy of the United States* (University of Chicago Press, 1993).

11 Paul A. Samuelson and William D. Nordhaus, *Economics*, 15th ed. (New York: McGraw-Hill, 1995), p. 645.

7 members, each with 14 year terms. The chairman is renewed every four years. The Board meets every six weeks to determine whether to make changes in the discount rate, the Federal Reserve Bank Funds Target Rate, or open market operations. The Federal Reserve Bank Open Market Committee (FOMC) meets at the same time (every six weeks). It consists of 12 members, 7 from the board of governors and 5 of the 12 regional bank presidents, one of whom always is chairman of the Federal Reserve Bank of New York, where open market operations are carried out. The FOMC determines the level of buying and selling of government securities—that is, the growth rate of the money supply, as explained below.

## THE FEDERAL RESERVE BANK'S MONETARY TOOLS

Today the Federal Reserve Bank, like other central banks, has two missions: (1) to promote as much as possible a stable growing economy with low inflation and low unemployment, and (2) to provide liquidity to counter a threatening national or global monetary/economic crisis.

Central banks conduct monetary policy by changing either the price of money (interest rates) or the quantity (money supply). The Federal Reserve Bank has the following tools available to accomplish these goals:

1. **Open market operations:** the purchase and sale of Treasury bonds. Open-market operations by the Federal Reserve Bank of New York are the most direct way of creating money and credit in the banking system.

2. **Interest rates:** The Federal Reserve Bank determines the discount rate, defined as short-term loans to member banks, and the Federal Reserve Bank Funds Target Rate, which is the rate charged for overnight loans between member banks. The Federal Reserve Bank Funds Target Rate affects other short-term interest rates, such as the Treasury bill rate and yields on money market funds.

3. **Reserve requirements:** Central banks can change the availability of credit by changing the bank reserve requirements. Currently banks are required to keep 10% of their demand deposits (checking accounts) available for withdrawals. The rest can be lent to banks and individuals. An increase in the reserve requirement reduces the bank's ability to lend money; a decrease in reserves increases its ability to lend money. (Developing countries, such as China, depend on changes in reserve requirements more than developed nations.)

4. **Emergency powers** to lend funds directly to financial institutions, and to purchase financial assets, including stock index futures, foreign debt, and mortgage securities. This tool is used sparingly, only in times of major crises. During the financial crisis of 2008-9, central banks took extraordinary measures to counter the deflationary collapse in real estate and a deep global recession. In the United States, the Fed made direct purchases of $300 billion in Treasury bonds, bought $700 billion in mortgage securities, and loaned money to investment banks. The Bank of England bought private debt to boost the quality of credit, and the Bank of Japan bought Japanese stocks and public debt. The Swiss National Bank intervened in the currency markets.

Let's look at each of these tools and how they can affect the financial system.

## HOW THE BANK MULTIPIER EXPANDS THE MONEY SUPPLY

**First, open-market operations.** By purchasing government bonds from commercial banks, the Federal Reserve Bank injects cash into the banking system, and through the bank multiplier, the money supply expands. By selling their bonds to the Federal Reserve Bank, banks replace long-term bonds with cash or demand deposits, thereby increasing the money supply.

Let's see how this works under a fractional reserve system. Suppose the government buys $10 billion worth of government bonds from commercial banks. Commercial Bank A now has $10 billion of additional cash, or demand deposits (checking accounts) on hand. Under current bank reserve requirements, the bank must maintain 10%, or $1 billion, on reserve, and can loan out $9 billion.

Let's suppose the $9 billion is lent to a retail outlet that uses the money to sell their products to the public. Upon receiving the loan, the company deposits $9 billion in its checking account at Commercial Bank B. Now Bank B has added $9 billion to its demand deposits, and it can lend 90% of it, or $8.1 billion.

You can see where this is going. Eventually, the $10 billion created by the Federal Reserve Bank's buying of government bonds causes the money supply to increase by $100 billion, according to the following formula:

M = $10 billion + $9 billion + $8.1 billion + $7.3 billion + ……

Or more generally,

$$M = \frac{1}{R} \times P$$

Where,

M = money supply
R = reserve requirement
P = net purchases of bonds by the Federal Reserve Bank.

Thus, if the Federal Reserve Bank purchases $10 billion in Treasury bonds, and the bank reserve requirement is 10, eventually $100 billion in new money is created:

$$M = \frac{1}{10\%} \times \$10 \text{ billion} = \$100 \text{ billion}$$

In this example, the bank money multiplier is 10. However, even though the bank reserve requirement today is 10%, the money multiplier has proven statistically to be around 4-5 in the real world. [Why is it less than 10?]

## MEASURING THE MONEY SUPPLY

There are several ways to measure the money supply, and economists differ on what constitutes money. In general terms, money is defined as funds available for immediate use to pay for goods, services, and debt reduction. The definitions are as follows:

**Monetary base**: Coins, currency (banknotes), and bank reserves (funds on deposit at Federal Reserve bank accounts)

M1 = monetary base + demand deposits and treasury checking accounts
M2 = M1 + money market funds + small time deposits
M3 = M2 + large time deposits (certificates of deposit)

Time deposits are a controversial measure of money, because technically they are not liquid funds. A penalty is imposed if time deposits are redeemed before maturity. Generally, M2 is regarded as the best broad measure of the money supply.

## CLASSICAL THEORY OF INFLATION

Price inflation — defined as a general rise in the price level, or a general decline in the purchasing power of the dollar — has always been the biggest challenge facing central banking since going off the gold standard. Examine figures 19.2 and 19.3 again. Note that during the classical gold standard, 1816-1914, there was an overall stability in the price level, excluding war time, and in fact, a slight deflationary trend as gold reserves were unable to keep up with the growth of real output or GDP.

However, since 1914, when the world gradually shifted away from the classical gold standard to a gold exchange standard (1921-71), and off the gold standard completely (after 1971), note the dramatic problem of inflation and occasional monetary crises. Without the discipline of gold, there appears to be a tendency to depreciate the currency, and the answer to any monetary crisis — whether it be a country unable to finance its debts (Mexico in 1982), a stock market crash (Wall Street in October 1987), a currency collapse (Asia in 1997), the imminent bankruptcy of a major hedge fund (Long Term Capital Management in 1998), a sudden drop in industrial output (January 2001), a terrorist attack (September 11, 2001), or mortgage credit crunch (2007-08) — the answer is always the same: A bailout with more liquidity.

Whether the Federal Reserve Bank is financing an ever-growing Leviathan or providing instant liquidity during a crisis, the result is a constant and often excessive expansion of money and credit, causing persistent inflationary pressure on prices. And this inflation occurs despite the efforts of the private sector to create new technologies and new production processes that increases output and decreases prices. There seems to be a constant battle between the inflationary forces of government and the deflationary forces of the market. Most of the time, the government seems to be winning.

## THE QUANTITY THEORY OF MONEY

What is the cause of persistent price inflation? Some public officials blame companies for raising prices, or labor unions for raising wages. But economists have long recognized the role of excessive monetary inflation as the chief cause of inflation.

The theory that links a rising price level with the money supply is known as the **Quantity Theory of Money**. The quantity theory has been recognized by economists including David Hume, David Ricardo, John Stuart Mill, Irving Fisher, and Milton Friedman. Friedman is famous for his statement, "Inflation is always and everywhere a monetary phenomenon."

The 20th century Yale economist Irving Fisher is often called the father of the Quantity Theory of Money, based on his mathematical formula for the Equation of Exchange:

$$M \times V = P \times Q$$

where

> $M$ = money supply
> $V$ = velocity of money
> $P$ = price level
> $Q$ = quantity of goods and services

The Equation of Exchange, $M \times V = P \times Q$, is nothing more than an accounting identity. The right-hand side of the equation represents the transfer of money, the left-hand side represents the transfer of goods. The value of goods must be equal to the value of money transferred in any exchange. Similarly, the total amount of money in circulation (M) multiplied by the average number of times the money changes hands in a year (V) must equal the dollar amount of goods and services produced and sold during the year (P x Q). If the money supply amounts to $500 billion in a nation, and this $500 billion circulates from one person to another an average five times a year, total spending in the economy equals $2.5 trillion all the goods and services produced and sold in that year, and the value of the total output purchased by consumers (or sold by producers) should equal $2.5 trillion. Hence, by definite $M \times V = P \times Q$.

The Equation of Exchange is not a theory, but a definition. However, Fisher turned the equation of exchange into a theory. He assumed that both V (velocity) and Q (real output) remain relatively stable, and changes in the price level must be directly related to changes in the money supply. As Fisher stated, "The level of prices varies in direct proportion with the quantity of money in circulation, provided that the velocity of money and the volume of trade which it is obliged to perform are not changed."[12]

Fisher advocated a "crude" Quantity Theory of Money. He believed that in the long run, inflation is neutral ("does not affect any real variable"). Real wages and real interest rates stay the same.

---

12 Irving Fisher, *The Purchasing Power of Money*, 2nd ed. (New York: Augustus M. Kelley, 1963 [1922]), p. 14.

## PRICE STABILIZATION OR MONETARY RULE?

As a Quantity theorist, Fisher argued that the Federal Reserve Bank's primary goal should be price stabilization. He was a leading advocate of the "stable money" movement in the 1920s. Since money supply figures as M1 or M2 were not available in his day, he focused on the price level. If the price level (P) was stable, Fisher concluded that there were no major economic problems. Fisher, in fact, is the father of price indexes. He wrote an entire book on the subject, and his indexes form the basis of today's Consumer Price Index and Producer Price Index.

Focusing strictly on broad price levels was Fisher's Achilles heel. Since prices were relatively stable in the 1920s, the New Era monetarists like Fisher thought everything was fine in 1929, even on the eve of the stock market crash and the Great Depression. Fisher failed miserably to anticipate the 1929-33 debacle. He was worth approximately $10 million at the height of the bull market on Wall Street (due to inventing today's equivalent of the Rolodex) but he lost it all and died a poor man.

Milton Friedman and modern-day monetarists focus on monetary aggregates (M2) more than the price level (P) to determine the condition of the national economy. Friedman in particular has advocated a **monetarist rule**, i.e., increasing the money supply (M2) at a steady rate equal to the average long-term growth rate of the economy. For example, if the U. S. has a long-term real growth rate of 4%, the Federal Reserve Bank should expand M2 at a 4% rate through open-market operations.

Modern-day Keynesians believe that monetarism is insufficient to stabilize the business cycle. In the equation of exchange, they emphasize that V (velocity) and Q (real output) may be unstable. Keynes argues that during a downturn or depression, an increase in M may not stimulate recovery because V will decline at the same time. It may be necessary to encourage Q (real output) through government spending and public works. Friedman disagreed with the Keynesians. According to his empirical studies, M and V tend to move together, not in opposite directions. As Friedman explains, "Empirically, however, it turns out that the movement of velocity tends to reinforce those of money instead of offset them. When the quantity of money declined by a third from 1929 to 1933 in the United States, velocity declined also. When the quantity of money rises rapidly in almost any country, velocity also rises rapidly."[13]

Austrian economist Ludwig von Mises also takes issue with Fisher and Friedman. They agree with the crude form of Fisher's Quantity Theory of Money, that if the quantity of money is increased, the value of the currency will fall. But by how much? Here Mises digresses from Fisher. He said the important question is, "Who gets the money first?" The creation of new money through open-market

---

13 Milton Friedman, *Monetarist Economics* (Oxford: Basil Blackwell, 1991), p.10.

operations does not enter the banking system equally, he said. Monetary inflation is "non-neutral" — it raises prices but it also distorts the structure of the economy. Or in the case of the Federal Reserve Bank lowering interest rates, the change in rates does not affect every part of the economy equally, but benefits some industries (especially the capital-intensive sector) more than others. In sum, monetary inflation causes an inflationary boom that is unsustainable and will eventually turn into a deflationary bust. This Austrian theory of the business cycle will be discussed in more detail in chapter 25.

## THE FEDERAL RESERVE BANK'S TARGETING OF INTEREST RATES

The second method the Federal Reserve Bank uses is targeting short-term interest rates through the Discount Rate and the Federal Funds Target Rate.

Historically, the Federal Reserve Bank has focused primarily on targeting interest rates. During World War II and the Korea war, the Federal Reserve Bank pegged interest rates to government securities to help finance the war efforts. The goal was always to keep rates low. In 1951, during the Korean conflict, the Federal Reserve Bank and the US Treasury reached an accord that allowed the Federal Reserve Bank to be independent.

Following World War II, Congress passed the 1946 Employment Act, which stated that the objectives of fiscal and monetary policy were to achieve full employment and price stability. Since then the Federal Reserve Bank's objectives have been three fold: maximize employment, stabilize prices, and moderate long-term interest rates. Initially, the Federal Reserve Bank worked to keep interest rates relatively low, and in fact, real interest rates (after inflation) were negative throughout the 1970s.

In 1979, under the direction of Federal Reserve Bank chairman Paul Volcker, the Federal Reserve Bank decided to focus primarily on monetary aggregates (the money supply) rather than to control interest rates. Milton Friedman had long argued that the Federal Reserve Bank should control the money supply, but all prices and interest rates should be set by market forces. In an attempt to control inflation, Volcker and his Federal Reserve Bank stabilized M2, following Friedman's Monetarist Rule, and allowed interest rates to fluctuate in an unregulated environment. Interest rates had been regulated prior to this time, and under conditions of double-digit inflation, short-term interest rates soared, with the prime rate reaching 21% in the early 1980s. Volcker was successful in breaking the inflationary psychology, but by 1982, the Federal Reserve Bank's tight money policy threatened the viability of foreign loans, and the Federal Reserve Bank had to abandon its liquidity squeeze during the Mexican debt crisis in the summer of 1982.

By the mid-1980s, with the deregulation of the banking system, the Federal Reserve Bank found that monetary aggregates were hard to measure, and since the dollar had become a worldwide currency, setting monetary targets proved ineffective and illusive in providing a stable market economy. From the mid-1980s on, Federal Reserve Bank policy sought to increase M2 on a fairly steady basis (a quasi-monetary rule), and focused primarily on setting short-term interest rates as a stabilization tool. Injecting new liquidity into the system is limited to monetary crises that might develop from time to time (as discussed earlier).

The Federal Reserve Bank now meets every six weeks, and all eyes are on the meetings held by the Federal Reserve Board and the Federal Reserve Open Market Committee. After the meeting, the Federal Reserve Bank issues a statement about the direction of the economy and inflation, and either raises, lowers or keeps the discount rate the same. The discount rate is the interest rate the Federal Reserve Bank charges member banks to borrow money from its 12 regional banks.

The Federal Reserve Bank also controls the Federal Funds Target Rate, which is the rate member banks charge for overnight loans to each other to help balance reserve requirements. The Federal Funds Rate fluctuates daily, while the discount rate varies only when the Federal Reserve Bank officially changes it. If the Federal Reserve Bank is concerned about inflationary pressure, it might raise the discount rate and Federal Funds Target Rate. If the Federal Reserve Bank is worried about a deepening recession, and even deflation, it may reduce these short-term rates. Or it may think the economy is in a stable non-inflationary growth pattern and not change rates at all.

It is important to point out that the Federal Reserve Bank does not have direct control over long-term interest rates, except indirectly through open-market operations, the trading of bonds. Long-term interest rates are determined by the supply and demand for credit in the mortgage and bond markets. it easier for the Federal Reserve Bank to manipulate short-term interest rates than long-term rates.

A major concern over the years has been the discretionary power of the Federal Reserve Bank to manipulate interest rates. Since the 1980s, Federal Reserve Bank interest-rate policy has been particularly volatile. For example, figure 19.5 shows the changes in short-term Federal fund rates during the Greenspan era, from 1987 until 2006.

As you can see, the Federal Reserve Bank changed monetary policy seven times during Greenspan's 19 years as chairman. The Federal Reserve Bank favored "tight money" (raising rates) when they feared a return of inflation (such as 1994 and 2000) and "easy money" (reduced rates) when they feared recession (1991, 2001) or various financial crises (the Asian currency crisis in 1997, the Russian economic crisis in 1998, the Y2K computer glitch threat in 1999, the terrorist attacks in late 2001, and the financial crisis of 2008).

**Figure 19.5.** *Short-term Federal Reserve Bank Funds Rate Changes, 1987-2009.*

## THE TAYLOR RULE

The **Taylor rule,** developed by John Taylor (Stanford University), is a guide to set the Federal funds target rate, based on the slack in the economy and the inflation rate.

If GDP is in line with the economy's capacity and inflation is equal to the central bank's target, then interest rates should be at a neutral level. If GDP outstrips long-run capacity, or inflation rises above the target level, rates should be set above neutral. If there is slack in the economy, or inflation dips, the central bank should ease and lower interest rates.

The Taylor rule is defined as,

The Federal Funds Target Rate = Inflation + Real equilibrium Federal funds rate + Inflation gap + Output gap

where

Inflation = CPI (average annual rate), and

Real equilibrium Federal funds rate = Federal funds rate consistent with long term full employment

Inflation gap = difference between current inflation and target rate

Output gap = Percentage difference between real GDP and estimated full employment level

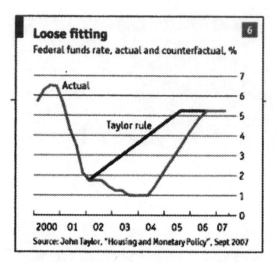

**Figure 19.6.** *Taylor Rule versus Federal funds rate, 2001-07.*
*Source: The Economist, October 18, 2007.*

Historically, the Taylor rule has worked out as follows: During the 1970s (under Arthur Burns and other chairmen), the Federal Funds Target Rate fell below the Taylor rule, and the result was inflationary. In the 1980s (under Volcker), the Target Rate exceeded the Taylor rule, and the effect was disinflationary. In the 1990s (under Greenspan), the Target Rate was close to the Taylor rule, and the result was relatively stable growth without much inflation. From 2000-2006 (under Greenspan and Bernanke), the Target Rate has been both below the Taylor rule, especially in 2004, when the Federal Reserve Bank pushed rates to 1%, and slightly above the Taylor rule by 2006. The result has been a period of volatility in the economy and the stock market.

## PRO'S AND CON'S OF INFLATION TARGETING

Another way to control inflation is through "inflation targeting." Recently, central banks have fallen back on this old Fisher concept, that is, setting a numeric price inflation goal (around 2% a year) for the public that the board would pledge to meet through its actions.

According to studies by Federal Reserve Bank members Ben Bernanke and Richard J. Mishkin, countries that have adopted "inflation targeting" have seen their core price inflation rates drop significantly: New Zealand since 1990; Canada since 1991; and United Kingdom since 1993. New Zealand in particular has been successful (see figure 19.5 below). Prior to inflation-targeting goals, the New Zealand price inflation rate varied from 10-15%. Now the CPI rate in New Zealand is less than 3% a year.

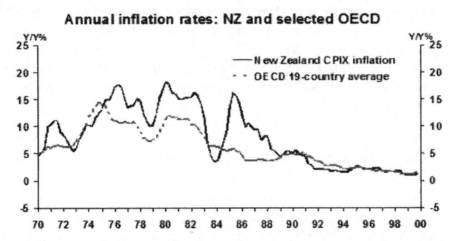

**Figure 19.7.** *Inflation Rates in New Zealand, 1970-2000, noting 1990, when inflation targeting began.*

The danger of "inflation targeting" is that the definition of inflation may be too narrow. During the 1920s, top economists such as Irving Fisher and John Maynard Keynes limited their definition of price inflation to general consumer or producer price indexes. By ignoring the impact of other prices, such as stocks and real estate, Fisher and Keynes failed to anticipate the 1929-33 crisis and were ruined financially.

Excessive price index aggregation may be the problem again if the Federal Reserve Bank only looks at the CPI or PPI to measure "inflation." If they ignore inflation of the money supply, commodities, or real estate, they may fail to anticipate a crisis in asset bubbles that could lead to a collapse in real estate or the stock market (2008-09 being an example).

## GOLD PRICE TARGETING: IS THIS THE GOLDEN MONETARY RULE?

Supply-side economists Art Laffer, Paul Craig Roberts, and Steve Forbes have urged central banks to use the price of gold as a monetary rule in deciding whether to change directions to control inflation. According to this formula, if the price of gold goes above a certain figure, say $900 an ounce, the Federal Reserve Bank should tighten the money supply and raise rates; if the price falls below $900 an ounce, the Federal Reserve Bank should expand the money supply and reduce rates. The goal is to maintain a stable gold price around $900 an ounce (or whatever the target price is).

There are several advantages and disadvantages: (1) the Federal Reserve Bank adopts an independent rule that takes the decision making out of the hands of authorities; (2) historically, gold has been a good indicator of global inflation, war, and crises; (3) a steady gold price demonstrates a stable economic and geo-political environment.

CHAPTER 19 • INFLATION, CENTRAL BANKING AND MONETARY POLICY

On the negative side: (1) other factors, such as technology, may influence gold price as well; (2) rising commodity prices do not necessarily lead to general consumer price inflation; and (3) there is the strong possibility of overshooting one's target. Gold doesn't just hit $900 an ounce and stay there. It may keep going to $1,000 or more before the Federal Reserve Bank can switch gears and impose a tight money policy. Or it may overshoot on the downside.

## THE FEDERAL RESERVE BANK AS LENDER OF LAST RESORT

The last and in some ways the most important role of central banking is to respond to banking and economic crises. The United States as an example. Since its inception, the Federal Reserve Bank has played a significant role in the following critical examples:

**1929-33**: While the Federal Reserve Bank made feeble attempts to provide liquidity to failing banks, it made its worse blunder by failing to bail out the official sounding Bank of the United States in December, 1930, causing another run on commercial banks.

**1982:** Mexican economic crisis. The U. S. government, in conjunction with the Federal Reserve Bank, bailed out Mexican foreign debt, and avoided a Mexican bankruptcy that would have been felt worldwide.

**1987**: stock market crash on Black Monday, October 19. For the inside story of how Federal Reserve Bank chairman Greenspan handled the 87 crash, see this excerpt of Bob Woodward's *Maestro*:
http://www.washingtonpost.com/ac2/wp-dyn/A1742-2000Nov11?language=printer

**1997**: Asian currency crisis. Southeast Asian countries had simultaneously linked their currencies to the dollar and inflated their currencies at high rates, causing a speculative run.

**1997:** Federal Reserve Bank arranged a $4 billion bailout with commercial banks for Long term Capital Management, a troubled giant hedge fund.

**1998:** Federal Reserve Bank helped bail out Russian economic collapse.

**1999**: Federal Reserve Bank injected billions in liquidity in anticipation of the Y2K computer glitch problem.

**2001**: On September 11, terrorist attacks in New York and Washington caused the Federal Reserve Bank to inject more than $30 billion in new liquidity to stave off a possible Wall Street panic.

**2008-09**: The mortgage credit markets collapsed, due to higher interest rates and falling real estate prices in previously hot markets, and the credit crunch spread into the stock market and the banking system. The Fed acted quickly cutting interest rates and injecting new money into the monetary system.

In every crisis, the solution has been the same: increase liquidity. Expanding the monetary reserves through open-market operations has always provided a short-term solution to the problem, whether it be a stock market crash, currency crisis, or a troubled corporation. Under emergency powers, the Federal Reserve Bank can even buy assets, such as index futures and mortgage securities, if that's what it takes to bail out Wall Street or a foreign market. Will there come a time when increasing liquidity fails to stem the tide and rebuild public confidence in the world banking system? Today's increasingly laissez faire financial environment coupled with an inherently unstable fractional reserve banking gives investors and institutions the capability of moving billions in assets by the click of a computer, or a telephone call. A global panic could eventually wreck havoc. Can any central bank counter such an unexpected event? Perhaps that is why most central banks are wisely holding on to gold, in the unlikely case that paper assets fail.

## WHAT ARE THE LESSONS: RULES, AUTHORITY, OR LAISSEZ FAIRE?

What is the ideal monetary policy? Which monetary system would best achieve the following goals:

1. Stable, low interest rates

2. Little or no price inflation, or perhaps even a gentle falling price level.

3. Low unemployment; ability to find or change jobs with little trouble or waiting.

4. No boom-bust cycle; steady economic growth and a rising standard of living, without the threat of recessions or depressions.

5. Widespread freedom to work, think, and act independently without fear of a monetary/economic crisis.

All monetary systems including the classical gold standard; the "golden rule" (a form of gold exchange standard); Friedman's monetary rule; interest rate targeting; and price inflation targeting have their strengths and weaknesses.

## ARE THERE BETTER BANKING SYSTEMS ABROAD?

According to the Global Competitiveness Report issued annually by the World Economic Forum, the US ranks 40th among banking systems in the world.

The world's most stable banks are in Canada, Australia and New Zealand. For example, Canadian banks received the highest ranking, 6.8, out of a possible 7.0 (healthy, with sound balance sheets). The lowest ranking of "1" means insolvent and a possible government bailout.

Canada, Australia and New Zealand almost completely avoided the subprime lending scandal and the home foreclosure mess, and have not required any bank bailouts so far in 2009.

Canada, Australia and New Zealand are all commodity-based economies, but are more conservatively managed than their American counterparts. They have far fewer commercial banks and the ones they do have are national in scope, with branches throughout the country, thus making them less susceptible to downturns. They have a large numbers of loyal depositors and a more solid base of capital. They are more tightly regulated than their US counterparts, more liquid and less leveraged.

## WHAT ABOUT FREE BANKING?

George Selgin and Lawrence White, two economists who advocate "free banking," are supportive of nationwide branching in the United States and elsewhere, which they argue would help stabilize the banking system.

But Selgin and White go further than encouraging nationwide branching. They define free banking as follows: "There is no government control of the quantity of exchange media. There is no state-sponsored central bank. There are no legal barriers to entry, branching, or exit of commercial banks....There are no reserve requirements....There are no government deposit guarantees."[14] The authors even suggest that banks should be allowed to issue their own currency. Competition would save the monetary world from excessive inflation and "wild cat" banking. Even Milton Friedman and Anna J. Schwartz are sympathetic to free banking: "Our own conclusion — like that of Walter Bagehot and Vera Smith — is that leaving monetary and banking arrangements to the market would have produced a more satisfactory outcome than was actually achieved through government involvement."[15]

Selgin and White point to the historical example of 18th century Scotland, which had a system of free banking, with complete free entry and minimal government regulation. But was it stable? Selgin and White say it was, Milton Friedman and Murray Rothbard say it wasn't.

14 George Seldin and Lawrence White, "How Would the Invisible Hand Handle Money?" *Journal of Economic Literature* 22 (December, 1994), pp.1718-19.
15 Milton Friedman and Anna J. Schwartz, "Has Government Any Role in Money," in Anna J. Schwartz, *Money in Historical Perspective* (University of Chicago Press, 1987), p. 311.

## SUMMARY

Chapter 19 covered these main points:

1.  Central banking came out of two needs: to provide a lender of last resort during a banking crisis, and to facilitate the growth of government power.

2.  Central banks grew out of national banks with special government monopoly power, such as the Bank of England, the Bank of France, and the Reichsbank in Germany.

3.  The international gold standard (1816-1914) provided a largely stable price level and strong economic growth, except in war times, when nations temporarily went off the gold standard.

4.  When countries went off the gold standard, they frequently depreciated their currencies and some engaged in outright hyperinflation, which was economically destabilizing. Examples include the hyperinflations of Germany in the early 1920s and hyperinflation of Yugoslavia in the early 1990s.

5.  Despite the positive case for the gold standard, nations gradually abandoned it in favor of a fiat monetary system because of gold's limitations on government power and its ability to inflate the money supply. Monetary authorities and academic economists also thought that a central bank could provide a more stable monetary environment than the classical gold standard. But their goal turned out to be more elusive than ever, with central banks failing to provide stability in the past hundred years. The Great Depression turned out to be the Federal Reserve Bank's greatest blunder.

6.  Since the Great Depression, central banks in major industrious nations have reduced the chances of another economic collapse, but have done so by encouraging monetary inflation. Inflationary boom-busts remain a common characteristic of modern-day economies.

7.  In the past 10 years, more central banks have focused on subduing price inflation as a monetary target. They use several tools to manipulate the economic system: open market operations, targeting interest rates, and acting as lender of last resort during a panic.

8.  Economists use the quantity theory of money to measure inflationary pressures on the economy. By increasing the money stock at a fairly steady rate, approximately equal to real economic growth, a nation can enjoy a growing non-inflationary economy.

9.  Rather than relying on the money supply or the price of gold, most central banks focus on targeting short-term interest rates as the primary monetary tool because in today's global economy it's difficult to monitor the size and effect of monetary aggregates.

10. Central banks still rely on their emergency powers of injecting liquidity and providing credit facilities during any kind of national or international emergency, whether it be a currency crisis, stock market crash, natural disaster, or major war.

## IMPORTANT TERMS

Assignats

Austrian economist

Austrian theory of the Bank of
  the United States cycle

Bank of France ("Napoleon's Bank")

Bank of North America

Bank of the United States (B. U. S.)

Bundesbank

Classical gold standard

Continental currency

Crude quantity theory of money

Currency crisis

Discount rate

Easy money

Elastic currency

Equation of exchange

Federal Reserve Bank

Federal Funds Target Rate

Federal Reserve Bank Act of 1913

Federal Reserve Board

Liquidity

Mississippi bubble

Monetarist rule

Monetarists

Monetary aggregates

Monetary base

Monetary policy

Money multiplier

Money supply

Multiplier

Napoleonic wars

Open market operations

Output gap

Peel Act of 1844

Price level

Federal Reserve Open Market Committee (FOMC)

Fiduciary money

Free banking

Gold exchange standard

Gold price targeting

Gold rush

Gold standard

Gold Standard Act of 1900

Greenbacks

Hard money

Hume-Ricardo specie-flow mechanism

Hyperinflation

International gold standard

Inelastic currency

Inflation

Inflation gap

Inflation targeting

Keynesians

Lender of last resort

Price stabilization

Quantity theory of money

Real equilibrium Federal funds rate

Real output

Rediscounting

Reichsbank

Reserve requirements

Second Bank of the United States

Stable money

Sound money

Specie flow mechanism

Sterilization of gold inflows/outflows

Real bills doctrine

Taylor rule

Velocity of money

Welfare state

## MILTON FRIEDMAN AND MONETARISM

### Name: Milton Friedman (1912-2006)

**Background:** Milton Friedman was the premier free-market economist of the 20<sup>th</sup> century. He grew up in New York, the only son of eastern European Jewish immigrants, and attended Rutgers University. In 1932, at the depths of the depression, he won a scholarship to study economics at the University of Chicago. There he met George Stigler, who became his lifelong colleague, friend, and counterpart, known as "Mr. Micro" in combating the Cambridge model of imperfect competition. (See Stigler's biography at the end of chapter 8.) At Chicago he met his future wife, Rose Director, sister of economist Aaron Director. They had two children. In the war years, he worked for the Treasury in Washington, D. C., and the Statistical Research Group at Columbia University, where he earned his Ph. D. He wrote for the National Bureau of Economic Research (NBER) and major professional journals. He won the highly sought after John Bates Clark Award (given to the brightest economist under the age of 40). In 1946, he began a long-career teaching at the University of Chicago. In 1967, he was elected president of the American Economic Association, and in 1976, he won the highest honor of the profession, the Nobel Prize.

**Major contribution:** Friedman's most important contribution was in monetary policy and history. In their major work, *A Monetary History of the United States, 1867-1960*, Friedman and his co-author Anna J. Schwartz demonstrated beyond doubt that government ineptitude by the Federal Reserve Bank, not free-enterprise capitalism, caused the Great Depression, when the Federal Reserve Bank allowed the money supply to collapse by over a third. This book marked the beginning of a counterrevolution—away from the Keynesian view that the welfare state and big government were beneficial. Now government was seen as the *cause* of our problems, not the cure, and monetary policy was important. Textbooks replaced "market failure" with "government failure." And Friedman made it happen. In other books, such as *Capitalism and Freedom* (1962) and *Free to Choose* (1980), Friedman advocated practical solutions to improve government policy and the standard of living, including a stable monetary rule to reduce inflation and the business cycle, freely floating exchange rates, elimination of the military draft, privatization of Social Security, and school vouchers to improve education. He retired from the University of Chicago in 1976, after winning the Nobel Prize, and he and Rose lived in San Francisco for the rest of their life. He was a senior researcher for the Hoover Institution.

445

**Quotations:** "The fact is that the Great Depression, like most other periods of severe unemployment, was produced by government mismanagement rather than by any inherent instability of the private economy....It is now widely agreed that the Keynesian proposition is erroneous on the level of pure theory....There always exists in principle a position of full employment equilibrium in a free market economy." (*Capitalism and Freedom*, 1962, p. 38).

## PROBLEMS TO PONDER

1. We noted that in 1900, the fixed exchange rate between the British pound and the U. S. dollar was £ equals $5. What is the exchange rate today? Whose currency has gained the most in purchasing power? What caused this dramatic change in the exchange rate?

2. Suppose the Federal Reserve Bank had adopted a strict Taylor Rule through the 1990s and 2000s. How would this be different from what the Federal Reserve Bank actually did? Would the Taylor Rule have been better for the economy?

3. If you were Federal Reserve Bank chairman, which monetary policy would you suggest the government adopt?

    A. Return to the classical gold standard

    B. A gold price targeting policy

    C. A monetary rule, i. e., increase the money supply (M2) at a steady rate equal to the long-term real GDP growth rate, and allow interest rates to fluctuate without interference.

    D. Price inflation targeting, i. e., set a maximum price inflation target, based on the Consumer Price Index or another broad-based price index, of 2% or less.

    E. Taylor rule.

    F. Switch to a more stable banking system (Canada, Australia, New Zealand).

## ADDITIONAL READING

* Andrew Dickson White, *Fiat Money Inflation in France* (Caxton Printers, 1974)
* Murray N. Rothbard, *What Has Government Done to Our Money?* 4th ed. (Ludwig von Mises Institute, 1990)
* Milton Friedman and Anna J. Schwartz, *A Monetary History of the United States, 1869-1960* (Princeton University Press, 1963)
* Mark Skousen, *The Economics of a Pure Gold Standard*, 3rd ed. (New York: Foundation for Economic Education, 1996)
* Richard Timberlake, *Monetary Policy of the United States* (Chicago: University of Chicago Press, 1993).

# Chapter 20

# FISCAL POLICY AND THE ROLE OF GOVERNMENT

*"Little else is required to carry a state to the highest degree of opulence from the lowest bar-barism, but peace, easy taxes, and a tolerable administration of justice."*

—ADAM SMITH (1776)

*"If everyone enjoyed the unrestricted use of his faculties and the free disposition of the fruits of his labor, social progress would be ceaseless, uninterrupted, and unfailing."*

—FREDERIC BASTIAT (1850)

In 1788, Benjamin Franklin wrote a friend expressing his desire to live in the 21st century. "I have sometimes almost wished it had been my destiny to have been born two or three centuries hence, for inventions of improvement are prolific, and beget more of their kind. The present progress is rapid," he said.[1]

Certainly Franklin, as a scientist and economist, would have been impressed with the technological advances in science and a $14 trillion American economy. He would have marveled at the uses of electricity, the advent of telephones, television, computers, cars, and airplanes, and the fact that almost all citizens, rich and poor, enjoy these material blessings. The American standard of living is perhaps a hundred times better today than the colonial days of the founders.

Franklin and the other founders of America would also be shocked by the size and scope of government. For the federal government alone, the budget amounts to $3.9 trillion for fiscal year 2009, or 27% of GDP; counting welfare transfers, government spending represents over 35% of GDP. The executive branch of government has 15 major cabinet departments. There are over a hundred federal agencies, and Washington has a national debt of $11.2 trillion, or approximately $36,000 per person.

Franklin said, "A virtuous and industrious people may be cheaply governed."[2] But today, government is anything but cheap, and most of us work until May to pay for federal, state and local taxes. The cost of the welfare/warfare state adds up.

---

1 *The Compleated Autobiography by Benjamin Franklin*, compiled and edited by Mark Skousen (Washington, DC: Regnery, 2006), p. 376.
2 *The Compleated Autobiography by Benjamin Franklin*, p. 189.

## THREE VITAL QUESTIONS IN POLITICAL ECONOMY

This chapter focuses on the role that government plays at the federal, state and local level and addresses three vital questions.

1. What is the proper role of government?
2. How should government be financed?
3. How can economic principles eliminate bad government and make good government better and maybe even smaller?

What is the proper role of government? Should there be limits to state authority? Most nations have moved far beyond the basic necessities of public expenditure, a legal system, and regulation. This chapter will focus on expansionary government policies, and how best to eliminate waste and state activities that harm economic performance.

## THE PROPER ROLE OF GOVERNMENT IN A FREE SOCIETY

There are three basic institutions that form the economic foundation of our nation: business, the nonprofit sector, and government.

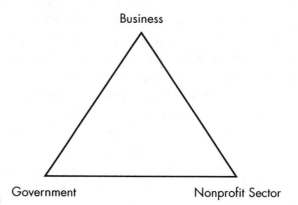

Business consists of firms and individuals producing goods and services and persuading individuals to buy them. Business represents the voluntary sector of the economy. Another non-compulsory part is the nonprofit sector, including churches, clubs, charities, foundations, and non-government organizations (NGOs). NGOs employ 10% of workers in the United States, 3% in France. Although both private for-profit companies and nonprofit organizations are subsidized directly through grants or indirectly receive tax breaks, neither institution can force customers to buy their products or contribute to their causes.

Government is different from the market and voluntary organizations. Government is based strictly on compulsion, or the threat of police power. Those who refuse to pay their taxes are subject to civil and criminal penalties. Many of the actions performed by government agencies would not be carried out if they had to be done in a voluntary society without the threat of sanctions. Why is force necessary?

To answer this question and determine the ideal size and scope of the state, let's begin with a *tabula rasa*, a blank slate that assumes no government at all. What activities require the creation of a force that imposes its will on citizens?

## THE LIBERTARIAN POSITION

Political philosophers have debated for centuries the legitimate purposes of government. Libertarians argue that the state should be strictly limited to serve one purpose only: to sanction and defend life, liberty, and property, John Locke's trilogy. As Frederic Bastiat states in *The Law*: "Law is the organization of the natural right to legitimate self-defense: to guarantee security of person, liberty, and property rights."[3] According to this view, in a free society, all citizens have the right to do anything they want as long as they do not act against others. Society has the right to organize a system of justice to defend rights; to pass laws against theft, stealing, lying, fraud, murder; and to defend against attacks from foreign foes. A legitimate state establishes the rules of law, a court system, and a police department to enforce the laws and protect citizens.

According to Bastiat, the law has been perverted by two causes, "stupid greed" and "false philanthropy." Greed causes the public to plunder the fruits of others: "The law takes property from one person and gives it to another." Bastiat gives many examples of legal plunger, "the seductive lure of socialism": slavery, tariffs, subsidies, progressive taxation, public schools, guaranteed jobs, minimum wages, a right to relief, and free credit.

Bastiat also warned against "false philanthropy." He opposed all forms of forced welfare, education and religion. Charity should be strictly voluntary, education should be private, and there should be no state religion.

To critics, Bastiat's position is nothing more than "the constable plus anarchy," to quote Thomas Carlyle. Adam Smith, the founder of modern economics, expanded Bastiat's list to include the following government programs:

3  Frederic Bastiat, *The Law* (New York: Foundation for Economic Education, 1996 [1850]), p. 2.

1. A well-financed militia for national defense.

2. A legal system to protect liberty and property, and to enforce contracts and payment of debts.

3. Public works — roads, canals, bridges, harbors, and other infrastructure.

4. Universal public education for youth.

## THE SOCIAL DEMOCRAT VIEW

For today's generation of social democrats, the purpose of government is three fold:

1. Allocation: to provide public goods that the private sector cannot or does not provide.

2. Distribution: to redistribute wealth and institute social justice.

3. Stabilization: to stabilize an inherently vacillating capitalist economy.

If a nation adopts all three of these purposes, there appears to be very few limits restraining government power.

However, most political philosophers agree with the first cardinal principle of legitimate government: The state should engage in beneficial activities that the voluntary market cannot achieve on its own. Milton Friedman states, "Government may enable us at times to accomplish jointly what we would find it more difficult or expensive to accomplish severally."[4]

──────────────── CASE STUDY ────────────────

## THE BATTLE FOR DIAMOND HEAD:
## A CASE OF MARKET FAILURE?

"Hawaii's great and beloved landmark . . . is too precious an asset to be sacrificed."

—*Honolulu Advertiser* editorial (1967)

Should government protect a local landmark from commercial development? Are zoning laws and other building restrictions necessary in a free society to stop "greedy" speculators and "fast buck" promoters from creating "urban sprawl" and unsightly commerce?

4  Milton Friedman, *Capitalism and Freedom* (University of Chicago Press, 1962), p. 2.

## THE STORY OF DIAMOND HEAD

Why does the string of high-rise apartments and hotels halt abruptly along the Diamond Head shoreline? In the late 1960s Diamond Head was the center of a fierce debate between developers and conservationists. After Hawaii attained statehood in 1959, tourists flocked to the paradise of the Pacific, and Waikiki Beach, sandwiched between downtown Honolulu and Diamond Head, became the hottest real estate market for resort hotels and condominiums. Honolulu newspapers ran photos of a rapidly disappearing view of Diamond Head, and local citizens became alarmed. A grassroots organization, the Save Diamond Head Association, was formed in 1967. This association demanded a halt to the construction of more skyscrapers along the shoreline.

Why save Diamond Head? In the nineteenth century, British sailors found crystalline rocks on its slopes and mistook them for diamonds. Conservationists argue that Diamond Head is a symbol of paradise, the mid-Pacific's most famous beacon. One visitor wrote during the debate, "I found Diamond Head, which has been declared a state monument, in imminent danger of turning into a monument for the fast buck, its craggy profile threatened with disappearance behind a palisade of tall concrete buildings."

Here's the conflict: Hawaii's natural beauty and delightful climate attracted millions of new tourists in the 1960s. The tourist boom in turn created a rush in real estate development. But the high-rise buildings, along with enormous billboards, blocked out the natural beauty that attracted tourists in the first place.

The fight between the developers and environmentalists came to a head in December of 1967. After a packed four-hour public hearing, five members of the nine-member city council voted against further commercial development of Diamond Head. The other four members abstained. Diamond Head was designated an official national landmark in 1968.

## IS THERE A MARKET SOLUTION?

Could the market have planned for a growing Hawaii without destroying its natural beauty and aloha spirit, or must government intervene?

Sometimes the market faces a difficult choice between two conflicting goals. In the case of Diamond Head, the conflict was the battle between development and those wishing to keep Diamond Head as a landmark symbol. Unfortunately events like these give capitalism a bad name. Could private developers have approached the issue differently? Could it have been in their own self-interest to limit the height of hotels and condos and preserve Oahu's historic skyline while still making a profit? Can progress and profit go together?

What do free-market economists have to say about zoning and building codes? In *The Constitution of Liberty*, F.A Hayek notes that local governments have often done a poor job of city planning and committing administrative despotism. He cites rent controls, zoning regulations, and excessive taxation as examples. Nevertheless, he does support "some regulation of buildings permitted in cities," including minimum building codes.[5]

Economists have often been critical of zoning laws as an infringement of property rights. Tom Bethell asserts that zoning laws hurt the poor, cause urban sprawl, and invite political corruption. He points to Houston as an example of a dynamic city which has grown without zoning regulations.[6]

If conservationists wanted to save Diamond Head, could they have purchased the shoreline property and kept developers out? Could they Save Diamond Head Association have raised the capital to stave off builders? Since 1953, Nature Conservancy, a nonprofit environmental organization with 900,000 members, has been buying and preserving land and habitats (now totaling over 10 million acres in the United States). Of course, such a plan would have been costly, with Waikiki property prices around $1 million an acre in 1967–68.

Property rights should include the right to be left alone from noise and air pollution. Should these rights also include the right of original owners to view Diamond Head?

---

5 F.A. Hayek, *The Constitution of Liberty* (Chicago: University of Chicago Press, 1960), p. 355. Hayek devotes an entire chapter to "Housing and Town Planning."
6 Tom Bethell, *The Noblest Triumph: Property and Prosperity Through the Ages* (New York: St. Martin's Press, 1998), pp. 297–99.

---

From an economist's point of view, government should not do what the market or voluntary organizations can do better. To have the state engage in activities that the private sector can do better is wasteful and redundant and violates the efficiency principle of economics.

What activities can government do better than the private sector? The list might include the following:

1. **National defense:** defend our borders.

2. **Justice system and rules of the game:** establish government as rule-maker and umpire; develop a court system, regulate against business fraud, deception, and bankruptcy; defend rights of minorities

3. **Public works:** build roads, utilities, bridges, and other forms of infrastructure that would be too costly for the private sector to provide.

4. **Monetary system:** stabilize the economy

5. **Social welfare system:** provide a safety net to assist those less fortunate.

What's interesting about this traditional list of government services is that these services can, to one degree or another, be provided by the private sector, and have historically been carried out by volunteer organizations. There have been private armies, and today many private police forces working for businesses and gated communities. Private firms have built roads, bridges, and even lighthouses. Private mints and banks have produced quality coins and banking services. For-profit firms have developed methods of self-regulation. Churches and charitable organizations have been providing welfare services to the needy for centuries, long before government took over this role.

## TWO CASE STUDIES IN LITTLE OR NO GOVERNMENT

Can the private sector do a better job than government?

The Articles of the Confederation were the basic law of the land from their adoption in 1781 until 1789, when they were replaced by the U. S. Constitution. The Articles limited the authority of the Federal government to conducting foreign affairs, making treaties, declaring war, maintaining an army and navy, coining money, and establishing post offices. But the government could not collect taxes, had no control over foreign or interstate commerce, could not force states to comply with its laws, and was unable to pay off the massive debts incurred during the Revolutionary War. States were already putting up trade barriers between states, striking a serious blow to free trade, and the economy struggled. After the U. S. Constitution became law, the United States flourished because of improved government finances, protection of legal rights, and free trade between the 13 states.

## "NO STATE" SOMALIA: THE COASE THEOREM IN ACTION

A modern-day example of too little government is Somalia. This country, located east of Ethiopia and Kenya, existed without any centralized governmental authority between 1991 and 2006. Lack of a centralized governmental authority made life in Somalia difficult. For example, drivers had to pass numerous checkpoints, each run by a different militia, on the way to the capital. At each of these "border crossings" vehicles were forced to pay an "entry fee" ranging from $3 to $300, depending on the value of goods being transported. To move cash a few miles between Mogadishu, Somalia's lawless official capital, and Jowhar, the seat of its transitional government, a local money-vendor had to pay $6,000 for an armored lorry, 30 gunmen, and three jeeps with heavy machine-guns.

Somalia pirates have attacked dozens of ships off the coast. The Somali shilling, the country's currency, has been used for years without the backing of a central bank or monetary reserves of any kind supporting the currency. Competing warlords vied for control of the countryside. There have been frequent collapses into civil war, leaving at least 300,000 dead. Only an estimated 15% of children attended school, compared to 75% in neighboring states.

A recent report by the World Bank indicates that despite these serious problems, the private sector flourished in Somalia during this time. This phenomenon vindicates the **Coase theorem**, named after Chicago economist Ronald Coase, which argues that in the absence of government authority, the private sector will step in to provide alternative services, depending on the transaction costs.[7] The central Bakara market began to thrive, where all kinds of consumer goods, from bananas to AK-47s, were readily sold, mobile phones and internet cafes prospered, and the US dollar became the currency of choice. Sharp inflation in 1994-96 and 2000-01 destroyed confidence in the three local currencies, and the US dollar became the common currency. But with no public spending, the roads and utilities began to deteriorate. Private companies did not step in to build roads and collect fees; the transaction costs were apparently too prohibitive. Access to public water sources was limited to urban areas. Although water was not considered safe to drink a private system extended to all parts of the country as entrepreneurs built cement catchments, drilled private boreholes, or shipped water from public systems in the city. 15 airline companies provided service to six international destinations, and airplane safety was inspected at foreign airports. After the public court system collapsed, disputes were settled at the clan level by traditional systems run by elders and with the clan collecting damages. But there was still no contract law, company law, or commercial law in Somalia.

7  See Ronald H. Coase, "The Problem of Social Cost," *The Journal of Law and Economics* 3 (October 1960), reprinted in *The Firm, the Market, and the Law* (University of Chicago Press, 1988), pp. 95-156.

The World Bank concludes, "The achievements of the Somali private sector form a surprisingly long list. Where the private sector has failed — the list is long here too — there is a clear role for government intervention. But most such interventions appear to be failing. Government schools are of lower quality than private schools. Subsidized power is being supplied not to the rural areas that need it but to urban areas, hurting a well-functioning private industry. Road tolls are not spent on roads. Judges seem more interested in grabbing power than in developing laws and courts. Conclusion: A more productive role for government would be to build on the strengths of the private sector."[8]

These two historical examples drive home two points: (1) Government plays a critical role in making the economy run efficiently; and (2) The private sector can do more than most people realize when it comes to social services. The question remains "Can the private sector provide public services better than a well-run government?"

Today citizens frequently lament the consequences of big government. They say that government is less a defender of freedom and more a Hobbesian leviathan that over regulates, over taxes us, and undermines prosperity. Limited government is often seen solely as a necessary evil. George Washington best summarized this cautious view: "Government is not reason; it is not eloquence; it is force! Like fire, it is a dangerous servant and a fearful master."

## THE VITALITY OF GOOD GOVERNMENT

The possibility of *too little* government, and the case of societies or countries that may not have enough good or legitimate government exists. In the never-ending battle against big government, it might be well to consider what constitutes "good government" as a measuring rod to see how far practice is from the proper role of the state.

James Gwartney, professor of economics at Florida State University and co-author of the Fraser Institute's annual *Economic Freedom of the World Index* has attempted to measure the right amount of government. Over the past 10 years, he and his colleagues have compiled an economic freedom index based upon five major areas of government activity in over 100 countries. The index is based on:

- size of government
- legal structure
- sound money
- trade
- regulation

8  Tatiana Nenova and Tim Harrford, "Anarchy and Invention: How Does Somalia's Private Sector Cope Without Government?" Public Policy Journal 280 (World Bank, November, 2004).

Gwartney was surprised by the importance of the legal structure as the key to peak performance of an economy. "It turns out," he said, "that the legal system — the rule of law, security of property rights, an independent judiciary, and an impartial court system — is the most important function of government, and the central element of both economic freedom and a civil society, and is far more statistically significant than the other variables."[9]

Gwartney points to a number of countries that lack a decent legal system, and as a result suffer from corruption, insecure property rights, poorly enforced contracts, and inconsistent regulatory environment, particularly in Latin America, Africa, and the Middle East. "The enormous benefits of the market network — gains from trade, specialization, expansion of the market, and mass production techniques — cannot be achieved without a sound legal system."[10]

## THE LEGITIMATE ROLE OF THE STATE

Milton Friedman identifies the legitimate roles of the state: "The scope of government must be limited. Its major function must be to protect our freedom both from the enemies outside our gates and from our fellow-citizens: to preserve law and order, to enforce private contracts, to foster competitive markets. Beyond this major function, government may enable us at times to accomplish jointly what we would find it more difficult or expensive to accomplish severally."[11] Adam Smith suggests that this "system of natural liberty" will lead to a free and prosperous society. As Smith declares, "Little else is required to carry a state to the highest degree of opulence from the lowest level of barbarism, but peace, easy taxes, and a tolerable administration of justice."[12]

Figure 20.1 suggests the symbol of a mountain peak to represent the division between the positive and negative role of government. In the diagram on the next page, we have on the vertical axis "socio-economic well being," some general measure of quality of life in a free and civil society. For empirical studies, economists might want to use changes in real per capita income, but this criterion may be too confining.

On the horizontal axis we have "government activity." At point O, we have zero government, and as we move along the horizontal axis, the size and scope of government activity increase. The ultimate extreme is the totalitarian regime, which institutes "total government," but I would hesitate to label this "100%" government, since no government can control all activity.

9  James Gwartney, quoted in Mark Skousen, "The Necessary Evil," *Liberty* magazine (September 2005), p. 32.
10 James Gwartney and Robert Lawson, *Economic Freedom of the World 2004 Annual Report* (Vancouver, BC: Fraser Institute, 2005), p. 35.
11 Milton Friedman, *Capitalism and Freedom* (University of Chicago Press, 1962), p.2.
12 Adam Smith, quoted in Clyde E. Danhert, ed., *Adam Smith, Man of Letters and Economist* (Exposition Press, 1974), p. 218.

## Optimizing Government Power

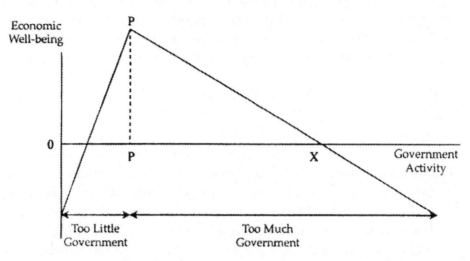

**Figure 20.1.** *The size of government in relation to economic well-being.*

## TOO LITTLE VS. TOO MUCH GOVERNMENT

Does the performance of a country under varying levels of state involvement looks like a mountain peak? As a society moves from zero government to point P, representing Smith's system of natural liberty, economic well-being increases to a peak performance. As government adopts a larger and more intrusive government, its growth diminishes, and can even turn negative if government becomes too burdensome and controlling. Too much government and the economy chokes. Too little, and it cannot function. Is there a Golden Mean?

The area to the left side of the mountain, point O (zero government) to point P (optimal government), constitutes "too little" government. This area graphically illustrates a nation spending too few resources on personal protection, property rights, and government administration. Increasing the size and scope of government activity initially leads to increased well-being, as measured by individual freedom and prosperity. Point P represents the right amount of government and the optimal amount of expenditures necessary to fulfill its legitimate functions. Point P forms a mountain peak, illustrating that this amount of government activity maximizes the well-being and performance of a civil society. This is the ideal of the minimalist state. Any point to the right of P represents too much government. In this area the central authority becomes a burden rather than a blessing. From the right of the peak a gradual downward slope indicates the decline in performance, even to the point X where government is so large and so intrusive that it results in negative performance of the economy and society.

## QUANTIFYING THE RIGHT AMOUNT OF GOVERNMENT

Can P, the optimal size of government, be quantified? Several economists have attempted to determine the ideal level of government spending as a percentage of GDP. In the 1940s, Australian economist Colin Clark said that the maximum size of government should not exceed 25% of GDP. Anything higher would hurt economic growth.[13] The work of the late Professor Gerald W. Scully (University of Texas at Dallas) for various countries suggests that the tax rate ought not to exceed 23%. World Bank economists Vito Tanzi and Ludger Schuknecht analyzed 17 countries during the period 1870 and 1990 and concluded that public spending in newly industrialized countries should not exceed 20% and in established industrialized countries not more than 30%. Any higher level results in diminishing performance.

How much faster could the United States and other nations have grown if they had enjoyed an optimal level of government, not exceeding 23%? According to Scully's econometric model, annual real GDP growth would have been 5.8% instead of 3.5%, the average from 1950 to 2004. Real GDP for the United States would have reached $37 trillion by 2004, more than three times greater than it was with the higher tax burden. In other words, the average American family would have more than three times as much real income today as the family actually has.[14]

Is optimal government (point P) the same for every country? Do the differences in culture and economic-sociological circumstances suggest more governmental influence in some nations than in others. If all nations were featured together on the diagram above would the various points P constitute a fairly narrow mountain range.

Almost every country in the world today is functioning to the right of Point P and could grow faster and enjoy a higher quality of life by reducing the size and scope of government. Countries from China to Ireland to Chile have demonstrated how dramatically the economy can improve by downsizing the state.-According to the latest surveys of economic freedom by the Fraser Institute, countries on average are becoming more free, and not surprisingly, the world's economic growth rate is rising. After noting that government represents 40-50% of GDP in most developed nations, Tanzi and Schuknecht conclude, "we have argued that most of the important social and economic gains can be achieved with a drastically lower level of public spending than what prevails today."[15]

13  Colin Clark, *Taxmanship* (Hobart Paper 26, Institute of Economic Affairs, 1964).
14  Gerald W. Scully, *Taxes and Economic Growth* (National Center for Policy Analysis, 2006).
15  Vito Tanzi and Ludger Schuknecht, *Public Spending in the 20th Century: A Global Perspective* (Cambridge University Press, 2000), p. 34.

## FIVE MEASURES OF GOVERNMENT ACTIVITY

To determine the degree of economic freedom for each country, the Fraser Institute draws upon five criteria:

1. Size of government: expenditure, taxes, and enterprises
2. Legal structure and security of property rights
3. Sound money (inflation)
4. International trade
5. Regulation of credit, labor, and business

Using these measures, the Fraser Institute created a single statistic of economic freedom for each country. Figure 20.2 demonstrates a strong correlation between economic freedom and a nation's standard of living, according to per capita income in purchasing power terms.

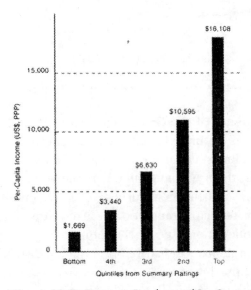

**Figure 20.2.** *Economic Freedom and Per Capita Income.*
*Source: The Fraser Institute, "Economic Freedom of the World," 2006 Annual Report, p. 22.*

## THE GROWTH OF GOVERNMENT

If the evidence supports the conclusion that less government leads to higher growth rates and a higher standard of living, why has government grown steadily since the early 20th century?

Figure 20.3 shows the expansion of government in major five countries.

**Figure 20.3.** *Growth of Government in Five Countries. Source:* The Economist.

There are two major causes of secular growth in government spending:

> **First, the influence of the Great Depression, 1929-33**: The Great Depression caused governments around the world, and especially in the West, to create a Welfare State providing social insurance, food stamps, and other social services to citizens. Keynesian theory, which gained credence during this period, favored an expanding state beyond the first purpose of government, i.e., to provide public goods that the private sector could not. These new functions focused on a stabilization policy. This policy attempted to: (1) stabilize an inherently vacillating capitalist economy; (2) to implement a distribution policy redistributing wealth; and (3) to create a system supporting social justice.

> **Second, the impact of war on the economy**: The size of government ballooned during World War II. War tends to make the state bigger. When a war ends the government does not return to the pre-war size.

## THE GROWTH OF THE WELFARE-WARFARE STATE: A SHORT HISTORY OF INCREASING GOVERNMENT AUTHORITY

Today government influences everything done by businesses, consumers, and investors. What were the origins of government-mandated social and health insurance, regulatory agencies, income taxes, and monetary controls?

Historically government has taken upon itself broad-based powers to pass laws, redistribute wealth, declare war, impose taxes, pass price and wage controls, regulate money, and provide welfare for its citizens. Edward Gibbon's classic work, *The Decline and Fall of the Roman Empire*, refers frequently to a variety of state actions: increased taxation, currency devaluation, welfare systems, subsidized food and housing, and artificially low interest rates. As a result of these policies, Rome suffered from war, bureaucracy, hyperinflation, bankruptcies, soaring relief roles, and economic collapse.

Chapters 18 and 19 discussed the critical role government plays in the monetary policy. The state has been equally involved in fiscal matters. State-run welfare originated with the passage of the Elizabethan Poor Law in 1601. This act imposed a compulsory tax to be levied on property owners in every English parish.

In the 1880s, state-run socialism became a popular perspective in Europe. Chancellor Otto von Bismarck implemented the first state-supported social insurance program paying retirement benefits in 1889 in Germany. The system was universally applied to all citizens and was funded with payroll taxes paid by the employee and the employer, along with contributions from the government. This program also included a disability benefit. Implementing the social insurance program was the beginning of modern welfare programs that are now common among developed countries.

Under the influence of the Fabian socialists, the first contributory pension program was enacted in 1911 in the United Kingdom. The pension program was endorsed by Winston Churchill, who described the social insurance principle as "bringing the miracle of averages to the rescue of the millions." During World War II, Sir William Beveridge in his famous Beveridge Report of 1942, proposed a comprehensive, universal scheme covering all the main social needs.

In the United States, the New Deal of President Franklin Roosevelt ushered in a variety of government programs. Roosevelt described the ideal social insurance system as one which provided economic protection from the cradle to the grave. The Social Security Act became law in 1935. This act provides benefits for retirement, disability, and death, and was, like Bismarck's program, applicable to all, rich and poor. The first taxes were collected on Social Security in 1937.

Medical coverage (Medicare) was introduced in the United States in 1965, along with Food Stamps and other "Great Society" programs of President Lyndon Johnson.

Regulatory agencies were created in the early 20th century. The Federal Trade Commission (FTC) was established in 1914 by President Woodrow Wilson to fight trusts and anti-competitive businesses, and to protect consumers against unsafe products. The Securities & Exchange Commission (SEC) began during the Great Depression to regulate the financial markets. The Food and Drug Administration was created in 1906 to protect public health and insure the safety of food. The mission of the Environmental Protection Agency (EPA), initiated by Richard Nixon in 1970, is to safeguard the natural environment (air, water, and land).

State and local governments and their agencies have grown even faster than the federal government. While the federal government employs 2.4 million workers, states now employ 12.2 million employees. State and local governments have increased dramatically their spending on public education, infrastructure, health and welfare for the poor, and prisons and law enforcement.

Total Federal and Combined State and Local Spending per Household.
1965-2007 estimate

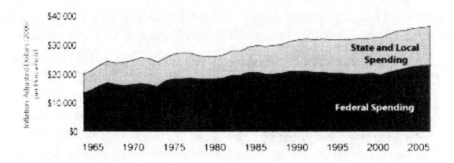

**Government Spending, All Levels, Nearly Doubled Since 1965.**

**Figure 20.4.** *The expansion of government spending at all levels since 1962. Source: http://www.heritage.org/research/features/budgetchartbook/charts_S/s11.cfm*

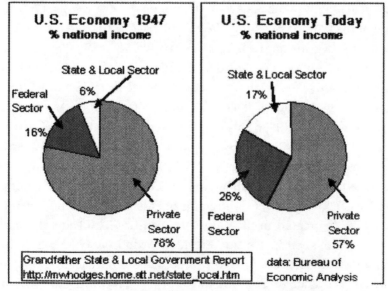

*Source: http://mwhodges.home.att.net/state_local.htm*

## PUBLIC CHOICE ECONOMICS AND GOVERNMENT POLICY

Government has grown rapidly in the past 100 years as a result of depression and war. Can the principles of economics help reverse the trend toward big government, so that the size and scope of the state reaches a point (P) that maximizes economic performance?

Public choice economics developed in the post-war era to help analyze the behavior of government and public officials. It was developed by James Buchanan and Gordon Tullock when they were at the University of Virginia in the late 1950s and early 1960s (now they are both at George Mason University). In their original work, *The Calculus of Consent* (1962), Buchanan and Tullock explained why government had a tendency to grow, and spend more than is taken in.

According to public-choice economists, politicians, like businesspeople, are motivated by self-interest. They set policies in order to be reelected, for example. By nature, politicians are encouraged by citizens to spend elaborately on local projects while discouraged by taxpayers to impose taxes to pay for those projects. Thus, without an outside discipline such as a balanced budget law, Congress is likely to run deficits. The incentives and discipline found in the marketplace are often missing from government. Voters have little incentive to control the excesses of legislators, who in turn are more responsive to powerful interest groups. As a result, government subsidizes the vested interests of commerce and other groups while it imposes costly, wasteful regulations and taxes on the public. As Peter Drucker states, by nature "government is a poor manager….It has no choice but to be 'bureaucratic'…..Modern government has become ungovernable."[16]

## MARKET PRINCIPLES FOR LEGISLATORS

What policy changes could be made to make government better and cheaper? Public-choice economists have made several recommendations:

1. **Constitutional rules of management**: Buchanan and Tullock make the case for limitations on government power and spending through balanced budget laws, requiring super majorities (two-thirds vote) to raise taxes; protecting minority rights (the Bill of Rights); and returning legislative and regulatory power to local governments; to increase competition among government units.

2. **Profit motive and incentives:** The private sector reinforces efficiency through the profit motive. By constantly searching for ways to eliminate waste and keeping costs down while fulfilling the needs of consumers,

16  See chapter 10, "The Sickness of Government," in Peter F. Drucker, *The Age of Discontinuity* (New York: Harper & Row, 1969), pp.220, 229, 23.

private companies maximize their profits and can grow. With increasing retained earnings, companies can invest in better products and better workers. Unfortunately, government often does not operate like a business. Government agencies and public employees frequently do not enjoy these incentives. Workers are paid a wage or salary irrespective of whether they serve the customer or not.

There are several ways government can improve. One way is to use **cost-benefit analysis**, if it can be measured. Another way is to **outsource or privatize** government services, and to require **competitive bidding** by private companies to build roads, run prisons, collect garbage, or educate students. Privatization is a growth industry among state and local governments. (We will discuss privatization more in chapter 27, "Development Economics: Capitalism, Socialism and Democracy.") Choice and competition give consumers more satisfaction, and keep costs down.

## THE WELFARE PRINCIPLE

3. **Welfare:** Another important principle of economics is known as the welfare principle, and it's equally important in the voluntary sector (private and non-government sectors) as in government. It suggests that a civil society should help those who need help, but not those who don't need help, and put a limit on so-called "entitlement" programs.

Churches and charities operate according to the welfare principle. For example, religious organizations such as Catholic Charities, the Welfare Program of the Latter Day Saints (Mormons), and the Salvation Army help the needy, but discourage assistance to the independent and the rich, or those who defraud the system. These organizations will ask those who seek assistance if they have exhausted other means of meeting their needs first. This may seem uncharitable, but to help every person, no matter what the circumstances, would easily overwhelm the scarce resources these charities have to help the truly needy.

For example, suppose that a minister announces one Sunday that instead of helping only the needy, the church has decided to help everyone in the congregation, rich and poor, healthy and unhealthy. In a gesture of good will he exclaims, "Come to us, one and all, and we'll pay your rent, your medical bills, your car payments." The audience is delighted with this new found liberalism at their church, and many members take him up on his offer. Word gets around and the next week, the pews are filled to overflowing with new members seeking assistance.

The minister is delighted with his new welfare program, which has filled up his church with smiling, grateful faces. A few weeks later, he stands up and announces, "Brothers and Sisters, because of the unprecedented demand for our new welfare services, we have suddenly run out of money. I'm sorry, but I'm going to have to ask you to dig deeper in your pockets and if you don't mind, triple your weekly contributions as we pass the plate. Thank you."

A universal welfare system that helps everyone, including the healthy and the financially independent, threatens the financial well-being of the charitable organization and forces members to pay substantially more in contributions. This program wastes valuable resources. Furthermore, helping the independent and subsidizing the rich create disincentives and destroys initiative. No church or charity could last long adopting a universal welfare plan.

## SOCIAL SECURITY AND MEDICARE: SAFETY NET OR DRAGNET?

Since Bismarck's introduction of social insurance in 1889, governments have offered a variety of welfare plans for virtually all their citizens. Instead of a social safety net for the needy, national welfare programs cover the entire population, rich and poor. In the industrial world, the vast majority of workers make mandatory payments into a government retirement system and medical program, which provides retirement income and medical assistance at or around age 65. Whether you are a pauper or a millionaire—at age 65, you qualify for Social Security (approximately $2,000 a month, depending on several factors) and a Medicare card to help pay your medical and hospital bills.

Not surprisingly the cost of Social Security and Medicare have risen steeply. FICA payroll taxes have jumped from 1% of wages/salaries in 1936 to 12.4% of income in 2009 (counting contributions by both employer and employee).

There is a growing threat of unfunded liabilities in Social Security and Medicare. As more Americans reach the age of 65, the cost of these universal plans could bankrupt the system unless taxes are raised sharply or benefits are cut. Figure 20.5 estimates the growing burden of Social Security and Medicare.

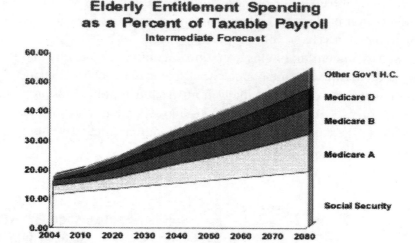

**Figure 20.5.** *The growing burden of Social Security and Medicare.*
*http://www.ncpa.org/pub/ba/ba476/*

## MEANS-TEST ALTERNATIVES

Not all welfare plans are universal. For example, Medicaid and the food stamp program in the United States are aimed for the needy only, and there is a means test to determine who qualifies.

Social Security and Medicare are compared with the Food Stamp program, as shown in figure 20.6 below.

Figure 20.6
U. S. SOCIAL WELFARE PROGRAMS

| Program | Total Coverage (in millions) | Current Recipients (in millions) | Total Annual Expenditures |
|---|---|---|---|
| Social Security | 153.8 | 52.2 | $491.5 billion |
| Medicare | 157.5 | 40.0 | $297.4 billion |
| Food Stamps | 23.9 | 23.9 | $ 27.0 billion |

*Sources: Social Security Adminstration; US Department of Agriculture; US Budget.*
*Coverage data for Social Security and Medicare is for 2002. All other data is for 2004.*

There is a difference between a universal plan (Social Security and Medicare) and a means-tested program (food stamps). Social Security and Medicare have become entitlements, and citizens have become benefit corrupted. They pay into these progams and they demand their benefits, whether they are rich or poor.

Food stamps are only provided to those who meet specific eligibility requirements. The food stamp program grew rapidly since it was introduced by President Lyndon Johnson as part of his Great Society program. Since the Welfare Reform Act of 1996 under President Bill Clinton, this program has started to shrink. A robust economy moves more people into the workforce where they are able to provide for their needs.

When the state violates market principles, such as accountability, welfare, and profit incentives, the result is shortages and surpluses, waste and fraud, cost overruns, corruption and privilege seeking, budget deficits, and excessive burdens in the form of taxes, and regulations. When the state adopts market principles, the result is greater efficiency, lower costs, and better service.

## SOCIAL SECURITY REFORM: LESSONS FROM THE PRIVATE SECTOR

The private sector often provides lessons on how government can better manage its finances. In particular, business offers a solution to the unfunded liability problem facing Social Security.

After World War II, major U. S. corporations added generous pension plans to the employee-benefit programs. These "defined benefit" plans largely imitated the federal government's Social Security program. Companies matched employees' contributions; the money was pooled into a large investment trust managed by company officials; and a monthly retirement income was paid out to company retirees age 65 and over, funded by the trust fund.

By the 1980s, corporate executives recognized a growing gap between contributions from current employees and income paid to retirees. They confronted huge unfunded liabilities as retirees lived longer than expected and money managers invested too conservatively in government bonds and blue-chip stocks. Newer employees were also angered when they changed jobs or were laid off and didn't have the required "vested" years to receive benefits from the company pension plan. Unlike Social Security, most corporate plans were not transferable. The Employment Retirement Income Security Act (ERISA), passed in 1974, imposed regulations on the industry in an attempt to protect pension rights, but the headaches, red tape, and lawsuits grew during an era of downsizing, job mobility, and longer life expectancies.

How to solve this problem of unfunded liabilities? The new corporate solution was a spinoff of another legislative invention—the Individual Retirement Account (IRA). The 401k rapidly became the business pension of choice, and there is no turning back. These "defined contribution" plans solve most of the headaches faced by traditional corporate "defined benefit" plans. Under 401k plans, employees, not companies, bear the burden of saving and controlling their own investments, by choosing among a variety of mutual funds. Corporations no longer face unfunded liabilities, because there is no guaranteed projected benefit. And workers and executives have complete mobility; they can move their 401k savings to a new employer or roll them over into an IRA.

According to the U. S. Labor Department statistics, many of the major Fortune 500 companies have switched to defined-contribution plans or hybrid "cash-balance" plans. New-economy companies, such as Microsoft, AOL, and Home Depot, offer 401k plans only, and older companies such as IBM are gradually making the switch.

The government's Social Security program faces the same dilemma that major corporations had to confront in the 1980s and 1990s: unfunded liabilities due to retirees living longer and the Social Security Trust Fund under performing. In fact, the underfunding of Social Security benefits is even more acute, because the government program is more a pay-as-you-go system than a true defined-benefit plan, where most of the funds go into a corporate managed trust fund. As a result, the unfunded liability, or payroll-tax shortfall, is expected to exceed $20 trillion over the next 75 years. To pay for so many current and future recipients, Congress has had to raise payroll taxes repeatedly, and according to some estimates, will need to raise them another 50% by the year 2015 to cover the growing shortfall. Few corporate plans require such high contribution levels.

Moreover, the Social Security trust fund invests only in T-bills and is poorly managed. Experts indicate the annual return on Social Security is 3.5% for single-earner couples and only 1.8% for two-earner couples and single taxpayers.

What is the solution? Using the accountability and welfare principles, Social Security could follow the model offered by business, and convert to a "defined-contribution" plan, gradually eliminating the unfunded liability burden. It should also consider means testing. There is no reason why the government should provide a retirement income to wealthy individuals who can provide for themselves, but the currently mandated participation in the government program gives all taxpayers, whether rich or poor, a sense of entitlement. Self-directed, defined-contribution plans would eliminate this entitlement mentality, while protecting the truly poor.

## DRUCKER'S SOLUTION:
## PRIVATE CORPORATIONS AS THE PREFERRED SOCIAL INSTITUTION

Peter Drucker (1909-2005), the management guru, has long argued that the large corporation should be the conduit through which economic stability and social justice would be established. According to Drucker, the private corporation is the only "free, non-revolutionary" alternative to big government, whether democratic, fascist, or communist. Only big business could afford to assume social responsibilities such as job security, training and educational opportunities, and other social benefits.

After the war, Drucker was hired as a consultant to General Motors, which gave him the opportunity to develop his thesis more fully. His exhaustive study of GM culminated in the 1946 publication of *Concept of the Corporation*. Drucker came to the unshakable conviction that the large corporation should be the "representative social institution" of the postwar period and that major American companies such as GM should take the lead in building the free industrial society.

Drucker maintains that a company is more than an economic entity. "Even more important than economics are the psychological, human, and power relationships which are determined on the job rather than outside it. These are the relationships between worker, work group, task, immediate boss, and management." A company's administrators have a moral purpose and social responsibility beyond making short-term profits. Drucker envisions the large corporation as the social institution, far superior to government in providing a retirement income, healthcare, education, childcare, and other benefits. He argues that corporate welfare should replace government welfare. Drucker acknowledges that such social activity could undermine economic performance, but he rejects Milton Friedman's admonition that business' only legitimate responsibility is to increase its profits. A lethargic government has created a "vacuum of responsibility and performance" which big business must fill.

## SUMMARY

1.  In today's world, there are three basic institutions that form the economic foundation of our nation: business, the nonprofit sector, and government.

2.  There are two views of government responsibility: the first is the libertarian view that limits government to protecting citizen's life, liberty, and property, and to engage in activities that the private sector cannot do efficiently. The second is the social democrat's view that government should be responsible for citizens' well-being by providing a welfare state, redistributing wealth and income through progressive taxation, regulating business, and intervening when economic crises arise.

3.  Most citizens favor government involvement in (a) national defense, (b) justice system establishing rules of law, (c), public works, (d) a monetary system, and (e) social welfare system providing a safety net to assist those less fortunate.

4.  There is an optimal level of government for each society, with a few examples of too little government, but more examples of too much government. War and the Great Depression are the two major causes of the excessive welfare/warfare state since the 1930s.

5. Public choice economists show how government can be reduced to its legitimate purposes and act more efficient through the adoption of market principles, such as (a) constitutional rules of management, (b) profit motive and incentives, (c) cost-benefit analysis, (d) competition, and (e) the welfare principle (not helping those who don't need help).

6. Means testing is an example of applying the welfare principle in government. Food stamps is means tested, but Social Security and Medicare are not. As a result, while the food stamp program has been fairly limited in its expansion, Social Security and Medicare have grown rapidly and created massive unfunded liabilities. Means testing, generous deductibles, and privatization would go a long way to limit the cost of today's welfare program.

7. The private sector business world is a better social organization than government to provide for the welfare needs of its citizens — retirement, healthcare, education, and other social needs.

## IMPORTANT TERMS

Allocation

Articles of Confederation

Coase theorem

Competitive bidding

Cost-benefit analysis

Defined benefit plan

Defined contribution plan

Distribution

Economic Freedom Index

Employment Retirement Income
Security Act of 1974 (ERISA)

Efficiency

Federal Trade Commission (FTC)

FICA taxes

Hobbesian leviathan

Individual retirement account (IRA)

Means testing

Non-government organization (NGO)

Occam's razor

Optimal government

Outsourcing

Privatization

Public choice economics

Securities & Exchange Commission (SEC)

Self-regulation

Stabilization

Unfunded liabilities

Vested benefits

Welfare Reform Act of 1996

## INFLUENTIAL ECONOMISTS

**James Buchanan, Gordon Tullock and Public Choice**
**Names: James Buchanan (1919- ) and Gordon Tullock (1922- )**

**Background:** James Buchanan and Gordon Tullock are considered the founders of the public choice school, an economic analysis of political decision making. Buchanan was born in Tennessee, and received his J. D. from University of Chicago. When he was an economics professor at the University of Virginia, he met up with Gordon Tullock and together in 1962 they authored *The Calculus of Consent*. Buchanan went on to teach at UCLA, Florida State University, and Virginia Polytechnic Institute. He won the Nobel Prize in economics in 1986. Today he resides at the Center for the Study of Public Choice at George Mason University.

Gordon Tullock was born in Illinois and received his J. D. from the University of Chicago in 1947. He has taught at the University of Virginia, Virginia Polytechnic Institute, and University of Arizona, and has published more than 150 papers and 23 books. He is the founding editor of the academic journal *Public Choice*. Currently he is a professor of law and economics at George Mason University.

**Major work:** *The Calculus of Consent* (1962), co-authored by James Buchanan and Gordon Tullock, and *Democracy in Deficit* (1977), co-authored by James Buchanan and Richard E. Wagner.

**Major contribution:** *The Calculus of Consent* (1962), co-authored by Buchanan and Tullock, is considered one of the classic works that founded the discipline of public choice, a melding of economics and political science. Their basic thesis is that the incentives and discipline found in free enterprise is frequently lacking in government. For example, legislators set policies in order to get reelection, which means a reluctance to raise taxes (unpopular) while supporting local spending projects (popular). The result is a tendency to run deficits. For government to act more responsibly, public-choice economists favor a series of constitutional rules to alter the misguided public sector into acting more responsibly. These rules include (1) imposing severe limitations on legislators' ability to raise taxes, such as requiring supermajorities (two-thirds vote); (2) protecting minority rights, such as the U. S. Constitution's bill of rights and state voting referendums; and (3) returning legislative and regulatory power to local governments, to increase competition among government units. Tullock also invented the

471

term "rent seeking" to describe monopolistic gains (excessive rents or high profits) obtained by a firm or industry through the use of political influence (lobbying) in excess of the competitive price. Examples include farm subsidies, taxi licensing, central banks, and radio and television licenses. Perhaps an alternative term would be "privilege seeking."

## PROBLEMS TO PONDER

1. What if government fails to provide essential activities? What does the "Coase theorem" say? Can you name examples of private initiative that have stepped in and replaced the void left by government failure?

2. After taking this course in economics, you are asked by the local newspaper to outline a formula for making your local government "better and cheaper" for its citizens. What recommendations would you make?

3. Social commentators Jean-Benoit Nadeau and Julie Barlow state that the French view the role of government differently from the Americans, and see a broader, more positive role of the state in their lives. According to Nadeau and Barlow, in the United States and Canada, "Federal governments are only supposed to do what the states or provinces, cities or towns, communities or neighborhoods or school boards can't, at least in principle, whereas the French see the State as responsible for the population's well being." (*Sixty Million Frenchman Can't Be Wrong*, p. 136). Which political philosopher is better, in your judgment, and why?

4. How would you respond to the following statement: "Government is better than private enterprise because it can provide services without a having to make a profit, and can therefore lower prices and pass on the savings to consumers."

5. Studies show that students who pay their own way through college (a) choose their majors sooner, (b) get better grades, and (c), graduate sooner. Using the principles you learned in this chapter, why is that?

6. Which of the following government activities fulfill, or violates, the principles of (1) profit incentive, (2) accountability, and (3), welfare?

   A. New York wants to build a new Jets stadium and wants to finance it with a tourist tax.
   B. The President proposes a national defense poll tax (flat fee for each resident) to pay for a war against terrorism. (Who benefits, who pays?)
   C. Medicare
   D. Social Security
   E. Food Stamp programs

7. In 2002, John Henry, a commodities trader worth $300 million and owner of the Florida Marlins baseball team, tried to push through the Florida state legislature a bill to tax cruise-ship passengers to help fund a new Miami ballpark. Which of the market principles discussed in this chapter does Henry violate? If you were a state legislator, how would you suggest the new ballpark be funded?

8. Name private alternatives to the following public services: (a) freeways, (b) food stamps, (c), public housing for poor people, (d) police, (e) firestation. In each case, which service performs better?

9. The U. S. Postal Service maintains a monopoly on first class mail. Could private enterprise (UPS, Fedex, etc.) provide this service? What effect would it have on the cost of a first class letter? In major cities? In rural areas? How would this new competition affect the financial strength of the US Post Office? Why are postal employees usually against "privatization" of the Post Office?

10. Do you agree or disagree with the following statement, and why? "It's hard enough for government to run essential services—police, courts, and utilities—let alone running hotels, steel mills, and airplanes. Government should not be the business of running businesses. It is beyond their expertise."

11. Observe in the next national elections how often the issues of Social Security and Medicare come up during the debates. Then note how often food stamps are raised as an issue. Why is it that Social Security and Medicare are hotly debated, but you don't hear much about food stamps?

12. Suppose a new "progressive" president comes into office and declares a war on poor nutrition, and introduces legislation into Congress called "Food Care." Since good nutrition is even more vital to each American citizen than health or retirement, he argues, the food stamp program should be expanded and universalized, like Social Security and Medicare, so that everyone qualifies for food stamps. The new "Food Care" program would be paid for through a special "food stamp" tax imposed through withholding. Thus, instead of 20 million Americans on food stamps, suddenly 200 million or more begin paying the "food stamp" tax and collecting food stamps, representing perhaps 10% of the household budget. What effect do you think this universal "Food Care" plan would have on the food industry? Would we face increased costs, red tape, abuse and fraud associated with the more comprehensive "Food Care"?

13.. In his 1971 book, *The Theory of Justice*, Harvard philosopher John Rawls (1921-2002) argued that the good society was the society in which a principal goal was the well-being of those worst off. Influenced by Rawls, economists have focused on the effects economic freedom and growth has one the bottom 10% or 20% of income earners. In the Fraser Institute's most recent "Economic Freedom of the World" report, professor James Gwartney concludes that the amount of income going to the poorest 10% of the population is much greater in nations with the most economic freedom and growth, than those with the least. However, the share of income by the poorest 10% of the population is unrelated to the degree of economic freedom in a nation. Why do you think this is?
(go to freetheworld.com/2007/1EFW2007ch1.pdf)

[Exhibits 1.9 and 1.10 from "Economic Freedom of the World" 2007 Annual Report]

14. Having studied this chapter, are there any flaws in this statement by Amnesty International's campaigns under "Poverty and Human Rights": "Everyone, everywhere has the right to live with dignity. That means that no one should be denied their rights to adequate housing, food, water and sanitation, and to education and health care." How can these "positive" rights be extended without violating individual "negative" rights, such as the taxation of property and income?

15. For years Paul Samuelson used the lighthouse as an example of a public good that the private sector could not provide. Then Chicago economist Ronald Coase found that the largest lighthouse in England, Trinity House, was originally privately funded and privately run, and paid for by imposing tolls on ships docking at nearby ports. To what extend can public infrastructure be funded and operated by private firms, such as roads, bridges, and water systems?

## FOR ADDITIONAL READING

- Milton Friedman, *Capitalism and Freedom* (University of Chicago Press, 1982 [1962]). Friedman's best philosophical work.

- Friedrich A. Hayek, *The Constitution of Liberty* (University of Chicago Press, 1960). This great Austrian economist outlines the case for a limited government.

- Vito Tanzi and Ludger Schuknecht, *Public Spending in the 20th Century: A Global Perspective* (Cambridge University Press, 2000). An excellent analysis of the growth of government, and the optimal size of government.

- Mark Skousen, "Persuasion vs. Force" (Eagle Publishing, 1992, 2006). www.mskousen.com/Books/PvF/pvftext.html.

# Chapter 21

# GOVERNMENT REVENUES AND TAX POLICY

*"A virtuous and industrious people may be cheaply governed."*

—BEN FRANKLIN (1778)

In 1990, President George H. W. Bush and the Congress pushed through a 10% luxury tax on yachts, jewelry, furs and expensive automobiles in an effort to reduce the national deficit. Congress and the President considered it a modest tax proposal and revenues were expected to close the deficit gap. Congress was certain the luxury tax would not affect the poor; the planned tax was a "Robin Hood" tax — a burden on the rich only.

But when the tax was imposed, the results surprised everyone. Wealthy customers stopped buying new yachts, or they bought foreign yachts or used ones, which were exempt from the 10% surcharge. Demand for new jewelry, furs and expensive cars suddenly declined sharply, demonstrating income elasticity (Chapter 5). As a result, middle-class employees who worked building luxury boats or selling in expensive jewelry stores were laid off. Now the middle class and the poor were being hurt by the tax. The public complained loudly.

Congress quickly repealed the tax on everything except automobiles. Even the "Robin Hood" tax on high-priced cars was phased out over a seven-year period after President Bill Clinton signed the *Small Business Job Protection Act* of 1996.

In 1997, President Clinton and Congress faced another tax policy question. Should the government reduce the capital gains tax rate on stocks, bonds, real estate and other assets sold during the year? Critics, especially Keynesians, warned President Clinton that the tax cut was simply a break for the rich and would hurt efforts to balance the budget. Others, known as "supply siders," argued that a capital gains tax cut would boost the stock market, stimulate economic growth, create jobs, and increase government revenues at the same time. President Clinton ignored his critics and joined with the Republican Congress to cut the capital gains tax rate from 28% to 20%. In 1996, the year before the tax rate cut went into effect, total taxes paid on assets sold was $66.4 billion. A year later, even though rates were lower, tax receipts jumped to $79.3 billion, and in 1998, they increased again to $89.1 billion. The capital-gains tax rate reduction played a major role in the 91% increase in tax receipts collected from capital gains between 1996 and 2000, and may have been partially responsible for the creation of numerous jobs and the financial wealth in the late 1990s.

These two stories raise some of the principal fiscal issues debated today:
- How should government programs be paid for?

- What principles of economics and tax theory can be employed to make government more efficient?

- Can the American theme of "cheaper and better" be applied to government, both on the national and local level?

- What is the best way to fund government operations without wasting too much of the taxpayers' money?

- Does it make any difference whether government raises funds by taxation, borrowing, or printing money?

## THE SCOPE AND SIZE OF TAXATION

This chapter addresses the issues of taxes and tax policy. Chapter 20 discussed the size and scope of government, and found that today's welfare state is expensive and large. Big government requires an extensive array of funding and bureaucracy. Figure 21.1 shows a breakdown of the federal government budget by spending and revenue for fiscal year 2006.

**Federal government spending**

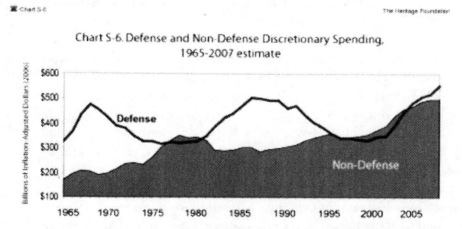

**Figure 21.1.** *Breakdown of Federal government spending and income, 1965-2007 (est). Source: U.S. Treasury..*

## Federal revenues

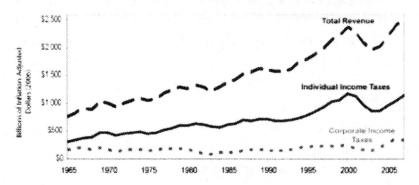

**Figure 21.1.** *Breakdown of Federal government spending and income, 1965-2007 (est). Source: U.S. Treasury..*

Government spends the majority of its income on its Social Security and Medicare programs, military spending, and interest on the debt. Where does government obtain the funds to pay for these programs? 32% comes from social insurance (FICA) taxes, 37.8% from individual income taxes, and 8.6% from corporate taxes.

The 50 states and local governments raise funds differently. According to the Tax Foundation, in fiscal year 2004, state and local governments earned revenues from the following:

| | |
|---|---|
| Federal government | 22.5% |
| Sales taxes | 19.1% |
| Property taxes | 16.8% |
| Individual income taxes | 11.4% |
| Corporate income tax | 1.8% |
| Non-tax charges and miscellaneous fees | 30.2% |

## THE ACCOUNTABILITY OR BENEFIT PRINCIPLE: USER PAYS

Which principles of economics can be applied to tax policy? Consider the following:

1. **Accountability or benefit principle, also known as "user pay"**: This principle links the taxpayer and the beneficiary. The importance of accountability or the "benefit principle" was discussed in Chapter 6, "Supply and Demand." In the marketplace, individuals who benefit from a good or ser-

vice usually pay for the good or service. If someone consume a loaf of bread, he is usually the one who pays for it. If he buy two loaves of bread, he pays twice as much. A clear link exists between the user and the payer. Because of this benefit principle, consumers are more accountable. Because they are paying out of their own pockets, they are more aware of prices and value. They notice differences in prices and shop around between stores. Knowing that consumers have choices, retailers keep prices as low as they can to attract shoppers. Thus, waste is minimized at all levels. The users are cost-conscious.

One of the hurdles facing the benefit principle is that users are sometimes difficult to isolate. For example, it's fairly easy and convenient to identify who uses major thoroughfares, and impose a toll to link users and payers, but what about city driving, where tolls would be inconvenient and cause traffic backups? Linking those who use a service and those who pay for the service is much more difficult.

Suppose the city government wishes to improve the roads in the city. Who should pay for the improvements? Everyone? Or just those who drive the roads? According to the accountability principle, those who use the road should pay for the road. Establishing toll roads ensure that those who use the road pay for the road since only those who use the roads pay the toll fee. Yet a solution of this type would be impractical within city limits. Perhaps a more pragmatic solution would be to impose a sales tax on gasoline. The government could impose a 5 cent local gasoline tax on all pumps within the city limits, and use the proceeds to fix the roads. The solution must take into account both the need for revenue and the means by which revenue will be collected.

Of course, if one town imposes a user fee and the next town does not, drivers might leave their own town to fill up at a cheaper pump. This sometimes happens when local communities charge different sales taxes. But usually the convenience and time cost will outweigh the tax differences.

Suppose the state government creates a Fish and Game Department to control and monitor hunting and fishing in the state. How should the state pay for this department, according to the benefit principle?

A. From general revenues.
B. From a real estate tax.
C. From fishing and hunting licenses.

What is the correct answer, based on the benefit principle?

## CASE STUDY

## SAN FRANCISCO BUILDS A NEW BASEBALL STADIUM: WHO PAYS?

Sports stadiums are traditionally built by the city using public funds, and leased to private sports franchises. But there have been a few exceptions to this traditional funding process. In 1962, Dodger Stadium was built by Walter O'Malley and his investors, who moved the Dodger franchise from Brooklyn, New York. The stadium remains privately-owned and is one of only a handful of baseball stadiums not named after a corporation

The most recent example of private funding is AT&T Park, home of the San Francisco Giants. After Bay area voters rejected four separate ballot initiatives to raise public funds to replace the windy and poorly attended Candlestick Park, Peter Magowan, a Safeway and Merrill Lynch heir, teamed up with local investors to buy the club. With the help of a $155 million Chase Securities loan, Magowan built the new stadium for $319 million. The owners also acquired huge sponsorships from Pacific Bell, Safeway, Coca-Cola, and Charles Schwab. The Giants did receive a $10 million tax abatement from the City, but otherwise, the funds were privately acquired.

The private ballpark has been a huge success, selling a league-leading 30,000 season tickets for the 41,000-seat stadium. Most home games are sold out. Other team owners, whose stadiums are heavily subsidized, are skeptical of private ownership and funding, but a dozen team owners have visited the park operations to study what they've done.

## ECONOMISTS CRITICIZE PUBLIC FUNDING OF SPORTS STADIUM

Perhaps the recent interest in private funding of major league sports facilities has been influenced by studies by professional economists attacking publicly subsidized sports arenas. In *Major League Losers*, Mark Rosentraub of Indiana University studied stadium financing in five cities and concluded that pro sports produces few jobs and little ripple effect in the community. Sports facilities take away businesses from suburban entertainment and food venues, and often leave municipalities with huge losses. A Brookings Institution study came to similar conclusions. After reviewing major sports facilities in seven cities, Roger G. Noll (Stanford) and Andrew Zimbalist (Smith College) found they were not a source of local economic growth and employment, and the net subsidy exceeded the financial benefit to the community.

A more complex example involves funding for the local police department. Most citizens of the community would reject the idea that only those who use the police (in responding to an emergency or an accident) should pay for the service. The police provide security for everyone, and everyone should pay something for the benefits of police protection. The cost of security could be achieved through a tax on retail sales, real estate, or some other general revenue system. More creatively, each household could be charged an annual "insurance" fee to cover police, fire protection, and other public services.

Fire protection has traditionally been a public service supported by taxes, but some localities, looking forward to save money, have considered contracting with a private company to provide fire service. Scottsdale, Arizona, for instance, has had a private, for-profit fire protection service since the city was first incorporated. The company, Rural/Metro, has received nationwide praise for its service and efficiency. Similarly, thousands of rural communities across America are served by volunteer fire departments, representing another kind of private-public partnership.

## THE FAIRNESS PRINCIPLE

2.  **Equity or fairness principle**: Another cardinal principle of taxation is that taxes should be simple, fair and equitable. Variations on this theme are:

    A.  Those who benefit more should pay more.
    B.  Taxes should be paid according to "ability to pay" or the "sacrifice" principle.
    C.  Similar taxpayers should be taxed equally.

## PROGRESSIVE TAXATION: SHOULD THE RICH PAY MORE?

Both A and B above are often used to justify progressive taxation, that is, charging a higher tax rate on the rich. According to the benefit principle, if the rich benefit more from government services, justice demands that they should pay more. If they have a larger house or own a factory that employs thousands of workers, do they not benefit more from the services of police, public utilities, and national defense? Probably so.

To understand progressive taxation, look at the case below. Suppose the tax schedule is such that the following holds:

| Income Level | Taxes Paid |
|---|---|
| $50,000 | $10,000 |
| $100,000 | $15,000 |

In the above example, the tax structure meets the "benefit" test. The more income, the more benefits—ergo, the more tax. Yet the above example demonstrates regressive taxation! The tax rate on the individual earning $50,000 is 20%; the tax rate on the $100,000 income earner is 15%. To make it progressive, the $100,000 income earner would have to pay more than $20,000.....If, for instance, he paid $30,000 in taxes, he would be paying a tax rate of 30%. That would be progressive.

The most practical policy would be to make the tax rate proportional. A **flat tax** would always fit the benefit principle. If you earn more income, you pay more tax. The benefit principle does not necessarily justify progressive taxation. It only means that the more income you earn, or the greater your wealth, the more tax you should pay. But progressive taxation requires not only that benefits increase with income but they increase more rapidly than income.

What about the ability-to-pay or sacrifice principle? The sacrifice principle reflects the idea that each taxpayer should face "equal sacrifice" or burden in paying for government. British economist A. C. Pigou argued that higher income individuals are so much better off than lower income people that they should sacrifice more. The ability to pay argument is similar. It's easier for the rich to pay than the poor, because only a small percentage of their income goes toward essential needs. Thus, a rich person can more easily afford or can more easily sacrifice his income than a middle class or poor person, and therefore, a progressive tax is appropriate.

But even the "ability to pay" argument may be ambiguous or fuzzy. With higher incomes, households often increase their standard of living by purchasing a larger home or buying a new car, and it may be just as much a burden for the rich person to pay a 20% tax rate as a middle class or poor person. Admittedly, wealthier people tend to have more "surplus" wealth, but should this essential source of capital investment and charitable contributions be taxed away?

Perhaps 19th century economist John Ramsey McCulloch (1789-1864) was right when he concluded: "The moment you abandon…the cardinal principle of exacting from all individuals the same proportion of their income or their property, you are at sea without rudder or compass, and there is no amount of injustice or folly you may not commit."[1]

3.  **Efficiency:** The third principle of fiscal responsibility is that taxes should be administered efficiently, easily and fairly, and they should minimize the distortion of economic activity. To fulfill the efficiency goal, most economists agree that:

    A.  Taxes should be easy to understand and administer;
    B.  Taxes should be low enough to reduce the incentives to smuggle and engage in black markets; and

---

1  J. R. McCulloch, *Taxation and the Funding System* (1845), quoted in Walter J. Blum and Harry Kalven, Jr., *The Uneasy Case for Progressive Taxation* (University of Chicago Press, 1953), p. 45.

C. Competition between tax jurisdictions is good (state by state, country by country), because if one jurisdiction increases taxes too much, citizens of one area will move or shift businesses to another. This healthy tax competition keeps taxes from getting out of hand.

Probably the most efficient tax system is a flat tax imposed across the board, with few exemptions.

--- CASE STUDY ---

## CIGARETTE TAXES, BLACK MARKETS, AND CRIME: LESSONS FROM NEW YORK CITY'S 50-YEAR LOSING BATTLE

by Patrick Fleenor

As large state government budget gaps have opened in the past year, lawmakers across the country are turning to cigarette taxes for added revenue. 26 states raised cigarette tax rates in 2002, and more hikes may be on the agenda during state legislative sessions in 2003. Proponents of high cigarette taxes portray them as innocuous levies that improve public health. Yet those taxes have long been known to have a dark side. Since the first state cigarette taxes were imposed in the 1920s, black markets and related criminal activity have plagued high-tax jurisdictions. Such activity has proven to be resistant to law enforcement curtailment efforts.

Thanks to recent city- and state-level tax hikes, New York City now has the highest cigarette taxes in the country—a combined state and local tax rate of $3 per pack. Consumers have responded by turning to the city's bustling black market and other low-tax sources of cigarettes. During the four months following the recent tax hikes, sales of taxed cigarettes in the city fell by more than 50% compared to the same period the prior year.

New York has a long history of cigarette tax evasion. Former governor Malcolm Wilson dubbed the city the "promised land for cigarette bootleggers." Over the decades, a series of studies by federal, state, and city officials has found that high taxes have created a thriving illegal market for cigarettes in the city. That market has diverted billions of dollars from legitimate businesses and governments to criminals.

Perhaps worse than the diversion of money has been the crime associated with the city's illegal cigarette market. Smalltime crooks and organized crime have engaged in murder, kidnapping, and armed robbery to earn and protect their illicit profits. Such crime has exposed average citizens, such as truck drivers and retail store clerks, to violence.

The failure of New York policymakers to consider the broader effects of high cigarette taxes has been a mistake repeated across the country in the stampede to maximize tax revenue from this demonized product. Too often, policymakers do not consider these effects in the erroneous belief that people do not respond to government-created economic incentives. The negative effects of high cigarette taxes in New York provide a cautionary tale that excessive tax rates have serious consequences—even for such a politically unpopular product as cigarettes.

*Patrick Fleenor has been chief economist of the Tax Foundation and senior economist at the Joint Economic Committee of Congress.*

Source: Cato Policy Analysis No. 468, February 6, 2003. Reprinted with permission.

## DIFFERENT KINDS OF TAXATION

Throughtout history, state officials have developed dozens of ways of taxing their citizens. Major forms of taxation are presented below:

1. **Poll tax.** The "poll" or "head" tax is defined as a set amount of tax, say $100, imposed on all citizens to help pay for government services. The poll tax is consistent with the market "law of one price" (see Chapter 6). For example, The price of bread is a fixed amount. Everyone pays the same amount, no matter whether they are rich or poor, white or black, male or female.

    A minimum head tax may be appropriate for every resident of a country to pay for basic government services, but it would not be an appropriate tax to cover all state expenditures, since wealthier citizens tend to benefit more from government services than poorer citizens.

    Many Southern states enacted a poll tax that discriminated against the poor and minorities in their right to vote. This practice was outlawed in 1964 by the 24th Amendment to the U. S. Constitution.

2. **User fees.** User fees are an excellent way to finance government services efficiently in accordance with accountability or benefit principles. Examples include electric and water utilities; garbage collection; bus fares; state fishing licenses, toll roads, and entry fees to museum and parks. According to this principle, those who fish should pay for the state agency that takes care of lakes and rivers. Why should citizens who don't visit the park have to pay for those who do? Moreover, when you have a market fee to visit a part, park visitors are likely to take greater interest in keeping the park like it is.

Similarly, museums should charge visitors to see the exhibits. If the museum is "free," all the taxpayers end up paying, including a large number who never visit the museum. Free entrance to museums may cause overuse, and failure to appreciate their value. User fees ensure that those who use services pay for those services and may provide the added benefit of ensuring that users take more interest in and care of the service.

─────────────── CASE STUDY ───────────────

## USING TOLL ROADS TO REDUCE CONGESTION

By Robert Poole, Jr.

Los Angeles (August 31, 2006) – How bad is your commute going to get? A lot worse. Traffic delays will increase 65 % and the number of congested lane-miles on urban roads will rise by 50 % over the next 25 years.

Los Angeles, home to the nation's worst traffic today, will continue to have the longest delays, with trips during peak hours taking nearly twice as long as they do when roads are free-flowing. But LA will not be alone. Several cities face the dubious honor of having Los Angeles-like gridlock.

By 2030, drivers in 11 metro areas – Atlanta, Baltimore, Chicago, Denver, Las Vegas, Miami, Minneapolis/St. Paul, Portland, San Francisco-Oakland, Seattle-Tacoma, and Washington, D.C. - will be stuck in daily traffic jams that are as bad as or worse than today's infamous bottlenecks in Los Angeles, according to a new Reason Foundation study. In those cities it will take at least 75 % longer to make a trip during peak hours than off-peak periods. So, for example, a trip that is supposed to take 30 minutes would take over 52 minutes.

Today, only four cities (LA, Chicago, San Francisco, and Washington, D.C.) experience travel time delays of even 50 %. But because road capacity is failing to keep up with demand and population growth, the Reason study finds that a whopping 30 cities will be experiencing daily delays that make rush hour trips 50 % longer than off-peak journeys. Los Angeles and the other 11 cities listed above will be joined in congestion purgatory by Austin, Boston, Bridgeport-Stamford (CT), Charlotte, Dallas-Fort Worth, Detroit, Houston, New York City-Newark (NJ), Orlando, Philadelphia, Phoenix-Mesa, Riverside-San Bernardino, Sacramento, Salt Lake City, San Diego, San Jose, Tampa-St. Petersburg, and Tucson.

Even in smaller cities, traffic congestion will worsen substantially over the next two decades. Boise, Idaho, for instance, will see its congestion more than double and Albany, New York, will experience almost triple its current congestion levels.

To prevent or relieve the severe congestion that seriously threatens the economy, U.S. freeways and arterials need 104,000 additional lane-miles of capacity (about 6 % more than current lane-miles), at a total cost of $533 billion over 25 years, according to the Reason report.

The good news is that this investment would save drivers a stunning $7.7 billion hours annually. Current traffic - and the looming congestion - can be reduced with just a fraction of the money we are already committing to transportation projects.

The $533 billion price tag breaks down to more than $21 billion per year, but that figure represents just 10 to 15 % of the money projected to be spent as part of the highway program over the next 25 years. This amount is also 28 % of planned spending in existing long-range plans of major urban transportation agencies, and works out to about $2.76 per hour of delay saved, just 1/10 the cost of federally funded transit lines.

"Contrary to conventional wisdom, it is possible for America to 'build out' of severe congestion, and it is relatively inexpensive to do so," said David Hartgen, the study's lead author and a professor of transportation studies at the University of North Carolina at Charlotte. "The bottom line is that if we want to reduce congestion, or even simply maintain our current levels of traffic, we will need to seriously reexamine what is presently planned for our roads."

"We will be spending billions on transportation projects in the coming years, but after population growth and increased truck traffic our congestion will actually be far worse, if we spend those billions as now planned," said Robert Poole, director of transportation at Reason Foundation and the study's project director. "We must prioritize and focus our transportation funding where it can do the most good. We know the vast majority of Americans need to drive cars and that truckers haul 80 to 90 percent of our economy's goods. Unless we take significant action to add capacity where commuters have shown they want and need it, our economy and quality of life will take a pounding from congestion."

The study highlights how a number of metro areas seem to be ignoring the commuting and transportation trends in their areas. Instead of reducing congestion by adding capacity on the roads and freeways used by taxpayers, many planners are crossing their fingers and hoping to get people to shift behavior and leave their cars behind. In highly decentralized Los Angeles, where just 4.8 percent of people use transit to commute, over half of the long-range plan money - $66.9 billion – is being spent on transit. The transit spending is nearly identical to the money ($67.7 billion) needed to relieve the area's severe congestion.

Likewise, cities such as San Jose and Salt Lake City, where transit's share of commuting is less than 3% are committing over half of their long-range transportation funds to transit.

"Increased capacity is the most important need. Toll roads and variable-priced lanes, traffic signal optimization, improved accident management, and – where justified by ridership numbers – better transit, should all be part of our transportation solution mix," Hartgen added. "It is vital that all transportation projects be evaluated on cost effectiveness and hours of delay saved."

The Reason Foundation study uses national congestion figures, detailed transportation data provided by 32 cities, and sophisticated, state-of-the-art computer modeling to calculate traffic statistics for 403 U.S. cities.

2.  **Excise taxes (federal and state).** Governments are increasingly turning to excise taxes on specific products to raise revenue. These include taxes on gasoline, highway tires, trucks, firearms, bows and arrows, telephone/water/utility fees, international airport ticket, airport security fee, air freight, wagers, foreign insurance policies, coal sales tax, crude oil tax, jewelry, hotel tourist tax, alcohol and tobacco taxes, and other goods and services.

    Government officials often ignore the secondary effects of excise taxes, and think they can raise the excise to any level. As demonstrated in the case of the cigarette tax, smuggling and black markets can occur when the excise is excessive. The effect of excise taxes on the supply and demand for these products is shown in Figure 21.2.

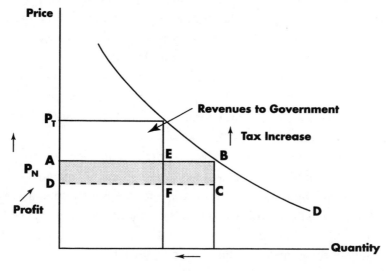

**Figure 21.2.** *Effect of excise tax on a product.*

As Figure 21.2 indicates, the price increases by the amount of the tax. This increase has three effects:

1. The increase reduces the demand for the product. Consumers cutback use as a result of the higher price.

2. The higher price cuts into the profit margins of the suppliers/producers. Normally, a higher price increases profit margins, but in this case, the new revenues go to the government, and the profits to the producers falls from rectangle ABCD to rectangle AEFD, a substantial drop.

3. Producers/suppliers see an increase in incentive to go underground and sell their product in the black market, where the tax is avoided altogether.

In many ways, the excise tax causes an artificial market for the product, with an unusually high price in relation to its cost of production. Thus, the profit margin may increase from, say, 10% under normal conditions, to 30% in the black market. If the established producers do not enter this black market, new suppliers will enter the market—illegal suppliers who engage in high risk criminal activity (smuggling, theft, etc.) to take advantage of the system.

Authorities can respond in two ways: (1) increase penalties and police resources to discourage black markets and the illegal activity; (2) reduce or eliminate the excise tax. The latter is the preference of most economists, but politicians are reluctant to give up excise taxes as a lucrative source of revenue.

3. **Sales taxes (state and local).** These are sales levies as a percentage of the price of retail purchases. Most foreign countries impose an indirect sales tax known as a Value Added Tax (VAT), discussed below. In the United States, sales taxes are the most popular way to raise state and local revenue, ahead of taxes on property and income taxes, corporate income taxes, and user fees.

Five states (Alaska, Delaware, Montana, New Hampshire, and Oregon) do not collect general sales taxes at the state level. The remaining 45 states rely heavily on sales taxes, and have a tendency to increase the rate whenever there's a fiscal crisis (usually caused by a recession). Rates have risen from 3% to 4% to 5% ……States with the highest tax rates are: California (8.25%), Mississippi (7.0%), New Jersey (7.0%), Tennessee (7.0%), Rhode Island (7.0%), Minnesota (6.9%), Nevada (7.5%), and Washington (6.5%). Many cities and counties have the option of imposing an additional local option sales tax. For instance, in Tennessee some cities add as much as 2.75%. Nevada's sales tax varies by county and can be as high as 7.75%.

Most states exempt prescription drugs from sales taxes. Some also exempt food and clothing purchases and a few also exempt non-prescription drugs.

4. **Value Added Taxes (VAT).** Value added taxes, a type of indirect sales tax, are most popular outside the United States, especially in Europe, Latin America, and Asia. In some countries, including Australia, Canada, New Zealand and Singapore, this tax is known as "goods and services tax" or GST; in Japan the tax is known as "consumption tax." VAT is an indirect tax, in that the tax is collected from the seller rather than the consumer. VAT is intended as a tax on consumption; exports are usually not subject to VAT, and foreigners are given a refund when they leave the country.

VAT was invented by a French economist in 1953. Maurice Lauré, joint director of the French tax authority (TVA) imposed a VAT on large companies, which was extended over time to all business sectors. In France, this tax is the most important source of state revenue, accounting for approximately 46% of state revenues. The VAT is levied at each stage in the economic chain of supply (recall our 4-stage model of production), and thus is a tax on the value added to a firm's products. Most of the cost of collecting the tax is borne by business, rather than by the state.

VAT was invented because very high sales taxes and tariffs encourage cheating and smuggling. By imposing a relatively small amount of tax at each stage of production, the incentives for tax evasion decline. VAT is a hidden tax, allowing the government to charge more without a citizen rebellion. As a result, European governments have been able to raise the total sales tax bill to double digit rates, much higher than American tax rates, which are single digit. Today, while US state sales tax rates are between 5-8%, European VAT schedules are between 15% (Luxembourg) and 25% (Sweden and Norway). It's 19.6% in France, and 17.5% in the UK. One of the debates going on in the European Union (EU) is an attempt to unify the tax system. This would be a mistake, however, based on the "efficiency" principle of taxation, mentioned above. Tax competition between countries, especially in the EU, which has freedom of trade, is good because it keeps countries from raising rates, and losing business to other countries with lower tax rates.

5. **Real estate taxes.** Taxes are imposed almost universally on the value of land, houses, and commercial buildings. In the United States, property taxes are used primarily to finance local government and public schools. Some cities and counties impose two real estate assessments, one for general purpose spending by the local government unit, and another specifically for public schools.

Real estate taxes are collected annually and are assessed as a percentage of assessed value. Some states prohibit the assessed value from rising by more than 1-3% a year until the property is sold. Proposition 13 in California is the most famous example of a citizens revolt against high property taxes. The "tax revolt" initiative, led by Howard Jarvis, was passed by the voters of California in 1978, resulting in a cap on property tax rates, reducing them by an average of 57%. Prop 13 also required a two-thirds majority in both legislative houses for future increases, including income taxes, but Californian legislators found ways to raise other levies to offset the decline in property taxes. Under Proposition 13, the real estate tax on a parcel of residential property is limited to 1% of its assessed value, until the property is resold, when the cap comes off. This has resulted in artificial imbalances, as the tax rate for identical houses in the same neighborhood may vary greatly.

6. **Tariffs and duties**. Import duties were the primary source of revenue in the beginning of the United States, but after the introduction of other sources, especially taxes on income and real estate, import duties have declined sharply. Figure 21.3 shows the history of duties in the United States since 1820. Despite temporary setbacks, such as the "Tariff of Abominations" in 1828 and the Smoot-Hawley Tariff in 1930, the downward trend in import duties is clear. At the beginning of the republic, tariffs represented nearly 100% of the new government's revenues. By 1910, they brought in only 50% of revenues, and today they are less than 2% of the government's budget. International free trade, as advocated by Adam Smith, David Ricardo, and other economists, has gradually won the day, not only in the United States but in many countries around the world.

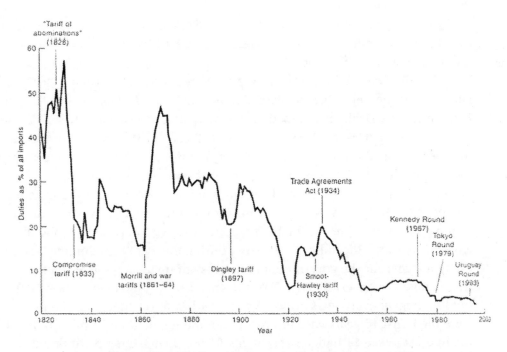

**Figure 21.3.** *Tariffs and Duties on the United States since 1820.*

However, protective tariffs still remain in many foreign countries, and demands even in the United States to raise the cost of imported foreign goods. Protectionism is an excuse to encourage import substitution, so that products such as automobiles and appliances are built domestically instead of imported. For example, some governments in Latin America impose a 300% duty on imported U. S. cars in order to encourage their citizens to buy cars built in their own country. Not surprisingly, any time import duties become prohibitive, smuggling and black markets are not far behind. (For more information on protectionism and free trade, see Chapter 26.)

6. **Federal, state and local income taxes.** Nothing has fueled the growth of government more than the introduction of the income tax and withholding. In the 19th century, the United States relied on internal taxes on distilled spirits, sugar, tobacco, and corporate bonds; excise duties on gold and jewelry; and tariffs on imported goods.

In 1862, during the Civil War, President Abraham Lincoln introduced the first income tax, and later added sales, excise, and inheritance taxes. The income tax was abandoned after the war in 1872. It was renewed in 1894 under President Grover Cleveland but was ruled a "direct" tax and thus unconstitutional by the U. S. Supreme Court. In 1913, the 16th Amendment was passed, making the individual and corporate income tax a permanent part of the U. S. tax system. At the time it was introduced the maximum tax rate was 7%, and the first $20,000 was exempt. Only the very rich had to file a tax return.

War changed all that. To finance the Great War, the maximum tax rate was raised to 17% in 1916 and rose to an astonishing 77% by 1918, when the Federal government collected over $1 billion.

After the war, the tax rate was gradually reduced, until it fell to 24% by 1929. Hoover and the Republicans raised the rates to 25% in 1930, then to 63% in 1932. Under the New Deal, rates leaped to 79% on marginal income in 1936, 81% in 1940, finally reaching 94% in 1944–1945. In 1944, President Franklin Roosevelt seriously proposed a "maximum wage" of $25,000 by requiring a 100% tax rate on any earned income above $25,000 a year. Congress wisely rejected his proposal.

World War II witnessed the beginning of income tax withholding at source of payment, a convenience invented in Europe and imitated in the United States. (Milton Friedman, known for his libertarian views, proposed withholding while working as a tax official for the Treasury during the war.) Withholding, like the VAT, made it easier for the government to increase dramatically the level of taxation on the average citizen. Prior to World War II, only the rich paid income taxes. After withholding began, everyone started paying. In 1940, fewer than 15 million tax returns were filed. Just 10 years later in 1950, the number would be 53 million. In 1939 the income tax raised $1 billion in revenues. 16 years later this tax would raise $19 billion.

With marginal tax rates exceeding 90% in the 1950s, clever tax accountants developed a variety of tax shelters and loopholes to evade progressive taxation, including the establishment of foundations, charitable trusts, and offshore companies. Some economists and public officials recognized the inefficiency of such a system, and recommended a sharp curtailment in the tax rates. The Kennedy-Johnson Tax Cut of 1964 reduced the highest tax rate to 77%, and this was followed by a tax cut passed under President Ronald Reagan that reduced the rate to 50% (considered the largest tax cut in U. S. history) and to 28% under the Tax Reform Act of 1986, which at the same time sharply curtailed a variety of tax shelters. Rates were then raised to 31% under George H.W. Bush, and increased again in 1993 to 39.6% under Bill Clinton. In 2001, George W. Bush pushed through a tax cut that reduced the maximum rate to 36%, but Barack Obama has proposed raising the maximum rate back up to nearly 40% for wealthy Americans.

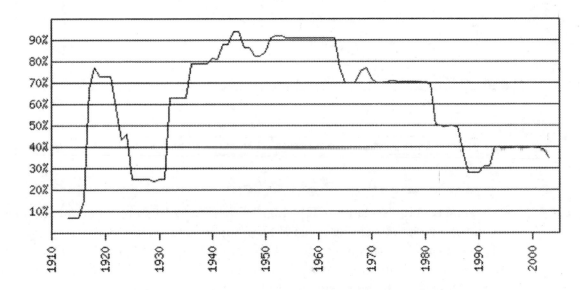

**Figure 21.4.** *Top marginal tax rate in the United States, 1913-2007.*

## INCOME INEQUALITY, THE LORENZ CURVE, AND PROGRESSIVE TAXATION

One of the traditional arguments for progressive taxation is that it helps reduce income inequality, an alleged flaw of unfettered capitalism. John Kenneth Galbraith reflects the conventional critical view: "The modern market economy accords wealth and distribution income in a highly unequal, socially adverse and also functionally damaging fashion."

Critics of market capitalism are often misled by conventional measures of economic well-being, in particular the Lorenz curve, which measures income distribution. See figure 21.5 below. The Lorenz curve measures the percentage of a nation's total income as earned by various income classes. Typically, there are five income groups. In the United States, the highest fifth (the highest income earners) usually receive 40% of the nation's income, while the lowest fifth (the lowest income earners) receive around 5%. Using the Lorenz curve, U.S. income appears to be poorly distributed, now the extreme case among the major industrial countries, says Galbraith.

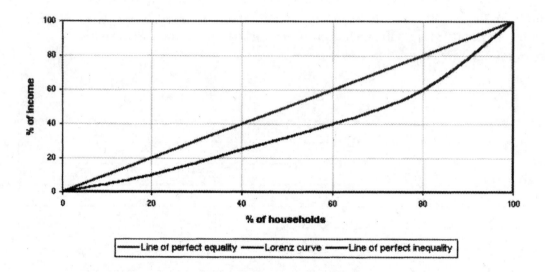

**Figure 21.5.** *The Lorenz curve.*

Some economists criticize the Lorenz curve for establishing an unfair and misleading guide for measuring social welfare. Suppose, for example, that an ideal line of perfect equality is achieved on the Lorenz curve, i.e., the highest fifth (top 20% of income earners) only receive 20% of the nation's income, while the bottom fifth (lower 20%) increase their share to 20%. What does this ideal mean? The ideal means that everyone—the teacher, the lawyer, the plumber, the actor—earns the same amount of income!

Since few economists think equal wages for everyone is an ideal situation, why do they think moving toward perfect equality on the Lorenz curve is appropriate? Moreover, the Lorenz curve is unable to show an increase in a country's standard of living over time. It merely measures distribution of income. To measure changes in social welfare, economists often rely on a second measure—average real income. This, too, has its shortcomings. A single statistic may mask improvements in an individual's standard of living over time.

For example, average real income in the U. S. shows hardly any change since the mid-1970s. Yet other measures of well-being, such as consumer expenditures and the quantity, quality, and variety of goods and services, show remarkable advancement over the past 20 years. (See Chapter 1 for statistics on consumer spending.) Consumer spending rose a dramatic 40% per person in real terms during this period. As Professor Richard Vedder says, "How many Americans in 1975 had VCRs, microwaves, CD players, and home computers?"

Stanley Lebergott, professor emeritus of economics at Wesleyan University, has probably done more work in this area than anyone else. Instead of relying on general measures such as average real income, he uses a more common sense approach—looking at individual consumer markets in food, clothing, housing, fuel, housework, transportation, health, recreation, and religion. For example, he developed the following table to measure improvements in living standards from 1900 to 1970, largely before the United States established a comprehensive welfare system.

| Percentage of Households with | Among all families in 1900 | Among poor families in 1970 |
|---|---|---|
| Flush toilets | 15% | 99% |
| Running water | 24% | 92% |
| Central heating | 1% | 58% |
| One (or fewer) occupants per room | 48% | 96% |
| Electricity | 3% | 99% |
| Refrigeration | 18% | 99% |
| Automobiles | 1% | 41% |

**Figure 21.6.** *Living Standards in the United States, 1900-70.*
*Source:* Stanley Lebergott, *The American Economy* (Princeton, 1976), p. 8.

In *Pursuing Happiness*, Lebergott demonstrates repeatedly how American consumers have sought to make an uncertain and often cruel world into a pleasanter and more convenient place. Medicines and medical facilities, artificial lighting, refrigeration, transportation, communication, entertainment, finished clothing—all have advanced living conditions. Regarding women's work, Lebergott notes that weekly hours for household and family chores fell from 70 in 1900 to 30 by 1981. The 1900 housewife had to load her stove with tons of wood or coal each year and fill her lamps with coal oil or kerosene. Central heating also reduced the housewife's tasks. She no longer had to wash the carbonized kerosene, oil, coal, or wood from clothes, curtains, and walls, nor sweep floors and vacuum rugs as persistently. Automated and mechanical equipment reduced her labor further. . . . By 1950, over 95% of U.S.

families had central heating, hot water, gas, electric light, baths, and vacuum cleaners. Regarding water, Lebergott comments, "The average urban resident consumed about 20 gallons of water per day in 1900. Rural families had virtually no piped water; 55 percent did not even have privies. . . . By 1990, American families devoted two days' worth of their annual income to get about 100 sanitary gallons every day, piped into the home."[2]

## THE DECLINE OF PROGRESSIVE TAXATION

What has led to the decline in progressive taxation? These are some of the major factors leading to the decline in progressive taxation:

1. The triumph of entrepreneurship and the efficiency of capitalism: Cutting taxes stimulates economic growth by transferring more funds from the public sector, which is viewed as relatively inefficient and wasteful, to private enterprise, which is considered more productive. Growth in the economy was seen as more beneficial to the average worker than wealth redistribution schemes. Even John Kenneth Galbraith admitted: "It is the increase in output in recent decades, not the redistribution of income, which has brought the great material increase, the well-being of the average man."[3]

2. With extremely high tax rates (at one point exceeding 90%), cutting the marginal tax rates is easier than reducing the average tax rate. In fact, by closing loopholes, the reduction in marginal rates can be offset by higher revenues and an average tax burden that remained the same, or at times increased. Cutting marginal tax rates has been a win-win situation for the politicians. Ironically, while cutting marginal rates, tax revenues rose.

3. Cutting marginal tax rates was considered a good trade off for eliminating wasteful and inefficient tax shelters, and reducing black-market activities. Excessively high rates had caused armies of accountants and attorneys to discover new ways to circumvent the tax man. As a result, huge new industries had been created just to avoid the tax man, in real estate, foundations and offshore trusts. Reducing the marginal rate decreased the need for these tax shelters, as many people decided it was more economical to pay the tax.

The tremendous growth of an untaxed underground economy is one measure of excessive taxation and bloated, over-regulated government. Some economists estimate that half of Italy's economy goes unreported. Growth in the underground economy should be a danger sign that taxation is excessive. Unfortunately, too often

---

2 Stanley Lebergott, *Pursing Happiness: American Consumers in the Twentieth Century* (Princeton University Press, 1993), pp. 117-118.

3 John Kenneth Galbraith, *The Affluent Society* (Boston: Houghton Mifflin, 1958), p. 96.

it is taken as a sign that government needs to get tough and crack down more on those who aren't paying their "fair share" by increasing the penalties and hiring more IRS agents to catch tax evaders. However, many economists suggest that imposing a reasonable tax rate would make evasion less attractive and would result in increased voluntary compliance. After studying the underground economy, economist Dan Bawley concludes, "If the IRS were to make every effort to collect every cent due to it, America would be much closer to being a police state."[4]

4.  Taxes distort incentives. Economists William Baumol and Alan Blinder ask, "What would happen if we tried to achieve perfect equality by putting a 100 percent income tax on all workers and then divided the receipts equally among the population? No one would have any incentive to work, to invest, to take risks, or to do anything else to earn money, because the rewards for all such activities would disappear."[5]

Supply-side economist Paul Craig Roberts argues that high progressive taxes are a strong disincentive to work, to invest, and to save. "Supply-side economics brought a new perspective to fiscal policy. Instead of stressing the effect on spending, supply-siders showed that tax rates directly affected the supply of goods and services. Lower tax rates mean better incentives to work, to save, to take risks, and to invest. As people respond to higher after-tax rewards, or greater profitability, incomes rise and the tax base grows, thus feeding back some of the lost revenues to the Treasury. The saving rate also grows, providing more financing for government and private borrowing."[6]

Supply-siders refer to the Laffer curve to support their contention that cutting marginal tax rates can stimulate economic growth and under the right circumstances, increase tax revenues. The Laffer curve (figure 21.7) shows a theoretical relationship between the tax level and revenues. It was invented by Arthur B. Laffer, a former economics professor at the University of Chicago and University of Southern California, who drew the famous curve on a napkin at a Washington, D. C., restaurant in the late 1970s to prove his point that tax cuts could potentially increase tax revenues.

According to the Laffer curve, an increase in tax rates will generate more revenues as long as the rates aren't too high. But once the tax rate exceeds X, further increases in tax rates will shrink revenues because higher tax rates discourage work effort and encourage tax avoidance and even illegal evasion. In figure 21.7, if tax rates have reached a prohibitive range, a tax cut ($t_a$ to $t_b$) could increase revenues (from $r_a$ to $r_b$). Supply-siders point to capital gains tax cuts in 1978 and 1996 in the

---

4  Dan Bawley, *The Subterranean Economy* (New York: McGraw Hill, 1982), p. 135.
5  William Baumol and Alan S. Blinder, *Economics: Principles and Policies*, 4th ed. (New York: Harcourt Brace Jovanovich, 1988).
6  Paul Craig Roberts, *The Supply Side Revolution* (Cambridge: Harvard University Press, 1984), p. 25.

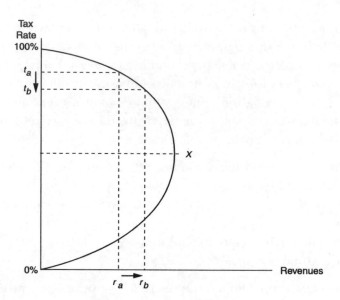

**Figure 21.7.** *The Laffer Curve: A tax cut can increase tax revenues.*

United States, where tax cuts increased revenues to the U. S. Treasury from capital gains (as noted in the beginning of this chapter).

Keynesians and other critics of the Laffer curve dispute where we are on the Laffer curve. For example, they point out that when taxes were cut under President Reagan in 1981, the deficit became worse, not better. Conversely, in 1994, when President Clinton pushed through Congress an increase in the federal income tax rate to 39.6%, supply-siders contended that tax increase would reduce revenues, similar to what took place with the luxury tax, but revenues rose during an expansionary boom. There are many variables at work in the marketplace.

Supply-side economics has largely been associated with the tax-cut movement, specifically with efforts to slash high marginal tax rates. Progressive taxation coupled with growing inflation in the 1960s and 1970s created "bracket creep," which moved middle-class income earners into higher tax brackets. "As tax rates rise one will get less saving, more consumption, less work, and more unemployment," Bruce Bartlett observes.[7] Supply-siders advocate a sharp reduction in marginal tax rates on income, capital gains, and other forms of wealth as a way to unleash entrepreneurship, innovation, and risk-taking, and to discourage investors and business people from engaging in wasteful "tax shelter" loopholes.

Supply-side economics has been closely associated with the Republican administrations of Ronald Reagan and George W. Bush, who advocated a sharp reduction in marginal tax rates on personal and corporate income, capital gains, and dividends. Many other nations around the world have adopted "supply side" tax cuts to stimulate economic activity.

7  Bruce Bartlett, "Supply-Side Economics and Austrian Economics," *The Freeman* (April, 1987)

## THE FLAT TAX MOVEMENT

In the preface to his study on the underground economy, Bawley recommends that "the free society substantially reduce and simplify taxation rates." That seems to be the direction many countries are taking. Supply-siders advocate a single low tax rate with a limited number of personal exemptions as the ideal tax system. The movement to eliminate the current complex, loophole-ridden, wasteful tax system in the United States and replace it with a simple one-rate flat tax is closely linked to the supply-side revolution. Following the publication of *Low Tax, Simple Tax, Flat Tax* by Robert E. Hall and Alvin Rabushka (1983), the movement to set one simple low income tax rate has gained support, especially in former Communist countries like Russia, Latvia, and Estonia.

For example, in the early 1990s, post-Soviet Estonia was facing 1,000% annualized inflation rates and an economy contracting by 30% over two years. Under Estonian Prime Minister Mart Laar, the small nation adopted a single tax rate for individuals and a zero corporate tax rate on reinvested profits, along with a deregulated economy. The results have been spectacular so far, with real GDP growth rates of 8% per year.

Hong Kong has also enjoyed a flat 18% tax on individual income for many decades, and no tax on capital gains. Other tax havens have adopted a zero income tax system, while compensating with other taxes on imports and corporate fees. However, so far no major industrial nation has adopted a flat tax system, although several nations have reduced the number of brackets.

There seems to be no ideal tax system toward which every nation is gravitating. Competition forces countries to change tax rates and ways of raising revenues. Europe, Asia and Latin America have adopted a high VAT and income tax system, but competition in the EU has forced several countries to slash corporate tax rates (Ireland's is down to 12.5%). American states vary in their tax strategy: most impose sales and income taxes, but others choose a sales tax but no income tax (for example, Washington, Nevada, Texas, Florida) while others have an income tax but no sales tax (Oregon, Delaware). New Hampshire has neither an income nor a sales tax, but makes up for them with a high real estate tax.

## CORPORATE INCOME TAXES AND DOUBLE TAXATION

Corporate income taxes have been part of the tax system since the early 20th century. Today the U. S. corporate tax rate is just shy of 40% when adjusted for state income taxes. This is the second highest rate among the world's most developed countries. Only Japan's is higher. In Europe, there has been a movement to slash corporate tax rates, especially after Ireland cut its rate to 12.5% to attract foreign capital.

Corporate taxes have always been viewed as a form of double taxation. Corporations pay the tax on total earnings, then individuals pay federal and state income taxes on corporate dividends. But dividends are not deductible as a corporate expense. Many economists have urged Congress to eliminate the corporate income tax entirely. Instead, Congress recently reduced the tax on dividends to 15%.

## TAXES ON CAPITAL ASSETS

One final debate is over taxes on investments, such as stocks, bonds, real estate, jewelry, art and collectibles. Governments impose a variety of taxes on these assets in the form of excise, capital gains, estate, and inheritance, either at the time of purchase, sale, or death of the investor or business owner.

Capital gains taxes are imposed when stocks, bonds, mutual funds, collectibles and real estate are sold. For example, today the federal government imposes a 15% tax rate on the profits of any assets (except collectibles) that have been held for more than one year. If the investment is sold in less than a year, the tax rate is equal to the individual's income bracket, and could go as high as 36%.

Suppose that you bought 1,000 shares of IBM stock for $70 and sold it a year later for $150 a share. How much would you owe the IRS?

```
Selling price.......................$150,000.
Purchase price (cost basis)...........$70,000
_____
Long-term profit....................$ 80,000
Capital gains tax (15%)...............12,000
_____
Retained profits by investor..........$68,000
```

In recent decades, the capital gains tax has declined from 40% (in the 1970s) to 15% today, resulting in increased revenues to the government. Why? Because a high capital gains tax inhibited investors from selling. When investors sell a stock and buy another one, they pay a capital gains tax that reduces their gains. Investors have an aversion to sending money to Washington, knowing that they will never see that money again. By reducing the rate, the government simultaneously encourages more investors to sell. Not surprisingly, after every cut in the capital gains rate, the government has earned more revenue, as investors unload their stocks and other assets and invest their funds in more productive areas.

Some countries, especially in Asia, impose no tax on capital gains, because they realize that taxes on assets inhibit liquidity and keep capital from going to its most productive use. A capital gains tax is a tax on capital investment.

The same could be said about estate or inheritance taxes, another favorite tax in industrial nations. The "death" tax is a tax on capital that has been accumulated over the years from surplus earnings and is then imposed at the time of death. These assets have already been taxes as income, and now is taxed again as wealth. Wealthy business leaders have long used trusts, foundations and corporate structures to avoid the tax. In the United States, many citizens complained that they had to sell businesses or family farms to pay the federal estate tax within 9 months of the death of the owner or business partner. Congress responded by raising the exemption level and reducing the tax rate, ultimately eliminating the "death" tax in 2010.

## SUMMARY

1. Government uses an array of taxes to fund its programs: on individual and corporate income, sales, property, and user fees.

2. Several economic principles apply to tax policy. The accountability or benefit principle is the idea that those who benefit should pay. User fees are an example of the benefit principle.

3. The fairness principle is the idea that taxes should be simple, fair and equitable.

4. Social democrats support progressive taxation — that wealthier people should pay a higher tax rate — according to "ability to pay" or the "sacrifice" principle.

5. Excessive taxes lead to an untaxed illegal underground economy. Cigarette taxes have become so high in some states that black markets have developed in cigarettes.

6. Tolls can provide more efficient use of roads and bridges, and can reduce congestion during high traffic periods.

7. Federal and state excise taxes on specific products (gasoline, highway tires, alcohol, tobacco, airport tickets) have become an increasingly important source of revenues.

8. Sales taxes are popular in the United States, value added taxes (VAT) are popular in Europe, and can sometimes be as high as 25%. Sales tax rate continues to rate in the United States.

9. Protectionism, tariffs and duties have gradually declined as the world has moved gradually toward "free trade."

10. Average income tax burden has increased in the United States, but marginal tax rates have fallen sharply, from 91% to 35%. Progressive taxation was a popular measure to redistribute wealth from the rich to the poor, and thus reduce inequality, but more economists and political leaders think that stimulating economic growth through tax cuts is a superior tool to progressive taxation.

11. The Laffer curve, named after economist Art Laffer, demonstrates that tax levels can be too onerous, leading an underground economy and lower government revenues. A tax cut can theoretically increase government revenues by encouraging economic growth. As a result, there has been a movement toward a flat tax, or a flatter tax.

12. Most economists agree that the corporate income tax is an inefficient form of taxation, causing "double taxation" of corporate profits and dividends. In recent years, taxes on dividends, interest and capital gains have been reduced sharply.

## IMPORTANT TERMS

Ability to pay principle
Accountability principle
Benefit principle
Black markets
Bracket creep
Capital gains tax
Direct taxation
Double taxation
Efficiency
Equity principle
Excise tax
Externalities
Fiscal policy
Flat tax
Indirect taxation
Kennedy-Johnson Tax Cut of 1964
Keynesian economics

Laffer curve
Lorenz curve
Marginal tax rates
Piguovian taxes
Poll tax
Progressive taxation
Proposition 13
Protectionism
Sacrifice principle of taxation
Small Business Job Protection Act of 1996
Smoot-Hawley tariff of 1930
Supply-side economics
Tariff of Abominations of 1828
Underground economy
User fee
Value added tax (VAT)
Welfare economics

## INFLUENTIAL ECONOMISTS

**Pigou, Laffer and the Art of Taxation**

**Names: Arthur C. Pigou (1877-1959) and Arthur B. Laffer (1940 - )**

**Background:** The two Arthurs are famous for their views on taxation. Arthur C. Pigou (prenounced pig-goo) is the father of welfare economics. Born in 1877 in the Isle of Wright in Britain, he went to King's College in Cambridge University, where he studied under Alfred Marshall, succeeding him as professor of political economy in 1908. He fought in the First World War, which turned him into a recluse. His neo-classical views were attacked by John Maynard Keynes in his book *The General Theory* (1936). Pigou retired in 1943, and died in 1959.

Art Laffer, one of the founders of supply-side economics, was born in 1940 in Youngstown, Ohio, and graduated from Yale University in 1963. He received an MBA at Stanford University in 1965 and a Ph. D. in economics in 1971. Afterwards, he taught for several years at the University of Chicago. He has taught at Pepperdine University and University of Southern California. He is the father of six children. He was a member of President Reagan's Economic Policy Advisory Board and later California governor Arnold Schwarzenegger's advisory board. He now resides in Nashville, Tennessee, where he is a institutional money manager and advisor.

**Major works:** Arthur C. Pigou, *The Economics of Welfare*, 4th ed. (London: Macmillan, 1932 [1920]); Arthur B. Laffer for inventing the "Laffer Curve."

**Major contributions:** Pigou is famous for two contributions, welfare economics and a critique of Keynesian economics. In *The Economics of Welfare* (1920), Pigou contended that the laissez-faire market mechanism necessarily failed to achieve efficient allocation of resources. One example was road congestion. Suppose, he said, that there are two roads connecting two cities. One road is cheap but badly surfaced, the other is narrow but well graded (with more costly upkeep). Pigou concluded that the better road will be overused and overcrowded. The solution to this market failure (what economists call "externalities") would be to impose a tax equal to the difference between the average cost and marginal cost on the well-surfaced road. Since then economists have criticized Pigovian taxes, as they are called. For example, Chicago economist Frank Knight made a seminal criticism of Pigou's social welfare thesis, showing that if roads were privately owned, road owners would set tolls that would reduce congestion, and therefore, no government tax was required to establish an efficient use of resources. On a broader scale, Knight's pioneering essay demonstrates that a free competitive environment can allocate resources efficiently as long as property rights are

501

clearly identified. Knight's seminal article encouraged disciples, including Buchanan, Armen Alchian, and Ronald Coase, to study property rights and externalities.

Pigou also revealed a flaw in Keynesian "liquidity trap" doctrine. Keynes feared that the economy could be trapped indefinitely in a deep depression where interest rates are so low and "liquidity preference" so high that reducing interest rates further would have no effect. The man who first countered the liquidity-trap doctrine was Arthur C. Pigou, ironically the straw man Keynes vilified in *The General Theory*. In a series of articles in the 1940s, Pigou said that Keynes overlooked a beneficial side-effect of a deflation in prices and wages: Deflation increases the real value of cash, Treasury securities, cash-value insurance policies, and other liquid assets of individuals and business firms. The increased value of these liquid assets raises aggregate demand and provides the funds to generate new buying power and hire new workers when the economy bottoms out. This positive real wealth effect, or what Israeli economist Don Patinkin later named the "real balance effect" in his influential *Money, Interest and Prices* (1956), did much to undermine the Keynesian doctrine of a liquidity trap and unemployed equilibrium.

Art Laffer is most famous for the invention of the Laffer curve and one of the founders of supply-side economics. The key to prosperity, according to Laffer, is to focus on incentives to increase saving, investing, capital formation, technological advances, and productivity, and this can best be achieved through tax cuts, deregulation, free trade, and other incentives, by which countries can grow faster and improve the lot of all citizens. The major drawback to supply-side economics is a refusal to recognize the ill effects of excessive deficit spending. According to Laffer and other supply-siders, tax cuts will be sufficiently productive that rising revenues from a growing economy will be large enough to reduce or eliminate deficits. But with fiscal discipline, higher tax revenues only feed the out-of-control big spenders in Washington. Thus, more conservative public-choice economists such as James Buchanan favor a Constitutional amendment barring deficits as well as limits on taxing power.

## PROBLEMS TO PONDER

1. Printed on the front of the IRS building in Washington DC are the words of Chief Justice Oliver Wendell Holmes, "Taxation is the price we pay for civilization." How would you reconcile this statement with that of British philosopher Alfred North Whitehead, "The resource to force, however unavoidable, is a disclosure of the failure of civilization"? Who is right? Is increasing the level of taxation a sign of success or failure of a civilized society?

2. Which of the following is a regressive (R), flat (F), or progressive (P) tax?

   A.  Poll tax (for example, each voter pays $10 to vote)

   B.  6% sales tax

   C.  Income earner pays $10,000 on $50,000 income, and another income earner pays $20,000 on $200,000 income.

3. A 1992 presidential candidate, Ross Perot, suggested that the Federal government impose a 50 cent gasoline tax to pay for the federal budget deficit. Which principles of economics discussed in chapters 20 and 21 does this policy prescription violate? Are there better ways to reduce the deficit?

4. After taking this course in economics, you are asked to do a study for the local county on the best, most efficient way to finance primary and secondary education. Which of the following financial options best reflects the accountability (benefit) and welfare principles of economics?

   A.  Schooling should be financed by real estate taxes.

   B.  Education should be financed strictly by parents of children in school.

   C.  Local schools should be financed largely by the federal government since they set the national educational standards.

   D.  The state government should pay for each child's education through state revenues from sales and real estate taxes.

5. Prepare a report on the benefits and disadvantages of private vouchers as a way to improve public school education. The proposal is that every parent/guardian should be given a voucher for each child that can be used to pay for the child's education at either a public or private school. Include in your report a discussion of the economic principles of (a) accountability, (b) welfare, (c), competition. Why are most teacher's unions opposed to the private voucher system, while minorities are in favor?

6. Should homeowners with no children have to pay for the schooling of children? In *Capitalism and Freedom* (1962), Milton Friedman argues that education is a public good with positive "neighborhood effects" and requires that everyone pay. He states, "the imposition of a minimum required level of schooling and financing of this schooling by the state can be justified by the 'neighborhood effects' of schooling." Do you agree that education has positive externalities? Are there ever any negative externalities in education (bad teaching leading to bad public behavior)?

7. In *The Wealth of Nations*, Adam Smith argued that children get a better education if students or their parents pay for their education instead of the state. Instead of the government paying teachers, teachers are paid directly by the students or their parents. Studies show that students who pay for their own college education choose their majors quicker, get better grades, and graduate sooner. Why should that be the case?

8. A growing campaign is to replace the federal income tax with either (a) a national consumption tax (a retail sales tax) that exempts saving and investment, or (b) a one-rate flat income tax. Evaluate the pro's and con's of both proposals and determine which is better.

9. Greg Mankiw (Harvard), Gary Becker (Chicago), and other economists have joined the "Pigou Club" — British economist A. C. Pigou advocated taxation as a way to combat negative externalities — and support a $1 gasoline tax to reduce the federal deficit, dependence on foreign oil, and global warming. Taxes on cigarettes, alcohol and traffic congestion are examples of Pigovian taxes. What are the pro's and con's of such a measure?

10. To pay for a local freeway, the city leaders choose to impose a sales tax on all retail purchases — a general sales tax. Does this violate the accountability principles? If so, what alternative financing would you propose?

11. In 2007, Mayor Joseph Delfino of White Plains, New York, proposed a 7% tax increase, justifying the tax hike on the grounds that "we are simply catching up with the tax level in other nearby cities." Does the competitive spirit between cities and states cause taxes to increase or decrease?

12. Hong Kong has enjoyed the same simplified tax system for decades, but the United States makes significant changes in its tax code every couple of years. Which system is better for long-term planning for individuals, estates, and businesses?

## ADDITIONAL READING

- Walter J. Blum and Harry Kalven, Jr. 1963. *The Uneasy Case for Progressive Taxation*. Chicago: University of Chicago Press.

- Robert E. Hall and Alvin Rabuska, *Low Tax, Simple Tax, Flat Tax*, (McGraw Hill, 1983)

- Gerald W. Scully, *Taxes and Economic Growth* (National Center for Policy Analysis, 2006).

# Chapter 22

# DEFICIT SPENDING AND THE NATIONAL DEBT

*"More recently, the emphasis has been on government expenditures as a balance wheel.
Unfortunately, the balance wheel is unbalanced."*

— MILTON FRIEDMAN
*Capitalism and Freedom* (1962)

In 1940, a year before entering World War II, the United States was still suffering from the worst depression in its history. Unemployment had stayed stubbornly high at 10 million Americans, the economy was weak, and the stock market was anemic. The "New Deal" under President Franklin D. Roosevelt had expanded its role during the Great Depression, but the federal deficits remained relatively small compared to GDP, and the economy seemed to be stuck in an everlasting depression. Economists were looking for new solutions and new theories. In 1936, British economist John Maynard Keynes (1883-1946) introduced a new model where the government played a key role in the business cycle. His book, *The General Theory of Employment, Interest and Money*, energized a new generation of economists, but political leaders and the established professors were skeptical of Keynes's argument that an activist government running deliberately high deficits could end the depression.

Then the Japanese attacked Pearl Harbor in December, 1941, and the United States declared war on both Japan and Germany. The massive war machine drove the deficit from $6 billion in 1940 to $89 billion in 1944. Government expenditures on goods and services, running at about 15% of GDP during the 1930s, skyrocketed to 46% by 1944.

An expansionary fiscal policy seemed to work in ending the depression. Industrial production rose dramatically, 10 million of the unemployed found work in short order (primarily as soldiers), and the unemployment rate fell to an unbelievable 1.2% of the civilian labor force. In addition, the massive deficit spending did not raise interest rates. Bond yields fell to a minuscule 1% during the war. The apparent ability of large government deficits to cure the world of depression caused a large majority of the economics profession to convert to the new school of

Keynesian economics. The "new economics" of Keynes — discussed in detail in this chapter — suddenly became the predominant theoretical and political model of the next generation.

## ARGENTINA, CONVERTIBILITY, AND DEFICIT SPENDING

In the late 1980s Argentina faced huge debts as a result of military dictatorships and a bloated centralized state. The economy collapsed and inflation reached 200% per month. Carl Menem, a member of the populist Peronista party, took office in 1989, and surprised everyone by instituting trade liberalization, labor deregulation, and privatization of state companies. To curb inflation, Menem in 1991 established a currency board and fixed the Argentine peso on par to the U. S. dollar. Anyone could go to the bank and ask for any amount of cash in pesos and convert them into dollars. To secure this convertibility, the central bank of Argentina was bound to keep its dollar reserves equal to the cash in circulation. For every peso, there had to be a U. S. dollar or equivalent in the government's vaults.

The convertibility law worked like a charm at first. Foreign investment flowed back into Argentina. Inflation dropped sharply, interest rates stayed low, and the economy boomed. If the Menem regime had maintained fiscal sanity, the country could have become the model for the rest of Latin America. Unfortunately, it became extremely expensive to live in Argentina as the Menem regime failed to control its budget and corruption ran rampant. Government spending continued on a high level and its massive deficits were financed by borrowing from foreigners at favorable rates because of the convertibility law and currency board. The International Monetary Fund (IMF) kept lending money to Argentina and postponing its payment schedules. Menem lost his reelection bid in 1999, and by 2001, Argentina started losing the confidence of investors as the flight of money to foreign investments began in earnest. The government froze bank accounts, causing popular protests (banging pots and pans), including the destruction of buildings owned by banks and American corporations, and Coca Cola billboards.

In January 2002, the fixed exchange rate with the dollar was abandoned, Argentina defaulted on its debt, foreign investment fled the country, and the capital flow into Argentina come to a halt. The economy collapsed and is only now starting to recover.

These two stories of America in World War Two and Argentina in the past two decades reflect the growing debate over deficit financing and the national debt. Is the national debt a blessing or a curse? Does deficit spending stimulate the private sector or does it crowd out private investment? Is chronic deficit spending a leading cause of inflation? Should states and the Federal government adopt a balanced budget amendment? What principles of economics can be applied to the debate over fiscal responsibility?

## CLASSICAL MODEL OF FISCAL RESPONSIBILITY

The classical model of fiscal policy was developed succinctly by Adam Smith in the 18th century. The classical model consists of five major elements:

1. Thrift, savings, and Say's Law (supply creates demand; production is more important than consumption).

2. International gold standard.

3. Laissez Faire: limited government

4. Balanced budget

5. Free trade

The first four principles were discussed in chapters 14-20. The issues of free trade will be discussed again in Chapter 26, "Globalization, Protectionism, and Free Trade."

The first four principles of classical economics encourage discipline, both as a household and as a nation. Thrift means economizing and avoiding excessive debt. The gold standard places severe limits on the ability of the state to inflate the money supply beyond gold and silver reserves. Limited government suggests avoiding waste, over-regulation, and a bloated bureaucracy. A balanced budget means living within one's means.

Adam Smith and other classical economists recognized the occasional need to go into debt, especially during war, depression, or other emergency. But after the crisis has passed, they advocate paying off the national debt. For example, when Alexander Hamilton proposed his scheme for creating the national debt to manage the war debt, he also urged Congress to create a sinking fund to pay it off, which was accomplished by 1830. By contrast, France failed to live up to classical principles of debt repayment, and suffered the negative consequences (see below for a comparison between the American and French monetary experiments).

## THE AMERICAN REVOLUTION VS THE FRENCH REVOLUTION: A STUDY IN MONETARY CONTRASTS

While Alexander Hamilton's financial scheme proved successful in the newly created United States, the plan hatched by the newly created French Assembly during the French Revolution turned out to be a disaster. What made the difference between success and failure?

George Washington, as first president of the United States, appointed Alexander Hamilton to be the first Secretary of the Treasury. In his 1789 *Report on Public Credit*, Hamilton proposed a financial plan based on the Bank of England model. He urged Congress to sell new government bonds that would absorb all state war debt, and to gradually pay down the national debt with a sinking fund that would depend on customs duties and postal revenues. The controversial proposal was opposed by Thomas Jefferson and James Madison, but was finally approved after a famous dinner meeting in Philadelphia where Washington and Hamilton agreed to move the nation's capital to Maryland/Virginia (to be named Washington, D. C.) in return for support in Congress for the Hamilton plan.

The Hamilton scheme was hugely successful, the bond issue was heavily oversubscribed, and the economy boomed under the stable monetary model.

## A DIFFERENT ENDING: THE FRENCH REVOLUTION (1789-1799)

During this era, France faced a similar national economic crisis. As a result of financial and military support for the American revolution and never-ending wars with England, the French court faced bankruptcy. A famine-induced bread shortage combined with the fiscal crisis led to a French revolution. Following the riots of Bastille Day on July 14, 1789, and the establishment of the National Assembly, the French Court found itself facing a national debt of 2400 million livres with little means to pay the debt off. The wealthy, the aristocrats and the Catholic Church were largely exempt from taxation, and this created a monstrous inequality among the citizens then in power. In April 1790, the National Assembly turned to the printing presses, creating a first issue of 400 million livres of paper money, backed by the confiscated property of the Catholic Church. To attract investors, the government agreed to pay 3% interest. But with no sinking fund, and with little taxing authority, the only recourse was to print more money. In September 1790, they issued an additional 800 million livres in bills, and in June, 1791, 600 million livres more. Supporters of the paper money scheme, such as Mssr. Matrineau, were unconcerned: "Paper money under a despotism is dangerous; it favors corruption; but in a national constitutionally government, which itself takes care in the emission of its notes, which determines their number and use, that danger no longer exists."

France attempted to stem the tide of rapid inflation by imposed heavy duties on foreign goods, but the depreciated currency destroyed savings, and encouraged the corruption of officials and legislators. The economy collapsed. As Andrew Dickson White comments, "Commerce was dead; betting took its place." It wasn't long before the monarchy was overthrown and the Reign of Terror began in earnest. Thousands of citizens were executed by the guillotine, culminating in the death of Louis XVI and Marie Antoinette in 1793. The Law of the Maximum was passed, imposing price, wage, and profit controls. This was followed by the outlaw of gold and silver as exchange, and the closing of the stock exchange.

When Napoleon came to power in 1799, financial conditions were appalling. "The government was bankrupt; an immense debt was unpaid. The further collection of taxes seemed impossible…War was going on in the East, on the Rhine, and in Italy, and civil war, in La Vendee," reports White.[1]

The French had listened to Benjamin Franklin when he was US ambassador to France in 1776-83, when they made a series of expensive loans to the American cause. Unfortunately, they didn't listen to the counsel of Alexander Hamilton a decade later.

The classical position toward the national debt continued until the Great Depression era. During war or a national crisis, it was permissible under classical economics to go temporarily off the gold standard, run deficits, and even print money, but when the war or crisis ended, it was considered sound financial policy to pay off those debts, balance the budget, and return to gold. The United States followed this cycle during the American Revolution and the Civil War, although the government continued to accumulate a national debt following the Civil War and World War I. But the debt did not grow dramatically until World War II.

As figure 22.1 indicates, the classical model was largely followed in the United States until World War II. The debt level has grown dramatically since then, in part because of the Keynesian revolution that led to greater government spending and a change in attitude toward deficit spending.

## POST-WORLD WAR II GLOBAL ECONOMY: THE AGE OF KEYNES

The Keynesian revolution countered the classical macro model in the 1930s with its own five principles:

1. **"Paradox of thrift" and the rejection of Say's law:** An increase in savings can contract income and reduce economic growth. Consumption is more important than production in encouraging investment, thus reversing Say's law to Keynes's law: "Demand creates its own supply."

2. **Deliberate deficit spending:** The federal government's budget should be deliberately kept in a state of imbalance during a recession. Fiscal and monetary policy should be highly expansionary until prosperity is restored, and interest rates should be kept permanently low.

3. **Big government and the welfare state:** Government should abandon its laissez-faire policy of limited government and intervene in the marketplace whenever necessary. According to Keynes, in desperate times it may be necessary to return to mercantilist policies, including protectionist measures ("fair trade" instead of "free trade").

1  Andrew Dickson White, *Fiat Money Inflation in France* (New York: Foundation for Economic Education, 1959), pp. 27, 100-01, 110.

**National Debt as % of GDP.**

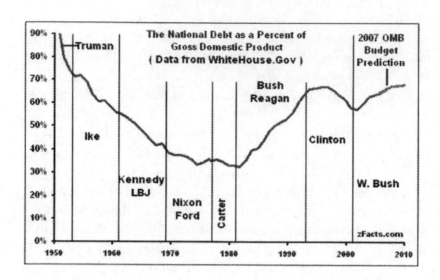

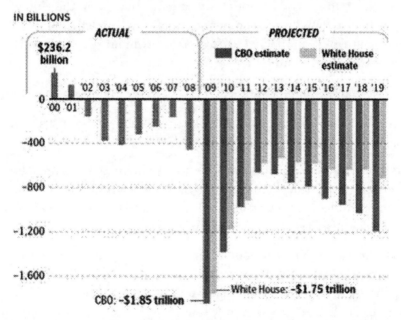

**Figure 22.1.** *National Debt and Deficit Spending in the United States, 1950-2019 (estimated).*

4. **Activist monetary policy:** The gold standard is defective because its inelasticity renders it incapable of responding to the expanding needs of business. A managed fiat money is preferable. Keynes held a deep-seated disdain for the gold standard and was largely successful in dethroning gold as a worldwide monetary numeraire.

## KEYNESIAN ECONOMICS: IS CAPITALISM INHERENTLY UNSTABLE?

Keynesian economics grew out of the Great Depression. John Maynard Keynes (1883-1946) sought to develop a model that could explain how an economy could remain "in a chronic condition of sub-normal activity for a considerable period without any marked tendency either toward recovery or toward complete collapse."[2]

Keynes rejected the classical notion that the capitalist system is self-adjusting over the long run. *The General Theory* was written specifically to create a model based on the view that the market system is inherently and inescapably flawed. According to Keynes, capitalism was unstable and could be stuck indefinitely at varying degrees of "unemployed equilibrium," depending on the level of uncertainty in a fragile financial system. Paul Samuelson correctly understood the intent of Keynes: "With respect to the level of total purchasing power and employment, Keynes denies that there is an invisible hand channeling the self-centered action of each individual to the social optimum."[3]

Keynes explained what he meant by "unemployment equilibrium," but used no diagram to illustrate it. Today's textbooks provide a diagram to demonstrate aggregate supply (AS) and aggregate demand (AD). See Figure 22.2.

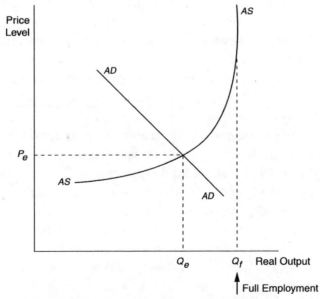

**Figure 22.2.** *Aggregate Supply (AS) and Aggregate Demand (AD) model from a Keynesian perspective.*

In the above figure, Aggregate Demand (AD) and Aggregate Supply (AS) look similar to the demand and supply schedules developed in Chapter 6 for individual products. Instead of a single price on the vertical axis, there is the combined price

2 John Maynard Keynes, *The General Theory of Employment, Interest and Money* (London: Macmillan, 1936), p. 249.
3 Paul Samuelson in Seymour E. Harris, ed., *The New Economics* (New York: Knopf, 1947), p. 151.

level (such as the GDP Deflator). And instead of a single quantity bought and sold, there is the output of all goods and services in real terms. As the price level declines in the Aggregate Demand schedule, the public can afford to buy more goods, and thus aggregate output (Q) increases. The AD curve is downward sloping. The Aggregate Supply (AS) schedule is upward sloping. As the price level rises, producers have a greater incentive to produce more goods.

However, note that the AS curve rises steeply at the end of its curve. That area reflects the limits of full production, or what economists call "full employment" GDP, that is, the full use of resources ($Q_f$).

Figure 22.2 demonstrates the Keynesian case of an economy at equilibrium (where AS = AD) at less than full employment. According to Keynes's model, the classical model only applies when the economy reaches full employment ($Q_f$), while the Keynesian general theory applies at any point along the AS curve where it intersects with the AD curve, such as $Q_e$ above.

## WHO'S TO BLAME? IRRATIONAL INVESTORS!

Keynes blamed the instability of capitalism on the bad behavior of financial markets. *The General Theory* presents a macroeconomic model based on an hypothesis of financial instability. As Keynesian economist Hyman P. Minsky declares, "The essential aspect of Keynes's *General Theory* is a deep analysis of how financial forces—which we can characterize as Wall Street—interact with production and consumption to determine output, employment, and prices."[4] Other economists agree that Keynes's theory of employment and output was not related to rigid wages as as much as to expectations and uncertainty in the investment and capital markets. Numerous passages in *The General Theory* support this view.

Keynes complained of the irrational short-term "animal spirits" of speculators who dump stocks in favor of liquidity during such crises. Such "waves of irrational psychology" could do much damage to long-term expectations, he said. "Of the maxims of orthodox finance none, surely, is more anti-social than the fetish of liquidity, the doctrine that it is a positive virtue on the part of investment institutions to concentrate resources upon the holding of 'liquid' securities." According to Keynes, the stock market is not simply an efficient way to raise capital and advance living standards, but can be likened to a casino or game of chance. "For it is, so to speak, a game of Snap, of Old Maid, of Musical Chairs—a pastime in which he is victor who says Snap neither too soon nor too late, who passes the Old Maid to his neighbor before the game is over, who secures a chair for himself when the music stops."[5]

---

4   Hyman P. Minsky, *Can "It" Happen Again? Essays on Instability and Finance*, (New York: ME Sharpe, 1982), p. 100.

5   John Maynard Keynes, *The General Theory of Employment, Interest and Money* (London: Macmillan, 1936), pp. 155-56.

Keynes was speaking from experience. He reasoned that the 1929–32 economic crisis destroyed his portfolio without any rational economic cause—the panic was due to Wall Street's irrational demand for cash, what he termed "liquidity preference" and a "fetish of liquidity."

## THE CULPRIT: UNINVESTED SAVINGS

In Keynes's model, the key factor in causing an indefinite slump is the delinking of savings and investment. If savings fail to be invested, total spending in the economy will fall to a point below full employment. If savings are hoarded or left in excessive reserves in the banks, as was the case in the 1930s, the fetish for liquidity would make national investment and output fall. Thus, thrift no longer served as a dependable social function.

In *The General Theory*, Keynes argued that as income and wealth accumulate under capitalism, the threat grows that savings won't be spent. He introduced a "psychological law" that the "marginal propensity to save" increases with income. That is, as individuals earn more income and become wealthier, they tend to save a greater percentage. There is a strong tendency for savings to rise disproportionately as national income increases. But wouldn't a growing capitalist economy always be under pressure to invest those increased savings? Keynes responded, "Maybe, maybe not." If savings aren't invested, the boom will turn into a bust. In Keynes's mind, saving is an unreliable form of spending. This process is only "effective" if savings are invested by business. Savings that are hoarded under a mattress or piled up in a bank vault are a drain on the economy and on aggregate demand.

Only effective demand counts. What consumers and businesses actually spend determines national output. Keynes defined effective demand as aggregate output (Y), which is the sum of consumption (C) and investment (I).

$$Y = C + I$$

Y, or aggregate "effective demand," is called gross domestic product (GDP). As noted in chapters 14 and 15, GDP is defined as the value of final output of goods and services during the year. Simon Kuznets, a Keynesian statistician, developed national income accounting in the early 1940s as a way to measure Keynes's aggregate effective demand. Keynes effectively demonstrated that if savings aren't invested by business, GDP does not reach its potential; recession or depression indicates a lack of effective demand.

513

## KEYNES'S LAW: DEMAND CREATES ITS OWN SUPPLY

What was Keynes' solution to recession? Increase effective demand! By stimulating demand through additional spending, more goods would have to be produced and the economy would recover. In this sense, Keynes turned Say's law upside down. Demand creates supply, not the other way around.

To increase Y (national output), the choices are limited in a recession. During a downturn, the business community might be afraid to risk its capital on I (investment). Equally, consumers might be unwilling to increase consumption (C) due to the uncertainty of their incomes. Both investors and consumers are more likely to pull in their spending habits when left to their own devices.

## ADDING G TO THE EQUATION

Encouraging government to start spending is the only way of stimulating the economy, according to Keynes. Keynes adds G (government) to the national income equation, so that

$$Y = C + I + G$$

Keynes sees government (G) as an independent agent capable of stimulating the economy through the printing presses and public works. An expansionary government policy can raise "effective demand" when resources are underutilized without hurting consumption or investment. In fact, during a recession, a rise in G would encourage both C and I and thereby boost Y.

## KEYNES ENDORSES AN ACTIVIST FISCAL POLICY

Keynes overturned the classical solution to a slump, which had been to cut prices, wages, and wasteful spending while waiting out the slump. During a recession, he recommended deliberate deficit spending by the federal government to jump-start the economy. He endorsed an even more radical approach during a deep depression like that of the 1930s: Government spending could be totally wasteful and it would still help. "Pyramid-building, earthquakes, even wars may serve to increase wealth," he proclaimed. Of course, "It would, indeed, be more sensible to build houses and the like," but productive building wasn't essential.[6] According to Keynes, spending is spending, no matter what the objective, and it has the same beneficial effect—increasing aggregate demand.

6  Keynes, *The General Theory*, p. 129.

## KEYNES FAVORS PUBLIC WORKS OVER MONETARY INFLATION

Keynes believed that tinkering with fiscal policy (changes in spending and taxes) was more effective than monetary policy (changes in the money supply and interest rates). He lost faith in monetary policy and the Federal Reserve in the 1930s, when interest rates were so low that reducing them wouldn't have made much difference. (See Figure 22.3.) Inducing the Federal Reserve to expand the money supply wouldn't be very effective either, because banks refused to lend excess reserves anyway. Keynes called this a "liquidity trap." The new money would just pile up unspent and uninvested, because of "liquidity preference," the desire to hold cash during a severe depression.

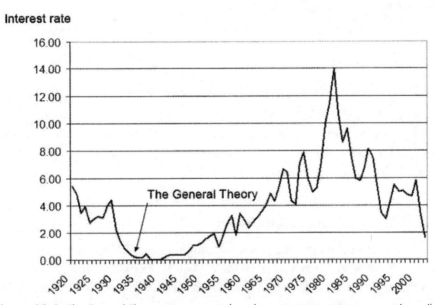

**Figure 22.3.** The General Theory *was written when short-term interest rates were at their all-time lows.*

## HOW THE MULTIPLIER GENERATES FULL EMPLOYMENT

Public works would serve several benefits. Public works are positive spending, putting people to work and money into business's pockets. Moreover, they have a multiplier effect, based on the nation's marginal propensity to consume.

The multiplier, a concept introduced by Richard Kahn, was a powerful new tool in the Keynesian tool box, demonstrating that a "small increment of investment will lead to full employment." Suppose in a recession that the government hires construction workers and suppliers to construct a new federal building costing $100 million. These previously unemployed workers are now getting paid. In the first round of spending $100 million is added to the economy.

515

Now suppose that the public's marginal propensity to consume is 90. These workers spend 90 cents of every new dollar earned. Their marginal propensity to save is 10%. In the second round of spending, $90 million is added to the economy.

After the workers spend their new money, that $90 million becomes the revenues of other businesses—shopping malls, gas stations, supermarkets, car dealerships, and movie theaters. These businesses may in turn hire new workers to handle the new demand paying them more wages, too, and these workers also spend 90% of that income. They receive an additional $81 million (90 percent of $90 million) of spending power. Ultimately, the public investment has a multiplier effect that generates round after round of gradually declining spending. By the time the new spending has run its course, and the aggregate spending has increased tenfold. Keynes's formula for the multiplier k is,

$$k = \frac{1}{1 - MPC}$$

where MPC = marginal propensity to consume

Since MPC = .90 in the example above, k = 10. As Keynes stated, "the multiplier k is 10; and the total employment caused by . . . increased public works will be ten times the primary employment provided by the public works themselves, assuming no reduction of investment in other directions."[7]

## KEYNES MAKES A MISCHIEVOUS ASSUMPTION

Note that in the Keynesian model, only consumption spending generates additional income and employment in the economy. Keynes assumes that saving is sterile, that it aborts into cash hoarding or excess bank reserves. Thus, the Keynesian model as originally proposed is considered a "depression" model. This was a crucial mistake that led to much mischief and misunderstanding in economics in the postwar era.

## A TURNING POINT IN TWENTIETH-CENTURY ECONOMICS

Two factors created the right atmosphere for the Keynesian revolution to sweep the economics profession. First, the depth and length of the Great Depression seemed to justify the Keynesian-Marxian view that market capitalism was inherently unstable and that the market could be stuck at unemployed equilibrium indefinitely.

7  Keynes, *The General Theory*, pp. 116-17.

Economic historians noted that the only countries that appeared to make headway in eliminating unemployment in the 1930s were totalitarian regimes in Germany, Italy, and the Soviet Union. Keynes himself acknowledged in the German introduction to *The General Theory* that his theory "is much more easily adapted to the conditions of a totalitarian state, than is the theory of the production and distribution of a given output produced under conditions of free competition and a large measure of laissez-faire."[8]

Second, World War II came along right after the publication of *The General Theory*, giving strong empirical evidence of Keynes's policy prescription. Government spending and deficit financing increased dramatically during World War II, unemployment disappeared, and economic output soared. War seemed "good" for the economy, just as Keynes suggested. The following quote from a popular textbook repeated what other textbooks were saying in the postwar period: "Once the massive, war-geared expenditure of the 1940s began, income responded sharply and unemployment evaporated. Government expenditures on goods and services, which had been running at under 15 percent of GNP during the 1930s, jumped to 46 percent by 1944, while unemployment reached the incredible low of 1.2 percent of the civilian labor force."[9]

## THE UPS AND DOWNS OF KEYNESIAN ECONOMICS

Keynesian economics reached its zenith in the early 1960s, when Keynesian economists Paul Samuelson, Walter Heller, and John Kenneth Galbraith became advisors to President John F. Kennedy and helped steer through Congress the Kennedy-Johnson tax cut of 1964, a Keynesian program designed to stimulate economic growth through deliberate deficit financing. This program appeared to work and the economy flourished through the mid-1960s. By that time, Samuelson's textbook reigned atop the profession, selling more than a quarter of a million copies a year. When the Nobel Prize in economics was established in 1969 by the Bank of Sweden, the first prize—after the required nod toward Scandinavian economists—went to Paul A. Samuelson.

Keynesians proclaimed that the economy could be fine-tuned with tax and spend policies, and that a little inflation was necessary to keep unemployment low. They relied on the Phillips Curve, a concept popularized in the 1960s that was based on empirical studies on wage rates and unemployment conducted in Great Britain by economist A. W. Phillips. (See figure 22.4). Many economists were convinced that a trade off between inflation and unemployment was unavoidable. Samuelson said that if society desired lower unemployment, it must be willing to accept higher inflation. Between these two tough choices, Keynesians considered unemployment a

8 Keynes, "Introduction to the German edition," *The General Theory* (London: Macmillan, 1973 [1936]), p. xxvi.
9 Richard Lipsey, Peter Steiner, and Douglas Purvis, *Economics*, 8th ed. (New York: Harper & Row, 1987), p. 573.

more serious evil than inflation. They quickly incorporated the Phillips curve to justify a liberal fiscal policy; to them, inflation could be tolerated if it meant lower unemployment. A little inflation could do no harm and considerable good, and they pursued a deliberate pro-inflationary policy in the 1960s.

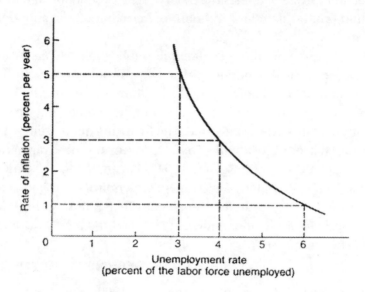

**Figure 22.4.** *Phillips Curve showing a trade-off between unemployment and price/wage inflation.*

However, in the 1970s and 1980s, the idealized Phillips trade-off fell apart. Western nations found that higher inflation did not reduce unemployment in the long run but made it worse. The emergence of an "inflationary recession" — lower real output and higher prices — caused economists to question the simplified Phillips trade-off and challenge for the first time their textbook models.

## FRIEDMAN TAKES ON THE PHILLIPS CURVE

Chicago economist Milton Friedman was one of those who questioned the authorized view. In his presidential address to the American Economic Association, published in 1968, Friedman introduced the "natural rate of unemployment" concept to counter the Phillips curve. Friedman argued that "there is always a temporary trade-off between inflation and unemployment; there is no permanent trade-off." Accordingly, any effort to push unemployment below the "natural rate of unemployment" must lead to an accelerating inflation. Moreover, "the only way in which you ever get a reduction in unemployment is through *unanticipated inflation*," which is unlikely. Friedman concluded that any acceleration of inflation would eventually bring about higher, not lower, unemployment. Thus, efforts to reduce unemployment by expansionary government policies could only backfire in the long run as the public anticipates its effect. In the late 1960s, Friedman even predicted that unemployment and inflation could rise together, a phenomenon now known as "stagflation."[10]

By the late 1970s, Friedman was proven right. The Phillips curve became unrecognizable as inflation and unemployment started rising together, opposite to what had happened in Britain in the 1950s. In a famous statement in 1977, British prime minister James Callaghan confessed, "We used to think you could spend your way out of a recession....I tell you, in all candor, that that option no longer exists; and that insofar as it ever did exist, it only worked by injecting bigger doses of inflation into the economy followed by higher levels of unemployment at the next step. This is the history of the past twenty years."[11] In his Nobel lecture, Friedman warned that the Phillips curve had become "positively inclined," with unemployment and inflation rising simultaneously. See figure 22.5.

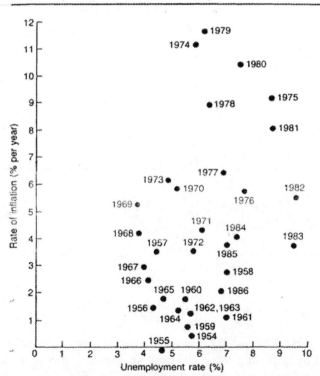

**The Phillips Curve—Historical Reality**

Source: From *Economics Today*, 6th Edition by Roger Leroy Miller, p. 397. Copyright © 1988 by Harper & Row, Publishers, Inc. Reprinted by permission of the publisher.

**Chart 2. Acceleration of Prices versus the Unemployment Rate: 1974-90.**

**Figure 22.5.** *A modern version of the Phillips Curve.*

10 Milton Friedman, "The Role of Monetary Policy," *American Economic Review,* March 1968; See also Friedman's Newsweek column of October 17, 1966.
11 Quoted in Mark Skousen, ed., *Dissent on Keynes* (New York: Praeger, 1992), p. 12.

The Phillips curve controversy resulted in creation of the "rational expectations" school, led by Robert Lucas, Jr., who won the Nobel Prize in 1995. Rational expectations undermine the theory that policymakers can fool the public into false expectations about inflation. Accordingly, government policies are frequently ineffective in achieving their goals.

## KEYNESIAN ECONOMICS MAKES A COMEBACK: THE CREATING OF AGGREGATE SUPPLY AND DEMAND

Yet Keynesian economics was able to make a surprising recovery with the discovery of a new tool that could explain the crises of the 1970s: Aggregate Supply and Demand or AS-AD. When Bill Nordhaus signed up as coauthor of the twelfth edition (1985), Samuelson's *Economics* added the new AS-AD diagrams. Samuelson and other Keynesians used AS-AD to explain the inflationary recession of the 1970s (see Figure 22.6).

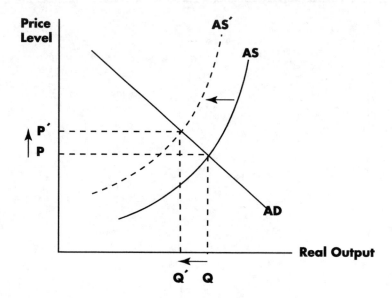

**Figure 22.6.** *Explanation of an inflationary recession using Aggregate Supply (AS) and Aggregate Demand (AD) model.*

Using the AS-AD model, Keynesians concluded, "Supply shocks produce higher prices, followed by a decline in output and an increase in unemployment. Supply shocks thus lead to a deterioration of all the major goals of macroeconomic policy."[12]

Alan Blinder, a leading Keynesian, also used AS-AD to explain the contortions in the traditional Phillips curve. According to Blinder, prior to the 1970s, fluctuations in aggregate demand had dominated the data. Due to energy shortages in the 1970s, however, aggregate supply dominated, and the result was stagflation. Prices rose

12 Paul Samuelson and William Nordhaus, *Economics*, 16th ed., (New York: McGraw-Hill, 1998), p. 385.

and real output fell. "That inflation and unemployment rose together following the OPEC shocks in 1973–74 and in 1979–80 in no ways contradicts a Phillips-curve trade-off."[13]

Thus, Keynesian economics recovered from the 1970s crises and AS-AD diagrams filled the pages of modern textbooks. In the words of G.K. Shaw, modern Keynesian theory "not only resisted the challenge but also underwent a fundamental metamorphosis, emerging ever more convincing and ever more resilient." The remaining Keynesian precepts achieved a certain kind of "permanent revolution."[14]

## POST-KEYNESIAN ECONOMICS TODAY

Was Keynesianism a permanent revolution, as G. K. Shaw says, or an unfortunate interlude, as Leland Yeager calls it, a temporary "diversion" from the neo-classical model? Keynesian economists still hold fast to a central belief that the system of Adam Smith is inherently precarious, especially under a laissez-faire global financial system, and require government intervention (expansionary fiscal and monetary policy) to maintain a high level of "aggregate effective demand" and full employment. Paul Krugman recently identified four Keynesian ideas that permeate today's economics:

1.  Economies often suffer from a lack of aggregate demand which leads to involuntary unemployment.

2.  The market (laissez faire) response to shortfalls in demand is often slow and painful.

3.  Government policies can make up for this shortfall in demand and reduce unemployment at the same time.

4.  Monetary policy may not always be sufficient to stimulate private sector spending; government spending must at times step into fill the gap.

Keynesianism still permeates the economic way of thinking. Keynesianism is demonstrated in everyday events such as the media warning watchers that falling consumer confidence is a threat to the economy, or when politicians promise that their tax cuts will create jobs by putting more spending money in people's pockets, or when consumers are warned that saving their tax rebate won't stimulate the economy.

13 Alan Blinder, *Hard Heads, Soft Hearts* (Reading, MA: Addison-Wesley, 1987), p. 5.
14 G.K. Shaw, *Keynesian Economics: The Permanent Revolution* (Hants, UK: Edward Elgar, 1988), p.5

## A SHORT CRITIQUE OF KEYNESIAN ECONOMICS

Many economists have criticized the Keynesian model for several reasons: unrealistic assumptions about the role of saving, the overly simplistic model of the economy, and for failure to recognize the importance of monetary policy, to name a few.

Milton Friedman was the first prominent economist to challenge Keynes's interpretation of the Great Depression. He and Anna J. Schwartz came out with *A Monetary History of the United States, 1867-1960*, published by the National Bureau of Economic Research and Princeton University. His study thoroughly contradicted the Keynesian view that monetary policy was ineffective. According to Friedman's study, quite the opposite was true. He demonstrated the unrelenting power of money and monetary policy in influencing the ups and downs of the U. S. economy.

Friedman had a two-fold mission in researching and writing *Monetary History*. First, he wanted to dispel the prevailing Keynesian notion that "money doesn't matter," the belief that an aggressive expansion of the money supply during a recession or depression amounted to "pushing on a string" and cannot be effective. Friedman and Schwartz showed that monetary policy had indeed been effective in both expansions and contractions. Friedman's work on monetary economics became increasingly important and applicable as inflation headed up in the 1960s and 1970s. Friedman's most famous line is "Inflation is always and everywhere a monetary phenomenon."[15]

## FRIEDMAN DISCOVERS THE REAL CAUSE OF THE GREAT DEPRESSION

That money mattered was an important proof, but the research by Friedman and Schwartz revealed a deeper truth. One startling sentence in their 860-page book changed forever how economists and historians would view the cause of the most cataclysmic economic event of the 20th century:

**From the cyclical peak in August 1929 to the cyclical trough in March 1933, the stock of money fell by over a third.**[16]

For 30 years an entire generation of economists had not known the extent of the damage the Federal Reserve had inflicted on the United States economy from 1929 to 1933. They believed that the Federal Reserve had done everything humanly possible to keep the depression from worsening but were impotent in the face of overwhelming deflationary forces. According to the Federal Reserve System nothing would stop the economic collapse.

Friedman radically altered this conventional view. "The Great Contraction," as Friedman and Schwartz called it, "is in fact a tragic testimonial to the importance of

15 Milton Friedman, *Dollars and Deficits* (New York: Prentice-Hall, 1968), p. 105.
16 Milton Friedman and Anna J. Schwartz, *A Monetary History of the United States, 1867-1960* (Princeton University Press, 1963), p. 299.

monetary forces." On another occasion, Friedman explained, "Far from being testimony to the irrelevance of monetary factors in preventing depression, the early 1930s are a tragic testimony to their importance in producing a depression." The government had acted "ineptly," in turning a garden-variety recession into the worst depression of the century by raising interest rates and failing to counter deflationary forces and bank collapses.[17]

One of the reasons for this ignorance about monetary policy is that the government did not publish aggregate money supply figures until Friedman and Schwartz developed the statistical concepts of M1 and M2 in their book in 1963. Friedman commented, "If the Federal Reserve System in 1929 to 1933 had been publishing statistics on the quantity of money, I don't believe that the Great Depression could have taken the course that it did."[18]

## IS FREE-MARKET CAPITALISM UNSTABLE?

On a more philosophical scale, Friedman's monetary research countered a core assumption behind Keynesian economics, i.e., that free-enterprise capitalism was inherently unstable and could be stuck at less than full employment indefinitely unless the government intervened to increase "effective demand" and restore its vitality. As James Tobin put it, the "invisible" hand of Adam Smith required the "visible" hand of Keynes. Friedman concluded differently: "The fact that the Great Depression, like most other periods of severe unemployment, was produced by government mismanagement rather than any inherently instability of the private economy." Furthermore, he wrote: "Far from the depression being a failure of the free-enterprise system, it was a tragic failure of government."[19] From this time forward, thanks to the profound work of Friedman and Schwartz, the textbooks would gradually replace "market failure" with "government failure" in their sections on the Great Depression.

Friedman came to the conclusion that once the monetary system is stabilized, if prices and wages remain flexible, Adam Smith's system of natural liberty could flourish. Contrary to Keynes' belief, Friedman faithfully maintained that the neoclassical model represents the true "general" theory and only a monetary disturbance by the government's central bank can derail a free-market economy. In short, according to Friedman, the business cycle is induced by the government, not the market, and monetary stability is an essential prerequisite for economic stability.

17 Friedman, *Dollars and Deficits*, pp. 78-79.
18 Milton Friedman and Walter Heller, *Monetary vs. Fiscal Policy* (New York: W. W. Norton, 1969), p. 80.
19 Milton Friedman, *Capiitalism and Freedom* (University of Chicago Press, 1962), p. 38.

## ANTI-SAVING MENTALITY

A second problem with Keynesian economics is its anti-saving mentality, which we discussed in chapter 17. The idea that consumption spending has a multiplier effect, but savings retards economic activity, is bogus—even during a downturn. Saving may be a better form of spending because it offers a potentially infinite pay-off in future productivity (thus Franklin's refrain, "A penny saved is a penny earned"). If the public saves more generally, the pool of savings enlarges, interest rates decline, old equipment is replaced, and more research and development, new technology, and new production processes evolve. The future benefits are incalculable. Funds spent on pure consumer goods are used up within a certain period, or depreciated over time.

The Keynesian multiplier k is higher as the public consumes more. But proponents assume that the savings remain uninvested, a false assumption under normal conditions. In truth, both components of income—consumption and savings—are spent. Thus, the multiplier k is infinite! The saving component also has a multiplier effect in the economy as savings are invested in the intermediate production stages. Moreover, the savings k is theoretically more productive than the consumption k because savings k is not used up as fast.

## THE IMPACT OF DEFICIT SPENDING

Today economists question the simulative effect of deficit spending, and do not assume that government spending automatically increases a country's well being during a recession.

Deficit spending can have three distinct effects, depending on who finances the deficit (thanks to Roger Garrison for this insight). Deficits can be financed by:

1. Domestic savers.
2. The Federal Reserve, or central bank.
3. Foreign investors.

If the deficit is financed by domestic savers, the effect is "crowding out" and the raising of interest rates. When the Treasury sells bonds in the capital markets, it means less investment capital for private business. Therefore, private firms must offer higher interest rates to attract the capital they need. As N. Gregory Mankiw states, "The increase in government purchases must be met by an equal decrease in [private] investment....Government borrowing reduces national saving"[10]

The second way to finance the deficit is for the government to borrow from its own bank—the central bank. This is known as debt monetization. When the Federal Reserve buys Treasury securities, it creates new money. It does this through "open

20 N. Gregory Mankiw, *Macroeconomics*, 2nd ed. (New York: Worth, 1994), p. 62.

market operations," that is, it buys Treasury bonds and bills from commercial banks. The Fed pays for the Treasuries by drawing on its own bank account, which has unlimited reserves (like having an unlimited overdraft bank account). Excessive monetary expansion puts pressure on prices to rise, and the value of the currency is depreciated. Not only does this inflation cause rising prices, but it also causes a boom-bust business cycle, asset bubbles, and other distortions in the economy (see chapter 25 on the business cycle).

The third way is for the Treasury to sell their debt to foreigners on the world capital markets. This has several advantages: it keeps the government from having to borrow from its own citizens, it keeps inflation in check, and it keeps interest rates low. But there is a cost of exporting government debt: a growing trade deficit. Instead of buying U. S. exported goods and services, foreigners are buying interest-bearing Treasury securities, giving rise to the twin deficit problem: the federal deficit and the trade deficit.

## CONTRIBUTION BY PUBLIC CHOICE ECONOMISTS

The deficit debate has also been addressed by "public choice" economists. For example, James Buchanan and Richard E. Wagner wrote a book on the subject entitled *Democracy in Deficit*, in which they tried to answer the question, Why is the federal budget chronically out of balance? Buchanan and Wagner point out that a democracy lacks fiscal discipline because representatives are chosen by the ballot box and have to worry about reelection. Raising taxes is usually unpopular, while spending money on pet projects in their district is usually crowd-pleasing. As a result the government budget is out of balance, running deficits instead of surpluses. Even in times of full employment and prosperity, government leaders have difficulty in restraining spending, or in raising taxes to close the gap.

Public-choice economists compare Congress to a business where every representative — all 535 — has a credit card with a maximum limit on total spending by Congress, but no credit limit on each individual's credit card. Each representative has an incentive to spend as much as possible so that all 535 representatives will share equally in paying the bill. Under such an arrangement, individual Congressmen are unlikely to limit spending.

Public-choice economists recommend several institutional limitations to state and federal budgets to solve this dilemma:

1. **Constitutional balanced budget amendment**: The majority of the 50 states are required to balance their budgets every year, or face automatic shutdowns of vital state services. This often forces states to cut programs suddenly or raise taxes, but it also puts pressure on them to become fiscally responsible. The balanced budget requirement is the primary reason state budgets are usually balanced, but the federal is not.

2. **Limitation on tax increases:** When states face the choice of either cutting programs or raising taxes, taxes generally rise. Over the years, for example, state sales taxes have gradually increased. To limit tax increases, public-choice economists often favor super-majorities (two thirds vote) in the state legislature to pass a tax increase.

3. **Rainy Day Fund:** Budget stabilization funds, or rainy day funds as they often are called, are now common in most states. This type of funding was set up to smooth over the budget in the normal business cycle. Without a rainy day fund, states facing a revenue shortage and a Constitutional balanced budget have little choice but to raise taxes or cut programs. (Unlike the Federal government, they do not have the power to print money.) A rainy day fund requires the state to build up reserves in the fund to be drawn upon during a recession. Forty-five states and Puerto Rico have created rainy day funds. The only jurisdictions without such funds are Arkansas, the District of Columbia, Hawaii, Illinois, Montana, and Oregon.

So far the federal government has not followed the example of state governments in adopting any of these three policies. Not surprisingly, the government budget has become bloated over the years, especially since the financial crisis of 2008.

## CAN A SOVEREIGN STATE GO BANKRUPT?

The final issue to consider regarding deficit spending and a large national debt is the possibility of national bankruptcy. Is this possible? Keynesian economist Campbell McConnell states, "It is difficult to conceive of governmental bankruptcy when government has the power to create new money by running the printing presses!"[21] However, while debt can indeed be floated perpetually, the risks increase dramatically when the government resorts to the printing presses instead of the traditional outlets of taxation and borrowing. Bondholders expect to receive something of value when their bonds mature, and if the risk increases significantly that the bonds will be worthless through inflation, they will sell off their holdings in a panic. Under conditions of rapidly rising inflation, governments have often resorted to issuing short-term debt. And excessively high inflation has caused foreign bond markets to collapse—in Latin America, Europe, and the Middle East. This is no far-fetched scenario. Creating new money to cover the government deficit results in runaway inflation, at rates of hundreds and thousands of percent per year, devastating countries such as Argentina, Brazil, Bolivia, and Israel. As late as 2008, Zimbabwe hyperinflated its currency.

11  Campbell R. McConnell and Stanley L. Brue, *Economics*, 11th ed. (New York: McGraw Hill, 1990), p. 296.

## DISADVANTAGES OF BALANCING THE BUDGET

**The Keynesian case for deficit spending and a large national debt:**

1. During an economic downturn, deficit spending stimulates the economy. "Crowding in" — deficit spending can stimulate economic growth if government spends money on capital investments and infrastructure.

2. Deficit spending is essential during a war.

3. Treasury securities provide a large stable liquid market for securities.

4. The national debt is not a burden because "we owe it to ourselves."

5. The federal government can never go bankrupt as long as it has the power to tax and print money.

6. Many major corporations borrow large amounts of money without any financial difficulties. Why can't Washington?

7. As long as the deficit and the debt are reasonable as a percentage of GDP, the deficit is manageable.

8. The deficit is beneficial if used to build necessary infrastructure.

## FOR A BALANCED BUDGET

**The classical case against deficit spending and a large national debt:**

1. Crowding out: deficit spending raises interest rates and reduces the amount of investment capital available to the private sector.

2. "Risk free" Treasury securities hurt the market for "high risk" corporate securities (below investment grade or "junk" bonds), forcing good companies to pay higher interest rates in the capital markets.

3. Deficit financing redistributes wealth from taxpayers (middle class) to the rich (bondholders).

4. No discipline: Deficit spending creates a political climate of irresponsible spending and out-of-control government programs. It leads to big government and a welfare state.

5. Deficit spending sends the wrong message to citizens: If the government doesn't have to pay its debts, why should we?

6. Deficit spending leads to monetary inflation by putting pressure on the central bank to expand the money supply.

7. Deficit spending leads to higher taxes on future generations.

8. Deficit spending is a way of not saving and leaves the government vulnerable to a financial emergency.

## SUMMARY

The main points covered in Chapter 22 are:

1. The classical economists (Adam Smith, David Ricardo, John Stuart Mill, Alfred Marshall and Ludwig von Mises) supported the virtues of saving, laissez faire, free trade, balanced budgets and a stable money through the international gold standard.

2. The American and French revolutions are a study in contrast. The United States was able to establish a sound monetary system by creating a fair tax system and a sinking fund to service the national debt, while the radical French government inflated the currency in a vain effort to pay off their war debts, resulting in corruption, depression, and despotism.

3. The Keynesian revolution was born in the midst of the Great Depression and the popular belief that market capitalism was inherently unstable. During periods of unemployed resources, Keynes rejected the classical model and Say's law, and adopted an anti-saving, pro-deficit spending, easy-money prescription for economic recovery. After World War Two, the Keynesian model was accepted by most of the profession.

4. Modern day Keynesians have created the Aggregate Supply - Aggregate Demand model to explain unemployment equilibrium, inflationary recession, and unsustainable inflationary booms in the global economy.

5. According to Keynesian economists, market economies cannot guarantee full employment because of the inherent instability of financial capitalism and savings, which can result in long periods of unemployed resources. Only government spending, especially on public works, and easy money policies (low interest rates, growing money supply) can assure the recovery to full employment.

6. The Phillips curve was introduced in the 1960s to demonstrate a trade-off between price inflation and unemployment. Keynesians believed that unemployment was worse than inflation, and were willing to tolerate some inflation if it meant full employment Milton Friedman countered that there is no trade-off in the long run, and any effort to reduce unemployment below the "natural rate" would lead to inevitable inflation and unemployment simultaneously.

7. In the 1970s, the world experienced a major "inflationary recession," with rising prices and increasing unemployment at the same time, as Friedman had predicted. Keynesian economists created the AS-AD diagram to explain how prices could rise while real output fell. According to Keynesians, the energy crisis of the 1970s and early 1980s caused Aggregate Supply (AS) to shift backwards. Thus the Keynesian mechanics of AS-AD remained a permanent feature of standard economics textbooks.

8. Free-market economists (supply siders, Austrians, and Chicago school advocates) has chipped away at the Keynesian monolith. Milton Friedman demonstrated that it was the Fed, not free enterprise, that caused the economy to collapse in the 1930s; a relatively free economy under a stable monetary system is likely to maintain full employment. Market economists, including public choice advocates, have offered a variety of ways to reduce waste in government through privatization, competitive bidding, deregulation, and constitutional limitations. Yet it's difficult to reduce deficit spending and the size of government. One seems to be able only slow its growth.

## IMPORTANT TERMS

| | |
|---|---|
| Aggregate demand (AD) | Marginal propensity to consume |
| Aggregate effective demand | Marginal propensity to save |
| Aggregate supply (AS) | Monetarism |
| "Animal spirits" | Multiplier |
| Classical economics | Natural rate of unemployment |
| Convertibility | Neo-classical model |
| Effective demand | Paradox of thrift |
| Fair trade | Peronista |
| Fiscal policy | Phillips curve |
| Free trade | Post-Keynesian economics |
| Full employment GDP | Public choice economics |
| Inflationary recession | Rainy day fund |
| International monetary policy | Rational expectations school |
| Invisible hand | Say's law |
| Junk bonds | Sinking fund |
| Keynes's law | Stagflation |
| Liquidity preference | Unemployment equilibrium |
| Liquidity trap | |

## INFLUENTIAL ECONOMIST

**John Maynard Keynes and the Keynesian Revolution**

**Name: John Maynard Keynes (1883-1946)**

**Background:** John Maynard Keynes (pronounced "Canes"), born the year Marx died, was destined to create his own school. He was born in Cambridge to John Neville Keynes, who taught economics at Cambridge University, and Florence Ada Keynes, who became mayor of Cambridge. Keynes attended Eton and King's College, Cambridge, where he earned his degree in mathematics in 1905. He studied under Alfred Marshall and Arthur Pigou, and beginning in 1908, became a lecturer at Cambridge. During the First World War, he worked at the Treasury Department, and participated in the Versailles Treaty. Disgusted with the draconian requirements imposed on the defeated Germans, he resigned and wrote a scathing critique in *The Economic Consequences of the Peace* (1920), which became a bestseller. Keynes was a speculator, and managed funds for himself and several institutions, including King's College. (He was wiped out by the 1929-32 crash and Great Depression, but managed to recover and died quite wealthy.) In 1925, Keynes married a Russian ballerina, but never had children. His wrote his revolutionary work, *The General Theory of Employment, Interest and Money*, in 1936. During the Second World War, he served again as an advisor to the Treasury and was made Lord Keynes. After the war he served as one of the architects of the Bretton Woods Agreement, which established a fixed exchange rate system based on gold and the dollar, and created the International Monetary Fund (IMF) and the World Bank. Two years later, in 1946, he died of a heart attack.

**Major works:** *Economic Consequences of the Peace* (New York: Harcourt, Brace, 1920), and *The General Theory of Employment, Interest and Money* (London: Macmillan, 1936).

**Major contribution:** Keynes turned classical economics upside down by insisting that his macroeconomic theory was the "general" theory and classical laissez faire economics was only a "special" case that applied only during times of full employment. (Keynes borrowed these ideas of "general" and "special" theories of macroeconomics from Einstein's "general" and "special" cases of relativity.) Otherwise, governments should deliberately run deficits and engage in "easy money" policies. Thus Keynesian economics became the theoretical underpinning of big government and the welfare state, and the idea that the federal government should be activist in responding quickly to any crisis and providing liquidity to buoy up the system. This form of Keynesian economics is still very much in vogue today among central bankers and government leaders. The belief is that the government should encourage a high level of spending at all times, by consumers, businesses and government, even if it means enduring some degree of inflation.

Classical economists, such as Milton Friedman, Friedrich Hayek and supply-siders, have countered the Keynesian model with the thesis that a high degree of economic freedom under conditions of a stable monetary system and fiscal responsibility will avoid most crises and depressions. The monetary free-market counterrevolution has been so effective that Harvard economist Gregory Mankiw has returned to the traditional view: that the classical model of Adam Smith is the "general" theory, and the Keynesian model of interventionism is the "special" case to be applied only during times of crisis — the very opposite approach of Keynes.

**Strength:** Keynes's activist policies offered hope to macroeconomists and political leaders who felt helpless in the face of dire depression and unemployment. He developed a financial instability hypothesis that stressed the fickle "animal spirits" of investors and how their attitudes can destabilize real economic activity during a crisis. He emphasized the need to maintain basic government services as a built-in stabilizer during a severe downturn, and for the federal government to respond quickly to a growing panic. His focus on the stability of consumption expenditures was under appreciated by economists before Keynes.

**Weakness:** Keynesian economics led to an overemphasis of debt, consumption, and wasteful government spending over the classical virtues of saving, productivity, and responsible fiscal policy. Big government, the welfare state, consumerism, easy money, inflation, and an anti-saving mentality are the effects of modern Keynesian thinking. Keynesianism also overemphasizes macro aggregates rather than the micro sectors of the economy.

**Quotation:** "There is no subtler, no surer means of overturning the existing basis of society than to debauch the currency. The process engages all the hidden forces of economic law on the side of destruction, and does it in a manner which not one man in a million is able to diagnose." (*Economic Consequences of the Peace*, p. 236)

## PROBLEMS TO PONDER

1.  Evaluate the following statement by Keynesian economist Robert Eisner in favor of a national debt and deficit spending: "The greater a person's debt, given his assets, the less his net worth; [but] the great the government's debt, the greater the people's net worth....Government's debt is the liquid assets of the American people." How is this possible?

2. Economists debate what caused the boom in the economy following the Kennedy tax cut of 1964. Keynesians argue that the cause was a stimulate fiscal policy of deficit spending. Monetarists say it was a liberal expansion of the money supply. And supply siders point to increased productivity by the tax transfer of resources from the public to the private sector. Who is right?

3. Respond to the following Keynesian statement: "The national debt is not a burden because we owe it to ourselves." Apologists for the national debt say that all that is happening is that the taxes are paid by some Americans, and interest is received by others. Therefore, the national debt cannot be properly called a burden on all citizens. "It's like taking money out of one pocket and putting it in the other. The net effect is zero. Therefore, the national debt is not a problem." Do you agree? Does this mean that it shouldn't matter whether the government pays 5% interest on its debt or 20%? Are the taxpayers who pay the interest on the debt the same as the bondholders who receive the interest income? Is there a redistribution of income and wealth occurring because of the deficit and national debt?

4. Comment on the following statement by Murray N. Rothbard in *Man, Economy, and State*: "The ingenious slogan that the public debt does not matter because 'we owe it to ourselves' is clearly absurd. The crucial question is: Who is the 'we' and who are the 'ourselves'? Analysis of the world must be individualistic and not holistic. Certainly people owe money to certain other people, and this fact that makes the borrowing as well as the taxing process important. For we might just as well say that taxes are unimportant for the same reason."

5. Discuss how Keynesian economics has made a comeback as a result of the financial crisis of 2008-09.

## ADDITIONAL READING

- John Maynard Keynes, *Economic Consequences of the Peace* (New York: Harcourt Brace, 1920). A lucid, powerful indictment of the Versailles Peace Accords after World War One. Keynes at his best.

- Robert Skidelsky, *John Maynard Keynes: Economist, Philosopher, Statesman* (New York: Penguin, 2005). The best biography ever written on this fascinating economist.

- James Buchanan and Richard E. Wagner, *Democracy in Deficit: The Political Legacy of Lord Keynes* (New York: Academic Press, 1977)

- *The Cato Handbook on Policy* (Cato Institute, 2005). Recommendations for eliminating government waste and corporate welfare.

# Chapter 23

# GOVERNMENT REGULATIONS AND CONTROLS

*"No arbitrary regulation, no act of the legislature, can add anything to the capital of the country; it can only force it into artificial channels."*

— J. R. McCULLOUGH
*Principles of Political Economy*
(new ed., Part 1, Ch. VII, p 219)

In 2002, President George W. Bush signed into law one of the most sweeping regulatory laws in history, "The Public Company Accounting Reform and Investor Protection Act of 2002." The signing of this regulatory law followed the collapse of the high technology and dot.com boom of the 1990s, and the corporate and accounting scandals of companies including Enron, Tyco, and Worldcom. Today the law is called the Sarbanes–Oxley Act, or Sarbox for short. The act is named after its two sponsors, Senator Paul Sarbanes (D–Md.) and Representative Michael G. Oxley (R–Oh.). The Act was approved by the House, 423-3, and in the Senate 99-0.

Sarbox created a new quasi-public agency, the Public Company Accounting Oversight Board. The law made corporate presidents criminally liable for the accuracy of their company's annual financial statements, and established costly, bureaucratic rules controlling all U.S. public company boards, management, and public accounting firms.

When this financial legislation became law, it was hailed as a necessary defense against an excessively "laissez faire" regulatory environment in the financial markets. Some major accounting firms and board members of large corporations lauded the new legislation as a way to uncover fraud and provide better evaluation of company operations. On the other hand, security analysts criticized Sarbox for imposing excessive red tape and massive new costs on business.

One provision of the law (the infamous section 404, which imposed new internal controls on company accounting) cost the average company $4.36 million in 2005. Total compliance during the year came to $6.1 billion for public companies overall. Sarbox has made it possible for the four largest accounting firms to raise their fees between 78% and 134% over the past three years. One academic study calculated that Sarbox has resulted in a cumulative loss of $1.4 trillion in shareholder value since going into effect, an average loss of $460 for every person in America. The law has had other negative effects: Initial Public Offerings (IPOs) have had to postpone going public due to increased compliance costs.

More publicly-traded companies have decided to go private, thus avoiding the cumbersome new rules. Other US companies are outsourcing and going overseas to reduce the costs of compliance. Sarbox has apparently caused a dramatic fallout in the number of foreign companies listing their shares in New York and an increase in their listings in London and other world exchanges, another costly form of out-sourcing.

Such are the unintended consequences of popular legislation.

## THE ABCs OF ECONOMIC REGULATION

The Sarbanes-Oxley case introduces us to the vital topic of government regulation of the economy. This chapter focuses on these issues:

- What is the extent of market failure?
- What are the costs and benefits of government controls?
- What are the market alternatives to state regulation?
- Is deregulation a good idea?

Sarbanes-Oxley is one of numerous examples of state control in the economy. Previous chapters discussed forms of government controls, such as wage-price-rent controls (see Chapter 6, "Supply and Demand") and minimum wage legislation (see Chapter 10, "Wages and the Productivity of Labor"). This chapter will provide more detail about these artificial methods of controlling market behavior and other forms of government intervention.

There are many examples of state regulation. The following examples of federal regulatory agencies are found in the United States:

- Bureau of Alcohol, Tobacco and Firearms (ATF): Regulates the sale and use of alcoholic beverages, tobacco and guns. State and local governments also impose restrictions and prohibitions on these items, such as establishing a minimum age for drinking alcoholic beverages and smoking tobacco.

- Consumer Protection Safety Commission: Protects consumers from harmful toys, electronic equipment, and other consumer products.

- Drug Enforcement Agency (DEA): Enforces prohibitions against and regulations of illegal and harmful drugs.

- Equal Employment Opportunity Commission (EEOC): Imposes rules against discrimination on the basis of race, religion, gender, and disability.

- Federal Communications Commission (FCC): Regulates and licenses radio and television stations and programming.

- Food and Drug Administration (FDA): Accepts or denies applications for distribution of new drugs and medical devices in the marketplace.

- Federal Energy Regulatory Commission (FERC) and Nuclear Regulatory Commission (NRC): Control and enforce rules for nuclear power and other energy sources.

- Federal Deposit Insurance Corp. (FDIC): Insures individual bank account deposits against bankruptcy of the financial institution.

- Federal Trade Commission (FTC): Regulates advertising and products.

- Environmental Protection Agency (EPA): Enforces and regulates the Clean Air Act, the Clean Water Act, fuel efficiency, and other environmental laws.

- Immigration and Naturalization Service (INS): Processes travelers to the United States and limits the number of legal immigrants into the United States.

- Occupational Safety and Health Administration (OSHA): Sets standards and enforces safety and health rules in the workplace.

- Securities and Exchange Commission (SEC): Establishes rules and regulates the stock market and securities firms.

## CAN THE MARKET REGULATE ITSELF?

The increasing number of regulatory agencies leads to the question: Is there sufficient market failure to justify all these regulatory agencies? The fact that new regulations and laws are constantly being passed implies that a free marketplace is incapable of fully protecting the legitimate needs of customers, employees, community and environment. Prices are too high, products are too shoddy or unsafe, wages are too low, benefits are inadequate, income and wealth are not fairly distributed.....the list of complaints about business is almost endless. Joseph Stiglitz concludes, "The market is everywhere imperfect" and needs to be regulated. Or are legislators overreacting to frauds and failures in the business world, and do government agencies actually make things worse?

## THE ADAM SMITH MODEL OF COMMERCE

Adam Smith, the founder of market economics, contends that the "system of natural liberty" — a laissez faire economy — would function well if three conditions exist:

1. Freedom to pursue one's own interests (the profit motive)
2. A system of justice
3. A competitive environment

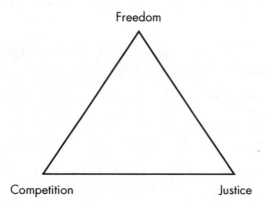

**Figure 23.1.** *Adam Smith's system of natural liberty: a trinity of freedom, competition, and justice.*

In the *Wealth of Nations* (1776), Smith describes the ideal model of economic laissez faire: "Every man, as long as he does not violate the laws of *justice*, is left perfectly *free* to pursue his own interest in his own way, and to bring both his industry and capital into *competition* with those of any other man, or order of men."[1]

Smith argues that a commercial society with all three elements — freedom, justice and competition — would maximize human achievements without undue interference by government. The "invisible hand" (Smith's symbol of free enterprise) would check unbridled greed and moderate the passions. Commerce, he said, encourages people to become educated, industrious and self-disciplined, and to defer gratification. It is the fear of losing one's customers "which retrains his frauds and corrects his negligence."[2] In other words, a properly balanced free-market economy controlled by the rule of law and encouraged by a competitive environment would minimize — though not eliminate — frauds, negligence and failure.

1 Adam Smith, *The Wealth of Nations* (New York: Modern Library, 1965 [1776]), p. 651. Emphasis added.
2 Ibid., p. 129.

## THE COASE T

In the early 1960s, Ronald Coase (University of Chicago) proposed the C
Theorem with regard to market regulation: In the absence of government controls,
the market would create its own solution to market defects. For example, without
any Federal Trade Commission, the marketplace could police itself and curb fraudulent and deceptive business practices. How? Over the years several voluntary non-
government organizations have been established by business to address these social
issues:

- *The Better Business Bureau* (BBB) deals with consumer complaints about
  local businesses. Founded in 1912, the BBB is supported by more than
  300,000 local business members nationwide. It is dedicated to fostering fair
  and honest relationships between businesses and consumers, instilling
  consumer confidence and contributing to an ethical business environment.
  Over 70% of all complaints are resolved by the BBB.

- *Good Housekeeping*, a women's magazine, established standards for products advertised in its magazine, long before government agencies were
  established. For example, it advocated truth in advertising as early as 1905,
  before the passage of the 1906 Pure Food and Drug Act. It prohibited the
  advertising of cigarettes in the magazine in 1952, 12 years before the
  Surgeon General's warning labels were required. In 1912, it created the *Good
  Housekeeping Seal of Approval*, an award granted to approved advertisers. It
  tested the accuracy of product advertising and promised a refund within
  two years if a product is proven defective.

- *Underwriters Laboratories* (UL) is a private institution in charge of product
  compliance. Benefiting a range of customers - from manufacturers and
  retailers to consumers and regulating bodies - UL has tested products for
  public safety for more than a century.

- *Consumer's Union* is a non-profit organization devoted to a fair and safe
  marketplace for consumers. With headquarters in Yonkers, New York, it publishes *Consumer Reports*, which has 5 million paid subscribers. It conducts
  independent research, and tests the safety and reliability of new automobiles, appliances, and other consumer products. It has also studied the risks
  of smoking, water pollution, and other national concerns.

Despite the efforts of business organizations and nonprofits, legislatures still find it necessary to protect the consumer from a variety of business ills. It appears that private initiative has not curtailed commercial abuses. The increasing number of commercial abuses results in constantly increasing regulation. One of the legitimate purposes of government (as noted in Chapter 20) is "at times to accomplish jointly what we would find it more difficult or expensive to accomplish severally."[3] Perhaps this is one area where government needs to supplement the private sector. Is there an optimal level of regulation?

## WHO PROTECTS THE CONSUMER?

When considering government intervention, government economists often measure the costs against the benefits. As Milton Friedman states, "Many people want the government to protect the consumer. A much more urgent problem is to protect the consumer from the government....The government solution to a problem is usually as bad as the problem."

## FOOD AND DRUG ADMINISTRATION: SAFETY, BUT AT WHAT COST?

Following the publication of Upton Sinclair's novel *The Jungle*, which exposed unsanitary conditions in the Chicago slaughtering and meat-packing houses, consumer protection became a major concern of government. The Food and Drug Administration (FDA) was established in 1906 in response to the outcry for greater control over how food was processed. (For more, see insert, "Is Unfettered Capitalism a Jungle?") The 1938 Food, Drugs and Cosmetics Act gave the FDA additional power to approve all pharmaceuticals and medical devices before they can be marketed. All drugs — with the exception of dietary supplements and vitamins — must go through a series of clinical tests before being approved by the FDA. Completing the development, testing, and approval process can take up to 10 years. Some analysts estimate that the cost of bringing a new product from conception to market is around $400 million.

Defenders of the FDA argue that this government approval process is essential to keeping unsafe drugs off the market. The most famous example of government protection occurred in the early 1960s, when the FDA refused to allow Thalidomide in the United States. Thalidomide was a popular drug being sold throughout Europe that diminished morning sickness in pregnant women. The FDA insisted there was not enough evidence of the drug's safety. In 1961, Germany was forced to remove Thalidomide off the market after several thousand newborns suffered grave deformities, and the FDA in the United States was vindicated.

---

3  Milton Friedman, *Capitalism and Freedom* (University of Chicago Press, 1962), p. 2.

Critics of the FDA point to severe human costs associated with failure to bring out efficacious drugs in a timely fashion. As the Cato Institute states, "every day that the FDA delays approving a product for market, many patients who might be helped suffer or die needlessly.[4]" Dr. Louis Lasagna, director of Tuft University's Center for the Study of Drug Development, estimates that the 7-year delay in the approval of beta-blockers as heart medication costs the lives of as many as 119,000 Americans who could have been saved by using the unapproved drugs. What the public sees is the government protecting citizens from potentially harmful drugs; what they don't see is the government's failure to allow beneficial new drugs to be used because of the costs involved in getting FDA approval. The FDA has recently adopted a "fast track" system if a drug appears promising and has an important impact.

The Cato Institute recommends that nongovernmental agencies be allowed to certify new drugs and label them anywhere from "risky" to "approved." Private firms already test drugs according to FDA requirements. A dual testing practice might be a good alternative to the overly regulated system currently in place.

---

## Is Unfettered Capitalism a Jungle?

Upton Sinclair's 1906 bestseller *The Jungle* was an expose on unfettered capitalism written by a socialist who advocated wholesale regulation of the economy. The book's most important revelation was the alleged unsanitary conditions in the meat packing industry. Publication led to the passage of the Meat Inspection Act and the Pure Food and Drug Act of 1906, which established the Food and Drug Administration.

Upton Sinclair relied on his imagination and hearsay support from market critics to write about the allegedly horrendous conditions of the meatpacking industry in his novel. He implied that there was no government inspection of meat packing facilities before his novel was written in 1906, but in fact federal and local officials had been inspecting meat for a decade. Theodore Roosevelt wrote of Sinclair in a letter to William Allen White in July 1906, "I have an utter contempt for him. He is hysterical, unbalanced, and untruthful. Three-fourths of the things he said were absolute falsehoods. For some of the remainder there was only a basis of truth."[5] The Meat Inspection Act of 1906 did have the effect of eliminating small businesses and reducing competition in the industry, however.

---

4   Michael F. Cannon and Michael D. Tanner, *Healthy Competition* (Washington, DC: Cato Institute, 2005), p. 7.
5   Roosevelt to William Allen White, July 31, 1906, Elting E. Morison and John M. Blum, editors, *The Letters of Theodore Roosevelt*, 8 vols. (Cambridge: Harvard University Press, 1951- 54), vol. 5, p. 340.

## Should Government Control Prices?

The first effort to control prices and regulate an industry occurred in 1887 when the Interstate Commerce Commission (ICC) was established to regulate the railroads. The railroads expanded rapidly following the Civil War. Competition between railroad companies was fierce, freight and passenger rates were constantly cut, and pool operations often broke down. Populous movements pushed for regulating the railroads, and the ICC was born. The first commissioner was a lawyer who had represented the railroads for many years. Under his direction, competition was limited, rates were fixed, and routes were assigned. One of the first acts of the commission was to raise the rates on long-haul trips. Regulation became a boon to existing companies and made it more difficult for new companies to start up.

The artificially high freight rates maintained by the ICC for railroads allowed a whole new form of transportation, the trucking industry, to flourish. By the 1920s, trucks became a threat to the railroads. Instead of decontrolling the railroads and allowing them to compete directly with the trucking industry, the Motor Carrier Act of 1935 brought trucking under the control of the ICC. Thus, the ICC acted to protect the railroads, not the consumers. It wasn't long before the trucking industry followed the path of the railroads: trucking companies were licensed, rates were set, and routes were assigned. Not surprisingly, the number of trucking companies declined and competition was discouraged. Consumer prices for final goods reflected the higher delivery costs.

A similar commission was established in 1938, The Civil Aeronautics Board, to act as a public utility, setting fares, routes, and schedules for the 19 licensed airlines. As a result, the number of licensed airlines declined and rates remained high, while the prices of dozens of other consumer goods fell over time. Like other government control boards, the CAB began to be controlled by the industry it was intended to regulate; directors of these regulatory bodies came from the companies themselves, and their primary goal was to set rates so that the airlines would earn a "reasonable" rate of return. Airlines favored this system that virtually guaranteed them a profit.

The CAB also created a bureaucratic nightmare. Airlines encountered lengthy delays when applying for new routes or fare changes. In the late 1960s and early 1970s, airlines like World Airways and Continental Airlines applied for low fares and new routes, a boon to consumers but a threat to existing airlines. Their rate and route changers were delayed for six years or longer, and they were often denied approval. In 1977, following the energy crisis and a period of double-digit inflation, President Jimmy Carter appointed Alfred E. Kahn, a professor of economics at Cornell University, to be chair of the CAB. Kahn pushed through a bill to deregulate the airline industry and phase out the CAB's regulation of fares and routes, culminating in the Airline Deregulation Act of 1978. This was the first act of a modern industrial state to eliminate a government agency. The CAB finally closed its doors on January 1, 1985.

The deregulation of the airlines has been highly controversial. On the positive side, fares have declined sharply, new routes have appeared, and new airlines and mergers have been ubiquitous. On the negative side, profits have declined and many old-line airlines, such as Pan American and Braniff, have disappeared, while other mainstream airlines, such as Continental, Delta, and United, have declared bankruptcy and reappeared after filing Chapter 11 reorganization. After two decades of deregulation, the airline industry appears to be nowhere near a point of competitive equilibrium, but is near a point of creative destruction. More people are flying than ever before. Both price and quality of service have decined.

## THE CASE FOR DEREGULATION

Since the early 1980s the global economy has experienced a period of dramatic deregulation of various industries under the influence of the Reagan administration in the United States and the Thatcher regime in Great Britain. Journals such as the *Journal of Law and Economics,* published at the University of Chicago beginning in 1958, and the *Bell Journal of Economics and Management Science,* started in 1970, have devoted articles to the topic of regulation. As a general rule economists have found that government regulation of industries harms consumers, often gives monopoly power to producers, and makes it difficult for new companies to enter the marketplace.

Chicago economist George Stigler (see biography at the end of Chapter 8) was the single most important academic contributor to this movement. He sought to answer the question, "Did governments regulate industries, as many had believed, to reduce the harmful effects of monopoly?" In a seminal article, "The Theory of Economic Regulation,"[6] published in 1971, Stigler argued that government regulatory agencies end up being "captured" by the industry they are supposed to regulate. Stigler called his discovery the "capture theory." For his work on industrial organization and regulation, Stigler won the 1982 Nobel Prize for economics.

Some of these findings were the catalyst for the deregulation of the transportation, natural gas, and banking industries, a solution that gained momentum in the Carter administration and continued through the Reagan administration. In transportation, decision making has been turned over to the marketplace to determine prices, routes, and schedules for airlines, trucks, and railroads. The FAA (Federal Aviation Administration) still controls security and air traffic, but it does not get involved in pricing and route selection.

6  George J. Stigler, *The Theory of Economic Regulation*, Bell Journal of Economics (Spring, 1971)

In the banking, insurance, and securities industries, deregulation has led to competition in brokerage commissions, interest and fee charges for checking account, credit cards, and consumer and investment banking. Low cost term insurance is now available due to insurance competition.

Worldwide, the financial industry is much freer today than it was a generation ago, when dozens of countries, including Great Britain, imposed foreign exchange controls and would not allow citizens to leave the country with substantial sums of money. Until the late 1970s, it was illegal to carry cash valued at £100 pounds or more out of Great Britain! Margaret Thatcher abolished exchange controls in 1979. The international monetary system is more laissez faire now and it is easier to transfer capital between countries. As a result the globalization of markets has increased. Privatization of industries that had been under previous government control was a main form of deregulation in Britain throughout the latter years of the last century. Some argue that although privatization led to increased choice in services, commercial standards have declined and wages and employment have been reduced.

For many years professions such as doctors, lawyers, and pharmacists considered advertising to be undignified and unnecessary. Regulatory services made it illegal, arguing that it was a wasteful expense carried on by monopolistic firms. In a classic study of advertising by optometrists, economist Lee Benham found that the prices of eyeglasses were $20 higher (in 1963 dollars) in states that banned advertising than in those that allowed advertising. After states passed laws allowing the advertising of eyeglasses, prices fell dramatically and choices have increased. In another case, economist Al Ehrbar found that gasoline prices are higher (about 6%, net of excise taxes) in communities that prohibit large price signs being displayed in gas stations. Today most states require large price signs for gasoline.

One area where there has been little progress toward deregulation is in small business. The World Bank's *Doing Business* database collects data from nearly 150 countries on the costs of regulation in certain areas, such as starting a business. For example, it takes a minimum of 19 working days to start a business in the OECD, compared to 60 in Sub-Saharan Africa; the cost of regulation as a percentage of GDP (not including bribes) is 8% in the OECD, and 22% in Africa.

## THE ECONOMICS OF WAGE, PRICE AND RENT CONTROLS

History is replete with stories of governments imposing wage, price and rent controls at times when inflation and the cost of living are rising. European governments in medieval times fixed the maximum price of bread. In recent times the government has limited the price of gasoline, controlled rents charged by landlords, and imposed minimum wages. During World War II, England and the United States established controls on prices in general and issued ration coupons for meat, gasoline, and many other consumer goods. Violators were punished by fines and jail sentences.

Chapter 6 presented a case study of the energy crisis in the mid 1970s, when the price of crude oil went from $5 a barrel to over $40 in less than a year. The government set price ceilings on gasoline and oil products to protect the consumer and prevent what was called "price gouging." Figure 23.2 illustrates the impact of this legislation:

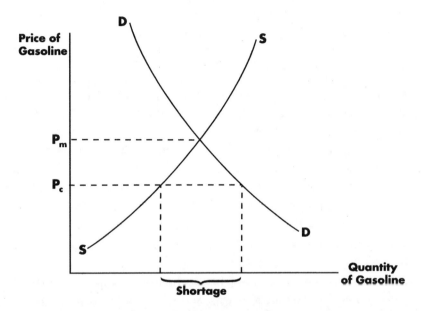

**Figure 23.2.** *Effect of price ceiling on gasoline.*

In 1974-75, local governments responded to the increases in gasoline prices by rationing gasoline. As noted in figure 23.2, a price ceiling of $P_c$ was imposed, below the market price, $P_m$. Under the below-market price, demand exceeds supply and a shortage arises. Long lines formed at gas stations, and some gas stations ran out of gasoline by 10 am every day. Stations could sell only a certain amount of gas each day. Black markets developed, sending profits to unscrupulous dealers. Oil companies were deprived of much needed revenue they could have used to find new oil fields and increase production in the future.

There is nothing dirty or unfair about the natural market sending prices higher. It gives consumers a natural incentive to self-ration by using less, and it sends the oil producers a strong signal to start looking for more oil.

Price controls have been draconian at times. Chapter 18 talked about the debasement of gold and silver coins in Rome. Following Caesar's reign, coins were constantly debased as the state took on more burdens—the expense of the

Roman army, welfare and subsidies, and the cost of public buildings. Diocletian declared several price controls and rationing schemes with the penalty of death for violators in his famous "Edict of Prices" in 301 AD. But not even the death penalty could stop the rampant inflation, where the gold solidus became 30 million denarii by the mid-4th century.

Chapter 10 presented the minimum wage controversy, and indicated that when governments impose a minimum wage, unemployment can result, especially among minorities and unskilled workers, and may cause companies to cut back employment in favor of machines, or outsourcing. Often there are unintended consequences to seemingly good government policies.

## PRICE CONTROLS DURING A NATURAL DISASTER

When hurricanes hit Florida or snowstorms blanket the northeast, consumers prepare for power outages, transportation lockdowns, and housing damage by stocking up on basic supplies. Store owners often respond by raising the price of tools, plywood, gasoline and generators. Some call this practice "price gouging," because they are taking advantage of a consumer in a crisis. Others see this as the market regulating itself. For example, suppose Home Depot has 20 heaters available for sale, and the usual price is $400. At this price, the first customers to arrive at the store may buy two of them, one for upstairs and one for downstairs. Home Depot will run out of heaters after 10 customers. If Home Depot raises the price to $800, customers will think twice before buying more than one. Some customers may decide to share the cost with a neighbor. The price is higher, but the heaters will be available for everyone who wants one. Home Depot earns more than usual, but the higher price will encourage them to stock enough goods for emergencies. Price controls may seem at first to be fair to customers, but a low price for a scarce or nonexistent product can result in misery for all.

—————————————————— CASE STUDIES ——————————————————

## RENT CONTROLS IN NEW YORK CITY

*"In many cases rent control appears to be the most efficient technique presently known to destroy a city — except for bombing."*

— ASSAR LINDBECK, *Swedish economist*

The War Emergency Tenant Protection Act was passed by the New York State legislature during the grim, panicky days between the attack on Pearl Harbor in December, 1941, and America's move to a full wartime economy in 1943. According to legislators, housing was just another market to be regulated, alongside rubber, gasoline, coffee and meat. Wartime controls were meant to be temporary; indeed, after the war was over, by 1947, controls on other commodities were eliminated and most cities scrapped rent controls. New York City, the capital of capitalism, was an unfortunate exception. Today, more than half a century after the end of World War II, only one-third of New York City's two million rental apartments are free of some kind of price restraint. A city board sets annual increases and administers a complicated bureaucratic system. In some buildings, people living in similar apartments pay wildly different levels of rent. The oldest controls cover pre-1947 buildings, some in fashionable districts. Controlled rents average only $500 a month, while control-free apartments rent for $3,000 or higher.

Rent control, like price controls, is a law placing a maximum price or a "rent ceiling" on what landlords are allowed to charge tenants. In virtually all cases, the maximum rent is below what the market would charge if landlords were free to establish the rent. Figure 23.3 shows the impact:

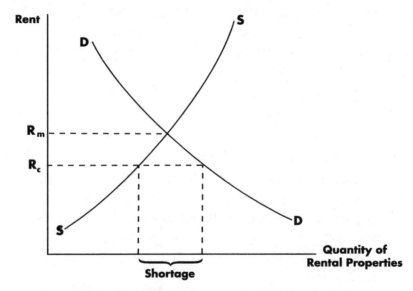

**Figure 23.3.** *Effect of a maximum rent price (Rc) below the market rent (Rm).*

When rents are set at less than their equilibrium levels, demand naturally exceeds supply, and a shortage of rental housing arises.

Supporters of rent control in New York include two classes of individuals: (a) tenants living in rent controlled apartments, and (b) government officials who warn that decontrolling housing would impose an unacceptable burden on poor residents.

However, here is another example of Adam Smith's unintended consequences. After doing extensive studies on New York housing under "rent stabilization," economists have discovered unexpected effects of long-time rent control in New York City:

1. With rents failing to keep up with the costs of upkeep, landlords gradually reduce the supply of tenant services. They cannot afford to paint and make repairs, make capital improvements, or provide other services.

2. Rent control has made it unprofitable for landlords to take care of their buildings, leading to decay and abandonment of buildings throughout the entire five boroughs of the city. Entire sections of housing in the South Bronx have been destroyed. An estimated 30,000 New York apartments were made unlivable by the lack of maintenance and were abandoned annually from 1972 to 1982, a loss of almost a third of a million units in this 11-year period.[7]

3. "Old lady effect": As a family grows up and the children move away, the parents and eventually the surviving widow have a strong incentive to stay in the low-cost apartment, even though it is larger than one person needs. Without rent control she would likely move to a smaller, less expensive apartment. Instead she lives alone and may even close off two or three rooms to save on heating and cleaning. Repeal of rent control would free up thousands of rooms for families.

4. The poor do not benefit most from rent controls. According to recent surveys, the lucky tenants who benefit most from rent controls are relatively wealthy individuals, especially in lower and mid-Manhattan.

5. A vast bureaucracy has grown up to administer the controls, supported by volunteers and litigators. Landlords and tenants find themselves in poisonous relationships. Unscrupulous landlords use questionable techniques to evict tenants in order to raise rents. New York City responds by imposing excessively strict tenant-protection laws that make it almost impossible to evict deadbeats. Black markets and bribery thrive.

While no one denies that inequities have arisen in the rental market in New York, few want to change the system, arguing that to do so would lead to chaos and evictions. How difficult would a transition to an unregulated real estate market be in New York? According to the most recent example, in Cambridge, Massachusetts, less painful than imagined. Cambridge lifted rent controls in 1994 after 23 years. According to a study by Henry Pollakowski, an economist at the MIT Centre for Real Estate, Cambridge experienced no dire consequences. Rather, spurred by the promise of market rents and reasonable profits, there was a huge surge in housing investment, and better accommodations for nearly everyone.

7 Walter Block, "Rent Control," *The Fortune Encyclopedia of Economics* (New York: Warner Books, 1993), p. 423.

## PATIENT POWER:
## THE NEW CONSUMER-DRIVEN MEDICAL PLAN

*"In health care today, fundamental principles of the marketplace do not apply. Prices are not determined by supply and demand ..."*

—*"America's Economic Outlaw: The U.S. Health Care System,"*
*The New York Times* (October 26, 1993)

*"Our health care is a hodgepodge of limited free market, all types of government intervention and regulations, and it is increasingly failing....But Health Savings Accounts (HSAs) are the solution that could solve the entire health care problem."*
—*John Mackey, CEO, Whole Foods Market*

As health care became a national issue, *The New York Times* ran a cover story in 1993 contending that America's health care system "operates with almost total disregard for basic economic principles" and therefore deserves special treatment by government. "Prices are not determined by supply and demand or by competition among producers. Comparison shopping is impossible. Greater productivity does not lower costs," the reporter claimed. Health care costs are rising rapidly in the United States, and now represent 15% of national income, the highest of any nation.

Are medical services really that different from soap, cars, or baseball tickets?

Contrary to *The Times's* statement, supply and demand are working all too well in the health care industry. The fact is that medical costs are rising rapidly and many people are failing to get decent coverage precisely because the economic principles outlined in chapter 6 are not allowed to function as they should. The level of competition, incentives, and accountability is not as high as it should be in a free economy.

Why is the cost of health care rising so rapidly? In general, supply isn't keeping up with demand. There are several reasons: first, increasing demand from "free" Medicare and Medicaid, which today accounts for 65 percent of all medical expenses; second, restrictions by the American Medical Association on the number of students admitted to medical school and limitations on what services nurses and paramedics are permitted to perform; third, the third party pay system, which separates the beneficiary from the payer.

The biggest failure facing the health care market is accountability. The natural relationship between beneficiaries and payers has been de-linked to a large extend. The user principle states that those who benefit from a service should pay for it. (If you buy one loaf of bread, you pay $1. If you buy two loaves, you pay $2.) When people don't pay for the services or products they are using, there is a tendency to overuse the benefits and less incentive to keep costs down. The connection

547

is obvious: If you use a doctor's services, you should pay for them. If you use more, you pay more. And if you use less, you shouldn't have to pay the same amount as someone who uses more.

Unfortunately, the link between payers and beneficiaries is breaking down. In more and more cases, Medicare patients are not paying the bill, taxpayers are. Customers of medical services and doctor visits are not paying the bill, the company's insurance company is. A major source of trouble is the pervasive use of employer-paid medical insurance to pay for even routine doctor visits. When employees know that someone else—the insurance company—is going to foot the bill, there is less incentive to shop around and to limit the number of visits to the doctor or the hospital's emergency room. Fortunately, the insurance companies do attempt to maintain some form of cost control on hospitals and doctor services, but the current system is less than optimal.

## IS UNIVERSAL HEALTH CARE THE SOLUTION?

Many influential pundits and politicians advocate adopting what most other countries have: universal health care and a single-payer system. In essence, this policy would mean that everyone would carry health insurance under a single plan run by the Federal government. It's called "single payer" because the Federal government writes the checks for the medical bills. According to supporters, a single-pay universal system would actually reduce costs and red tape.

Universal health care violates the second half of the welfare principle in economics: it offers a taxpayer benefit to people who don't need coverage. Should taxpayers foot the medical bills of Bill Gates, David Rockefeller, or for that matter anyone making more than, say, $100,000? Most people would say no, we shouldn't subsidize the rich. Yet that is precisely what a "universal" health care system does—forces everyone to be on the program and to pay for it (through their taxes), even those who can easily afford their own medical health insurance.

## HOW GOOD ARE THE BRITISH AND CANADIAN HEALTH CARE SYSTEMS?

Supporters of the single-pay system often look to Britain and Canada for successful alternatives. The British National Health Service (NHS) was instituted by the socialists when they took power after World War II. Under the NHS, patients do not pay directly for medical or hospital services; it's paid by the British government. For many years it was regarded as one of the world's best health care systems, but no longer. With unlimited demand at a zero marginal price, medical services at state hospitals and doctor's offices are rationed. In some London hospitals, patients routinely wait more than 12 hours to see a physician.

Total administrative staff at the NHS has skyrocketed to 3.1 staff for every patient, but it still hasn't helped the shortage problem, mainly because they are part of the bureaucracy and not assigned to the treatment of patients. Since 1948, the number of bed per thousand people have fallen in half. The British newspapers regularly feature stories of bungled operations and patients left untended in hospital hallways.

What about Canada? Some supporters point to Canada as an ideal single-pay plan. The government picks up the entire tab of medical expenses for Canadians. Their system is considered low cost. Canada devotes only 9.5 percent of its national income to health care, compared to 15% in the United States.

But the low cost is largely due to a failure to keep up with medical technology and the latest medical devices and procedures. It ranks in the bottom third of developed countries in terms of availability of technology, such as magnetic resonance imaging (MRI) machines or kidney dialysis machines. As Figure 15.1 shows, there are long waiting times for treatment by a specialist in Canada.

### Median Waiting Time for Treatment by Specialist in Canada

| Specialty | Average Waiting Time (weeks) |
|---|---|
| Orthopedics | 32.2 |
| Plastic Surgery | 28.6 |
| Ophthalmology | 30.0 |
| Gynecology | 15.3 |
| Otolaryngology | 16.4 |
| Urology | 13.0 |
| Neurosurgery | 20.1 |
| General surgery | 10.3 |
| Internal medicine | 11.1 |
| Cardiovascular | 14.1 |

*Source: The Fraser Institute, Vancouver, BC, Canada*

Not surprisingly, Canadians who need specialized treatment and surgery go south to the United States, where waiting time is minimal.

Whenever you hear a candidate or political leader say, "We need universal health care," you know that person doesn't understand sound economics.

## THE MARKET SOLUTION:
## LOWER COSTS, HIGHER QUALITY, AND NO WAITING

To show how health care could work if market principles were followed, consider the two examples: laser eye surgery and cosmetic surgery. Most health care products and services have become more expensive, but not laser eye surgery. Lasik surgery has been performed more than three million times in the past decade, and it has gotten better over time. The Lasik process has the highest patient satisfaction of any surgery. In 1998, the average price of laser eye surgery was about $2,200 per eye. Today the average has fallen to $1,350 per eye, a decline of 38 percent. Why has the laser eye surgery case represented the standard market model of "cheaper and better," while other forms of health care have not? Simple. Laser eye surgery is not covered by third-party private insurance, Medicare or Medicaid. Laser eye surgery is one of the few health procedures in a true free market of price competition and consumer choice.

Cosmetic surgery is another example of where choice and competition has delivered lower prices and higher quality over time. Patients pay out of their own pockets for elective surgery, and therefore weigh the costs and benefits of each procedure. Consequently, inflation-adjusted prices have fallen every year from 1992 to 2001.

## WHO'S TO BLAME?

The author of the *Times*'s article blames the market for America's health care problems, but the real cause is the government's failure to let the market operate fully. Even employer-paid medical insurance is, in a way, a government creation. High corporate taxes encourage businesses to offer a wide variety of fringe benefits, which are tax-deductible to corporations and tax-free income to employees.

Contrast the health care industry with the dental industry. The dental market does not suffer from the problems facing the medical industry (spiraling costs, bureaucracy, long waits at medical facilities) largely because (1) most dental services are paid for directly by the patient, and (2) the number of dental students is not restricted. These two factors, patient accountability and expanding supply, have worked to keep the price of dental care down. Despite *The Times*'s dire pronouncement, market principles do work.

## HOW TO RESOLVE THE HEALTH CARE PROBLEM

What should be done to improve the situation? Imitating national health programs in Canada and Europe won't do because they violate market principles. (If you want to know the weaknesses in each country's health care system, analyze each according to market principles.) Hillary Clinton's health care plan, briefly introduced in 1993, wouldn't work either. The Clinton plan made the cost of medical services vary according to income; beneficiaries wouldn't pay directly for medical services; and a new federal agency would impose cost controls on drugs and other medically related services. The result would be shortages, bureaucracy, higher costs, reduced services, and less research and development. Fortunately, the plan was aborted.

## INTRODUCING HEALTH SAVINGS ACCOUNTS (HSAs): THE WHOLE FOODS STORY

Health Savings Accounts (HSAs) are a practical solution to the medical crisis. Congress enacted Health Savings Accounts (HSAs) in 2003 as part of the Medicare reform package. Earlier, they were called Medical Savings Accounts. They were signed into law by President Clinton in 1996.

HSAs are tax-deferred accounts that allow you to save money for medical expenses.

An example from one of the most successful companies illustrates how an HSA works. Whole Foods Market is the world's fastest growing natural food chain and ranked as #5 in the Fortune Top 100 Best Companies to Work For. Until 2003, Whole Foods Market had a generous cafeteria plan in health insurance. The plan was costly with no incentives to economize. Whole Foods was faced with a $7 million deficit in 2003, and were forced to raise premiums by nearly 35 percent. Employees (known as "team players") were not happy with Whole Foods' medical plan.

Whole Foods was one of the first companies to try a Health Savings Account for its employees. To emphasize a positive approach to health care, the company actually calls them "Personal Wellness Accounts." The company pays 100 percent of the premiums for all-full time workers, who are automatically enrolled. However, there is a high deductible of $3,500: $1,000 in medical costs, $500 deductible for prescription drugs, and $2,000 in co-pays (both company and worker co-pay for costs). Each team member is given a MasterCard debit card which they can access for "health and wellness" expenses. (The company tracks carefully MasterCard expenses to make sure they are only used for medical-related items.)

If employees don't use all of the deductible, the remaining funds are placed into a HSA, which builds up tax-free until withdrawn. Under the new law, HSAs are portable, so workers can take the account with them if they move to another company. HSAs create an incentive for workers to become smart health-care consumers because they can keep money that is left over. They have two options for handling unspent HSA funds:

1. They can save money (tax-free) for future medical expenses and the interest that also accrue tax-free; or

2. they can withdraw money from the HSA at the end of the year, but would need to maintain a minimum balance.

Nonmedical withdrawals would be fully taxed and subject to a 15 % tax penalty. "Some of our team members are going to have $8,000, $9,000, and even $10,000 tucked away in their accounts," states CEO John Mackey. "They don't have to worry about going bankrupt due to medical problems."[8]

The results have been phenomenal. The turnover rate has plummeted to around 20%. Company medical costs have dropped substantially. 45 percent of employees don't use their HSA at all. Why not? Because they were healthy, not sick; 74% spend less than $500 on their HSA.

Now, for the first time, Whole Food Market employees have an incentive to shop around for medical services. The high deductible encourages them to shop around and find the best deal. They are encouraged to eat healthy foods and to exercise. By reducing the number of visits to doctors and hospitals, they can save money in their HSA. John Mackey calls it "an empowered model."

According to Forrester Research, by 2010 24% of the health insurance market will be consumer-driven health plans (HSAs). It is the future of American health care.

## SUMMARY

Chapter 23 covered these main points:

1. Government regulatory power has increased dramatically over the past 100 years in all nations.

2. Self-regulation exists in the private marketplace, as evidenced by the Better Business Bureau, Good Housekeeping, Underwriters Laboratories, and Consumer's Union.

3. Government regulation has benefits and costs. For example, the long testing period for new drugs required by the Food and Drug Administration (FDA) keeps potentially harmful drugs off the market, but the long delays also keep good drugs from being used by consumers, resulting in the early death of thousands.

8 John Mackey, "Whole Foods Markets' Consumer-Driven Health Plan," speech at the State Policy Network meeting, October 2004, Austin, Texas.
http://www.worldcongress.com/news/Mackey_Transcript.pdf

4.  Controlling prices and production raises costs, creates shortages, and reduces the quality of goods and services. Excessive government controls has led to deregulation and decontrol of markets, resulting in lower prices and higher quantity and quality in most cases. Markets that have been deregulated in the United States include the transportation, natural gas, and banking industries. Allowing advertising by doctors, lawyers, dentists and pharmacists have been found to reduce prices for consumers.

5.  Governments have engaged in wage-price-rent controls during times of inflation and war, and have resulted in shortages, black markets, corruption, and loss of quality control. Rent controls still exist in New York City, although rent controls are gradually loosening.

6.  Health care costs have been rising rapidly in the United States because of government intervention in medicine. Often patients, doctors and health-care providers lack incentives to economize. Health Saving Accounts (HSAs) will help alleviate the rising cost of health care.

## IMPORTANT TERMS

Bureau of Alcohol, Tobacco and Firearms (ATF)
Chapter 11 bankruptcy
Coase theorem
Consumer Protection Safety Commission
Deregulation
Drug Enforcement Agency (DEA)
Equal Employment Opportunity
  Commission (EEOC)
Environmental Protection Agency (EPA)
Federal Communications Commission (FCC)
Federal Deposit Insurance Corp. (FDIC)
Federal Energy Regulatory Commission (FERC)

Federal Trade Commission (FTC)
Food and Drug Administration (FDA)
Food, Drugs and Cosmetics Act of 1938
Health Saving Accounts (HSAs)
Immigration and Naturalization Service (INS)
Nuclear Regulatory Commission (NRC)
Occupational Safety and Health
  Administration (OSHA)
Price gouging
Productivity of labor
Sarbanes-Oxley Act of 2002
Securities & Exchange Commission (SEC)

## INFLUENTIAL ECONOMIST

### RONALD COASE AND THE COASE THEOREM

**Name: Ronald H. Coase (1910-    )**

**Background:** Ronald Coase was born in Middlesex, Britain and earned his bachelor's degree in economics in 1931 at the London School of Economics, and a Ph. D. at the University of London in 1951. He emigrated to the United States, where he taught at the University of Buffalo and the University of Virginia. In 1964, he moved to the University of Chicago, where he now enjoys emeritus status.   He received the Nobel Prize in economics in 1991.

**Major Work:** Coase is unusual in publishing only a small number of papers that have had a significant impact. His primary focus has been the private sector and its surprising ability to perform better than the public sector in areas traditionally dominated by the state. For example, in 1974, he wrote a paper on the lighthouse disputing the establishment view held by Paul Samuelson and other interventionists that the lighthouse was a public good. As Samuelson stated in his famous textbook, "Its beam helps everyone in sight. A businessman could not build it for a profit, since he cannot claim a price for each user." (*Economics*, 6th ed., p. 59).   In other words, since one cannot prevent the light from being seen by all ships, regardless of whether the ship has paid for this valuable service, no one would pay without being forced through government taxation or harbor fee.   But Chicago economist Ronald Coase revealed that numerous lighthouses in England were built and owned by private individuals and companies prior to the nineteenth century. They earned profits by charging tolls on ships docking at nearby ports. The Trinity House was a prime example of a privately owned operation granted a charter in 1514 to operate lighthouses and charge ships a toll for their use. The cost of the lighthouse was simply bundled into the port-docking fee. Samuelson recommended that lighthouses be financed out of general revenues. According to Coase, however, such a financing system has never been tried in Britain: "the service [at Trinity House] continued to be financed by tolls levied on ships." [See "The Lighthouse in Economics" in *The Firm, the Market, and the Law* (Chicago: University of Chicago Press, 1988), p. 213.]

Earlier, in 1960, Coase wrote an even more influential paper, "The Problem of Social Cost" in the *Journal of Law and Economics*. Prior to this article, economists accept A. C. Pigou's argument that if, say, cattle rancher A's cows destroyed his neighbor B's crops, the only way to right this wrong would be for the government to step in and prohibit A's cows from crossing over into B's farm, or to penalize A with penalties and jail time. But Coase challenged this view, countering that without government, it would pay rancher A to negotiate a mutually beneficial deal with farmer B. When Coase's theorem, as George Stigler dubbed it, was presented to the faculty at the University of Chicago, it was initially objected to as heresy, but after a two hour discussion, it was embraced as a stunning insight. Coase's paper has been cited ever since, and was a primary factor is awarding Professor Coase the Nobel Prize in 1991. We've noted several cases in this textbook of the Coase theorem in action, where the private sector has provided much needed services when the government was not around to act (see the example of Somalia in chapter 20 and private regulatory agencies in this chapter).

## PROBLEMS TO PONDER

1.  The Securities & Exchange Commission was created by Congress in the 1930s to curtail stock market abuses and protective the public from fraud and deception. However, in 2008, despite repeatedly warnings from Wall Street security analysts, the SEC failed to uncover the largest Ponzi scheme in history, when New York money manager Bernie Madoff confessed to embezzling up to $60 billion in accounts for hundreds of clients, many of them non-profit charities and wealthy celebrities. Questions: Are there any costs or unintended consequences to having the SEC protect the public? Does the existence of the SEC create a false sense of security? If the SEC did not exist, what private alternatives would exist to protect investors from fraud and deception?

2.  Should the Food, Drugs and Comestics Act of 1938 be amended to allow nongovernmental agencies to test and approve new drugs as an alternative to the lengthy and costly FDA system? Is the risk of allowing some dangerous drugs in the marketplace worth the benefits of introducing good drugs sooner and at lower cost? Do a cost-benefit analysis of a deregulated drug marketplace.

3.  For many years cigarettes have been banned in television and print advertising. What are the unintended consequences or costs associated with this ban?

4.  Make a list of products and services which are least satisfactory and have shown the least improvement over time. How many of these are produced by government? Do you agree or disagree with this statement by Milton Friedman: "Postal service, elementary and secondary schooling, railroad passenger transport would surely be high on the list. Ask yourself which

products are most satisfactory and have improved the most. Household appliances, television and radio sets, hi-fi equipment, computers and, we would add, supermarkets and shopping centers would surely come high on that list." (*Free to Choose*, p. 192).

5.  On August 15, 1971, President Richard M. Nixon closed the gold window and declared a 90-day freeze on wages, rents and prices. What effects did this executive order have on the economy in terms of quantity, quality and variety of goods and services? Did it create any shortages or surpluses? Did business, landlords, workers, and consumers find ways to get around these regulations?

6.  Twenty-seven states and the District of Columbia have laws or regulations against "price gouging" in a declared disaster. After a massive hurricane hit New Orleans and the Gulf Coast in 2005, shortages of basic commodities became common. Prices doubled and tripled for plywood, drinking water, and generators. The media complained about "price gouging" and state and local authorities cracked down on the law breakers, imposing fines and even jail sentences. An entrepreneurial young man from Kentucky came to Louisiana with a dozen generators and was jailed for "price gouging." On the other hand, many economists contend that these higher prices are necessary in order to attract entrepreneurs to provide scarce supplies quickly to desperate consumers. Do you agree that price gouging should be illegal during a natural disaster, or should such laws be ignored or repealed?

## ADDITIONAL READING

•   *Regulation* magazine (Cato Institute) scrutinizes the effects of regulatory policies on our lives and livelihoods. Since its first publication in 1977 it has examined every market, from agriculture to health and transportation, and nearly every government intervention, from the regulation of interstate commerce to labor law and price controls. Each issue features articles by leading experts at the cutting edge of regulatory reform.

# Chapter 24

# ENVIRONMENTAL ECONOMICS

*"We know that the environment is not in good shape . . . .*
*My claim is that things are improving."*

— BJORN LOMBORG
*The Skeptical Environmentalist*

Early in the 19th century, an estimated 60-100 million American buffalo (technically bison) roamed the West and served as the primary food source for the Plains Indians. But by the mid-1880s, the buffalo had become almost extinct and surviving species amounted to less than a thousand head. The primary cause was commercial hunting. Skins were in heavy demand for industry, clothing, and rugs both in the United States and Europe. Old West buffalo hunts were often a big commercial enterprise, involving thousands of teams of professional hunters, skinners, gun cleaners, cooks, blacksmiths, security guards, and numerous horses and wagons. Hides sold for anywhere from $3 to $50, depending on condition. The commercial take varied from 2,000 to 100,000 animals per day; Buffalo Bill Cody is said to have killed over a hundred animals in one day.

The federal and state governments did nothing to protect these animals from extinction. It was James "Scotty" Philip, a rancher in South Dakota, who came to the bison's rescue. In 1899, he purchased a small herd of five buffalo and took them back to his ranch on the Cheyenne River to breed them. By 1911, at the time of Scotty Philip's death, the herd had grown to an estimated 1,000 to 1,200 head. Other ranches followed suit and developed their own privately owned herds. Two Montana ranchers spent more than 20 years assembling a large collection of purebred buffalo, and after the U. S. government declined to buy the herd, they shipped most of the animals to Canada. With large herds on both private and public lands growing rapidly the bison population is now estimated to exceed 400,000 and bison are no longer considered an endangered species. Most current herds, however, are crossbred with cattle. The only wild bison herd in the United States exists within Yellowstone National Park.

To commemorative the unique nature of the American bison, the United States Mint issued its famous "buffalo" nickel from 1913 to 1938 and began issuing a popular 1-ounce American buffalo gold coin in 2007.

## "THE TRAGEDY OF THE COMMONS"

The American buffalo story is a classic example of the "tragedy of the commons." In a 1968 issue of *Science*, Garrett Hardin, professor emeritus of biological sciences at the University of California at Santa Barbara, wrote a seminal article arguing that a resource tends to be overexploited when owned by the public and not by private individuals. If no one owns a piece of grazing land for example, each herdsman has an incentive to add another animal to the herd until the land is overgrazed. Without individual ownership of the land a herdsman bears only a fraction of his real costs. As a result, "Freedom in a common brings ruin to all."

In the case of the American buffalo, since no one owned the bison herds they were overused to the point of practical extinction. Only when property rights were reestablished — private ranchers owning their own herds for breeding — were the American buffalo herds allowed to grow.

## THE GHOST OF MALTHUS

Environmentalists complain that unrelenting emphasis on economic growth under unfettered capitalism and big business leads inevitably to overuse and exploitation of resources and environmental degradation. This view, first voiced by the Reverend Thomas Malthus in his 1798 *Essay on Population*, builds on the fears that resources are vanishing, or that resources can't keep up with a growing population and its material demands. Figure 24.1 illustrates the Malthusian dilemma.

According to Malthus, the unlimited demands of a growing population tend to put pressure on the earth's limited resources. His conclusion is a fatalistic pessimism of poverty, misery, war, and human mismanagement of earth's resources. Environmentalists worry about air and water pollution, extinction of animals, destruction of forests, strip mining, global warming, and over use of non-renewable resources. Excessive growth and market failure contribute to the problems. Many environmentalists are alarmists. For example, as the Worldwatch Institute stated in 2002: "The bright promise of a new millennium is now clouded by unprecedented threats to humanity's future."[1] Concern over global warming and potential melting of the ice caps increased following the release of Al Gore's film, *An Inconvenient Truth*. According to his followers, the solution to control over global warming is government regulation and establishment of sustainable growth.

1  Worldwatch Institute, *The State of the World 2002* (New York: Norton, 2002), p. xvii.

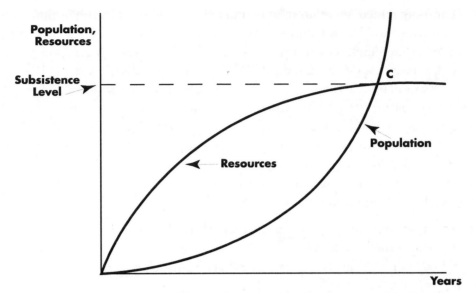

**Figure 24.1.** *Malthusian prediction of population, resources, and subsistence.*

## ANGRY PLANET OR BEAUTIFUL WORLD: THE FREE MARKET RESPONSE

Bjørn Lomborg, a Danish professor of statistics who was an environmental activist and member of Greenpeace, accepted the Malthusian views expressed by Paul Ehrlich, Lester Brown, and groups such as the Worldwatch Institute, Greenpeace, and the Sierra Club that the world was running out of renewable resources, clean water, and forestland, that the earth was becoming more polluted, and that population growth was exploding. Julian Simon, an American economist from the University of Maryland, challenged Lomborg's thinking. Simon had published several books and papers supporting his view that life was getting better, that air in the developed world was becoming less polluted, that fewer people were starving, and that population growth was slowing.

Simon made two arguments against the pessimists: First, natural resources are virtually unlimited in the long run because higher prices, reflecting scarcity, encourage the discovery of additional reserves and the use of substitutes. In addition, entrepreneurs and inventors are developing new technologies and cost-cutting techniques allowing more resources to be discovered and developed. Second, a large and growing population leads to a higher standard of living because it increases the stock of useful knowledge and trained workers.

Lomborg decided to test Simon's statistics. In the fall of 1997, he and a group of students examined Simon's data. Their conclusion: Simon was right. Lomborg reversed course and published his findings in *The Skeptical Environmentalist*, creating a furor within the environmentalist community.

Lomborg joined Simon in refuting most of the claims of the environmentalists: global forests have increased in size since World War II, although the world's population (over six billion) continues to expand. The population growth rate peaked in 1964 and has since declined. Only 0.7% of species have disappeared in the past 50 years. Fewer people in the world are denied access to water, incidence of infectious disease is still on the decline worldwide, the number of extremely poor/starving people is also declining, and air pollution is less in many parts of the world.

But what about global warming, the overriding concern that the capitalistic lifestyle is changing the climate and could do permanent damage to the ecosystem? The evidence is clear that temperatures have been rising slightly in the past century, but the questions remain:

- How much of the temperature increase is man-made?
- How much is natural?
- What is the best course of action to control global warming?

Many economists are skeptical of the dire predictions of environmentalists such as Al Gore and believe that they have exaggerated the environmental problems that do exist.

## THE WEALTH EFFECT

Free-market economists question the argument that economic development is responsible for environmental degradation. In fact, they observe just the opposite. There appears to be a link between national income and concern over the environment which is called the wealth effect. According to one study, in countries where rising incomes reached between $6,000 and $8,000 per year in 2001 dollars, air pollution began to decline.[2] Another study suggests that spending on a better environment is a positive good: demand for a better environment increases with income. Interestingly, members of the Sierra Club have incomes almost twice as high as the average American.[3]

This close link between income and ecological concern creates an interesting paradox: developing nations should maximize economic growth, yet in order to grow faster, they will probably pollute more before they can afford to pollute less. To reduce pollution in the long run, they need to pollute more in the short run!

Lomborg states, "environmental development often stems from economic development—only the sufficiently rich can afford the relative luxury of caring about the environment."[4] Milton Friedman and other free-market economists have

2  Richard L. Stroup, *Eco-nomics* (Washington, DC: Cato Institute, 2003), p. 14.
3  Jennifer Hattam, "Sierra Readers, by the Numbers," January/February 2005, http://www.sierraclub.org/sierra/200501/bulletin.asp
4  Bjorn Lomborg, *The Skeptical Environmentalist: Measuring the Real State of the World* (Cambridge University Press, 2001), p. 33.

been less pessimistic about environmental problems. Friedman states, "Private industry tends to reduce pollution…..But without modern technology, pollution would be far worse. The pollution from horses was much worse than what you get from automobiles….The air today is cleaner in most of the United States."[5] In the 1980s, Albert O. Hirschman commented, "There's a tendency to blame capitalism for environmental damage, but now we find that in the socialist bloc the situation is much worse."[6] These economists have publicized government failure in the debate about the environment. Recent studies have revealed that less-developed countries, including the former Soviet Union, have more pollution, lower health standards, and more environmental hazards than industrialized nations. Economists Terry Anderson and Donald Leal point to several examples of government mismanagement: National parks such as Yellowstone are in major disrepair, the U.S. Park Service is notoriously wasteful (it once built a $330,000 outhouse), the Canadian government destroyed the cod industry, and Brazil and Indonesia forced migrants to burn once-pristine rain forests to plant crops.[7]

## WEALTH CREATION, WASTE AND EXTERNALITIES

How can the economy grow and standards of living increase without destroying the air, polluting the water, cluttering up the environment, and creating global warming? Chapter 1 demonstrated that waste is a required consequence of wealth creation. When unfinished resources are transformed into usable final goods and services — the very definition of wealth — the economic process results in some form of waste at virtually every stage of production.

A serious problem arises when the producer does not pay the full cost of waste and pollution. Negative externalities occur when a person's actions affect neighbors adversely without their permission or without providing them compensation for the adverse effects. For example, a steel plant emits pollution into the air or a local river without permission and the company owning the plant does not pay the neighbors or community for the cost of cleaning the pollution up. The challenge is to find ways to minimize that waste without hindering the wealth creation process. These tools are:

1. **Using property rights** to provide the proper incentives to develop a successful stewardship of the earth's resources and atmosphere.

2. **Implementing reasonable institutional rules and regulations** in cases where property rights cannot be established.

5 Quoted in Carla Ravaioli, *Economists and the Environment* (London: Zen, 1995), pp. 9-12.
6 Quoted in Ravaioli, *Economists and the Environment*, p. 32.
7 Terry L. Anderson and Donald R. Leal, *Free-Market Environmentalism*, 2nd ed. (New York: Palgrave, 2001, pp.47-48.

3. **Establishing prices** as an optimal method of rationing to avoid wasteful overuse of scarce resources, and to encourage new technology as a way to minimize resource use.

In this chapter, economic analysis is applied to the problems of the environment — air and water pollution, overuse of renewable and non-renewable resources, and global warming. The principles of sound economics including incentives, price theory, marginal analysis, property rights can be useful in solving environmental issues.

## GOVERNMENT REGULATION VS PROPERTY RIGHTS?

The phenomenon called the "tragedy of the commons" it describes the unintended destruction that occurs when property is held in common. The traditional solution to the tragedy of the commons and to environmental problems is to regulate the market. Regulations can include passing a law to prohibit the hunting of endangered species and the pollution of water or air, nationalizing forested and mining areas, and imposing fines for automobile manufacturers building cars that pollute the air.

The American buffalo story provides another alternative: establishment of some form of property rights over the misused resource which encourages owners to maintain and expand an asset. There are many examples of how this private solution to a public environmental problem can work.

For example, commercial loggers stand accused of serious crimes against the environment. They are charged with the extinction of tens of thousands of species, the deforestation of vast areas of the earth, and the total and irreversible destruction of the ecosystem.

When forests were first opened up by the Federal government in the 19th century, commercial loggers often practiced clear-cut logging and had no plans for regeneration for the areas cut. Planting and nurturing new trees is expensive. Because the loggers did not own the land they had no incentive to do anything to sustain the forests. They cut down thousands of acres of forests, and then moved on, leaving behind an environmental disaster that caused flooding and destruction of the ecosystem. A public outcry led to government regulation of commercial lumber companies, requiring them to plant trees and to avoid clear-cut logging. Regulation worked to some extent but the market provides another solution: By granting tree companies the right to own the forest land, commercial firms now had an incentive to create a sustainable lumber business that would conserve trees and provide the wood products of the future. Companies such as Weyerhaeuser have developed sophisticated forestry methods and have become self-sustaining companies while exercising sound environmental practices.

## CONTROLLING POLLUTION

Pollution and other environmental problems get out of hand when property rights are not enforced or do not exist. When the rights to use and sell resources are well established and can be defended, all individuals and corporations have an incentive to avoid or minimize pollution problems. If a privately owned home or stream is polluted the owner has a right to sue in court and to seek damages. Economist Richard Stroup points out that in England and Scotland (unlike the United States), private citizens can own fishing rights in local ponds and streams. Owners vigorously defend their property, and have formed small anglers' clubs and other associations that are ready to go to court when their lakes and streams are polluted.[7]

In the United States, government regulation is a more common approach to preventing air and water pollution. In 1970, Congress under President Richard Nixon created the Environmental Protection Agency (EPA) and passed the Clean Air Act Amendments of 1970, unleashing a torrid of standards and regulations upon states, cities and businesses. Today the EPA has 18,000 employees, 10 regional offices, and 17 laboratories across the nation.

One of the most costly federal policies is the EPA motor vehicle emission standards, officially called Corporate Average Fuel Economy (CAFE). Automobiles sold in the United States must meet these strict CAFE standards based on tests by the EPA and administered by the National Highway Traffic Safety Administration. Federal and state governments have gradually raised their standards to increase fuel efficiency and reduce air pollution in major cities, and auto makers who do not meet these standards must pay a "gas guzzler" tax, although large pick up trucks and vans are exempt. Today most automobile manufacturers meet these standards especially with hybrid vehicles that run on both gasoline and electric-powered batteries, and air pollution has declined sharply in American cities.

CAFE standards have been criticized by some economists at the Heritage Foundation and Competitive Enterprise Institute for encouraging car makers to make unsafe, light weight cars in order to meet the increasingly stringent fuel economy tests. They cite a correlation between increased CAFE standards and increased highway deaths, a case of unintended consequences.

---

7  Richard L. Stroup, *Eco-nomics* (Washington, DC: Cato Institute, 2003), p. 22.

## MARKET-BASED APPROACH TO POLLUTION CONTROL

Many economists are opposed to the "command and control" programs of the Federal government, which they regard as inefficient, costly and haphazard. Under their influence, two forms of market incentives have been introduced to enhance environmental rules:

1. Pollution fees, and
2. Marketable permits.

Pollution fees are taxes imposed on polluters, penalizing them in proportion to the amount of pollutants they discharge into the air, waterway, or local landfill. Such taxes are common in Europe but not in the United States. They provide a strong incentive to reduce pollution. The less European companies pollute, the less tax they pay. Fines are a more common punitive action used against polluters in the United States.

The Clean Air Act allows the EPA to issue "emissions permits" for certain pollutants, such as sulfur oxides. These permits can be traded among polluters. Emissions trading is also known as "cap and trade" because the government agency sets a limit or cap on the amount of a pollutant that can be emitted. Polluting companies are given credits which represent the right to emit a certain amount of pollutant. The total amount of tradable credits or permits cannot exceed the cap. Companies that pollute beyond their credits are allowed to buy credits from those who pollute less than their allowances. As a result all the companies have an incentive to reduce pollution: the heavier polluters face higher costs (paying for the credits), and can save money by reducing their emissions, while companies that receive the credits can use these additional funds to reduce their emissions even further and thereby sell more credits in the next go-around.

In many cap-and-trade systems, environmental groups can also participate by buying up credits and thereby causing a net reduction in the emissions cap. Sometimes corporations will retire pollution credits by donating them to a nonprofit organization. Government agencies can always reduce the size of the cap.

Tradable permits have been successful in many states and cities in the U. S. and in the European Union. Studies indicate that tradable permits have reduced sulfur oxides in the United States by 50% or more since 1990. Critics complain that "cap and trade" systems have been abused and costly to taxpayers.

─────────────── CASE STUDY ───────────────

## THE LOVE CANAL SCANDAL, 1978
By Richard Stroup

Liability for pollution is a powerful motivator when a factory or other potentially polluting asset is privately owned. The case of the notorious waste dump, Love Canal [near Niagara Falls, New York], illustrates this point. As long as Hooker Chemical Company owned the Love Canal waste site, it was designed, maintained and operated (in the late forties and fifties) in a way that met even the Environmental Protection Agency standards. The corporation wanted to avoid any damaging leaks, for which it would have to pay.

Only when the waste site was taken over by the local government — under threat of eminent domain, for the cost of one dollar, and in spite of warnings by Hooker about the chemicals — was the site mistreated in ways that led to chemical leakage. The government decision makers lacked personal or corporate liability for their decisions. They built a school on part of the site, removed part of the protective clay cap to use as fill dirt for another school site, and sold off the remaining part of the Love Canal site to a developer, without warning him of the dangers as Hooker had warned them.[8]

## ENVIRONMENTALISTS VS BIG CORPORATIONS

We often see battle lines drawn between environmentalists and major corporations on such issues as cutting down forests and oil drilling. It's often a debate over jobs and profits versus saving the environment or the whales. How to decide which is more important?

One way is to look at the economics. The Audubon Society is adamantly opposed to oil drilling in the Arctic National Wildlife Refuge. "A wildlife refuge is no place for an oil rig!" says one of its flyers. "It would be an environmental disaster!" Traditionally, environmental groups have lobbied for Congress to prohibit or regulate big business from exploiting natural resources. But why not choose another option — buying the property and managing it themselves?

For years private individuals and environmental groups have preserved wildlife habitats and scenic lands around the world. Nearly 300 such land trusts can be founded in most states of the union. National groups such as the Nature

8 Free-Market Environmentalism," by Richard Stroup in David R. Henderson, ed., *The Fortune Encyclopedia of Economics* (Warner Books, 1993), p. 443.

Conservancy and the Audubon Society own numerous plots of land. The Nature Conservancy, founded in 1951, is the largest group in the world aimed at protecting lands and lakes in all 50 states and more than 30 countries. With more than 1 million members and 10,000 volunteers, it owns more than 117 million acres of land and 5,000 miles of river around the world. It also operates more than 100 marine conservation projects in 21 countries and 22 states.

Here are some other land trusts:

- **American Land Conservancy** - Dedicated to the preservation of land and water as enduring public resources, to protect and enhance our nation's natural, ecological, historical, recreational and scenic heritage.

- **Center for Ecological Management of Military Lands (CEMML)** - Supports the national defense mission by providing professional services and technical support to the Department of Defense in conservation, environmental protection, and natural and cultural resources management.

- **Delta Land Trust** - Nonprofit conservation and sustainable development organization based in Madison, Mississippi with operations throughout the Mississippi River Alluvial Valley portions of Arkansas, Louisiana and Mississippi.

- **Equestrian Land Conservation Resource** - Nonprofit organization founded to promote national awareness of the importance of land conservation for equestrian sports and activity. Guide, directors, council, calendar of events, library, equestrian partners, contact, and links.

- **The Forest Guild** - A land trust and stewardship organization in the American Southwest serving foresters, forest-dependent rural communities and businesses, policy makers, and public agencies with research and education on sustainable forestry.

- **Great Rivers Land Trust** - Seeks to promote, for the benefit of the public the preservation and improvement of natural resources principally in, but not limited to, the watershed of the Mississippi River.

- **Habitat Trust** - USA land trust and conservation project. Manages donations of land and money.

- **Northern Prairies Land Trust** - Provides landowners with information to protect lands that are significant for agriculture, ranching, fish and wildlife habitat, water resource enchancement and open space.

- **Southern Plains Land Trust** - Dedicated to preserving and restoring the short grass prairie ecosystem, including key species such as the black-tailed prairie dog, swift fox, and others.

- **The Trust for Public Land** - A U.S. national, nonprofit organization that conserves land for people to enjoy as parks, gardens, natural areas and open space.

- **Wilderness Land Trust** - Has acquired over 180 private holdings in 35 National Wilderness Areas in Arizona, California, Colorado, Montana, New Mexico and Washington.

- **Wildlife Land Trust** - Protects and preserves habitat for wildlife and provides sanctuary for wildlife by prohibiting commercial and recreational hunting and trapping. Affiliate of The Humane Society.

Private ownership of land and water provides proper incentives and farsighted behavior that government ownership often lacks. For example, at the turn of the 20th century, Seattle's Ravenna Park was privately owned and operated by W. W. Beck and his wife, who had developed the park into a family recreation area that attracted thousands of people a day. It was famous for its magnificent tall Douglas firs. However, the city leaders, concerned that the park might not be cared for properly, condemned it and then purchased it in 1911. With no one taking personal responsibility for maintaining the park, it gradually deteriorated, and the tall trees started disappearing soon after the city bought it. The theft of trees was brought to the attention of the city, but nothing was done, and by the early 1970s, Ravenna Park had become a dangerous hangout for drug users.

Compare the Ravenna Park story with Beaverhead Ranch in southwestern Montana, which is owned by Koch Industries. Beaverhead is largely a cattle ranch, but has found a way to make a profit and still work closely with local environmentalists to make sure their business interests work with public concerns about wildlife and the environment. It has sharply reduced worker injuries while winning seven environmental awards. It became the first ranch in the country to be certified by the Wildlife Habitat Council for rebuilding wild animal populations.

## GLOBAL WARMING: TRAGEDY OF A GLOBAL COMMONS?

Global warming, or the "greenhouse effect," is a complicated process whereby the earth is gradually becoming warmer. An increase in the concentration of atmospheric gases (carbon dioxide, methane, nitrous oxide, and chlorofluorocarbons) causes the earth to absorb more sunlight and thus becoming warmer. According to environmental economist and Nobel laureate Thomas C. Schelling, carbon dioxide has increased about 25% since the onset of the industrial revolution, and may have contributed to the increase in temperatures lately (on average 1 degree worldwide in the past 50 years). Some environmentalists such as Al Gore are predicting dire consequences if something isn't done.

The greenhouse effect is a tragedy of global commons. Because no one owns the atmosphere, individuals and businesses lack the incentives to reduce carbon dioxide and other emissions. What solutions can government and private enterprise propose to this threat?

The Kyoto Treaty, organized by the United Nations in Kyoto, Japan, in 1997, is a prominent government response. It imposes limitations on greenhouse gas emissions by nations who signed the treaty, while allowing tradable emissions permits. National limitations range from 8% reductions for the European Union to 7% for the US, 6% for Japan, and 0% for Russia. It permits increases of 8% for Australia and 10% for Iceland. But what are the costs? As of 2007, 169 nations had ratified the Treaty, with the notable exceptions of the United States and Australia, which regard the Kyoto limits are too severe on the economic growth. Recently Canada decided to renege on the treaty, arguing that to enforce it would mean doubling the taxes on gasoline, which was thought to be too costly on its economy.

**Other possibilities include:**

- a worldwide program of slowing or stopping deforestation, since trees absorb carbon and emit oxygen.

- International actions to reduce chlorofluorocarbons (CFCs)

- Adopting energy conservation methods

- Increasing energy efficiency through technological advances and upgrading to more efficient energy use

- Switching from high carbon to low carbon or non carbon sources, especially nuclear energy

- Economists have proposed a universal carbon tax, and tradable permits.

## SUMMARY

Most environmental problems arise when property rights cannot be reasonably established, causing overuse of limited resources and pollution — what biologist Garrett Hardin calls a "tragedy of the commons."

Reverend Thomas Robert Malthus was the first economist to raise concerns about whether the earth's limited resources are sufficient to keep up with the growing demands of an ever increasing population. Malthus is the father of gloomy and fatalistic forecasts about the environment and economic sustainability, and the mentor of social engineers who advocate population control and limits to economic growth. Malthusian advocates highlight threats of environmental degradation and global warming, and advocate strong government intervention and regulation of "unfettered" capitalism.

Market economists are more optimistic about the ability of humankind, what Julian Simon calls the "ultimate resource," to discover new technologies that multiplies the supply of resources to meet ever growing demands. They also contend that market prices provide the best incentive to adopt energy conservation, increase new supplies, and discover alternative energy resources. They point to recent successes, such as the slowing of population growth, curtailment of air and water pollution, increasing standards of living, and a sharp reduction in world poverty.

To reduce pollution and the overuse of limited resources, economists advocate the establishment of property rights whenever possible, and pollution fees and marketable permits.

Private companies and non-government agencies have increasingly entered the environmental field to preserve wildlife habitats and scenic lands around the world.

## IMPORTANT TERMS

Clean Air Act Amendments of 1970
Corporate Average Fuel Economy (CAFE)
Environmental Protection Agency (EPA)
Emission permits
Externality
Global warming
Greenhouse effect
Malthusian

Marketable permits
National Highway Traffic Safety Administration
Negative externality
Positive externality
Sustainable growth
Tragedy of the commons
Wealth effect

## INFLUENTIAL ECONOMIST

### JULIAN SIMON, ENVIRONMENTALISM, AND THE ULTIMATE RESOURCE

**Name: Julian L. Simon (1932-98)**

**Background:** Simon was born in 1932, and earned a BA from Harvard in 1953, and an MBA and Ph. D. in business economics at University of Chicago in 1961. He taught economics and business at University of Illinois, 1969-1983, and University of Maryland from 1983 until his death in 1998.

**Major works:** *The Ultimate Resource* (Princeton University Press, 1981, 1996); *The State of Humanity* (Cato Institute/Blackwell Publishers, 1995).

**Major Contribution:** Simon is best known for his optimistic work on population, natural resources, and immigration. In the 1960s, he was a young economics professor at Illinois worrying about overpopulation and nuclear war. In studying population growth, he discovered that the standard pessimistic Mathusian view didn't fit the evidence. He concluded that there was neither an unsustainable population nor a plundered earth. On the supply side, natural resources are virtually unlimited in the long run. Higher prices of scarce non-renewable resources encourage new discoveries and technological breakthroughs. Entrepreneurs are making new discoveries all the time, increasing the level of known resources of natural resources, or finding new cost-cutting techniques that allow more resources to be developed. The law of diminish returns can be postponed indefinitely because land, labor, capital, and technology are not fixed in the long run. In sum, "every forecast of the doomsayers has turned out to be flat wrong. Metals, foods, and other natural resources have become more available rather than more scarce throughout the centuries."

On the demand side, a large and growing population means a higher standard of living because it increases the stock of useful knowledge and trained workers. The "ultimate resource" is people. "Human beings are not just more mouths to feed, but are productive and inventive minds that help find creative solutions to man's problems, thus leaving us better off over the long run." According to Simon, an increasing population spurs the adoption of new and existing technology.

In 1980, Simon made news when he bet Stanford biologist Paul Ehrlich, author of the alarmist book, *The Population Bomb*, $1,000 that the price of five commodities would be lower in 10 years. Ehrlich lost the bet, but luck was on Simon's side because commodity prices collapsed in the 1980s. In 1995, Simon began a wager with David South, professor of the Auburn University School of Forestry, that timber prices would be lower in five years. Simon was losing the bet when he died in 1998, and timber prices have continued to increase since then.

**Quotation:** "We have in our hands now—actually in our libraries—the technology to feed, clothe, and supply energy to an ever-growing population for the next 7 billion years. Most amazing is that most of this specific body of knowledge was developed within just the past two centuries or so, though it rests, of course, on basic knowledge that had accumulated for millennia. Indeed, the last necessary additions to this body of technology—nuclear fission and space travel—occurred decades ago. (*The State of Humanity*, 1995)

## PROBLEMS TO PONDER

1.  Because the oceans are not owned by any single private company, tragedy of the commons is….common. Today many areas of the ocean are being over fished. Identify government and market solutions to this over fishing problem. Is it possible to create identifiable private property in the oceans?

2.  Governments continue to allow "clear-cut" logging in Canada and in the Amazons in Brazil. What is the rationale for this policy, and should it be prohibited?

3.  Why did the buffalo nearly become extinct while the cow did not?

4.  Who should pay for national parks, the general taxpayer or park visitors? Survey several national and state parks and see where their revenues come from.

5.  Do a cost-benefit analysis of the Endangered Species Act, and look at specific examples of how landowners have been hurt by this act, and who has benefited. In your answer, consider this comment from economist Richard Stroup: "Many environmental policies erode property rights. When they do, they often work against the very environmental protection they are intended to protect. The Endangered Species Act, intended to save species thought to be in danger of extinction, is an example. Only 13 of the approximately 1,800 listed species have recovered since the act was passed in 1973…..The far reaching powers vested in federal agencies to control the landowners' use of their properties have sometimes worked to protect endangered species, but often have had the opposite effect."[9]

6.  Having studied this chapter, how will you celebrate the next Earth Day?

## ADDITIONAL READING

*   Julian L. Simon, *The Ultimate Resource 2* (Princeton University Press, 1996).

*   Terry L. Anderson and Donald R. Leal, *Free-Market Environmentalism*, 2nd ed. (New York: Palgrave, 2001).

*   Richard L. Stroup, *Eco-nomics: What Everyone Should Know about Economics and the Environment* (Washington, DC: Cato Institute, 2003)

9  Richard L. Stroup, *Eco-nomics* (Washington, DC: Cato Institute, 2003), p. 55.

*Chapter 25*

# EXPANSION AND CONTRACTION: WHAT CAUSES THE BUSINESS CYCLE?

*"The fact is that the Great Depression, like most other periods of severe unemployment, was produced by government mismanagement rather than by any inherent instability in the private economy."*

— MILTON FRIEDMAN
*Capitalism and Freedom*, p. 38

## MEASURING THE BUSINESS CYCLE

Many citizens worry about job security, income, bank accounts, inflation, and the value of their investments and real estate. Nations go through a general business cycle, or more accurately, fluctuations in economic activity. A business cycle is defined as the ups and downs of the economy as defined by gross domestic product (GDP), employment, and corporate profits. An expansion can be characterized by rising GDP, increased employment, higher wages, and more corporate profits, while a contraction will see job layoffs, falling profits, rising bank-ruptcies, and falling GDP. Often the economic indicators of the business cycle move together. Figures 25.1 illustrates the general business cycle.

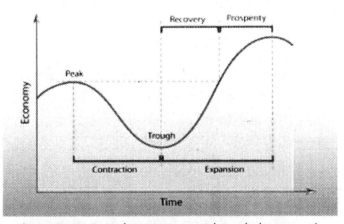

**Figure 25.1.** *General economic activity during the business cycle.*

Economic indicators of nations are measured in many ways. Chapter 15 introduced Gross Domestic Expenditures (GDE), a measure of annual total spending in the economy, and Gross Domestic Product (GDP), the value of final goods and services produced in a year. Real GDP adjusts output for price inflation.
Figure 25.2 shows the changes in real GDP since 1869.

**Graph #1: Real GDP Fluctuations, 1869–1992**

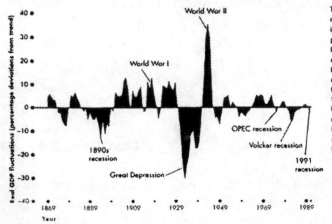

Real GDP fluctuations (percentage deviations from trend)
40
30
20
10
0
-10
-20
-30
-40
1869
1889
1909
1929
1949
1969
1989
Year
World War II
World War I
1890s recession
Great Depression
OPEC recession
Volcker recession
1991 recession
The uneven pace of increase of real GDP is illustrated by tracking its fluctuation measured as the percentage deviation of real GDP from trend. Rapid expansion of real GDP, which occurred during both world wars, puts real GDP above trend. Decreases in real GDP, which occurred during the 1890s recession, the Great Depression, and the three most recent recessions, puts real GDP below trend. The real GDP fluctuations describe the course of the business cycle.

Source: 1869–1929: Christina D. Romer. "The Prewar Business Cycle Reconsidered: New Estimates of Gross National Product, 1869–1908, *Journal of Political Economy* 97. (1989) 1–37; and Nathan S. Balke and Robert J. Gordon, "The Estimation of Prewar Gross National Product: Methodology and New Evidence," *Journal of Political Economy* 97, (1989) 38–92. The data used are an average of the estimates given in these two sources. 1929–1958: *Economic Report of the President,* 1991. 1959–1992: *Economic Report of the President,* 1993. The data for 1869 to 1958 are GNP and those for 1959 to 1992 are GDP. The difference between these two measures is small and is explained in Chaplet 23, pp. 619–520.

**Figure 25.2.** *Changes in Real GDP, 1869-1992.*

The rate of real GDP growth varies sharply from year to year and volatility of real economic growth seems to have slowed since World War II (from 1945 onward).

**Question: Why has the US economy tended to be less volatile since World War II?** (See question #1 at the end of this chapter.)

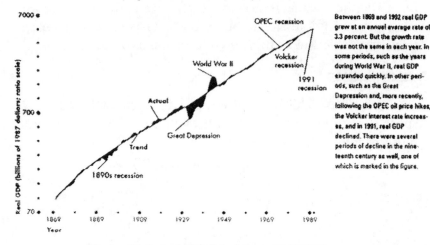

**Figure 25.3.** *Real GDP, United States, 1867-1992.*
*Source: Michael Parkin, Economics, 2nd ed., p. 595.*

Figure 25.3 measures real GDP rather than a change in real GDP.

In Figure 25.2, the US economy appears extremely unstable, but in Figure 25.3, which measures total real GDP, the US economy appears healthy and growing. How can two charts that rely on the same data give two different impressions?

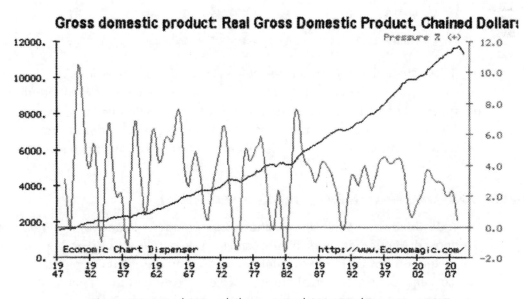

**Figure 25.4.** *Real GDP and Changes in Real GDP, United States, since 1947.*

Figure 25.4 looks at real GDP (the line that is gradually rising) and changes in real GDP (the line that is highly volatile) since 1947. Clearly, showing *changes* in real GDP gives the impression of instability and volatility, while real GDP itself appears relatively stable and rising. Everything depends on perspective.

## PINPOINTING RECESSIONS

Figure 25.5 highlights quarterly growth in real GDP since 1947. Note the shaded space from time to time, such as 1948-49, 1974-75, 1988-82, 1990-91, 2000-01, and most recently 2008-09.

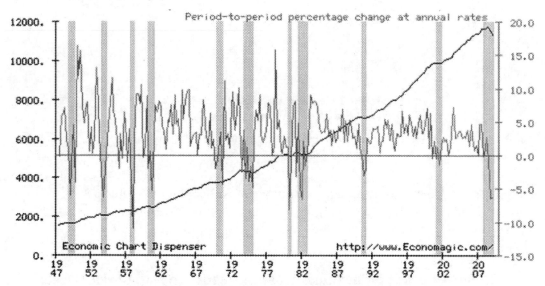

**Figure 25.5.** *Quarterly Growth in real GDP at annual rates.*

These shaded areas are periods defined officially as "recessions" or downturns as determined by the National Bureau of Economic Research (NBER), a nonprofit organization of professional economists. A recession is defined as a decline in real GDP for one or more consecutive quarters of negative real economic growth. NBER officially determines the dates of the peaks and troughs of the business cycle.

## EMPLOYMENT AND UNEMPLOYMENT DURING A RECESSION

A decline in real GDP affects other sectors of the economy that should not be overlooked. Major indicators in the business cycle tend to move together. During an expansion, output and employment rise and the unemployment rate falls. During an economic contraction, real output falls, the creation of new jobs may slow, and unemployment increases. Chapter 10 introduced the subject of unemployment beyond the "natural" rate of unemployment. In a dynamic economy it is normal for workers to change jobs and for companies to hire and fire workers. Most economists agree that a "natural" rate of 3-4% is possible in the United States, and any attempt to reduce it below this rate might be counterproductive and inflationary.

Figure 25.6 illustrates the unemployment rate in the US since 1948 (recessions are noted in gray).

The unemployment rate rises during each recession.

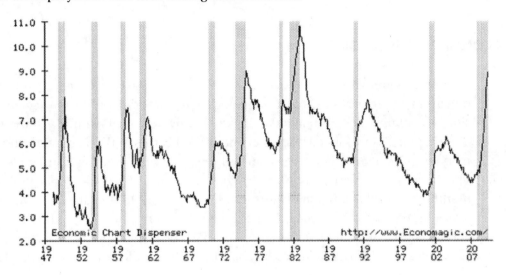

**Figure 25.6.** *Civilian Unemployment Rate: Percent: SA.*

Corporate profits also move up and down during a business cycle. See Figure 25.7 below for changes in corporate profits since 1980.

Figure 25.7 shows corporate profits and changes in corporate profits since 1980 (with recessions in gray).

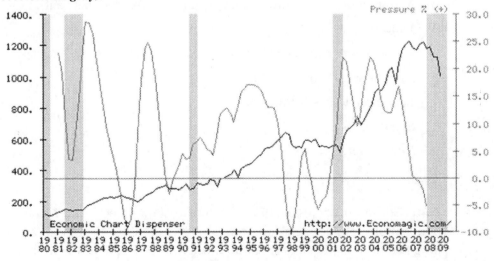

**Figure 25.7.** *Corporate Profits.*

As this chart shows, corporate profits are a "leading economic indicator." Note that corporate profit rates usually fall before a recession is officially announced, and once the recession is in full swing, suddenly corporate profits start picking backup, which inidicates that the recession is ending.

## LEADING ECONOMIC INDICATORS

Can economists predict recessions? One way to do so is by observing the growth rate of corporate profits. Often a sharp decline in corporate profits is a sign of recession — declining real output and rising unemployment (as Figure 25.7 shows).

Chapter 17 introduced leading economic indicators in the discussion about the relative influence of late-stage consumption vs. early-state investment sectors. The Conference Board, a nonprofit organization based in New York, publishes a monthly index of leading indicators for nine countries: In the Americas, the United States and Mexico; In Europe, France, Spain, Germany, and the United Kingdom; and in Asia-Pacific, Japan, Korea and Australia. The Conference Board also publishes coincident and lagging indicators, but the leading indicators are of most interest.

In the United States, the Conference Board lists 10 leading indicators:

1. Building permits.
2. Manufacturers' new orders for nondefense capital goods.
3. Manufacturers' new orders for consumer goods and materials.
4. Vendor performance.
5. Average weekly initial claims for unemployment insurance (inverted).
6. Average weekly manufacturing hours.
7. Real money supply (M2).
8. Stock prices.
9. Interest rate spread.
10. Index of consumer expectations.

**Note:** Corporate profits are not listed by the Conference Board in the 10 leading economic indicators because corporate profits are reported quarterly, and the U. S. Leading Economic Indicators are announced monthly. The only country to include corporate profits in its leading indicators is Japan, which collects data monthly.

## HOW VALUABLE IS THE CONSUMER EXPECTATIONS INDEX?

Consumer Expectations are listed last because it is apparent from the list above that all the other indicators above are located in the early and intermediate stages of production — not the final consumer stage. They are in the manufacturing and wholesale stage, not the retail stage. Yet the Conference Board, perhaps under the influence of a Keynesian mindset that consumer spending drives the economy, highlights the one index that appears to be linked to consumption: the Index of Consumer Expectations.

Upon further analysis, however, this it might not be just a consumer spending index after all. Statisticians surveys 5,000 households each month with questions about their outlook for business, jobs, and income, and plans to purchase automobiles, homes, and major appliances — all expensive durable consumer goods. The only question related to current consumption relates to vacation plans. The survey asks no questions about spending for food, clothing, entertainment, and other immediate consumption goods. The Index of Consumer Expectations is more like an Index of Business Expectations, and should be renamed.

## CAUSES AND CURES OF THE BUSINESS CYCLE

Discussion of the major factors involved in the structure of economy – money, technology, entrepreneurship, and government rules and regulations – provide the basis for answering two important questions:

What causes the economy to rise and fall, the standard of living to ebb and flow, and the markets to boom and bust, in a seemingly endless cycle?

Can the business cycle be controlled or negative impacts to the cycle minimized?

Many theories of the business cycle have been proposed. The ebb and flow affecting the cycle has been blamed on monetary policy, asset bubbles, under consumption, external shocks like OPEC, geo-political events, and even sunspot theories. The most promising theories have been limited to two: 1. government intervention in the economy through monetary and fiscal policy, and 2. external shock catalysts such as an energy crisis, war, or technological revolution, also known as the "real business cycle theory."

## MONETARY THEORY OF THE BUSINESS CYCLE

Monetary theory is considered by many economists as the most influential factor in determining whether a country is in the expansion or recession stage of the business cycle. The Chicago school of Milton Friedman and the Austrian school of Ludwig von Mises and Friedrich Hayek have advocated this theory. The theory proposes that the ups and downs of the economy are largely caused by changes in the money supply and interest rates.

The work of Milton Friedman has been prominent and influential. Friedman gradually changed the mind of the profession regarding the role that money and monetary policy plays in the economy. The shift has been unmistakable. During the Great Depression, John Maynard Keynes and many other economists believed that monetary policy was relatively ineffective in stimulating the economy, and that injecting new money into the system or lowering interest rates through the discount window would be like "pushing on a string." Therefore, conclude the Keynesians, the only effective mechanism for jump starting the economy is to increase "effective aggregate demand" through fiscal policy — by increasing public works, cutting taxes, and running deficits. As evidence they point to the government policy during World War II that pulled the U. S. out of the Great Depression.

What about monetary policy? Keynesians have shifted their views over the years. In 1955, Keynesian economist Paul A. Samuelson wrote in his popular textbook, "Today few economists regard federal reserve monetary policy as a panacea for controlling the business cycle."[1] As a result of this attitude, monetary policy was reduced to a permanent "cheap money" technique for keeping interest rates as low as possible to accommodate government borrowing. The burden of controlling the business cycle fell largely on fiscal policy, through varying the rate of government spending and taxation. Inflation was largely viewed as a "cost-push" phenomenon, and as such, an "incomes policy" (wage/price controls) might be useful in controlling inflation.

However, Friedman's research changed this attitude. In his work *A Monetary History of the United States, 1867-1960*, co-authored by Anna J. Schwartz, Friedman painstakingly gathered a wide variety of statistics on money, credit, interest rates, and the policies of the Federal Reserve for over 100 years, demonstrating conclusively that monetary policy was effective in both expansions and contractions. Friedman concluded that the business cycle, both ups and downs, is linked primarily to expansion and contraction of the money supply (broadly defined). Easy money causes a boom and inflation, while tight money a bust and deflation. At the same time, Friedman acknowledged that monetary policy has little to do with the long-term growth rate of a nation, which is determined by private savings, investment, and technological growth. Furthermore, he states, "I have never believed that fiscal policy [tax cuts or deficit spending by the government], *given monetary policy*, is an important influence on the ups and downs of the economy."[2]

Friedman argued that the reason the war economy recovered from the Great Depression was largely due to an expansionary monetary policy. The money supply increased at a 20% rate during World War II. Critics dismiss Friedman's views by claiming that Friedman believes that "only money matters."

---

1  Paul A. Samuelson, *Economics*, 3rd ed. (New York: McGraw-Hill, 1955), p. 316.
2  Milton Friedman, quoted in *Supply-Side Economics in the 1980s* (Federal Reserve Bank of Atlanta, 1982), pp. 53-54.

Over time, more economists and government officials have come to accept Friedman's monetarism. During a period of double-digit inflation in the 1970s, Paul Samuelson changed his tune about the importance of monetary policy: "Both fiscal and monetary policies matter much."[3] By 1995, Samuelson and co-author William Nordhaus had switched entirely to the side of Friedman: "Fiscal policy is no longer a major tool of stabilization policy [for controlling the business cycle] in the United States. Over the foreseeable future, stabilization policy will be performed by the Federal Reserve monetary policy."[4] As a result the Federal Reserve Chairman is considered more important today than the Treasury Secretary, or even the president of the United States, when it comes to business cycle policy. Central banks around the world give credit to Friedman for encouraging nations to control the money supply as the primary technique of reducing inflation and stabilizing the economy.

## CASE STUDY

### IRVING FISHER, FATHER OF MONETARY ECONOMICS

Irving Fisher (1867-1947) is the father of monetarist economics. Fisher was a brilliant Yale graduate who devoted his entire life to the study of money, the economy and the stock market. Highly skilled in mathematics, he created the first price index. He taught mathematics at Yale, married and had children. Born in upstate New York in 1867, he overcame tuberculosis and invented an index file system that later became the Rolodex. After selling his invention to Remington Rand he became a wealthy man, and by the height of the stock market boom in the 1920s, his fortune exceeded $10 million. He was one of the few professors to enjoy a chauffeur-driven limousine.

At Yale, Fisher developed the first econometric model to predict the future of the economy and the stock market. He was an advisor to world leaders and corporate executives, and was frequently quoted in newspapers as the "Oracle on Wall Street." Observing a booming economy and the introduction of many new consumer goods, including the automobile, refrigerators, telephones, and radio, Fisher was a "New Era" optimist and predicted permanent prosperity in the Roaring Twenties. He firmly believed that the new tools of the Federal Reserve would avert any crisis or depression. His "quantity theory of money" indicated that no serious depression could develop if prices were relatively stable, which they were in the 1920s. On October 16, 1929, two weeks before the stock market crash, Fisher made the soon-to-be-immortal prediction that "stock prices have reached what looks like a permanent plateau."[5]

3  Paul A. Samuelson, *Economics*, 9th ed. (New York: McGraw-Hill, 1973), p. 329.
4  Paul A. Samuelson and William D. Nordhaus, *Economics*, 15th ed. (New York: McGraw-Hill, 1995), p. 645.
5  Irving Fisher, quoted in *The New York Times*, October 16, 1929.

## FISHER AND THE GREAT DEPRESSION

Irving Fisher was mistaken. By the end of the year, the Dow Jones Industrial Average had lost half its value, and by 1932, the Dow had dropped to 40 points, a 90% collapse. Starting in 1930, the U. S. economy went into a tailspin and not long after, Europe and the rest of the world followed suit in what became the greatest economic catastrophe of the 20th century.

By traditional measures of economic performance, the 1929-33 era was a disaster: Industrial output fell by over 30%. Real GDP declined by 25%. Nearly half the commercial banks failed. Unemployment soared to over 30%. In some cities, such as Detroit, half the adult population was out of work. In addition, the recovery in the 1930s was slow and uneven. Unemployment remained high, above 15% until the armaments race heated up in the early 1940s.

Sadly, Irving Fisher never recovered personally. Fisher's stock portfolio was wiped out, and he was forced to juggle heavy debts, failing assets, and to fight terrible battles with the federal tax authorities over his previous earnings for the rest of his life. When he was unable to make mortgage payments, Yale University agreed to buy his home and rent it back to him. He lost his battle with cancer and died in disgrace in 1947. It would take another generation to recover his reputation. Today Noble laureate James Tobin calls him "America's greatest economist" because of his seminal contributions to monetary theory (the quantity theory of money) and price indexing formulas. See Chapter 16 for more information.

---

## AUSTRIAN THEORY OF THE BUSINESS CYCLE

A more sophisticated monetary model of the business cycle is provided by the Austrian school, as developed by Ludwig von Mises and Friedrich Hayek. The Austrian theory is useful in explaining asset bubbles and structural imbalances in the economy that occur due to artificial manipulation of the money supply and interest rates. Austrians argue that bank credit expansion does more than stimulate short-term commercial activity and raise prices. Bank credit expansion distorts the very structure of interest rates and price signals, creating over investments (or malinvestments) in certain markets that are not sustainable and can lead to serious damage to the economy. Talk of real estate bubbles, unsustainable growth in capital-intensive industries, irrational exuberance in stock markets, and other structural problems has led to a revived interest in the Austrian theory of the business cycle.

To understand the Austrian viewpoint, we begin with an economy in macro equilibrium, as illustrated in Figures 25.8 and 25.9. (These concepts and graphs were introduced in Chapters 11 and 14).

First, let's look at macro equilibrium in the credit and capital investment markets, as shown in figure 25.8.

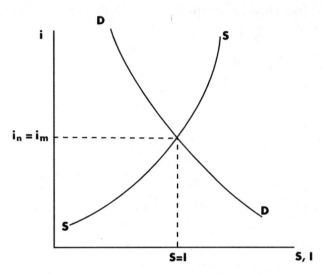

**Figure 25.8.** *Macro equilibrium in supply and demand for credit and capital investment markets.*

In this "evenly rotating economy," as Mises calls it, the "market" rate of interest ($I_m$) is equal to the "natural" rate of interest ($I_n$). Thus the time preference of individual consumers is equal to the demands of credit by investors and capitalists. In other words, savings (S) is equal to investment (I) at interest rate ($I_n$).

We can also show macro equilibrium in the Aggregate Production Structure (APS). In figure 25.9, the Aggregate Supply Vector (ASV) and the Aggregate Demand Vector (ADV) are parallel and equal at each stage of production.

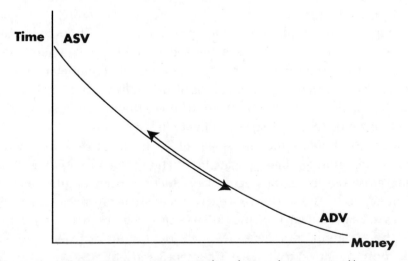

**Figure 25.9.** *Aggregate Supply and Demand in Macro Equilibrium.*

Now suppose the Federal Reserve decides to adopt an "easy money" policy by expanding the money supply and artificially reducing interest rates ($I_m$) below the natural rate ($I_n$). Figure 25.10 illustrates the initial effects of the "easy money" policy.

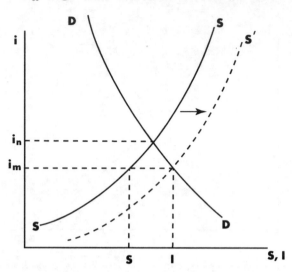

**Figure 25.10.** *The initial effect of the Fed's "easy money" policy on the credit markets.*

As noted above, the supply of loanable funds increases as the market rate of interest ($I_m$) falls below the natural rate of interest. Lower interest rates encourages capital investment (I), but discourages new savings (S).

Can artificially low interest rates (below the natural rate) last? Not according to the Austrian model. When the central bank artificially cuts interest rates and expands the money supply, it creates an artificial boom and structural imbalance in the capital-good industries and in capital assets that cannot last. Recall that in the Austrian model, the macro economy involves a time structure, with goods undergoing a lengthy and complex production process. Thus, changes in interest rates and injections of new money affect some sectors more than others. "Who gets the money first?" is a question Austrians always ask, while monetarists such as Milton Friedman assume that the new money is distributed evenly, like a helicopter spreading cash equally to all citizens. Those who get the money first benefit more than those who get the money last, according to the Austrians.

Figure 25.11 shows the four stages of the business cycle as a consequence of monetary inflation on the Aggregate Production Structure (APS). ASP measures the annual gross output of all stages of production, from natural resources to final consumer goods. The vertical axis measures the time or stages it takes for goods and services to be produced, from the earlier basic resources to the final consumer stage, while the horizontal axis measures the gross output or revenue at each stage of production. We introduced ASP in Chapters 3 and 14.

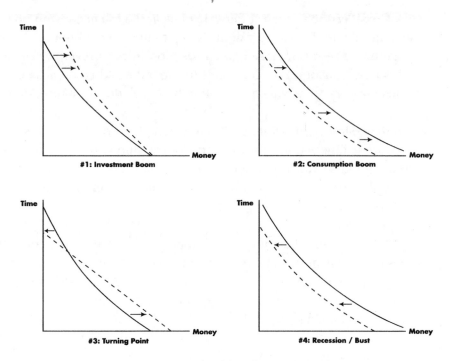

**Figure 25.11.** *Four stages of the inflation-induced business cycle.*

A review of these stages from an Austrian perspective shows:

**Stage 1: The capital-goods boom.** If the Federal Reserve cuts interest rates and expands the money supply, industries such as construction, housing, and capital-intensive industries — which are more interest-rate sensitive — will benefit more than grocery stores, where food purchases are usually not sensitive to interest rates. Most people don't borrow money to buy food, but they do take out mortgages to buy a house, and finance businesses with borrowed funds to expand their operations. Final consumption goods that are consumed in a fairly short period are hardly affected by interest rates and monetary policy. Food, clothing, gasoline, and entertainment are examples of consumables that are not normally sensitive to interest rate changes. However, demand for durable capital goods, such as machinery used in mining or manufacturing, is highly volatile. When machines, tools and other forms of capital are financed, raising or lowering the interest on the loans can dramatically affect the long-term cost of this capital.

**Stage 2: Consumption boom.** The capital-goods boom spills over into the consumption phrase as profits are spent for more consumption goods—new cars, appliances, travel, entertainment, second homes, art and collectibles. Stage 2 represents the full expansion phase.

**Stage 3: Credit crunch.** Interest rates ($I_m$) rise in the full expansion phase to above the natural rate ($I_n$), causing diminishing returns in the booming economy. The Fed must raise rates, causing a contraction in the previously most profitable industries. Consumption continues to expand but the cutbacks in the capital-goods markets offset the consumption boom, leading to a recession.

**Stage 4: Recession/depression.** This is the bust phase of the business cycle, where all sectors of the economy are falling. Consumption does not fall as much as the capital-good sector. Eventually, with interest rates falling back down to their "natural" rate($I_n$), the economy returns to macroeconomic equilibrium (where ASV equals ADV).

Figure 25.12 below illustrates what happens to the economy in between the two extremes of the business cycle. Throughout the cycle, the early stages of production (capital goods industries, stocks, real estate, and other assets) tend to expand and contract on a magnitude much greater than that experienced by the later stages of production (consumer goods industries). Note that output, prices, employment and inventories in capital goods industries and assets tend to be more volatile than those in the consumer good industries. Note that BC/AC is substantially smaller than EF/DF.

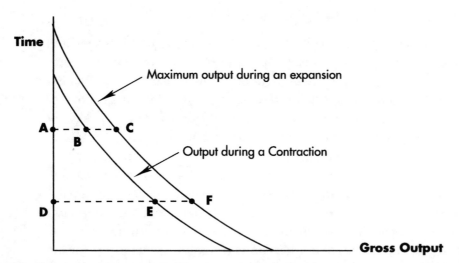

**Figure 25.12.** *Output in an expansion and contraction in the Aggregate Production Structure (APS).*

The Austrian model explains why investment, real estate, stocks, commodities, and manufacturing tend to be more volatile than consumption, retail sales, and groceries, and why asset bubbles in real estate, the stock market, and other investment sectors occur.

Evidence of Austrian-type asset bubbles and unsustainable industrial booms are clearly demonstrated in the business cycles over the years. (See box for historical examples.) Capital-intensive goods and industries, including real estate, manufacturing, and mining, are far more cyclical than consumer-goods and government-oriented industries. Austrian capital theory predicts that the further removed the production process is from final consumption, the more volatile prices, employment, inventories, and output will be, due to the time value of money (interest rates). Research on a variety of U. S. prices from 1952-84 reveals that "raw industrial materials prices proved to be the most volatile, consumer prices the most stable, and producer prices somewhere in between."[6] Empirical work and time-series evidence uncovered by Frederick C. Mills at NBER in the 1930s and 1940s and Charles Wainhouse's doctoral dissertation at NYU confirms significant malinvestment, structural imbalances, and intertemporal volatility in the real economy throughout the business cycle. The most recent 1995-2003 experience in the high-tech economy supports the relevance of the Austrian model. (See box, "Case Studies in Austrian Business Cycle.")

Mises suggests that an increase in the quantity of money can affect either consumer goods, producer goods, or both, depending on "whether those first receiving the new quantities of money use this new wealth for consumption or production."[7] Hayek adds, "Everything depends on the point where the additional money is injected into circulation (or where the money is withdrawn from circulation), and the effects may be quite opposite according as the additional money comes first into the hands of traders and manufacturers or directly into the hands of salaried people employed by the State."[8] Lately money has entered the economy through banks, mortgage companies, and Wall Street, and the effects have been seen in real estate and stock indexes.

## —————— CASE STUDY IN AUSTRIAN BUSINESS CYCLE ——————

Many historical examples confirm the Mises-Hayek theory of the business cycle. For example, in the U. S., monetary inflation was relatively modest throughout the 1950s and early 1960s, and so was the business cycle. But when monetary inflation picked up its pace and grew much more rapidly in the late 1960s and 1970s, the result was a much more volatile economy. The expansions were greater and the contractions were more severe, just as Mises-Hayek would have predicted.

---

6  Mark Skousen, *The Structure of Production* (New York University Press, 1990, 2007), pp. 58-60, 292-93.
7  Ludwig von Mises, *On the Manipulation of Money and Credit* (New York: Free Market Books, 1978), pp. 124-25.
8  F. A. Hayek, Prices and Production, 2nd ed. (London: Routledge, 1935), p. 11.

A look at Japan in the 1980s and 1990s reveals some insights as well. If the Bank of Japan had adopted the Friedman monetarist rule, increasing the money supply steadily at 3-4% a year, the Austrians would have predicted only a mild inflationary build-up and subsequent recession. But the Bank of Japan engaged in an extremely liberal money policy in the 1980s, expanding the monetary base by 11% for four straight years and keeping interest rates artificially low. The result was (1) dramatic economic growth in the late 1980s, followed by (2) a crash and prolonged depression in the 1990s. Japanese economist Yoshio Suzuki accepts the Austrian interpretation of his nation's boom-bust cycle: "As Hayek teaches us, easy money does not always raise the price of goods and services, but always creates an imbalance in the structure of the economy, particularly in the capital markets....This is exactly what happened in Japan [in the 1980s]."[9] Suzuki also adds an important footnote, "In my 40 years' experience as a monetary economist, I have never felt as strongly as I do today the need to bring back to life the essence of Hayek's trade cycle theory."[10]

The third example is the boom-bust cycle of the late 1990s and early 2000s. What fueled the "irrational exuberance" of the high tech boom and stock bubble of the late 1990s, beyond the genuine technological advances in telecommunications and computers? The Austrians point to the Federal Reserve, which deliberately cut interest rates and injected large amounts of liquidity into the banking system between 1995 and 2000, prompted by the Asian financial crisis in 1997, the Russian economic collapse in 1998, and the Y2K fears of 1999. When the Y2K disaster was averted, the Fed sopped up liquidity by squeezing the money supply and raising short-term interest rates sharply in 2000. Consequently, the economy came unglued and Wall Street, especially the high-tech dominated Nasdaq, suffered its worst bear market since the Great Depression, lasting three years. *The Economist* (September 28, 2002 issue) was one of the first to acknowledge that the Austrian business cycle theory, long out of fashion, offers a plausible explanation of the 1995-2003 boom-bust cycle. Prior cycles had been explained by an exogenous oil-price shock, policy mistakes, or productivity changes, but "this cycle was different.....It was an investment-led boom that carried the seeds of its own destruction. The recent business cycles in both America and Japan displayed many 'Austrian' features."

The fourth example is the real estate bubble in 2000-2006. Austrian economists blame the Federal Reserve for reducing interest rates to 1% in 2004, encouraging mortgage companies and banks to lend funds to individuals who would not normally qualify to buy a house. Housing prices skyrocketed, especially in California, Nevada and Florida, and then prices fell sharply in 2007-09, precipitating a worldwide credit crisis that required massive intervention by central banks and governments around the world.

---

9 Yoshio Suzuki, quoted in Mark Skousen, *Vienna and Chicago, Friends or Foes?* (Washington, DC: Capital Press, 2005), p. 179.
10 Ibid.

## POLITICAL BUSINESS CYCLE

The political election cycle is often a major factor in the economic cycles of many countries. The business cycle is often influenced by the manipulation of fiscal and monetary policy by incumbent politicians hoping to stimulate the economy just prior to an election and thereby improve their own and their party's reelection chances. Expansionary monetary and fiscal policies create politically popular consequences in the short run such as tax cuts, falling unemployment, falling interest rates, or new government spending on services for special interests.

Mexico, for example, often goes through a 6-year cycle based on its presidential election cycle. When first elected, the new administration typically adopts a policy of restraint and retrenchment, but as the election nears, the party in power increases spending and expands the money supply to gain public support for its reelection.

In the United States, investment analysts often refer to the four year presidential election cycle on Wall Street. The pattern is quite clear. The last two years (pre-election year and the election year) of the 43 administrations since 1833 produced a total net market gain of 746%, compared to only 228% gain in the first two years of these administrations following the election. Presidential elections every four years have an impact on the economy and the stock market. As *The Almanac Investor* states, "Wars, recessions, and bear markets tend to start or occur in the first half of the term; prosperous times and bull markets, in the latter half....In an effort to gain reelection, presidents tend to take care of most of their most painful initiatives in the first half of their term and 'prime the pump' in the second half so the electorate is most prosperous when they enter the voting booths."[11]

## EXTERNAL SHOCKS AND THE "REAL" BUSINESS CYCLE

"Real" business cycle theory is a relatively new addition to the interpretation of economic fluctuations. In a broader sense, advocates blame "real" world external factors rather than monetary and fiscal policies for domestic troubles: world wars, the regional wars in Vietnam and Middle East wars, the oil embargoes of 1973-74 and 1979-80, and the terrorist attacks in September, 2001 are examples. Another example of "real" effects on the business cycle is technological innovations, such as the computer revolution, or the Internet.

The "real" business cycle (RBC) theory was introduced by Finn Kydland and Edward Prescott in their seminal 1982 work "Time to Build and Aggregate Fluctuations," for which they won the Nobel Prize in Economics in 2004. According to their model, technological shocks can generate random fluctuations in the productivity level that shifted the economic growth trend up or down. Examples of such shocks include product innovations, bad weather, imported oil price increase, or stricter environmental and safety regulations. Such shocks affects the decisions of

11 Jeffrey A. Hirsch and J. Taylor Brown, *The Almanac Investor* (New York: Wiley & Sons, 2006), p. 98.

workers and firms, who in turn change what they buy and produce and thus eventually affect output. RBC models predict time sequences of allocation for consumption and investment, given these shocks. They conclude that little can be done to counter the cycle. Their prescription is largely laissez faire; government intervention can only makes things worse.

Critics complain that the RBC theory ignores other important factors in the business cycle, such as monetary and fiscal policy, and imperfections in institutions and markets.

## CURES OF THE BUSINESS CYCLE

Under the influence of Keynesian economics, Congress passed the Employment Act of 1946, which mandated the U. S. government to use its monetary and fiscal tools — spending, taxation, and the money supply — to stabilize the economy. Most economists are convinced that the amplitude and duration of recessions have been reduced, but certainly not eliminated, by this method. During the 1950s and 1960s, Keynesian economists strongly believed that the government had the tools with which to control the business cycle, and even banish it through fine-tuning. Monetarists, too, assured the world that depressions were a phenomenon of the past. Milton Friedman gave a speech in Sweden in 1954 entitled, "Why the American Economy is Depression Proof," in which he argued that between strong monetary authority to inject liquidity at any time and federal bank deposit insurance, the chances of another Great Depression were virtually nil.[12]

The inflationary recessions of the 1970s dispelled any pretension that economists had all the answers. Certainly as Friedman predicted, we have avoided another Great Depression, but there have been numerous booms and busts along the way. The central bank's frequent policy of switching between "easy money" and "tight money" has not helped to maintain a stable monetary environment.

What can be done to minimize the ups and downs of the economy? Most economists now endorse several principles:

1.  Maintain a relatively stable monetary policy, both in terms of increases in the stock of money (broadly defined, which usually means M2) and interest rates.

2.  Keep government regulations on labor, capital and business to a minimum so that adjustments to new economic conditions can occur quickly and smoothly.

3.  Keep borders relatively open in terms of trade, capital, money, and immigration. Closing off an economy from the outside world can make it more vulnerable to natural disasters, government policy, and human error.

## MONETARY POLICIES TO CONSIDER

Economists have considered five possible solutions for controlling inflation and the business cycle.

12  Milton Friedman, *Dollars and Deficits* (New York: Prentice-Hall, 1968), pp. 72-96.

## A MONETARIST RULE

Monetarists favor a "monetary rule," where a broadly-defined money supply (usually M2) is increased at a steady rate equal to the long-run real GDP growth rate. Milton Friedman has advocated this monetary rule since the 1950s. However, it has never been implemented because (a) it has been difficult to define the proper money supply, and (b) it rules out discretionary authority for central bankers to intervene and inject liquidity into the markets during a crisis. Austrians also complain that a 4-5% monetary inflation would still cause structural imbalances and asset bubbles in the economy, depending on who receives the money first.

## GOLD PRICE TARGETING

Some Austrians and supply-side economists support some form of gold standard and free-banking solution. Supply-siders Art Laffer, Paul Craig Roberts, Steve Hanke, and Steve Forbes favor a central bank policy called "gold price targeting." Suppose the target price of gold is around $900 an ounce. According to their approach, central bankers should therefore, seek to maintain the price of gold close to $900. If gold exceeds this target price, the Federal Reserve should restrict credit until the price declines to $900. If the price falls under $900, the Federal Reserve should loosen and expand the money supply until the price goes backup to $900. Critics complain, however, that gold is too volatile to use as a price target, as it would be easy to overshoot in both directions.

## FREE BANKING

What is free banking? According to George Selgin and Larry White, economists who have done considerable research in this area, free banking is a form of an "invisible hand" or free trade in money. According to this approach, government's involvement in the monetary sphere would be entirely laissez faire: "There is no government control of the quantity of exchange media. There is no state-sponsored central bank. There are no legal barriers to the entry, branching, or exit of commercial banks....There are no reserve requirements....There are no government deposit guarantees."[13]

Will free banking without government guarantees and without reserve requirements and other forms of supervision deteriorate into chaotic "wild cat" banking? How could citizens be assured that a stable, non-inflationary monetary framework is achievable under free banking? Here advocates such as Selgin and White rely primarily on historical evidence. Based on studies of free banking in Scotland and Britain in the 18th century and 19th century, they contend that for over a century and a half, when Scotland had free entry and minimal government interference with

---

13 George Selgin and Lawrence White, "How Would the Invisible Hand Handle Money?" *Journal of Economic Literature* 22 (December, 1994), pp.1718-19.

the banking system, virtually all the bank notes of different banks circulated at par, and there were few bank failures. Furthermore, they say, competition among bank note issuers assures a variety of choices in banking and minimize the risk of insolvency. Advocates concur that free banking would not be destabilizing, competition would keep banks from overissuing their bank notes, and monetary inflation would be minimized. Although gold is not necessary as a numeraire to the free-banking system (silver may serve as a good substitute), the free-market system would be "self-regulating."

According to critics, the major drawback to free banking is the high degree of faith in the market required by the public to accept this kind of laissez faire framework. Without any government regulation or reserve requirements, the degree of uncertainty in the system is far greater than a system based on 100% reserves in specie, or a Monetarist Rule. And who wants uncertainty in the money system when other secure systems are available? On a practical level, who wants to deal with potentially dozens of different kinds of privately issued bank notes? Presumably under free banking there would be no official national bank notes, and the wide variety of private notes might be intimidating.

## CANADIAN/AUSTRALIAN BANKING MODEL

A fifth possibility is to imitate the Canadian, Australian and New Zealand banking model. According to the Global Competitiveness Report issued annually by the World Economic Forum, the world's most stable, profitable banks are in Canada, Australia and New Zealand. Not a single Canadian bank failed during the Great Depression, or in the financial crisis of 2008-09. They have far fewer commercial banks and the ones they do have are national in scope, with branches throughout the country, thus making them less susceptible to downturns. They have a large numbers of loyal depositors and a more solid base of capital. They are more tightly regulated than their US counterparts, more liquid and less leveraged.

## PRICE INFLATION TARGETING

Keynesians tend to support a flexible form of "inflation targeting" as their long-term monetary tool, allowing the central bank's flexibility to respond to monetary crises by injecting liquidity to maintain order. Under this model, the monetary goal is to stabilize the price level, such as the consumer price index (CPI) or GDP deflator.

Inflation Targeting is relatively new in the evolution of Fed policy. It focuses on controlling the rate of price inflation rather than interest rates. Until the late 1970s, the Fed's plan was to implement a "low interest rate" environment so that the government could easily finance its deficits. That changed from 1979 to 1982, when Paul Volcker was called in to fight inflation. He immediately changed the rules in favor of "monetarism," focusing on controlling the money supply and letting interest rates fluctuate freely. Volcker slammed on the monetary brakes, breaking the inflationary psychology, but interest rates skyrocketed to 21% before gradually declining again. Volcker's experiment in monetarism ended in the mid-1980s when the relationship between the money supply and the global economy broke down, due to the deregulation of the banking system and the globalization of the economy.

For the next 20 years, under the leadership of Alan Greenspan, the Fed switched back to a policy focusing primarily on interest rates – raising them to fight inflation, and cutting them to fight recession. Greenspan was largely successful, even though his Federal Reserve changed policies seven times during his 19-year reign (1987-2006). Greenspan's successor, Ben Bernanke, sought to change Fed policy again by adopting "inflation targeting," which would set a numeric CPI goal (around 2% a year) that the board would pledge to maintain through its monetary authority.

According to studies by Ben Bernanke and Frederick Mishkin, countries that have adopted inflation targeting have seen their core inflation rates drop significantly:

- New Zealand since 1990
- Canada since 1991
- The United Kingdom since 1993

New Zealand has been successful. Prior to inflation-targeting goals, its inflation rate varied from 10% to 15%. Now the CPI rate in New Zealand is less than 3% a year. See Figure 25.13 below.

Chairman Bernanke seeks to imitate the success in New Zealand, Britain, and other Western nations. The financial crisis of 2008-09 postponed the return of inflation targeting as a tool.

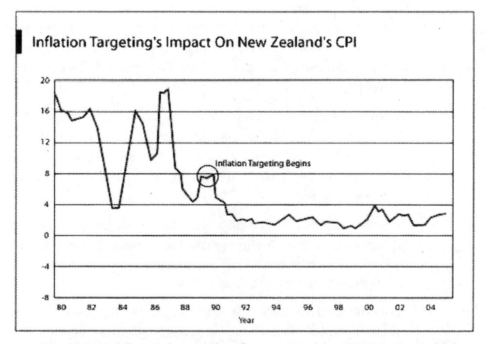

**Figure 25.13.** *Inflation before and after inflation targeting began (1989) in New Zealand.*

## SUMMARY

Chapter 25 covered these main points:

1. A business cycle is defined as the ups and downs of the economy as defined by GDP, employment, and corporate profits.

2. Since World War II, the volatility of real GDP growth appears to have slowed.

3. The National Bureau of Economic Research (NBER) in Boston, Massachusetts, determines officially the beginning and end of recessions (defined as two or more consecutive quarters of negative real GDP).

4. The Conference Board in New York seeks to predict recessions using its Index of Leading Economic Indicators, which is published monthly. However, the Index of Leading Economic Indicators omits corporate profits, one of the best leading indicators, because corporate profits are published quarterly.

5. The Index of Consumer Expectations, which the media and Wall Street watch closely, is a misleading guide of consumer behavior. The Index of Consumer Expectations is more a "business" expectations index.

6. Several popular explanations of the business cycle exist. One important explanation is central bank monetary policy — easy money creates an artificial boom, and tight money causes an economic downturn. The Austrian theory of the business cycle is a more sophisticated model that focuses on asset bubbles and structural imbalances as a result of the central bank's easy money policies.

7. Another business cycle theory is the political election cycle. Wars, recessions, and bear markets on Wall Street tend to occur in the first half of the presidential term; prosperous times and bull markets in the last half, when presidents seeking reelection tend to "prime the pump" and engage in excessive spending.

8. According to the "real" business cycle theory, booms and busts are linked to random fluctuations due to unexpected "shocks" to the system, including technology, energy crisis, natural disasters, or government regulations, rather than monetary and fiscal policy.

9. Economists offer a variety of ways to tame the business cycle, including a monetarist rule, price inflation targeting, gold price targeting, free banking, and institutional improvements (the Canadian/Australian banking system).

Aggregate Production Structure (APS)
Aggregate demand vector (ADV)
Aggregate supply vector (ASV)
Austrian theory of the business cycle
Business cycle
Capital-goods boom
Conference Board
Consumer Price Index (CPI)
Consumption boom
Easy-money policy
Effective aggregate demand
Employment Act of 1946
Evenly rotating economy
Fiscal policy
Free banking
GDP Deflator
Gold price targeting
Gross Domestic Expenditures (GDE)
Incomes policy
Index of Consumer Expectations
Index of Leading Economic Indicators
Inflation targeting
Invisible hand
"Irrational exuberance"

Laissez faire
Market rate of interest
Monetarism
Monetary policy
Monetary rule
National Bureau of Economic Research
    (NBER)
Natural rate of interest
"New Era"
Nominal GDP
Organization of the Petroleum
    Exporting Countries (OPEC)
Presidential election cycle
Price inflation targeting
"Pushing on a string"
Quantity theory of money
Real business cycle (RBC)
Real GDP
Recession
Specie
Technological shocks
Tight-money policy
Wild-cat banking

**INFLUENTIAL ECONOMIST**

**FRIEDRICH HAYEK AND THE AUSTRIAN THEORY OF THE BUSINESS CYCLE**

**Name: Friedrich A. Hayek (1899-1992)**

**Background:** Friedrich Hayek, one of the founders of the modern Austrian school of
    economics, was born in Vienna, Austria, and earned two doctorates at the
    University of Vienna. He worked under Ludwig von Mises (see biography in
    chapter 2) as director of the Austrian Institute of Economic Research. He was
    one of the few economists to anticipate the 1929-33 Great Depression, and
    because of his foresight, became a professor at the London School of Economics
    until the late 1940s, where he was known as John Maynard Keynes's chief rival.

During World War Two, Hayek wrote *The Road to Serfdom* (1944), his most popular book. He had two children from his first marriage, and after a bitter divorce, married his childhood sweetheart, and joined the faculty at the University of Chicago as a member of the Committee on Social Thought in the 1950s. There he wrote *The Constitution of Liberty* (1960). In 1962, he left Chicago for the University of Freiberg, where he continued to work on a three volume work, *Law, Liberty, and Legislation* (1973-79). In 1974, Hayek was the first free-market economist to receive the Nobel Prize in economics for his work on business cycle theory and the importance of knowledge in the economy. After winning the Nobel Prize, he began writing once again on economic issues—socialism, inflation, and monetary reform, culminating in his final book on a lifetime theme, *The Fatal Conceit: The Errors of Socialism* (1988). He died in 1992.

**Major works:** *Prices and Production* (London: Routledge, 1931); *The Road to Serfdom* (University of Chicago Press, 1944); *The Constitution of Liberty* (University of Chicago Press, 1960)

**Major contributions:** His book, *Prices and Production* (1931), introduced the Austrian theory of the business cycle, which he learned from Mises. It provided a counter argument to the Keynesian revolution. During World War II, he wrote a classic on political philosophy, *The Road to Serfdom* (1944), warning that the world's movement toward welfare statism and national dictatorship could lead countries down a dangerous "road to serfdom" and the loss of political and economic freedom. His book became a bestseller after *Reader's Digest* condensed it. Hayek followed this book with a seminal article, "The Use of Knowledge in Society," broadening his critique of socialist central planning. The article explains that prices communicate vital information to consumers and producers, and that specialized knowledge, vital to economic growth, is decentralized and local, and thus cannot be duplicated by industrial planners and technocrats. As Hayek states, "To assume all the knowledge to be given to a single mind....is to disregard everything that is important and significant in the real world." Hayek saw the market economy more as an organism that coordinates activities, which differed significantly from Keynes and most other economists who saw the economy as a machine that has broken down from time to time.

**PROBLEMS TO PONDER**

1.  Review Figures 25.2, changes in real GDP in the US over time. Which of the following explains the fact that since World War II (1945), the economy seems to have become less volatile compared to pre-1945. Is it because:

    A.  Government provides a "built in stabilizer" and has become larger as a percentage of GDP since 1945.

    B.  Federal Reserve monetary policy has learned its lesson from the Great Depression and has adopted a more stable monetary system since 1945.

    C.  Western economies such as the US have benefited from new technologies and a more integrated global economy, so that economic growth in the United States have grown more smoothly since 1945.

    D.  We have not had another world war since 1945.

    E.  The apparent discrepancy is largely due to improved statistics. Prior to 1945, data on unemployment, real GDP, and industrious production has been incomplete and often misleading. Since World War II, the statistics have been more carefully and consistently applied to make it appear that the business cycle has smoothed since 1945. As Christina Romer concludes after comparing the use of data between the two eras, "These comparisons show essentially no decline in the severity of cycles between the prewar and postwar eras."

Contact several economists and ask them what they think.

2.  One of the major debates among economists is whether a free-market economy is inherently stable or unstable. Followers of Adam Smith argue that free-market economies are relatively stable, and the source of instability, if any, is caused by government intervention. Socialists and Keynesians argue that the economy and financial markets are inherently unstable. In looking at Figures 25.2, changes in real GDP in the US, does the chart support the Adam Smith stability argument for capitalism, or the Keynesian/Marxist instability hypothesis?

    Now look at Figures 25.3, total real GDP over time in the US. Does this chart support Adam Smith or Keynes/Marx? Although the data is the same for both charts, perception of the data will vary.

3.  Are economic cycles predictable? Do they occur on a regular basis, say, every 50 years? Economist Ravi Batra wrote a bestseller in the late 1980s called *The Depression of 1990*, based on his theory that business cycles occur every sixty years. Do they? Why was Batra proven wrong?

4. Which of the following indicators is not included in the Conference Board's Leading Economic Indicators, even though the indicator is acknowledged to be one of the best measures of future economic performance? Why?

A. Sunspots

B. Corporate profits

C. Retail spending

D. Stock prices

E. Housing starts

5. Why was Irving Fisher unable to forecast the stock market crash and Great Depression? What was missing from his monetary model? Why was stable price inflation insufficient to predict the future? Was the Great Depression predictable?

6. In 1974, in the middle of an oil crisis and inflationary recession, Friedman was asked a very "Austrian" question: "What is the possibility that a process of inflation, by producing a misallocation of resources and malinvestment, will raise the natural rate of unemployment?" Friedman responded, "If the inflation is open — if there are no restrictions — there is no reason why it should produce malinvestment." Do you agree with Friedman? Why or why not?

7. Milton Friedman frequently advocated increasing the money supply at a steady rate fairly equal to real GDP growth, and let interest rates fluctuate freely. But since the deregulation of the banking system in the early 1980s, it has become difficult if not impossible to determine exactly what constitutes the "money supply." Survey some economists on how they would measure the money supply (M1, M2, what?), and if this is impossible, what kind of alternative monetary policy would they advocate? Would they use a gold price monitor, inflation targeting, or what?

8. During a recession, which is more flexible in finding new employment: labor or capital goods?

9. Why did unemployment stay so high during the 1930s, in double digit levels? Why is unemployment so high today in Europe compared to the United States?

10. Who was responsible for the global financial crisis of 2007-09? Free-market capitalism, government interventionism, or a combination of both? Identify the causes of the crisis, the steps the private and public sector took to resolve it, and what leaders should do to keep it from happening again.

## FOR ADDITIONAL READING

- Milton Friedman, *Monetarist Economics* (Blackwell Publishers, 1991). Excellent summary of Friedman's views on money and its influence on the economy.

- Murray N. Rothbard, *America's Great Depression*, 5th ed. (Mises Institute, 2000 [1963]). A lucid introduction to the Austrian theory of the business cycle.

- *The Austrian Theory of the Business Cycle and Other Essays*, by Ludwig von Mises, Friedrich Hayek, and other Austrian economists (Mises Institute, 1996). Several important essays on the Austrian model.

- Joseph H. Ellis, *Ahead of the Curve: A Commonsense Guide to Forecasting Business and Market Cycles* (Harvard Business School Press, 2005)

- Thomas E. Woods, Jr., *Meltdown: A Free-Market Look at Why the Stock Market Collapsed, the Economy Tanked, and Government Bailouts Will Make Things Worse* (Regnery, 2009)

*Chapter 26*

# GLOBALIZATION, PROTECTIONISM AND FREE TRADE

*"In our age of international division of labor, free trade is the prerequisite
for any amicable arrangement between nations."*

— LUGWIG NOV MISES
*Omnipotent Government*

O ne of the most radical free-trade experiments in history began on January
1, 1994. The North American Free Trade Agreement (NAFTA) created an
open market between two first-class economies — the United States and
Canada — and a struggling third world nation, Mexico. NAFTA eliminated duties on
the majority of tariffs between products traded among the United States, Canada
and Mexico, and gradually phased out other tariffs, over a period of about 14 years.
Import restrictions were to be removed from many categories, including motor
vehicles and automotive parts, computers, textiles, and agriculture. The treaty also
protected intellectual property rights (patents, copyrights, and trademarks), and
outlined the removal of investment restrictions among the three countries.

Supporters contended that NAFTA would expand trade and jobs among all three
countries, and considered the agreement to be a bold attempt to demonstrate the
power of globalization to turn a developing nation into a modern economy.
Proponents argued that with wages and jobs rising in Mexico, the demand for illegal
immigration would decline. On the other hand critics said that NAFTA would
destroy manufacturing jobs in the United States as companies moved into Mexico to
take advantage of cheap labor; Presidential candidate Ross Perot famously
predicted, "You're going to hear a giant sucking sound of jobs being pulled out of this
country."

Who was right? On the tenth anniversary of NAFTA, *Business Week* concluded,
"The grand experiment was a smashing success on many levels."[1] American and for-
eign investment in Mexico rose $12 billion a year to take advantage of cheap wages.
Trade grew threefold, from $52 billion to $161 billion today. Mexico's per

1  *Business Week*, December 22, 2003.

capita income rose 24%, to just over $4,000 — which is roughly 10 times that of China. "NAFTA gave us a big push," Mexican President Vicente Fox told *Business Week* at the time. Mexico's economy went from No. 15 to ninth-largest in the world. "It gave us jobs. It gave us knowledge, experience, and technological transfer."[2]

What about the United States? It turns out that there was no significant drain of manufacturing jobs. Throughout the 10 year period (1994-2004), U.S. civilian employment grew from 120.3 million to over 150 million and the unemployment rate fell steadily. Meanwhile domestic manufacturing output accelerated significantly since NAFTA's ratification. Imports did hurt some sectors, such as the Maine shoe industry and the South Carolina apparel industry, but lower consumer prices meant more money for consumers to buy other things, which boosted jobs elsewhere. People may have lost jobs making shoes, but they could find other manufacturing or service jobs. As demonstrated in Chapter 10, overall job creation has exceeded job destruction over time.

Mexico still faces many challenges — low wages, underemployment, and competition from the Chinese, to name a few. The latter is ironic, since it was the success of NAFTA that spurred the global free-trade movement, including the Uruguay round of global trade talks in the mid-1990s and China's entry into the World Trade Organization in 2001.

## TRADE, GLOBALIZATION, AND CURRENCIES

This chapter discusses several issues:

1. How important is trade between countries?

2. Why do most economists support free trade? What are the costs and benefits of eliminating economic barriers between nations?

3. How is a country affected by a rising or falling currency?

4. Does a trade deficit matter?

## THE SIZE AND SCOPE OF INTERNATIONAL TRADE

International trade is big business, and has been growing faster than domestic output. As nation after nation has relaxed exchange controls and reduced import duties, trade has boomed. Studies have even demonstrated that more trade increases the number of nations. (See box, "Does Free Trade Lead to Political Separatism?")

Figure 26.1 shows the growth of international trade in relation to domestic GDP growth.

2 Ibid.

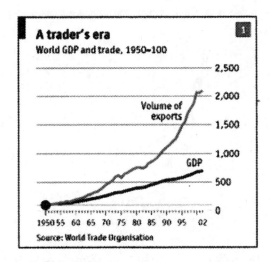

**Figure 26.1.** *Growth of World GDP and International Trade. Source: The Economist.*

The size and impact of foreign trade varies significantly among countries. Here's the most recent breakdown:

| Country | Imports as a % of GDP (as of 2006) |
|---|---|
| Brazil | 9.4% |
| United States | 14.3% |
| Argentina | 15.5% |
| Hong Kong | 17.6% |
| India | 22.8% |
| United Kingdom | 25.7% |
| France | 24.5% |
| China | 29.8% |
| Germany | 32.4% |
| Canada | 32.7% |

U. S. imports relatively little compared to other nations. However, the trend is clearly up, as Figure 26.2 demonstrates.

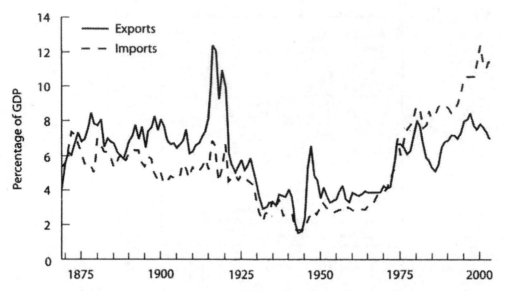

**Figure 26.2.** *Merchandise Exports and Imports in the U. S. as a Percentage of GDP.*[3]

In the 1950s, the U. S. imported only about 4% of GDP — today the percentage has risen to over 12% .

──────────────────── **CASE STUDY** ────────────────────

## DOES FREE TRADE LEAD TO POLITICAL SEPARATISM?

STANFORD, Calif.—(BUSINESS WIRE)—Jan. 29, 2001—The world became a crowded place during the 20th century. There was also an explosion in the number of new countries, many of them small. Among them: Sri Lanka, Cambodia, Burundi, and Djibouti. Why are so many new countries forming and surviving? In a recent research paper, Stanford Graduate School of Business economist Romain Wacziarg explains that free trade makes small countries economically viable. More new countries will form as trade replaces central planning. Wacziarg and research coauthors Alberto Alesina of Harvard and Enrico Spolaore of Brown argue that the globalization of markets goes hand in hand with political separatism.

Reviewing a half-century's worth of nation building, the researchers found that the number of countries in the world nearly tripled between 1946 and 1995, from 74 to 192. 87countries had fewer than 5 million inhabitants, 58 had fewer than 2.5 million, and 35 had fewer than 500,000. "More than half of the world's countries have fewer people than the state of Massachusetts," says Wacziarg, who is assistant professor of economics. What makes this even more interesting is that in the same five decades, the volume of imports and exports as a share of world GDP increased by roughly 40% in a sample of 61 countries.

3  Douglas A. Irwin, *Free Trade Under Fire* (Princeton University Press, 2005), p. 8

Examining the political and economic landscape between 1870 and the present, economists uncovered a strong association between the number of countries in the world and free trade. They also found the reverse was true during periods of protectionism. For example, tariff rates slowly increased between 1870 and the 1920s, while the number of countries was stable or decreasing.

---

## THE BENEFITS OF EXCHANGE AND TRADE

Chapter 2 discussed the production process, how resources are transformed into finished goods and services that consumers and business can use. Many products can be produced without exchange, trade, or money, and some societies and communities have attempted to do so: ancient Egypt and China, the Incas in South America, monasteries, medieval manors, feudal estates, tribal communities, and frontier farms. These societies tended to be authoritarian.

Exchange and trade develop naturally in society. For example, in a agricultural community, farmers often produce more commodities than they can consume. They then sell their surplus wheat, eggs or flowers at a farmer's market to customers who need them. In a sense, all trade is the result of surplus production.

## THE MUTUAL BENEFITS OF TRADE: THE CANDY BAR EXAMPLE

If a transaction is voluntary and all information is disclosed, trade benefits both buyer and seller as shown in this example:

The teacher brings to class a candy bar and offers it for sale for $1. "Would anyone like to buy this candy bar for $1?" he asks students. One raises his hand. The teacher goes over to the student and asks "Which would you rather have—the $1 bill or the candy bar?" The student answers, "The candy bar."

The teacher responds, "You prefer the candy bar, but I'd rather have the $1."

Every transaction involves a **reverse inequality of values** during the exchange of goods or services. The student prefers the candy bar over the $1, while the teacher values the $1 over the candy bar. Similarly, there must be an *inequality* of values in society! People trade and barter precisely because they naturally differ in resources and tastes.

The more transactions, the more satisfaction is achieved in each trader's condition. Standards of living increase because of trading goods and services.

Exchange and foreign trade offer many benefits to business, consumers, and society:

1. **Economic Growth**: Buyer and seller/producer and consumer situations improve (they achieve their goals) through exchange and trade.

2. **Specialization**: Trade encourages individuals, companies and nations to specialize.

3. **Efficiency**: Increased competition between communities, states and nations keeps costs and prices down, and increases volume of transactions.

4. **Social welfare** ("invisible hand" doctrine of Adam Smith): Law of comparative advantage suggests that less qualified individuals can survive and prosper in the marketplace. Trade increases comparative advantage of relatively poor nations.

## THE LAW OF COMPARATIVE ADVANTAGE

Chapter 2 briefly introduced the theory of comparative advantage, the idea that two nations can benefit from trade even if one has a lower relative cost of producing some product. What matters is not the absolute cost but the opportunity cost. The Law of Competitive Advantage was elucidated by David Ricardo, British classical economist (1772-1823), using a celebrated example of English cloth and Portuguese wine. Let us look at this example:

Number of Labor Hours to Produce

|                | England | Portugal |
|----------------|---------|----------|
| 1 unit of cloth | 50      | 25       |
| 1 unit of wine  | 200     | 25       |

In the above example, England does not have an absolute advantage in either good; everything is cheaper to produce in Portugal. In England it takes 50 work hours to produce a unit of cloth, while it takes 200 work hours to produce a unit of wine. In Portugal, everything is easier to accomplish. It takes only 25 work hours to produce cloth or wine.

Clearly, Portugal is more efficient in producing cloth and wine. The casual observer might conclude that Portugal should export both items to England. However, Ricardo brilliantly demonstrated that specialization and trade still makes sense for Portugal and England. Here's why: Suppose Portugal took 25 work hours from the production of cloth and employed that effort in producing wine. The result would be an increase of one more unit of wine, and one less unit of cloth in Portugal. If at the same time England took 100 work hours from the wine industry, and applied them to making cloth, England would gain two more units of cloth, and lose half a unit of wine. If the total output of both countries after this act of specialization is added up, there would be one more unit of cloth and one-half more unit of wine produced in the aggregate as a result of trade.

Ricardo concluded that trade between two countries increases total output, even when one country has a natural advantage over the other. Therefore, free trade benefits both countries.

## THE CASE OF A DOCTOR AND A SECRETARY

A more modern example (repeated from Chapter 2) may make the point clearer. Suppose a top medical surgeon is also the fastest typist in town. She can type 150 words per minute and is an excellent organizer. Clearly she has an absolute advantage in medical services and in typing/secretarial work. Yet even though the surgeon is an excellent typist, it pays for her to hire a secretary to type and organize her appointments. Why? Because she can make more money by not doing secretarial work. Suppose she could make $500,000 a year working full time as a surgeon. If she spends half her time doing secretarial work, she would make only $250,000. The lost income from her medical practice is her opportunity cost, which is substantial. She can reduce her costs dramatically by hiring a secretary, even though the secretary is not as efficient as she is. By hiring a secretary for perhaps $50,000 a year, she can earn a net $450,000 ($500,000 minus $50,000, the cost of hiring a secretary). In sum, the medical doctor has a comparative advantage in performing surgeries, while her secretary has a comparative advantage in secretarial work. By specializing and hiring a secretary, both the MD and the secretary benefit.

## MOST ECONOMISTS SUPPORT FREE TRADE

Because of the benefits of lower prices, specialization, and increased trade, most economists support a liberalized trade policy. In *The Wealth of Nations*, Adam Smith made the case for free trade and relaxing restrictions between countries. "If a foreign country can supply us with a commodity cheaper than we ourselves can make it, better buy it of them," he writes. "By means of glasses, hotbeds and hot-walls, very good grapes can be raised in Scotland," but it would cost 30 times more to produce Scottish wine than to import wine from France. "Would it be a reasonable law to prohibit the importation of all foreign wines, merely to encourage the making of claret and burgundy in Scotland?"[4] Smith opposed mercantilist policies

4  Adam Smith, *The Wealth of Nations* (New York: Modern Library, 1965 [1776]), p. 425.

that favored only the domestic producers at the expense of domestic consumers. He spoke out against the monopoly power of manufacturers who were protected against foreign competition. "But in the mercantilist system, the interest of the consumer is almost always constantly sacrificed to that of the producer."

Ideas have consequences. Smith, Ricardo and the classical economists gradually convinced legislators to lower tariffs and other trade barriers. In France, Frederic Bastiat, an indefatigable advocate of free trade, began a nationwide free trade association. In 1846, he wrote his most famous fable, "The Petition of the Candlemakers," as a satire of protectionists. Using a ridiculous case, he attacked the notion that the French candlestick makers could enrich themselves by passing a law requiring the closing of all windows and shutters to keep out their greatest rival: the sun!

In that same year, 1846, the British Parliament repealed the Corn Laws, the high tariffs imposed on wheat and other agricultural products. The repeal could not be entirely claimed as a theoretical victory of the classical economists. It was passed mainly to bring relief to Ireland, many of whose citizens were starving due to the potato famine.

Figure 26.3 shows the history of the declining influence of duties in the United States since 1820.

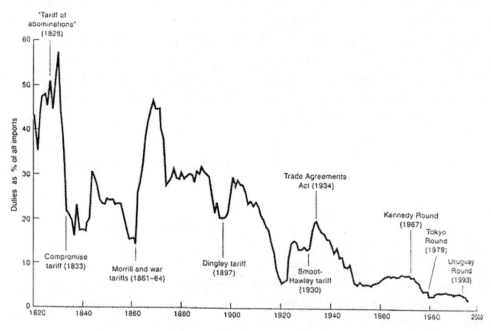

**Figure 26.3.** *The Gradual Decline in U. S. Tariffs, 1820-present: Duties Calculated as a Percentage of Dutiable Imports* [5]

5  Paul Samuelson and William D. Nordhaus, *Economics*, 17th ed. (New York: McGraw-Hill, 1998), p. 708.

Despite temporary setbacks, including the "Tariff of Abominations" in 1828 and the Smoot-Hawley Tariff in 1930, the downward trend in trade duties is clear. At the beginning of U. S. history, tariffs represented nearly 100% of the new government's revenues. By 1910, tariffs brought in only 50% of revenues, and today they provide less than 2% of the government's budget.

Free trade has won the day, not only in the United States but in Europe and around the world. The creation of the European Union during the postwar period has now produced a remarkable situation where capital, labor, and money flow between two dozen European nations with little restriction or regulation. Free-trade agreements flourish among nations in North America, South America, Asia, and Europe. In addition, many economists are convinced that Japan, Hong Kong, and the rest of Asia were able to grow rapidly in the postwar period because the United States opened its doors to cheap products from abroad.

Economists agree on the principle of free trade. Several surveys of professional economists show that over 95% support free trade, the highest percentage of agreement in any category.

## WHO SAYS AMERICA DOESN'T EXPORT MANUFACTURED GOODS ANYMORE?

A common complaint among pundits in the media is that America is losing its manufacturing base and isn't exporting televisions or cars, only wheat and Hollywood movies. Not so! Here's a partial list of American exports:[6]

|  | Value $million (2005) |
|---|---|
| Agricultural commodities | $63,139 |
| Manufactured goods | $685,398 |
| Airplanes and airline parts | 47,829 |
| Cars and trucks | 71,747 |
| Chemicals | 120,132 |
| Cigarettes | 1,202 |
| Clothing | 4,129 |
| Footwear | 508 |
| Furniture | 4,415 |
| General industrial machinery | 38,902 |
| Iron and steel mill products | 10,430 |
| Jewelry | 3,029 |
| Metal ores, manufactures, and machinery | 31,024 |
| Paper | 11,457 |

6 *Statistical Abstract of the United States, 2007*: 1289 - U.S. Exports And General Imports, By Selected SITC Commodity Groups: 2002 to 2005.

| | |
|---|---|
| Photographic equipment | 3,343 |
| Power generating machinery | 41,296 |
| Printed materials | 5,445 |
| Pulp and waste paper | 5,093 |
| Records/magnetic media | 5,142 |
| Rubber tires and tubes | 2,778 |
| Scientific instruments | 34,544 |
| Ships, boats | 1,913 |
| Specialized industrial machinery | 33,144 |
| Televisions, VCRs, and electronics | 20,974 |
| Textile yarn and fabric | 11,516 |
| Toys/games/sporting goods | 3,756 |
| Wood manufactures | 1,818 |
| Crude oil, propane, gas and other fuels | 26,488 |

The United States imports most of its televisions, cars, clothing, footwear, and oil products — but it also surprisingly exports billions of dollars worth of these same items.

## THE CASE FOR PROTECTIONISM

Despite almost universal support for free trade among economists, some organizations and government officials support various forms of protectionism. Protectionist measures include the following possibilities:

- **High tariffs** on goods that compete directly with domestic producers.

- **Quotas** to limit cheaper foreign goods that could overwhelm the domestic market.

- **Import substitution**: Some countries, especially in developing nations, prohibit foreign goods such as cars, shoes and toothpaste, in order to promote domestic industrialization.

- **Subsidies** to protect existing businesses from foreign competition.

- **Anti-dumping** measures that prohibit foreign products from being sold domestically at below cost.

- **Special tax breaks** for domestic producers to export certain goods. For example, many countries offer 5 year tax exemptions to their exporting companies.

- **Exchange rate**: Some governments keep their currency's exchange rate low to encourage exports.

## ARGUMENTS FOR TRADE RESTRICTIONS

What drives protectionist measures? These include the following arguments and economists' responses:

**Argument #1: Infant industries.** Nascent industries do not enjoy the economies of scale or business acumen of more mature foreign competitors; why not give them a chance? By imposing tariffs or other restrictions on foreign products, governments give new or infant industries the time to develop a significant market before facing stiff competition from abroad.

**Response**: By taking advantage of tariffs or subsidies, fledgling industries may never gain the incentive to become competitive. Besides, if a nation has a natural comparative advantage in a new industry, why can't foreign capitalists enter the market and finance this new market?

**Argument #2: National security.** Oil, platinum and other commodities may be vital for a nation to keep functioning during a war or national emergency. If foreign imports are allowed, domestic industry will not be capable of providing essential products during a national crisis, when the essential import may suddenly be restricted. Journalist Pat Buchanan states, "The United States ought not to surrender any weapon in its arsenal of defense for vital U.S. economic interests."

**Response:** Most economists believe that stockpiling essential commodities and importing foreign products for day to day use is a more efficient way to protect the national economic interest than through protectionist measures.

**Argument #3: Protection against lost jobs and lower wages at home**. Businesses and labor unions lobby legislators to provide relief from foreign competition to prevent jobs from going overseas, or cheap labor from undercutting high union wages. Representing this view, economist Alan Tonelson in *Foreign Affairs* magazine (July/August 1994) states, "Five major American industries—automotive, steel, machine tool, semiconductor, and textile—received significant relief from imports through intelligently structured trade laws. Those industries have confounded the predictions of laissez-faire economic ideologies by gaining market share at home and in some cases abroad, contributing to job creation and reinvigorating American competitiveness."

After Tokyo agreed to voluntary import limits in 1981, American auto makers achieved an astonishing comeback. The Big Three introduced new products such as the minivan and compact utility vehicles. Investments in new plants and equipment resulted in a substantial increase in both productivity and the quality of U.S. cars. Similarly, after Reagan negotiated bilateral agreements limiting imports of finished steel in 1984, investment and worker productivity in the U.S. steel industry soared, making the U.S. one of the lowest-cost producers in the world. Import curbs on machine tools, semiconductors, and textiles saw similar results—increased research and development, investment, cost-cutting, job creation, and retooling. The U.S. improved its competitiveness in all these markets. As Pat Buchanan concluded, "The conventional wisdom was wrong."

## COST-BENEFIT ANALYSIS OF PROTECTIONIST MEASURES

**Response:** But is this the whole story? Buchanan and Tonelson do not mention the environment in which these five industries performed so well. The reality is that virtually all industrial groups expanded sharply during the "Seven Fat Years" of the Reagan era of the 1980s, as Robert Bartley calls it. The free-trade critics have committed the classic *post hoc, ergo propter hoc* argument. Just because an event (import restrictions) occurs simultaneously with another event (economic recovery) one cannot assume that one is the primary cause of the other. There may be more powerful forces at work. Indeed, in the midst of a sharp recession (1981), Congress cut tax rates substantially for individuals, corporations, and investors, thus stimulating a "supply-side" revolution. Furthermore, in the summer of 1982, the Federal Reserve reversed its tight money, high-interest-rate policy in favor of easy money and lower interest rates. This low-interest rate, tax-cutting environment continued almost throughout the 1980s, factors which most likely dwarfed the impact of import restrictions. One should also not ignore the impact of currency exchange and the falling dollar on the improvement in U.S. exports and foreign competition since 1985.

The steel-related industries may have revived primarily because of the economic boom and "supply-side" revolution of tax cuts, deregulation, and an accommodating monetary policy—not necessarily because of protectionism alone. At least Buchanan and Tonelson provide little evidence that the protected industries outperformed all other industries.

This is not to say that U.S. producers didn't benefit from import relief. Undoubtedly, they did benefit. Yet the benefits may not have been all that significant. The auto, steel, and textile industries would probably have done almost as well without the import restrictions. Even before the import quotas were imposed in the 1980s, most of the leaders in these industries had recognized that the world was rapidly moving toward global free trade. Ford, for example, had already decided to face the Japanese and the Germans head on in building high-tech automobiles. Gradually more of the components of "American" products are being made in foreign countries. Despite all kinds of restrictions and regulations in the textile and apparel industries, more shoes and clothing are being made in Asia and Latin America—by American-based companies. Global free trade is a simple fact of life and any manufacturer in the United States who doesn't recognize its inevitability is headed straight for bankruptcy court.

## WHAT ABOUT THE CONSUMER?

In his book *Economics in One Lesson*, Henry Hazlitt says that a good economist looks at how a policy affects all groups, not just one group. Let's apply this "one lesson" to the free-trade debate. Yes, import relief helps the 21 highly protected sectors of the U.S. economy. It maintains thousands of American jobs in these industries. It keeps prices and wages higher than what they would be otherwise. But what about other groups in the economy—are they helped or hurt by import restrictions? Let's look specifically at the consumers. According to a study by the Institute for International Economics in 1990, American consumers paid $70 billion more for goods and services as a direct result of import protection in 1990. Now, in a $6 trillion dollar economy (GDP at the time), that may not seem like much. In fact, it demonstrates the high degree of free trade which already exists in the U.S. Nevertheless, the consumer cost per job saved averages about $170,000. Economists Hufbauer and Elliott conclude: "This is far higher than the average annual wage in the protected industries and far more than any current or proposed labor adjustment program would cost."[7]

Tariffs and quotas affect the U.S. economy in many obscure, subtle ways. For example, the voluntary import quotas on Japanese cars agreed to in the early 1980s resulted in a substantial increase in the importing of higher-priced, larger Japanese cars. Since the profit margin was higher on the more expensive models, Japanese manufacturers exported them to the United States. Import limits on finished steel forced U.S. automobile companies to pay higher prices on their inputs. Consumers were hurt. According to a 1985 study by the International Trade Commission, American consumers paid $15.7 billion in higher prices on Japanese car imports since 1981.

Clearly, most producers benefit from tariffs and quotas, while consumers are hurt. Why don't consumers complain more loudly? Probably because they don't realize the connection. As public-choice economists demonstrate, industry and labor are much better lobbyists than consumers. Moreover, consumers are also producers and may work in protected industries as well. The protectionist story is the same everywhere, in the U.S., Japan, or Germany. Everyone favors promoting exports but not imports.

## AN ALTERNATE SOLUTION

While the debate over protectionism rages on, some economists and journalists offer another alternative to encourage domestic production: eliminate the corporate income tax in order to encourage a more productive manufacturing sector. One of the primary reasons the auto, steel, and textile industries have had difficulty com-

---

7 Gary Clyde Hufbauer and Kimberly Ann Elliott, *Measuring the Costs of Protection in the United States* (Washington, D.C.: Institute for International Economics, 1994), back cover.

peting in the world economy is that they lack the capital investment to adopt the latest technology and rebuild their markets. Imagine the impact on American industry if the corporate income tax and the capital gains tax were eliminated and red tape and regulations were streamlined. It could do much more to increase productivity and reduce consumer prices than the standard response of calling for protectionism and fair trade.

## THE LERNER SYMMETRY THEOREM: SHOULD DEVELOPING COUNTRIES PROMOTE EXPORTS OR ADOPT A FREE-TRADE ZONE?

Adopting a "pro-export" policy, promoting exports through tax breaks, subsidies, and tariffs, and at the same time discouraging imports through taxes, duties, or quotas, is a common practice among emerging markets and developing nations. Many Asian and Latin American countries have adopted this "pro-export" program for years. Is this mercantilist policy wise, or should they adopt a free-trade zone along the lines of Hong Kong, which does not impose limitations or duties on imports or exports?

Abba Lerner wrote a paper on the subject as a graduate student at the London School of Economics in the mid-1930s, known as the "Lerner Symmetry Theorem." He discovered a fundamental principle of trade: When a government adopts a policy to encourage exports, it cannot help but expand the volume of imports. Equally, any restraint on imports will act to restrain exports. Moreover, any reduction in import duties will act to encourage exports.

The data supports Lerner's Theorem. It turns out that exports and imports tend to move together, no matter what the trade restrictions. Figure 26.4 demonstrates this fact in the case of China.

Why is this? Basically, the link occurs through the foreign exchange market. When exporters send goods abroad, they are paid in a foreign currency. The foreign currency in turn gives exporters the ability to buy imported goods. An imbalance of exports will lead to an overabundance of foreign currency reserves, driving the price of the currency down and making imports more attractive. Let's look at it another way. Suppose Japan reduces its duties of American imports. Japanese consumers will now buy more American goods at lower prices. American exporters will see an increase in their business, for which they are paid Japanese yen. With more yen they can in turn buy more Japanese goods. Thus an increase in Japanese imports leads to higher Japanese exports.

Studies show that countries benefit the most if they have a "free trade" zone that enjoys no duties or restrictions on imports or exports. Hong Kong and Panama are two examples of countries with "free trade" zones.

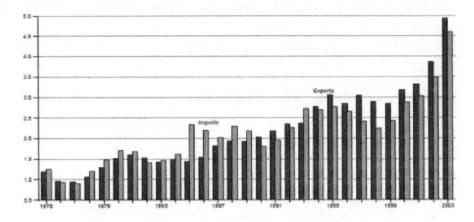

**Figure 26.4.** *Imports and exports in China.*

## DOES THE TRADE DEFICIT MATTER?

Another concern in international trade is the fear that a growing deficit in trade (goods only) and current account (goods and services) is a danger that should somehow be avoided. As Figure 26.5 shows, the United States has suffered a growing current-account deficit since the 1970s.

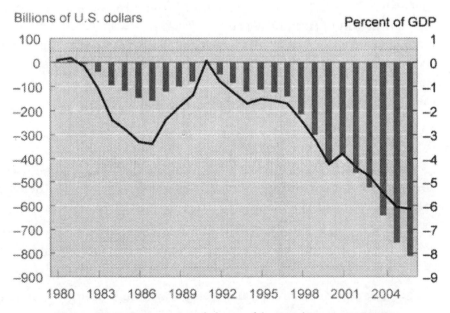

**Figure 26.5.** *Current account balances of the United States, 1980-2004.*

It is important to note that when one country experiences a current-account deficit, other countries are enjoying a surplus. For years, Japan has enjoyed a trade surplus. More recently, China's current account is in heavy surplus (see Figure 26.6 below).

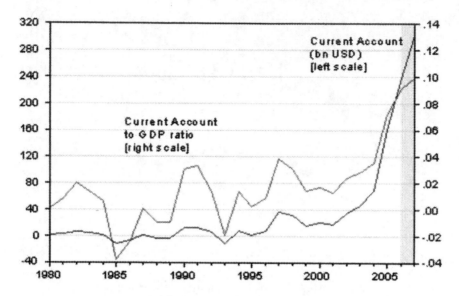

**Figure 26.6.** *China's current account surplus.*

Are trade imbalances between the United States and China (and other countries) something to be concerned about? Economists point out that natural trade imbalances within countries occur — New York has a trade deficit in oranges, and Florida has a trade surplus in oranges, but neither state sees this as a threat to its economy. Yet politicians and journalists frequently complain about the growing trade deficit with China or some other country. Should Americans be worried that their country is "the world's largest debtor nation"?

## THE BALANCE OF PAYMENTS

Any analysis of trade imbalances must begin with a general accounting of a country's international transactions. The balance of payments depends on three measures, defined as follows:

1 **The trade balance:** exports minus imports of goods only. If exports exceed imports a trade deficit exists; if imports exceed exports, a trade surplus exists.

2. **The current account balance:** exports minus imports of goods and services only.

3.   **The capital account**: all transfers of assets, either portfolio or direct investments.

The first accounting lesson in international finance is this: the balance of payments always balances; that is, it sums to zero. A current account deficit indicates a capital account surplus somewhere else. In other words, if America is running a current-account deficit, exporting more goods and services than it's importing, there must be a net capital inflow into the United States from abroad.

Consider your own situation. If you spend more money than you make in income, you have to borrow money or sell some assets to pay the difference. The same concept works in international finance. Countries like the United States with currency account deficits are borrowing from or selling assets to other countries. Countries with current account surpluses are buying assets from the rest of the world, or using their savings to lend money abroad.

A fundamental equation of international finance is this:

Exports - Imports = Savings - Investment.

Countries running trade surpluses (such as China and Japan) have domestic savings in excess of domestic investment. This excess savings is invested or lent abroad, where it appears as a capital account deficit. The United States has a capital account surplus, meaning that the country is saving less than it is investing. In the 1980s, Japan used its savings to buy U. S. real estate and corporations, bringing yen into the United States. Now China is going down the same path. Most economists do not consider the trade deficit a problem as long as foreigners find the United States an attractive investment.

**Question: What would be the impact if foreigners lose faith in investing in the United States due to domestic instability, a dollar crisis, or better opportunities elsewhere?**

## THE RISE AND FALL OF THE DOLLAR AND FOREIGN CURRENCIES

International finance and the balance of payments are also closely related to the changes in the value of currencies. Prior to 1971, the international financial system was based on a fixed rate currency system that came out of the Bretton Woods Agreement in 1944. Under this international agreement, all major currencies were linked to the U. S. dollar at a fixed rate, and the dollar in turn was linked to gold at the fixed rate of $35 an ounce. That system worked well until the U. S. engaged in inflationary policies in the 1960s and circulated an excess amount of dollars overseas. Gold drained from the U. S. Treasury as foreigners demanded gold with cheap dollars. On August 15, 1971, President Richard Nixon imposed a 90-day freeze on wages and prices, closed the gold window to foreign buyers, and the U. S. dollar was allowed to float (sink) against foreign currencies.

Since then as Figure 26.7 shows (see below), the U. S. dollar has been in a long-term decline against most major currencies. Only in Latin America is the dollar considered a good value.

**Figure 26.7.** *Value of the U. S. dollar against major foreign currencies.*

Why has the U. S. dollar been in a long-term declining market? These factors determine the value of currency?

1.  **Monetary inflation**: If a country inflates its money supply faster than other countries adjust theirs, over time its currency will lose value. Monetary inflation is probably the most important factor affecting the long-term value of a currency. The euro has been stronger than the U. S. dollar since the mid-1990s because the European central bank has been less inflationary than the Federal Reserve.

2.  **Interest rates**: Central banks can affect the short-term strength of a currency by raising or lowering short-term rates. Governments sometimes attempt to stave off a currency crisis by raising interest rates sharply.

3.  **Economic growth**: A strong non-inflationary growth rate in GDP is usually viewed favorably by currency traders, while a recession is viewed negatively.

## PURCHASING POWER PARITY THEORY

According to the purchasing power parity theorem, a currency must have the same purchasing power in all countries. A dollar should be able to buy the same quantity of goods in the United States as it does in England. If not, business people would take advantage of this opportunity to make sizeable profits. For example, if a DVD costs $20 in the United States, and $40 (£20 at today's exchange rate) in London, it would be highly profitable for American exporters to buy DVDs in the United States and sell them in London, and double their money. At the present time, however, the dollar's purchasing power in London is half what it should be for most items — clothing, food, movies, real estate, etc. And it has been that way for years. Why?

One of the most popular ways to compare purchasing power between countries is the Big Mac Index, published annually by the Economist since 1986. (See box, "The Big Mac Index.")

**————————— CASE STUDY —————————**

### THE BIG MAC INDEX
Feb 1st 2007
From Economist.com

*The Economist*'s Big Mac index is based on the theory of purchasing-power parity (PPP), which states that exchange rates should adjust naturally to equalise the price of a basket of goods and services around the world. In order to be accurate, the goods or services should be identical as possible. Our basket is a burger: a McDonald's Big Mac. The contents are virtually identical in every country, but the number of dollars required to purchase a Big Mac varies from country to country, and provides a fairly accurate picture of the value of the dollar in that country.

The table below shows by how much, in Big Mac PPP terms, selected currencies were over- or undervalued at the end of January. Broadly, the pattern is much as it was last spring, the previous time this table was compiled. The most overvalued currency is the Icelandic krona: the exchange rate that would equalize the price of an Icelandic Big Mac with the price an American Big Mac is 158 kronur to the dollar, but the actual rate is 68.4, making the krona 131% too dear. The most undervalued currency is the Chinese yuan, at 56% below its PPP rate; several other Asian currencies also appear to be 40-50% undervalued.

The index is supposed to give a guide to the direction in which currencies should, in theory, head in the long run. The index is only a rough guide, because its price reflects non-tradable elements—such as rent and. For that reason, the index is probably more accurate when comparing countries at roughly the same stage of

## A feast of burgernomics
The Big Mac index

| | Big Mac prices | | Implied PPP* of the dollar | Actual dollar exchange rate Jan 31st | Under (-)/over (+) valuation against the dollar, % |
|---|---|---|---|---|---|
| | In local currency | in dollars | | | |
| United States† | $3.22 | 3.22 | | | |
| Argentina | Peso 8.25 | 2.65 | 2.56 | 3.11 | -18 |
| Australia | A$3.45 | 2.67 | 1.07 | 1.29 | -17 |
| Brazil | Real 6.4 | 3.01 | 1.99 | 2.13 | -6 |
| Britain | £1.99 | 3.90 | 1.62‡ | 1.96‡ | +21 |
| Canada | C$3.63 | 3.08 | 1.13 | 1.18 | -4 |
| Chile | Peso 1,670 | 3.07 | 519 | 544 | -5 |
| China | Yuan 11.0 | 1.41 | 3.42 | 7.77 | -56 |
| Colombia | Peso 6,900 | 3.06 | 2,143 | 2,254 | -5 |
| Costa Rica | Colones 1,130 | 2.18 | 351 | 519 | -32 |
| Czech Republic | Koruna 52.1 | 2.41 | 16.2 | 21.6 | -25 |
| Denmark | DKr27.75 | 4.84 | 8.62 | 5.74 | +50 |
| Egypt | Pound 9.09 | 1.60 | 2.82 | 5.70 | -50 |
| Estonia | Kroon 30 | 2.49 | 9.32 | 12.0 | -23 |
| Euro area§ | €2.94 | 3.82 | 1.10** | 1.30** | +19 |
| Hong Kong | HK$12.0 | 1.54 | 3.73 | 7.81 | -52 |
| Hungary | Forint 590 | 3.00 | 183 | 197 | -7 |
| Iceland | Kronur 509 | 7.44 | 158 | 68.4 | +131 |
| Indonesia | Rupiah 15,900 | 1.75 | 4,938 | 9,100 | -46 |
| Japan | ¥280 | 2.31 | 87.0 | 121 | -28 |
| Latvia | Lats 1.35 | 2.52 | 0.42 | 0.54 | -22 |
| Lithuania | Litas 6.50 | 2.45 | 2.02 | 2.66 | -24 |
| Malaysia | Ringgit 5.50 | 1.57 | 1.71 | 3.50 | -51 |
| Mexico | Peso 29.0 | 2.66 | 9.01 | 10.9 | -17 |
| New Zealand | NZ$4.60 | 3.16 | 1.43 | 1.45 | -2 |
| Norway | Kroner 41.5 | 6.63 | 12.9 | 6.26 | +106 |
| Pakistan | Rupee 140 | 2.31 | 43.5 | 60.7 | -28 |
| Paraguay | Guarani 10,000 | 1.90 | 3,106 | 5,250 | -41 |
| Peru | New Sol 9.50 | 2.97 | 2.95 | 3.20 | -8 |
| Philippines | Peso 85.0 | 1.74 | 26.4 | 48.9 | -46 |
| Poland | Zloty 6.90 | 2.29 | 2.14 | 3.01 | -29 |
| Russia | Rouble 49.0 | 1.85 | 15.2 | 26.5 | -43 |
| Saudi Arabia | Riyal 9.00 | 2.40 | 2.80 | 3.75 | -25 |
| Singapore | S$ 3.60 | 2.34 | 1.12 | 1.54 | -27 |
| Slovakia | Crown 57.98 | 2.13 | 18.0 | 27.2 | -34 |
| South Africa | Rand 15.5 | 2.14 | 4.81 | 7.25 | -34 |
| South Korea | Won 2,900 | 3.08 | 901 | 942 | -4 |
| Sri Lanka | Rupee 190 | 1.75 | 59.0 | 109 | -46 |
| Sweden | SKr32.0 | 4.59 | 9.94 | 6.97 | +43 |
| Switzerland | SFr6.30 | 5.05 | 1.96 | 1.25 | +57 |
| Taiwan | NT$75.0 | 2.28 | 23.3 | 32.9 | -29 |
| Thailand | Baht 62.0 | 1.78 | 19.3 | 34.7 | -45 |
| Turkey | Lire 4.55 | 3.22 | 1.41 | 1.41 | nil |
| UAE | Dirhams 10.0 | 2.72 | 3.11 | 3.67 | -15 |
| Ukraine | Hryvnia 9.00 | 1.71 | 2.80 | 5.27 | -47 |
| Uruguay | Peso 55.0 | 2.17 | 17.1 | 25.3 | -33 |
| Venezuela | Bolivar 6,800 | 1.58 | 2,112 | 4,307 | -51 |

Sources: McDonald's; *The Economist*
*Purchasing-power parity: local price divided by price in United States
†Average of New York, Atlanta, Chicago and San Francisco  ‡Dollars per pound
§Weighted average of prices in euro area  **Dollars per euro

development and labor costs. Perhaps the most telling numbers in this table, therefore, are those for the Japanese yen, which is 28% undervalued against the dollar, and the euro, which is 19% overvalued resulting in the European finance ministers' discouragement with the low level of the yen.

In the Big Mac index, the *Economist* seeks to compare the purchasing power of a Big Mac sandwich sold by the McDonald's fast food restaurant chain. The index is available to a common specification in many countries around the world, with local McDonald's franchisees negotiating local prices of ingredients. Thus, the index allows a comparison between many countries' currencies. The Big Mac PPP exchange rate between two countries is obtained by dividing the price of a Big Mac in one country (in its currency) by the price of a Big Mac in another country (in its currency). This value is then compared with the actual exchange rate; if the value is lower, then the first currency is under-valued (according to PPP theory) compared with the second, and conversely, if the value is higher, then the first currency is overvalued. As the latest comparison chart indicates, Europe is deeply overvalued, while Asia and Latin America are the most undervalued.

---

## SUMMARY

Chapter 26 covered these main points:

1. International trade is growing faster than domestic output. As nation after nations has relaxed exchange controls and reduced import duties, trade has boomed.

2. Free trade tends to increase business and economic growth in both countries that adopt free-trade agreements.

3. Exchange and foreign trade offer a variety of benefits: (a) higher economic growth, (b) specialization, (c), efficiency, and (d) improved social welfare.

4. The law of comparative advantage demonstrates that all countries, even those not naturally endowed with certain talents or resources, can benefit from trade.

5. Several arguments exist in favor of protectionism, including national security for critical resources, and concern over job loss and lower wages as a result of foreign competition. Most economists agree that these arguments are misguided. There is no evidence that NAFTA and other trade agreements have hurt the countries involved. If anything, both business and consumers have benefited.

6. The Lerner Symmetry Theorem, named after Abba Lerner, demonstrates that exports and imports always move together.

7. Most economists do not consider the trade deficit an alarming problem as long as foreigners are willing to invest capital in the United States. But if they lose confidence in the U. S., it could spell serious trouble for the United States and the dollar.

8. The purchasing power parity theory suggests that a currency should ultimately have the same purchasing power in all countries. The Economist published the Big Mac Index as an estimate of the purchasing power party between most countries. It takes years, however, before nations change their purchasing power.

## IMPORTANT TERMS

| | |
|---|---|
| Balance of payments | Invisible hand doctrine of Adam Smith |
| Big Mac index | Law of comparative advantage |
| Capital account | Lerner symmetry theorem |
| Corn laws | North American Free Trade Agreement (NAFTA) |
| Cost-benefit analysis | Opportunity cost |
| Current account deficit | Purchasing power parity |
| Free-trade zone | Reverse inequality of values |
| Import substitution | Trade deficit |
| Infant industries | |

## INFLUENTIAL ECONOMIST

### ROBERT MUNDELL, FREE TRADE, AND GLOBALIZATION

**Name: Robert A. Mundell (1932- )**

**Background:** Columbia professor Robert Mundell is an influential advocate of globalization, free trade, supply-side tax cuts, and the benefits of the European Union and single currency, the euro. Born in Canada in 1932, Mundell is a graduate of the University of British Columbia in Vancouver. He earned his Ph. D. from MIT in 1956. He has had an amazing professional career, having attended, taught, or worked at over a dozen universities and organizations, including MIT, University of Washington, Chicago, Stanford, Johns Hopkins, the Brookings Institution, London School of Economics, Graduate Institute of International

Studies in Geneva, Remnin University of China (Beijing), and the International Monetary Fund. Before going to Columbia in 1974, he was a professor at the University of Chicago and editor of *The Journal of Political Economy*. Thus the Chicago school can once again claim a Nobel, although Mundell differs markedly from the monetarist school. Mundell won the Nobel Prize in economics in 1999. In addition to teaching at Columbia University, he lives part-time at a second home in Italy, with his second wife and son.

**Major Contribution:** Robert Mundell is one of the theoretical founders of supply-side economics and globalization. In the 1970s, he offered a creative solution to stagflation (inflationary recession): impose a tight-money, high-interest rate policy to curb inflation and strengthen the dollar, and slash marginal tax rates to fight recession. Mundell's prescription was adopted by Reagan and Fed chairman Paul Volcker in the early 1980s. "There's been no downside to tax cuts," he told reporters recently.

Mundell strongly believes that cutting marginal tax rates and slowing government spending can reduce the deficit, lower interest rates, and stimulate long-term economic growth. He states, "Monetary policy cannot be the engine of higher noninflationary growth. But fiscal policy—both levers of it—can be . . . . The U.S. tax-and-spend system reduces potential growth because it penalizes success and rewards failure."

Mundell favors spending on education, research and development, and infrastructure rather than government welfare programs. He advocates reducing top marginal income tax rates, slashing the capital gains tax, and cutting the corporate income tax. Such policies would sharply raise saving rates and economic growth—"an increase in the rate of saving by 5% of income (GDP), say from 10% of income to 15%, would increase the rate of [economic] growth by 50%, i.e., from 2.5% to 3.75%," he predicts.

Mundell also take a different approach to monetary policy. Unlike the monetarists, supply-siders like Mundell resolutely favor increasing the role of gold in international monetary affairs. "Gold provides a stabilizing effect in a world of entirely flexible currencies," he told a group of reporters in New York after winning the Nobel Prize in 1999. According to Mundell, gold plays an essential role as a hedge against a return of inflation. He did not foresee central banks selling any more gold. "Gold will stay at center stage in the world's central banking system," he said.

In awarding Mundell the prize, the Bank of Sweden recognized Mundell as the chief intellectual proponent of the euro, the currency of the European Community. He considers the euro a super-currency of continental dimensions that will challenge the dollar as the dominant currency. The benefits of a single currency include lower transaction costs, greater monetary stability, and a common monetary policy. Mundell advocates an open global economy, expanded foreign trade, and fewer national currencies. Ultimately, he envisions a universal currency backed by gold as the ideal world monetary system. Under a strict gold standard, "real liquidity balances are generated during recessions and constrained during inflations." Mundell is an optimist and bullish on the global stock markets, the gold standard, globalization, and downsized government.

## PROBLEMS TO PONDER

1. Suppose two countries, the United States and Japan, produce food and cars per month according to the following table:

|  | Cars | Food |
|---|---|---|
| Japan | Two | One ton |
| United States | Three | Two tons |

   Which country has an absolute advantage in the production of cars and food?

   Which country has a comparative advantage in cars? In food?

   Should Japan export cars or food to the United States?

   Should the United States export cars or food to Japan?

2. Supporting an "America First" doctrine, political commentator Pat Buchanan declared in 1994, "The dogma of free trade does not stand up....Import relief in the 1980s saved America's industrial base — and countless jobs — at tiny cost."[8] He was referring to the federal government's imposition of "voluntary" import limits in 1981 on Japanese automobiles. Do a cost-benefit analysis on the car import restrictions in the 1980s: What were the costs? What were the benefits? On the whole, was import quotas a good or bad idea?

3. Montesquieu observed in *The Spirit of the Laws* (1748) that "commerce cures destructive prejudices." To what extend does trade between the East and the West, or between the Middle East and the United States, encourage tolerance and peace between countries and cultures? Is free trade a partial solution to war in the Middle East?

---

8  Pat Buchanan, "How the Rust Belt Was Revived," *Washington Times*, July 20, 1994.

4.  A financial "hard money" guru recently predicted, "Our days as the dominant economic power are numbered. The dollar is going to collapse, and Americans are going to experience stagflation on an unprecedented scale in the form of recession and hyperinflation." What could cause such monetary chaos in the United States? What could keep it from happening? Is the United States depression proof? What are the chances of this doomsday scenario occurring?

5.  Comment on the following: "I can understand maintaining barriers between the United States and Mexico, whose countries differ dramatically in culture and economic development, but not between the United States and Canada. The border between Canada and the U. S. is artificial and should be eliminated."

6.  Which protectionist measure causes the least damage economically, import quotas or tariffs?

7.  Nobel laureate economist Gary Becker suggests that immigrants should be allowed to purchase the right to immigrate into the United States. What advantages would there be to offer tradable immigrant permits?

## ADDITIONAL READING

- Douglas A. Irwin, *Three Simple Principles of Trade Policy* (Washington, DC: American Enterprise Institute, 1996)

- Douglas A. Irwin, *Free Trade Under Fire*, 2nd ed. (Princeton University Press, 2005)

*Chapter 27*

# DEVELOPMENT ECONOMICS: CAPITALISM, SOCIALISM AND DEMOCRACY

*"The government of India regulates nearly everything, so there's very little progress; whereas in Hong Kong the government keeps its hands off . . . and the standard of living has multiplied."*

— JOHN TEMPLETON

During the 1930s, the mutual fund magnate John Templeton traveled around the world, noting in particular the extreme poverty in two Asian nations under British control, India and Hong Kong. 40 years later, in the 1970s, Templeton returned. Once again he witnessed the poverty in India. But Hong Kong had changed tremendously. "The standard of living in Hong Kong had multiplied more than tenfold in forty years, while the standard of living in Calcutta has improved hardly at all," he wrote.[1]

Today neither country is under British rule, but the contrast between the two countries is more pronounced. Hong Kong enjoys the greatest concentration of wealth in the world. India, despite its recent progress, still suffers the greatest concentration of poverty in the world.

Development economist P.T. Bauer once wrote an essay in which he pondered, "How would you rate the economic prospects of an Asian country which has very little land (and only eroded hillsides at that), and which is indeed the most densely populated country in the world; whose population has grown rapidly, both through natural increase and large-scale immigration; which imports all of its oil and raw materials, and even most of its water; whose government is not engaged in development planning and operates no exchange controls or restrictions on capital exports and imports; and which is the only remaining Western colony of any significance?"[2]

Bauer was discussing Hong Kong. For decades, the economic prospects for Hong Kong were dismal. At the end of World War II, Hong Kong was a dirt-poor island with a per-capita income about a fourth of Britain's. Yet by making cheap

1 John Templeton, quoted in William Proctor, *The Templeton Prizes* (New York: Doubleday, 1983), p. 72.
2 P. T. Bauer, "The Lesson of Hong Kong," in *Equality, The Third World, and Economic Delusion* (London: Weidenfeld and Nicolson, 1981), p. 185.

627

products for export to the faraway West, Hong Kong managed to become the powerhouse of Southeast Asia. Today the income of Hong Kong's citizens rivals Britain's, and in Asia the income is second only to Japan, despite the teeming seven million people crowded into 400 square miles in Hong Kong. What broke the vicious cycle of poverty? According to Bauer, Hong Kong's economic miracle did not depend on having money, natural resources, foreign aid, or even formal education, but rather on the "industry, enterprise, thrift and ability . . . of highly motivated people."[3] Hong Kong's "overpopulation" turned out to be an asset, not a liability.

Equally important, Britain did not interfere in private decisions. Thanks largely to a British civil servant, John Cowperthwaite, Hong Kong adopted a laissez-faire economic policy, except in the area of subsidized housing and education. Cowperthwaite called it "positive noninterventionism." The success of laissez faire in Hong Kong was a major factor in Communist China's pursuing a largely noninterventionist approach when it took over in 1997. The island continues to flourish with a stable currency, free port, and low taxes. Hong Kong's maximum income tax rate is 18% without capital-gains tax. The Fraser Institute Economic Freedom Index has always ranked Hong Kong number one in the world.

## WEALTH AND POVERTY IN INDIA

India is an entirely different story. India's population of one billion remains relatively poor, although a middle class is starting to flourish, largely as a result of outsourcing. Unlike Hong Kong, India has valuable natural resources including forests, fish, oil, iron ore, coal, and agricultural products. India has achieved self-sufficiency in food since gaining independence in 1947, yet deep poverty persists.

Some commentators blame India's anti-capitalist culture, the fatalistic caste system, overpopulation, and the hot and humid climate (it reaches 120 degrees or more in summer) for the economic problems. But Milton Friedman identified another cause when he wrote, "The correct explanation is . . . not to be found in its religious or social attitudes, or in the quality of its people, but rather in the economic policy that India has adopted."[4] Indeed, in the decade after independence, Jawaharlal Nehru and other Indian leaders were heavily influenced by Harold Laski of the London School of Economics and his fellow Fabians, who advocated central planning along Soviet lines. Like the USSR, India adopted five-year plans, nationalized heavy industries, and imposed import-substitution laws. They perpetuated the British civil-service tradition of exercising controls over foreign exchange and requiring licenses to start businesses.

3  P. T. Bauer, *Equality, The Third World, and Economic Delusion*, p. 189.
4  Milton Friedman, *Friedman on India* (New Delhi: Centre for Civil Society, 2000), p. 10.

Even today, India is a bureaucratic nightmare. *The Economist* (June 3, 2006) reported that a lorry transporting goods must pass 12 toll booths and 14 inspection points to travel between two of India's "metros," Kolkata and Mumbai (1,340 miles). Due to long lines and transportation delays, it takes a week to travel this distance. Parth Shah, an economist and head of the Centre for Civil Society, describes how he recently returned to India and toiled to find an apartment in New Delhi (thanks to rent controls), then spent half day standing in line to pay his first telephone bill and another half a day to pay his electricity bill. "Corruption has become the standard among those who are in public service at every level,"[5] reports Gita Mehta, a well-known Indian writer. India has ranked around number 100 on the Fraser Institute's index of economic freedom.

In 1991, facing default on its foreign debt, India abandoned four decades of economic isolation and planning, and freed the nation's entrepreneurs. India sold off many of its state companies, cut tariffs and taxes, and eliminated most price and exchange controls. As a result, India became one of the world's fastest-growing economies in the 1990s and 2000s, averaging nearly 10% growth per year. This progress has not been made at the expense of the poor. While the rich have gotten richer, poverty rates have also fallen sharply in India.

Can India ever catch up to Hong Kong? Western Economists have urged India to cut its government deficits (currently 10% of GDP); reduce tariffs and taxes further; privatize state enterprises; eliminate red tape; and restore honesty in government. If these goals are achieved, India might be able to reach what Adam Smith called "universal opulence which extends itself to the lowest ranks of the people."[6]

## INTRODUCING DEVELOPMENT ECONOMICS

The story of modern India and Hong Kong is a good introduction to development economics. This chapter seeks to answer the following questions:

1.  What are the key elements for developing nations to break out of a "vicious circle of poverty" and achieve strong economic growth and a higher standard of living for their citizens?

2.  What can advanced economies do to speed up the development process?

3.  Have foreign aid, the World Bank and the International Monetary Fund benefited or hurt the growth of developing countries?

4.  Can a centrally controlled socialist economy thrive in a global economy?

5  Gita Mehta, *Snakes and Ladders: A Modern View of India* (London: Minerva, 1997), p. 16.
6  Adam Smith, *The Wealth of Nations* (New York: Modern Library, 1965 [1776]), p. 11.

## CENTRAL PLANNING AND SOCIALISM

Chapter 17 focused on the classical model of economic growth and the positive role of savings, productive investment, and technology played in achieving a higher standard of living.

Prior to the Great Depression in the 1930s, the classical theory of capitalist development was preeminent among economists and political leaders. However, in 1917 the Communists took over Russia and began an experiment in socialist central planning with wholesale nationalization of Russian industries and farms. Could a full-blown socialist state prosper without private property, exchange, and competition? Austrian economists Ludwig von Mises and F. A. Hayek charged that socialist central planning could not work. In a book called *Socialism*, Mises argues that a socialist economy could not calculate prices and production efficiently. He used the example of building a railroad. "Should it be built at all, and if so, which out of a number of conceivable roads should be built?[7] In a competitive and monetary economy, this question should be answered by monetary calculation." But under a socialist regime? "There is only groping in the dark. Socialism is the abolition of rational economy," he concluded. [8]

Then the Great Depression hit in the 1930s and economists and political leaders questioned the benefits of a free economy, while witnessing what appeared to be economic success stories in the Soviet Union and Nazi Germany. While the "free" Western economies suffered depression and massive unemployment, Germany and Russia looked like economic miracles. The United States and Europe eventually recovered from the Great Depression, but only after World War II, when governments expanded rapidly and engaged in massive public works and war production. Oskar Lange, a Polish economist, and Fred M. Taylor, president of the American Economic Association, countered Mises and Hayek by suggesting that central planning boards could determine prices through "trial and error." Under a wartime footing, central planning could achieve economic miracles. Even fellow Austrian Joseph Schumpeter declared, "Can socialism work? Of course it can," adding, "The capitalist order tends to destroy itself and centralist socialism is a likely heir apparent."[9]

Mises and Hayek appeared to have lost the debate with the socialists in the 1930s and 1940s. After World War II, the British government nationalized its coal, gas, rail, shipbuilding, and steel industries. European and Latin American countries began experimenting with socialism on a gigantic scale, nationalizing industry after industry, restricting foreign investment, raising taxes, imposing wage-price controls, inflating the money supply, and creating national welfare programs.

7  Ludwig von Mises, *Economic Calculation in the Socialist Commonwealth* (Auburn, AL: Mises Institute, 1990 [1920]), p. 24.
8  Mises, Economic *Economic Calculation in the Socialist Commonweath*, p. 26.
9  Joseph Schumpeter, *Capitalism, Socialism, and Democracy*, 2nd ed. (New York: Harper & Row, 1950), pp. 61- 167.

## THE ALLEGED SOVIET ECONOMIC MIRACLE

Economists were convinced by data from the U. S. Central Intelligence Agency in the 1960s and 1970s that Soviet-style socialist central planning had produced high levels of economic growth, even faster than that experienced by market economies in the West. Influenced by these reports, Paul Samuelson reported in his popular textbook that the Soviet Union had grown faster than any other industrial economy since the 1920s. As late as 1989, Samuelson claimed, "The Soviet economy is proof that, contrary to what many skeptics had earlier believed, a socialist command economy can function and even thrive."[10]

A generation later, following the collapse of the Berlin Wall and Soviet communism in 1989–91, economists discovered that much of the success of socialist economies was a sham. These economies may function and even thrive temporarily during a wartime environment, but they are no match for a free economy in producing goods and services for consumers. Robert Heilbroner, a professor at the New School of Social Research, shocked his colleagues in the socialist world by boldly declaring that the long-standing debate between capitalism and socialism was over. "Capitalism has won," he confessed. "Socialism has been a great tragedy this century."[11] Furthermore, Heilbroner was forced to change his mind about Mises and the debate over socialism. Following the unexpected collapse of communism, Heilbroner admitted, "It turns out, of course, that Mises was right." And it wasn't long before Paul Samuelson did an about-face in his textbook, labeling Soviet central planning "the failed model."[12]

Based on research at the Soviet archives, historian Sheila Fitzpatrick wrote a pioneering account of everyday Russian life in the 1930s: "With the abolition of the market, shortages of food, clothing, and all kinds of consumer goods became endemic. As peasants fled the collectivized villages, major cities were soon in the grip of an acute housing crisis, with families jammed for decades in tiny single rooms in communal apartments. . . . It was a world of privation, overcrowding, endless queues, and broken families, in which the regime's promises of future socialist abundance rang hollow. . . . Government bureaucracy often turned everyday life into a nightmare."[13] This was a sharp contrast to Samuelson's glowing account of the Soviet economy.

10  Paul A. Samuelson and William D. Nordhaus, *Economics*, 13th ed. (New York: McGraw-Hill, 1989), p. 837.
11  Robert Heilbroner, "The Triumph of Capitalism," *The New Yorker* (January 23, 1989), p. 98.
12  Paul A. Samuelson and William D. Nordhaus, *Economics*, 17th ed. (New York: McGraw-Hill, 1995).
13  Sheila Fitzpatrick, *Everyday Stalinism* (New York: Oxford University Press, 1999), cover.

———————————————— CASE STUDY ————————————————

## SINGAPORE VS HONG KONG
## LAISSEZ FAIRE AGAINST CENTRAL ECONOMIC PLANNING – WHO IS WINNING?
## A NEW ZEALAND HERALD COMMENTARY
May 23, 2002.

Since the inception of the Index of Economic Freedom, Hong Kong and Singapore have ranked at the top of the economic freedom scale.

It is instructive to understand what they might have in common that produces such exemplary performance, as well as he differences that enable the editors to place one above the other.

In his 1992 article on these two city-states, Massachusetts Institute of Technology professor of economics Alwyn Young chronicled the modern evolution of Hong Kong and Singapore. He noted their obvious similarities. Both had once been British colonies that served as trading ports. Each country developed a flourishing manufacturing sector after World War II and a financial services sector during the 1980s. In 1960, their economies had similar per capita GDP, which grew at approximately the same rate thereafter. Further, both countries experienced heavy immigration from Southern China.

The similarities end there, however, and the differences between the two have come to define them. As Young observed, "While the Hong Kong government has emphasised a policy of laissez faire, the Singaporean government has, since the early 1960s, pursued the accumulation of physical capital via forced national saving and the solicitation of a veritable deluge of foreign investment."

Since the two city-states consistently rank at the top of the Index of Economic Freedom and both have shown remarkable economic growth, do the differences matter? The editors of this year's Index suggest both that they have mattered and that they will matter even more in the future. Singapore's economic growth, which has not been systematically greater than Hong Kong's, has come at much greater cost.

While Hong Kong's investment rate has been fairly constant over the period at 20% of GDP, Singapore's rose from 11% of GDP in 1960 to 42% in 1984; in 1992 it was approximately 36% Since Singaporean growth rates were no higher despite all the compulsory investment required of its citizens, it is fair to say that the government effectively dissipated all the forced savings.

The questions are how and why. The savings were squandered over the years by Singapore's policy of "industrial targeting." As Young put it, "Singapore is a victim of its own targeting policies, which are increasingly driving the economy ahead of its learning maturity into the production of goods in which it has lower and lower productivity."

Young found that Singapore "has had one of the most rapid rates of intra-manufacturing structural change in the world economy." He also found that as a consequence, "Singapore had one of the lowest returns to physical capital in the world. The days in which Singapore can continue to sustain accumulation driven growth are clearly numbered." Over the years, Singapore's government has massively transformed the economy, developing new sectors more rapidly than anywhere else, but at the cost of lower and lower total factor productivity and returns on investment.

Young's study paints a picture of a kind of dilettante central planning in which the authorities strive to be first but at the cost of efficiency and the ultimate well-being of the people. Industrial targeting is only one of several Singaporean policies that cause concern.

For example, the government occasionally "gazettes" periodicals' including *The Asian Wall Street Journal* and its sister publication, *The Far Eastern Economic Review*, which limits their circulation for violations of Singapore press law. This practice is troublesome from the perspective of the rule of law and predictably, has drawn criticism from advocates of free speech. Limiting the circulation of print media also constitutes a straightforward infringement on commercial activity. Moreover, it has profound effects that go beyond the publishing industry. A modern market economy depends on the free flow of economic and commercial information. Particularly in asset markets (for example, stock and bond markets), up-to-date information is crucial to efficient operation. Interference with the flow of economic and financial information becomes one of the most problematic and costly forms of intervention. Even if it were Singapore's policy to censor only political material, in a modern economy it would be impossible in practice to censor the political without inhibiting the economic flow of information and opinion.

As financial services become more important to Singapore, the inner contradictions of promoting that sector while censoring the information that flows to it will become more evident. One of these two policies' if not both will need to give way.

Though not without its faults, Hong Kong's more laissez-faire policy has made its economy once again the freest in the world. At the same time, Hong Kong has achieved enviable economic growth without compulsory saving, industrial targeting, or other policies that not only impinge on economic freedom but also do nothing in the long run to foster growth.

*(Published in New Zealand Herald on May 18, 2002.)*

## NEW STUDIES DEMONSTRATE THAT FREE ECONOMIES GROW FASTER

Since the collapse of the Soviet model, economists have attempted to determine scientifically what drives economic growth in the developing world. According to work by James Gwartney (Florida State) and Robert Lawson (Auburn University), countries with the greatest level of economic liberty enjoy the highest standard of living. See Figure 27.1.

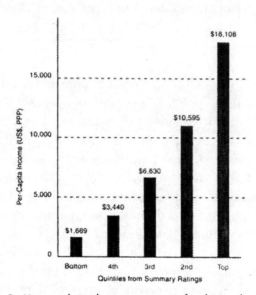

**Figure 27.1.** *Positive correlation between economic freedom and per capata income, 2008.*[14]

Gwartney and Lawson define economic freedom as follows: "The key ingredients of economic freedom are personal choice, voluntary exchange, freedom to compete, and protection of person and property." They use 38 components in five basics areas to construct the economic freedom index for 123 countries:

1.  Size of government expenditures and tax policy.

2.  Legal structure and security of property rights.

3.  Access to sound money.

4.  Freedom to trade internationally.

5.  Regulation of credit, labor, and business.

14 James Gwartney and Robert Lawson, *Economic Freedom Around the World*. Vancouver: Fraser Institute, 2008

According to their study, the following countries rank in the top 10 in terms of economic freedom:

1. Hong Kong 8.7 (out of 10)
2. Singapore 8.6
3. New Zealand 8.2
4. Switzerland 8.2
5. United Kingdom 8.2
6. United States 8.2
7. Australia 7.9
8. Canada 7.9
9. Ireland 7.8
10. Luxembourg 7.8

Their major findings confirm the Adam Smith model:

1. Economically free countries grow more rapidly.

2. Low income nations with high levels of economic freedom tend to grow faster than low income nations with low levels of freedom.

3. A legal structure that secures property rights and enforces contracts and rule of law is essential if a country is going to grow and achieve a high level of income. Gwartney concludes: "It turns out that the legal system — the rule of law, security of property rights, an independent judiciary, and an impartial court system — is the most important function of government, and the central element of both economic freedom and a civil society, and is far more statistically significant than the other variables."

   Gwartney pointed to a number of countries that lack a decent legal system, and as a result suffer from corruption, insecure property rights, poorly enforced contracts, and inconsistent regulatory environment, particularly in Latin America, Africa, and the Middle East. "The enormous benefits of the market network — gains from trade, specialization, expansion of the market, and mass production techniques — cannot be achieved without a sound legal system."

Their overall conclusion: "This research has found that economic freedom is positively correlated with per-capita income, economic growth, greater life expectancy, lower child mortality, the development of democratic institutions, civil and political freedoms, and other desirable social and economic outcomes."[15]

15 James Gwartney and Robert Lawson, *Economic Freedom of the World 2004 Annual Report* (Vancouver: Fraser Institute, 2004), summary.

## THE WINDS OF CHANGE IN DEVELOPMENT ECONOMICS

The shift from pro-government activism to pro-market solutions would not be seen in development economics until the late twentieth century. Following World War II, economists focused on the fate of poor nations in Asia, Africa and Latin America, dubbed the "Third World," or officially the "less developed countries" (LDCs). Generally, they experienced low literacy rates, high unemployment, rapid population growth, and commodity-based economies. Many suffered from high rates of inflation, shortages, black markets, internal conflict, and capital flight. How could poor nations participate in Adam Smith's goal of universal opulence?

After the 1930s had discredited capitalism and the postwar Marshall Plan had demonstrated the efficacy of government aid, the new economic orthodoxy became state-driven growth. International development organizations such as the World Bank, the International Monetary Fund, and the Alliance for Progress were established to assist LDCs.

In 1960, MIT's W. W. Rostow wrote his "noncommunist manifesto," *The Stages of Economic Growth*, which quickly became the standard bearer for Third World planning. Rostow categorized all societies into five categories according to economic growth:

1. Traditional society.

2. Preconditions for take-off.

3. Take-off.

4. Drive to maturity.

5. Age of high mass-consumption.

Rostow identified capital investment and what he termed "social overhead capital" (roads, bridges, ports, and other infrastructure) as key issues for development. For Rostow, a traditional economy, which on average had a 5% rate of investment, could "take off" if it invested 10% of national income. He was influenced by the Soviet example under Stalin, "a nation surging, under Communism, into a long-delayed status as an industrial power of the first order." The Keynesian/Rostow approach to development was embodied in the Harrod-Domar model of economic growth, named after Roy Harrod and Evsey Domar. According to this model, economic growth is simply a function of the national capital-output ratio, so that the growth of fixed capital generates increased profits and economic growth. The Harrod-Domar model emphasizes almost exclusively the need to expand the capital stock and technology as the keys to growth — either through an increase in domestic saving, foreign aid, private investment, government spending, or monetary inflation. Their model virtually ignores the role of entrepreneurs using capital and new ideas to create wealth. Since LDCs suffered from a "vicious circle of poverty" and could not internally generate growth, Rostow and other development economist insisted that the state break the vicious cycle through massive investment projects using government funding and foreign aid.

## THE SOLOW GROWTH MODEL

In 1956, Robert Solow helped develop a growth model that questioned the positive contributions of capital investment to the economic growth of a nation. For this work, Solow received the Nobel Prize in 1987.

To understand the Solow growth model, see Figure 27.2.

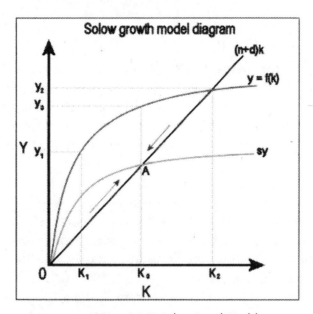

**Figure 27.2.** *Solow Growth Model.*

Figure 27.2 begins with a neoclassical production function, where output per worker is a function of per capita investment (or capital). Thus,

$$y = f(k),$$

which is represented as the higher curve on the graph. In Figure 27.2,

n = population growth rate
d = depreciation
k = capital per worker
y = output/income per worker
L = labor force
s = saving rate

Solow came to two major conclusions, based on his research using data in the United States:

1. Capital investment and savings suffer from diminishing returns. An increase in saving and investment will stimulate the economy, but higher doses of saving and investment will increase economic growth at a lower rate.

2. Technology plays a more important role in economic growth than saving/investment.

According to Solow, increasing saving and capital investment, even with aid, isn't enough to stimulate economic growth; the adoption of technology is essential.

## DISSENT ON FOREIGN AID

One ardent critic of the development orthodoxy was P. T. Bauer of the London School of Economics. In the postwar period, Peter Bauer waged a lonely battle against foreign aid, comprehensive central planning, and nationalization of industries. He noted that industrial nations such as Britain refuted the "vicious cycle of poverty" thesis, adding, "Throughout history innumerable individuals, families, groups, societies, and countries — both in the West and the Third World — have moved from poverty to prosperity without external donations."[16] He denied that advanced capitalist countries had progressed at the expense of poor ones and argued that foreign investment is a key ingredient to development of the Third World. State planning is not a benevolent program of growth, according to Bauer, but a concentration of power in the hands of a political elite that would inevitably lead to corruption and abuse.

In one of his classic articles, "The Story of Hong Kong," Bauer wrote how this Asian colony rose from the severe poverty of its largely Chinese immigrant population to become the second most prosperous enclave in the Pacific Basin, and how this feat was accomplished with limited natural resources.

By 1993, following the collapse of the Soviet socialist model, the World Bank issued a major report on the East Asian economic miracles, concluding, "The rapid growth in each country was primarily due to the application of a set of common, market-friendly economic policies, leading to both higher accumulation and better allocation of resources."[17]

16 P. T. Bauer, quoted in James A. Dorn, Steve Hanke, and Alan Walters, eds., *The Revolution in Development Economics* (Washington, DC: Cato Institute, 1998), p. 27.
17 The World Bank, *The East Asian Miracle* (New York: The World Bank, 1993), p. vi.

——————— **CASE STUDY** ———————

## MICROLENDING TO THE POOR AND THE GRAMEEN BANK

*"The able bodied poor don't want or need charity. . . .*
*All they need is financial capital."*

—MUHAMMAD YUNUS,
Winner of the Nobel Peace Prize (2006)

For years free-market economists have protested the waste and abuse of foreign aid programs, International Monetary Fund loans, and World Bank projects. P.T. Bauer has been in the forefront as a dissenter against government development programs. For the past 50 years, he has argued forcefully that government assistance in developing nations only retards economic growth.

But if IMF lending, foreign aid, and the World Bank are abolished, what should be done to alleviate poverty? Bauer and other classical liberals advocate reducing trade barriers; increasing foreign investment; establishing property rights, the rule of law, and a stable monetary policy; encouraging free markets, and limiting government domestically.

## PRIVATE-SECTOR MICRO LENDING

Market advocates have been surprisingly silent on a burgeoning private-sector success story known as "micro lending," the lending of extremely small amounts of money to self-employed entrepreneurs in the Third World by independent banks and institutions. The most famous of these micro-lenders is the Grameen Bank, founded by Muhammad Yunus in Bangladesh, the world's poorest country, in 1983. Yunus is an economics professor at Chittagong University in Bangladesh. In 2006, he shared the Nobel Peace Prize with the Grameen Bank for his revolutionary work.

The Grameen Bank lends only $30 to $200 per borrower. Applicants don't have to read or write to qualify. No collateral or credit check is required. Amazingly, the Grameen Bank has made these micro loans to millions of poverty-stricken people in Bangladesh, $2.5 billion so far. These loans are not interest-free; the Grameen Bank is a for-profit private-sector self-help bank that charges 18% interest rates. The default rate? Less than 2%. This remarkable record is due to the requirement that borrowers must join small support groups. If anyone in the group defaults, no one else in the group can borrow more. This puts social pressure on the individual to satisfy debts.

The bank lends to entrepreneurs, overwhelmingly female, who need only a few dollars to buy supplies and tools. Borrowers might be makers of bamboo chairs, sellers of goat's milk, or drivers of rickshaws. By avoiding the outrageous rates charged by other money-lenders (often 20% a month), these people are finally able to break the cycle of poverty. Their small businesses grow, and some use their profits to build new homes or repair existing ones (often using a $300 Grameen house loan). Thousands of Grameen borrowers now own land, homes, and even cell phones. And they are no longer starving. Yunus plans to issue private stock and eventually go public with his antipoverty program

His bank has been so successful that other micro-lending institutions have sprung up throughout the world. The concept has gained credence everywhere, to the point that even the World Bank and other government agencies have gotten into the million-dollar micro-loans business.

## SAYING NO TO THE WORLD BANK

Yunus won't have anything to do with the World Bank. In his autobiography, *Banker to the Poor*, Yunus decries the World Bank: "We at the Grameen Bank have never wanted or accepted World Bank funding because we do not like the way the bank conducts business." Nor does he much like foreign aid: "Most rich nations use their foreign aid budgets mainly to employ their own people and to sell their own goods, with poverty reduction as an afterthought. . . . Aid-funding projects create massive bureaucracies, which quickly become corrupt and inefficient, incurring huge losses. . . . Aid money still goes to expand government spending, often acting against the interests of the market economy. . . . Foreign aid becomes a kind of charity for the powerful while the poor get poorer."[18] Peter Bauer couldn't have said it better.

## FROM MARXISM TO MARKETISM

Yunus's statements are all the more amazing given that he grew up under the influence of Marxist economics. But after earning a Ph.D. in economics at Vanderbilt University he saw firsthand "how the market [in the United States] liberates the individual" and rejected socialism. "I do believe in the power of the global free-market economy and in using capitalist tools. . . . I also believe that providing unemployment benefits is not the best way to address poverty."[19] Believing that "all human beings are potential entrepreneurs," Yunus is convinced that poverty can be eradicated by lending poor people the capital they need to engage in profitable businesses, not by giving them a government handout or engaging in population control.

[18] Muhammad Yunus, *Banker to the Poor* (New York: Public Affairs, 1999), pp. 145-46.
[19] Muhammad Yunus, *Banker to the Poor*, p. 205.

His former Marxist colleagues call it a "capitalist conspiracy." "What you are really doing," a communist professor told him, "is giving little bits of opium to the poor people. . . . Their revolutionary zeal cools down. Therefore, Grameen is the enemy of the revolution." Precisely.

---

## DENATIONALIZATION: THE STORY OF PRIVATIZATION

With the collapse of Eastern Bloc communism, the paramount question became how to dismantle the socialist state and reestablish a liberal democratic capitalist system. The watchwords became denationalization, privatization, and deregulation. Peter Drucker, the Austrian-born management guru, wrote about privatization as early as 1969, but it wasn't until Prime Minister Margaret Thatcher advocated the selling off of national industries in the late 1970s that it became a reality. She started with British Petroleum in 1979. The real trailblazer came in 1984 with the sale of British Telecom (BT). Millions of British citizens were encouraged to buy shares at low prices, and public support for privatization rose dramatically when stock prices skyrocketed as BT went public. Moreover, telephone service improved dramatically. Prior to privatization, the British telephone system was antiquated. It took months to get a new telephone, and many out-of-service public phones went unrepaired for months. That all changed quickly after BT went public on the London Stock Exchange.

Since then support for privatization, both in the United States and around the world, has widened considerably as workers and customers became shareholders, government revenues increased, and companies became more profitable. Privatization has been particularly expansive in foreign lands, where it has become a full-blown global industry. According to the magazine *Privatisation International,* an estimated 100,000 medium and large-size firms have been divested around the world, generating proceeds of more than $1 trillion. Everything under the sun has been sold off by the state: oil companies, utilities, telephone companies, banks, post offices, hotels, restaurants, airports, railroads, mines, garbage collection, prisons, fire departments, taxi services, farms, supermarkets, churches, even movie theaters. Almost every country on every continent, including India, Russia, China, Vietnam, Mexico, and Peru, has privatized some or most state-owned businesses.

Privatization in Russia following the demise of the USSR was especially controversial. Tens of thousands of state-owned enterprises, from small retail shops to major industrial enterprises, were turned into privately owned companies. Under harsh new competitive conditions, most of these enterprises collapsed financially and were forced to layoff workers. Even the ones that did flourish did not enrich the workers. Corrupt officials and influential businessmen became the primary shareholders of the new companies. For years thereafter, privatization became a dirty word in Russia.

## PRIVATIZING SOCIAL SECURITY

Nevertheless, privatization has continued to expand worldwide. One area in particular that is gaining support is privatization of government retirement plans, or social insurance against old age. In the early 1980s, the Chilean state-run, pay-as-you-go pension system collapsed due to economic depression, and was replaced by an individual retirement program for workers under the direction of José Piñera, the Chilean labor minister.

The Chilean privatized pension system, the world's first, proved a huge success in deepening the nation's capital markets, boosting its saving rate, and stimulating economic growth (an average 5.4 percent since 1982). Today, 93% of Chile's labor force is enrolled in 20 separate private pension funds. Government pension experts from around the world have studied the Chilean pension program to see how the private sector has built a better social retirement program than the government. According to José Piñera, 30 countries have now adopted some form of privatized retirement system, and he believes China is the next big nation to make the change. However, the financial crisis of 2008-09 has dampened enthusiam for social security privatization.

## SUMMARY

Chapter 27 covered these main points:

1. Until the Great Depression of the 1930s, most economists and government leaders accepted the classical model of economic growth, stressing the virtues of saving, capital formation, free trade, sound money, and limited government.

2. Following the alleged economic success stories of the Soviet Union and Nazi Germany, many developing countries adopted a Soviet-style command economy involving nationalization of major industries, import substitution, wage-price controls, monetary inflation, and five year plans.

3. Since the collapse of the Soviet social model in the early 1990s, many economists have found that broader economic freedom — free trade, denationalization, deregulation, control of the money supply, and tax cuts — leads to strong economic growth and a reduction in poverty.

4. The Solow growth model has replaced the Harrod-Domar model of economic growth: Artificially stimulating capital formation through foreign aid, government spending, or monetary inflation does not necessarily lead to sustainable economic growth; adoption of private foreign capital and technology is essential.

5. Private sector micro credit loans to poor people, as exemplified by the Grameen Bank, has led to a substantial elimination of extreme poverty in many developing countries.

6. Privatization of public industries and government services (including social insurance for retirement) has expanded rapidly in developing countries.

## IMPORTANT TERMS

Harrod-Domar model
International Monetary Fund (IMF)
Import substitution laws
Less developed countries
Microlending
Positive non-interventionism

Privatization
Rostow stages of economic growth
Solow growth model
Third world
Vicious circle of poverty
World Bank

## INFLUENTIAL ECONOMISTS

### KARL MARX, MUHAMMAD YUNUS AND WORLD POVERTY

**Name: Karl Marx (1818-83)**

**Background:** Karl Marx is the most famous critic of market capitalism. Born in Trier, Germany, in 1818, to Jewish parents who converted to Christianity. In college, under the influence of philosophers George Hegel and Ludwig Feuerbach, he rejected his religious roots and became a fiery radical for socialist causes. He earned his Ph. D. from the University of Jena in Greek philosophy. In the 1830s, he encountered his lifelong friend and financial supporter, Friedrich Engels, in Paris, and together they wrote *The Communist Manifesto* in 1848, which advocated the abolition of private property and the violent overthrow of Western democracies. Marx was exiled from Continental Europe, and moved to London in 1849, where he and his wife Jenny would reside for the rest of their lives. They had three children, and suffered from serious illness, premature death, and desperate poverty (though not from want of money; Marx was subsidized heavily by Engels and other friends). He worked part-time jobs, and engaged in communist politics, but most of the time he spent writing his magnum opus, *Capital*, published in 1867 at the age of 49. He studied a variety of topics and constantly updated his book, but never finished the next two volumes of *Capital*; they were published posthumously by Engels. March died in 1883 and was buried in Highgate Cemetery in London.

**Major work:** *The Communist Manifesto*, co-authored by Friedrich Engels (1848); *Capital* (1867).

**Major contributions:** Marx is most closely associated with socialism and totalitarian communism, though he wrote little on how socialism works. Above all, Marx was a harsh critic of market capitalism. While recognizing the explosive growth of goods and trade under industrial capitalism, he pictured free enterprise as alien, exploitative, and crisis-prone. For all the horrors committed in Marx's name, the German philosopher struck an inspirational chord among workers and intellectuals disenfranchised by globalization. Today sociologists see value in Marxist thinking when it comes to issues of monotonous work in the workplace; the problems of greed, fraud, overwork, materialism, and lack of community in a money-seeking capitalist society; inequality of wealth, income, and opportunity; and conflicts over class, race, feminism, discrimination, and the environment. Marx also introduced the idea of economic determinism, that legal, political, religious and commercial "superstructure" of national culture is geared to the vested interests of economic forces of society.

**Weaknesses:** Most of Marx's predictions have failed to materialize, and his labor theory of value and other ideas have been proven wrong. Marx failed to recognize the incentive system built into the capitalist model—consumer choice and the profit motive of the entrepreneur. The irony is that capitalism, not socialism or Marxism, that has liberated the worker from the chains of poverty, monopoly, war, and oppression, and has better achieved Marx's vision of a millennium of hope, peace, abundance, leisure, and aesthetic expression for the "full" human being. Robert Heilbroner correctly recognized this conclusion when he wrote in 1989, "Less than seventy-five years after it officially began, the contest between capitalism and socialism is over: capitalism has won. The Soviet Union, China, and Eastern Europe have given us the clearest possible proof that capitalism organizes the material affairs of humankind more satisfactorily than socialism: that however inequitably or irresponsibly the marketplace may distribute goods, it does so better than the queues of a planned economy; however mindless the culture of commercialism, it is more attractive than state moralism; and however deceptive the ideology of the business civilization, it is more believable than that of a socialist one."

**Yunus, the Grameen Bank, and the Micro Credit Revolution**

**Name: Muhammad Yunus (1940 - )**

**Background:** Muhammad Yunus, co-winner of the 2006 Nobel Peace Prize, is the founder of the Grameen Bank and father of the micro credit revolution. Born in Bangladesh, Yunus was offered a Fulbright scholarship in 1965 to study in the United States, where he earned a Ph. D. in economics from Vanderbilt University (1969). He returned to Bangladesh to teach at Chittagong University, and began fighting poverty after witnessing the famine of 1974. In 1976, he come up with the idea of making small loans to poor people. Professor Yunus noticed that poor people borrowed money from loan sharks at high usury rates. His first loan of $27 was to 42 women in a small village near Chittagong University to make bamboo furniture. Yunus realized that making tiny loans at more reasonable rates could benefit large numbers of poor people, but traditional banks were not interested because of the risks and the small size of the loans. In the late 1970s, Yunus began the Gramean Bank to make micro credit loans, and by 1982, had 28,000 members. Today over 100 million poor people have benefited from micro credits from the Grameen Bank and many other micro banks. For his work in reducing poverty, Muhammad Yunus and the Grameen Bank won the Nobel Peace Prize in 2006.

**Major work:** *Banker for the Poor* (New York: Public-Affairs, 1999; paperback, 2003); *Creating a World Without Poverty* (New York: Public Affairs, 2007).

**Major contribution:** For decades, the World Bank, the International Monetary Fund, and Western governments have granted billions of dollars in aid to fight poverty without success. Now Muhammad Yunus and his Grameen Bank have demonstrated how a commercial for-profit bank can help alleviate poverty around the world. How do they do it? The secret is to ensure repayment of the loans by using a system of "solidarity groups." These small groups apply together for loans and if one defaults, they all are financially responsible. This encourages support for each other's businesses, and the default rate is less than 5%. The bank also makes money by charging interest on the loans (20% or so). Micro credit has been extended to all sorts of projects, including housing and education. More than 96% of Grameen loans have gone to women. Yunus states, "I do believe in the power of the global free-market economy and in using capitalist tools....I also believe that providing unemployment benefits is not the best way to address poverty....All human beings are potential entrepreneurs."

## PROBLEMS TO PONDER

1. In 1945, at the end of World War II, Japan was a poverty-stricken, war-torn island with massive unemployment, food and housing shortages, and a devastated economy. Much of the country was destroyed by Allied bombing. There were no skyscrapers, no wealthy banks, no automobile and electronics industries. Yet within a single generation, Japan became an economic powerhouse, the second largest economy in the world. How did it achieve this remarkable economic miracle? What role did General Douglas McArthur and its American occupational forces play, if any? Was the Japanese miracle financed domestically or from foreign capital?

2. Give three reasons why the Four Tigers (Hong Kong, Taiwan, Singapore, and South Korea) have enjoyed their own economic miracles. To what extend did any of these countries benefit from the leadership of a single individual? In your research, consider a controversial article, "The Myth of Asia's Miracle" (*Foreign Affairs*, November/December 1994), where economist Paul Krugman argued that the Four Tigers largely imitated the Soviet model of authoritarian central planning: "Singapore grew through a mobilization of resources that would have done Stalin proud," Krugman contends. What are the similarities and differences between the Soviet model and the Singapore model?

3. To maintain a stable monetary system, should developing countries adopt (a) a currency board, where the local currency is backed 100% by foreign currencies and gold, (b) establish a fixed exchange rate with the currency of its largest trading partner, (c), establish its own currency and create its own central bank to manage it, or (d) abolish its local currency and simply use the currency of its largest trading partner or the U. S. dollar (known as "dollarization")? What are the pro's and con's of each approach?

4. Thousands of years ago Egypt was the birthplace of one of the world's greatest civilizations, with remarkable advances in architecture, astronomy, mathematics, and economics. The pharaohs ruled the world for centuries. But today Egypt is a fallen nation, and Cairo, the capital, suffers from undrinkable water, dire poverty, noisy traffic, teeming millions, incessant vendors, and dust everywhere. Although Egypt has tremendous resources (oil, cotton, some of the best fertile land in the world along the Nile Valley, a first rate irrigation system, the Suez Canal, and a huge labor force), unemployment is 20%, the illiteracy rate is 66%, and it imports half its food. What is the cause of this economic malaise? Is it cultural, religious, political or economic?

## ADDITIONAL READING

- P. T. Bauer, *The Development Frontier* (Cambridge, Mass.: Harvard University Press, 1991), *Equality, the Third World and Economic Delusion* (Cambridge, Mass.: Harvard University Press, 1981), and *Dissent on Development* (Cambridge, Mass.: Harvard University Press, 1976).

- James A. Dorn, Steve H. Hanke, and Alan A. Walters, eds., *The Revolution in Development Economics* (Washington, D.C.: Cato Institute, 1998).

- William Easterly, *The Elusive Quest for Growth* (Cambridge: MIT Press, 2001) and *The White Man's Burden: Why the West's Efforts to Aid the Rest Have Done So Much Ill and So Little Good* (New York: Penguin, 2006)

- Muhammad Yunus, *Banker for the Poor* (New York: Public-Affairs, 1999; paperback, 2003)

# Chapter 28

# WHAT DO ECONOMISTS DO?

*"Economics is experiencing…a golden age of discovery.*
*This is not an exaggeration. Empirical economists are charting the economy*
*and society with a wealth of detailed applied results that truly bear comparison*
*with other epochs of discovery in other sciences."*

—DIANE COYLE
*The Soulful Science*

We ended chapter 27 highlighting Muhammad Yunus, the founder of the Grameen Bank and the micro-credit revolution, who in 2006 became the first economist to win the Nobel Peace Prize. Since the Sixties, the Nobel committee has awarded dozens of Nobel prizes in economics, but only one Nobel *Peace* Prize has gone to an economist. It is a watershed event, symbolic of the new prowess of the profession. Establishing peace through commerce and micro-credit is a new solution to eliminating severe poverty, one of the world's most persistent challenges, and the Nobel committee recognized the connection between commerce and peace.

When British economist John Maynard Keynes wrote his optimistic essay "Economic Possibilities for our Grandchildren," in 1930, at the beginning of the Great Depression, he hoped economists would come down from their ivory towers and become useful, competent people "on the level with dentists."[2] Many economists have indeed become useful practitioners, but Keynes did not realize how far-reaching and influential the new frontiers of economics would expand. He had no idea that, for example, beyond his lifetime, economists would be telling investors to reduce their risk and maximize their returns by diversifying into a variety of stock index funds, that government officials could save millions by changing the way they auction off their debt, that religious fanaticism and strife could be curtailed through free competition among a large number of rival faiths, that legislators could reduce crime by authorizing concealed weapon permits, or that they could clean up the environment by auctioning off pollution permits.

---

1  Diane Coyle, *The Soulful Science: What Economists Really Do and Why It Matters* (Princeton University Press, 2007), p. 232.
2  John Maynard Keynes, "Economic Possibilities for Our Grandchildren," *Essays in Persuasion* (New York: W. W. Norton, 1963 [1930]), p. 373.

## A CAREER IN ECONOMICS?

For most professional economists, the work they do may not be as creative, but it can be rewarding. According to the Labor Department, in 2004 there were approximately 13,000 economists working in the United States with a median salary of roughly $72,780. The majority work for the government, but other fields include academia, major corporations, and Wall Street. Most jobs require economists to be familiar with advanced methods in statistics, mathematics, and computer programming. In working for the government or a large corporation, they may collect and study data and statistics to spot trends, estimate growth in industries or countries, help set prices for products and services, and analyze policies and proposals.

Today economics is a popular major in college, and thousands of graduates go on to careers in economics and such related fields as business, finance, international affairs, and government service. Many CEOs, security analysts, and government officials have benefited from majoring in economics, and are applying their theories in the real world by running businesses, consulting companies, and improving government policies.

Not all economists are engaged in practical advice. Many go on to teaching economics and doing theoretical research. In fact, I would guess that only a minority of academic economists are attracted to applied economics. The majority of academicians, especially in the graduate schools and Ph. D. programs at major universities, focus largely on highly abstract mathematical modeling, divorced from real-world problems. It may not be for you.

To teach economics in high school, only a bachelor's or master's degree may be required, but at the college and university level, a Ph. D. is essential. To teach at an ivy league university such as Yale or Stanford, most professors need to earn a Ph. D. from one of the top ten schools in the United States or Europe, and must be willing to spend countless hours writing papers for peer-reviewed journals that only a small number of colleagues will read. Being a popular teacher on campus or writing a bestseller do not count as much as getting published in the top economic journals. It takes a uniquely dedicated and bright individual to reach the top echelons of academia. Teaching and writing at a small liberal arts college may be more rewarding for most budding economists.

## MAJORING IN ECONOMICS

Should you major in economics? I highly recommend it for several reasons. It is a broad based major that touches many other interests, including mathematics, statistics, money, the stock market, business, journalism, and politics. You may find that economics is useful in your career, even if you decide to do something else.

650

You should also consider joining the American Economic Association (www.vanderbilt.edu/AEA), and attending its annual meeting, which is always held the first weekend in January, usually in New York or other major city. As a member, you will receive the flagship publication *The American Economic Review*, as well as the *Journal of Economic Literature* and the *Journal of Economic Perspectives*. The latter is now the most popular journal because the articles are written for intelligent laymen without advanced mathematical jargon. You might also enjoy regional conferences held by the Southern, Western or Eastern economic associations.

The wide-ranging nature of economic thinking is what attracted me in my youth, and I found it so fascinating that I earned a bachelor's, master's, and Ph. D. in economics in the 1970s! I found having a degree in economics opened up many options for me, and I've worked for and consulted with the government, private corporations, and non-profit foundations during my career. With a master's degree in hand, my first job out of college was as an economic analyst for the Central Intelligence Agency, where I did research and wrote intelligence briefing for the White House and other federal agencies. During this time, I began my Ph. D. work at George Washington University. Then I shifted over to the private sector and was managing editor of a financial newsletter and was introduced into a new world of high finance in the inflationary seventies. My understanding of monetary policy and international trade helped me be a better security analyst. I traveled around the world, and started writing books on economics and investment based on what I had learned. Eventually, I struck out on my own and started a publishing business that was sufficiently successful that my wife and family moved to the Bahamas in 1984-85, and then bought a flat in London, where we spent many summers touring Europe. When I returned to the United States, I began teaching at Rollins College in Winter Park, Florida (near Orlando), and started writing textbooks and financial "how to" books that combined theory and experience. This textbook, *Economic Logic*, came out of this endeavor. Then, after 18 years of teaching at Rollins College and writing my investment newsletter, I was invited to be the president of a non-profit organization, the Foundation for Economic Education, in New York in 2001. Here again my training in economics proved to be valuable. And a few years later, the writing of *The Making of Modern Economics*, the story of the great economic thinkers from Adam Smith to the present, landed me a position as an adjunct professor at Columbia Business School in 2004. So you can see how majoring in economics can lead one down many unpredictable and rewarding paths.

## FROM THE DISMAL SCIENCE . . .

Economics itself has come a long way over the centuries. During the 20th century it was popular to label economics the "dismal science," a term of derision coined by English critic Thomas Carlyle in the 1850s. Carlyle lashed out against the classical economists who predicted poverty, crisis, and the iron law of subsistence wages. Even a century later, in the 1970s, when global economies suffered from a combined bout of rising inflation and rising unemployment, economists were criticized for having a terrible record of forecasting interest rates, inflation, or the next recession. In accepting his Nobel Prize in Economics in 1974, Friedrich Hayek reflected the somber mood of most economists when he confessed, "We have indeed at the moment little cause for pride: as a profession we have made a mess of things."[3]

During the early 1990s, economists went through a period of narcissist self-incrimination. For example, during the 1991-92 recession, Harvard professor Robert J. Barro had this to say about the economy: "Why is the economy weaker than expected? How will the economy do over the next year? What should the government do to help? As a first approximation, the right answers to questions like these are: 'I don't know,' 'I don't know,' and 'nothing.'"[4] Not to be outdone, Herbert Stein, a former chairman of the Council of Economic Advisors, admitted, "I am more and more impressed by my ignorance….I don't know whether increasing the budget deficit stimulates or depresses the national income. I don't know whether it is M2 or M1 that controls the level of spending. I don't know much a 10 percent increase in the top rate of individual income tax will raise the revenue….I do not know how to pick winning stocks."[5] A year later, Princeton professor Paul Krugman, who won the coveted John Bates Clark Medal (given bi-annually to the brightest economist under the age of 40), asserted that economists "don't know how to make a poor country rich, or bring back the magic of economic growth when it seems to have gone away….Nobody really knows why the U.S. economy could generate 3 percent annual productivity growth before 1973 and only 1 percent afterward; nobody really knows why Japan surged from defeat to global economic power after World War II, while Britain slid slowly into third-rate status."[6] And this quote comes from a man whom *The Economist* has called "the most celebrated economist of his generation."

3 Friedrich A. Hayek, "The Pretence of Knowledge," Nobel Prize Lecture (December 11, 1974).
4 Robert J. Barro, "Cut Taxes," *Wall Street Journal* (November 21, 1991)
5 Herbert Stein, "The Age of Ignorance," *Wall Street Journal* (June 11, 1993)
6 Paul Krugman, *Peddling Prosperity* (New York: W. W. Norton, 1994), pp. 9, 24. His previous book, *The Age of Diminishing Expectations*, came out in the early 1990s, just when Third World nations began throwing off socialism and Marxism, and sensed rising expectations for the first time. The decade of the 1990s turned out to be an explosion in economic and stock market growth.

### . . . TO A NEW IMPERIAL SCIENCE

Fortunately, this professional self-defeatism has been reversed in the past decade. The 21st century has given way to a more optimistic can-do attitude. Economics, no longer dismal, has come a long way toward reinventing itself and expanding into new territories so rapidly that another phrase is needed to describe this new golden age of discovery. Like an invading army, the science of Adam Smith is overrunning the whole of social science — law, finance, politics, history, sociology, environmentalism, religion, and even sports. Therefore, 21st-century economics might appropriately be dubbed the "imperial science." We've introduced this expanding approach throughout this textbook.

Who started this trend? Some historians point to Kenneth E. Boulding, long-time professor at the University of Colorado in Boulder, who died in 1993, as the father of interdisciplinary science. Boulding published over 1,000 articles on more than two dozen eclectic subjects, ranging from capital theory to Quakerism. But Boulding's vision of interdependence between disciplines isn't exactly what has happened. Instead, economics has started to dominate the other professions. In my judgment, much of the credit for this new imperialism should go to Gary Becker, the Chicago economist who holds positions in the departments of sociology, business and economics. Becker, who won the Nobel Prize in 1992, was one of the first economists to branch into what were traditionally considered topics in sociology, including racial discrimination, crime, family organization, and drug addiction. His ubiquitous approach continues at Chicago under the direction of a younger generation, led by Steven Levitt. Many departments in economics and business are establishing problem-solving research centers, such as the new Applied Economics Workshop at Chicago's Graduate School of Business. Economists are becoming more empirical than ever before. (See "influential economists" in chapter 6 of this textbook.)

### SEVEN POWER TOOLS OF ECONOMICS

In writing about economics over the past decades, I've been amazed by the powerful and diverse ways in which economic analysis can influence the worlds of finance, business, law, religion, politics, history, and the other social sciences. Economics can change people's and nation's lives, for better or for worse, depending on how closely they adhere to or violate basic principles. Economic policy can change the course of history.

What are these basic concepts? Below are seven essential principles that, when applied to a wide variety of problems, can transform the world. You have encountered them over and over again in in this course, and this list of "seven power tools of economics" can serve as a review.

1. **Accountability**: Economics is all about accountability. In a market economy, those who benefit from the fruits of labor ought to pay for them. The user-pay concept encourages discipline, industry, thrift, and other virtues. If someone else pays, the user doesn't pay much attention to the cost. When consumers don't pay for the products they use, the results are high costs, waste, and fraud. Ownership rights, therefore, are essential to accountability. Nobody spends someone else's money as carefully as he spends his own. What belongs to you, you tend to take care of; what belongs to someone else, or to no one, tends to fall into disrepair or overuse. As William Graham Sumner states, "A fool is wiser in his own house than a sage is in another man's house." This principle applies at home, in the workplace, and in the halls of government.

2. **Economizing and cost-benefit analysis**: In a world of scarcity and choice, one must economize. The most successful households, businesses and governments are those that invest for a better tomorrow, live within their means, and avoid excessive debt. Thrift is a virtue. Competition and the profit motive are the best systems ever devised to keep costs low and avoid losses. Measuring costs and benefits helps determine the best, most efficient use of resources.

3. **Saving and investment:** Saving and investment are critical elements in achieving long-term success in business and life in general. As a sign posted outside one business states, "You can't do today's work with yesterday's machines if you expect to be in business tomorrow." It's time to discourage the consumer-society mentality of excessive debt, overspending, and waste, and to encourage thrift and the productive use of investment resources.

4. **Incentives. Incentives matter.** The law of the downward sloping demand curve demonstrates that if you encourage something, you get more of it; if you discourage something, you get less of it. The profit motive promotes economic growth by creating better products at cheaper prices. A freely competitive price system is also the best solution to an economic crisis. Shortages are eliminated more quickly because higher prices discourage consumption and encourage the expansion of new supplies naturally, without government interference. Taxes can also have a significant impact on incentives. As Calvin Coolidge stated, "You can't increase prosperity by taxing success."

5. **Competition and choice:** Economic freedom leads to choice and opportunity—the freedom to move, obtain a better education, compete in a new business, find a new job, hire and fire, and buy and sell. The best way to achieve prosperity is to produce what people want. In Latin the phrase is

*do ut des*, "I give in order that you should give." The fastest way to earn more is to produce more of what the customer wants, as a worker, or as a business entrepreneur.

On the other hand, monopoly leads to higher prices and less service. Competition levels the playing field — it leads to lower prices and even the principle of "one price," that is, everyone paying the same low price for a product, no matter what your financial or social status (known as the principle of non-discrimination). The secret to ending poverty is equal opportunity, not state-mandated equality of wealth or income. Free people are not equal in wealth or income, and equal people are not free. As Winston Churchill once said, "The inherent vice of capitalism is the unequal sharing of blessings; the inherent virtue of socialism is the equal sharing of miseries."

6. **Entrepreneurship and innovation:** Success for individuals as well as for nations depends on entrepreneurial skills and strategies that often go contrary to the conventional wisdom. Where will technological advances originate from? Joseph Schumpeter wisely contends that "economic progress, in capitalist society, means turmoil," the "creative destruction" of the market place — and it is the entrepreneur who performs this essential function in search of excessive profits. Society must embrace change, sometimes dramatic change, that comes with innovation and entrepreneurial skills.

7. **Welfare:** The welfare principle states that you should try to help those who need help. This is the virtuous principle of all good religions, and good economists. Nobel laureate Muhammad Yunus put this into practice through his Grameen Bank loans. But they were not handouts. We must not forget the other side of the welfare principle: officials have an obligation not to help those who don't need help. To help the independent is to destroy their initiative. This policy applies to the household, churches and government programs. If a government institutes a welfare program for everyone, irrespective of their financial condition, it opens the community up to slothful behavior, and costly and inefficient operations on a massive scale. Imagine if everyone in a parish, rich or poor, were eligible for church assistance. A government program that concentrates on helping the needy demonstrates a caring society, but one that offers benefits to everyone for free or at a very low cost, discourages self-discipline and makes things worse.

The principles of accountability, economy, competition, incentives, investment, opportunity and welfare apply to all peoples and all nations. As Leonard E. Read, founder of the Foundation for Economic Education, stated, "Let everyone do what they please as long as it's peaceful." The role of government in every nation is to keep the peace, and to defend everyone's right to ~~life, liberty and property.~~ Good government enforces ~~contracts, prevents injustice,~~ provide a stable monetary and fiscal system, and ~~encourage good relations with~~ its neighbors. Benjamin Franklin correctly observes, "~~No nation has ever been ruined by trade.~~" Moreover, a sound economy cannot be founded ~~on an unsound monetary~~ system. Keynes rightly states, "There is ~~no subtler, no surer way of overturning the existing~~ basis of society than to debauch the currency." ~~Sound policy also requires that government~~ officials consider ~~the economics of legislation on all people in the long run, and not~~ just in the short run. ~~Frederic Bastiat observes,~~ "~~Countries which enjoy the~~ highest level of peace, happiness and prosperity ~~are the ones where the law least~~ interferes with private affairs." And the great Chinese philosopher ~~Lao-Tzu wisely notes,~~ "Governing a large country is like frying a small fish. ~~You spoil it by too much poking.~~" ~~These seven~~ great principles constitute the power of economic thinking. The future belongs to sound economics.

## ECONOMISTS' POWERFUL METHODS

~~Economics~~ has developed powerful tools of investigation that have led to many discoveries. Their toolbox includes ~~empirical work, data mining,~~ simulations, experiments, institutional incentives, and the use of ~~statistical methods~~ to test the validity of theories. ~~Empiricism~~ and ~~econometric work~~ are relatively new phenomena that have gradually changed the profession, especially with the availability of cheap computer power for calculations of complicated mathematical models. There has always been a lively debate about the best tools for achieving n~~ew knowledge~~ and building better policies. ~~Should economists engage in~~ the abstract methods of pure ~~deductive reason and high theory~~, or should they engage in concrete testing of hypotheses and the mining of data? Both have their value, but in my judgment, those who combine the two have made the most significant contributions.

The new field of ~~behavioral economics~~ has also created some valuable tools, largely borrowed by the ~~principles of psychology,~~ to achieve the ~~goals of individuals~~ and society. This is one of the few examples where economics has borrowed from another social science, rather than the other way around. The results have been impressive, especially in analyzing the financial crisis of 2008-09.

By focusing on solving many of the world's problems, applied economists are being recognized as never before. Let's look at some recent examples of the triumph of economics.

## CAN INVESTORS BEAT THE MARKET?

One of the first breakthroughs in applied economics came in finance theory. Harry Markowitz, a graduate economics student at the University of Chicago, wrote an article on portfolio theory in the March 1952 issue of *The Journal of Finance*. It was the first attempt to quantify the economic concept of risk in stock and portfolio selection. Out of this work came modern portfolio theory, which advances three principles: (1) investors cannot expect to achieve above average profits without taking higher risks; (2) diversification will increase returns and reduce risk; and (3) the markets are relatively efficient, that is, short-term changes in stock prices are virtually unpredictable and it is extremely difficult if not impossible to beat the market averages over the long run. This view, known as the Efficient Market Theory, was a revolutionary but now accepted doctrine among academics, although as we shall see in the first part of this book, behavioral economists are finding ways to improve on these initial findings and have discovered a few ways to beat the market—for now anyway.

These "ivory tower" researchers were greeted with scorn by Wall Street professional managers, but numerous studies by financial economists since Markowitz's initial paper have confirmed modern portfolio theory. Stock Market index funds, the economists' favorite way to profit from the efficient market theory, are now the largest type of mutual fund sold on Wall Street.

## PUBLIC CHOICE THEORY: NEW AND IMPROVED GOVERNMENT

James Buchanan and Gordon Tullock, both at the University of Virginia, published *The Calculus of Consent* in 1962 and forever changed how political scientists view public finance and democracy. Today public-choice theory has been added to the curriculum of every economics department.

Buchanan and other public-choice theorists contend that politicians, like businessmen, are motivated by self-interest. They seek to maximize their influence and set policies in order to be re-elected. Unfortunately, the incentives and discipline of the marketplace are often missing in government. Voters have little incentive to control the excesses of legislators, who in turn are more responsive to powerful interest groups. As a result, government subsidizes vested interests of commerce while it imposes costly, wasteful regulations and taxes on the general public.

The public-choice school has changed the debate from "market failure" to "government failure." Buchanan and others have recommended a series of constitutional rules to require the misguided public sector to act more responsibly by protecting minority rights, returning power to local governments, imposing term limits, and requiring super-majorities to raise taxes.

## ECONOMICS ENTERS THE COURTROOM

In 1972 Richard A. Posner, an economist who teaches at the University of Chicago Law School and serves as chief judge of the U.S. Seventh Circuit of Appeals, wrote *Economic Analysis of Law*, which synthesized the ideas of Ronald Coase, Gary Becker, F. A. Hayek, and other great economists at the University of Chicago. Today centers of "law and economics" are found on many campuses. Judge Posner states, "Every field of law, every legal institution, every practice or custom of lawyers, judges, and legislators, present or past—even ancient—is grist for the economic analyst's mill."[7]

Economists apply the principles of cost-benefit and welfare analysis to all kinds of legal issues—antitrust, labor, discrimination, environment, commercial regulations, punishments and awards. In chapter...., former Chicago law professor John R. Lott's extensive work on the relationship between gun ownership and crime is discussed and debated. He applied the incentive principle to demonstrate the controversial claim that well-armed citizens deter crime.

Chicago's Gary Becker has been in the forefront of applying price theory to contemporary social problems, such as education, marriage and divorce, race discrimination, charity, and drug abuse. Not surprisingly, he calls his book for the general public *The Economics of Life*. But Becker warned, "This work was not well received by most economists," and the attacks from his critics were "sometimes very nasty."[8] Now, decades later, Becker's work is being imitated everywhere by those who seek ways to solve social problems.

Economists have made significant improvements in other disciplines — in accounting, history, religion, management, public infrastructure, sociology, and even auction design. This textbook offers dozens of examples how these tools are being applied to solve problems for individuals, communities, and the nation, whether the theme be personal financial matters, business management, and domestic and international issues. Economists are even improving their ability to predict the future, as evidenced by the recent forecasts by behavioral economists Jeremy Siegel at the Wharton School and Robert Shiller at Yale on the stock market and real estate.

---

7  Richard A. Posner, *Law and Literature*, 2nd ed. (Cambridge: Harvard University Press, 1998), p. 182.
8  Gary S. Becker and Guity Nashat Becker, *The Economics of Life* (New York: McGraw-Hill, 1997), p. 3.

## TODAY'S CHALLENGES

What kind of new dynamic economic philosophy will dominate the new millennium? What about the future? The financial crisis of 2008-09 has been a setback for the economics profession and its ability to solve macroeconomic problems. As the Business Week cover story wrote, "Economists mostly failed to predict the worst economic crisis since the 1930s. Now they can't agree how to solve it. People are starting to wonder: What good are economists anyway? To be fair, economists can't be expected to predict the future with any kind of exactitude. The world is simply too complicated for that. But collectively, they should be able to warn of dangers ahead. And when disaster strikes, they ought to know what to do. Indeed, people pay attention to economists at times like this precisely because of their bold claim that they know how to prevent the economy from sliding into a repeat of the Great Depression. But seven decades after the Depression, economists still haven't reached consensus on its lessons."

Hopefully, you will find some answers in this textbook. Countries such as Canada, Australia and New Zealand demonstrate that stable monetary and banking systems do exist and can teach us important lessons about achieving macroeconomic stability. See especially chapters 19 and 25 and monetary policy and the business cycle.

Ultimately, we have reason to be optimistic. As John Maynard Keynes wrote in his famous essay, "Economic Possibilities for Our Grandchildren," written in the depths of the Great Depression, "in the long run mankind is solving its economic problem." He anticipated a "far greater progress" than we had ever imagined, that within a hundred years the human race would be so far advanced economically that the real problem would be simply this: "how to use his freedom from pressing economic cares, how to occupy the leisure, which science and compounded interest will have won for him, to live wisely and agreeably and well."[9]

In sum, the future for economics and economists looks bright. And if indeed we solve the "economic problem" in the next hundred years, who can we thank? The answer may be found in these poetic words by the great Swiss economist Leon Walras: "If one wants to harvest quickly, one must plant carrots and salads; if one has the ambition to plant oaks, one must have the sense to tell oneself: my grandchildren will owe me this shade."

9  John Maynard Keynes, "Economic Possibilities for Our Grandchildren," *Essays in Persuasion* (New York: W. W. Norton, 1963 [1930]), pp. 366-67.

# MARK SKOUSEN

Mark Skousen is a professional economist, investment expert, university professor, and author of over 25 books. He earned his Ph. D. in monetary economics at George Washington University in 1977. Currently he holds the Benjamin Franklin Chair of Management at Grantham University. He has taught economics and finance at Columbia Business School, Columbia University, Barnard College, Mercy College, and Rollins College. Since 1980, Skousen has been editor in chief of *Forecasts & Strategies*, a popular award-winning investment newsletter. He is a former analyst for the Central Intelligence Agency, a columnist to *Forbes* magazine, and past president of the Foundation for Economic Education (FEE) in New York. He has written for the *Wall Street Journal*, *Forbes*, and the *Christian Science Monitor*. His bestsellers include *Economics on Trial* (Irwin, 1991), *Puzzles and Paradoxes on Economics* (Edward Elgar, 1997), *The Making of Modern Economics* (M. E. Sharpe, 2001), and *The Big Three in Economics* (M. E. Sharpe, 2007). In 2006, he compiled and edited *The Compleated Autobiography, by Benjamin Franklin* (Regnery). His latest book is *EconoPower: How a New Generation of Economists is Transforming the World* (Wiley & Sons, 2008). In honor of his work in economics, finance and management, Grantham University renamed its business school, "The Mark Skousen School of Business."

He and his wife, Jo Ann, have five children, and have lived in Washington, DC; Nassau, the Bahamas; London, England; Orlando, Florida; and New York.

| | |
|---|---|
| **Websites:** | www.markskousen.com |
| | www.mskousen.com |
| | www.worldlyphilosophers.com |
| | www.freedomfest.com |
| **E-mail:** | editor@markskousen.com |
| **Address:** | P.O. Box 2488 |
| | Winter Park, FL 32790 |